The Phenix:

OR, A

REVIVAL

OF

Scarce and Valuable Pieces

SR Scholarly Resources Inc.
Wilmington, Delaware · London

SCHOLARLY RESOURCES, INC.
Wilmington, Delaware • London

Reprint edition published in 1974
First published in 1707 for F. Morphew,
London

Library of Congress Catalog Card Number: 72-83168
ISBN: 0-8420-1425-X

Manufactured in the United States of America

The Phenix:

OR, A

REVIVAL

OF

Scarce and Valuable Pieces

From the Remoteſt Antiquity down to the Preſent Times.

BEING

A COLLECTION of Manuſcripts and Printed Tracts, no where to be found but in the Cloſets of the Curious.

By a Gentleman who has made it his Buſineſs to ſearch after ſuch Pieces for Twenty Years paſt.

All Men receive their Birth from other things,
But from Himſelf the PHENIX *only ſprings;*
From his own Cinders, balm'd in coſtly Spices,
A Second PHENIX *like the Firſt ariſes:*
O happy thine own Heir! What ruins all,
Adds Strength to thee, reſtor'd by Funeral.

Dryden.

LONDON, Printed for *J. Morphew* near Stationers Hall.
M. DCC. VII.

PREFACE
By the Undertakers.

THE Nature and Extent of this Deſign being explain'd ſufficiently in the Title-Page, it's needleſs to inſiſt on it here; and the Uſefulneſs of the Work being obvious to every Intelligent Reader, it's equally needleſs to enlarge upon it.

A Deſign partly of the ſame nature, was begun in *Holland* by the Learned and Induſtrious Mr. *Le Clerc* in 1703. which has met with ſuch Approbation, that it is ſtill continu'd and publiſh'd there in *French*, in a ſmall Volume in 12°. once in half a year, under the Title of *Bibliotheque Choiſie*, i. e. *The Select Library*. But whereas that Author mixes new Books as they come out, with thoſe of an older date, our Deſign is only to give ſuch as are antient or ſcarce; not by way of Abridgment as he does (except they be very bulky) but the Pieces themſelves: And becauſe many don't underſtand *French*, we ſhall from time to time inſert ſuch of Mr. *Le Clerc*'s Extracts as are Valuable and ſute our Deſign, when we can't meet with the Books. But for thoſe newly publiſh'd, either abroad or at home, we leave them to the *Works of the Learned*, becauſe we would not interfere with the Proprietors of that uſeful Book. And tho we ſhall take all poſſible care to invade no Man's Property, yet we ſhall be ready, if any ſuch thing happens, to give all reaſonable Satisfaction, upon a reference to Indifferent Perſons.

A Work of this nature requires Impartiality; and as we mix nothing of our own Judgment in it, no man has reaſon to be offended that we don't make the Humour of any Party a Rule for our Collection; ſince in this matter we have no regard to our own Sentiments, which is the ſureſt Teſt of Impartiality.

The Gentleman who laid the Groundwork of this Deſign, has look'd over all the late Mr. *Miller*'s curious Collection of Pamphlets; and ſince Dr. *Seaman*'s Auction, which was the firſt, he has attended moſt that have been in *London*; where he purchas'd ſuch curious Pieces as he thought fit for his purpoſe: beſides what he has had from his particular Friends, and other Perſons who were willing to promote this Undertaking. And that nothing may be wanting to make it compleat, ſuch Gentlemen as have any thing Scarce and Curious to impart, and will be pleas'd to ſend it, directed for the Undertakers of the *Phenix*, to be left at *Fellows*'s Coffee-Houſe *Alderſgate-ſtreet*, or give notice where they may be attended, we ſhall be ready to wait upon them, and hear their Propoſals. In the mean time 'tis thought fit to give this publick notice, That we are already Maſters of a Valuable Collection for ſeveral Volumes, and ſhall go with all poſſible ſpeed upon another, if this meet with a favourable Reception; which we can ſcarce doubt of, ſince this is the only method for preſerving and making publick ſuch Valuable Pieces, as would otherwiſe be utterly loſt, or at leaſt confin'd to the Cloſets of the Curious: Whereas they may at one time or other be uſeful and inſtructive to Men of all Ranks and Facultys, and by conſequence anſwer the End of the firſt Publiſhers or Compoſers.

The

The ſeveral TRACTS contain'd in this VOLUME.

Phenix I.

A Letter of Resolution concerning ORIGEN *and the chief of his Opinions.*

Written to the Learned and most Ingenious C. L. *Esq; and by him publish'd.*

To the READER.

I'N *conformity to Custom, which sends few Books into the World, be they never so mean, without some fair bespeaking of the Reader, or giving him an account of the Author or his Work, it was thought convenient that some little thing in that kind shou'd be prefix'd to these few Sheets, and that I shou'd do it, who may reasonably be presum'd to have a greater Knowledg and Interest in this Affair than any other. Know therefore, Reader, that some while ago, upon a certain Occasion, which would be to no purpose here to mention, there was begot in me a Curiosity to know the Opinions of that pious Father of the Church, the learned* Origen: *and being neither by natural Temper, nor the way of my Studies, nor condition of Life, either so punctually inform'd what was in general Esteem accounted* Orthodox, *or much aw'd by the word; I suffer'd that Curiosity to grow so great in me, that I was even afflicted till it was satisfy'd.*

But having neither Time enough to ſpare from my own ſecular Imployments, nor Philoſophy enough to pierce into thoſe recondite Myſteries, I quickly perceiv'd I could not by my own Induſtry and Meditation come to the end of my Deſires. I therefore wrote unto a Friend of mine, competently well enabled with thoſe Advantages of Leiſure and metaphyſical Knowledg, conjuring him, by our long Acquaintance and Friendſhip, to give himſelf the Trouble of ſending me an account of ſome Queries I there put to him, tending to my Contentment and Satisfaction in this Particular. He, by good hap, having juſt before finiſh'd a Treatiſe, which may one day ſee the Light to the benefit of the Church, and having nothing new in the Forge, pity'd my Anxiety, and promis'd to do ſomething for the Eaſe of my Mind, and accordingly ſhortly after did me the Honour to ſend me the following Papers. Thou may'ſt eaſily imagine I receiv'd ſo obliging a Preſent with all due Reſentment, and entertain'd the fair Conceptions in it with extraordinary Emotion of Spirit: For really ſeveral Things before lay ſo croſs and ſcurvily in my Soul, that I took no pleaſure to look into it, nay I was ſenſibly pain'd and prick'd when I had the Hardineſs ſo to do: But I quickly felt all thoſe Unevenneſſes begin to wear away, and every thing to range it ſelf in its right Place and Order, Principles and Concluſions fairly accorded, and a laſting Peace and Calm (for ſo I boldly preſag'd) poſſeſs'd me throughout. Having receiv'd ſo great a Benefit my ſelf, and conjecturing that in this inquiſitive Age, the Minds of other Men, as well as mine, might need, and would joyfully receive Relief by the ſame means which miniſtred to my Tranquillity, and having by Trial aloof off, upon ſome capable Perſons, found that my Conjecture was real, I thought I ſhould be envious if I did not endeavour to obtain leave of my Friend to make his Papers publick. Whereupon, after ſome time, I reſolv'd to give him a Viſit at his Hermitage *(as he is wont to call the Place of his Retirement) for the effecting of my purpoſe. Where amongſt many learned and pleaſant Entertainments, the clear Witneſſes of a benign Nature, an innocent Conſcience, and ſatisfy'd Underſtanding, I mov'd my Deſign unto him. He with an amaz'd Look, ask'd me what I meant? I plainly told him that I meant to do what was in me, that others might receive that Eaſe and Benefit which I my ſelf had felt by his Labour; for others there were in the World, I doubted not, in the ſame Condition I was then in, when I requeſted his Aſſiſtance; and in exchange for his Queſtion, I ask'd him, why he ſhou'd be ſo unwilling to it as his Looks ſhew'd him to be? To which, after ſome little Recollection, The Queſtions diſcuſs'd in thoſe inconſiderable Papers you talk of (reply'd he) are great and bold, and you miſtake the World if you imagine they will find an equal Hearing; but are certainly much out in your account, if you think Men will be convinc'd of their Truth by ſo mean an handling as mine is. For tho I thought that wou'd be enough to entertain your Curioſity a little till the Fit was over, and to offer ſome Hints to your more deliberate Meditations;*

Meditations; yet I did not then while I was scribling of them, much less now in my cooler Thoughts, conceive them convictive to any who were not in a very forward Preparation to the Belief of them already. For neither are the Foundations of my Reasonings laid low enough, nor firmly settled (being I was to follow Origen *rather than my own Invention) nor is the Order of my Conceptions upon any of the Opinions such as it ought to be: for I remember very well upon my reading the Papers over after I had finish'd them, I discern'd some things in the entrance of a Question or an Argument, which by the right Laws of Discourse ought to have come behind; and others I saw were cast into the close of it, which wou'd have done better service more forwardly plac'd. To tell you the Truth, I did not scrupulously set my self any method, but took all Thoughts that came, and as they came (if homogeneous to the whole) and there upon the spot fetter'd them in Words, lest they might not have been at hand when I needed them, nor I been able to recal such fugitive Things when their Turn came. My Answers to Objections have the same Carelesness in them, no applying this or that to such or such a Proposition, but a diffuse speaking to the whole; being loth, as it shou'd seem, to lose any good Words that came in my Mind, which must needs render my Answer weak and obscure to strict Logical Readers. Many of my Interpretations of Scripture are rather extravagant or pleasant, than the serious Confirmations of a weighty Cause, and which affect to make the Holy Penmen of Sacred Writ speak Notions where in all likelihood they never meant it. I am also much too short in most of the Points debated: Which Faults, tho they be pardonable in a private Letter to a familiar Friend, will be sottish and ridiculous in a publish'd Piece. Do you then impartially judg whether so short a Discourse, full of so many and such monstrous Defects, pretending the Defence of high and rais'd Mysteries against strong inveterate Prejudices, be not a thing rather to be laugh'd at, than receiv'd as useful to any better Purpose. To this I smilingly reply'd, that he might be as bold as he pleas'd with his own; yet if he wou'd that I shou'd be of his Mind for the present, and acknowledg with him these Faults (as he call'd them) I was content, upon condition that he wou'd take his Papers back, and mend them in all the Particulars he was pleas'd to say they were defective in, and then give me that leave which I then came to beg. This I press'd him to with all earnestness possible, hoping that either he wou'd do it, and so I might receive his second and (as the Proverb says) better Cogitations, whose first pleas'd me so much; or else that he wou'd be forc'd out of Civility to grant my first Request, if he was resolv'd to deny the second. And it fell out according to my Hope; for being obstinately set against all Review, partly because he was now more seriously imploy'd, partly because that wou'd look like an Approbation of* Origen's *Opinions, he at last unwillingly permitted me to do what I wou'd with that I had. Which I here offer to thy candid Acceptance, being confi-*

dent thou wilt not be offended with any thing in it, if thou be'st of my Humour, to think no Opinion formidable which does Honour to God, renders him most amiable to Men, and a sure Object of our Faith and Hope, which justifies the Ways of his Providence, and reconciles them with his most precious Attributes, Equity and Benignity. Farewel.

C. L.

A Letter of Resolution concerning ORIGEN *and the chief of his Opinions.*

SIR,

IF the partial Judgment which your Friendship makes of me, and the heat of your commendable Curiosity would suffer you equally and coolly to consider the Undertaker and his Work; you would, out of Pity to me, and Honour to the great Personage you enquire of, expect no other Letter from me at this time than one of humble Thanks, for releasing me from the Burden your Commands had laid upon me: For verily I much need your Pity and Relief, who am combated with two mighty contrary Passions; the one an infinite Desire to do the Father Right, the other as great a Despair of doing it, from the most certain Consciousness of my own Inability. And tho by my undertaking of it I shall reap this Fruit of having given you an evidence of what Authority your Commands are with me, and how ready I am in the greatest Disadvantages to obey them; yet I shall neither satisfy you nor my self in the Performance, and possibly be injurious to his venerable Name, in adding more Envy to his Opinions thro my unskilful Representation of them. But to be bold with you upon the warrant of our Friendship, I think you are not at present capable of any equitable consideration as to this Particular; and therefore I do resolve to bear the Necessity, as well as I may, hoping it will prove a Benefit to me, and Security for the future: for certainly you will not be very forward to impose a second Task of this nature upon me, who have so ill acquitted my self in the first. And to shew you how little Power I have over my own Inclinations and Actions, where you are pleas'd to direct them, I shall, even contrary to my own Judgment, omit nothing of the Method you have set me, but give you an Account, such as it will be, of all the Particulars you desire to know, and according to the Order they are in in your Letter; tho otherwise, being left free, I should certainly have wav'd the first

† of

of them, and poſſibly the ſecond. Five Things then you enquire of:

1. What Opinion the Antients had of the Worth, Spirit and Temper of his Perſon.
2. What they thought of his Doctrine.
3. What his *Dogmata* are.
4. By what Arguments he aſſerted them.
5. By what his Adverſaries endeavour'd to confute them, and how I imagine an *Origeniſt* would anſwer to their Objections.

IN anſwer to the firſt, be pleas'd to receive this Advertiſement in the firſt place, which may ſerve to arm you againſt the Entertainment of a too forward Prejudice againſt him. Thoſe that are skill'd and well-read in the antient Writers of the Church, tell us, that there are very few Records left of him, but ſuch as muſt be had out of thoſe Writings which were on purpoſe compos'd to refute his Opinions; or at leaſt out of ſuch as collect and amaſs together his Opinions without their Confutation, with deſign to bid Men beware of them and deteſt them. Wherefore it is not to be wondred at, if the Heat of Diſputation, or Zeal for what they were perſuaded was the Truth, make them ſometimes, in ſo pardonable a Paſſion, ſpeak ſomething more harſhly and tartly of his Perſon and Opinions, whom they imagin'd the Adverſary and Subverter of it. But to the buſineſs: 'Tis laid to his Charge that he was carry'd away with too curious an Endeavour of letting no part of Holy-Scriptures, how hard ſoever, go unexplain'd, which prov'd his Ruin: That he was very temerarious, and in his Interpretations ſaid any thing careleſly what he pleas'd; that he was κομπώδης καὶ δοκήσει σοφός, a Searcher of Things unſearchable, ἐκβιβαστὴς τῶν ἀπερευνήτων, who fill'd all the World with his Toys and Nugacity, a Fanatick, ἐθελόσοφος, a Caviller and Jeerer at the Simplicity of true Believers, one who thro his carnal Mind and Reaſonings could not receive the Grace of the Spirit, an Unbeliever, and the greateſt of Unbelievers, a pitiful vain-glorious Man, perverted by his great Skill in the Greek Learning. The Unpleaſantneſs of the Argument tires me already, and my Reverence to the Cenſurers makes me abſtain from their Names: But I ſhall recreate your Mind with his more advantageous Picture, which they drew for him in a direct View of him, without ſo oblique a Caſt upon his Opinions. And here they repreſent him as one who, both in his Youth and afterwards, willingly and courageouſly ſuffer'd many Perſecutions and much barbarous Uſage for the Name of Chriſt, and the Holy

Doctrine of Faith, being many times drag'd thro the Streets of the City, reproachfully us'd and revil'd, enduring Tortures unsufferable, envy'd and hated by those in Power for his eximious Piety and Learning, who overthrew and confuted all the Heresies that were in the Church in his time; very well skill'd in the Natures and Properties of Animals and other natural things; who liv'd an Ascetick Life, and thro his excessive Strictness, spare Diet, and Abstinence from Animals, 'tis reported, τὴ ϑώρακα αὐτοῦ πεπηγωκέναι· whom none but the Ignorant and Unskilful can deny to have been the Master of the Churches after the Apostles, so well vers'd in the Holy Scriptures, that he had them all without book; and his Knowledg in them was so great, that even his Adversaries wish'd to have had it, tho with the Envy of his Name; whose continual Study Night and Day was to understand them, and to explain them to others; and innumerable Treatises of that kind he publish'd for the good of all Men, besides a multitude of other Writings, to the number of 6000 Volumes in all; who writ more than other Men can read: and all this Divine Knowledg he had in conjunction with the perfect understanding of the profoundest Mysteries of the best and noblest Sects of Philosophy, before whom *Plotinus* himself was asham'd to continue his Lecture, so much did he revere this holy and learned Father. And to be short, I refer you to the Encomium given him by *Vincentius Lirinensis*. This is a Draught of him from those who otherwise were not apt to favour him. And you in taking a view of it, cannot but clearly discover these two things, the Ingenuity and Integrity of those who were Enemies to his Doctrine, in that they did not, like the Disputers of After-ages, make all Men ignorant and impious who were not of their Mind; and the stupendious worth of *Origen*, which drew such fair Testimonies of his personal Perfections even from them, who thro their Dislike of his Opinions, could not possibly be his profess'd Encomiasts. And if I should add what Intimations I find of the Esteem had of him by such as did not disapprove his *Dogmata*, you would then say that he was little less than an Apostle; but because the witness of Friendship is so apt to be partial, and so less credible, I will wave it, and here make an end of the first Query.

THE second is, What they thought of his Doctrines?

They say his Heresy, tho entertain'd by the most eminent Christians, and such as profess'd a Monastick and Anchoretick Life and Poverty, yet was it πασῶν τῶν παλαιῶν μοχθηρότερα· That his *Dogmata* concerning Faith and matters of higher

higher Speculation, are the most absurd of any that ever were before or after him, those only Opinions of other Sects excepted, which countenanc'd impure and filthy Practices: That his Doctrine of the Resurrection, beside the Nugacity of it, was indeed mere Unbelief; a deceitful Opinion, not maintain'd by Faith, but Syllogisms and Ratiocinations, subverting the Confession of our Faith, ἐκ τῆς κατὰ φύσιν ἡμῖν συμβαινόντων· Madness, and Ignorance, and Blasphemy; a putative Resurrection, and only in Appearance, for he did only in Words confess that Article, but in Deed and in his Mind deny'd and subverted it. His Opinion concerning *Pre-existence*, and the happier State of the Soul before she was thrust down into these inferior parts of the World, they say, is τερατισμὸς καὶ τραγικολογία, without Sense or Understanding, the Conceit of bad Men, Blasphemy and Stolidity: That the Author of it did imitate the Craft and Deceitfulness of the Devil, that old Serpent, who of old deceiv'd *Eve*, and still does the Minds of the Simple: That his Doctrine in general is absurd and pernicious, a Serpentine deadly Poison, which he vomited into the World to his own Destruction, and theirs who adhere to him. His Doctrine of the Holy Trinity, they say, is manifest Blasphemy, and he by it was the Father of *Arianism*, and the Root whence all other like Heresies sprang; so nearly symbolizing not only with *Arius*, but with *Eunomius* and *Manichæus* also, that they who have written against them have with the same Labour answer'd to his Impieties: An Enemy of God and the Church for his most hateful Opinions; and one professes, in the Word and Faith of a Christian, that his *Dogmata* are poisonous and contrary to Scripture. His Opinion concerning the happy Restitution of all Things, and the Liberation of the Punish'd, whether Men or Dæmons, is such, that they cannot tell whether they shou'd be griev'd or laugh at it. What hath been produc'd upon this second Inquiry, I think is sufficient, to let you see what Opinion some pious and learned Persons of the Church had of *Origen*'s Doctrines. I cannot here, as in the former Query, oppose to this severer Censure one more favourable in his behalf, because the more antient Authors, I make use of in this whole matter, were profess'd Enemies to his *Dogmata*, and I have heard of no other extant which befriend them. Yet something you may gather from the first Testimony produc'd in this Particular, and add to it, that he hath not wanted such as have apologiz'd for him, and defended the Catholickness of his Doctrine; Men very eminent in the Church for Place and Dignity, and also for their learned Writings, some whereof are still extant, and in great esteem in the World. One of them is by his Adversaries themselves confess'd to be Catholick in the grand Heresy of all, to wit, that of the Holy Trinity: A second was so good a Christian, as to confirm the Truth of his Faith by Martyrdom. That I may not add that some later Writers, but very learned Men, have defended him too: for I know with some Men it will be exception enough against their Authority to say they are Modern; with others against their Reason to say, This Man was a Philosopher, that a Papist, a third a Jesuit, the worst of Papists; for the Holy Father hath found Defenders amongst all these sorts of Men. But instead of such Testimonies of antient Writers, which do as much cry up the Truth and Nobleness of his *Dogmata*, as those others I have produc'd do reprove their Falseness and Contrariety to the Faith of the Gospel: What if I should give you a short History of their Quarrel against him and his Opinions? May not this possibly somewhat lessen the Credit of their harder Censure? I will be very brief in it, because I know you would rather hear what his Opinions are, than see the Contentions among the venerable Fathers of the Christian Church. *Origen*, according to the Philosophicalness of his excellent Spirit, had asserted God to be purely incorporeal and immense, and that it was an impious derogation to his most perfect Essence to be limited by any form whatever, and therefore not by human Shape; however the Scripture does ascribe to him the several Parts of human Bodies. And this he did with some Zeal and Earnestness, because some unlearned Monks of *Egypt* had advanc'd the contrary Opinion, for which they were call'd by him *Anthropomorphites*. Now as it commonly happens, and as we see in the *Roman* Church, that the same Orders constantly transmit the same Opinions to all their Successors; so was it amongst these ignorant Monks, for the same false Conceit was preserv'd and strenuously maintain'd amongst them almost two hundred years after. At which time *Epiphanius*, one of that Profession, had imbib'd the Error, or at least was not much averse from it; for tho he was without doubt a very pious Man, yet it is apparent enough that he had not much Learning, and therefore was very obnoxious to that dull Hallucination: for his Piety would make him very much revere the plain Declarations of Scripture which countenance it, and his little Learning could not rescue him from the Fallacy. But as tenaciously as the Monks of his time kept their old *Mumpsimus* which their Predecessors had taught them; so with no less care did other more learned Christians retain the true and more reasonable Doctrine of *Origen*. And it is no wonder

der if there was much Contention amongst them, and many hard Words given, to the mutual provoking and inflaming one another. It happen'd about this time that *Theophilus* Bishop of *Antioch*, an *Origenist*, and one who had in publick Writings call'd *Epiphanius* an *Heresiarch*, had ordain'd one *Dioscorus*, an *Origenist* too, Bishop of *Hermopolis*, and committed to two of his Brothers the whole management of the Affairs of his own Church: but they being as pious as learned, did much dislike the Temper and Practices of *Theophilus*, who was a proud, revengeful, covetous, crafty and turbulent Man; and out of this disgust left him, and retir'd to their Monasteries again, from whence he had call'd them. He smelling out what it was that displeas'd them, instead of mending his Manners, was resolv'd to be reveng'd of them; and therefore besides his sending several Monkish *Anthropomorphites* into those Parts whereto they had retir'd, to kindle that Controversy afresh, to bring *Dioscorus* and his Brothers into what Danger and Envy he could, as holding the blasphemous Opinion of *Origen* (for so he impiously and against his Conscience call'd it) he also persecuted them by the arm'd force of Soldiers; so that they poor Men were constrain'd to save themselves by flying to *Constantinople*, where St. *Chrysostom* was Bishop. And tho this holy and wise Prelate would not communicate with them till the whole Cause was heard and judg'd according to Ecclesiastical Form; yet the proud *Theophilus* having nothing in his Eye but Violence and Revenge, was resolv'd to be reveng'd on him too for giving shelter to his Enemies. And therefore, thro his malicious Craft, he abus'd the simple and unwary Zeal of *Epiphanius*, and instigated him to call a Synod in his See for condemning the Books of *Origen*; signifying to him withal, that tho he had formerly been of another Mind, yet now he had renounc'd that pernicious Doctrine, and was wholly come over to his Opinion. By this Device he knew he should be even with all his Enemies together, who all admir'd and reverenc'd the Name and Works of that learned Father. And by the same great Craft of his, it is thought he drew in St. *Jerom* also into the same Confederacy: Which he might not difficultly do, he being naturally of a very hot and eager Disposition, and tho a very learned Man, yet scarce beyond the bounds of Philology. The Synod was call'd, and the Books condemn'd, according to *Theophilus*'s Project, who did the same in his own See too, and made *Epiphanius* write to *Chrysostom* to follow their Example. But as it seems this Holy Father was not so forward in the Business, and therefore the restless Spirit of *Theophilus* instigated *Epiphanius* to go to *Constantinople*, car-

rying

rying the Decree of the Synod with him, to have it ſubſcrib'd there. But St. *Chryſoſtom* refus'd to ſubſcribe, judging it very hard and unequal, and not according to the manner of Eccleſiaſtical Cenſures, that a Perſon of ſo great Learning and Piety, who had been ſo ſerviceable to the Church, who liv'd two hundred Years before, whoſe Books no Council had condemn'd, ſhould now be condemn'd by a ſmall pack'd Synod of his profeſs'd Enemies. But *Epiphanius* was reſolv'd to go thro with his Work, being abetted in it not only by the falſe and implacable *Theophilus*, but alſo by the Empreſs her ſelf, and ſome potent Men in the Court, and ſeveral licentious Prieſts, who had a pique againſt *Chryſoſtom* for his free reproving of their Faults; and therefore in the moſt invidious manner he could, before all the People, he recited the Decree, expreſly naming ſome of the *Origeniſts*, to wit, thoſe whom the wrathful *Theophilus* ſo cauſeleſly perſecuted, with oblique Reflections alſo upon *Chryſoſtom* as the Patron of them. And this fervent Zeal of his for the Truth, as he conceiv'd, was the more eaſily boil'd up to this irregular height becauſe of ſome Diſciples of *Arius*, who ſince the Condemnation of their Maſter and his Doctrine, not daring to avow his Hereſy under that Title, craftily and moſt falſly endeavour'd to propagate it under the unmeet Cover of the plauſible name of *Origen*. If I was concern'd in the Opinions of *Origen* more than barely to give you an hiſtorical Account of them, or took ſo great an Intereſt in his Quarrel, as to be an Adverſary to his Adverſaries, I could mention to you, that *Chryſoſtom* gently ſnubbing *Epiphanius* by *Seraphion* for this pragmatical Deſign of his (as ſome would call it) and meddling ſo much where he had ſo little to do, and kindly bidding him beware leſt from the Stir and Commotion he had put the People in any danger ſhould redound to himſelf; the good Man forthwith upon this advertiſement haſted from *Conſtantinople* to his own See, but died by the way. I could alſo tell you what befel *Cyrinus* Biſhop of *Chalcedon*, a bitter Enemy of *Chryſoſtom's*, when the pack'd Biſhops were there who were to compoſe another Synod againſt that pious Father. There are not wanting who draw ſuch Accidents into Argument againſt their unrighteous Proceedings againſt two ſuch excellent Perſons, and think they were the Rebukes of Providence: But ſuch Events are of too lubricous a conſideration to be taken notice of by any but an Adverſary and an Orator; but I am neither in this Work you have impos'd on me. Only this you may plainly gather from what I have now related, that the great Heat and Bitterneſs againſt the Opinions of *Origen* had ſuch beginnings as no Man now would dare to own, *viz*, the

ſatisfying

ſatisfying the Revenge of an impious Diſſembler, and the diſcountenancing a Doctrine which almoſt all the Chriſtian World believes for true. But the eager Contention againſt this one Opinion would neceſſarily diſcover many others which were like to be ſuſpected likewiſe; for *Origen*'s rais'd Genius could not but light on ſuch Concluſions as were of an higher and more remote Speculation, which to Heads unus'd to ſuch Theories, would firſt appear ſtrange, and then falſe; becauſe we are very unwilling that any thing ſhould be true which we never heard of before, and which we do not now underſtand. Many of which Concluſions fagotted together by ſome malicious or quarrelſom Reader of his Works, would make ſuch a ſhow to his Diſadvantage in the Judgment of the Simple and Unlearned, that without any ſcruple they would be ſet againſt him as a Man of moſt monſtrous Conceits.

YOur third Query is, What his *Dogmata* are?

By which Queſtion I preſume you do not mean all the Doctrines that are in his Writings, which cannot be found in the common compendious Creed of the Chriſtian Church, nor amongſt the Articles of particular Churches, no nor yet in the uſual Syſtems of Theology; for it would be as hard to tell you what his Opinion is in all thoſe Queſtions he propounds and diſcuſſes in his Books, as it is unworthy in him who hath heap'd up ſeveral of them together as his Opinions, when yet he profeſſes of them that he does not propound them as the Sentiments of his own Mind, but only as noble and illuſtrious Arguments of our Contemplation, very well worthy to be further enquir'd of: but your meaning, I ſuppoſe, is of the moſt material of them, and which moſt offend our otherways taught Ears. Thoſe of this ſort may be reduc'd to theſe Six.

1. His Doctrine concerning the Holy Trinity, among the Hypoſtaſes whereof, they ſay, he puts an Inequality.

2. That the Souls of Men do pre-exiſt.

3. That thro their Fault and Negligence they appear here Inhabitants of the Earth cloth'd with Terreſtrial Bodies.

4. That the Myſtery of the Reſurrection is this, that we ſhall be cloth'd with heavenly or æthereal Bodies.

5. That after long periods of time the Damn'd ſhall be deliver'd from their Torments, and try their Fortunes again in ſuch Regions of the World as their Nature fits them for.

6. That the Earth, after her Conflagration, ſhall become habitable again, and be the manſion of Men and other Animals; and this in eternal Viciſſitudes.

These are the chief Matters wherein *Origen* is conceiv'd to have mightily transgress'd; and of which *Jerom* says, *Cum hæc rejeceritis & quasi censoriâ virgulâ separaveritis a fide Ecclesiæ, tuto legam cætera: nec venena jam timebo, cum antidotum præbibero.*

HOW he asserts these, and upon what Grounds and Reasons, is your fourth Query, which in order comes now to be answer'd.

Concerning the First of them, whether *Origen* ever us'd the very Term *Inequality* or *Inequal* in his Speculations of that mysterious and blessed Essence, I cannot say. Sure I am, I never met with it in his Writings; and, what is a better Argument that he us'd it not, none of those object it to him who have made Collections of his Errors and dangerous Speeches. And therefore if the thing it self be laid to his Charge, it must be infer'd from such Passages as these they take notice of, and have excerpted out of his Writings, *Pater non videtur a Filio, Pater non comprehenditur a Filio, Filius, qui est imago invisibilis Patris, comparatus Patri non est Veritas, &c.* But if he did hold a kind of Inequality amongst the blessed Hypostases of the most Sacred Trinity, a Man would probably guess from what he finds in his Writings that his Grounds were these.

1. The Difference of their Essential Characters and *Idiomata*, which is such as might easily induce him to think that the Divine Hypostases, which substantially were those *Idiomata* or Properties, did also differ one from another according as the Perfections differ'd signify'd by those Essential Properties. They are these, Original Goodness, or first Plenitude of Life and Being, All-comprehensive Wisdom or Reason, and Demiurgical Love; which tho they all be truly and properly universal Natures, yet there is manifestly in the two latter and derivative Hypostases a verging towards Particularity, if compar'd with the first Primitive Fountain of the Deity; and this drawing towards Particularity is greater in the Third than in the Second. For all things are in the First in such an indistinct manner, and in such Exuberances flow from him, that our Minds cannot particularly set out this and that: but emptying himself into the Second, we then find them, according to his Name and Nature, limited and bounded and divided into their respective Reasons and Ideas, but without destroying his Essential Unity, for he is them all; from whom they being further carry'd down to the Third, are by his Almighty and never-failing Power distinctly brought forth into visible Life and Existence, exactly according-

ing to thoſe eternal Reaſons and Ideas which ſhone into him from the Second, and faithfully govern'd the Operations of his Power. And if we deſcend from this higher Metaphyſical Speculation, and take a view of theſe three Excellencies, not as they are Subſtances in the Deity, but as Diſpoſitions and Qualities in created Beings; we cannot but pronounce that there is ſuch plain difference in their Notions, that if they were from their accidental Nature exalted into Subſtantial life, they would there alſo ſtill retain their difference.

2. There ſeems ſuch a Neceſſity of Nature, that all Effects and Productions whatever, whether voluntary or emanative, ſhould decline ſomething from the ſupereminent Excellency of the Cauſe and Producer, that it is ſcarce poſſible to keep our Minds from thinking but that the Rule holds alſo in the Divine Emanations; eſpecially when the very Names of *Father* and *Son*, and the Modes of Derivation, *being begot by the Father*, and *proceeding from both*, do ſo fairly countenance the Truth of it.

3. Tho the Divine Hypoſtaſes be acknowledg'd Three in reſpect of their proper Eſſences, (for ſo, for more plainneſs, I ſhall crave leave to ſpeak) and thoſe three different, or *alius atque alius*; and not only ſo, in regard of three different Names, or a threefold Order (as the Church hath rightly determin'd, againſt *Sabellius*, I take it:) yet if we abſtract from them in our Minds their Names and Order, and barely contemplate thoſe Eſſences, we can find nothing in them (according to the Hypotheſis of the Equaliſts) why one ſhould be call'd the *Father* or *Son* rather than another: which muſt needs have ſeem'd very harſh to *Origen*'s contemplative Spirit, if not derogatory to him who is ſimply Firſt in that ever-bleſſed *Triad*.

4. The ſtrict *Equaliſts* could not give him any reaſon why the Deity was not rather multiply'd into an Infinity of Hypoſtaſes, than have its Progreſſions ſtop'd at Three. Nay, it ſeems neceſſary by their Hypotheſis, that the Multiplication ſhould be Infinite. For the firſt Original Good communicating of himſelf to his firſt Productions, according to the emanative fertility of his own exuberant Fulneſs, if they did as fully receive his Life and Power, as he their Author was himſelf poſſeſs'd of it, the Third would be as able, and by the neceſſity of equal plenitude, would be as much conſtrain'd (as I may ſo ſpeak with reverence) to produce Three more, and ſo on perpetually. And for them to ſay that the Number was limited to Three by explicit Will and Counſel, is to hazard the neceſſary Exiſtence, and conſequently the Divinity of the two latter Hypoſtaſes, and to induce ſuch an Indifferency into

to the first and earliest Operations of the Author of all things, as is inconsistent with infinitely-full Goodness. Wherefore *Origen* was forc'd to conclude that the Number was limited in a *Triad* by their unequal Declension from the First, in such a measure and proportion that those Three did perfectly comprehend and make up together in their Essential *Idiomata*, whatever Perfection goes to the constituting the entire τ̀ Θεῖον, or Divine Essence.

5. Since God is an Essence infinitely perfect, and since all the Perfections worthy of the Divine Nature, as Goodness, Wisdom, Power, *&c.* are neither of the same Nature, nor of the same Worth and Excellency; if every Hypostasis be essentially all those Perfections, they are three Gods; if one be one of them, another be another, they are not essentially equal.

6. He was encourag'd to think these his Reasons good, and his Conclusion true, from the fair Confirmations of it in Holy Scripture: *ex. gr. My Father is greater than I. I live by the Father. The Son can do nothing of himself. I can of my self do nothing. The words that I speak unto you, I speak not of my self.* And of the Holy Ghost it is said, that *he proceeded from the Father, and is sent into the World by him.* That *he is the Spirit of the Son.* That *he shall not speak of himself. He shall receive of mine.* All which places, that I may name no more, do most naturally imply some kind of inequality; and after the Reasons given, may pass for an evident Testimony of the Truth of *Origen*'s Doctrine; which some Men say is necessary to be establish'd and believ'd, lest otherwise we be as sacrilegious to the Honour and Majesty of the *Father of all things*, as the antient Hereticks were impudently injurious to the other two blessed and ever-to-be-ador'd Hypostases. And if the temerarious and confounded Conclusions of the meddlesom School-men be receiv'd with a like temerity, they think there will be as much need to multiply Councils in this latter Age of the Church, to assert the Honour due to *God the Father*, as there was of old to restore the *Son* and *Holy Ghost* to their deserv'd Dignity of Nature in the Beliefs of Christians, from whence the saucy Ignorance and Impiety of some bold Men had detruded them. Thus, Sir, you have some of those Reasons upon which *Origen* founded his Doctrine of Inequality. Which Hypothesis of his he hath so warily and judiciously form'd, that it hath been said by some, that neither the subtiler Attacks nor more rude and boisterous Shocks of his Adversaries have been able hitherto to shake or disorder it, much less utterly to destroy the Reasonableness and Concinnity of it. And what some have too hastily fancied, and as clamorously pronounc'd, *viz.* that it made the

two

two latter Hypoſtaſes Creatures, and render'd ſome main parts of the Oeconomy of Chriſtianity leſs reaſonable and decorous, and was not conſiſtent with many places of Scripture; have been like ill-planted Ordnance, which made a great noiſe and rattle indeed, but never touch'd the Fort their murtherous Load aim'd at.

It is not my buſineſs here to give you a perfect Explication of the Trinity after the *Origenian* way; but by that little hath been now ſaid, with what I may have poſſibly ſome time or other more largely diſcours'd unto you, your piercing Judgment cannot but plainly ſee and be ſatisfy'd, that there is nothing in that bleſſed *Triad* he deſcribes which can be call'd *Creature.* Is not every one of them eſſentially, immutably and independently on any Will endow'd with ſuch perfection, and in ſuch a degree as is truly and properly Divine? Are not the Two latter unſpeakably-cloſely united with the Firſt? and by their ſo near approach to him, who is the pureſt Spirit poſſible, are not they neceſſarily ſuſceptive of what he Eſſentially is in a degree infinitely beyond the Comprehenſion of a Man; as likewiſe for the ſame Reaſon of what one another are? Are they not alſo by the Divine Excellency of their Natures, the true and adequate Cauſes of all Creatures? How needleſs then and unskilful is their Fear, that they are not by his Hypotheſis truly and properly God? And therefore the higheſt Parts they bear in the moſt wiſe and gracious Oeconomy of the Goſpel, of being ador'd, worſhip'd, invocated, obey'd, truſted in, and the like, do rightfully belong unto them, not only by a Temporary Conſtitution of the Father, but by the Eſſential and Eternal Dignity of their Nature. And the Nature of every Hypoſtaſis, and their incomprehenſible-near Union one with another conſider'd, they will neceſſarily have but one Will, and conſequently be of equal Power; and the greateſt Honour and Service any Creature can poſſibly perform, being manifeſtly due to the two latter Hypoſtaſes, they are all truly of equal Glory. Thoſe places of Scripture which (I ſuppoſe) they mean, *There are Three that bear witneſs in Heaven, the Father, Son, and Holy Ghoſt, which three* ἕν εἰσι; *I and the Father* ἕν ἐσμεν; *I am in the Father, and the Father in me,* and the like, are ſo ſolely congruous to his Hypotheſis, that thoſe Phraſes of ἕν εἰσι and ἕν ἐσμεν are very improper, if every Hypoſtaſis was perfectly like and equal to the reſt, and each of them Eſſentially endow'd with all thoſe Perfections which intirely conſtitute the Deity or τὸ Θεῖον. And leſt any Man ſhould yet be ſuſpicious of *Origen*'s Mind, beſide what he hath more than once in that very Book of his which moſt offends, *That the Son is coeternal with the Father, and inſeparably united with him,* and that *the*

the Holy Spirit is not a Creature; I dare wager my Credit and your Friendſhip, than which there are very few things more valuable to me, that in his excellent Treatiſe againſt *Celſus*, he twenty times joins together theſe words Θεὸς λόγος, and in ſeveral of them adds ὄντως or ἀληθῶς Θεός. For that impious Epicurean gave him very frequent occaſion ſo to do by his fooliſh Cavilling and Jeering at our Bleſſed Saviour, whoſe Glory, as of the only begotten Son of God, his foul and impure Eyes could not diſcern through the Veil of his Humiliation and Crucifixion. But I am to beg your pardon, Sir, for my heedleſneſs in anſwering Objections out of place; for by your Method that is not to be done till the fifth Query. But my Pen, I know not how, grew warm, and was got ſo far before I perceiv'd it was out of the way. If you pleaſe therefore to transfer ſome few of theſe laſt Lines to their proper place in the fifth Query, I ſhall take care hereafter not to preoccupate the Order you have ſet me. This is all I ſhall now ſay of his Firſt *Dogma*.

His Second is, *That the Souls of Men do præexiſt.*

Before I ſay any thing of this, I am to put you in mind of two Things which concern both this and his other Opinions which follow. The Firſt is, that I ſo interpret your Commands to me to write you an Account of theſe Matters, not as if you expected from me a ſtrict and accurate Diſcourſe of them from their firſt and loweſt Principles, and thoſe Principles philoſophically prov'd and confirm'd, and then orderly advanc'd to the very Concluſions aſſerted by the Father: but only ſuch general Touches at thoſe Principles, *Phyſical* or *Metaphyſical*, in the lax and diffuſe way of a *Letter*, as may put you upon a more cloſe and methodical Conſideration of them; or re-mind you of conſulting ſuch Treatiſes where they are purpoſely and exactly handled. And therefore you will find many things concerning the Nature of the Soul and her Operations, her Union with Matter, with many other incident Speculations, not prov'd by me, but ſuppoſed, becauſe they are fully and excellently diſcuſs'd in the Writings of that learned Gentleman Mr. *More* of *Cambridge*: whom ſince I have here nam'd, I think I ſhould be highly ungrateful, if I did not acknowledg the infinite Obligation I have to you for giving me the firſt Notice I had of ſo worthy an Author; whoſe lately-publiſh'd Book of the *Immortality of the Soul*, I unluckily not having by me at the preſent, the Account I ſhall ſend you of thoſe things you enquire of, which with all helps and advantages would have been imperfect, is for that reaſon like to be only not contemptible. The Second Thing I am to mind you of, is out of the *Holy Father*, in the beginning of of his Book Περὶ ἀρχῶν· where setting down an immutable Canon of necessary Truths, which the Blessed Apostles and Founders of the Christian Faith had plainly taught, and the Church receiv'd; and the contrary to which cannot be admitted, but with the lopping off an Essential part of our Religion; he then instances in many worthy Objects of Contemplation, concerning which there is no determinate Declaration in the divinely-inspir'd Writings of Holy Scripture: but the Truth in such things, he says, was purposely conceal'd by the Holy Spirit, to excite the Study and Industry of the Lovers of Truth, and to reward their honest Labour and pious Disquisition, with the finding so rich a Jewel, and so precious a Treasure. Of this last kind, he says, is this present Question concerning the Soul, *Whether she be traduc'd*, or upon occasion *then first created by God*, or *præexist*; as also several other of his *Dogmata*, which are behind. And to do him right, he propounds all such disputable Matters doubtfully, and discusses them variously, and explicitly tells his Reader that he only exhibits to him several Phantasms, that he may use his Judgment about them, and take which he thinks is truest. Which singular Modesty and Fairness in this learned Father, may seem to every candid and ingenuous Man, Apology enough for him where he is conceiv'd to err, and more than enough where he offers, beside such probable Reasons, as he does in behalf of those Opinions which the World will needs father on him. For the Reasonableness of this Opinion which is now before us, I find these things in him.

1. That the Nature of the Soul is such as makes her capable of existing eternally backward, as well as forward: For her spiritual Essence, as such, makes it impossible that she should either through Age or Violence be dissolv'd, part from part, as it happens in Bodies, where there is no *Vinculum* passing through the very Substance of them to tie and retain one part to another; and therefore either through the stiller insinuation of other Bodies near them, they insensibly melt away and decay, or by the ruder dashes of such as knock against them, are broken all to pieces: Whereas the Soul, as a Spirit, by the advantage of that formal Power and Property of hers, whereby she is distinguish'd from Matter, cannot only penetrate her self and other Substances to the preserving her own Continuity; but also by her gradual Derivation of part from part, is in her whole Substance ultimately connected to her indivisible Head and Centre, as *Plotinus* speaks. Which Centre, being in its very Substance intellectual, does plainly shew who is the Father of it, to wit, the Essential Mind and Wisdom of God, whose univocal Productions (as I may so speak) are ac-

cording to their measure and capacity what their Parent is in the most perfect and most infinite degree conceivable, Life it self, or eternal Life: and therefore whatever other parts of the Substance of the Soul necessarily proceed and flow from this, can no more be cut off from it, than Indivisible can be divided; nor no more perish, than Life it self can die. We have then here an Essence capable of eternal Existence: and since the Powers and Operations of Life are not such things as can at pleasure be put on and off, like loose-hanging Adjuncts, but are intrinsecally made up into the essential Contexture of the Substance they are in; so vital and active a Substance as the Soul is, is as capable of acting according to her Nature, and consequently of feeling and enjoying the pleasure of her Life and Actions from eternal Ages, as she is of bare Existence throughout that long Period of Duration. So that nothing now is wanting to her actual Existence, but his good pleasure, from whom she and all things else proceed. I appeal therefore to your own candid Breast, and that noble Benignity of Mind which is in you, what Reason or Cause can you think of, worthy of God, which will manifestly assure us that she did not actually exist of old? If you pitch upon the *Platonick* way, and assign the production of all things to that exuberant Fulness of life in the Deity, which, through the blessed Necessity and Constraint of his most communicative Nature, emptied it self into all Possibilities of Being, as into so many capable Receptacles, you must then pronounce her Existence in a sense necessary, and after a sort coeternal with God. But if such Expressions seem too bold, and the Heats of an Enthusiastick Fancy, take that more sober Hypothesis, which is built upon the more conceivable Attributes of God, his infinite Goodness and Benignity, arm'd with equal Power, and directed by no less Wisdom, beside which nothing can be thought on to fit one for Action; and then ask your self, whether if the Subject in question be capable of existing and enjoying some part of that infinite Goodness, it be not evident from those Attributes that it will be made to exist? that which is infinitely Good, as certainly doing by a *Logical Necessity* every thing that is good, (no other Attribute gainsaying) as infinite Fire will necessarily burn whatever is combustible, if put to it. Wherefore unless God act by such arbitrary Humours, as we mortal Men are asham'd of, as Weaknesses and Imperfections in our selves, there is no doubt to be made but that this Conclusion is true, That the Souls of Men did exist and act before this present World was fitted for their Habitation; at least, before they were born upon Earth. I have heard some Men seriously profess, that there

there was a Light and Power in this Argument far more vigorous and convincing to their Minds, than in the plainest Demonstration in *Euclid*'s *Elements*. But yet they wonder'd not that others were not mov'd by it, because it requir'd a peculiar Disposition of Spirit to feel the force of it. For there are Moral Axioms *Noematically* true, as well as *Geometrical:* and as if you imagin a Man so miserably confounded in his Mind, that the common Notions of *Geometry* appear'd not certain to him, he must necessarily be insensible of the Evidence of any Proposition in that Science ; so in like manner will it happen to him whose Soul is so much out of her natural Order, as to have lost or dull'd, or silenc'd by what way soever her discriminative Sense of what is good, worthy, congruous, and decorous ; all Argumentations proceeding upon those κοῖναι ἔννοιαι of a diviner Sense, which to others are Demonstrations, will affect him no more than an Ape is taken with the Air of Moral Beauty.

2. The Actions of Providence will not otherwise correspond to those holy Attributes in the Deity, *Righteousness* and *Benignity*, according to which he governs and orders the Affairs of all the World. This Argument he makes use of two ways, in his Book against *Celsus*, and in his Περὶ ἀρχῶν, *viz.* in respect of the Place and Time wherein we are born, and of the Temper and Disposition of the Body wherewith we are born. As to the First of these, there is no Man doubts but that Education, Institution and Company are of wonderful moment to the making us good or bad. For it is manifest enough that few are born into this World in any higher condition than a possibility (as I may so speak) or capability of being made good and vertuous ; which Capability is perfected and actuated by good Instruction and wholesome Precepts assiduously inculcated to us, and by exhibiting and commending to us daily Examples of Vertue and Honesty : So that when or where either these are wanting, or of little credit and esteem, or the contrary more in use and practice, there seems little less than a Necessity of our running into all Wickedness and Vice. And if we call to mind the sad Accounts we have met withal in History, of Times and Places almost all the World over, over-run with all manner of Barbarity and Lust, adopted even into their Laws, and practised in their most solemn Religions, how can we but think that the Soul then and there born and living, is inevitably condemn'd to all Iniquity and Impiety? What Father will care for instructing his Children in such things as are of no use, and small regard in the place he lives in ; especially when they will certainly unlearn what he teaches them, by the stronger and more pleasing Impressions of publick

 Practice?

Practice? And indeed what Father will be fit to teach them ſuch things, who himſelf hath all his life long, in all probability, done the contrary, being carried away in his younger years, as his Children are now, by the popular Stream of his Country's Vices? Certainly there is very little likelihood he ſhould prove a benign, loving, compaſſionate, or a juſt and upright Man, who by the Laws of the City where he was born, is eſpecially train'd up in his earlieſt years to the ferity and rage of War, and the ſleights of Theft and Cozenage. And as ſmall hope is there of his Purity and Chaſtity, who is ſo ſolemnly led, by his Father, it may be, to behold impudent Strumpets ſtrip themſelves, and wind their rotten Bodies into all unclean and laſcivious Geſtures; and who with great Devotion ſacrifices to an allow'd Deity his foul Embraces of mercenary Harlots. It would be very eaſy for me to be copious in this Argument: The Hiſtories of all Countries of old, all the Apologies and Diſputations of the Primitive Fathers againſt the *Gentiles*, the latter Deſcriptions of the Religions and Manners of ſeveral Barbarous and Idolatrous Parts of the World, not long ſince diſcover'd or viſited, would afford me too plentiful Matter to fill up a very ſad Catalogue of all manner of Iniquity, which hath and doth ſtill reign amongſt them with little or no controll. For God therefore to ſend out of his pure and holy Hands an immaculate Soul, capable of living elſewhere, and fit for all Vertue and heavenly Wiſdom, leſt the Luſt of two brutiſh Perſons poſſibly ſhould come to nothing, and condemn it to an Habitation in ſuch Parts of the Earth, where reigns nothing but groſs Ignorance and Vice, by which ſhe cannot fail, without a Miracle, to be overborn (having ſuch a Principle in her, vivid and vigorous, to which thoſe brutiſh Depravities are natural and hugely pleaſing; and that better principle of Life which ſhould defend her from them, being ſcarce in a poſſibility of being awakened into any conſiderable degree of Power and Energy in ſuch an Education and ſuch Converſe, and amongſt ſuch Examples as are above deſcrib'd) what is this, ſays the Father, but to betray his own Offspring (for he is the Father of Spirits) unto unavoidable Miſery; and to put off the chief Excellencies of his moſt bleſſed Nature, Goodneſs and Righteouſneſs, and to govern the World with leſs Juſtice than an ordinary upright Man would do? You may, if you pleaſe, taking occaſion from what hath been ſaid, carry this Firſt Part of his Argument from Providence further, and enquire how it came to paſs that ſo many whole Nations both of old, and at this preſent day, were ſo over-run with all kind of Barbarity, Ferity, and Beſtial Luſt, ſo utterly eſtrang'd from the knowledg of

† God

God and the love of Vertue, so abus'd and tyranniz'd over by the accursed Rebels of the Airy Principality, the Kingdom of Darkness; lastly, so quite estrang'd from themselves and human Nature, that they seem to have left themselves nothing whereby they might be distinguish'd from downright Brutes, save Speech, and a something larger and more methodical Wit and Craft to compass the satisfaction of their degenerate Appetites. Truly, Sir, if you would form the Idea of human Perfection in no greater Glory, or set the Attainments of a reasonable Soul at no higher pitch than the certain Knowledg of some of your own vertuous Friends will warrant you to do, in whom (as you have oft with joy and wonder related to me) appears so pure and Angelical an Understanding, so firm and radicated a Life of all Holiness and Sanctity, Love and hearty Benignity to all the World, of Justice and Purity, and whatever is truly Divine: and if you then consider the vast Dissimilitude between this Idea, and the Spirit of so many whole Nations in the World; I make no doubt but you will say, that the Life of Man upon Earth is too short so far to abuse the capacity of what he might come to, as to put him in so low a degree of Degeneracy as those forlorn People contentedly live in. But not only the degree of their Apostacy from a divine and intellectual Life, and of their Immersion in the brutish and sensual, is so wonderful; but their continuance also in that wretched Estate for so many Ages together, without any remarkable appearance of Providence for their Deliverance, nay rather with her perfect leaving them to the insolence, subtilty, and conduct of the Devil, is a *Phænomenon* inexplicable without the *Origenian* Hypothesis. For since whole Nations and their continuance are but the Aggregate of single Souls born into the World in successive Generations; and since every particular Soul comes into such or such parts of the Earth with so vast disadvantages as is above declar'd: If beside this, the crafty and malicious Serpent hath such free Scope to tamper with them, who at the best are very deceivable; it can seem to you little less than necessary but that they should be wrought into that enormous lapse from God, which History and too sad Experience witness they are and have been. Now since the two great and most proper Objects of the gracious and beneficent Providence of God are the vertuous and faultlesly-calamitous (of which latter Order those miserable Nations would in great measure be, if Souls did not præexist) who can doubt but that Providence would very early have appear'd for their Rescue, or rather taken such care, that they should not so much have needed any extraordinary Assistance from her? But since we see She hath done neither, and yet are ſure that all her ways are gracious and equal, it will be very hard for us to keep our ſelves from concluding, That all thoſe wretched Souls had of old, by their long Revolt from God, and the Laws of his Righteous Kingdom, highly deſerv'd this Scourge from him, to be ſo put out of his Care, as it were, and given up to the barbarous Domination of the Devil, the Head and Prince of the unrighteous and rebellious Empire of Darkneſs; and whom they by Choice and Affection fell off to, in other Regions of the World, that him and his Tyranny they ſhould here upon Earth ſtill ſuffer, whether with or againſt their Wills. *Exedendum eſt tibi quod tute intriſti*, is a piece of warrantable Juſtice. And ſince there is poſſibility and hope that the preſent ſad part of the *Drama* may end, and a more chearful Cataſtrophe cloſe up all, the Benignity of Providence may in due time be as illuſtrious as her Juſtice hath been conſpicuous.

I know there are many Men who, part out of Piety and Humility, part from a Parrot-like talking ſuch words as their Books and Education have taught them, would make no bones of this Difficulty of the Holy Father, but can with very great eaſe and ſatisfaction of Mind reſolve all into the Pleaſure and Sovereignty of God, who being the Creator and Lord of all Men, may (they ſay) diſpoſe of them how and where he pleaſes. But it would be very well if they were as zealous Patrons of the more excellent Attributes of God, as they are peremptory Aſſertors of his abſolute Will and Power. For then they would both render his Exiſtence and Government in the World ſo deſirable to all Men, that none but the extremely-guilty would wiſh either his not-being, or his non-concerning himſelf in the Affairs of Men; and alſo cut off many ſcandalous Occaſions of Atheiſm and Epicuriſm, and ſpoil the Profeſſed of thoſe execrable Myſteries of thoſe over-plauſible Pretences they now have and craftily manage againſt the Truth. For tell me, Sir, if the Frame of the Bodies or the Paſſions and Affections of Men or Beaſts in whole Regions of the Earth, or of many in every Region, were ſuch as did plainly ſerve for nothing but to incommodate or cruciate them, or make them an inevitable Prey to others; could you with any reaſonable Confidence affirm, that the Goodneſs and Providence of a wiſe Mind did preſide over their Generations? or think you could reaſonably ſatisfy the Exceptions of an Atheiſt, or an Epicurean, taken from ſuch manifeſt Phenomena, by ſaying God might make them as he pleaſed which were his own voluntary handy-work,? I am glad, for my own particular, all things are ſo made, that there is no occaſion given for any ſuch Exception; for, believe me, if if there was, I know not how I ſhould behave my ſelf in ſo croſs a rencounter. And may not theſe Men with the ſame plauſibility of Reaſon, maintain the ſame Concluſion from the odd Frame of Things in the Moral World, were it ſuch as the Deniers of Præexiſtence muſt needs make it? I think they might do it with far juſter Reaſon; foraſmuch as a Man is a far nobler Creature, and the intereſt of his Mind and immortal Spirit much greater and more laſting, and therefore a more proper Object of the Care and Providence of God, if any Providence there be. Or are they ſo little peremptory in their Aſſaults, as to be beaten off by ſuch painted Fire, ſuch hurtleſs lambent Flames as are caſt againſt them, by thoſe who oppoſe to their Arguments nothing but the Will and Sovereignty of God? For they profeſs themſelves well aſſur'd, that if God be at all, he is infinitely Good and Wiſe, as well as Powerful and Uncontrollable; and therefore by the neceſſary Conſequences of Reaſon, wherever he is pretended by any to intermeddle either as to the making or diſpoſing of any thing, they expect to find the Impreſſes and Indications of thoſe Attributes: but if inſtead thereof they find all things quite contrary, it is not in their power to think that God hath had any thing to do there. But whatever ruin their Argumentations from ſuch ſubſtantial Grounds may threaten to the ill-built Fabrick of ordinary Theology, the Houſe of Wiſdom and Truth, which hath made Præexiſtence one of her Pillars, ſtands as firm as a mountainous Pyramid; and by that Hypotheſis, the great Phænomenon of Providence we have been ſpeaking of, is clear and righteous. Neither hath the Atheiſt or Epicurean any thing conſiderable to ſay againſt the Truth of it, either as it is a ſingle Propoſition by it ſelf, or as an Hypotheſis to ſalve the *Phænomena* of Providence. Which ſtraits of theirs they plainly enough confeſs by their either only gravely ſmiling at it as an Extravagance, or with a more ſolemn Brow chaſtiſing it as a dangerous Paradox. And truly a dangerous one it is to their pretended and boaſted Wiſdom: but to the genuine Plants of heavenly Truth and Divine Knowledg, 'tis as agreeable and ſalutary as Showers and Sun-beams are to the growing Spring.

The Second Part of the Father's Argument from Providence, is much-what the ſame with the firſt, *mutatis mutandis.* For the experience of moſt Men can bear witneſs, that there are not ſtronger Allurements from without to all manner of Viciouſneſs, than we find Incitations to the ſame from our own intrinſick Conſtitution: which (according to the common Hypotheſis) is not properly our Fault, nor any Fruit of it, nor was it in our power to prevent it; yet we are ſo fatally intangled in it, that it is next to a Miracle to rid our ſelves in any good meaſure of its Chains. Is not the World diſorder'd, and Society poiſon'd, and Mens own particular Peace and Honour miſerably violated with the baleful Effects of the four Elements of our Terreſtrial Compoſition? whilſt ſome live even in this World, in a perpetual Fire, and are tormented before their time through Wrathfulneſs and Strifes, Contentiouſneſs and injurious Zeal, which their Choler kindles in them; others on the contrary are drown'd in ſottiſhneſs and ſtupidity, and an utter ineptneſs to all things worthy of a Man, by the overflowing of ſtupifying Phlegm; a third ſort toſs'd about like feathers with light-mindedneſs and admiration of trifles, or wafted into the foul Lake of bodily Pleaſures by the guſts of reeking Blood; a fourth conſum'd by that ſlow-devouring Demogorgon in the Earthy Melancholy, in which lodg anxious Fear, dark Suſpicion, and fretting Envy. And tho you poſſibly may have heard ſome Men talk of Liberty and Free-will, and a Sovereign Power in us to keep all theſe rebellious humours in good order, and that with much eaſe, if we would but give our Minds to it; yet if you but conſider whence it is that they talk in that high ſtrain, you will begin to think they reckon without their Hoſt, and againſt Experience. Such Men have a ſort of Adverſaries, who from the aſſurance of their very Senſes, that there is a great Lapſe and Degeneracy in Univerſal Mankind, do, without all ceremony, bluntly caſt the Cauſe upon God, or at beſt aſſign ſuch a Reaſon of it as their Antagoniſts think comes to the ſame; who therefore out of an abhorrency to ſuch Blaſphemy (as they call it) think it better and more pious to deny the Truth of a manifeſt Obſervation, than to make God the Author of ſo calamitous a *Phænomenon*. Where, by the way, you may obſerve, that both ſides, by their earneſt contention, making good half of their reſpective Opinions, have, to the free Enquirer and Lover of Truth, facilitated his finding out the true Cauſe, which neither contradicts Experience, nor is injurious to the Glory of the Almighty. But granting to theſe Contenders for Free-will, that ſomething of what they plead for is true (as indeed it cannot be deny'd) I yet would aſk them, whether or no, the condition of our Nature conſider'd, the ſtrong inclinations in us naturally to that which is evil, and theſe ſtrengthen'd and further confirm'd for ſeveral years before we can come to have any conſiderable uſe of our Reaſon, or arrive to any Command over our ſelves; laſtly, the way and manner how the Elections of our Will are perform'd, which we never find free where there is a Cuſtom or Paſſion againſt it, and how corporeal Motions determine the Thoughts and Paſſions of of our Mind: I ask them whether, these things being consider'd, it be not hundreds to one odds, that we shall chuse the ways of Vice rather than Vertue? Or let the disproportion be as little as they can with any colour pretend, they cannot clear the Goodness and Rectitude of Divine Providence by their Hypothesis, which thrusts pure and immaculate and most innocent Spirits into so great danger of being defil'd and corrupted by the Passions of the Body, and of soundly smarting for it hereafter. But for my own part, I think the Observation of their Adversaries is much the truer, that the disproportion is exceeding great: For since the ways of Holiness and Vertue are so full of Peace and unspeakable Contentment, and shine with so enravishing and irresistible Pulchritude to prepar'd Minds, and do so perfectly correspond to all the Senses of so happy a Temper, that we are fully assur'd our Soul is then as she should be, and in conjunction with her most proper Good; I cannot see why Men should universally take the contrary course, and that with so much passion as they do, jeering at those who have made the better choice, as Mad-men or Fools, if there was any Liberty in them worth speaking of, to Vertue or Piety. 'Tis true indeed, there is great variety, as to degree, in the backwardness of Men to Goodness and Vertue, and proneness to that which is Evil; yet those who have the care and nurture of Youth, Fathers, Schoolmasters and Tutors, do with one consent affirm, that they not seldom have some in their charge, who from their earliest years are of so inexpugnable a propension to that which is naught, so wretchless and insensible of all wholesome Counsels, and have their Eyes so perfectly seal'd up, and their Hearts so frozen to all impressions of Vertue and Sobriety, that you may as well read Lectures of Temperance to a Goat or a Boar, and as successfully teach Goodness, Pity and Kindness to a Bear rob'd of her Whelps, or a Tyger inrag'd with Hunger, as think to fasten any such things upon their blind and obdurate Minds. Whence is this strange Phænomenon? If the Soul was not in the World before she was born upon Earth, it is not conceivable how she should in so little a time contract so peremptory an affection to Vice, amidst those continual chidings and reproofs, those sharp and painful corrections, those several ways of ignominious punishments she meets with, those advantageous representations made to her of that which is good and laudable, those many and earnest invitations and allurements of her to embrace it, with all other methods of a good and prudent Institution. That she comes pure and undefiled out of the hands of her Creator, all grant; and be this Pureness what it will, whether with or without

those

those Natural Notions of what is good and honest, the business will be much-what the same as to our present purpose. For if the latter way be the Truth, even this Negative Purity will leave her in an Indifferency to Vertue or Vice; and therefore if her first Precepts and earliest Inculcations be good and vertuous, she would be form'd unto Vertue: which yet we see is so far from happening to some (tho the very same instruction to others proves successful) that they on the contrary, impatient of every Curb and Rein, and deaf to all Calls and Charms, run headlong into all iniquity. If the former way be true, it would be still more wonderful how her first-appearing Inclinations should so eagerly carry her to that which is vicious, contrary to the positive Restraint of her inward Light. But if they say (as they generally do) that the Soul her self is pure and immaculate, but that she contracts this unreclaimable proclivity to Vice from the Body she is put into, beside the ignorance they discover by so saying, in the speculation of things, in joining such ill-agreeing Mates together into one vital Composition, where Sympathy and Congruity is the only *Vinculum*, the Father asks them how it is consistent with the Goodness and Righteousness of God, the blessed Spring of all Vertue and Holiness, and tender Lover of all his Creatures, to put such innocent Souls into such foul and untam'd Bodies, which so fatally and necessarily hurry them to that which alone of all things in the World he disapproves of, and which he knows will be their utter bane and miserable ruin. And therefore upon the whole of this Second Part of his Argument from Providence he concludes, That since so great a part of our pitiable bondage to Vice and Passion, in the judgment of all sides, proceeds from these Bodies of ours; if the Soul was merely passive in being born into this World, and was not before she was born here, much of the calamity she suffers from Vice, for which she must suffer more hereafter, must in his judgment be cast upon God: which he thinks is impious to affirm, and utterly contradictious to his holy Attributes.

A Third Argument of his I find in St. *Jerom*, from the misbecomingness of the contrary Position, which makes the blessed Majesty of Heaven and Earth diligently wait upon the unclean Embraces of lawless Persons, even to the degenerate vileness of Incest and Buggery with Beasts, and by a special Act of Providence carefully to perfect their impure Rudiments of Life. Which monstrous *Indecorum*, tho coarser Spirits are not sensible of, and think they have answer'd the Argument by those mean Comparisons of the Sun's shining upon Dunghills as well as flowery Meads, and stollen Seed's growing as well as that which the Sower came justly by; yet it was ex-

ceedingly

ceedingly harsh to the more delicate sense of *Origen's* Mind, and not to be put off by such slight and ill-fitting Similitudes. 'Tis a shrewd sign that Soul is much discompos'd in her Harmonical Nature, who hath so far lost her sense of proportionateness and congruity, as either not to think this is a very humble Office to the Supreme Deity; or if it be so, not to feel in her self a great Reluctance, to the making God so particular an Executor of it. If they imagin'd all things were made and order'd by such settled Laws of Nature as might in some sense be call'd Necessary, this Indecorum would be more tolerable; but to make God work all things in an express and voluntary way, and with his own hands, as it were, and yet to fancy so special an interposal of his Will and Power in so abhor'd an occasion, is to be very bold with the Sovereign Majesty on High, and to make him do that which they themselves, were it in their power, would be asham'd to do. And what contrariety would it be to any of the Divine Attributes, or what loss to the World, if God did not appear in such unlawful Inchoations of life, but let them come to nought in the end, as they were without his Approbation begun? But the true Judgment of this Argument, as I intimated above, is the inward Touch of a Man's Mind; which in you I know to be so comely and graceful, that at the first Proposal you felt the force of it, and need not that I further inlarge upon it.

4. Tho Scripture no-where particularly and plainly teaches us when the Soul was first produc'd and came into Being, yet there are some passages in it which favour her Præexistence. *I have glorify'd thee on Earth; I have finish'd the Work thou gavest me to do. And now, O Father, glorify thou me with thine own self, with that glory I had with thee before the World was.* In which Text these two Things are plainly enough intimated, the Existence of the Subject of this Glory pray'd for before the World was, and an Intercision of this Glory for a while, and Recuperation of it again; the former whereof, tho it be true of the Divine Λόγος, yet the latter is incompetible to him. And the Event plainly shews the Subject of this Glory: for he that humbled himself to the Death of the Cross, was exalted by God to be the Sovereign Prince of Men and Angels; and he that was made in the Likeness of Man, or sinful Flesh, in a vile Body, was invested with Power to change our vile Bodies into the Similitude of his glorious Body. *I came forth from the Father, and am come into the World: again, I leave the World, and go to the Father. His Disciples said unto him, Lo, now speakest thou plainly, and speakest no Parable.* For the opinion of Præexistence, but in a special manner of the Soul of the Messiah,

ſiah, was the common Doctrine of their Nation; and that Key eaſily unlock'd our Saviour's meaning. *Let this mind be in you which was in Chriſt Jeſus, who being in the form of God, did not*, like *Lucifer, think equality with God a prey or ſpoil* to be invaded by him, in that ſenſe that *Cicero* ſays of *Verres*, lib. 5, *Omnium bona prædam ſuam duxit*; but was ſo far from aſſuming that which was not his own, that on the contrary he made himſelf leſs than indeed he was, *and emptied himſelf by taking the form of a ſervant*, which conſiſted in his *being made in the likeneſs of Man*, or of one of the Sons of *Adam*; *and being found in faſhion as a Man, he humbled himſelf yet further, becoming obedient even to death.* If this place be to be underſtood of the Humanity of Chriſt, nothing can be more plain than that his Soul præexiſted: for otherwiſe to be born, tho but in the Likeneſs of a Terreſtrial Man, would have been a gain to him, not a diminution; ſince there is no good at all in *not being*, ſave to thoſe who are extremely miſerable. And that it is ſo to be underſtood, will be very probable, if we but take notice of the importance of the Phraſes here us'd, and compare them with others in Holy Scripture. Ἐν μορφῇ Θεȣ̃ ὑπάρχων, is as much as if he had ſaid, θεόμορφος, or, after the more *Attick* Purity, θεοειδὴς, or θεοείκελος ὢν, or ὑπάρχων· even as St. *Mark*, in the ſtory of the Woman which had the Iſſue of Blood, ſays after the *Jewiſh* way, ȣ̃σα ἐν ῥύσει αἵματος, but St. *Matthew* more elegantly αἱμοῤῥοȣ̃σα. St. *John*, after the *Seventy*, διδακτοὶ Θεȣ̃, but St. *Paul* Θεοδίδακτοι· a very uſual Hebraiſm in theſe Holy Writers. The thing ſignify'd by the Phraſe in hand is Chriſt's Angelick Purity both in Body and Spirit. This is that Image of God according to which we were all at firſt made, and which Chriſt had not loſt as the reſt of his degenerate Brethren had; and this is the Divine Nature we ſhall again be made partakers of, when we ſhall have eſcap'd the Corruption that is in this World: for the Sons of the Reſurrection are truly the Sons of God, and like unto God. But tho the Humanity of Chriſt was ſo truly Deiform, yet he emptied himſelf of this Fulneſs of Life and Glory by taking the Form of a Servant, μορφὴν δȣ́λȣ. What this means, the Apoſtle tells us in another place: *The Creature*, i. e. Man in the Jewiſh Language, *ſhall be manumitted from the ſervitude of corruption*, and aſſerted *into the glorious liberty of the Sons of God*, i. e. Angels, or Angelick Souls, *by the redemption of his Body*. So that μορφὴ δȣ́λȣ is a mortal corruptible Body, which the Soul of Chriſt voluntarily took upon her, by which he became like unto us mortal Men, as he immediately adds, ἐν ὁμοιώματι ἀνθρώπων· which he otherwhere calls ὁμοίωμα σαρκὸς ἁμαρτίας, and εἰκόνα τȣ̃ χοϊκȣ̃. And being by this his Servile *Schema* made lower than the Angels, he was

put

put in a capacity of being obedient even unto Death, and of tasting Death for every Man; and was thereby made perfectly like unto his Brethren, partaking of Flesh and Blood as they did, that he might by Death destroy him who had the power of Death, as the Apostle to the *Hebrews* speaks. For without this exinanition of himself, and descent from his Æthereal or Angelical condition, it was not possible for him to die. I might further add, for the justifying of this interpretation, that it is not conceivable how the Eternal Λόγος, who is what he is by an unchangeable and undiminishable necessity of Nature, can be said *to empty* himself; especially since the several parts and degrees of the Humiliation here describ'd, are spoken of the same person: but certainly he that is *Life it self* cannot be said to die, or become obedient to the Death of the Cross. Neither is it proper nor usual in Scripture to propound the Deity to us as an Example of Humility; tho nothing is so frequent there, nor more congruous than to exhort us to be conformable to him in Love, Goodness and Purity. I shall say no more upon this place but this, That if *being in the form of God*, be to be expounded of the Soul of Christ, as in Physical Union with the Divine Λόγος, yet still our Argument for the Præexistence of his Soul will be every whit as good; as is plain at first sight. I have been something long upon this Text, but will make amends for it in only pointing to the rest which countenance this Opinion of Præexistence, as all those many Texts most naturally do, which say Christ *came down from Heaven.* For every other Interpretation of this Phrase *coming down from Heaven,* will either be *Socinian* as to the Notion, and a mere Violence as to the Words; or else will make the Λόγος alone to be the *Christ*, and him that *fills all things* to quit a place.

And certainly something in favour of this Opinion may be made of that question of the Disciples to our Saviour concerning the Man that was born blind; for either he approv'd of the common Opinion as true, or at least thought it very harmless, if false; since having so fair an occasion of rectifying the common Belief, he yet said nothing against it. I know indeed that the Silence of Scripture and the Arguments from thence, which they call *Negative*, are esteem'd of little force in Disputation, unless in some certain Cases. But he that shall seriously consider how great a Change does necessarily follow in the whole Frame of Christian Religion, from the beginning to the end of it, by the taking in or leaving out this Opinion of Præexistence, may possibly be induc'd to think that our Saviour's saying nothing on so apt an occasion, is one of those Cases wherein Silence is almost as argumentative as a positive Approbation.

Para-

Parables likewise will not be taken for Arguments: which is no ill Rule, if understood of the minute Circumstances of them, and of such parts as the *Decorum* of an Apologue requires; but certainly the whole will argue as well as instruct. But I lay no stress upon them, because they may have other true and sober Interpretations; yet I thought good to cast them in for variety sake, that you may see how congruously they may be apply'd to the Doctrine we are upon. The Prodigal Son's leaving his Father you know is describ'd by his *going into a far Country*, and there wasting his Substance with riotous Living: and in his return, his Father says of him, This my Son *was dead*, but is *alive again*; was lost, but is found. *The Son of Man is come* [from Heaven] *to save that which was lost. If a Man have an hundred sheep, and one of them go astray, doth he not leave the ninety and nine, and goeth into the mountains, and seeketh that which is gone astray? For ye were as sheep going astray, but are now return'd unto the Shepherd and Bishop of your Souls. I am the good Shepherd, not an hireling, whose* own *the sheep are not.* You may consider these places also, tho they do not all belong to this head of Parables: *I am not sent, but* εἰς τὰ πρόβατα τὰ ἀπολωλότα—— *and not for that Nation only, but that he should gather together in one* τὰ τέκνα τοῦ Θεοῦ τὰ διεσκορπισμένα—— *and having made peace by the blood of his Cross, by him to reconcile all things unto himself, whether things* in Heaven, *or things* in Earth. *Dearly belov'd Brethren, I beseech you as* Strangers *and* Pilgrims, *abstain from fleshly lusts which war against the soul*—— *And confess'd that they were* Strangers *and* Pilgrims upon Earth.

Lastly, The History of the Creation, *cabbalistically* interpreted, confirms the Truth of *Origen*'s Opinion. And that the Word may not fright you, nor you think I mean by it *fancifully* and *extravagantly*, I will more particularly tell you my meaning; which is this: So interpreted as becomes the Majesty of that Spirit which dictated it; the profound Wisdom and Science of *Moses* who wrote it; the Natures of those things whose production is there deliver'd; lastly, so as may answer that form of delivery which it manifestly pretends to. For do but read it over, and then tell me whether it does not plainly aim at a Philosophical Method of completely teaching us the Natures and Order of God's universal Creation: and then apply the literal sense to this design, and see whether that alone does not infinitely fall short of it. Therefore necessarily some higher sense must also be added: which if it be so manag'd as to contain nothing but what is Great and True, answering the Title of the Sacred Story, and continuedly applicable to the Letter; I should not be very difficult to grant that this is the very thing intended by the Holy Spirit and his Pen-

Pen-man *Moses*. And that this hath been so done with all these Conditions observ'd, and that the *Praexistence of Souls* is found amongst the other noble Doctrines of that great Physiologer, *Moses*, I refer you for satisfaction to the most judicious and ingenious Essay of the learned Gentleman above-nam'd. This may serve to let you see that the Father had very probable Reasons for his Second Opinion.

His Third is this, That these præexisting Souls, through their Fault and Negligence, became Inhabitants of the Earth in Terrestrial Bodies.

Which Opinion he grounds upon these Considerations.

1. That that infinitely full Goodness, the first blessed Spring and Original of all things, communicated of himself in their production to all possible varieties and degrees of Life, which his essential and eternally-assistant Wisdom judg'd best for the things produc'd, and most fitting and decorous in it self, so as they might neither incommodate one another, nor yet be unhandsomely crowded together without due distance and discrimination of their Natures. In which long Chain of Life and Being, propagated from the highest to the lowest of all, from the most incorporeal Deity to Matter it self, 'tis not to be wonder'd at, nay, 'tis necessary, that many of the intermediate Essences should partake of both the Extremes, and so there be brought into light Spirits incorporate. But since few Spirits after the First and Best are of immutable Purity, and since every different degree of their changeable Purity is proportion'd to a correspondent degree of Purity in Matter; and since Matter is actually existent in the World according to all degrees of Purity, 'tis not to be wonder'd at neither, that the same individual Spirit, or same Order of Spirits, should be sometimes united with one sort of Matter, sometimes with another. But whatever happen'd to them afterwards through the Mutability of their Nature, we may be assur'd from that infinite Goodness which produc'd them, that they were at first join'd to the purest Matter, and plac'd in the best Regions of the World, that the highest Life and Purity of Essence they then had made them then fit for. The Souls of Men are one Order of these essentially-incorporate Spirits, as both their deep Immersion into Terrestrial Matter, the Modification of all their Operations by it, and the heavenly Body promis'd us in the Gospel, as the highest Perfection of our recover'd Nature, do sufficiently argue. And therefore if our Souls did exist before they appear'd Inhabitants of the Earth, the Sediment of the corporeal World, they did exist in a purer Element, to which an higher degree of Life and purer Operations, and consequently greater Happiness, did belong. Who then

then ſhould turn them out of that better condition, in which the Order and Courſe of Nature, and the internal Congruity of their own Eſſence had plac'd them? Certainly not He whoſe overflowing Goodneſs firſt brought them into Life and Being, and who, no doubt, in the firſt moment of their Exiſtence, ſet them to exerciſe thoſe Powers of Life he had given them, in thoſe Parts of the World as were moſt advantageous for the Happineſs they were capable of. And tho they ſhould through the Lapſability of their Nature fall from this eminent pitch of primitive Felicity, to a ſtate leſs happy and perfect: yet this State being not the loweſt and worſt of all, and that ſame Goodneſs which firſt made them, and always governs them, being undiminiſhable; it is almoſt as harſh to think he would precipitate them from this ſomething better condition into that which is the moſt miſerable of all, as that he did originally create them in ſuch a condition as was far worſe than what he then judg'd them capable of. And to think that any other external Cauſe could do it by Force and Violence, is very unphiloſophical, ſince there is an inward Maturation of vital Congruity to be firſt wrought, before they be ſo much as capable of uniting with this or that Element, much leſs of living in it as a Seat and Habitation of a durable Life. beſides, it ſeems inconſiſtent with that moſt wiſe and gracious Providence which governs the World, that any thing ſhould have a power of diſpoſing of any Being in it, παρὰ τὴν ἀξίαν. What then remains, but that through the faulty and negligent uſe of themſelves, whilſt they were in ſome better condition of Life, they rendred themſelves leſs pure in the whole Extent of their Powers, both Intellectual and Animal, and ſo by degrees became diſpos'd for the ſuſception of ſuch a degree of corporeal Life, as was leſs pure indeed than the former, but exactly anſwerable to their preſent diſpoſition of Spirit; ſo that after certain Periods of Time they might become far leſs fit to actuate any ſort of Matter than the Terreſtrial; and being originally made with a capacity to join with this too, and in it exerciſe the Powers and Functions of Life, it ſeems neceſſary, according to the Courſe of Nature, that they ſhould ſink into it, and ſo appear Terreſtrial Men? And that this is a very probable Cauſe of their becoming Inhabitants of the Earth, the learned Father thinks cannot be doubted, if we conſider the neceſſary Mutability in created Eſſences, the Freedom of Will in humane Souls, and the great Sympathy there is betwixt the Parts of the Soul, (for he, according to the *Platonick* Doctrine, thinks the Soul heterogeneous, and nothing is more eaſy than to prove ſhe is ſo.) For as he often inculcates, Goodneſs and Truth are not

Eſſential

Effential or Subftantial in thefe inferior Natures, fo as that they fhould be in a perpetual Contemplation of them, and under that moft happy Conftraint of never lofing the fight of their glorious Forms, and of never fwerving from their Laws; but do in a more accidental way belong unto them, and are efficacious in them only upon certain terms and conditions. From which imperfection of their Nature arifes the *αὐτεξούσιον*, (for this, in fome fenfe, is no perfection) and by the too great liberty of that power it eafily happens, that they obferve not thofe terms and conditions, being drawn away from a prefs and careful attendance to them, by converting to the delightful Motions of their congenite Bodies: which delight is both natural, and in fome degrees allow'd; but all corporeal Pleafure having fomething of Confufion and Difturbance in it, together with a ftrong magical Devocation of the Animadverfion to the fenfe of it, they might, in this dark huddle, eafily lofe the fight of thofe Bounds and Limits beyond which they ought not to proceed in the enjoyment of thofe Pleafures they reap from corporeal Life. For it is very hard for the Soul, under the prefent actual Fruition of what is delightful to her, and meeting with nothing in this her freer indulgency, which by its fharpnefs may check her, not to be tempted a little and a little further, fhe feeling a freedom in her accompanying this her fecret defire and inward prefages all along. This unwarrantable Liberty is not at firft fo free, while the Principle of the more divine and intellectual Life is more intire: but this by little and little is weakned by thofe Permiffions we make unto our felves, in favour of our natural Propenfions to corporeal Joy; and fo the fuperior Life extinguifhing by degrees, and the inferior more eagerly kindling, we rufh at laft, without Bounds and Meafure, to take our fill of thofe Pleafures, which the lawlefs Motions of the Body we are then united with, offer to our corrupted Senfe. But whatever Aberrations we make from the Laws of intellectual Life, the ill effect of them is not confin'd to that chief and principal part of our Soul wherein that Life is feated, but defcends from thence, and fpreads its impure Contagion through all the Seats of inferior Life, by reafon of that clofe Continuity which is in all the parts of the Soul. And whatever happens to her principal part, as the Centre of all the reft, does in a correfpondent manner affect thefe which ray from that: For as thefe, in their firft Emanation, were determinately fuch or fuch only, becaufe that from whom they proceeded was of fuch or fuch a degree of Purity and effential Power; fo in all the After-mutations which happen, they conftantly fympathize with one another. For if the inferior Parts of the Soul deftin'd unto her meaner Functions, do so punctually obey the most still and silent Volition or Imagination of that which is Supreme, as we plainly find they do in Passions and spontaneous Motion; what Wonder is it if the present Frame, Habit and Temper of that supreme Part (which is certainly more powerful than a single transient Command) does mould and form them into a suitable Temper with it self? And therefore if that Central part, by forsaking the Laws of a better Life, become so impure, that her Operations in this degenerate condition, would not exceed those which may be expected from an Understanding in conjunction with Earthly Matter; the parts Derivative will necessarily be chang'd into a correspondent Feculency, and so the whole Soul will sink into Terrestrial Matter, for which alone it is now fit, and by her Seminal Reasons, proper to this State, shape it into the Fabrick of a Terrestrial Man.

2. And the Father further thinks we ought not to wonder at any thing in this procedure, if we do but read and understand what the Holy Scripture teaches us of the sinning Angels; That they kept not their primitive Excellency, but left their proper Habitations in the Regions of heavenly Light, and are therefore bound ἐν πέδαις τοῦ ταρτάρω, with the Chains of fuliginous Air. For what greater Wonder is it that *aereal Genii* become Terrestrial Men, than *æthereal* Angels *aereal Dæmons*? But this parity of Reason is not all the assistance which *Origen* conceiv'd the Scripture afforded him in this Assertion. For the Sacred Story of *Man* in *Genesis* plainly describes a Transgression, for which he was turn'd out of Paradise, and became Mortal, as the Text says. Which History St. *Paul* carries further in his Epistle to the *Romans*, and says, That *as by one Man sin entred into the World, and by sin death and mortality; so also did this death and mortality go through all Men, because*, or *so far as, all have sinned*; or in his own words more elegantly, ὥσπερ δι' ἑνὸς ἀνθρώπου ἡ ἁμαρτία εἰς τὸν κόσμον εἰσῆλθε, καὶ διὰ τῆς ἁμαρτίας ὁ θάνατος· καὶ οὕτως εἰς πάντας ἀνθρώπους ὁ θάνατος διῆλθεν, ἐφ' ᾧ πάντες ἥμαρτον. And again to the *Corinth. As by Man death*— and, *As in Adam all die*—— By which places it appears that *Adam* sin'd, and as a consequent thereof became Mortal; his Sons also sin'd, and Mortality pervaded them too. Now who this Mortal *Adam* is, whose Image all that bear are likewise Mortal, the Apostle tells us in the same Chapter, to wit, ἄνθρωπος ἐκ γῆς, χοϊκός. Therefore we all become χοϊκοὶ, or Terrestrial Men by sin. But since we are such from our first coming into this World, and the fault must needs be before the consequents of it, that Sin and Transgression by which we became such, must be look'd for higher, or in some former State. I know this conclusion would not be thought by many

Men rightly deduc'd from these places of Scripture: but this ought to be no prejudice against it, if you but remember that the gainsayers are of two sorts of Divines; the one those who deny this Original and general Depravation of Mankind; the other those who ascribe all to the Will and Sovereignty, or mistaken Justice of God, upon occasion of the personal miscarriage of the First Man that dwelt upon this Earth. The first of these do manifest Violence (in my apprehension) to Scripture, and contradict Experience: the latter grosly pervert the Nature of Things, and rudely dishonour the Divine Attributes; as might with much ease be shewn, if I thought it necessary to your sagacious Judgment.

But lest I should expose this Doctrine of the Holy Father, we have been debating, to a suspicion of greater inconcinnity than as he himself asserted it; I am to give you notice (if I have not already sufficiently done it) that this passing of the Soul through several States of Life, and different Elements, is neither perform'd in a short time, nor ever descends so low as to destroy her Rational Nature, or put off Humane Form; both these are expresly deny'd by him. What the length of her better States of Life is, he only can truly judg who knows the internal Frame and Constitution of our Nature, and how vital every Congruity of Life is which he implanted in the Soul, or he who is a present Inhabitant in that State of which the question is ask'd. But for us Terrestrial Animals, so perfect an Oblivion hath seiz'd on us through the great Change we underwent in our descent hither, where we now are, (that I may name no other reason) that we are utterly disabled to make any certain Answer to so curious an Enquiry. Only upon that Hypothesis, that to every remarkable difference of Purity in the Essence of created Spirits, there is a difference in Matter exactly answering and fitted thereto; and by how much more pure they are, by so much more durable is their Life, as approaching nearer to, and more fully partaking of the first and purest Fountain of Life: Upon this Hypothesis, I say, we may probably guess that the ordinary duration of Aereal Life does as far exceed the common Limits of the Terrestrial, as the subtilty and tenuity of that Element does the coarseness of that Matter which the Soul does especially actuate in our Terrestrial Bodies; and the Aereal Period falls as far short of the Celestial, as the blended Atmosphere of the pure lucid *Æther*. But these are mere guesses, and let them go with you for no more. This only we know, what the Life of Man upon Earth commonly is in this Age of the World, and to what length it was drawn out in the days of old, when all the Elements were in their Spring and whole-

 some

ſome Verdure, and before the fiery Principle was grown ſo potent and copious as now it is; and the Goſpel aſſures us, that the days of the heavenly or æthereal Life are ſo numberleſs, that it is call'd Eternal. The other part of my Advertiſement was, That the Soul never deſcends below her rational Nature, and humane Form. Which I therefore take notice of, becauſe I perceive the Adverſaries of *Origen* have been ſomething forward to draw this into the heap of their Criminations, that he did hold the contrary. But the Father was not ſo ſlight a Contemplator as to believe the Truth of it; and knew better what was the meaning of the Fable in the *Pythagorick* Doctrine, and could not but have obſerv'd after what manner *Plato* talks of it in the Cloſe of his *Timæus:* who tho he do not (as far as I remember) call it a Fable; yet it is plain he handles it ſo careleſly, compar'd with the other parts of the Dialogue, that there is little doubt to be made but that he held it for one in the literal ſenſe. Which will be more probable, if you obſerve, that he in that excellent Dialogue does punctually follow the Method and Opinions of *Timæus Locrenſis* in his *De Anima Mundi*, who does expreſly call it Fabulous. Beſide, the learned Father, where he does mention it, diſertly affirms, that it is not an Opinion which he believes, but was propounded by him only for the *Copia* and variety of diſputation. And that he may not ſeem to have ſaid this in a colour, and cautiouſly for his own ſecurity, as St. *Jerome* very charitably would have him, he does in ſeveral places upon St. *Matthew*, and in his *contra Celſum*, dogmatically declare, that there is no ſuch μετενσωματώσεις.

His Fourth *Dogma* is, That the Myſtery of the Reſurrection is this, That we ſhall be cloth'd with heavenly or æthereal Bodies, properly ſo call'd, and in a phyſical ſenſe.

What is the Truth in this Opinion, muſt be learn'd from the Faith and Doctrine of the Goſpel, whereof it is ſo eminent an Article, the great βραβεῖον of our holy Faith and Obedience; and the whole Evangelical Myſtery, ſo far as it reſpects our Good and Advantage, is for the recovery of Mankind to this high pitch of Felicity: and the pious Father does moſt willingly reſolve his Belief in this Opinion, into the ſentence of thoſe infallible Writings. But that you may have a more orderly and demonſtrative Underſtanding of what they teach us in this matter, you are to recall to your Memory ſomething of what I have before diſcours'd out of the Father, that ſo you may with one View ſee how coherent his Speculations are, and how much they confirm, and are confirm'd, by the Doctrine of the Goſpel. We have out of him affirm'd, That the Souls of Men are Spirits eſſentially incorporate;

That such Spirits depend much in all their Operations on that Body they are united with; That the Elements of our Terrestrial composition are such as almost fatally intangle us in Vice, Passion and Misery; That these Souls did exist and act (for to what purpose else did they exist?) before they became visible Inhabitants of the Earth; That therefore they then had at least aereal Bodies; That the purer the Body is the Soul is united with, the purer, more perfect and happy is her Life and Operations; besides, that Supreme Goodness which made all things, assures us, that he made all things best at first: And therefore his recovery of us to our last Happiness (which is the design and purpose of the Gospel) must restore us to our better Bodies, and more happy Habitation. In the declaration of which recovery, if it be found that he promises us Celestial Bodies, 'twill be both according to what our Reason would expect in so gracious a design; and does also not obscurely intimate, that Earth was not the first Element wherein we did exist. Upon these Principles the Father establishes the present *Dogma*, some whereof we have already largely endeavour'd to prove; the rest are plain of themselves, and confess'd by all, or you know where to have the accurate proofs of them, if you think they can be doubted of: and therefore I shall leave you to make the best of them for the advantage of the Father's present Assertion, betaking my self to see what Scripture says in the business, after I have taken two Arguments in my way, which I shall offer to your consideration in a more careless and popular manner.

1. He that is a Christian and Disciple of the Son of God, hath given up himself to the Observation of such Laws as require of him perfect Holiness and Purity, universal Abstinence from all Wrong and Injustice, hearty and unfeigned Love and Good-will to all Mankind; and all this in the inward Affection of his Mind, so as that they become his Nature, and the very Life of his Spirit. He is by the Tenour of that Holy Institute to mortify every inordinate Affection, to be dead to the sense of bodily Delights, not to be carried away with Self-conceit, and the tickling Air of Fame and Honour from Men, not to be transported with Anger, to have no esteem of those things the World so much admires, and so eagerly pursues, Power and Wealth: but cut off from all things that are without, and perfectly commanding all the allow'd Motions and Desires of his Natural Spirit, he is solely to live the Life of God with intire Subjection to his Will. But do not all the World complain of the extreme difficulty of the Task? That it is as cruel to their imagination when they think of it, and as painful to their sense when they go about it, as the violent dis-

cision of their very Life would be, could it be forcibly torn in pieces? Not but their Minds are very well satisfy'd of the reasonableness and justness of such an undertaking, and their most inward Light cannot but pronounce, that the possession of that Life they are call'd to, by the Counsels and Exhortations of the Gospel, would be a State of most desirable Felicity: so that if the Law of their Mind had a perfect Sovereignty over the whole Man, the business was done. But alas! they are drawn away by the pleasing Force of the Magick of the Flesh, and in despite of all the Succour which their Mind, Reason and Conscience bring them, are willingly led Captive by an Enemy whom they love. This is the *Law in the Members*, whose very Nature is warring and opposition to the *Law of the Mind*: it is also call'd the Will, Sense, or *Affection of the Flesh*, which hath such an essential Enmity to God, and whatever is divine, that it can *by no means be made subject to his Law*. For the *Body of Death*, or the mortal Body, is, according to St. *Paul*, *sinful Flesh, in which dwells nothing that is good*, and the Law of it is the *Law of Sin and Death*. And that *Members*, *Flesh*, *Body*, *Death*, are to be taken plainly and literally, both St. *Paul*'s Discourse makes evident enough, and the Experience and Confessions of Men confirm; who palpably feel, that their Transgressing the Laws of God and the Mind, proceeds from the Motions of the Earthly Body they are cloth'd withal. Now these Motions being as natural to it as Descent is to heavy Bodies, and as necessarily affecting us with the Sense of Sin, as Fire does with Warmth and Heat; it follows, that our Establishment in a truly divine and sinless Life, which is the End of Christian Religion, cannot be effected but by our obtaining such a Body, as is farthest remov'd from the Nature of our present *Body of in*, that is, an heavenly or æthereal One.

2. You cannot but have observ'd, even in those who are Instructors of the People in Knowledg and Piety, Men otherwise learned, and of good capacity, a strange fatal proneness to such Opinions, as are as plainly repugnant and contradictious to the most easy and natural Ideas of our Mind, as any can be: which Opinions, many of them, are concerning such Subjects, whose Worth and Excellency should make us very careful what we think of them, and hugely tender that we pronounce nothing of them which is injurious or mean; as God, his Works, and Counsels, what is Holy, Righteous, Comely, Equitable, and the like: whose Natures rightly known, and according to Truth, bring the greatest Ease and Satisfaction, ineffable Peace and Quiet, and the most pure and inravishing delight that our Minds can receive from any knowledg whatever, and govern all the Purposes and Enter-

prizes

prizes of our Soul, all the Actions of our Lives consistently, quicken and encourage us to all growth and progress in Vertue, and whatever is good and laudable, and with unshaken Firmitude support our Hope, that our Labours shall not be in vain; lastly, which are also with abundant Clearness defined in those holy Oracles, which we all believe infallible. Whence is it then, that all that Light which should direct us to the Truth of such Objects, is not seen? That we are so easily content to want all that Pleasure and Peace arising from the Knowledg of their Truth; and patiently endure to live, act, and expect at random, without any sufficient Grounds, or coherency of Reason? If the Souls of Men were Essentially unlike one another, or the Ideas of Truth were not every-where the same, my Wonder would quickly cease: nay, if these erring Persons were but affected with their odd Conceits in that moderate degree of Prejudice which Authority is apt to beget in us, where we respect the Man who first deliver'd them to us, I could be content to look for the Reason of this *Phænomenon* in the modesty and humble deference of the Mind it self: but when I see them believe such gross Errors with such eagerness of Spirit, and with so settled an Affection, and from a congruity and sympathy of vital disposition, I am at a loss to find the Cause any where but in the complexional Impurity of their Earthly Bodies; whose foul Steams mixing with, and infecting that subtile Instrument the Soul uses in all her Senses and Perceptions, and by which all her Operations are modified, condemn them fatally to such gross Mistakes, and to an utter Insensibility of the contrary Truths, so long as they are condemn'd to see nothing but through such a coarse Medium, and to labour for Truth with such unqualify'd Instruments. And knowing that not only Vertue and Piety, but also Truth and Knowledg are the natural Accomplishments of the Soul, I conclude according to the Father, That that complete Perfection, which by the warrant of the Gospel we hope for in the Resurrection, cannot be wrought in us, unless we be possess'd of such a Body, whose Purity of Temper will be as subservient to Truth, as I find the Terrestrial one an hindrance thereto.

3. I said at the beginning of this *Dogma*, That the Truth of it must be decided by the Testimony of Holy Scripture, whereof it is so important a part, and that the Holy Father is most ready to be concluded by its decision; therefore, in the third place, he argues from thence. You know St. *Paul*, in his first Epistle to the *Corinthians*, hath a Discourse on purpose concerning the *Resurrection*; from thence therefore, if any where, we may very well hope to find a determination of the matter

in hand. The Apoſtle in that moſt excellent and learned Diſcourſe, having firſt prov'd the Reſurrection of our Ever-bleſſed Lord and Saviour, comes at laſt to anſwer the Objections of ſome incredulous or miſinform'd Men in that Church, which he gives us in theſe words, *How are the dead raiſed up? and with what bodies do they come?* In which, if there be any ſenſe or force to make it worthy of an Anſwer from the Apoſtle, it muſt be this, or ſome ſuch like; How is it poſſible that thoſe Bodies ſhould riſe again and be joyn'd to the Souls that formerly actuated them, which we ſee rotted in the Grave, diſſolv'd into Duſt, and ſcatter'd over the Face of the Earth, or evaporated into Air, and diſpers'd as far aſunder poſſibly as the Heaven is wide, and undergo Ten thouſand ſeveral Tranſmutations, and are adopted into as many ſeveral Bodies, whether Animals or others? To which the Apoſtle anſwers, not by ſaying the Power of God is infinite, and his Knowledg infinitely diſtinct, ſo as he can find out and recollect all thoſe wandring Atoms, and of them recompoſe that Building which once they made: but by calling firſt the Objector fool, for ſo groſly miſtaking the Queſtion, as if the Chriſtians expected the ſame individual Body, made of the ſame numerical Particles of Matter, which his Objection ſuppoſes; whenas their Doctrine of the *Reſurrection* is ſomewhat like that of a grain of Corn, which muſt firſt die before any thing ſpring of it, and that which does ſpring up from its Death, is another thing from that which was ſown and died. And then, Secondly, by further informing him, that the differences of Body and Matter are far more numerous than he takes notice of; ſo that it is ſo far from being neceſſary, that we ſhould have the ſame individual Bodies, that there is no neceſſity we ſhould have Bodies of the ſame ſort or kind: for the World is better ſtor'd than ſo, and contains Celeſtial Bodies as well as Terreſtrial, of different Worth and Excellency; and that God who gives us a Body as it pleaſes him, is graciouſly pleaſed to give us one in the Reſurrection of that kind which is moſt Excellent and Glorious, *viz.* Heavenly and Spiritual: and that tho we have born the *Image of the Earthly Adam*, having an Earthly Body as he had, yet it is not neceſſary we ſhall always do ſo; for there is an Heavenly *Adam* too, the *Lord*, whoſe *Image we ſhall bear*, having an heavenly and ſpiritual Body as he hath. And leſt we ſhould miſtake what he meant by *Earthly* and *Heavenly*, *Animal* and *Spiritual Bodies*, and transfer theſe words to Diſpoſitions in the Soul, or uſe them improperly any other way, to the countenancing any groſs or ſlow conceit, he gives us a key of his meaning by this plain and down-right Affirmation, That *Fleſh and Blood* (a Phraſe well known to ſignify the

the *Earthly Body*, and for its ſake *a Man in ſuch a Body)* cannot come to Heaven, or *the Kingdom of God*; for it is impoſſible that ſuch a Body, which is in its intrinſecal Nature corruptible, ſhould become incorruptible, or be fit to inherit incorruption. And further, you may poſſibly not think it a Remark altogether impertinent, that if the Apoſtle had been of the Mind of *Origen*'s Adverſaries, it would be very hard to imagine why he ſhould give ſo long, ſo diſtinct and particular an Anſwer to the Queſtion. For it may ſeem more ſuitable to the Authority of ſo great a Perſon, when captiouſly ask'd, *With what Bodies do they come?* roundly to have anſwer'd, *With the ſame they left behind them.*

Another Argument out of the ſame Apoſtle may be, that in his ſecond Epiſtle to the ſame *Corinth. For we know, that if our earthly Houſe of this Tabernacle was diſſolved, we have a building from God, an Houſe not made with hands, eternal in the Heavens. For in this we groan, earneſtly deſiring to be clothed upon with our Houſe which is from Heaven.* Where are plainly deſcrib'd two ſeveral Houſes, or Bodies, quite different one from the other in their Materials, Duration, and Benefit to the Inhabitant: the one is call'd *Earthly*, and a Tabernacle which ſhall be diſſolv'd, wherein we groan through the burdenſomneſs of it; the other *Heavenly*, and *Eternal*, and hugely advantageous and deſirable to us: the former Characters deſigning the Body we have here upon Earth, the latter that which we expect hereafter in Heaven. So that unleſs any thing may be any thing, and the ſame thing while the ſame be quite another thing, it is not poſſible but that that Body we look for in Heaven, or at the Reſurrection, ſhould be a quite different thing from that Body of Fleſh and Blood we are now clothed with, ſince it hath ſuch different Properties. For unleſs the coarſe Concretion of Earth, as Earth can be as liquid as *Æther*, or Heavenly Matter, and that which is in its own nature diſſoluble, be eternal, and be actually diſſolv'd only to be ſet together again, or that we groan through the Oppreſſion of that weight which we earneſtly deſire to be burdened with again, the Body which we have here cannot (according to the Apoſtle) be that which we hope to have hereafter. And all the Properties of the former Body will, from its eſſential Contexture, neceſſarily adhere to it wherever it be, and the Properties of the latter are the moſt genuine Reſults of æthereal Purity; ſo that if St. *Paul*, by the Building we are to have from God, by the *Houſe not made with hands*, deſcribes that Body God will give us in the Reſurrection of the Juſt, he ſays the ſame with the Holy Father, That the Myſtery of that happy Time and Change is this, That we ſhall then be clothed with heavenly or æthereal Bodies.

This

This is ſufficient for the proof of this Aſſertion out of Scripture: yet if you pleaſe you may over and above make trial, whether any convenient ſenſe can be made of thoſe ſo very frequent Phraſes of a *mortal* body, a *corruptible* body, a body of *death*, a *vile* body, an *inglorious* and *infirm* body, a *dead* body, the *fleſh of Sin*, and the like; if ſuch bodies may be incorruptible, immortal, eternally living, never to die more, refulgent with lucid Glory, like the Body of Chriſt, who is the *Adam* ἐπȣράνιος, in the ſame ſenſe that the other *Adam* was χοϊκὸς; and laſtly, be the Inſtruments of perfect Purity, Righteouſneſs and Holineſs. I perſuade my ſelf you will find it an hard Task to reconcile ſuch diſcordant Attributes. But to ſay, that whatever the Bodies we have upon Earth be in their own nature, God by his Omnipotent Power can make them ſuch as the Goſpel promiſes they ſhall be at the Reſurrection, and keep them by his Almighty Hand from Death or Decay, is to ſay, that Miracles are very cheap with him; nay further, it is to ſay, that God, where he intends us a benefit, will work a perpetual Miracle to keep us in a worſe ſtate than we might arrive to by the ordinary Laws, and Courſe of Nature. For it is demonſtrable from Philoſophy and Apparitions, that an aereal Body will neceſſarily fall to our ſhare upon the quitting of this we have; and where the Soul is more than ordinarily advanc'd in the progreſs of an holy and vertuous Life, that aereal Body of hers will be in great diſpoſition to an æthereal Purity: ſo that if the Providence of God would not interpoſe her ſelf, but leave things in that ſtate they come to by her eternal Laws, it would be much better for ſo perfect Souls to ſtay where they are, than to be again clothed with Fleſh and Blood. For this is plainly to climb downwards, and with pretence of Courteſy to remand the releas'd Man to his Priſon and Chains. And it is very childiſh to think, that Fleſh and Blood made gay without, by I know not what imagin'd Light and Glory, is one pin the better for it: For if the Houſe be ruinous in the Materials and Make of it, and ſluttiſh and unclean within, all the external Painting and Pargetting imaginable can neither ſecure the Inhabitants from its Fall, nor make their Dwelling one jot more wholeſome. The Moon, as bright as ſhe looks, is as very an Earth as this we tread on, contemn, and deſire to leave. But as hard as you will find it to make ſenſe of thoſe Phraſes above-nam'd, which characterize our Earthly Body, if this Earthly Body is to come to Heaven; juſt ſo eaſy and natural are the oppoſite Expreſſions which deſcribe that Heavenly Body, which ſhall certainly come thither. For both the Duration of it, its refulgent Glory, and its eximious Subſerviency to all Purity, Righteouſneſs and Truth, do as properly belong to a Body of æthereal Purity; and this only, as any natural Effect whatever, to its true and specifick Cause, as a very little Skill in Philosophy would satisfy any Enquirer. And what greater Assurance can any Man have, that he understands any thing he reads, than evidently to see that the Words are fit and apposite, and the very same that all Men use who write or speak perspicuously, and the Things asserted such as exactly answer to the Nature of Things?

Having Scripture so plainly on our side (for so for *decorum* sake I must speak, plainly the part of an *Origenist*) I think I may be bold to expostulate with the Adversaries, and ask them what it is they seek by their so eagerly-defended Fleshly Body, and what is the prop of their tenacious Confidence? For 'tis plain that we are nothing, and are concern'd in nothing more than what we are conscious of, feel and perceive; That the Soul alone is the Subject of all Sense, Perception, Memory, and Affections; That what she perceives by, is neither the Flesh nor Blood, no, nor the Brains themselves, nor any other gross part of our Bodies, but that purer and subtiler Matter in us which is call'd *Animal Spirits*; That if the Soul be an immaterial Substance, distinct from the Body, 'tis as easily conceiv'd, nay more easily, how she should unite with an whole Vehicle of such pure Matter, as with her whole Terrestrial Body; especially she giving us, even in this Body, a *Specimen* of that Capacity of hers, by being in her highest degree of Vitality united with some portion of that Matter already. What is it then that they expect from the most refin'd Flesh and Blood they can imagine, which they may not have with Usury and Advantage in a Body of purer Consistence? or what is the Scruple that makes them so backward in admitting such a Body? To the former Question I make no doubt they can answer nothing which will not be gross and ridiculous. To the latter I know they will say, that the Scripture says otherwise: we shall see that more particularly at the fifth Query. In the mean time consider, O ye fond Doaters on Flesh and Blood, what we have already produc'd out of that Sacred Treasury of Truth, contrary to your dull Pretensions: and further call to mind, that as Scripture calls those Bodies we hope for in the Resurrection of the Just, *Celestial* and *Spiritual*, and terms the place of our Abode at that blessed time, the Kingdom of Heaven, and the Inheritance in Light; so Philosophy and Astronomy can demonstrate, that the Matter of that happy Place is mere Light, and liquid Spirit or Æther. Why then do you pretend misinterpreted Scripture contrary to all Reason, Philosophy, and your own Benefit, against Scripture; having Philosophy, and your Advantage on its side? And since

our

our present Bodies, by which we are Inhabitants of the Earth, are of a Terrestrial Concretion, and consist of such Matter which arises from the Earth, and which after all its Transmutations, Elutriations and Filtrations in the Body, is not purg'd from the coarse Tincture it had from its Earthly Original; and since the Scripture says that Angels, the Inhabitants of Heaven, are Spirits, and a Flame of Fire, and are call'd Angels of Light, as Heaven it self is Light and Fire, and appear always in a lucid Form, and that the Devils or Dæmons are the Inhabitants of the Air (whom the Stories of Apparitions, and the Confessions of Witches, plainly prove to have Bodies of Air) what Crossness and Madness is it to believe we shall be Fellow-Citizens of the Angels in the Kingdom of Heaven, and have such a Body as the Apostle calls Heavenly and Spiritual, and yet to interpret that word *Heavenly* otherwise than in relation to the Subtilty and Tenuity of the Matter of Heaven? But to leave these φιλοσάρκεις, and let you further see that St. *Paul* did not only sit at the Feet of *Gamaliel*, (from whom Mr. *Gregory* conceives he learn'd the Analogy between the germination of a Grain of Corn, and the Resurrection of the Body) but had also been admitted into the *Pythagorick* ὁμακοεῖον, or rather that both he and the Divine *Pythagoras* were taught by the same Spirit of Truth and Holy Knowledg; I will give you a taste of that great Congruity of Phrase there is in the Delivery of their Doctrine. And not to trouble you with many Authors of that way, I will content my self with *Hierocles* in his Commentary on the *Golden Verses*, as they are call'd. The body of Flesh we have here upon Earth, he, with St. *Paul*, calls θνητὸν and ψυχικὸν· that which the pure and perfected Spirits in Heaven have he with him calls πνευματικὸν, as also φωτεινὸν and αὐγοειδές, which plainly answer to St. *Paul's* σῶμα τῆς δόξης· he likewise terms it ἀθάνατον, and ἀΐδιον, and αἰθέριον, which is exactly the same with St. *Paul's having put on Immortality, and Eternal, and Heavenly.* He says likewise, that in order to our Heavenly Journy, we must first τὴν τοῦ θνητοῦ σώματος φύσιν ἀποδύσασθαι, and that the σῶμα ψυχικὸν cannot ascend εἰς τὸν αἰθέριον τόπον. What is this, but that *Flesh and Blood cannot inherit the Kingdom of God?* And again,——τοῦ θνητοῦ ἡμῶν σώματος, ἐν ᾧ τὸ αὐγοειδὲς ἔγκειται προσπνέον τῷ ἀψύχῳ σώματι ζωήν. ζωὴ γὰρ ἐστι τὸ ἄϋλον σῶμα. Than which it is not possible to find a better Comment upon that of St. *Paul*——*Cloth'd upon with our House which is from Heaven, that Mortality might be swallow'd up of Life.* Again,——τὸ θνητὸν ἡμῶν σῶμα ἐκ τῆς ἀλόγου ζωῆς καὶ τοῦ ὑλικοῦ σώματος συγκείμενον, εἴδωλον ὂν τοῦ ἀνθρώπου, ὃς ἐκ λογικῆς οὐσίας καὶ σώματος ἀΰλου συνέστηκεν· St.

Paul's

Paul's outward and inward man, the Earthly and the Heavenly *Adam.* He ſays alſo that the Spiritual Vehicle of the Soul being perfected and purged from all material Unvitalneſs or Mortality, and the lucid Body being rendred pure and defecate, we are then fit to be admitted into the Company and Converſe of the pure Spirits which have æthereal Bodies, and are then arriv'd to the Angellick Nature; which in the Words of Scripture is, *But ye are come to the City of the Living God, the Heavenly* Jeruſalem, *to an innumerable Company of Angels, and to the Spirits of juſt men made perfect.*——*They are equal to the Angels, and are the Children of God* [θεοὶ in *Hierocl.*] *being the Children of the Reſurrection.*——*If by any means I might attain to* the Reſurrection of the Dead. *Not as if I had already attain'd, or was already perfected.* Laſtly, that I draw the Parallelism no further, in this Theory of Bodies he uſes the Words of ἐπεγείρειν and ἀναβιώσκεσθαι. I need not tell you, much leſs ſhew you, that he does not uſe ſuch Words alone. I ſhall trouble you with no more Examples, theſe being ſufficient, and clear, and appoſite enough (chiefly ſome of the firſt of them, which I eſpecially intended) to ſhew you the Agreement in Stile between St. *Paul* and *Hierocles.* Now the uſe I make of it is this: 'Tis notoriouſly known that the *Pythagorick* or *Platonick* Doctrine concerning the different ſtates of Spirits incorporate, is the ſame with *Origen*'s; and that the Words and Phraſes they uſe to expreſs the different nature of the Body by they are cloth'd with, are as fit and proper (if their Doctrine be true) as any that can be invented, is plain to every one that underſtands the uſe of Words. Now that St. *Paul* ſhould uſe the ſame in the ſame Matter and Argument, yet not in the ſame ſenſe, but a quite different one, is the moſt unlikely thing in the World; and beſides, renders all Endeavours of finding his Senſe and Meaning utterly fruſtrate, or deſperately uncertain. But if St. *Paul* us'd them in the ſame ſenſe with thoſe Philoſophers, then it is manifeſt that *Origen*'s Doctrine of the Reſurrection is the ſame with St. *Paul*'s, and therefore infallibly true. There is a reverend Doctor of our Church of eximious Piety and Learning (and long may he live to be a Light in this perverſe Generation, and the Envy of thoſe that are Adverſaries and Afflicters of our dear Mother) whom I have heard to be of Opinion, that this *Hierocles*, of whom we have been ſpeaking, was a Chriſtian; and who intends to increaſe the number of his learned and uſeful Writings, with a Diſſertation to prove the ſame. If this Report of him be true, I make no doubt but amongſt other Arguments which have perſuaded him to entertain this Paradox, the great Agreement in Doctrine and Phraſe betwixt the holy

Penmen

Penmen of Scripture and that Author, is not the leaſt. But to the verifying of my Conjecture, you muſt expect, till that reported Work of his ſee the Light.

I come now to the Father's Fifth Opinion, which is this, That after long Periods of Time, the Damned ſhall be deliver'd from their Torments, and try their Fortunes again in ſuch Regions of the World as their Nature and preſent Diſpoſition fits them for.

There are in ſome Men's Minds wonderful high reaches at great and unuſual Objects; that diſpoſition of Soul, whence ſuch extraordinary Offers proceed, you may not unproperly call the Magnificence of the Intellect, which often hath ſomething of Temerity in it, as the Moral Vertue of that Name not ſeldom hath ſome touch of Ambition. But as we are very favourable to this, and apt to pardon its ſmaller Extravagances for the ſake of thoſe high Deſigns and eminent Works to which they adhere; ſo by the ſame Reaſon and Juſtice ought that other to be candidly ſentenc'd by us when it ſeems to ſlip, becauſe of thoſe rais'd and concerning Diſcoveries it makes where it lights right and happily; eſpecially where it ſeems to have been betray'd by a forward and pious Endeavour of doing Honour to God. Which is *Origen*'s Caſe here, of whom his greateſt Adverſaries cannot in reaſon but confeſs, that the Error they conceive him fallen into, in this Opinion, proceeded from his over-great Solicitude of rendring the ways of Providence clear, righteous and benign. Yet this, as ſtrange as it looks, hath its Probabilities too, as well as the former. For he look'd upon God as making all things for their Good and Benefit, with this gracious Deſign, that they might be happy according to their Place and Order in the infinite Orb of Beings. Some whereof would neceſſarily be ſo far remov'd from the Stability of his bleſſed and immutable Perfection, that he plainly foreſaw and wondred not at their future Change and Deſcent from their Original Integrity; which tho it would not happen to them without their own fault, yet his moſt juſt and righteous Eyes could not but more favourably look upon the Miſcarriage, ſince it proceeded ſomewhat from that Incompoſſibility which his own hands had wrought in their Eſſential Contexture, and from a too free and careleſs uſe of ſuch natural Powers, and Enjoyment of ſuch Delights, as he himſelf had made and permitted to them in due Bounds and Meaſures. For it ſeems true and not diſhonourable to God, that Sin it ſelf proceeds from no Power of the Sinner's own making, neither is the Pleaſure of it from any Sutableneſs and Congruity which he deviſ'd; for he finds them both made ready to his hand; only he was ſo careleſs and

unhappy

unhappy as to transpose things from their due Places, and make such Combinations of them as were to his own damage in the Event, and such as were not primarily intended by that most wise and benevolent Mind which made and order'd all things to the best they were capable of. That Eternal Mind therefore making all things out of a Principle of infinite Love, and for the Good and Happiness of the Things themselves, and seeing what he had made, and how he had made them, and what was likely to be the Lot of some of them from the necessary Unperfectness of their Natures, if their future ill hap was like to be infinitely more sharp and dolorous, than all the good they should enjoy from him till that Calamity befel them, grateful and pleasant, his great Compassion certainly would have persuaded him quickly to annihilate them; or rather his Wisdom would have judg'd it more decorous never to have made them. For assuredly he needed them not in any respect, least of all as they were miserable. But we see such mutable Creatures made, and hear nothing of their Annihilation (as indeed it would be very strange we should; for this would be as much as to say, God had made such Beings as he could not continue in Being with Consistency with his own Attributes; that I may not add that possibly such was the manner of the production of all things, as makes Annihilation impossible) therefore we may be assur'd there are such Reserves in his most wise and gracious Providence, as will both vindicate his Sovereign Goodness and Wisdom from all just Disparagement, and take such Course with, and so dispose of all his Creatures, as they shall never be but in such a Condition, which, all things consider'd, will be far more eligible than never to have been. Amongst which Ways and Dispositions of Providence, wherein his Wisdom, Rectitude and Mercy all concur, Punishment is not the least, nor unprofitable to be punish'd. And this sharper kind of Favour hath a very just and righteous Place in such Creatures as are by Nature mutable. For this natural Mutability pass'd not into an actual Declination from their better Principles of Life without their Fault, and suffering a Possibility of being worse to prevail above an actual Power of continuing better. And therefore Providence hath interwove in the Natures of Things, and all States and Conditions of Life, such Acerbities and Incommodities, as may give check to them when they are descending lower than they ought, and seasonably remind them of the better Condition they have left. But if this gentler Smart and Uneasefulness will not reclaim them, but they for all that still further pursue forbidden and uncertain Pleasures, and think them not dearly bought, tho mix'd with Bitterness;

yet

yet we are not ſtraight to conclude that Providence hath given them over either as utterly unfit for her Care and Diſcipline, or degenerated beyond her power of Cure and Emendation. For beſide her ordinary and natural ways of Nurture and Correction, ſhe can and will, when it ſeems fit or neceſſary, with a ſeverer hand ſcourge theſe Rebels to her gentler Laws, and Contemners of her milder Rebukes. And ſuch will be that Day of fiery Vengeance, when the inferior Elements of Nature ſhall melt with fervent Heat, the Earth and all the Works thereon be burnt up, and the Air be fill'd with ſuffocating Smoke which ſhe ſhall ſend up from her inflam'd Entrails. Into which far-ſpreading Lake of ſlow-conſuming Fire and ſulphureous Stench, the unreclaimable Devils, and obſtinately wicked Men ſhall be by the righteous hand of God precipitated. A ſad pitiable Fate, and Torture unſufferable! but no doubt as juſt as great. Juſt, I ſay, not only according to the Eſtimation of modern Theology (which from an Exceſs of Complement to the Juſtice of God, becomes almoſt as rude and troubleſom as the Aſs in the Fable, who did not fawn upon, but invade his Maſter, and which tragically pronounces that the leaſt Peccadillo highly deſerves the greateſt Puniſhment conceivable) but alſo in the Compute and Judgment of that all-righteous Mind, which judges and orders all things by the living Law of Equity. But what tho it be ſo great and juſt? is it therefore ſo quite different from the reaſon of all other Puniſhments inflicted by God or Man, that there is nothing in it of that End for which they are inflicted? They are Curative, and for the Emendation of the Party ſuffering; but this, if it be Eternal, in the Scholaſtick Senſe of the Word, leaves no place for the bettering of the Sufferers, who are never to get out of this inexplicable Labyrinth of Woe and Miſery. Or becauſe this exceeds all other Puniſhments imaginable, muſt it alſo ſo infinitely tranſcend the very Meaſures and Proportions of this kind of diſtributive Juſtice? If not, why ſhould we think that the Pain and Smart of it ſhall be infinitely great and long, when the Pleaſure reap'd by the Tranſgreſſion which brought the Puniſhment is not in any degree equal; and when a ſhorter Torture may make the Puniſh'd change their Mind, or leave it very probable they would do ſo, were they out of their Torture, and in an Opportunity to ſhew it? And to imagine that God ſuffers any real Injury and Detriment from the Tranſgreſſions of a peccable Creature, which muſt (ſay they) be infinite, becauſe he is ſo, and therefore deſerve a Puniſhment in all reſpects infinite, is to talk of God very meanly, and too much after the manner of Men; and to ſet ſuch a Rule for the meaſuring the Demerit of a Fault by, as will make all Sins equal, and which they themſelves confeſs will not univerſally hold good towards any Perſon beſide God, and therefore may be juſtly ſuſpected to be a falſe one. Now to think theſe miſerable Souls are ſo far amiſs as to be beyond the Power of all Redreſs and Reſtitution, is to ſuppoſe God made ſome of his Creatures very untowardly; and that when he pronounc'd they were all very good, he look'd only upon the Primitive State they were in when they came freſh out of his gracious Hands, and was ſo taken with that, that he omitted to caſt his all-comprehenſive Eyes to all poſſible Conditions they might afterward fall into. For certainly if he had done ſo, and ſeen this never-to-be-ended doom of intolerable Pain and Anguiſh of Body and Mind, the infinite Compaſſionateneſs of his bleſſed Nature would ſcarcely have given ſo chearful an approbation to the Works of his Hands. For none of them are good to him as advantaging him ought; and thoſe of them he foreſaw would be ſo remedileſly calamitous as this Hypotheſis ſuppoſes, would have been ſo far from being good as to themſelves, that it would have been the greateſt Favour God could do them, never to have brought them into Being. But then to think they are not beyond the Power of Redreſs and Recovery, and that that great Puniſhment they ſhall undergo in the end of this World may contribute much thereto; and yet to imagine they ſhall for all this their better Diſpoſition be ſtill kept in it for ever and ever, is to fix ſo harſh a Note upon the Mercy and Equity of the righteous Judg of all the World, that the ſame Temper in a Man we ſhould for ever execrate and abominate. And that they are in a poſſibility of being better, if God ſo pleaſe and do not purpoſely hinder it, is not improbably concluded by the Father from hence, That Sin, wherein they are ſo obdurately ſettled, tho it hath extinguiſh'd or ſilenc'd the Divine Life in them, and for the preſent ſubjected them only to the Senſe, Reliſh and Exerciſe of the Natural or Animal; yet it hath left them their Reaſon and Underſtanding, ſuch as it is, Conſideration and Memory, which like mercenary Soldiers will fight on either ſide, and incline to and ſerve that Life which is moſt powerful: If therefore the vigorous Alliciency of the brutiſh Nature be abated, thoſe Powers will liſten to better Counſels, and reſume the Seeds and Inchoation of a better Life and Nature. And certainly a ſearching ceaſleſs Pain, ſpreading thro Soul and Body, will ſo abate and conſume all that Joy they formerly took in their brutiſh Rebellion, that any Offer of Releaſe will be welcome to them now the Tumult and Hurry of their former Luſts and eager Affections is ſlack'd, which alone before made them uncapable of better Advice; and their close-adhering Pain, which sticks to them and scorches them worse than *Hercules*'s Shirt, should methinks necessarily force them to take up strong and peremptory Resolutions and Indignation against those Courses whose Fruits they now feel so direful to them. What is it then that should make the merciful Governor of Heaven, and Earth, and Hell too, the compassionate Father of Spirits, either forcibly to keep off and prevent this natural course of things; or, which is worse, suffer those Offers and Preparations which it induces for the bettering the present Condition of so great and so considerable a part of his Creation, and for the putting of them in a way of return to what he at first made them, to come to nought? If we look but into the natural World, we shall find that no Disposition of Matter to the Susception of Life is rendred void and frustrate; but that there is always ready at hand so fruitful a Principle, as perfects and completes whatever is presented to its further Vivification: and yet this Principle is but the brute obscure shadow of that Almighty Goodness and exuberant Life which actuates and manages the moral and intellectual World. Surely then no Preparation happens here which is not carry'd onwards as far as it is capable; especially since this may be done, and yet these miserable Souls we are speaking of, pay soundly for their rebellious Transgressions by a very long, exceedingly great and intolerable Torture both of Body and Mind. And indeed by how much greater it is, by so much surer may we be that it will sometimes have an end by the necessity of Nature. *Si gravis, brevis*, takes place here too; for it being unconceivable how the Soul should suffer any Pain or Torture but by the harsh and discordant Motions of the Body wherewith she is vitally united, if this Union ever cease, she will become senseless; and this Union being conditional upon certain Terms on both sides, and the Conditions being such as are not necessarily at all times present to either of them, it may very well be thought that it may be dissolv'd. For if the Induction of an unnatural Foulness and Impurity, or an over-vehement agitation into the Blood and Spirits and other fluid Parts of the Body, if old Age it self can make the Soul quit her unfit Tenement; what shall we think she will do when it is all on fire, when all the Motions of it are but one continu'd great Pain? Which Disposition of Body, when come to its height by long Continuance, is certainly far more contrary to that vital Temper the Soul requires in the Body she will livingly join with, than either Coarseness of Blood or Consumption of animal Moisture. For as if an actually-perceiv'd Pleasure was that which tempted and drew out the Soul to join with her Body, no Man would ſay ſhe would ever unite with that Body; from whoſe croſs Conſtitution ſhe ſhould be affected with nought but Pain; ſo where that Congruity in her which diſpoſes her to that Union is more deeply pitch'd in her imperceptive Powers, a Man would be apt to think nevertheleſs that ſhe could not vitally take hold of any Body from Conjunction, with which ſhe ſhould after feel no Motions, but ſuch as would torture her. And we may eaſily perſuade our ſelves, that that Diſpoſition of Body which will not prolicite the Soul to join with it when ſhe is free, and her unfelt Appetite catching, cannot for ever tie her to it when forc'd upon her by her ſad Fate. And the Matter ſhe is then ſurrounded with being all of that unvital Temper, it ſeems neceſſary that ſhe ſhould ceaſe from all Life and Senſe. So that whitherſoever we look, whether to the gracious Providence of God, or the Neceſſity of the nature of things, we find ſome probable hope that the Puniſhment of the Damned, as it implies the ſenſe of Pain, ſhall not be eternal in the higheſt ſenſe of the Word. And the Scripture too may ſeem to favour us, in that it calls this dreadful doom by the name of *Eternal Death*, which one would think did very ſtrangely ſet out that State and Condition wherein is the higheſt and moſt pungent ſenſe; but it does very appoſitely expreſs the ſenſe of *Origen*'s Hypotheſis, explain'd after the latter and more probable way. But whether their Releaſe be by any change wrought in the Diſpoſition of their Spirits, but without Death, or whether by an Eſcape as it were by Dying to the Body ſo tortur'd, there is no doubt to be made but that both ways they may come into play again, and try their Fortunes once more in ſuch Regions of the World as Providence judges fit for them. For all things were made that they might have their Being; and ſuch of them as are capable of Life and Senſe, and yet never exerciſe it, had as good not be at all, for they would be uſeleſs both to themſelves and others: but certainly there never were, nor ever will be ſuch things in the World, which was created and is govern'd by that Eternal Mind, which does nothing fooliſhly and in vain. And tho that raging Fire which will, in the conſummation of all things, ſeize upon the Earth, will render it and the adjoining Atmoſphere unhabitable for the preſent; yet that this ruinous Defacement of Things will extend thro the whole Compaſs of Nature, is neither the Belief of Chriſtians, nor the Aſſertion of ſuch Philoſophers as were thro their Skill in the Conſtitution of the World fit to judg of ſuch Theories. And therefore if any Man can conceive any of theſe Souls which ſhall be puniſh'd in that ſulphurous Lake, fit to emerge out of it, he need not be at a loſs for Habitations

tions for them elsewhere. But if the other way be more probable, that there is no getting out but by Death, which is rather a Dying in it; yet since they therefore only die, because the Matter all about them is then such as they cannot livingly unite with it, tho their radical Principles of Vitality are still safe and unperishable; and since that Matter which for the present is so deadly, is as capable as ever of such Modifications as are vital and healthful, and will even by the Course of Nature, after long Periods of time, settle again into such a wholesome Temper; What should hinder but that these punish'd Souls, whom long vexing Pain drove from all Commerce with Matter, and cast them into a senseless Sleep, will after their long Inactivity awake again into Life and Action, when all things are become so fresh and fit to receive them? For if Providence hath been so favourable as to establish so gracious an Order in the Nature and Course of Things, as will lead those miserable Spirits to a Release at last, she certainly will not be unwilling that they should live again, when all things conspire to give them Life, and they continue capable of receiving it. But I am stepping, methinks, before I was aware, into the sixth and last Opinion of the learned Father, which is this:

That the Earth after her Conflagration shall become habitable again, and be the Mansion of Men and other Animals, and this in eternal Vicissitudes.

The Philosopher in his Politicks says, those Instruments are the best contriv'd, and do their Work best, which serve but one Effect and End. But surely it is an Argument of a larger and more comprehensive Wisdom, to make one and the same thing serve to several good Purposes; as we see Providence hath done both in the Bodies of particular Animals, and also of that great and universal one, the World. And the same Course she takes in the Conflagration of the Earth; for that one Fire will be the just and salutary Punishment of rebellious Spirits, and the Restoration of the Earth grown old and effete, unto an healthful genital Strength and Verdure. And so wonderfully sportful is she (as I may so speak with reverence) in the Government of the World, and the Ascents and Descents of her great Wheel are so unexpected, and so seemingly unlike one another (yet the same Hand and Counsel turns all, and to the same End) that that very Region of the World, and the Face of Things in it, which even now seem'd miserable and forlorn, and the Region of Malediction, a Delivery from which was thought well bought at the Price of Death and utter Insensibility; even this at the next succeeding Roll becomes a flourishing Paradise, thick set with vigorous Life, and adorn'd with all the Charms and Gaiety of fresh youthful Pleasure. For the Holy Father might think it no extravagant Conjecture, to imagine that the Process and Consequences of that great Fire will be somewhat the same with those we daily observe upon Earth in Bodies subjected to the Operation of Fire. Most of which consist of a twofold Principle, the one more dense and solid, the other subtile and tenuious; but when Fire is apply'd to the whole, and spreads its insinuating active Atoms thro every Commissure of Parts, where either it finds or can make its way, the finer and more agitable Particles by this new Heat and Motion got amongst them, issue out in Smoke and Vapour from those Places of Restraint where they before lay more still, into the free and open Air; but the more heavy and solid are left behind, as which the too subtile parts of Fire, notwithstanding all their Activity, could not carry away with them, being overpower'd by their Excess of Magnitude. And tho we observe not any further Progress in ordinary Fires, and care not what becomes of the evaporated Parts of the consum'd Body; yet where either Use or Curiosity leads our Observation on further, and we would not have those Parts dissipated and lost, we then find that they which steam'd forth in a vaporous Rarity, being kept in by fit Receivers, and falling in closely with one another, do at last fall down again in a watery Consistence, retaining the same nature they had before they were forc'd out of the Body they belong'd to. And if the Return of this descending Dew was so order'd, that it might have time enough to insinuate it self again equally thro all the Vacuities it made in the Body by its Departure, it would no doubt bind and consolidate the looser Parts thereof, and tincture the whole Concretion with its specifick Virtue and Qualities. For this is no more than letting Ground wrought out of heart, lie fallow for some Years, and it again will answer the Hopes, and reward the Labour of its Tiller. Tho this Example of the ordinary Operation of Fire and its Consequences, for many Reasons, falls short of those Advantages for Vitality and Fertility which may be expected from the Conflagration of the Earth; yet as it is, it lets us see in some measure what will be the necessary effect of that piece of Divine Chymistry, in which Seas and Rivers, and all the evaporable Parts of the upper Region of the Earth (for the metallick Regions below are too solid to be much concern'd in this Matter) and all things thereon, will in a thick confus'd Cloud mount aloft and cover the Face of Heaven, filling the Air with pitchy Darkness; but their own Gravity, and that Cause which limits the Extent of the Atmosphere, will necessarily keep them below the purer Regions of Heaven or

Æther: ſo that rolling up and down in the lower Vault of Heaven, and kept yet from deſcending by that ſmothering Heat that is amongſt them, that intenſe Fire under them, and the continual Aſcent of new vaporous Steams, they will at laſt, when theſ Cauſes abate, and themſelves become more crouded and confert thro their exceſſive Copiouſneſs, fall down in trickling dewy Showers, and mix again with that great Heap of Aſhes which covers the Face of the Earth, and make her fruitful and vegetative, and fill her empty'd Channels with wholeſome Streams; the Air alſo will be kindly cool'd and moiſtned by thoſe long-deſcending Showers which paſs thro it. So that ſo far as concerns material Preparations of Life, here may be a new World again, if God ſo pleaſe. And unleſs he purpoſely put a ſtop to the Courſe of Nature, the great Principle of vegetative Life will neceſſarily ſhape the Matter, when duly modify'd, into all kind of Trees, Plants, Herbs and Flowers: for the inferior Spirit of the World acts not by Choice, but fatally; and being eſſentially ſtor'd with an univerſal Seminality, will not fail to bring her Treaſure into view, when invited by congruous and ſequacious Diſpoſitions of Matter. And methinks 'tis very odd there ſhould be ſo fair and pleaſant a Garden, and none to enjoy the Fruits and Fragrancy of it. But if Philoſophy hath rightly determin'd that the Souls of Brutes are Spirits (which for my own part I think is done with demonſtrative Evidence) and therefore remain after all Fates whatever undiminiſhable and indiſſipable in their intire Subſtances, we need not fear thoſe pleaſant Fruits will grow up and die unenjoy'd. For let the conciliating Principle of Souls and Matter be what it will, either Spermatick only, or Senſitive too, the Souls of Brutes will not fail to unite with it now it is become ſo fit. If the former, their Expergefaction into Life will then be as neceſſary as the growth of Herbs and Flowers; if the latter, then ſince the Pleaſures of ſenſitive Life are the top of the Felicity they are capable of, and conſequently their ſtrongeſt Deſires are bent thitherward and without any check, they will as certainly unite with Matter whereby they may enjoy them, as they will eat Meat caſt to them when their Appetite is edg'd with a keen Hunger. But ſince the former is more rational, and is found in the Souls of Men and Dæmons, as well as Beaſts, what ſhould hinder it from having the ſame effect in all, and ſo both Earth and Air be again repleniſh'd with their reſpective Inhabitants? And for the Earth it may further be ſaid, that the *Decorum* and Congruity of the thing perſuades it. For ſince there ſeems little leſs than a neceſſity that ſhe ſhould be furniſh'd with all manner of Fruits and brute Animals, and

and that the greateſt part and chiefeſt kinds of thoſe Fruits are ſuch as are either little regarded or cannot be come at by the Beaſts, that I may not add how quickly the Soil where they grow, and the Plants that bear them, will decay and come to nothing without humane Culture; and further, ſince many Species of Beaſts themſelves ſeem ſo made with relation to Man, that without him they would be ill provided for, or too much expos'd to ſuch as would prey upon them, and the exerciſe of their chief Powers could not be call'd forth, and many Appetites and Affections, which hugely pleaſe them, would find little or no Gratification: This Congruity of Things, I ſay, would almoſt perſuade one that Man ought alſo to appear on the Earth, to be the Father of this great Family, the Lord, Governor, Patron and Defender of all the Creatures therein. And there is nothing in the Nature of God to make us doubt of the Truth of theſe pleaſant Conjectures, but much which favours them. For, for theſe better and more perfect Spirits to continue yet in being, and yet to be kept for ever dead and ſenſleſs, is to fill the World with that which is perfectly uſeleſs and in vain (as I intimated above) and to be capable not only of Life, but alſo upon a new Trial of their Fortune to be in more than a poſſibility of making a better Choice than that they paid ſo dearly for, and of returning in due time to that ſtate of Holineſs and Felicity God made them for (to all which worthy Purpoſes they may now have a fair Opportunity) and yet after all this to ſay that God is ſo far from furthering and helping on theſe hopeful Beginnings, that, on the contrary, by a peremptory Will and violent Hand he ſtrangles them, is at leaſt to ſay this, That there is no certain nor probable arguing from the Attributes of God, by which I, through a certain Infirmity of my Nature, was always the moſt ſtrongly convinc'd, that I was by any way of arguing whatever. But if a Man may with any probability argue from the Nature of God in ſuch Subjects, and about ſuch Effects as depend on his Operation; I, in the Perſon of *Origen*, deſire his Adverſaries briefly to compare the ſtate of things after the Conflagration of the Earth, with that which they ſay was before any thing was made. God was then infinitely good and kind, and by that his infinite Goodneſs was mov'd to create the World; ſuch is he ſtill, for his bleſſed Nature is immutable. The Things afterward created by him were not then in Being; here they are all in Being, and want only his permiſſive or ordering hand of Providence. They were then only in a poſſibility of being well and happily made; here they are in the very next ſtep to being ſo, even by the neceſſary Laws of Nature. Thoſe reaſonable Creatures he

 then

then made, were not indeed Sinners and Tranſgreſſors; yet they were made of ſuch a Nature, as they might very likely become ſuch afterward; and they have now ſoundly ſmarted for it, and have been afflicted even unto Death, and at this term Revenge it ſelf ſtops: Then certainly juſt and righteous Puniſhment, inflicted by the *Father of Mercies*, and Father of the puniſh'd, will not go beyond it; which if it do not, it will be very hard for them to give any tolerable Reaſon why the Earth ſhall not become habitable again after her Conflagration and Purification by Fire, and be the Manſion of Men and other Animals, as well as it was in the firſt Production of it. This is the firſt Part of the Father's Opinion. But if this Firſt was granted for true, and but one Reſtauration of the Earth, and re-planting of her with all her proper Inhabitants, was acknowledged; he that believes this, would find no difficulty in believing that eternal Viciſſitude, and infinite Repetition of Conflagrations and Re-productions, which in the Second Part of the *Dogma* he aſſerts. For ſince nothing periſhes out of the Compaſs of univerſal Nature, neither Spirit nor Matter; it is plain, there will be always ready at hand both the Materials and Inhabitants of the Thouſandth habitable Earth, as well as of the Second: and that moſt benign Principle which made and governs all things, is neither leſſened nor changed at that thouſandth Period, from what he was at the ſecond.

You may now poſſibly expect that the pious Father ſhould confirm his Doctrine out of Scripture, as in moſt of the former he did. But here he bids you call to mind the Advertiſement he gave you at the beginning of his ſecond *Dogma*, and conſider how neceſſary and decorous it was, that the Holy Penmen of Scripture ſhould not run out into ſuch abſtruſe natural Theories, which ſo few of thoſe they were to Chriſtianize would be capable of, but keep themſelves within the Bounds of thoſe few plain Articles which were neceſſary to the reforming the World, and begetting in the Minds of the ſimpleſt a firm hope of Life and Immortality hereafter, and deterring all Men from the Ways of Sin and Unrighteouſneſs by that ſad After-clap they muſt expect in the End of this World; leaving all further Conſiderations not repugnant to theſe, to the laudable Curioſity of ſuch as Nature and Education had fitted for ſuch Enquiries. Yet will he not wholly fruſtrate your Expectation, for I find him making uſe of theſe following places of Scripture in behalf of his Opinion: *Of old haſt thou laid the foundation of the Earth, and the Heavens are the work of thy hands. They ſhall periſh, but thou endureſt; yea all them ſhall wax old like a Garment: as a Veſture ſhalt thou change them, and they ſhall be changed;*

changed; but thou art the same. Where he says, such a Perishing is exegetically signified, both of the Earth and Regions of the Air, as is consistent with but a Change; but where there is only a Change, the Substance is not destroy'd. And this Change being as the Change of a Garment, worn out or decaying, supposes not only a Change for another (which it certainly does, unless he that hath worn out one Garment, and after goes naked, be said to change his Clothes) but also for a newer and better. Also that of St. *Paul, The fashion of this World passes away*, i. e. like a *turning Scene*, to exhibit a fresh and new Representation of Things; and if only the σχῆμα of this World, or the present outward Dress and Appearance of Things, go off, the Substance is suppos'd to remain intire. And that of the Prophet *Isaiah, Behold, I make new Heavens and a new Earth; and the former shall not be remembred, nor come into mind.* How exactly does this agree with his Hypothesis, whether you interpret the latter part of it concerning the Excellency of the vernant Youth and Spring of the renew'd World, above the squalid and decrepit Age of the old One, or concerning that perfect Oblivion in the Inhabitants of the New, that ever they liv'd before in the Old? And that *new Heavens* and *new Earth*, may be understood in a Physical sense, both St. *Peter* and St. *John* make it not utterly improbable. For tho our Translation seems to lay an Emphasis upon *We* in that place of St. *Peter*, as if the expected *new Heavens* and *Earth*, according to promise, were those Habitations of Glory which Christ shall give to his faithful Subjects in his heavenly Kingdom: yet there is nothing in the Greek which countenances such an Emphasis. The whole is plainly thus: *That fire shall melt and dissolve all the combustible Elements of Nature; yet for all that, according as he hath promised, we expect there shall be new Heavens and new Earth, or Heavens and Earth again, whose Inhabitants shall be better and more righteous than those of the decaying and corrupted World are.* And the Vision of a *new Heaven* and *new Earth* in St. *John*, does so immediately succeed the universal Judgment, and the casting of Death and *Hades* into the Lake of Fire, that it would almost persuade a Man that it is to succeed it also in Order of Time, since there is so great a congruity in the thing for it so to do. For suppose this Opinion true, and to have been a part of the Apocalyptical Visions, what fitter and more natural place could you assign it amongst them, than that it now hath, according to our present Interpretation? I will trouble you but with one Argument more, tho consisting of more Texts than one, but all in the same Epistle of St. *Peter: And spared not the old World, but preserved* ὌΓΔΟΟΝ ΝΩ͂Ε ΔΙΚΑΙΟΣΎΝΗΣ ΚΉΡΥΚΑ, *having brought the Flood upon the World of the ungodly.*

This

This they are willingly ignorant of, that there were of old Heavens and Earth consisting of, and placed amidst the Waters by the Word of God. By which constitution of things, the World that then was being overflow'd with Water, perish'd. But the Heavens and Earth which now are, by the same Word are kept in store, reserv'd for fire at the day of judgment and perdition of ungodly Men. To these Texts, add that which we cited before; *But we look for new Heavens, and a new Earth*; and then compare the several Passages in them one with another: For example; the *physical* State and Constitution of Things before the Flood, is call'd the *Old* or *Original World*, the *then World*, the *Heavens and Earth*, which were *of old*; that after the Flood is call'd the *Heavens and Earth*, which *now are*; and in respect of the former, might as properly be call'd the *new World*, as that is call'd the *old World* in respect of it: That which is to succeed the burning of this is (as we have conjectur'd) term'd *new Heavens* and a *new Earth* in respect of the Second. The First of these three Worlds is said to *perish*, or be destroy'd by Water for the punishment of the ungodly; yet so, as *Noah* was preserv'd to be a Preacher of Righteousness, as some Interpreters expound it. The Second is said to be reserv'd to the destruction of Fire for the perdition of ungodly Men, that so the Third may be the Habitation of Righteousness. Now since they are so distinctly describ'd as several Worlds; and since the Changes happening to them are call'd *Destructions* alike, and their Ends are the same, to wit, the punishment of the Ungodly: why should we imagine so vast a difference, that the Destruction of the First should be follow'd with a new Plantation of Mankind by *Noah* and his Sons, of Animals by the Pairs of each kind reserv'd in the Ark, and of all kind of Plants by their own fruitful Seminalities, but nothing follow upon the destruction of the Second, but a perfect irrecoverable Excision of all things? when yet the way that this is to be destroy'd by, does as naturally lead to a re-production, as that of the other, but after a far longer time. There is one thing more I am to put you in mind of, which I had from a very good hand, concerning one of the Texts above cited, to wit, about that odd disturb'd Order of Words in this Sentence, ἀλλ' ὄγδοον Νῶε δικαιοσύνης κήρυκα ἐφύλαξε· for such it must needs seem, according to that Interpretation which makes it ὄγδοον κήρυκα· and that other which makes him be call'd ὄγδοος, because he was one of the Eight sav'd in the Ark, is harsh, and without Example in Scripture, so far as I remember. What then if there be a Mystery in the business? (as you know Numbers have been commonly us'd to this purpose by the antient Wisdom, both holy and profane) And as *Enoch*, who was translated, is call'd the *seventh* from *Adam*, as a Type of that ex-

pected

pected Sabbatism in the last day of the *Millennial Hebdomade*, and of this World; so *Noah*, who begun the World again, is call'd the *Eighth*, (not from *Adam*) as a Figure signifying this, That the simply-last Period of this lower World, was not then then come to an End, but was still to be counted onward: and the production or drawing out of the Existence of Things being here *symbolically* taught, it would be more expresly done by reckoning upward in the Numeral Scale, than by beginging again at the First of that long *Hebdomade*. But enough of these fanciful Conjectures, as also of the Arguments from Scripture, to confirm this last Opinion of *Origen*. Unto all which, if you, in the Person of others, make answer, and say, That there is no Necessity that these places should be so interpreted as the Father interprets them, but that other convenient Senses may be put upon them, I am perfectly of your mind: but further reply, First, that they whose Answer you have form'd for them, are commonly so superstitious, that they will not admit of a Philosophical conclusion, tho warranted by the Attributes of God, and Necessity of Nature rightly understood, and be such as was not decorous nor becoming the simplicity of the Gospel, to be expresly and of set purpose taught by the holy Writers of Scripture, who were only to mind the greater and more necessary Doctrines of Christian Faith and Life, unless it also bring the Testimonials of Divine Writ. Secondly, Tho these Texts should have a more especial respect to some other Sense than that we have given them; yet why may it not be that Ours also was intended in some degree by the Holy Spirit? For since the holiest and most intellectual Persons would be very prone to fall into this Opinion, which they plainly saw so worthy of God, and consentaneous to Reason; but yet could not but with some fearfulness fully embrace it, because like to be unusual, and not in general vogue: It is not strange that some places of Scripture should be so contriv'd, as not obscurely to sing the same Note their own Thoughts had been harping on before, and so give boldness and assurance to their Conceptions; for a little touch or intimation would be enough for them so well prepar'd aforehand; and as for others, they either might not be fit for, or not deserve a plainer Instruction. Lastly, Whoever they be, in whose Name you have made this Exception, of what Church, Sect or Way soever, I doubt not they would have far fewer Articles in their Creeds and Confessions than they now probably have; and must profess the Belief of fewer Opinions than now 'tis likely they do, if so be they thought all groundless which were not built on such Texts of Scripture as would admit of no other tolerable and plausible Exposition than that they give of them. And therefore I demand of them in the Father's behalf, that which they in Equity ought not to deny him; That his Opinion ſtand as probably true, and the Scriptures cited by him as commodiouſly interpreted, till ſuch time as they bring better Arguments, more agreeing with the Nature of Things and the Attributes of God, and clearer places of Scripture for the Truth of the contrary.

I have now given you an Account of thoſe Reaſons and Grounds the learned and pious Father had for thoſe Six capital Errors ſome of the Antients have charg'd him with, and under which Attainder he ſtill lies from their Authority; and have therewith anſwer'd your Fourth Query. Wherein I have punctually obſerv'd your Commands, in giving you thoſe Reaſons only by which I find him to have maintain'd his Opinions; and have wav'd many other very material or plauſible Conſiderations for confirming the ſame, which ſome later Authors have uſed with much danger, I have fear'd, to their leſs-ſetled (or as they ſpeak now-a-days, free) Readers; and have alſo omitted thoſe Injections, rather than ſtudied Thoughts, which my own melancholy Fancy hath oft with too great importunity obtruded on my Mind: which ſometimes are ſo ſtrong in me (I will not to you diſſemble my infirmity) that all the Charms of Reverend Names, of Churches, of Articles, of Confeſſions, of univerſally-approv'd Syſtems, have had much ado to expel them, or ſo far abate their force, that I was not carried away by them from that ſtability and ſobriety of ſpirit, upon which I deſire to build all my Conceptions. Before I come to your Fifth Query, I muſt crave pardon of his venerable Aſhes, if I have any where diſadvantag'd his Cauſe, either by my unskilful Management of his Reaſons, or by omitting any more conſiderable and convincing than thoſe I have produc'd out of his Writings. For the general Opinion of the Learned, that the Tranſlations of them were ſo ſacrilegiouſly mangled, and perform'd with ſo little Judgment and Faithfulneſs, made me never care to look much into them, ſince I could not be certain whether I read the Mind of *Origen*, or ſome very mean Author; and therefore I was now forc'd, that I might obey your Commands in ſome meaſure, to tumble them over as my hand led me, and where by chance I ſpied any hopes that there was ſomething there handled proper for my purpoſe, to uſe the beſt judgment I had in conjecturing, which was likely to be the genuine iſſue of *Origen*'s contemplative Genius, and which the ſpurious Interpolations of another. In which tumultuary Labour, 'tis no wonder if ſeveral things eſcap'd me, far more fit to appear in his defence than theſe are, which by chance I light upon.

Your

YOur Fifth and laſt Query is, By what Reaſons and Arguments his Adverſaries oppugned his Opinions, and how I imagine an *Origeniſt* would anſwer to their Oppoſitions?

Truly, Sir, tho I muſt praiſe the Freedom and Prudence which appear in the firſt Part of this Query, and which plainly tell me (tho I well knew it before) that you are not willing to pronounce of any Propoſition under debate, till you have clearly ſeen through it from end to end; and that you are ſo diffident of your ſelf (a ſure ſign of true Wiſdom) that you care not to have a plauſible Opinion come near you, unleſs you alſo have an Antidote at hand: yet I crave leave freely to tell you, there is ſome iniquity in the ſecond Part of it, in that it impoſes a Perſon upon me which I am unfit to ſuſtain. But ſince I have already acted that part here and there, and am now more fully to do it only for your divertiſement, without the preſence and conſciouſneſs of any other Arbiter, I ſhall not be much ſollicitous what ineptneſs or *indecorum* I commit in it; for you cannot for ſhame laugh at the ill managery of it, when by your Commands alone I undertake it.

Againſt his firſt Opinion they object, That 'tis mere *Arianiſm*, an Hereſy condemn'd in the early Age of the Church, when Truth may be ſuppos'd to have been free from that Corruption or Obſcurity wherewith length of Time, and the improv'd Craft and Subtilty of intereſted Perſons might afterwards debaſe or entangle it.

To this heavy Charge, but laid on at random, I, according to my part, thus anſwer. You cannot but have oft obſerv'd how common a practice it is with Men, who either cannot diſpute, or begin to be tired with it, to make ſhort work with their Adverſaries by calling them *Hereticks*. And that I may not trouble you with many Examples, nor fetch them far, call but to mind how frequently you have read and heard two very conſiderable Parties in this Nation, both for Learning and Piety, call one the other in their Writings and Sermons, *Manichees* and *Pelagians*. And yet both of them diſown the Names which their Adverſaries would fix on them, and are aſſur'd they can demonſtrate it is invidiouſly, but improperly given them. And this the *Origeniſt* will ſay is his Maſter's Caſe. For by what I have ſaid above in this Opinion, it is manifeſt, that he will not, nor cannot ſay by his Hypotheſis, *That it ever was that the Son was not; that he was not before he was born; that he was made ἐξ οὐκ ὄντων, or that he is not of the ſame Subſtance or Eſſence with the Father, or is created, or is variable or mutable, or that he is not God of God, Light of Light, very God of very God.* So

that

that if a Man may be bold with, or without the leave of, mindless or heated Declaimers, to think himself free from Heresy, when neither the *Anathematisms*, nor the *Creed* of that Council which, if any, is to condemn him, do concern or touch him, *Origen* is then pure as Innocence and Truth her self from this Charge. Which I could very particularly demonstrate, if his Accusers had been pleas'd as particularly to charge him. They have been indeed very forward to catch at one word of his, to wit, γεννητὸς Θεὸς, and from thence infer what their humours pleas'd. One of them says, because he said γεννητὸς, therefore he denied the Son to be *begotten*; whenas he often calls the Divine Λόγος the *only-begotten Son of God*. Another of them as rashly concludes that he meant by it *created*, and yet confesses that there are ὁμολεξίαι καὶ ὁμωνυμίαι ἐν τῷ βίῳ, and that this same word might have been us'd by another in this matter κατ' ὀρθὴν διάνοιαν· but in *Origen* it must not scape so fairly, but *created* must by all means be understood by it, because he does in many places (yet none of them are produc'd) ἀπαλλοτριοῦν τὸν μονογενῆ Θεὸν τῆς τοῦ πατρὸς θεότητός τε καὶ οὐσίας. Which is manifestly false; for he every where calls the Λόγος God, and the Creator of all things; and, according to his Doctrine of the Holy Trinity, he is substantially, essentially and immutably such, and of the same Divinity and Essence with the Father, therefore certainly no Creature. And tho *Ruffinus* his Translations are of no certain credit, yet certainly his appealing to *Origen*'s Writings, then extant in their Original, and in the hands of his Adversaries, for his plain affirming the Father and Son to be of the same Substance or Essence, is a sufficient Argument that *Origen* did indeed think so: unless you will think *Ruffinus* such a Fool, as so confidently to appeal to such Testimonies out of his Writings, whom he would defend, as every one might convince of falsity. Nay, *Epiphanius* himself hath one quarrel with him for the inconsistency of his Doctrine, in that making the Son of the same Essence with the Father, he makes him also created; but this *created* is his own Inference from the word γεννητὸς (as I said before) not the Affirmation of *Origen*. And it may further be said in his Defence, as to the use of this word, what is for the Defence of all the Fathers before the *Nicene* Council, that they spoke less cautiously in the Doctrine of the Trinity. For till the Church had for the security of this Article determin'd, that the Belief and Confession of it should be in such certain conceiv'd Words, and had forbad the use of others which were obnoxious to such Interpretations as were injurious to the dignity of any Hypostasis in it, such interdicted Words might have been then harmlesly used, which could not afterwards,

without

without great Carelesness of Spirit, Neglect of the Governors of the Church, or Heretical Persuasion. And particularly this word γενητὸς, in its large sense, signifies no more than what is true of any thing whatever that hath a Cause of its Being and Existence; and therefore in those early Ages of the Church, which spoke more simply and intelligibly, might have been us'd without offence, but certainly did not raise such Tragedies in those days as afterwards, when Subtilty and Niceness about Words had made Men peevish. For that it is always the same with κτιστὸς and ποιητὸς, as *Epiphanius* would have it, no Critick will grant: for these do particularize the way of Production, and that such an one as is not competent to the Eternal Son of God, which that other does not necessarily. Neither did *Origen*, for ought that appears, use it often: I am sure *Epiphanius* takes notice of it only once, to wit, out of his Preface to his Exposition on the *Psalms*. And possibly he did never use it at all; for he himself complains that some Hereticks corrupted his Writings while he was yet living; What would they then do, think you, when he was not present, who could authentically convince them of their foul dealing? And it is well known in the Records of Ecclesiastical Story, that the *Arians* would have kept up their blasphemous Error by the venerable Authority of *Origen*. How easy then was it for them, a crafty and industrious Generation, and sometimes in great Power, to change γεννητὸς into γενητός? But why do I trouble you or my self with so tedious a Chase of a flitting word? The substantial Frame of *Origen*'s Hypothesis concerning the *Trinity*, is such in the nature of the thing, as makes it impossible there should be any place for suspicion that he thought the Son of God a Creature; unless he could think him a Creature, whom by that Hypothesis he acknowledges eternally Existent, and essentially and immutably endow'd with Perfections truly Divine in an infinite degree, and to be the Creator of all things. And therefore all those Expostulations of *Epiphanius* are lost, as to *Origen*, by being misapply'd. How is he adorable if he be a *made* God? Nothing *created* can be worship'd. Does Christ the Word ever say, God *created* me, or my Father *created* me? or does God ever say, I have *created* the Son, and sent him to you? How can he be *created* who says, I in the Father, and the Father in me, and we two are one? For these and such like Sayings I am not concern'd in, and therefore let those Hereticks, whether Antient or Modern, answer them (if they can) against whom they are truly levell'd.

His second and third Opinions are so conjunct, and his Adversaries Arguments against them, sever.l of them so indeterminate,

minate, that I think it beſt to join them both in one, and leave it to you to diſtinguiſh which Argument belongs to which Opinion. If his Opinion (ſay they) of *Præexiſtence* and *Lapſe* of ſuperior Beings into this inferior Life be true, where is then the Benediction to *Adam* and his Seed, *Increaſe and multiply, and replenish the Earth?* For it would be a Curſe rather than a Bleſſing, according to him who turns Angels into Souls, and makes them deſcend from their high pitch of Dignity to theſe inferior Habitations. As if God could not ſupply Humane kind with Souls, unleſs the Angels ſin'd, and there be as many Ruins in Heaven as Births on Earth. The Ambiguity of the word *Angels* being premis'd, and nothing underſtood here by it but *humane Souls* inhabiting ſome purer Regions of the World; I then anſwer, That this Objection proceeds upon a miſunderſtanding of *Origen*'s Hypotheſis, as if he made the Generations of Mankind to be ſupply'd by the Deſcent of ſuch Souls or Spirits into Terreſtrial Bodies, while ſuch, *i. e.* while by Congruity of Life, they were fit to be the Inhabitants of thoſe better Dwellings. This, I confeſs, would be a condition they may juſtly wonder God ſhould ſo ſpecially own and favour by his Benediction. But if through the neceſſary Incompoſſibility in created Natures incorporate, thoſe Spirits which were ſometimes Inhabitants of more happy places, and the Eyes and Ears of Providence, and inviſible Adminiſtrators of the Affairs of ſome Parts of her great Kingdom, become, by degrees, after long Periods of better Life, fit only for the Terreſtrial, which is the Father's mind: for theſe to be born upon Earth, and reap thoſe Pleaſures which the eternal Wiſdom and Goodneſs, who paſſes through all Things and Conditions, and hath left ſome Impreſſions of himſelf in all, hath imparted to that Life, is neither to make any violent Breach in Heaven, nor is any Curſe to thoſe deſcending Souls. For ſuch mutable Creatures may have ſo worn out ſome way or other their more perfect Vitality, that the diſorder'd Ruins of it may be very uneaſy to their ſenſe, and a pain rather than any ſatisfaction; and to be awakened into a Life, tho inferior in kind, yet ſtronger and fuller in the ſenſe of thoſe Delights it affords, than the meaneſt and loweſt Ruins of the ſuperior were, may be a releaſe and advantage. But if they be born into this World out of the dark Womb of Death and Inſenſibility, 'tis then a manifeſt Bleſſing to them. And God, who hath furniſh'd every kind of Life with its proper and ſutable Good and Pleaſure, may very truly and righteouſly be ſaid to impart his Benediction to thoſe Beings which are vivificated into it, when they were capable of no better. And whether he made them of ſuch a Nature, as to be capable only of one condition

condition of Life, and one place of Habitation, or of more, makes no matter, since by the eternal Laws of Nature or Demerit, they are now become fit only for one; and for this present Turn can perform their parts in it as well, and as sutably to the Ends of Providence, as if they had been originally made capable of this alone. Shall I call that an Argument, or a pitiful Mistake in St. *Jerom*, which he hath form'd with a great shew of subtilty and coherence, bringing his Adversary at last (as he imagin'd) to a gross Absurdity? His Words are these: *Si anima fuit antequam Adam in Paradiso* [the Terrestrial one] *formaretur, in quolibet statu & ordine, & vixit & egit aliquid; (neque enim possumus incorporalem & æternam in modum glirium immobilem torpentémque sentire) necesse est ut aliqua causa præcesserit, cur quæ prius sine corpore fuit, postea circundata sit corpore. Et si animæ est naturale esse sine corpore, ergo contra naturam est esse in corpore. Si contra naturam est esse in corpore, ergo Resurrectio corporis contra naturam erit. Sed non fiet Resurrectio contra naturam: ergo juxta sententiam vestram corpus quod contra naturam est resurgens, animam non habebit.* I know not what to make of this, nor how to interpret it so as it shall have any force at all; for if by being *without a Body*, he mean a Terrestrial one, I wonder why he should suppose that the *Origenists* neither had nor could assign a Cause, why the Soul, once without a Terrestrial Body, should afterwards be clothed with such a Body. For he himself takes notice out of *Origen* of very sufficient Reasons how this should come to pass, as I have before shew'd. And further, It is strange he should think it an Absurdity to an *Origenist* to deny the Resurrection of such a Body, whom he knows, and often affirms, makes the Mystery of the Resurrection to be our Vivification into an æthereal Life, and the obtaining of an æthereal Body. But if by being *without a Body*, he mean without *any body* at all, you may justly wonder at so great a Forgetfulness and Dormitation in so acute and diligent a Writer; who, amongst other of *Origen*'s Errors or Fancies (as he calls them) does more than once take notice of this: *That he makes all created Spirits have Bodies according to the Nature of those Regions of the World they live in, and to change them as oft as they do their Mansions, from the highest Heaven to Earth, the lowest Aboae of all, so as that they never will be without a Body* (if they be alive) *so long as there is any matter in the World.* So that howsoever you interpret him, the Objection will be pitifully precarious, or a gross carelesness and inadvertency. Hither must also be refer'd what *Epiphanius* and his two Assistants, *Proclus* and *Methodius*, keep such a stir about, to wit, the *Coats of Skins*, which God in the Story of *Adam* is said to make for him, which *Origen* interpreted *Terrestrial Bodies*, wherewith *Adam* and *Eve* were clothed upon their

their Transgression. But they think 'tis plain from the Order and Words of the History, that they had such Bodies before their Fall, even from their first Creation; for God is there said to form Man *out of the dust of the ground*, and make the Woman of *Adam*'s Rib; and when she was brought to him, he said, This is *bone of my bone, and flesh of my flesh.* But what a poor Attempt is this of theirs, to pass over those substantial Arguments, by which he maintains the Reasonableness and Concinnity of those two Opinions, of the *Præexistence* and *Descent* of Souls into *Terrestrial Bodies*, and to catch at an Interpretation of a word in such an History as the most Learned both of *Jews* and *Christians* have always acknowledg'd to contain more Senses than the plain and literal one? And in such mysterious Writings, which are to look more ways than one, and handle Subjects of much different nature; 'tis not strange if there be something in the Order wherein they are handled, which may seem perplex'd to those who are only for the Literal sense, and who have not the freedom and patience to observe the Continuity of the Allegory, but snatch at one single part of it, and disjoint it from the rest; and if they cannot fit it to that Order they have set to themselves in their Interpretation, presently reject the whole as a perturbed intricate Fancy. But how congruous all things are in the *Cabbala* of the Creation, and how naturally one part follows upon another, without Violence to the Letter, you may fully see in that learned Gentleman's *Cabbalistical Conjecture*, to whom I refer'd you before. And I dare appeal to the Fancy of any Man, tho but meanly capable of understanding what is proportionate, congruous and apposite, when he hears it, whether any thing can be more comely and more expressive of the Condition of the Soul fallen from her divine and intellectual State into an animal Condition, than to say she is then clothed with the *Skins of a Brute*. And methinks *Proclus*, if he understood himself, should have little reason to quarrel at *Origen*'s Allegory, who himself makes these Coats to signify τὴν ὑπὸ τοῦ λόγου τῶν ζώων νεκρότητα κατεσκευασμένην. They have another bout with him concerning this Matter, for affirming that we were turn'd out of *Paradise celestial*, before we came to dwell upon Earth. For 'tis plain (say they) that Paradise is a pleasant place upon Earth, appointed for the happy and quiet Habitation of the Saints, from the Rivers of it, *Tigris* and *Euphrates*, &c. For could the Earth bear the down-pouring Floods of so much Water, tumbling in such heaps from Heaven? Do you not smile at such Arguers? and I fear you would laugh at me if I should industriously set my self to answer them. I shall therefore only mind them of another

Paradise

Paradise ſpoken of in the Goſpels, where Chriſt promiſed the good Thief *he ſhould be with him*; *whither*, St. *Paul* in his Epiſtles ſays, *he was caught up*; which St. *John* alſo calls by the Name of the *Paradiſe of God*, ſomewhere within the compaſs whereof grows the *Tree of Life*, and whoſe Rivers are the *Water of Life*. I would know of them likewiſe what they would anſwer to the Authority of the beſt *Jewiſh* Writers, who generally ſay that *Paradiſe* is out of this World, and was created before this *lower World* was. Nay *Jerom* himſelf here helps *Origen*'s Cauſe with his Authority, concluding thus from the Words of the Text, *Ex quo manifeſtiſſimè comprobatur, quod priuſquam cœlum & terram Deus faceret, Paradiſum antè condiderat. Quæſt. in Gen.* But 'tis no wonder the *Objectors* ſhould talk at that rate they do; for they plainly affirm, that the eternal Habitation of the Bleſſed, after the Reſurrection, ſhall be upon Earth. St. *Jerom* hath other Texts of Scripture againſt *Præexiſtence*, which in his own Words are theſe: *Pater uſque modo operatur, & ego operor*; and that of *Iſaiah*, *Qui format ſpiritum hominis in ipſo*; and that in the Pſalms, *Qui fingit per ſingulos corda eorum*. By theſe places he thinks it appears, that God does daily, as there is occaſion, create Souls. To the Firſt I anſwer, by demanding what Neceſſity there is, that the *working* here mention'd ſhould ſignify *Creation* of Souls? Are not all the Works of his Providence in continuing Life, Motion, Order to the World, and every part of it, in governing and managing all by his Goodneſs, Power and Wiſdom, to their behoof and advantage, ſufficient to verify this Saying, That the *Father worketh hitherto?* And does not our Saviour's adding, *And I work*, with reference to that beneficent Miracle he had wrought on the Sabbath-day, plainly intimate what kind of Operation he meant in both? And if I ſhould confront *Jerom*'s Expoſition with that in *Geneſis*, *God reſted on the Seventh day from all his work*; or that of St. *Paul*, *His works were finiſh'd from the foundation of the World*; I am ſure I ſhould have Reaſon and Philoſophy on my ſide: and their Exception, that theſe places are to be underſtood of the Species of Things, is not ſo plainly gather'd from the words, as is my interpreting of *my Father worketh hitherto*, of his Works of Providence and continual Beneficence. His other two places mean no more than this, That God is the Creator and Father of Souls or Spirits, and by his Power over them, moulds, faſhions, and changes them as he pleaſes; both which are true, tho the Soul ſubſiſted from eternal Ages. You will aſk me then, Where lies the Father's Argument? Truly, Sir, it is ſo thin and evanid a ſubtilty, that your great Mind, made for, and uſed to great Objects, may very likely miſs it; but this it is, He reads the Words thus; *Who forms* in him *the Spirit of Man*, not *the Spirit of Man* which is *in him*. This would have been pretty, had he firſt prov'd by ſubſtantial Arguments, taken from the Nature of the *Soul* or *Providence*, that the Souls of Men could not exiſt before they inform'd a Terreſtrial Body; but having not done that, nor ſcarce endeavour'd it, his Argutenefs is ridiculous. For who can doubt, but that the *Prophet* meant the ſame with that more compleat and expreſs Form of Speech in St. *Paul*, Who knows the Things of a Man, εἰ μὴ τὸ πνεῦμα τῦ ἀνθρώπυ τὸ ἐν αὐτῷ; If I ſhould ſay of that elegant Watch you did me the honour to give me, that your own neat and curious Hand wrought and form'd all the Springs and Wheels in it, no Man would be ſo mad as to think I meant, that you wrought them within the Caſe: or if I ſhould tell you (which I may with Truth) that I have been ſo oft at *Alney-thorpe*, that I know all the Inhabitants in it, I hope you would not think that the Image of your noble Perſon was ſo ſeldom in my Fancy; or that I was of ſo fantaſtick a Memory, that I knew you, and the reſt of your Neighbours only, when I was there, but ſhould not know you at my own Hermitage, or any where elſe.

Theſe are all the Objections they have (ſo far as I remember) againſt theſe two Opinions of *Origen*, the *Præexiſtence* and *Deſcent* of the Soul into a Terreſtrial Body; unleſs you will give ſo much to the Authority of *Jerom* in a metaphyſical Argument, as to take that magnificent Bravado of his for another; *Quod vos miramini, olim in Platone contempſimus*. And do not you think now, Sir, that theſe *good Fathers* having ſo ſtrenuouſly and perſpicuouſly ſhewn, that theſe two *Dogmata* are inconſiſtent with the Attributes of God, and contrary to the Nature of Things; and having ſo plainly demonſtrated the Sophiſticalneſs of *Origen*'s Arguments, and the Inconſequence of his Illations; laſtly, having by ſo plain and cogent places of Scripture prov'd the contrary Poſitions to be true; do you not think, I ſay, that they had reaſon to call theſe Opinions of his περιλισμὸν καὶ τερατολογίαν, Nonſenſe and Stolidity? I leave you to judge.

But I paſs on to their Objections againſt his Fourth Opinion of the Reſurrection. Aud here they are more copious, I mean in Arguments taken out of Scripture; for I do not yet remember, that they make uſe of Ethnick and Secular Philoſophy (as they ſpeak) againſt it. And indeed, their Arguments are ſo numerous, that it is a prejudice againſt the Truth of their Cauſe: For tho a ſingle Text or two may probably eſcape the Obſervation, even of a diligent Reader; yet that ſuch a Multitude as they boaſt of and oſtentate, ſhould be all unmark'd by *Origen*, one ſo well vers'd in Scripture, that he had it all

without

without book; or that he should be so stubborn and pervicacious in his false Persuasion, who was so hearty and sincere a Christian, is a very wonderful thing. In many of their Arguments against him, they are so fanciful and allegorical, and do so toy and sport with a word or two in the Text, that if a Man did not know the persons, he would certainly conclude either such Argumentators, or the Question was not serious; or that they thought their Adversaries such Mushrooms, so soft and foolish, that they would be put off with any thing. Such Objections as these I shall not trouble you withal; the chief of the other, which have a better show and pretence, I will give you. They say then, With what Body our Saviour rose, and ascended into Heaven, with the like shall we be raised again, and live in Heaven with. But he rose with the very same Flesh and Blood he had before his Crucifixion, as is manifest from his shewing the Print of the Nails, and of the Souldier's Spear to St. *Thomas*, and ascended with the same to Heaven in the sight of his Disciples. To this *Origen* himself answers in the Words of *Jerom: Illud corpus aliis pollet privilegiis, quod de viri semine & carnis voluptate non natum est. Comedit post resurrectionem suam & bibit, & vestitus apparuit, tangendum se præbuit; ut dubitantibus apostolis fidem faceret resurrectionis. Sed tamen non dissimulabat naturam aerii corporis & spiritalis: clausis enim ingreditur ostiis, & in fractione panis ex oculis evanescit.* And in other places he adds his being not known of the two Disciples going to *Emmaus*, nor of *Mary* in the Garden, his walking on the Waters, his escaping from the Multitude, when they led him to throw him headlong from a Rock. Some of which passages at least verify *Origen*'s *illud corpus aliis pollet privilegiis*; and the Effects of these Privileges are such as naturally proceed from Tenuity of Body: For this Disposition is both easily mouldable into any Form and Shape by the Fancy, and other natural Powers, of its actuating Spirit; and also easily passes through such Bodies, as to others are impervious, and is devoid of Gravitation. But *Origen* no where says, that the Body of Christ upon Earth was not truly Flesh and Blood. For he knew well enough, that there is no other difference in Matter, than what it receives from such or such Modifications of its Parts; and that it is capable of all these Modifications, where a sufficient Cause works upon it; and such he very piously conceiv'd the Soul of our Saviour to be: which could as well fix and constipate the Matter of his Body into a Terrestrial crassness, as loosen it into a spiritual Tenuity; and when it was wrought into such particular Modifications as constitute the Form of Flesh and Blood, it was then as truly Flesh and Blood as that is which we mere mortal Men are clothed withal. And the

Oeconomy of his Evangelical Undertaking, both in his Life and Death, requiring ſuch a Body, he very rarely gave any publick Specimen of that mighty Power which was in his quickning Spirit; but was content to want the happy Privileges of that freer Life he might have enjoy'd, by exerting that his heavenly Power. For his humble and obedient Soul was reſolv'd to perfect what he had taken upon him, whatever debaſement, whatever inconvenience he ſhould endure from the weight and preſſure of his Servile *Schema*. And moreover, a firm hope of Life, and bleſſed Immortality of the whole Man, being the main End of the Chriſtian Myſtery, and the palpable Evidence thereof in the Perſon of our Lord, being neceſſary to make his Apoſtles and Diſciples with Boldneſs and Courage, and convictive Teſtimony, preach the Goſpel in the World, (whom we find ſo amazed at his Death and Crucifixion, that they knew not what to think of it;) it was therefore neceſſary that he ſhould exhibit himſelf to them again after his Reſurrection, in the ſame ſenſible manner of appearance that he did before his Death: and if with the Prints of his Wounds receiv'd at his Crucifixion, 'twould be the better, leſt their backwardneſs of Belief, in ſo ſtrange an Event, ſhould make any of them (as it did St. *Thomas*) ſo curious, as to demand or need ſo punctual an aſſurance; for this the Wiſdom of his Oeconomy requir'd, as well as the other parts of his Condeſcenſion. But for all this, ſome of thoſe Inſtances *Origen* takes notice of, as alſo his Transfiguration, do very fairly invite us to believe, that he had that in him which was of ſuch ſovereign Energy and Life, as could *ſwallow up what was mortal in Victory*, and *ſubdue every thing to it ſelf*. And the Exerciſe of this Power being only reſtrain'd for the performing his Temporary Diſpenſation upon Earth; that being ended, who can doubt but that it would then freely break forth, and melt his Body into ſuch a rarity and fineneſs, as would, like a *winged Chariot*, carry him from the Earth? And the Exertion of this Power being ſo temper'd, as not forthwith to make his Body pure *Æther*, he might as well, for ſome time in his Aſcent, be corporally beheld by his Diſciples, as *Ghoſts* and *Spectres* are, whoſe ſudden diſappearing does ſufficiently manifeſt, that they had not ſuch Bodies as we Terreſtrial Men have. Nay, *Epiphanius* himſelf, not wont to be very Philoſophical, tho he contend for Chriſt's riſing from the Dead with the ſame Body he had before; yet he preſently tells us what Sameneſs of Body he means, by acknowledging that his *raiſed Body* was changed into a *ſpiritual ſubtilty* and *tenuity*; by the advantage whereof he entred the Doors, when ſhut; which (he ſays) cannot be done by the Bodies we have here διὰ τὸ παχυμερὲς, and not having yet attain'd their ſpiritual

ſpiritual Tenuity. He affirms likewiſe, that the Body which Chriſt ſhew'd to St. *Thomas*, was the ſame which was crucified, but changed into a ſpiritual Tenuity; and that which was before παχυμερὲς, was then πνευματικὸν and λεπτομερές. How far this is from the *Origenian* Hereſy, I leave you to judge; and ſhall let his Adverſaries fight it out amongſt themſelves, ſince I perceive there is Diſſenſion amongſt them. For it is not the ſame individual Particles of Matter that we, in this Queſtion, principally deny or diſpute about, but the ſame Modification and Conſiſtency of Body with that which is in Fleſh and Blood. It may perhaps ſeem to ſome very ſtrangely done of us, (that I ſay no worſe) who read that the Deſcent of Chriſt from Heaven was his *Humiliation*, and his taking upon him the *form of a ſervant*, and being made in the *likeneſs of ſinful fleſh*, his *exinanition*; yet to be ſo deſirous to impriſon him ſtill in the ſame ſervile Condition, and to be unwilling that he ſhould reſume that antient Glory and Liberty which he had with God before his Incarnation. And if it was done out of half as much Malice as Ignorance, no Man would doubt to pronounce, that it was next to *crucifying our Lord afreſh, and putting him to perpetual ſhame.* After all this which hath been ſaid, it will not be neceſſary to give a formal Anſwer to the Objector's Syllogiſm. But inſtead thereof, I ſhall only point at two or three places of Scripture, and leave you to conſider them. *The firſt man Adam is* χοϊκὸς, *the ſecond man, the Lord, is* ἐπουράνιος. *But Chriſt being come, or made an High Prieſt of good things to come, by a better and more perfect Tabernacle,* οὐ χειροποιήτου, τουτέστιν, οὐ ταύτης τῆς κτίσεως, *enter'd into the holy places not made with hands, Heaven it ſelf. Fleſh and blood ſhall not inherit the Kingdom of God.* I cannot get it out of my fancy, but that there is an intimation of ſomething contrary to the Objector's pretenſions in theſe Texts which follow. —— *Jeſus the Chriſt come in fleſh.* Ἐν τῷ σώματι τῆς σαρκὸς αὐτοῦ —— Ὃς ἐν ταῖς ἡμέραις τῆς σαρκὸς αὐτοῦ, &c. Καὶ τελειωθεὶς, &c. I deſire you likewiſe to try if you can make any ſenſe of the Sixth of St. *John*, from the 32d Verſe, to the end; which ſhall ſo naturally agree to the Words, as that which we have aim'd at in our Anſwer to this Objection concerning Chriſt's Body. *I am the bread of life which truly came down from Heaven, which he that eateth thereof ſhall never die. The bread which I will give is* my Fleſh, *which I will give for the life of the World. He that eateth* my Fleſh, *and drinketh* my Blood, *hath eternal life, and I will raiſe him up at the laſt day. Many therefore of his Diſciples, when they heard this, ſaid, This is an hard ſaying, who can hear it?* But he anſwer'd them, *Doth this offend you? What and if you ſhall ſee the Son of Man aſcend up where he was before? The Spirit is that which quickens, the Fleſh profiteth nothing; the words which I have ſpoke unto you are* Spirit *and* Life. This Chapter is by ſome interpreted, of the ſymbolical Participation of the Body and Blood of Chriſt, in the Commemoration of his Death: which tho I acknowledg to be the higheſt, moſt ſolemn and moſt uſeful part of publick Devotion that the Chriſtian Church uſes; yet I think I may, without any irreverence to my deareſt Lord and Saviour, affirm, That the Effect aſcrib'd to the *Manducation* ſpoken of in this Chapter, i. e. *Eternal life*, is too great for the Cauſe aſſign'd. Others interpret it of *Faith in him*, and *Obedience to his Precepts*; but by ſo doing, they do that themſelves, which they cannot away with in others; to wit, depart from the Letter where there is no need. For the very Letter here is (as I may ſay) the greateſt Myſtery of the Goſpel; the Communion of the Body of Chriſt being truly Eternal Life, the End of our Faith, and the Reward and Crown of our Obedience. And if the word *Eating* be Tropological, 'tis the modeſteſt Trope that can be: For what other word could be uſed to expreſs our Participation of a Body, which was to give and prolong Life to him that is made partaker of it, even as our daily Food does to our mortal Fleſh? So that our Expoſition adjuſting the Cauſe and Effect, and yet keeping to the very Letter, may very deſervedly be look'd upon as the true and natural One: which if it be, I leave you to judge, whether we have not fully anſwer'd the Objection, and out of his mouth, who is *Truth it ſelf*, ſhewn, that it is a great Miſtake, and a diminution to his holy Perſon.

Secondly, They ſay that *Enoch* and *Elias* were tranſlated to Heaven in their Terreſtrial Bodies, and there live in the Fleſh and Members wherein they were tranſlated; therefore ſhall we likewiſe have the ſame kind of Body there, which we now have upon Earth. To this I anſwer, That that good Providence which governs the World, hath in all Ages been ſo gracious to Mankind, that ſhe hath from time to time raiſed up ſuch holy Men, as ſhould by their excellent Life and Doctrine, teach the Inhabitants of the Earth the Ways of Vertue and Godlineſs, ſuch as *Plato* calls *good Souls*; *who leaving their heavenly habitation, were content to deſcend* εἰς τόνδε τὸν τάρταρον; *and aſſuming terreſtrial Bodies, underwent all the calamities and diſadvantages* τῶν ἐν γενέσει, *out of kind Good-will to Men, to whom they gave Laws, and taught them Philoſophy.* Or if you ſuppoſe theſe holy Perſonages, *friends of God and Prophets*, to have deſcended ſomewhat from the Summity of their æthereal Life, and thereby to have had a nearer diſpoſition and fitneſs to actuate a Terreſtrial Body; yet it was not ſo much, but that they recover'd it again before they left the Earth; and therefore their departure hence (of ſome of them I mean) would not be after the ordinary way of Men: and the rather, becauſe the Terreſtrial Life, and the Pleaſures of our fleſhly Body, do ſo extinguiſh our Hope and Belief of ſomething to come, that we have always need of ſuch palpable pledges of continuance in life after this is ended; which therefore Providence mercifully afforded to the Generations of Men, in ſuch like Examples as the Objection inſtances in out of the *Jewiſh* Records. But to be ſhort, I ſay, that that moſt excellent and moſt energetical part in us which the Scripture calls *Spirit*, being throughly enlivened, hath a power to quicken any kind of Body it is united with, into a vigour and ſubtilty anſwerable to its own Might and Purity; and thoſe two holy Perſons, *Enoch* and *Elias*, by this advantage of their exalted Spirit, partaking of the like Power and Virtue in good meaſure, which we have before ſhewn to have been in our Saviour in a moſt eminent degree, they might leave the Earth, and aſcend to Heaven as he did; but with no more neceſſity, that this ſhould be in a Terreſtrial Body, as ſuch, than that Chriſt aſcended, and is glorified in ſuch a Body. And for *Elias*, the Chariots of Fire, and Horſes of Fire, mention'd in the Story of his Aſcenſion, plainly ſignify to the intelligent Reader in what kind of Vehicle he aſcended. His Faſting forty days, and raiſing the Widow's Son, by ſtretching himſelf upon him (that I may name no more of his miraculous Operations) are an Argument of ſome very efficacious Principle in him; like as it was in Chriſt to cure by a *touch*, who once ſaid, that he *perceiv'd Virtue was gone out of him.* Now wherein this miraculous Power did in great meaſure conſiſt, *Herod*, according to the Opinion of the *Jews*, informs us; who hearing of the Miracles that Chriſt did, ſaid, That *John the Baptiſt was riſen from the dead*; *and therefore wonder-working Powers did ſhew forth themſelves in him.* But *John* did no Miracle in his Life-time; and therefore this Inference of *Herod*'s is not from the Perſon of *John* at large, but from the Exaltation of Power and Virtue, which he believ'd naturally accru'd to him from the Excellency of the State of the Reſurrection. And ſomething like this may be ſaid alſo of *Elias*; that he had attained in ſome ſort to the *Reſurrection of the dead* in this life, which in the *Jewiſh* Notion is the ſame with the *Vivification of the Body* (as is plain in many places in St. *Paul*'s Epiſtles) and therefore cannot belong to the Body of Fleſh as ſuch, which he every where calls θνητὸν and νεκρόν.

Thirdly, They object out of St. *Paul*, *This corruptible muſt put on incorruption, and this mortal muſt put on immortality*; *not in general, mortal and corruptible, but* this *mortal and* this *corruptible.* This is *Epiphanius*'s Objection; but I think I have intimated already what kind of Individuation of Body he contends for, to wit, ſuch

ſuch as ariſes from the ſame numerical Particles of Matter, tho this ſame Matter be changed into what Tenuity you pleaſe. But this *ſameneſs of Body* does not oppoſe the Aſſertion of *Origen*, as we have deliver'd it in his fourth Opinion; which only affirms, that the Bodies we ſhall have in the bleſſed Reſurrection, will be of an æthereal ſubtilty, without thinking it worth the while to determine whether they ſhall become ſo tenuious by the change of that Matter which was once terreſtrial, into an æthereal Purity, or otherways. And if they can fancy any way whereby that may be done, in that great and neceſſary Flux of all Matter in the World, in that infinite diſperſion of thoſe Parts of Matter which did once meet together, and made up the Body of a Man, in their innumerable Aſſumptions and Adoptions into other Bodies; and this without making the Exerciſe of the Knowledg and Power of God nice and punctual to no purpoſe, and to no benefit and behoof of thoſe Souls for whom he is ſuppos'd to make thoſe Bodies; if they can fancy any ſuch way, they ſhall have my free leave (if St. *Paul* do not ſay otherwiſe) and may be *Origen*'s too, without much difficulty, who look'd at nothing ſo much in his Hypotheſis of the Reſurrection, as the Vivification of that Body we ſhall then have, into an æthereal Purity. Yet it is not amiſs, if they take the Advertiſement along with them, which he gives to ſuch as ſet themſelves to conſider this Article of our Faith, and to anſwer the Objections which ſimpler Men make againſt the true Notion of it, Χρὴ δὲ πάντα τὸν φιλαληθῆ κατ' αὐτὸν τούτοις τὸν νοῦν ἐπιστήσαντα περὶ τῆς ἀναστάσεως ἀγωνίζεσθαι, σῶσαί τε καὶ τὴν τῶν ἀρχαίων παράδοσιν, καὶ φυλάξασθαι ἐμπεσεῖν εἰς φλυαρίαν πτωχῶν νοημάτων ἀδυνάτων τε, ἅμα καὶ Θεοῦ ἀναξίων. But if any fear they ſhall loſe themſelves and their proper Perſonality in the World to come, unleſs the ſame individual Atoms of Matter meet again to conſtitute the Body they ſhall then have; or if they imagine that *Origen*'s way will induce that monſtrous Change they fear; *Origen* himſelf bids them take heart, and aſſures them there is no ſuch danger. For he thus ſpeaks in *Methodius*, Tho every body, which is continually taking in and letting out its Parts (as Plants and Animals) never hath the ſelf-ſame ὑλικὸν ὑποκείμενον for two days together, but like a River, is in perpetual change: yet *Peter* and *Paul* remain the ſame perſons, both as to their Souls, which are ſtable and without flux; and alſo as to the εἶδος χαρακτηρίζον τὸ σῶμα, and all ſuch Peculiarities thereof as individuate *Peter* and *Paul*, as to their Bodies. Which individuating εἶδος, he ſays, continues ſtill to the Body, even in the Reſurrection, but better'd and perfected. And again, Tho it be neceſſary (ſays he) that the Soul being in corporeal places, ſhould uſe a body a body sutable to the place she is in, as if we were to be aquatick Animals, and live in the Sea, we should have a body like to what the Fishes have: so tho for the same reason being to be Heirs of the Kingdom of Heaven, and Inhabitants of those excellent Regions, it be necessary that we have spiritual and heavenly Bodies; yet for all this, our antient εἶδος is not destroy'd, tho chang'd into greater Glory, as was the Form of *Jesus*, *Moses* and *Elias* in the Transfiguration. Lastly, Upon that place, *Flesh and blood cannot enter into the Kingdom of God*; he says, tho our Body there shall not be Flesh, yet the εἶδος of our corporal Person remains the same. For the Father knew that there is such a thing as humane Form, in what state or place soever the Soul happens to live, and that the particularizing or individuating Notes of it proceed from the particular *Seminal* or *formative Reason* in the Soul of every individual Man; which being a Power that works fatally, and without Animadversion, will work alike as to the main Strokes and Lineaments in every kind of Body it operates upon; but where the Matter is more pure and pliant, there no Strokes will miscarry, or be perverted, but the whole Impression will be exact, and faithfully answer the beautiful Idea, according to which the Plastick works. And the Truth of this he saw confirm'd by many credible Stories of the Apparitions of deceased Men, which punctually retain'd the well-known Forms they had when they liv'd upon Earth, even in their fluid Vehicles of Air. So that whether that τοῦτο in St. *Paul* mean the same individual Particles of Matter, but chang'd into an æthereal Consistency, as *Epiphanius* would have it; or the same Form, Character and Air, which particularize our bodily Person; the Opinion of *Origen*, according as we have asserted it, stands good and unshaken. But if any Man, out of Heedlesness or Prejudice, will venture to stretch the meaning of it further, as if it signified the same Modification and Consistence of the same Particles of Matter with that they are in, in the Body of Flesh; he must first ask our leave to transfer the τοῦτο to some other place, and disjoin it from the words of the Sentence where the Apostle hath placed it. For if he understand any thing of the Nature of Bodies, he cannot but know, that the Body we now have, is therefore corruptible and mortal, because it is Flesh; and therefore if it *put on incorruption* and *immortality*, it must *put off* it self first, and cease to be *Flesh*. For that which is Essentially such or such, is so at all times, and in all places. He that should take up in his hand some dirty piece of Wood, and tell a By-stander that he could make that Wood a pure bright Flame, would never persuade him that it should continue Wood still, be he ever so simple; I think

he

he would be more wiſe and wary than the Satyr was, and not imagine he could handle it now as harmleſly as he might before, nor put it to any of thoſe Uſes it was fit for, before it was laid on the Fire: for its Properties are changed, and it is become perfectly another thing. Laſtly, (that we may make an end of this) they that conſider how neceſſary it was for the Apoſtles, even in their moſt Philoſophical Doctrines, to uſe a groſſer and more palpable way of ſpeech, leſt otherwiſe their ruder and more unlearned Diſciples ſhould not be benefited, will eaſily ſatisfy themſelves, that this Objection does not ſo much as weaken their Opinion, who think it more congruous to the Nature of things to ſay, we ſhall not ſo much as have the ſame Particles of Matter (unleſs by chance) tho ſuppoſed to be changed into that æthereal Purity which *Origen* contends for. But this is more than our preſent Cauſe requir'd.

Their fourth Objection is this Text; *If the Spirit of him that raiſed Jeſus from the dead dwell in you, he that raiſed Chriſt from the dead, ſhall alſo quicken your mortal Bodies by his Spirit dwelling in you.* By *raiſing* and *quickning* (they ſay) the Reſurrection is underſtood, and the mortal Bodies to be raiſed, and our Bodies of Fleſh, which are truly Mortal; therefore in the Reſurrection we ſhall have Bodies of Fleſh. To this I anſwer, Firſt, that the Vivification here mention'd, is not the great Day of Reſurrection in the End of the World, as he that will take the pains to read from the beginning of the ſixth Chapter, to the end of the eighth, in which the Objection is, will plainly ſee. For in this diſcourſe St. *Paul* tells us of two Principles that are in us, the Spirit, Mind, or inward Man, and the Old Man or Fleſh; the Law of the firſt, is the Law of Life and Righteouſneſs, but of the ſecond, the law of Death and Sin. Theſe two Principles are ſo contrary, and their Laws ſo oppoſite to one another, that they cannot both live or reign together; hence therefore ariſes in us great Slavery or Diſtraction: but Chriſt was given us of God to free us from the latter, the Law of Death, and to ſave us by his Life, who is the *Spirit of Life*. From whence the Apoſtle, according to his wont, takes occaſion to teach us, that whatever happen'd to Chriſt, the Captain of our Salvation, to whoſe Image we are in all things to be conform'd, the ſame is myſtically to be wrought in us: ſo that as he was crucified and died, ſo that which is Mortal in us, the *Body of Death and Sin*, was to be crucified, and die likewiſe; and as he was raiſed up from the Dead by the Glory of the Father, ſo ſhould we alſo be to walk in newneſs of Life, and ſerve in the newneſs of Spirit, which then we ſhall do when that *Spirit of Life* and Power, which raiſed

raised Christ from the dead, shall so strengthen that better Principle in us, which he calls *Spirit*, and which he says is *Life*, that it with him become the cause of Life and Vivification to our otherwise mortal Body, and make us alive from the dead unto God. To which Interpretation the Apostle bears witness in giving Thanks to God, that he had *deliver'd him from the body of Death*, or the mortal Body; and in affirming afterwards, *that the Law of the Spirit of Life*, or quickning Spirit, *in Christ Jesus, had freed him from the Law of Sin and Death*, which is the Law in the Members of the mortal Body, the Body of Sin, or the Flesh of Sin: but certainly the Operations of the *Spirit of Life*, or quickning Spirit, are all vivificative; and if the Subject upon which they are exercised be the *Body*, it will thereby become quickned. Now St. *Paul* affirming they had passed upon him, does plainly inform us, that the *Vivification of the mortal Body*, mention'd in the Objection, is something that is wrought in us in this Life, contrary to what the Objectors pretend. And tho I am the least confident of any Man that heartily believes the Scripture, to establish the Sense and Interpretation of any part of it upon Tittles and Apices; yet having (as I think) given the Summary sense of the Apostle in these Chapters (of which taken altogether, a Man may be more assured) and conceiving it very agreeable to Reason, I think I may now be bolder to make my advantage of that, which single, and by it self I should make no great matter of. The words of the Objection are these; *If the Spirit of him that raised up Jesus from the dead dwell in you, he that raised up Christ from the dead*; ζωοποιήσει καὶ τὰ θνητὰ σώματα ὑμῶν, shall quicken even your mortal Bodies *by his*, or the same *Spirit dwelling in you:* i. e. the Spirit of Life and Righteousness shall exert his vivificative Energy upon these mortal Bodies of yours; and they which, without his enlivening Power, only *bring forth Fruit unto Death*, shall, by his Inhabitation in you, have such a *preparatory* Power and Virtue imparted to them, that *Sin shall not reign in them*, but *their Fruits shall be unto Holiness*, while you are constrain'd to be clothed with them, and the end and perfect completion of his Work shall be *eternal Life*. The thing it self, abstracted from all full and pregnant Authority of Scripture, is so reasonable to those who have considered and marked in themselves, with what dependance we act upon something in our Bodies, that the least intimation from so authentick Testimony, might be sufficient to assure them of the Truth of it. But this same holy Apostle, who in the very same Subject once said, *If ye be any otherwise minded, God will reveal this unto you*; hath himself taken further care, that this so true and so concerning

cerning a Notion ſhould be receiv'd by all with whom his Authority, or the reaſonableneſs of the thing, is of any value. Many places there are in his Epiſtles to this purpoſe; ſome of them, which I now remember, I ſhall give you. *And not only they, but we our ſelves alſo, who have* the firſt fruits of the Spirit; *even we our ſelves groan within our ſelves, waiting for the Adoption, the redemption of our Body——For we that are in this Tabernacle do groan, being burdened, ſo far as we would be (I do not ſay unclothed, but) clothed upon, that ſo that which is mortal in us might be ſwallowed up of Life. Now he that hath made, fitted or framed us for this very thing, this victory of Life, is God, who hath alſo given us, as a pledge and part thereof,* the earneſt of the Spirit.——*In whom after that ye believed, ye were ſealed with that holy Spirit of Promiſe, who is* the earneſt of our inheritance, *until the compleat Redemption of the purchaſed Poſſeſſion be effected. With which ſame Spirit the eyes of your underſtanding being enlightned, you will know what is the hope of his calling, and what the rich glory of his inheritance in the holy or heavenly places above, and what is the exceeding greatneſs of his power to us-ward who believe; even ſuch and ſo great as he wrought in Chriſt, raiſing him from the dead, and ſetting him at his own right hand in the heavenly regions.* Which places, if you mind them throughout, cannot but ſeem to you to intimate a certain Inchoation of the æthereal Life wrought in us by the holy Spirit, by which *the Life of Jeſus*, the heavenly *Adam* and vivificating Spirit, *is manifeſted even in our mortal Fleſh.* For what elſe can be the *firſt fruits of the Spirit*, where the whole *Harveſt* is the *redemption of our body from the bondage of corruption, into the glorious liberty of the Sons of God*, the angelick Inhabitants of the *free Æther?* And what elſe can be the *Earneſt of the Spirit*, where the whole Price is the *clothing of us with our houſe from Heaven, eternal and æthereal?* Or what the Earneſt of our Inheritance, (which ought to be homogeneous with the whole Sum) when the Inheritance is the Kingdom of Heaven, the Regions of Light and Glory? But, ſecondly, ſuppoſing the laſt and final Reſurrection in the conſummation of all things was meant by the Apoſtle, it would be ſo far from advantaging the Objector's pretenſions, that it would utterly deſtroy their Cauſe. For if the Body of Fleſh be a mortal Body, if it be quickned and made a living or immortal One, it muſt be made ſomething elſe intrinſecally than what it was; but it being Fleſh before, it muſt not be Fleſh when 'tis enlivened too. For if ſuch a Form of Speaking be allow'd, which can reconcile ſuch different Attributes and Affections to the ſame Subject, farewel all Philoſophy, and all intelligible Speech 'twixt Man and Man. The fabled Miſtakes at *Babel*, at this rate of ſpeaking, would not be Miſtakes; and by a far leſs Licenſe than they take to themſelves, it might be defended, that he did right, who being bid reach a *Trowel*, brought a *Pick-axe*; and the Fox fear'd more than the arbitrarious Power of the Lion, when he fear'd his *Ears* might be call'd *Horns*.

The Fifth Objection may be that known place in *Job*, which *Jerom* wonderfully triumphs in, and cannot tell what ground to ſtand on, for joy he had found an Argument, which ſo ſtrikes the matter quite dead. And tho Life and Immortality be brought to light through the Goſpel, yet he, in a jolly confidence, doubts not to ſay, *Nullus tam apertè poſt Chriſtum, quam iſte ante Chriſtum de Reſurrectione loquitur.* But I muſt confeſs he had great reaſon to be ſo glad of this place as he is; for that coarſeneſs of Spirit which dictated theſe words, *Is ſi non in ſexu ſuo reſurrecturus eſt, ſi non eiſdem membris quæ jacuere in ſtercore, ſi non eoſdem oculos aperiat ad videndum Deum, quibus tunc videbat vermiculos, ubi erit ergo Job? tollis ea in quibus ſubſtitit:* This Spirit, I ſay, had need of ſupport from ſuch an Interpretation as he gives this Text. But he that ſhall conſider how many ſeveral ways that place is tranſlated and interpreted by ſuch as are famous for their Skill in the Language, and how many Words they are fain to ſupply by mere gueſs, to make any ſentence in it intire and perfect; and with what ſuſpence of Mind they propound to their Readers, either this or that ſenſe ſo patch'd up by them, will be very difficultly drawn to believe the riſing again of Fleſh upon the Authority of *Job*, unleſs he be intereſted by a former Perſuaſion, and ſo think that all things he reads without, chime after the meaſures of his inward fancy. For the holy Man ſeems to ſay no more than this, That tho God had ſore afflicted and purſued him as his Enemy, even unto death, tho all his Kinsfolk and Friends had forſaken and abhorred him; yet ſtill would he truſt in God, who he knew was the Patron of the innocent and calamitous, who ever lives, and whoſe hand is not ſhortned, that he cannot ſave and deliver thoſe that hope in him. And tho for the preſent he had hid his Face from him, yet he would at laſt conſpicuouſly appear for his Reſcue and Redemption. And after my Skin be conſum'd, let that which remains of me be by piecemeals deſtroy'd likewiſe; yet I am confident that I ſhall ſee him again, who is now withdrawn from me, ſound and intire, and that with theſe languiſhing Eyes, which ſo long have ſeen nought but the Wounds of his Indignation. Now the Event exactly anſwering his Hope ſo deſcrib'd, would probably perſuade a Man, that the Paraphraſe we have given, or ſome other like it, is the true meaning of the words. For the *Lord* at laſt turn'd the Captivity of *Job*, and then all his Kinsfolk, and Friends, and Acquaintance, who had forſaken him

him before in his Calamity, flock'd to him again, to comfort him concerning all the Evil he had undergone, and to congratulate his deliverance. It may alſo ſeem a wonderful thing, if this place make ſo plainly for them as they brag, that the *Jewiſh* Writers ſhould not interpret it to that ſenſe; who, for want of any tolerable Arguments in their Scriptures for the proof of the Reſurrection, do pitifully and contemptibly catch at every Tittle and Apex of a Letter that looks that way. And the reaſon that ſome give of this their Omiſſion, to wit, that they were afraid of the word *Redeemer*, and ſo choſe to balk a Text, which would have much confirm'd the Opinion they would gladly have advanc'd, rather than by uſing it to that purpoſe, countenance ſuch a Notion of their *Meſſiah* as they lov'd not to hear of, is very ſlight. For certainly, here is not the leaſt intimation of an humble and meek Saviour, whoſe Kingdom is not of this World, whoſe Spirit and Laws put contempt upon all thoſe things which the natural Man ſo highly values, who was at laſt to be ignominiouſly crucified, and to leave the Civil State of the World juſt as he found it, and the *Jews* ſtill ſubject to an Idolatrous Yoke. This is the Scandal and Stumbling-block of the *Jews*, not the Title of *Redeemer*; for certainly the two Diſciples, to whom Chriſt join'd himſelf as they were travelling to *Emmaus*, ſpoke according to the common Phraſe and Opinion of the *Jews*, concerning their expected *Meſſiah*, when they ſaid, *We truſted it had been he which ſhould have* redeemed *Iſrael*. For *Redeemer* and *Redemption*, in the ſenſe of the Chriſtian Myſtery, is not only not inconſiſtent with, but neceſſarily requires Chriſt's being condemn'd to death, and crucified; and yet his Death and Crucifixion was that which made theſe Diſciples conclude he could not be the Redeemer of *Iſrael*.

I ſhall trouble you but with one Objection more againſt this Opinion, and it ſhall be that which is drawn from the Juſtice and Righteouſneſs of God; which, they ſay, cannot ſtand, unleſs the ſame Body of Fleſh riſe again, which was Partner with the Soul in all ſhe did, whether good or bad, and accordingly ſhare with her either in Reward or Puniſhment. For 'tis not equal that that Body which had been induſtrious, temperate and chaſte, ſhould be ſupplanted in its hopes by a new-comer, which underwent not any ſuch tedious Hardſhip and ſevere Self-denial; neither is it juſt, that that Body which had liv'd in all Debauchery, and Exceſs, and Violence, ſhould eſcape, and another far more innocent be whipped in its ſtead. Which Argument *Epiphanius* further carries on in ſuch ridiculous Schemes of Speech, as for his credit I ſhall not produce. That a young Man of a good Fancy, and choice Words, might handſomly

ſomly declaim in this Cauſe, I by no means will deny; but that there is any thing in it beſide empty Pomp, built upon Ignorance, I fear you would not grant. You are not wont to be ſo great a Friend to Mr. *Hobbes*, as to think that Matter, by what name ſoever it be call'd, *dead* or *living*, hath any ſenſe or perception at all, much leſs can it be vertuous or vicious. Yet, upon this ſuppoſal, their Objection is made and built; which being groſly falſe, and the wideſt Inlet that is unto Atheiſm, their ill-ſupported Edifice comes tumbling to the ground; and for the Intereſt of Vertue and Religion, they ought not to reſent the Ruin. Yet it would be very eaſy for me to ſhew moreover, from the continual flux and change of our Bodies, that their pretended Juſtice would not hold in their way neither; but the thing is obvious, and cannot eſcape your notice. He that prevents the Aſſaſſination of his Prince, by killing the treacherous Murderer, ought, by your Suppoſition, to riſe again with the ſame Sword by his ſide wherewith he did that laudable Action, as well as with the ſame Hands which diſtributed to the Wants of the Poor; for one is as much an Inſtrument of Vertue as the other, and as ſenſible of Reward. I believe the Matter that makes up the Vehicle of the Devil, is as well content with its Lot, as that which compoſes the beautiful Robe of an Angel of Light. But this is too much to be ſaid againſt nothing. And I know no other uſe can be made of this Objection than this, to let you ſee that their ſo eager and zealous oppoſing of *Origen* did probably proceed only from their not knowing the Natures of Things. For, for want of ſome true ſetled Notions in their Minds, which might guide their Expoſitions of Scripture aright, they were eaſily miſs-led by any words they read, and as eaſily blurted out very weak and ridiculous Things. Which defect I perceiving in them, gave ſo much to their unqueſtion'd Piety and Eminence in other kinds of Learning, as not rudely to preſs them in this Queſtion, with many Phyſical Conſiderations, which would overthrow the Opinion they contend for from the very Foundations. One whereof *Jerom* ſeems to have been aware of; and therefore, to ſecure the *Body of Fleſh* from Diſſolution in the æthereal Regions, he ſays, that *lutum carnis in teſtam excoquetur*; the beſt way I know to keep it unconſum'd in the Fire: and he ſeems hugely pleas'd with this conceit, and does more than once make uſe of it either as a Subtilty or an Elegance, in his Diſcuſſions of the *Origenian* Errors. If I had a mind to produce all the abſurd Paſſages I obſerv'd in him, *Epiphanius*, and his two Aſſiſtants, you would hardly forbear to ſay (as candid and equal a Cenſurer as you are) they were Men of ordinary Intellectuals.

But in ſuch Subjects as are beſt diſcern'd, and trulieſt pronounc'd of, from a moral ſenſe and reliſh of Spirit (which is a Perfection far more divine than the other) I do freely acknowledg them very excellent Perſons. And thus have I, after my lax careleſs way, anſwer'd to their chiefeſt Objections againſt *Origen*'s fourth Opinion.

Againſt the Fifth, *Epiphanius* ſays not a ſyllable, and I think does not ſo much as barely name it: and I remember nothing in *Jerom* about it but ſuch Admirations as theſe, That the Devils ſhould become Angels again, and *Judas* a Saint! And ſince he hath been pleas'd to ſay no more, I ſhall not ſay much, but only ask, What difference is there in the diſtance betwixt a *Devil* made an *Angel*, and an *Angel* made a *Devil?* I am ſure the advantage is on the aſcending-part, rather than on the deſcending: for the Mercy and Compaſſion of God to all the works of his hands, may reaſonably be ſuppos'd to help them up, tho undeſerving; but there is nothing in his moſt righteous Nature which would caſt them down, without their high demerit. But if St. *Jerom* wondred at this Reſtitution as certain, or eaſy, or of ſhort diſpatch, 'tis his own Miſtake he wondred at, not *Origen*'s Opinion, at leaſt in the two laſt Particulars. What *Methodius* diſputes from the Nature and Reaſon of Puniſhment againſt *Origen*'s making the Terreſtrial Body δεσμὸν καὶ πέδας, if it be apply'd to the final Puniſhment which God will inflict upon all the obdurately-wicked in the end of this World, will as much confirm this fifth Opinion, as he imagin'd through miſtake of the Father's Doctrine, and a pedantick Accuracy in the uſe of a word, it would weaken the Third: and ſo he really gives the Father as much with one hand, as he but thinks he takes from him with the other. For he very largely diſputes in his *Socratical* way, that all Puniſhment is curative, and for the Emendation of the Suffering-party. Some there are that think thoſe Phraſes of πῦρ αἰώνιον and κόλασις αἰώνιος, and the like, cannot be reconcil'd with *Origen*'s Opinion. But theſe Objectors ſeem to take the meaning of the word αἰώνιος from Scholaſtick Definitions, rather than from the true and lawful Maſters of Language, or the authentick Rule of its popular Uſe. For 'tis notoriouſly known that the *Jews*, whether writing in *Hebrew* or *Greek*, do by עולם and αἰὼν mean any remarkable Period or Duration, whether it be of Life, or Diſpenſation, or Polity. Any of which Periods, if plainly computable by a known time, they do then define it by a ſet number of years; but others, which are not ſo known, they ſimply expreſs by עולם or αἰὼν, leaving the length of them to be determined according to the Nature of the Subject matter; which, where

where it is ſuch as comprehends more than a ſingle determinable αἰὼν, they expreſs it in *Hebrew* by the Phraſe of לעולם יעד, in *Greek* by εἰς τὸν αἰῶνα καὶ ἔτι, or εἰς τοὺς αἰῶνας and εἰς αἰῶνας τῶν αἰώνων. But by none of theſe Forms do they mean a Scholaſtick Eternity, unleſs the Nature of the thing then expreſs'd require ſuch an interminable Duration. And hence the Period of this World is call'd αἰὼν οὗτος, when yet there is another to ſucceed it, αἰὼν ἐκεῖνος· and as theſe αἰῶνες differ, ſo would alſo the meaning of αἰώνιος be different, according as it was apply'd to the one or other of them. And ſo in the *plural* Chriſt is ſaid to appear and ſuffer ἐπὶ συντελείᾳ τῶν αἰώνων, when yet the longeſt αἰὼν of all was not then come. And he of whom it was ſaid, *Thy Throne, O God, is* εἰς τὸν αἰῶνα τοῦ αἰῶνος, is yet to *deliver up the Kingdom to God the Father, and to be ſubject himſelf to him who did ſubject all things to him:* ſo that here is plainly an end of that Reign, which is ſaid to be *for ever and ever.* And as ἀπ' αἰῶνος does not in Scripture ſignify *from all Eternity* in the ſenſe of the Schools, ſo by the ſame reaſon ought not εἰς αἰῶνα to ſignify *to all Eternity* in the ſame notion: and is not εἰς αἰῶνα and αἰώνιον all one? Every Lexicographer and Expoſitor will furniſh you with Authorities enough to confirm what I have ſaid; and I leave you to judg, whether the whole Subject matter in this periodical Doom, the Nature of that Fire and its fewel, the Powers of a Spirit incorporate, be not ſuch as will inforce us to make it ſhorter than ſome Men do; who having got eaſy ways of aſſuring themſelves it ſhall not be their portion, do as little pity thoſe calamitous Souls, whoſe Lot it may be, as they darkly fancy God himſelf does. But tho we from the reaſon of Things, and right uſe of Words, do make it ſhorter than they do; yet, according to our Hypotheſis, the whole puniſhment of Pain and Death will neceſſarily be ſo long, as may juſtly be call'd αἰώνιος in a very high ſenſe of the word. But if out of filial regard to the Authority of our dear Mother the Church of *England*, you are yet ſomething backward to give Aſſent to the Probability of *Origen*'s Doctrine; I would have you firſt to conſider, that all thoſe that write and preach in this Nation, are not her Sons, no more than they of *Geneva*, or *Scotland*, or *New-England* are. Secondly, I would fain know why ſhe, who in her 39 *Articles* does ſo punctually follow the Articles agreed upon in K. *Edward*'s Days, or with very little variation, ſhould wholly omit that Article which condemns the Reſtorers of this Opinion, if ſhe had thought it ought to have been condemn'd. And the ſame may be ſaid in behalf of the preceding Opinion; for ſhe hath quite left out that Article of K. *Edward*, wherein it is affirm'd, that *the dead ſhall be reſtor'd to their own bodies, flesh and bones*; very modestly and wisely contenting her self, to impose no more on the belief of her Sons in this particular, than what the Three *Creeds* say of it, which she approves of in her 8th *Article*: but they say no more, than that there shall be a *Resurrection of the Dead*, or *Resurrection of the Body*.

Epiphanius is also silent in the sixth and last Opinion, and *Jerom* says nothing against it. Nay, it seem'd so reasonable a Doctrine, that *Proclus*, by his Suffrage, confirms the Truth of it. For to *Aglaophon* the *Origenist*, in the Question about our future Bodies, arguing from the Conflagration of the World, and upon that demanding ἐν ποίᾳ διαγωγῇ τότε τὰ σώματα ἔσονται, when Earth and Air shall be utterly defac'd, he thus answers, That there shall indeed be a Conflagration, but not to consume things, but to perfect and renew them; for since it is better they should be than not be, (as is plain in that God made them to be, which he would not have done, had it not been the better) it is better they should ever be. And to this sense he interprets that of St. *Paul*, *The creature shall be deliver'd from the bondage of corruption*; and also that of *Isaiah*, *New Heavens and new Earth*. Which is just the same with that of *Sophocles*,

> Ἔσται γὰρ, ἔσται καινὸς αἰῶνος χρόνος,
> Ὅτ' ἂν πυρὸς γέμοντα θησαυρὸν χάσῃ
> Χρυσωπὸς αἰθὴρ, ἡ δὲ βοσκηθεῖσα φλὸξ
> Ἅπαντα τἀπίγεια καὶ μετάρσια
> Φλέξει μανεῖσα. ὅτ' ἂν δὲ, &c.
> Κἄπειτα σώσει πάνθ' ἃ πρόσθ' ἀπώλεσεν.

So that *Proclus* at least grants one new Habitation and Plantation of the Earth again after the Conflagration. And I esteem it a great Blessing that our Enemies are so far at peace with us, as either to say nothing against us, or in our behalf; especially in these two last Opinions of the Father, which seem the most bold and venturesome of all the rest. But it seems, that as all Truth was not discover'd in one Age, but something of her hid Treasures is purposely conceal'd to be the Price and Reward of After-inquirers, that so every Generation may have something of peculiar Excellency to equal it to those that went before: so neither is all Error detected and profligated by the Conduct and Courage of the Learned of one Age. And therefore those pious and learned Men, whom I have made use of for the Refutation of *Origen*'s Temerities, contenting themselves with their zealous Endeavours to correct some of them, have left the rest to be the

Spoil

Spoil of their victorious Successors: which, with what Success, and by what Arms they have done, is not my purpose now to shew. For truly, Sir, I am perfectly tired already, and your Commands, which alone made me hold out so long, by good hap confin'd my *Enquiry* to the more antient Writers; which now I have brought to an end: and having given you this Notice, that where I say St. *Jerom* is silent, or says little of this or that Question debated; my meaning is only, that he is so in such of his Writings, as were purposely compos'd concerning *Origen*'s *Dogmata* (for what he is occasionally in his other Works, I cannot tell, I neither having them, nor being in a place where I have opportunity to procure them) Having given you this Advertisement, it remains only, that I beg your pardon for the imperfect Resolution I have endeavour'd of your Queries, and for the carelesness you will discover in my Style, and the negligent tacking of Sentence to Sentence, even to the obscuring my Sense sometimes; Faults, I confess, which might easily be mended; but not being so, therefore need your Pardon more: For, to tell you the Truth, I was unwilling to render the whole illegible by too frequent interlining, and very loth to write so long a Letter over again. Which I desire you to accept of, such as it is, as a Testimony of that great Power your Commands have over me, which you see I have not detracted, even in an Argument where the Sentiments of my own Mind are not at all interested. For I am,

SIR,

Your, &c.

Phenix II.

God's first Sally out of Himself, in the Birth of the Universe.

The Motives which invited God to create the World.

THO GOD was what he is, and in the perfect Fruition of his Grandeur, before his omnipotent Hand had drawn the Creatures out of their Nothing; yet his Nature requir'd Homage, his Majesty Service, his Glory Admiration, his Goodness Acknowledgment, and his Beauty, Hearts and Affections. It was needful, tho he were independent of all Beings, Immense in his Extent, Eternal in his Duration, and Infinite in all his Perfections, that he should cause himself to be seen and felt by Emanations out of himself. It was not sufficient, (methinks) that God should contemplate himself in the Mirror of his Essence, and that without issuing out of himself, he should beget his Word in the Splendor which flows from his Light. It was not enough to love himself, and in loving himself to produce without Change, Loss, or Alteration, the sacred Fire of his Love. All these immanent and infinite Productions could not exhaust the Treasures of so fruitful a Nature: For in giving it self, it suffers no detriment, since amidst these Sallies and Emanations, the Father and the Son, in such sort, communicate their Nature and Perfections, the Father to the Son, and both to the Holy Ghost; that all Three by a Common power can act *ad extra*, or externally; and they needed to employ but one single word to create, not only a World, but even Worlds without end.

I fancy, that if Nature had had a Being, or could have spoke, she would have address'd the Almighty thus:

The Sighs of Nature.

Speak, O speak (Great God) stretch forth thy Arm, and cast thy Looks out of thy self; Issue forth of the Luminous Darkness, which forms Thee a Day without Night, and a Night more resplendent than the Day. Give some little passage to those Ejaculations and Flames, which from all Eternity are inclosed within thy Bosom, and which frame therein a Circle of Light and Love. Thou need'st but open thy Mouth, and immediately all Creatures will be obedient to thy Commands: The least of thy Irradiations will dissipate the Shadows, and open that Abyss in which they are buried. It is true, that nothing ought to disturb the Peace and Repose of thy Solitude; It is true, thou hast and possessest in thy self all that can ever be. But thou canst bring it to light, and art able, without noise and disorder, to break that eternal Silence, which hitherto hath made Thee heard but of thy self. In fine, thou art a God of Love, and this Love would be Captive, if it had not Sallies and Ejaculations. It was not satisfied to remain in thee by Eminence, and, as it were, in the Source of Beauty and Goodness; but having made its Folds within it self by numberless Revolutions, it must descend upon external Objects, to attain that Effect and Property which is natural to Love, (*viz.*) that amorous Exstacy, that prodigious Effusion, and that pompous and magnificent Shew, which, to speak properly, is the Torch of Love, or rather the Chariot of its Triumph. Upon which, God might have graciously spoke thus:

Well then, Creatures, come forth of the Mass in which you lie confused, Heaven, Earth, Sea, Stars, Trees, Fishes, Furnaces of Fire, and Flames; vast Extents of Air, Clouds, Abysses, Precipices; listen to the Voice and Command of God, of the Word, and of their Love. O God! O Power! O Love! what Word? what Speech? and what Voice? We must proceed in Order, and pursue the same which God himself has follow'd.

The first Alarm of Nature.

The Word was in God the Father, and this Word was God; from that beginning which could never begin, the Common Spirit of God animated the Father and the Son: But, in fine, this glorious and happy Moment, which saw the Birth of Times and Seasons, being arriv'd; the eternal God seeing no Object out of himself, which could deserve his Love; and besides, this Love being incited by a holy Desire of communicating it self, it was requisite to frame a Copy of the Intel-

Love the Architect of the World.

lectual Original, which was in his Idea, and in his heavenly Mind. From that instant the World, then but a lively *Vacuum*, but an universal Privation of Forms and Qualities, was chosen as the blank Table, whereon he resolv'd to draw the first strokes of his Goodness. That Nothing which hath but the bare name Men give it, became immediately a fruitful Abyss of Essences, and Nature was ingendred out of it by the sole Power of the Divinity.

First *Heaven*, *Earth*, *Water*, and Darkness appear'd in an instant, as the Field on which all the Effects of a most amorous and sage Prodigality were to be display'd. It was before any other thing that this dark Compound, this confused Medley, and this heap of Water and Earth, was the Object of him who alone was able to chase away its Shadows, and convert its Dust into Gold and Christal. This is the Throne on which the Title of *Sovereign Monarch* and Lawgiver shall be seen ingrav'd: But what! this Theater is too obscure to behold therein the Birth of the World; we must expect the Aurora, and the Rays of the Day.

The first Day of the Creation.

Nature awake, it is time for the World to rise; the Night hath preceded, and twelve Hours are, as it were, already past, since Heaven and Earth have been in obscurity. Behold the Break of Day; and those delightful Colours, which play upon the Waters, are the Companions of that Light, which in *Palestine* hath already opened the Doors and Windows of the East, and is going to spread it self upon another Hemisphere. Nevertheless, to finish this Career, to perfect this Course, and to go round the whole Globe twelve Hours more, are required; And then counting from Evening till Morning, and from Morning till Evening, you shall find all the Moments, which form the first Day, a glorious Day, a Day illustrious for having first receiv'd the Light, which gives Glory and Splendour to all Days. God himself made even a Stand to behold these Lights, and could not contain himself from praising the attractive Charms of this glistring and pompous Quality, which is as the Life of the Eye, and a most lively Representation of the Spirit.

The second Day.

The second Day was no less glorious: for it was that in which God chose to raise up the Firmament, like a Circle of Brass, or rather like a Globe of Gold and Azure, which might serve to divide the seven Orbs of the Planets from the Empireal Heaven. Now it was in the midst of the Waters that this admi-

admirable Work was form'd; whether they were neceſſary to temper the Rays and Orders of the Stars; or that the Courſe and Revolutions of a moving Body would be more even and free in an Element ſo pure and ſo pliable to all ſort of Motions; Or finally, whether it were for ſome other reaſon known only to the incomparable Architect, who caus'd his Power and Wiſdom equally to ſhine in the Fabrick of the Univerſe.

The third Day.

The next day God deſcended from Heaven upon Earth, and it was on this day he mark'd out Bounds and Limits to Rivers, Streams, Seas and Torrents; ſo that the Waters retiring, ſome on one ſide, and ſome on the other, juſt as they were ſhut up within their Banks, Clifts and Channels, the Earth appear'd, and immediately her Sides were found pierc'd with Caverns, and her Back loaden with Mountains and Rocks, which rais'd her in a ſtately manner. Inſtantly her Entrals were fill'd with Stones and Metals: and whilſt thoſe four great Portions of the Earth, which divide the World, and all the Iſlands of the Ocean and Seas, were level'd to ſerve for Empires and Poſſeſſions of Men; the Hand of God, as juſt as liberal, did in the Boſom of the Earth uphold the Arches of her Priſons and Dungeons, to the end, that if the Paradiſe of *Eden* was a Garden of Delights and Pleaſures, Hell, on the contrary, might be an Abode of Dread, Horror and Miſery. It was likewiſe very convenient, that as God had mix'd Light with Darkneſs, he ſhould create wild Places and Deſarts to render the Gardens, Fields and Meadows more delightful; and finally, having the very ſame Day given Plants, Herbs and Flowers for an Ornament to the Earth, his wiſe Providence mingled Thorns with Roſes, and the moſt wholeſom Herbs ſprung out of the ſame Soil with the *Mandrake* and *Aconite*.

The fourth Day.

The fourth Day having been, as it were, the Chariot of the Sun, Moon, Stars and Planets which ſhine in the Heavens, may, in ſome manner, be call'd the Day of Days; ſince it was the Origin of the Fires brightneſs and flames, which are the Soul of the Day.

Then were the frozen and condenſed Waters gather'd together with more Light and Heat to form the Body of the Planets: Next the Sun, Moon and Stars began their Courſes, Periods and Revolutions, and took the Tracks and Ways which were trac'd out to them from Eaſt to Weſt; they began likewiſe to caſt their favourable Aſpects, and from that time their Influences fell upon the Earth, and they receiv'd the Orders and Laws, which they have ſince obſerv'd ſo inviolably, and

with

with so great respect. But whilst these Torches rowl over our Heads, for fear lest our Eyes should be dazled at such luminous Objects,

The fifth Day. Let us turn them upon the fifth Day, wherein God created the Birds which fly in the Air, and the Fishes which swim in the Water. One must here represent unto his Thoughts some fair Summer's day, and imagine that he sits in the cool upon the Shore of some Island; from thence he must lift up his Eyes towards Heaven, and behold over head Thousands of little feather'd Bodies, cleaving the Air with their Wings, piercing the Clouds, and mingling with their Flight the sweet Harmony of their Warblings: He must afterwards behold at his Feet a River full of Fishes armed with Scales, some of which cut their Way near the Surface of the Water, and others through the midst of the Waves; some swim aloft against the Stream and Current, others are carry'd down at the pleasure of the Winds, and by the favour of so sweet and rapid an Element.

This is that which God took pleasure to see and do, five Days after the Creation of Heaven and Earth: This was the Day he chose to people the Air and Sea with their Guests, which were in so great Numbers, as since it hath not been necessary to create other Species of Birds and Fishes. But what! the Earth, which serves for a Basis and Foundation unto Sea and Air, would have some cause to murmur against both, and might with reason complain, as it were, of God her Creator, if she were abandon'd, and without Inhabitants. Soft, a little patience: It belongs not unto Creatures to prescribe Laws to their Creator.

The sixth Day. Scarce had the Morning brought news of the arrival of the sixth Day, but at the same instant the Earth opened her Eyes unto her Sun, and her Ears unto the Voice of her God. This dull, heavy and insensible Mass, not satisfied to have brought forth Flowers, Plants and Trees, yet farther display'd it self to produce all sorts of Beasts and Animals: Behold the World in her Cradle, and Nature in her Infancy; The unmoveable Earth, round about her Center, is sown with Flowers, tapistried with Turf and Verdures, beautified with Woods and Forests; She is stately in her Mountains, pleasant in her Valleys, delightful in her Meadows; She is rich in her Metals, fertile in her Fruits, and plentiful by her Rivers and Seas, which inviron her on all parts, and form her a thousand liquid Transparencies. The Air encompasses her on all sides, and serves her for a Veil to temper the over-humid Influences

ces

ces of the Moon, and the too ardent Rays of the Sun. The Heavens, like pendent Roofs and rowling Arches, are ſtrew'd with Flowers, Emeraulds and Rubies. What doth remain after all theſe Prodigies of Power, and all theſe Works of Love? O Power! O Love! I cannot condemn his Fancy who ſaid, that * *Love produc'd Heaven out of a Chaos, and the World out of a confuſed and undigeſted Lump.* Theſe are the Draughts of a powerful God, which were victorious over the Nothing: Theſe are the conquering Flames of his Love, who hath carried his Rays and Torch, even into the Abyſſes of an eternal Negation.

* Heſiod *in the Genealogy of falſe Divinity.*

The Errors of ſome Philoſophers.

The World then had not its Origination in the Water, as *Thales* ſuppoſed; nor was the Impreſſion of the Univerſe fram'd in the Air, as *Anaximines* affirm'd; *Heraclitus* was extravagant when he taught, that Fire was the Source and Origin of Nature; And *Democritus* was a mere Scoffer, and fitter to be laugh'd at himſelf, than to laugh at others; when he ſaid, that the World was form'd by an accidental concourſe and mixture of inviſible Atoms. No, no; the Beginning of Beginnings muſt be without Beginning. But the *Heavens, Air, Fire, Earth and Water, the World and Atoms*, cannot be from themſelves, and without a Producer; therefore grant, that God alone is the Fountain, Cauſe and Origin of the Univerſe.

Comfort of Creatures.

Ah then, let the Heavens, and all the Elements; Let the Sun and Stars, let the Plants and Herbs, let the Birds and Fiſhes for evermore praiſe and bleſs the powerful Hand of the increated Love, who form'd them all out of Nothing. Let the World never have any propenſion, inſtinct, or inclination, but to become pliable to the impulſes of its Author. Let the Morning and Evening Stars imitate him, conveying every where their Influences and Light. Let Rain be the Pledg of his Favours, and Dew the Symbol of his Graces. Let Thunder and Lightning be the Heraulds of his Juſtice, and the Miniſters of his Indignation. Let the gentle Weſtern Winds awaken our Hearts, to liſten to his moſt holy Inſpirations. Let his Threats be heard amongſt Storms and Waves. Briefly, let the World, and all Nature, be an Altar whereon Vows and Sacrifices may be continually offer'd to his Law; and let the *Feaſt of the ſix Days*, during which God created the Univerſe, be for ever celebrated. But what, O Lord? Who is it that hath hitherto ſpoken? From whence came this Voice? And where is the Perſon that can preſent Sacrifices unto thee? The World hath Altars, it hath Water, Fire, Wood and Victims:

Victims: But where is the Priest? There wants a Man upon the Earth; and without a Man, all thy Works seem not sufficiently perfect. Yes, my God; this Man, who is to be the Image of thy Essence, the Accomplisher of thy Commands, and thy Lieutenant upon Earth, well deserves the last Touches of thy Hand; to the end, that after his Creation thou may'st continue in the Repose of thy most holy Entertainments.

Man necessary for the World.

Eloquence of Self-love.

It is almost incredible how bold and eloquent Men are, when it concerns their own Praises: To hear them speak, would not a Man swear, all the Members of their Bodies are converted into Tongues, to publish, without blushing, the Advantages of their Nature, above whatever the rest of the World can boast of, as most rare and beautiful? The Earth, say they, is but an Abode, or rather a High-way, which shall be their Pilgrimage; The Air and Sea are but their Harbingers and Hosts; Lightnings and Celestial Flames form but a Plan, in which the Features of their Minds appear, as it were, rough-drawn: And Heaven it self is but the Haven and Shore, which after the Course of some Months and Years is to receive them all. Man, according to their Opinion, is the fairest Piece of the Universe, the All of All, and, as it were, the Soul of this World. *Anastasius*, in his Homily of Man's Creation, observes some Lines of Honour and Veneration in his Fabrick. *Clemens Alexandrinus* compares him to the *Thessalian* Centaur, by reason of the mixture of the Soul with the Body: And *Lactantius Firmianus*, speaking of the Composition of Man, saith, That he is a Work which may rather beget Admiration than Words. *Trismegistus* calls him the Interpreter of the Gods; *Pythagoras* looks upon him as the Measure of all things, in whom are found the Longitudes, Latitudes, Altitudes and Profundities of all Beings, *Plato* cries out, that he is the Miracle of all visible Miracles; *Theophrastus* considers him as the Copy of the Universe; *Synesius* calls him the Horizon of Creatures; And *Zoroaster*, as one transported, scarce finding Words to describe him, concludes at last, *That Man is the Portrait of an attempting and daring Spirit.* Are not these very excellent Terms and Expressions? which sufficiently evidence, that albeit those Learned Authors did speak of Man in general, yet all of them were interested therein as to their own particular. But whatever they have said, it is certain, that of all the

Excellent Conceptions of divers Authors.

Encomiums can be given to Man, the most Noble, the most August, the most Transcendent and High is, *That Man is the Image of God, the Character of his Substance, and the most faithful Copy of his Divinity.* I know he hath a Being common with Stones and Marble, a Life common with Plants, a Sense with Beasts, and an Understanding which equals him with the Angels: but he excels them in this, That he was created from God's Idea, as the most lively and sensible Representation of his Maker.

God deliberates upon the Enterprize of this Work, and the Council is held in the Conclave of the most Holy Trinity; the Three Persons are assembled; Power, Wisdom and Love take their Seats near the Paradise of *Eden.* But let us not deceive our selves; is it not peradventure God's intention to recall into favour those proud and rebellious Spirits, whom a shameful Revolt hath most justly precipitated from Heaven to Earth, where they wander as Exiles and Reprobates? At least would it not satisfy him to banish them from Heaven, and to grant them the World for a Paradise, after so long and fatal a Captivity? Nothing less, the Act is past, the Angels are lost without Redemption, and the Punishment their Insolence hath merited, will pursue them without relaxation, term, or pity.

It is concerning *Man and his Creation* that the Decree is past; It is on him God reflecteth, and it is he who must be substituted in the place of Angels. It is this Act which makes the World behold God's Master-piece, the Object of his Favours, and the most glorious Term of his Power. O Sun! stop here thy Course, and be witness of his Birth, who was the Cause and End of thine.

The Time of Man's Creation.

It was, as I conceive, about high Noon, when the Earth was resplendent with Light, that this *Animated Sun was born.* It was by the Light of Nature's greatest Bonfire that God vouchsaf'd to stoop so low as Earth to take Clay, out of which he form'd the Body of the first Man. This Wise and All-knowing Workman, to whom all things are possible, drew out of Dirt, Mortar and Dust, the Bones which were to be, not only the Piles, Pillars, Basis and Strength of the Body, but even the Instruments of all its Motions. He added to it Ligaments, Joynts, Cartelages, Nerves, and an Infinity of Fibres, or little Strings, which were to lock the Bones and Members within one another, to be serviceable to all Motions, to arm every Part, to keep in or draw superfluous Humors, or rather, to be assisting to its Nourishment. *The Body being thus rough-drawn,* or, as I may say, in its first draught, appear'd appear'd at the same Instant divided into three Parts, of which the highest and most elevated was the Head, the Bulk appear'd in the midst, and the Joynts link'd together, the Legs and Arms to become more useful to all the extreme Parts. Within these Joynts were, as inchased, all the Instruments of Life. Within the Trunk reign'd the Vital Parts, as the Heart, Lungs, and Liver; about which were found a thousand little Veins, and as many little Skins, which are the Channels of the Blood, and of all the Humours. O strange! this little Labyrinth was no ways confus'd. *The Heart*, tho Monarch and Sovereign in this Empire, disdains not to unite it self with the Liver, and to join by a mutual and reciprocal Agreement, its Virtue and Heat, to act with more force upon the Aliment. From thence issue a World of interlac'd Veins, which are to suck in the purest of the Chile, and to discharge the grosser part, which afterwards conveys it all at leasure into the Bowels: At the same time the Liver will separate the Blood, and divide the Humours; and whilst the Heart is distributing all the Spirits through the Arteries, lest it chance to be over-heated, the more light, humid, and spungy Lungs will give it air, and refresh it by such regular Intervals, as even amidst this palpitation it may receive from the Arteries its purest Blood, and its most delicious Nourishment. All the rest passes into the Brain, which is the Summit of this admirable Structure. It is cover'd outwardly with Skin and Hair, and wrapped up within two Panicles, which cover its Out-lets, its Substance, and the Source of all the Nerves. It is in this Fort or Dungeon where the Animal Spirits are to be form'd, which the Sensitive Soul distributes to the Five Senses; Spirits which are but Fire and Rays, that very often get loose, and escape from the Eyes like Lightnings, and so many Stars which appear to us at high Noon.

The Oeconomy of humane Bodies.

There is the Seat of the Common Sense, where all the Nerves of our exterior Senses meet, through which the Spirits slide, and is the way by which the Species pass, when they are the Messengers of their Objects. Well may this Part receive these Images, but cannot retain them. The Imagination then must be plac'd further within, which collecting and preserving the Species, will borrow part of their Name. *Behold the Body thus perfect, and accomplish'd*; but not to descry all the Bones naked, and a Flesh too lively and bloody, cover it with the whitest, smoothest and thinnest Skin that can be. Afterwards fix your Eyes upon his Face, behold his lovely Hair sweetly waving on his Shoulders; contemplate his

Fore-

Forehead ſmoother than Marble, and his Eye-brows forming an Arch of Ebony over his Eyes; conſider his Mouth ſurrounded with Coral; obſerve his Cheeks mix'd with Roſes and Lillies, and ſmell his Breath a thouſand times ſweeter than Ambergreaſe. In truth, are you not raviſh'd with the Aſpect of his Eyes, which are *the Windows of the Soul*, the Doors of Life, and the moſt faithful Interpreters of our Minds? What ſay you to the diſcloſure of this living Theater of Choler, of Vengeance, of Pity, of Hatred, of Fury and Love? Do you ſee by their Looks how they riſe and fall, how they flatter, how they excite, how they weep, how they ſmile, and how they ſhew upon their liquid and tranſparent Chryſtal, all that is diſcernable in the World? But who will wonder at this, ſince, in truth, theſe are *the two Suns of the Little World*, and the Mirror of the Great One, which is to be compriz'd and incloſ'd within the Humane Body?

Theater of Paſſions.

Should not the Eyes of all Nature open themſelves here to admire this Miraculous Body, and this Prodigy of the Univerſe? But the thing of greateſt Admiration is, that God hath cauſed the Soul of Hearts, and the Life of Bodies, to flow into his Mouth and Heart; and that *Heaven hath poured the Seed of Immortality into his Breaſt*. God, by a Divine Breathing, communicated this Fountain of Life, to wit, the *Soul*, which inſtantly made the Image and Pattern of the Divinity reflect on his Face. This heavenly Form, without noiſe or delay, diffus'd it ſelf entire into the Body, remaining nevertheleſs whole in every part. God alone knows with how many Lights the Underſtanding of Man was illuminated, with how many Ardors his Will was fired, and with how many Species his Memory was filled in a moment.

The Maſter-piece of Nature.

The ſole Source of Beauty, and of Operations.

The

Phenix III.

A Design about Disposing the Bible into an Harmony: or, *An Essay concerning the Transposing the Order of Books and Chapters of the Holy Scriptures, for the reducing of all into a continued History.*

To the Right Honourable the LORDS and COMMONS Assembled in Parliament.

THIS that I now humbly offer to your Hands, hath been long in my Thoughts; but much more since in my Attendance on his Majesty's Children, I have (under the Encouragements and particular Favours of the Right Honourable, my Lord, the Earl of Northumberland, *to whose Care You have intrusted those Royal Pledges) read thorow the whole Bible in an Expository way. I have high Thoughts of the sacred Authority of Scripture; I admire the Wisdom of the whole, and the admirable Consent of all the Parts of it; and do firmly believe, that the Majesty of it will triumph over the Attempts of all Anti-Scripturists to the contrary, till the Time of our Lord's coming again. 'Tis the Glory of Christian States to maintain and advance it, which was the meaning of those Learned Men, who have lately enrich'd the World with that Treasury of the King of* France *his Bible in Ten Volumes; where, in one Frontispiece, they have represented a Table of the Portraicture of Cardinal* Mazarine, *supported and mounted by Angels, as being a great Patron*

Patron of that renowned Labour. May your Names alſo be great unto Poſterity, whilſt you promote the Glory of God, and the ſaving Knowledg of Men, by Works of this nature. The learned Licenſer intimates the Difficulty of this, I alſo acknowledg it; but withal, I nothing doubt, but under ſuch an Influence as Yours it may grow to a full Maturity.

Your Honour's moſt humble,
and moſt devoted Servant,

SAM. TORSHELL.

The Authority of the Canon of Scripture. The Liberty of Interpreting it. A Complaint againſt the Abuſe of it. The Remedy.

IT is a receiv'd Principle, even among the *Turks* themſelves, *That God's Teſtimony ſufficeth*, (ſo the *Alcoran* ſpeaketh, cap. de Aranea, *Sufficit Dei teſtificatio*) and, *That God hath made known his Will in Books.* The *Alcoran* gives witneſs to both the *Teſtaments*, as we call them. And *Philip Guadagnoli*, the *Arabick Profeſſor* at *Rome*, in his *Apology for Chriſtian Religion*, againſt *Ahmed* the *Perſian*, hath produc'd clear Inſtances of ſome Paſſages, almoſt out of every particular Book in the whole Bible, expreſly quoted, or manifeſtly alluded unto, in many Chapters of the *Alcoran.*

Much more therefore, in the entrance of this Diſcourſe or Eſſay, which I have now undertaken, I will ſuppoſe it among *Chriſtians*, to be a *Principle* that needs not proof, and a thing conſtantly granted, that the whole *Scripture*, contain'd in the *Canon*, or Number of Books, which we call *Canonical*, is the Word of God, divinely inſpired, and left unto us to be the Rule of Faith and Manners. Under that *Title* or *Right*, the *Law* and the *Prophets* were deliver'd over from the *Jews*, the old and faithful Keepers of them, to the *Chriſtians*, by whom both *thoſe*, and the *Evangelical* or *Apoſtolical Writings* and *Declarations*, have been held in poſſeſſion, under the ſame Title, in the ſeveral Ages ſince, even down to theſe days. There was never, among the *Antients*, any publick Quarrel about that; only (which adds alſo to the weight and ſtrength of the *Scripture's Title*) there have been not a few Quarrels about the Senſe.

The *Arts* that have been us'd by the *Romanists*, for the setling and establishing *the Right of Interpretation* upon the *Bishop* of *Rome*, have been well known; whereby they have labour'd to make him the *Oracle* to the World, as the *Turkish Mufti* is (by the relation of *Busbequius*) in those Parts, finding it to be the most expedite way to gain the Opinion of the *publick* and *authoriz'd Interpreter*. But upon the experience of his own, and his Servants readiness, to make advantage of every thing that hath any *likelihood* to *advance* them, and to *wrest* and *abuse Scriptures* to the maintenance of their *Usurpations*; therefore so long as there are (at least) *reasonable* Men in the World, it will always prove a broken and entangled *Title* unto him.

Who then must be Judg? There are many that would give it to the *Fathers*, and that we must receive their *Sense*. But that were to make them not *Expounders*, but, in a manner, *Lawgivers*. I have spoken somewhat to this in my *Exercitation* upon *Malachy*, and in my *Historical Preface* before Mr. *Stock*'s *Commentary* upon that *Prophet*, from whence I shall transcribe a little: That we regard the *Fathers* highly, but yield them not the *Royalty* of a *Mint*, as *Mornay* speaks. In the very *Council* of *Trent*, a Saying of Cardinal *Cajetan*'s, *That a new sense of Scripture is not to be rejected, tho it be against the old Doctors, seeing Power is left now also to interpret*; was by some much commended, who thought it a *Tyranny* to forbid the *faithful* the use of their own proper *Ingeny*. Others indeed opposed that Saying, accounting *License* worse than *Tyranny*. Among others, *Richard* of *Mans*, a *Franciscan Fryar*, went so far as to say, That the *Doctrine of Faith* is now so *clear'd*, that we ought to learn it *no more* out of the *Scriptures*, which were heretofore *read* in the *Church* for *instruction*, but now only are read to *pray* by, not to *study*. There were not many that adhered to him; the better part deliver'd themselves, as *Dominick a Soto* did: *That it was fit to keep every Wit within limits for Matters of Faith and Manners, but else to leave them to their liberty for the sense.* Others of them yet more plainly: *That it was not fit to restrain the Understanding of the Scriptures to the Fathers only, whose Expositions were for the most part Allegorical, seldom Literal, and those fitted to their own times.* Seeing then the more *learned* and *sober* Party, even among the *Romanists* themselves, have been tender of taking away the Liberty of the *Faithful* to *judg* of what is written; far be it from us to be worse than they, or to erect a Tyranny, by putting the *Key* of *Knowledg* into the hands of any particular Order of Men.

But what way may be taken, to prevent, that this *liberty* prove not a *mischief*? Of late we have had too sad an experience, of the *boldness* of such as *pretend* to the Knowledg of

* Scriptures.

Scriptures. Besides what we hear of, deliver'd here and there in *corners*; there is too much witness in those *weak*, *senseless* and *triobolary Pamphlets*, which have *wasted* so much Paper, and have *unmannerly* intruded upon the *leisures*, yea the necessary *business* of all sorts of Men of late years; in which, what *childish* and *impertinent Allegations* of *Texts* have we found? what *raw* and *indigested Collections* from them? what *bandying* up and down of *incoherent Scripture-words* and *Sentences?* Many thorow a proud forwardness, venture *unripe* and *unexperienc'd* upon the *expounding* of the *Scriptures*; that, as *Eckius* said, he chose the Points of *Predestination*, that upon them he might *exercere juveniles calores*, make trial of his youthly Heat; so these take the *sacred Oracles* of God, upon which to make their *raw* and *imperfect Essays*. And ordinarily, as the most learned Men are *sceptical*, and but little *positive*; so the *weakest* Men are most *magisterial*, and cry out like the *Mathematician* at *Athens*, *I have found*, *I have found it*, when they light upon a *Notion* which seems *new* to them; but, it may be, might be had in twenty *Authors* which they know not.

But the most of those that are *unlearned* and *unstable*, do *wrest* the *Scripture*, as the *Apostle* speaks, thinking they find that in it which is not it. They bring an *Opinion* with them, and with that they read the *Bible* all along, imagining that they see it every where before them; like the *Man* of whom the *Philosopher* spake, who thought he saw his own *shape* before his Eyes at every step he took. A strong Imagination or Fancy will persuade very much, and beguile both the *Eye* and the *Ear*: As for instance; Some, when they look up to the *Racke*, or moving Clouds, imagine them to have the Form of *Men*, of *Armies*, of *Castles*, *Forests*, *Landskips*, *Lions*, *Bears*, &c. where none else can see such things, nor is there any true resemblance of such *shapes*. And for the *Ear*, when a Man hath somewhat that *rowls* and *tumbles* in his *thoughts*, he will think, that the *ringing* of *Bells*, the *beating* of *Hammers*, the *report* that is made by great *Guns*, or any other measured or intermitted Noise, doth *articulately* sound and speak the same which is in his Thoughts. In this same manner, many perswade themselves, that the *Scripture* represents to them such and such formed Opinions, while they *patch* and lay things together, without any reason; like *Children* looking upon a *Wall*, will fancy an *armed Man*, or some other thing, such a *spot* to be the *bulk* of the Body, such another *spot* to be the *Head*, some other *scratches* or *flaws* to be the *Legs* or *Arms* with *weapons*; while another perhaps, at the same time, imagines the same *spots* to resemble a *Dragon*, and a third that they resemble a *Ship*, or what else may indeed be most unlike a Man. We could not have thought what *vanity* there is in the *imagination* of Men, if somewhat had not been testified to us of old by the *Apostle*, who tells us of the *Gentiles*, how their *foolish hearts* were *darkned*, Rom. 1. ver. 21. and by the Antients, *Augustine*, *Philastrius*, and others, who have recorded the *strange* and *senseless Dotages* of many *Hereticks*; and of late in the *ridiculous Papers* that have flown about, and bring *Scripture* with them, but no *sense*; fancying the holy Word of God, to *strike*, to *ring*, or *chime* to their Tunes. The Apostles *Peter* and *Jude*, speak of *Dreamers*; sure there are many such now. A Man that is awake (we know) may think of a *golden House*, the way to which is *paved* with *Rubies* and *Saphires*, the Wall *plaister'd* with *Pearl*, and the Gate one entire *Diamond*: but his *external Senses* not being hinder'd with other witness and information, his *internal sense* gives judgment aright; but when the outward *senses* are lock'd up by *sleep*, then those vainest *fancies* are entertain'd without controul. Such danger is there, when (to use the *Apostle*'s Phrase, *Heb.* 5. 14.) Men have not their *Senses exercised to discern both Good and Evil.*

But yet a greater Mischief ariseth out of a corrupt and deprav'd Mind and Affection; according to that of St. *Paul*, 1 Tim. 6. 5. *Perverse disputings of Men of corrupt Minds.* When the *Appetite* or *Affection* is *eager*, and stays not the leisure of *deliberation*, but *out-runs* it, so as not to be recalled; then the *Mind* is drawn to be of the same Opinion with the *Appetite*, and takes up what is *fancied*, as *true*; and what is *affected*, as *warrantable*: that at length the *beguiled* Man *believes* himself. He that looks upon an *unlovely* thing with the *Eye* of *Love*, thinks it *lovely*; so that what is *false*, seems *true* to him that strongly *affects* it. He that is extreamly *a-thirst*, drinks down that with pleasure, which if he were not so *distemper'd*, would offend his tast, and very much *nauseate* his *stomach*.

I might instance in many the like *deceits* and *inconveniences*, growing partly from *depravedness* of Mind, partly from *ignorance*, partly from *instability*, *suddenness* and *haste*, when Men take a *snatch*, and *run* away with that which *looks* like the *sense* of *Scripture*, as if they had gotten somewhat that made much for them, and *weary* themselves about them; like the *Apes* in the *story*, who finding a *Glo-worm* in a cold Night, took it for a *spark* of *fire*, and heaped *sticks* upon it, to *warm* themselves. So do they lose their labour, who are busy about *sounds* of *Words*, and *incoherent Scripture-sentences*.

But I have not spoken all this with a mind to *defraud* the *faithful* of their *Right*, even their Right to *judg* of what is written. The Sentence of the great *Apostle* resolves and directs me in this, who applying himself to the *Community* of *Believers* at *Corinth*, saith even to all, *I speak as to wise men, judg ye what*

what I say, 1 Cor. 10. 15. And in after-times, the *Christians* held themselves in possession of it. *Theodoret*, in the Fourth Book of his *History*, cap. 19. gives us a notable Testimony. When *Euzoius*, the Governor of *Alexandria*, had thrust out *Peter*, the Orthodox Successor of *Athanasius*, and had placed *Lucius* an *Arian* in that Church; the People having been brought up under *Athanasius* Doctrine, perceiving contrary Food provided for them, they would not hear, but forsook the *Ecclesiastical Meetings*. That which God hath given to the *People*, let none presume to take from them. Let us rather renew the Earnestness of *Chrysostom*, and others of the *Antients*, to persuade and encourage them more to the *reading* and *examining* of the *Scriptures*. Take not away the *Book*, only *spread* it more open. The *Ministry Ecclesiastical* was appointed to this *end*, and to this *end* were *Gifts* given unto Men.

To this purpose many have profitably labour'd: The *Antients* fram'd their *Commentaries*, *Enarrations*, *Scholies*, *Glosses*, *Metaphrases*, *Paraphrases*, *Homilies*. In the several Ages there have been some or other (as I have particularly mention'd in my fore-nam'd *Historical Preface* to *Malachy*) that have apply'd themselves to this Work, but more abundantly in these later Times. Only, whereas the *difficulty* and *obscurity* of *Scripture* is in great part, because of the *Anticipations*, *Transpositions*, and *Dislocations* of whole *Books*, or some *parcels* of the *sacred Canon*; we are yet wanting to our selves, and to our clear understanding of the whole *Scripture*; that the *whole* hath not been digested into one *continued History*, according to the *Order* of *Times*, which would make the Work of *Commenting* and *Interpreting* much more easy, and the whole *Context* altogether more *clear*. This therefore is it, which I have humbly to offer:

1. To propose and open the Design about the Harmonizing of the whole Bible, or the bringing of both the Testaments into one continued History.
2. To shew the Usefulness or Benefit of such an Harmony.
3. To discover the Difficulty of such an Undertaking.
4. To enquire into some Helps towards it.
5. To commend it to the Allowance and Care of the Publick State.

An Essay of the Design.

THE *Design* is to lay the *whole Story* together in a *continued Connexion*, the *Books*, or *parts* of Books, and all the several *parcels* disposed and placed in their *proper Order*, as the continuance and *Chronical method* of the *Scripture-history* requires; so that no *sentence* nor *word* in the whole *Bible* be *omitted*, nor any thing *repeated*, or any word *inserted*, but what is altogether necessary for *Transition*. So as some *whole Chapters*, or *pieces*, be put into other places, yea great parts of some *Books*, and some *whole Books* to be *woven* into the *Body* of another Book. For the Illustration of my meaning, I shall only offer at a *general Draught*, or *imperfect Essay*.

It must necessarily begin with the first Book of *Moses*, which is *Genesis*, where such *anticipations* as may be found, are to be refer'd to their own place. As for Example: To make up the 27th and 28th *verse* of the *first Chapter* of *Genesis*, with the 7th, the 18th and 19th *verses*, &c. of the 2d *Chapter*, together into one *relation*. Then to continue, *Chap*. 1. *ver*. 29, 30, &c. after the end of the 2d *Chapter*. And to place the three first *verses* of the 2d *Chapter* at the *ending* of the 3d. And so throughout the *Bible*, where any thing is related by *Prolepsis* or *Anticipation*. And to place the whole Book of *Job* (digested also particularly, if there be any *Anticipations* in it) into the Body of *Genesis*, either after the History of *Nahor*; or next after the 33d *verse* of the 36th *Chapter* of *Genesis*, according as it shall be judged upon a learned *Examination*, that after the Opinion of the *Hebrews*, he was the *Third* from *Nahor*; or after the Opinion of the *Greeks*, and the *Genealogy* added in the LXX, at the end of *Job*, he were the *Fifth* from *Abraham*, and *Third* from *Esau*, and so the same with *Jobab*, mention'd *Gen*. 26. 33. Whether *Moses* wrote the *History* of *Job*, will not be material now to question: but however, the *Story* is to be *inserted* into that place that shall be found most unquestionably to agree to the *History* of his *time*.

In this manner to *digest* the *Books* of *Exodus*, *Numbers*, *Leviticus*, *Deuteronomy*, and to continue them to the *story*, placing the several *Exhortations* of *Moses* recorded in *Deuteronomy*, in their own proper times, when the Occasions of speaking them there were, if it may be found in *Numbers* the History of the *Removes*, when they were spoken. And into the History of *Moses*, to *insert* the 90th *Psalm*, if it shall be concluded to be writ by him, and (as to me it seems most likely) if it were pen'd upon occasion of that *threatning*, related *Deut*. 4. 31. then in that story to be conveniently placed. There

There are some particular *Anticipations* in *Joshuah*, and so in the Book of *Judges*; but those being *digested*, they are to be continued *successively* to the *story*. And for the whole Book of *Ruth*, it may seem fit to be put in the *story* of *Eli*, in the beginning of *Samuel*, if she be found to have liv'd under the time of his Judging *Israel*.

The *Books* of *Samuel*, *Kings* and *Chronicles*, will be next in their *order*, where the *History* of the *Kings* of the whole People, and after, of the two Kingdoms of *Judah* and *Ephraim*, being distinctly, and in one relation of their several Reigns, made up of the *circumstances* in the several Books brought together: here will be the greatest *variety* of *transposition* and *inserting*.

To distribute the *Psalms* (so many as are found to be *David*'s, and whose *argument* and *occasion* may be found) into the *Chapters* in *Samuel*, according to the several *estates* and *passages* of *David*'s *life*, that in his continued History we may hear him *singing* answerable to the *emergencies* of Providence, whereby we shall much better know his meaning. As for such *Psalms* as are thought his, but no *satisfaction* (so much as *conjectural*) concerning the *occasion*, those to be set at the end of his *Life* and *Reign*. The other *Psalms* to be *distributed* to the Time and Stories of their *Authors*; one to *Heman*, namely, *Psal.* 88. one to *Ethan*, where we find him mention'd in the *Kings*, namely, *Psal.* 89. some to *Asaph*; some haply to the *Sons* of *Korah*, that were of the *Quire* in *David*'s time, namely, *Psal.* 42, 43, &c. and haply some to King *Solomon*, at least *one*, namely, *Psal.* 72. being thought to be of his composing.

The *Books* of *Proverbs* (so many of the *Proverbs* as may be judged to be *spoken* or *collected* by *Solomon*,) *Canticles*, and *Ecclesiastes*, to be put into the *Body* of the *second Book* of *Kings*, according to the Times of *Solomon*'s Reign: If the Opinion of some *Rabbins* be thought to be followed, that the *Song* was made when he was *young*, at his *Marriage*, the *Proverbs* collected in his *maturity*, *Ecclesiastes* in his *age*; those *Proverbs*, ch. 25. ch. 26. ch. 27. ch. 28. ch. 29. to be placed in the Body of the *Chronicles*, at the end of the Reign of King *Hezekiah*.

The *Sermons* of the *Prophets*, to be disposed into the *times* of the *Reigns* of those *Kings* under whom they lived. So that if with industry and diligence the particular *times* and *occasions* can be found out, so accordingly to *refer* them; placing, it may be, a *Chapter* or *Chapters* of *one*, *two* or *more Prophets* contemporary, and prophesying of the same Subject, *together*. And so in order to the *Times*, without regard to the *order* of *Books*. And those *Prophecies*, whose *occasions* or *time* cannot be judged of, those to be placed at the *ends* of *Kings* under whom they lived.

Ezekiel and *Daniel* to be *inserted* about the *end*, or added after the *end* of *Chronicles*, as ſhall be maturely conſider'd.

Haggai and *Zachary* to be *interwoven*, with the continued Hiſtories of *Ezra* and *Nehemiah*, into which alſo the whole Book of *Esther* is to be wrought: And then *Malachy* to be placed in the order of his own *time*.

As for the *New Teſtament*, the *beginning* of it, namely, the *Hiſtory* of our *Lord's life* and *ſufferings*, recorded by *four* ſeveral *Evangeliſts*, is already brought together, by many *Learned Men* into an *Harmony*, but moſt diligently by *Chemnitius*, ſo far as he went, and then continued by *Lyſerus*, and after by *Gerhard*.

Into the Body of the *Hiſtory* of the *Apoſtles Acts*, are to be diſtributed the *Epiſtles* of *James*, *Peter*, and eſpecially of *Paul*, in another *order* than now they *lie*, according to the *times* wherein they were writ, which will be applied without much difficulty to his *Hiſtory* within ſeveral *Chapters* of the *Acts*. And the Writings of *John* will finiſh up the *whole Hiſtory*.

And whereas it may be objected, That the *Order* of *Books* and *Chapters* being ſo *alter'd* and *tranſpos'd*, we ſhall not know where to *find* any thing.

That may be eaſily help'd by *marginal Columns*, all along throughout, with the *Context*; and a *Table* or *Index* at the *end* of the *whole*. In moſt places there will need but *two Columns*, for a great part *none* at all, where the *Hiſtory* or *Book* runs along without *diſlocation* or *inſertion*; and in no place above *four*, as in the *Evangeliſts*, unleſs haply a *fifth Column* ſomewhere there, if it be judged fit to inſert *Jude's* Epiſtle, into the *Hiſtory* of the *Evangeliſts*; concerning which, for the preſent, I *Query*.

At the end may be an *Index* of *two Columns*: In the *firſt*, the *Books*, *Chapters* and *Verſes* in the *order* as they *lie now* in the *Bible*: And in the *other* the *Books* and *Chapters* of the *Harmony*, it being divided into ſo many *Books* and *Chapters*, as may be moſt for *eaſe*. Whereby may preſently be *found*, in what part of the *Harmony*, any *Chapter*, *Verſe*, or *Sentence* of the *whole Bible* lies. As for Example:

Geneſis.		*Harmony.*	
Ch.	ver.	Lib.	ch.
1.	1. to 27.	1.	1.

The *Harmony* being thus framed throughout, there may be ſome *marginal directions* where they are neceſſary, to give the *Reaſons* of the *Tranſitions*, *Inſertions*, *Tranſpoſitions*, and of the *whole Order*.

The

The Benefits.

THE *benefit* of ſuch an *Harmony* will be *greater* than we can fully comprehend, till we have the *uſe* of it. It will help much toward the making up an *exacter Scripture-Chronology.* It will ſerve abundantly to the clearing of the *genuine* and *hiſtorical meaning* of the *Text* every where. As for inſtance: The Sermons of the *Prophets*, tho they were *laid up* and preſerv'd by the *Sanhedrim*, are deliver'd unto us in a *body*, as the *learned Elders digeſted* them; yet they were *applied* at ſeveral *times*, in the ſeveral *emergencies* of affairs, of the *two Kingdoms* of *Judah* and *Iſrael*, and upon *ſeveral occaſions*; which being found out, will make us as it were *preſent Auditors* of thoſe *Prophets*, and in the *quality* of thoſe to whom they were *directed*. So the *Pſalms* were written by *ſeveral Men*, at *ſeveral times*, and thoſe of *David* not all at *once*. We ſhall know the *temper* of their *ſpirits*, upon what *motives*, upon what *rejoycings*, upon what *fears*, or *diſtreſſes*, or *accidents* they were *compoſed*. Take one Example; *Pſal.* 90. 10. The *Author* of that Pſalm *paſſionately complains* of the *ſhortneſs* and *miſery* of Man's *years*. *The days of our years are threeſcore years and ten*, &c. But it concerns not all *Men* and *Times*. Only *Moſes*, who ſeems to have been the *Author* of that *Pſalm*, complains upon an occaſion peculiar to that *Time*, and that *People* whom he govern'd. It was the Word of the *Lord* concerning that *generation*, when they *provok'd* him in the *Wilderneſs*, that none of them ſhould enter into his *reſt*, nor ſee the good Land, but that all their *carcaſes* ſhould *fall* in the *deſart*, that occaſion'd this complaint. A *ſtrange* and an *unuſual* thing, that of Six hundred thouſand Souls, Men of *able conſtitutions*, and lying under no *Epidemical diſeaſe*, none (except two perſons, *Caleb* and *Joſhua*) ſhould out-live *threeſcore* and *ten years*, or at utmoſt but *fourſcore*, that were *twenty years* of Age at their coming forth of *Egypt*. We may take another Example; *Pſal.* 27. 13. *I had fainted, unleſs I had believed, to ſee the goodneſs of the Lord in the land of the living.* What was that *Land* of the *living* that *David* ſpeaks of? When he made this *Pſalm*, he was forc'd from *Jeruſalem*, where he was wont to *live* in *ſociety* with *Men*, and now ſhifted up and down among *Grotts*, and *Caves*, and *ſolitary Holes*, as if his *dwelling* had been among the *Sepulchers* of the *dead*. The *occaſion* then *enlightens* the *Pſalm*, if we inſert it into that part of *David*'s ſtory. The *literal*, *hiſtorical ſenſe* of *Scripture*, we muſt firſt *build* upon; elſe in *Myſteries* and *Allegories*, we may ſooner be *fine* and *witty*, than *ſound*. *Jerom* confeſſeth his own *youthly vanity*, in interpreting *Obadiah*'s Prophecy. *When I*

was

was young (ſaith he) *I interpreted the Prophet allegorically, becauſe I was ignoraut of the Hiſtory. I thought then I could read a ſealed Book. No man can write ſo ill, but ſome will like it. Such an one praiſed it, but I bluſht. I now freely profeſs, that was the work of my childiſh Wit, this of my mature Age.* Many undertake *Scripture* as if they could *read* a *ſealed Book*, and perhaps many praiſe them for *lofty* and *raiſed Notions*; but where is their *Authority*, when they loſe the *genuine* and *literal meaning* of the holy *Pen-man*? *Iſidore Peluſiota* hath obſerv'd, That whereas the *Manichees* thought that no part of the *Old Teſtament* ſpake of *Chriſt*; ſome in his time went to the other *extream*, thinking all to be ſpoken of *him:* and ſo brought a *diſcredit* upon the *true Teſtimonies*, when *wrong* ones were *wreſted*. *Weakneſs* of *proof* brings the greateſt *prejudice* againſt the *Truth*.

Divines have given out ſome *Obſervations*, for the underſtanding how *Scripture* is *fulfilled*; either, 1. When the thing is *done* or comes to paſs, which was *meant* by the *Prophet* in his *literal* and *proper ſenſe*. Or, 2. When that comes to paſs which was *fore-ſhadowed* by the *proper* and *immediate ſubject* of the *Prophet's ſpeech*. Or, 3. When the thing that happens, was not *literally* and *properly pointed at*, nor *fore-ſhadowed*, but aptly and handſomely *applied* to, and compared with ſomewhat *like* it. Or, 4. When that which was *fore-told* or *fore-ſhadowed*, tho it have been already *done in part*, or have been *begun* to be *done*, is afterwards *done* more *fully*, or elſe more *conſtantly:* It being poſſible that the *ſame Scripture* may be fulfilled *often*, yea in the ſame *literal ſenſe*. Now an *Harmonious hiſtorizing* of the *Pſalms* and the *Prophets*, and the like, will lead us more clearly to know the *immediate Subject* of what was ſpoken, and give us *hints* to diſcern what was *higher* and *further* meant; yea, poſſibly *more* than what *themſelves* underſtood in the words that *themſelves* ſpake. For the *Scriptures* being given for the *inſtruction* and *uſe* of all *ſucceeding Ages*, it may be that the *Prophets* knew not all that they deliver'd, and which the *ſenſe* of their words might be afterwards *improved* unto. *Daniel* was a Man full of the Spirit of God, and much travelled in *Revelations*, yet he knew not the then approaching time of the *Jews* Liberty, till that in the firſt of *Darius*, he learned more than was *immediately inſpired* unto him, by *Books* that had been written by *Prophets* before him, *Dan.* 9. 2. *In the firſt year of Darius's reign, I Daniel underſtood by books the number of the years, whereof the word of the Lord came to Jeremiah the Prophet.* No doubt he diligently *ſatisfied* himſelf, unto what *Year* of *Jeremy*'s publick Miniſtry thoſe *Predictions*, Chap. 25. 11, 12. and Chap. 29. 10. were made. Some *Prophets* knew *more*, and ſome *leſs*. They ſaw *for* after-times, but often themſelves ſaw but what concern'd the *preſent times*,

places,

places, and *affairs*. It was ſaid to *Daniel* himſelf, *Chap.* 12. 4. *O Daniel, ſhut up the words, and ſeal the book even to the time of the end.* Theſe Myſteries were to be ſhut up till theſe *later times*, concerning which it follows in the ſame Verſe, *Many ſhall run to and fro, and knowledg ſhall be encreaſed*; namely, by reading thy Book, when the time of fulfilling comes. There is a *Manuſcript* that offers a *pleaſant Interpretation* of theſe words; *That the opening of the World by Trade and Navigation, and the encreaſe of Knowledg, ſhould meet in one Age.* The Lord *Verulam* embrac'd this *ſenſe*, if himſelf invented the *Frontiſpiece* to his *Inſtauratio magna*, where, in a quiet Sea, a *Ship* is pictured with *full-ſpread Sails*, and under it this ſame Sentence out of *Daniel*, *Multi pertranſibunt & augebitur ſcientia.* A little before *Luther*, when *Columbus* found out the *Indies*, there was alſo a general reviving of all *Parts of Learning*. And ſurely, as our *Age* hath much advanc'd above what *Antiquity* knew, ſo the *Ages* after us are likely to know *more*, even out of the *Scriptures*, concerning *themſelves*, and their *times*. Had *Moſes*, *Abraham* (of whom *Chriſt* ſaid, *He ſaw his Day, and rejoyced*) *David*, *Iſaiah*, *Micah*, *Malachy*, &c. lived; and had they been Ear-witneſſes of *Chriſt*'s words, and Spectators of his doings, they would better have underſtood *one anothers words*, yea, and their own too. But this is the *benefit* which the deſigned *Harmony* doth promiſe, that it will bring them *nearer together* in fellowſhip with themſelves, nearer unto *Chriſt* and to his *Apoſtles Writings*, whereby much that we knew not what to think of, will be *eaſy* to us.

But I will not undertake a further *commendation* of the *Benefit*, which I do not yet my ſelf ſo *fully* underſtand, nor can *apprehend*, as when, according to the *Deſign*, the thing it ſelf ſhall be *done*. They talk much of the *Glaſſes* of thoſe curious and excellent Men, *Galileus* and *Gaſſendus*, &c. that will rectify many of our *Errors* about the *Planets*; but thorow this *Glaſs* we ſhall ſee into the *Heavens* of the *Scriptures*, and every day enrich our ſelves with *new Diſcoveries* and *Obſervations*.

The Difficulty.

AS I have commended the *Benefit*, ſo I may not deny or conceal the *Difficulty* of the work. They that have labour'd in the *leſſer Harmony*, namely, that of the *Four Evangeliſts*, have found it to be no *mean labour*, nor could they ſoon put it out of their *hands*. The *Attempts* of many upon it, give Teſtimony of this *difficulty*. *Jacob. D' Auſoles a Lapeyre, in* 1610. reckon'd up *twenty* known Authors this way. *Renhard Lutz* (omitted in *Lapeyre*'s Catalogue) who compiled his *Harmony*, 1560. confeſſeth

confesseth he was often at a stand in it. *Calvin*, who compiled it, 1555. made his *way* the *easier*, by treading after *Bucer*, but yet sometime was forc'd to *part*, and go *another Tract.* Indeed *Andrew Osiander* was willing to persuade himself he had overcome the *Difficulties* of it: He saith, That *John Schopper*, an *Abbot*, had shew'd him two *Compilers* of it; one an *Anonymus*, the other was *Zacharias Chrysopolitanus*; but they stuck where *Ammonius* of *Alexandria*, and after him St. *Augustin*, had, namely, at the *cure* of *Peter's Wife's Mother*, whether it were *before* or *after* the *Sermon on the Mount.* And there he had *stuck* and *staid* too, but that our *Cranmer* (being at his House, as he was on his way, being *Embassador* from King *Henry* the 8th, to the *Emperor*) desir'd him to go on. He did so, and saith, he saw his *scarecrows* remov'd: but some *judg* of it, that he had better have *stuck*, than *plunged* over. All that did it, met with *censure. Vincentius Regius* finds fault with *Jansenius*, others with him. *John de la Haye* at *Doway*, and *Francis de Roia* at *Toledo*, find defects in all before them: tho some have professed more than ordinary diligence, as particularly *Tho. Beaux-amis* a *Carmelite*, professeth it was the *substance* of *twenty six years labour.* 'Tis done at length, indeed to good satisfaction, but not by one hand, but begun by *Chemnitius*, continued by *Polycarp Lyserus*, and again continued by D. *Gerhard.* It cannot then be expected, that this *Work* now *designed*, should on a sudden be *done*, or *done* by *one hand*, being so much more *large*, and abundantly more *difficult:* For in many things there will be need of an *Elias*, as the *Jews* are wont to speak concerning *knots* that they cannot *untie.* As for Example;

Not to speak of the *two Psalms* which *Amadeus* saith, it was reveal'd to him that they were *composed* by *Adam*, which are in the King of *Spain*'s Library of *Manuscripts* in the *Escurial:* It may notwithstanding, perhaps deservedly be put to the Question, Whether the 92d *Psalm* be to be inserted into *Adam*'s History, seeing many of the *Jews* thought it was his; and in the *Chaldee* it hath this Title, *The Praise and Song which the first Man spake for the Sabbath-day.*

Then, as for the 90th *Psalm*, I have spoken to it, as composed by *Moses*; and so the *Chaldee Title* speaks, *The Prayer which* Moses *the Prophet of the Lord prayed, when the people of the house of* Israel *sinned in the desart.* But if we should follow *Jerom*'s Rule, That all the *Psalms* which are without *Title*, are to be *ascribed* to the *same Author* that is mention'd in the *next fore-going*; then the 91st *Psalm*, and *nine* more that follow, should be *inserted* into *Moses*'s *History.* But that Rule will justly deserve to come under Question.

Then,

Then, Whereas the *Vatican Septuagint* do insert the *Proverbs of Agur* and *Lemuel*, Prov. 30. and 31. between *Chap.* 24. and 25. it will require an Examination, 1. Whether *Agur* were some wise and godly Man in *Solomon*'s time, or before; or rather, whether he were not *Solomon* himself, call'd *Agur*; *The Collector*, the Son of *Jakeh*, that is, *David*; *The Vomiter*, because as it was said of the *later Poets*, that they *licked up Homer*'s *vomit*, so *Solomon* gather'd up what *David* had let fall in many occasional Sentences; or else, *The Son of Vomit*, an *Hebraism (i.)* so *full*, that he could not *hold*, but must needs *vent* and *utter* what he had to say: according to that, *Psal.* 45. 1. *My heart is enditing*, or *boileth* and *bubleth up* a good matter: Or *Agur* (i.) *Solomon* the *Satyr*, so the Phrase is also us'd among the *Latins*, *Evomere aliquid in aliquem*. The Character of a great part of that 30th Chapter being *Satyrical*, may rather strengthen that Conjecture. But it is left to the Question, 2. Whether *Lemuel*, Chap. 31. be *Solomon*, who, they said, had *eight Names*, or else King *Hezekiah*, as it might seem, because the *Proverbs* of this Chapter are brought in *after*, and *in order* to those which his *servants copied out*, as is noted *chap.* 25. 1. But these, and an hundred more *Queries*, will require Solution to the framing of such a *work*.

The *Professor* of any *Faculty*, besides *Divinity*, may without much Skill in any Profession but his own, truly understand the *genuine* Rules or Precepts of it; all his Learning else, is but *Ornament* to him: As a *Physitian* needs not *History*, *Mathematicks*, &c. as necessarily to inable him to his *Faculty*. But the very *literal sense* of much in *Scripture* (which is the *Divines Canon*) cannot be rightly understood, without *variety* of Reading and Learning in other *Faculties* and *Sciences*. And to the *collating* of *Scriptures*, and reducing *parcels* to the *Order* of *History*, there will need both much *sagacity* and *industry*, and a competent knowledg in the *Rites* and *Customs civil* of all the neighbour Nations: together with *humane Histories*, of those and the succeeding Times; as likewise an acquaintance with the *Jewish* Laws; and haply the Time of some of the *Prophets* will be known only by the *Characterisms* of Language, peculiar to such and such different Ages.

The

The Helps.

THE *Helps* towards this Work, must be from such as have diligently written the *Ecclesiastical Chronology*, such as are vers'd in *Rabbinical* and *Talmudick* Learning. Among others, *Plantavitius* his *Florilegium Rabbinicum*, especially the *third Tome*, where we have the *Bibliotheca Rabbinica*. Such as have studied the *Jewish* Laws and Rites; *L'Empereur*, so far as he hath gone *De legibus Hebræorum Forensibus*; *Corn. Bertram de Politeia Judaica*; *Car. Sigonius de Republica Hebræorum*; M. *Selden* in many of his learned Books, will be of much use. And haply such as have confined themselves to particular Arguments, tending to the clearing of some *Scripture-Antiquities*, may be of service. *Peter Faber* his *Agonisticon* about *Sports* and *Olympick Games*. *Nicolaus Caussin* of *Hieroglyphicks* and *Ænigma's*. *Brissonius* and *Roa* for the *Customs* of Marriage, *&c.* *Janus Cornarus*, of Things belonging to *Vines*, according to the Scripture. *Georg. Longus* of *Milan*, concerning *signatory Rings*. Such as have writ of *Stones* and *Minerals*, of *Weights* and *Measures*, of *Treaties* and *Covenants*, of the *Jewish Kalendar*, and of the *Jubilees*, and many such other Arguments according to the Scripture. *Theodoret*, *Melanthon*, and *Moller* have done somewhat by way of *conjecture*, about the *occasion* of divers of the *Psalms*. *Petrus Aureolus* in his *Compendium Bibliorum*, *Georg. Ederus*, Counsellor to the Emperors *Ferdinand* the first, and *Maximilian* the second, in his *Oeconomia Bibliorum*; The *Tigurine Divines* in the Preface to their *Version*: *Solomon Glassius* in his *Tract de methodo S. Scr.* And *Eusebius Nierembergius*, *de Origine S. Scrip.* especially in his 9th and 10th Books; and divers Authors of that kind, have somewhat concerning the *Pen-men* of holy Writ, and their *times*. But whereas no Man hath yet thought of the *main design*, much less *attempted* any thing in direct *tendency* to it, it must be expected, that the way will be *rough* and *uneven*, full of *bracks* and *thickets*, and in which the Undertakers must be pardon'd, if haply they may sometimes lose their way.

The Recommendation.

BUT some *Helps* there are, and if the *State* may please to look upon it with *favour* and *encouragement*, somewhat may be done to the great Service of the Churches of *Christ*, not only for the Ease of the *Ministry*, which *Osiander* saith was the Reason why he set upon the *Harmony* of the *Evangelists*, but for the

the *abundant encrease* of saving Knowledg of all *Christians*, who will find the *benefit* of it being *done*, which, I doubt, I am not so *happy* in my *expressions*, as to make it *plain* enough in the *Design*. And the very *labour* and *search* will yield comfort all along, to such as may be employ'd in it, as *George Wyrth* professeth; that in his *Old Age*, when he had serv'd as a *Physitian* in *Brussels*, and in King *Philip* the Second's Court many years, he apply'd himself to the difficult *collating* of the *Evangelists* (being then turn'd Protestant) for his last Refreshments. Let the *State* only please to make it their *care*, after the *example* of some *Kings* and *Republicks* that have done such like Works of general use for the Advance of Learning and Divine Knowledg, and they will find some Men very learned of their own Order; besides, many in the Profession of Divinity, and others of private Quality, that will contribute much Assistance to it.

Perhaps it may be thought a daring and bold Design: I humbly submit it to the Judgment of Men *learned*, and *godly wise*, who will pardon an Error (if it be any) of *earnest affection* to the *advance* of *holy Scripture-knowledg:* which is the greatest *Treasury* of *heavenly Wisdom* and *Science*, that the whole Earth hath in *keeping*; and of which we cannot put too *high* a *value*. Let me, by way of *Conclusion*, add some just *Characters* of the *whole Bible*, and the particular *Books*; some of which I have gather'd from the *Antients*, and others, but many of them holding out their own Evidence.

The whole Bible. The Soul's food: so *Athanasius.*
The common Shop of Soul-physick: so *Basil.*
The invariable Rule of Truth: so *Iraneus.*
The Divine's Balance: so *Augustin.*

1. In respect of the dictating of it; It is,
The Library of the Holy Ghost.
Christ's Aphorisms.
The Acts and Statutes of the highest Parliament.
God's Mint-house.
The Signet of God's right-hand.
The Epistle of God to the World.
The Court-roll of God's Fines and Amercements.

2. In respect of its Worth; It is,
A stately Palace.
A fruitful Field.
The true Hesperides.
The inestimable Pearl.

3. In

3. In respect of its Use; It is,
The Touch-stone of Error.
The Key of the Sheep-fold.
The Glass of Life.
The Weather-glass.
The Christians Magazine.
The Armory.

Genesis. The Cabinet of greatest Antiquities.
Exodus. The sacred Rule of Law and Justice.
Leviticus. The holy Ephemerides.
Numbers. God's Arithmetick.
Deuteronomy. The faithful Monitor.
Joshuah. The holy War.
Judges. The Mirror of Magistrates and Tyrants.
Ruth. The Picture of a pious Widow.
Samuel. } Sacred Politicks.
Kings. }
Chronicles. The holy Annals.
Ezra. } An Idea of Church and State Reformation.
Nehemiah. }
Hester. The great Example of God's Providence.
Job. The School of Patience.
Psalms. { The Soul's Soliloquies.
The little Bible.
The Anatomy of Conscience.
The Rose-garden.
The Pearl-Island.
Proverbs. Divine Ethicks, Politicks, Oeconomicks.
Ecclesiastes. Experience of the Creature's Vanity.
Canticles. The mystical Bride-Song.
Isaiah. The Evangelical Prophet.
Jeremiah. The Pathetical Mourner.
Lamentations. The Voice of the Turtle.
Ezekiel. Urim and Thummim in *Babylon.*
Daniel. The Apocalypse of the Old Testament.
Hosea. Sermons of Faith and Repentance.
Joel. The Thunderer.
Amos. The Plain-dealing Reprover.
Obadiah. *Edom*'s Whip.
Jonah. The Prophetical Apostle of the Gentiles.
Micah. The Wise-men's Star.
Nahum. The Scourge of *Assur.*
Habakkuk. The Comforter of Captives.
Zephaniah. Preparation for sad Times.

Haggai.

Haggai. Zeal for God's House.
Zachariah. Prophetick Hieroglyphicks.
Malachy. The Bound-stone of the two Testaments.
Matthew. }
Mark. } The four Trumpeters proclaiming the
Luke. } Title of the great King.
John. }
Acts. The Treasury of Ecclesiastical Story.
Romans. The Principles of Christian Faith. The Catholick Catechism.
1 *Corinthians.* Apostolical Reformation.
2 *Corinthians.* A Pattern of just Apologies.
Galatians. The Epistle to the *Romans* Epitomiz'd.
Ephesians. The opening of the great Mystery of Salvation.
Philippians. An Apostolical Paræneſis.
Colossians. A brief Rule of Faith and Manners.
1 *Thessalonians.* Practick Theology.
2 *Thessalonians.* Polemick Theology.
1 *Timothy.* The sacred Pastoral.
2 *Timothy.* The Title of the Scripture pleaded.
Titus. *Agenda*, or Church-Orders.
Philemon. The Rule of Relations.
Hebrews. A Commentary upon *Leviticus.*
James. The golden Alphabet of a Christian.
1 *Peter.* A Theological Summary.
2 *Peter.* The Encouragement of a Spiritual Warrior.
1 *John.* The Glass of Love, or Charity.
2 *John.* The Pattern of a pious Matron.
3 *John.* The Mirror of Hospitality.
Jude. A Picture of false Prophets.
Revelation. *Daniel Redivivus.* The opening of the Treasury of future Events.

Phenix IV.

CHRIST's Birth Miss-tim'd;

OR

A Resolution of the Right Honourable the Lord Carew's Question, touching the true time of the Conception and Birth both of John Baptist, and also of our Saviour. Proving that Jesus Christ was not born in December. By R. S.

Sect. I. *The Preface.*

Right Honourable,

SEeing we all agree in the Substance, and differ only three Months in the Circumstance of Time, (premising that of *Tully's* *Loquendum ut vulgus, sentiendum tamen ut sapientes*) for that I am careful that the least Schism should be made in Christ's *Tunica*, which is seamless and *Unica*: I have sent your Honour this Resolution, not out of *Beroaldus*, *Bucholcerus*, and *Broughton*, but out of the *sacred Scriptures*, which we are commanded to search, especially in difficult Points.

Sect.

Sect. II.

The true Time of Christ's Nativity Evidenced.

THE Conception of *John Baptist* was in the Month of *June*, as the *Hebrews* reckon their Months; therefore Christ's Conception must needs be in the sixth Month following *June*, which is *December*, where we ignorantly make his Birth.

1. The Consequent of the Major is proved, for that *John Baptist* was six Months elder than Christ, as appears *Luke* 1. 36. *And behold thy cousin* Elizabeth, *she hath also conceived a Son in her old Age, and this is her sixth Month, which was called barren.* Now compare the 36. *v.* with the precedent 26. *v.* and it will appear that this sixth Month of *John*'s Age in his Mother's Womb, was the same sixth Month in which the Angel *Gabriel* was sent to the Virgin *Mary*, and in which she conceived Christ, as the words shew, *v.* 26. *And in the sixth Month*, (viz. in which *John* was six Months old) *the Angel* Gabriel *was sent from God to a City of* Galilee *named* Nazareth *to the Virgin* Mary, *&c.* And *v.* 31. his Message is declar'd to be this; *For lo thou shalt conceive in thy Womb, and bear a Son, and shalt call his name Jesus.* The Virgin then conceived *Jesus* in the same sixth Month of *John*'s Age, *John* was then six Months old at Christ's Conception: Therefore Christ was consequently conceived in *December* after, and not Born then, as the Calculation is (groundlessly) made.

2. Now that *John*'s Conception was in *June* (and not his Birth, as we make it) is proved by the Course of *Abia*, being the eighth Course of the twenty four Courses of the Priests, as is proved, 1 *Chro.* 24. 10. *The seventh Lot fell to* Hakkoz, *the eighth to* Abia. Now *Zacharias* the Father of *John Baptist* was of this eighth Course, or Lot of *Abia*, Luke 1. 5. *In the time of* Herod *King of* Judea, *there was a certain Priest named* Zacharias *of the Course of* Abia, *and his Wife was of the Daughters of* Aaron, *and her name was* Elizabeth, *and they had no Child*, v. 6. and v. 13. *The Angel* Gabriel, v. 19. told him; *Thy Wife* Elizabeth *shall bear thee a Son, and thou shalt call his name* John. And v. 23. *And when the Days of his Office was fulfilled, he departed to his own House.* And v. 24. *And after those days, his Wife* Elizabeth *conceived*, after the end of his eighth Course, in the beginning of *July*, after our Accompt; for their *June* contains part of our *July*. *And she hid her self five Months, saying.* And v. 25. in the sixth Month after *Elizabeth*'s Conception, the Angel was sent to *Mary* to tell her of her Conception of

 Christ.

Christ. Now for as much as the *Jews* did begin to reckon their Years from the Month of *Nisan* or *Abib*, part of our *March* and *April*, which was the first of the Months of the sacred Year since their going out of *Egypt*, as appears, *Exod.* 12. 2. *This Month shall be unto you the beginning of Months, it shall be unto you the first Month of the Year.* Now *Chap.* 13. 4. *Moses* tells you what Month he means (by this Month) *This day came ye out in the Month of* Abib; the Month Corn began to Ear, containing part of our *March*, and part of our *April*. Now begin thou thy reckoning from *Abib* or *March*, giving and allowing to every Lot or Course of the twenty four Courses of the Priests one Fortnight, (for there were twenty four Courses of Priests, and but twelve Months, therefore every Priest must needs serve a Fortnight for his Course, for twenty four Fortnights make twelve Months;) and so the eighth Fortnight or Course shall fall to *Abia*, of which *Zachary* was, which was in *June*, after the *Hebrews* accompt.

For two Courses in *March*, and two Courses more in *April* following, make four Courses, two more in *May* make six, and two more in *June* make eight. The eighth *Abia's* Course, of which *Zacharias* was. I conclude then *John*'s Conception to be in *June*, where we make his Birth, which in truth was in *March* following. And so consequently Christ's Conception was in *December*, six Months after *John*'s Conception, in which *December* we make Christ's Birth; which Birth of Christ was in truth in *September* following, in the *Feast of Tabernacles*, beginning at the fifteenth of *September*, and lasting eight Days, till the end of the twenty second Day; in which Feast time of eight Days, *Christ pitched in the Tabernacle of his Flesh amongst us*, as appears, *John* 1. 14. *And the word was made Flesh*, [ϰ) ἐσκήνωσεν ἐν ἡμῖν] *and pitched his Tabernacle amongst us: He became a Scænite.* Thus behold the sweet Harmony between the *Type* and the thing *typified*, for Christ came not to break the Law, but to fulfil it.

And thus desiring your Honour to vindicate my Credit from the unjust imputation that some, peradventure seeing this, may lay upon me as a Broacher of Novelties, in that I endeavour to wade further in the Originals, and paralleling of Scriptures than the Vulgar do, having written this to satisfy your Honour's request only, I rest now and ever,

Your Honour's obliged in all

Duty and Service,

R. S.

SECT.

Sect. III.

Of the occasion of this Error, the invalidity whereof is manifested.

POSTSCRIPT.

Saint *Chrysostom*, mistaking the Story of *Zachary*, *John*'s Father, was the occasion of this Error in Circumstance of Time. For he supposed that *Zachary* ministred in the Priest's Office in the seventh Month, which is *September*, and fourteenth Course of the Priests, and not in the fourth Month *June*, and eighth Course, which is the Truth; thus we following his Calculation, Christ's Conception was in *March*, and his Birth in *December*, as we commonly reckon. Now that which deceived the golden-mouth'd Father, (tho all is not Gold that glisters) was this: *Chrysostom* supposed, (as *Arias Montanus* the Popish *Spaniard* doth, that *Zachary* was the High Priest, and therefore the Course of his Ministry must needs be on the tenth of *September* the seventh Month, because on that Day only, called *(Iom Haccippurim)* יום הכפורים the *Day of Expiation of Sins* and Reconciliation, the High-Priest must go into the *Debyr*, the *Oracle*, or *Sanctum Sanctorum*, once a Year only. Now I will shew you *Chrysostom*'s ground for these two things that moved him to think, 1. That *Zachary* was High Priest. And 2. That therefore consequently he must on the tenth of *September* go into the *Sanctum Sanctorum*.

Drusius on *Luke* 1. 5. saith thus, *In Historia Hebraica Johannes Baptistes vocatur* (Cohen Gadol,) כהן גדול *hoc est magnus sacerdos: quæ vox æquè significat Pontificem maximum & Principem sacerdotum.* Therefore it's probable that *Zachary* was *Princeps Sacerdotum*, which he might be, and yet not *Sacerdos maximus*. For tho these two words *Sacerdos maximus*, and *Princeps Sacerdotum* be often promiscuously used one for the other, yet the distinction is plain in Scripture that *Princeps Sacerdotum* שר הכוהנים *(Sar Haccohanim,)* was the chief Priest only of every one of the twenty four Classes or Courses of Priests; and so it's likely that *Zachary* was the Prince of the Priests, of his eighth Course of *Abia*. But *Sacerdos maximus*, or *Pontifex*, is he that is Head of all the twenty four Classes and Orders of Priests, which *Zachary* was not; for these reasons.

First, Because he is called, *Luke* 1. 5. ἱερεύς τις, *a certain Priest*, therefore not *Pontifex maximus*; for had it been certain that *Zachary* had been High Priest, *Luke* wou'd have so stiled him, and not have spoken uncertainly of a certain and known Dignity in the Pronoun *indefinite*, [τις *quidam*] which indefinite Pronoun [τις] he presently defines, saying, *Of the course of* Abia. So v. 8. it's said of *Zachary*, that *while he executed the Priest's Office before God.* And St. *Luke* doth not stile him with the *High-Priest's Office*; which Title of Dignity to omit, had been an indignity offered by St. *Luke* to *Zachary*.

Secondly, for that it is said, v. 8. *that his Lot was to burn Incense when he went into the Temple of the Lord.* And v. 11. *that there appeared an Angel to* Zachary, *standing on the right side of the Altar of Incense.* For these two reasons *Chrysostom* and *Arias* think *Zachary* to be an *High Priest*, whereas all *Jews* know, that the *Candlestick, Table, and Altar of Incense* were without the *Sanctum Sanctorum*, (not within, as they suppose) and therefore being placed without, they were daily gone unto by *Zachary*, and other Sacrificers in their Courses. And thus much of *Chrysostom*'s and *Arias Montanus*'s Grounds, no solider than an *Irish* Quagmire to trust to.

Thirdly, Mr. *Broughton* saith, that *there was an Old Record in Greek found at* Rome (*as the* Romanists *say, but it is not now extant to be shewed*) *that mentioneth* Zachary *to have ministred in the seventh Month.* And thus all Error cometh from *Rome*, that bitter Star, *Wormwood*, cast into the Fountains of the Scriptures and Universities, to corrupt and *bitter* them, not to *better* them, as *Moses* Tree did the Waters of bitter *Marah.* Now I will add, after Confutation of the Error, a probable Confirmation of the Truth.

The *Rabbins* in *Midrash Rabba* conclude, *that the* Messias *must be born in the Month* Æthanim *or* Tisri; *that is, in* September, *the Month of Strengths, full of Feasts, to teach of the* Messias. And so agreeably we find in *Moses*, that the Three chief Anniversary-Feasts do foretel and typify out Christ's times.

1. Their *Passover*, and our *Easter*, prefiguring his Death, falls out fitly in the first Month for redemption from *Egypt*, and of our redemption by Christ.

2. Their *Feast of Weeks*, or Harvest, fifty Days after the Passover, or Joy of the Law, when the Fire of the Law was given *Israel*; jumps with our *Pentecost*, or *Whitsontide*, when the fiery Law of the Spirit was given by Jesus in cloven Tongues. *Acts* 2.

3. The

3. The *Feast of dwelling in Tabernacles* on the 15th of *September*, for eight Days, is suitable to our Lord's pitching in the Tabernacle of his Flesh amongst us, or his Nativity in *September*, the first Month after the Creation. The Feast of joyful Meditation of God's dwelling in the Cloud amongst *Israel*, is a Memorial of Christ dwelling in the Flesh with us, *John* 1. 14. *And the Word was made flesh, and he pitched his Tabernacle amongst us.* So in 1 *Kings* 8. 2. this is plainly typified. *Solomon* brings the *Ark* and *Tabernacle* into the Temple, in the seventh Month, call'd *Æthanim* or *September*, Month of Strength and Fruits; and the *Cherubims* spread their Wings over the Ark. This *Ark* and *Tabernacle* was the Type of the *Ark and Tabernacle of Christ's Body:* The bringing in of this Tabernacle into the Temple, the *coming of Christ into the World*, in the Temple of *Zorobabel*, under which he was born, preached, and wrought Miracles. And the Cherubims are the Angels, spreading their Wings of Protection over him, proclaiming him, singing at his Birth. And this was in the Month *Æthanim* or *September*, (the Month of Strengths, or Fruits and Feasts) wherein Christ was born, bringing Strength, and Fruits of Righteousness, into the World.

And thus having shew'd your Honour the sweet Harmony between the *Type* and the thing *typified*; The *Feast of Tabernacles in September*, and Christ in the same time pitching in this *Tabernacle of his Flesh*, amongst us; The Consent between the *History* and the *Mystery*: I conclude with that of the Apostle, *Great is the Mystery of Godliness, God manifest in the Flesh.* For the true Calculation of the Months, consult with *Munster's Calendarium Hebraicum.*

This tract was answered by Bp Pearson by another entitled "Christ's Birth not Misstimed" London 1649. reprinted in his Minor Theological Works Vol 2. p. 153.

Phenix V.

The Reformation *of the* Church *in* Ireland, *during the Reigns of King* Henry VIII. Edward VI. *and Queen* Mary.

Wherein are ſeveral material Paſſages (omitted by other Hiſtorians) concerning the Manner how that Kingdom was firſt converted to the Proteſtant Religion; and how by the ſpecial Providence of God, Dr. Cole, *a bloody Agent of Q.* Mary, *was prevented in his Deſigns againſt the Proteſtants there.*

Set forth in the Life and Death of George Browne, *ſometime Archbiſhop of* Dublin, *who was the firſt of the Romiſh Clergy in* Ireland *that threw off the Pope's Supremacy, and forſook the Idolatrous Worſhip of* Rome; *with a Sermon of his, on that Subject.*

GEORGE BROWNE, by Birth an *Engliſhman*, of the Order of St. *Auguſtin* in *London*, and Provincial of the Fryars of the ſame Order in *England*, being a Man of a meek and peaceable Spirit, was prefer'd to the Archiepiſcopal See of *Dublin* by King *Henry* the Eighth, and conſecrated before his Arrival into *Ireland*, by *Thomas* Archbiſhop of *Canterbury*, two other Biſhops aſſiſting him, viz. *John* then Biſhop of *Rocheſter*, and *Nicholas* then Biſhop of *Saliſbury*, on the 19th of *March*, *Anno* 1535.

The

The Reverend *James Usher*, late Primate of *Armagh*, amongst his Memorials of *Ireland*, gives this holy Father this Description. *George Browne* was a Man of a cheerful Countenance, in his Acts and Deeds plain down-right, to the Poor merciful and compassionate, pitying the state and condition of the Souls of the People, advising them, when he was Provincial of the *Augustin* Order in *England*, to make their Applications solely to Christ; which Advice coming to the Ears of *Henry* the Eighth, he became a Favourite, and upon the decease of *John Allen*, late Archbishop of *Dublin*, became his Successor. Within five years after that he had enjoy'd that See, he (much about the time that King *Henry* the Eighth began to demolish the Priories, Abbeys and Monasteries, formerly built by the Romish Clergy, within these His Majesties Dominions of *England* and *Ireland*) caus'd all Superstitious Reliques and Images to be remov'd out of the two Cathedrals in *Dublin*, and out of the rest of the Churches within his Diocess; he caused the Ten Commandments, the Lord's Prayer, and the Creed, to be placed, being gilded and in Frames, about the Altar in the Cathedral of *Christ-Church* in *Dublin*: he was the first that turn'd from the Romish Religion of the Clergy here in *Ireland*, to embrace the Reformation of the Church of *England*; for which Fact he was by Queen *Mary* laid aside, and his Temporality taken from him, yet he patiently endured Affliction for the Truth to the end.

Upon the Reformation of King *Henry* the Eighth in *England*, and at his Renouncing the Papal Power or Supremacy of *Rome*, the Lord *Thomas Cromwell*, then Lord Privy Seal, wrote unto *George Browne*, then Archbishop of *Dublin*, signifying from his Highness (then terming the King by that Title) that he was fallen absolutely from *Rome* in Spiritual Matters within his Dominion of *England*, and how it was his Royal Will and Pleasure to have his Subjects there in *Ireland* to obey his Commands, as in *England*; nominating the said *George Browne* Archbishop, one of his Commissioners for the Execution thereof, who, in a short space of time, wrote to the Lord Privy Seal, as follows:

My most Honoured Lord,

Your humble Servant receiving your Mandate, as one of His Highness's Commissioners, hath endeavour'd, almost to the danger and hazard of this Temporal Life, to procure the Nobility and Gentry of this Nation to due Obedience, in owning of his Highness their supream Head, as well Spiritual as Temporal; and do find much oppugning therein, especially by my * *Brother*

* *George Cromer* then Archbishop of *Armagh*.

Armagh,

Armagh, *who hath been the main oppugner, and so hath withdrawn most of his Suffragans and Clergy within his See and Jurisdiction; he made a Speech to them, laying a Curse on the People whosoever should own his Highness Supremacy; saying, that Isle, as it is in their* Irish *Chronicles,* Insula sacra, *belongs to none but to the Bishop of* Rome, *and that it was the Bishop of* Rome's *Predecessors gave it to the King's Ancestors. There be two Messengers by the Priests of* Armagh, *and by that Archbishop, now lately sent to the Bishop of* Rome. *Your Lordship may inform his Highness that it is convenient to call a Parliament in this Nation, to pass the Supremacy by Act; for they do not much matter his Highness's Commission which your Lordship sent us over. This Island hath been for a long time held in Ignorance by the* Romish *Orders; and as for their Secular Orders, they be in a manner as ignorant as the People, being not able to say Mass, or pronounce the Words, they not knowing what they themselves say in the* Roman *Tongue: The Common People of this Isle are more zealous in their Blindness, than the Saints and Martyrs were in Truth at the beginning of the Gospel. I send to you, my very good Lord, these things, that your Lordship and his Highness may consult what is to be done. It is fear'd* O Neal *will be order'd by the Bishop of* Rome *to oppose your Lordship's Order from the King's Highness; for the Natives are much in Numbers within his Powers. I do pray the Lord Christ to defend your Lordship from your Enemies.*

Dublin 4. Kalend. Decemb. 1535.

The Year following a Parliament was call'd in *Ireland*, the Lord *Leonard Grey* being then King *Henry*'s Vice-Roy of that Nation, in which *George Browne*, then being not many Months above a Year in his Archiepiscopal Chair in *Dublin*, stood up and made this short Speech following:

My Lords and Gentry of this His Majesties Realm of *Ireland*.

B*Ehold, your Obedience to your King, is the Observing of your God and Saviour Christ; for He, that High Priest of our Souls, paid Tribute to* Cæsar *(tho no Christian) Greater Honour then surely is due to your Prince His Highness the King, and a Christian one.* Rome *and her Bishops, in the Father's days, acknowledged Emperors, Kings and Princes, to be Supreme over their Dominions, nay Christ's own Vicars; and it is as much to the Bishop of* Rome's *shame, to deny what their precedent Bishops owned; therefore his Highness claims but what he can justify the Bishop* Elutherius *gave to St.* Lucius *the first Christian King of the* Britains; *so that I shall without scruple Vote his Highness*

King

King Henry *my Supreme over Ecclesiastick Matters as well as Temporal, and Head thereof, even of both Isles,* England *and* Ireland, *and that without Guilt of Conscience, or Sin to God; and he who will not pass this Act, as I do, is no true Subject to His Highness.*

This Speech of *George Browne* startled the other Bishops and Lords so, that at last, through great difficulty, it passed; upon which Speech Justice *Brabazon* seconded him, as appears by his Letter to the Lord *Thomas Cromwell*, then Lord Privy Seal of *England*; which Original is in that famous Library of Sir *Robert Cotton*, out of which Sir *James Ware*, that learned Antiquary, transcrib'd the same.

Within few years after that the Act of Supremacy had pass'd in *Ireland*, we do find a Letter written by *George Browne* to the Lord *Cromwell*, complaining of the Clergy how they fell off from what had pass'd, and how the Bishop of *Rome* had contriv'd Matters against the then Reformation: Collected by Sir *James Ware*, out of an old Registry, some time in the Custody of *Adam Loftus*, *Hugh Corwin*'s Successor, and also Archbishop of *Dublin*.

Right Honourable and my singular good Lord,

I Acknowledg my bounden Duty to your Lordship's Good Will to me, next to my Saviour Christ's, for the Place I now possess; I pray God give me his Grace to execute the same to his Glory and his Highness's Honour, with your Lordship's Instructions. The People of this Nation be zealous, yet blind and unknowing; most of the Clergy, as your Lordship hath had from me before, being ignorant, and not able to speak right Words in the Mass or Liturgy, as being not skill'd in the Latin Grammar; *so that a Bird may be taught to speak with as much sense as several of them do in this Country. These sorts, tho not Schelars, yet are crafty to cozen the poor Common People, aad to dissuade them from following his Highness's Orders:* George, *my Brother of* Armagh, *doth underhand occasion Quarrels, and is not active to execute his Highness's Orders in his Diocess.*

I have observ'd your Lordship's Letter of Commission, and do find several of my Pupils leave me for so doing. I will not put others in their Livings till I do know your Lordship's Pleasure; for it is meet I acquaint you first, the Romish *Reliques and Images of both my Cathedrals in* Dublin, *of the* Holy Trinity *and of* St. Patrick's, *took off the Common People from the true Worship; but the Prior and the Dean find them so sweet for their Gain, that they heed not my Words: Therefore send in your Lordship's, next to me, an Order more full, and a Chide to them and their Canons, that they might be remov'd. Let the Order be, that the Chief Governors may assist me in it. The Prior and*

Dean

Dean have written to Rome, *to be encourag'd*; *and if it be not hindred before they have a Mandate from the Bishop of* Rome, *the People will be bold, and then tug long before his Highness can submit them to his Grace's Orders. The Country Folk here much hate your Lordship, and despitefully call you, in their* Irish *Tongue, the* Blacksmith's Son.

The Duke of Norfolk *is by* Armagh, *and that Clergy, desir'd to assist them, not to suffer his Highness to alter Church-Rules here in* Ireland: *As a Friend, I desire your Lordship to look to your Noble Person*; *for* Rome *hath a great kindness for that Duke (for it is so talk'd here) and will reward him and his Children.* Rome *hath great Favours for this Nation, purposely to oppose his Highness: and so having got, since the Act passed, great Indulgences for Rebellion*; *therefore my hope is lost, yet my Zeal is to do according to your Lordship's Orders. God keep your Lordship from your Enemies here and in* England. Dublin *the 3d.* Kalends *April*, 1538.

To the Lord Privy Seal his Honourable good Lordship's,
Ex Autographo.

Your Lordship's at Commandment,

George Browne.

Soon after this Letter had been written, News came to the Castle of *Dublin*, that the Bishop of *Rome* had sent over a Bull of Excommunication of all those who had or shall own the King's Supremacy within the *Irish* Nation; which caused the Archbishop to write accordingly.

Right Honourable,

M*Y Duty premised, it may please your Lordship to be advertised, sithence my last there has come to* Armagh *and his Clergy a private Commission from the Bishop of* Rome, *prohibiting his Gracious Highness's People here in this Nation to own his Royal Supremacy, and joyning a Curse to all them and theirs, who shall not within forty days, confess to their Confessors, (after the publishing of it to them) that they have done amiss in so doing: the substance, as our Secretary hath translated the same into* English, *is thus.*

The Form of their Confession to their Popish Priest.

" I *A. B.* from this present hour forward, in the presence of " the Holy Trinity, of the Blessed Virgin Mother of God, " of St. *Peter*, of the Holy Apostles, Arch- " angels, Angels, Saints, and of all the Holy " Host of Heaven, shall and will be always " obedient to the Holy See of St. *Peter* of " *Rome*, and to my Holy Lord the Pope of

" *Rome*

" *Rome* and his Successors, in all things, as well Spiritual as " Temporal, not consenting in the least that his Holiness " shall lose the least Title or Dignity belonging to the Pa- " pacy of our Mother Church of *Rome*, or to the Regality " of St. *Peter*.

" I do vow and swear to maintain, help and assist the just " Laws, Liberties and Rights of the Mother Church of " *Rome*.

" I do likewise promise to confer, to defend and promote, " if not personally, yet willingly, as in ability able, either by " Advice, Skill, Estate, Mony or otherwise, the Church of " *Rome* and her Laws against all whatsoever resisting the " same.

" I further vow to oppugn all Hereticks, either in making " or setting forth Edicts or Commands contrary to the " Mother Church of *Rome*; and in case any such to be " moved or composed, to resist it to the uttermost of my " power, with the first convenience and opportunity I can " possible.

" I count and value all Acts made, or to be made, by He- " retical Powers of no force or worth, or be practised or " obeyed by my self, or by any other Son of the Mother " Church of *Rome*.

" I do further declare him or her, Father or Mother, " Brother or Sister, Son or Daughter, Husband or Wife, " Uncle or Aunt, Nephew or Neece, Kinsman or Kinswo- " man, Master or Mistress, and all others, nearest or dearest " Relations, Friend or Acquaintance whatsoever, accursed, " that either do or shall hold, for the time to come, any " Ecclesiastical or Civil Power, above the Authority of the " Mother Church, or that do or shall obey, for the time to " come, any of her the Mother of Churches Opposers or " Enemies, or contrary to the same, of which I have here " sworn unto: so God, the Blessed Virgin, St. *Peter*, St. *Paul*, " and the Holy Evangelists help, *&c.*

His Highness, Vice-Roy of this Nation, is of little or no power with the old Natives; therefore your Lordship will expect of me no more than I am able: This Nation is poor in Wealth, and not sufficient now at present to oppose them: It is observ'd, that ever since his Highness's Ancestors had this Nation in possession, the old Natives have been craving Foreign Powers to Assist and Rule them; and now both English *Race and* Irish *begin to oppose your Lordship's Orders, and do lay aside their National old Quarrels, which I fear will, if any thing will, cause a Foreigner to invade this Nation: I pray God I may be a false Prophet; yet your good Lord-* *ship*

ship must pardon my Opinion, for I write it to your Lordship as a Warning.

Dublin, May 1538. *Your humble and true Servant,*

To the Lord Privy Seal with speed. George Browne.

Upon the Feast of St. *John Baptist* following, the said *George Browne* seiz'd on one *Thady O Brine*, one of the Order of St. *Francis*, who had Papers from *Rome*, as follows, being sent to the Lord Privy Seal by a Special Messenger.

My Son *O Neal*,

Thou and thy Fathers were all along faithful to the Mother Church of Rome: *His Holiness* Paul, *now Pope, and the Council of the Holy Fathers there, have lately found out a Prophecy, there remaining, of one St.* Lacerianus, *an* Irish *Bishop of* Cashell; *wherein he saith,* That the Mother Church of *Rome* falleth, when in *Ireland* the Catholick Faith is overcome: *Therefore for the Glory of the Mother Church, the Honour of St.* Peter, *and your own Secureness, suppress Heresy and his Holiness's Enemies; for when the* Roman *Faith there perisheth, the See of* Rome *falleth also: Therefore the Council of Cardinals have thought fit to encourage your Country of* Ireland, *(as a sacred Island) being certified, whilst the Mother Church hath a Son of Worth as your self, and of those that shall succour you, and join therein, that she will never fall, but have more or less a holding in* Britain, *in spite of Fate. Thus having obey'd the Order of the most sacred Council, we recommend your Princely Person to the Holy Trinity, of the Blessed Virgin, of St.* Peter, *St.* Paul, *and of all the heavenly Host of Heaven.* Amen.

Rome 4 Kalend. May 1538. Episcopus Metensis.

Upon further Examinations and Searches made, this *Thady O Brine* was Pillory'd, and confin'd a Prisoner until his Highness's further Order for his Trial; but News coming over, that he must be hang'd, he made himself away in the Castle of *Dublin*, on the Eve of the Feast of St. *James*; yet his dead Corps was carried to the *Gallows Green* and hang'd up, and after there buried: But it was said, by the Register of St. *Francis's* Monastry of *Dublin*, that they brought him from thence and buried him in that Monastry.

George

George Browne having enjoy'd the See of *Dublin* seven years, or thereabouts, King *Henry* the Eighth, upon the Dissolution of the Abbeys, Priorys and Monastrys here in *Ireland*, chang'd the Priory of the *Blessed Trinity* of *Dublin* into a Deanery and Chapters; since which Mutation, it hath generally bore the Name of *Christ-Church*.

Upon this Alteration, as it appears upon Record, this Cathedral consisted of a Dean and Chapters, a Chanter, a Treasurer, six Vicars, Chorals, and two Singing-Boys, allowing to them two 45 *l.* 6 *s.* English (*durante beneplacito*) which Sum his Daughter Queen *Mary* confirm'd for ever, having confirm'd the Deanery, yet with Alterations, as she was a Romanist.

This Cathedral continued after this said Form (tho not in Popery) even until King *James*'s Days, who then alter'd all what King *Henry* and his Daughter had done; and upon this second Alteration he constituted a Dean, a Chanter, a Chancellor, a Treasurer, three Prebends, six Vicars, Chorals, and four Singing-Boys; ordering likewise, that the Archdeacon of *Dublin* should have a Place in the Choir, and a Vote in the Chapters. As for a further Description of this Cathedral, we shall omit it; having reserved the same for a large Narrative of the said Cathedral, in a Book which is ready for the Press, entituled, *The Antiquities of the City of* Dublin.

King *Henry* the Eighth deceasing, and his hopeful Offspring, King *Edward* the Sixth, succeeding within a short space after his Royal Father's Death, that hopeful Prince (by the Advice of his Privy Council) began to consider what good Effects the Translation of the Holy Bible had done, also how much it had enlightned the Understanding of his Subjects; they alter'd the Liturgy-Book from what King *Henry* had formerly printed and establish'd, causing the same to be printed in English, commanding the same to be read and sung in the several Cathedrals and Parish-Churches of *England*, for the common Benefit of the Nobility, Gentry and Commonalty; and that his Subjects of *Ireland* might likewise participate of the same Sweetness, he sent over Orders to his Vice-Roy Sir *Anthony St. Leger*, then being Lord Deputy of that Nation, that the same be forthwith there in *Ireland* observ'd within their several Bishopricks, Cathedrals and Parish-Churches; which was first observ'd in *Christ-Church* at *Dublin*, on the Feast of *Easter* 1551, before the said Sir *Anthony*, *George Browne*, and the Mayor and Bailiffs of *Dublin*, *John Lockwood* being then Dean of the said Cathedral.

The

The Translation of the Copy of the Order for the Liturgy of the Church of England, *to be read in* Ireland, *runs as follows.*

EDWARD by the Grace of God, *&c.*

" WHereas our Gracious Father, King *Henry* the Eighth " of happy Memory, taking into consideration the " Bondage and heavy Yoke that his true and faithful Subjects " sustain'd under the Jurisdiction of the Bishop of *Rome*, as " also the Ignorance the Commonalty were in; how several " fabulous Stories and lying Wonders misled our Subjects in " both our Realms of *England* and *Ireland*, grasping thereby " the means thereof into their hands, also dispensing with " the Sins of our Nations by their Indulgences and Pardons " for Gain, purposely to cherish all evil Vices, as Robberies, " Rebellions, Thefts, Whoredoms, Blasphemy, Idolatry, *&c.* " He, our Gracious Father King *Henry* of happy Memory, " hereupon dissolv'd all Priorys, Monastrys, Abbeys, and other " pretended Religious Houses, as being but Nurseries for " Vice or Luxury, more than for sacred Learning; He " therefore, that it might more plainly appear to the World, " that those Orders had kept the Light of the Gospel from " his People, he thought it most fit and convenient for the " Preservation of their Souls and Bodies, that the Holy " Scriptures should be Translated, Printed and placed in all " Parish-Churches within his Dominions, for his faithful " Subjects to encrease their Knowledg of God, and of our " Saviour Jesus Christ. We therefore, for the general Be-" nefit of our Well-beloved Subjects Understandings, when " ever assembled or met together in the said several Parish-" Churches, either to pray or to hear Prayers read, that they " may the better join therein, in Unity, Hearts and Voice, " have caus'd the Liturgy and Prayers of the Church to be " translated into our Mother Tongue of this Realm of *Eng-" land*, according to the Assembly of Divines, lately met with-" in the same for that purpose. We therefore Will and " Command, as also Authorize you, Sir *Anthony St. Leger* Knight, " our Vice-Roy of that our Kingdom of *Ireland*, to give spe-" cial notice to all our Clergy, as well *Archbishops*, *Bishops*, " *Deans*, *Archdeacons*, as others our *Secular Parish-Priests* within

" that

" that our ſaid Kingdom of *Ireland*, to perfect, execute and
" obey this our Royal Will and Pleaſure accordingly.

Given at our Mannor of *Greenwich*, *Febr*. 6. in the Fifth year of our Reign.

E. R.

To our Truſty and Well-beloved Sir Anth. St. Leger *Knight, our Chief Governour of our Kingdom of* Ireland.

Several Collections from Anthony Martin, *formerly Biſhop of* Meath.

BEfore Proclamations were iſſued out, Sir *Anthony St. Leger*, upon this Order, call'd an Aſſembly of the Archbiſhops and Biſhops, together with other of the then Clergy of *Ireland*; in which Aſſembly he ſignified unto them, as well His Majeſty's Order aforeſaid, as alſo the Opinions of thoſe Biſhops and Clergy of *England*, who had adhered unto the Order: ſaying, that it was His Majeſty's Will and Pleaſure, conſenting unto their ſerious Conſiderations and Opinions, then acted and agreed on in *England* as to Eccleſiaſtical Matters, that the ſame be in *Ireland* ſo likewiſe celebrated and performed.

Sir *Anthony St. Leger* having ſpoken to this effect, *George Dowdall*, who ſucceeded *George Cromer* in the Primacy of *Armagh*, ſtood up, who (through his *Romiſh* Zeal to the Pope) labour'd with all his power and force to oppoſe the Liturgy of the Church, that it might not be read or ſung in the Church; ſaying, Then ſhall every illiterate fellow read Service (or Maſs) as he in thoſe days term'd the word Service.

To this Saying of the Archbiſhop's Sir *Anthony* reply'd, No, your Grace is miſtaken, for we have too many illiterate Prieſts amongſt us already, who neither can pronounce the Latin, nor know what it means, no more than the Common People that hear them; but when the People hear the Liturgy in Engliſh, they and the Prieſt will then underſtand what they pray for.

Upon this Reply, *George Dowdall* bad Sir *Anthony* beware of the Clergy's Curſe.

Sir *Anthony* made anſwer, I fear no ſtrange Curſe, ſo long as I have the Bleſſing of that Church which I believe to be the true one.

The Archbiſhop again ſaid, Can there be a truer Church than the Church of St. *Peter*, the Mother Church of *Rome*?

Sir *Anthony* returned this Anſwer: I thought we had been all of the Church of Chriſt; for he calls all true Believers in him his Church, and himſelf the Head thereof.

The Archbiſhop reply'd, And is not St. *Peter* the Church of Chriſt?

Sir *Anthony* returned this Anſwer: St. *Peter* was a Member of Chriſt's Church; but the Church was not St. *Peter*'s, neither was St. *Peter*, but *Chriſt*, the Head thereof.

Then *George Dowdall*, the Primate of *Armagh*, roſe up, and ſeveral of the Suffragan Biſhops under his Juriſdiction, ſaving only *Edward Staples*, then Biſhop of *Meath*, who tarried with the reſt of the Clergy then aſſembled, on the Kalends of *March*, according to the Old Stile, 1551. But if we reckon as from the Annunciation of our Lady, which was the 25th of *March*, it was 1550.

Sir *Anthony* then took up the Order, and held it forth to *George Browne* Archbiſhop of *Dublin*, who (ſtanding up) receiv'd it, ſaying, This Order, good Brethren, is from our Gracious King, and from the reſt of our Brethren, the Fathers and Clergy of *England*, who have conſulted herein, and compar'd the Holy Scriptures with what they have done; unto whom I ſubmit, as Jeſus did to *Cæſar*, in all things juſt and lawful, making no queſtion why or wherefore, as We own Him our true and lawful King.

After this, ſeveral of the meeker, or moſt moderate of the Biſhops and Clergy of *Ireland* cohered with *George Browne*, the Archbiſhop of *Dublin*: amongſt whom *Edward Staples* Biſhop of *Meath*, who was put out from his Biſhoprick, for ſo doing, in Queen *Mary*'s days on the 29th of *June* 1554. *John Bale*, who on the ſecond of *February* 1552. was Conſecrated Biſhop of *Oſſory* for his Fidelity, and afterwards by Queen *Mary* expulſed. Alſo *Thomas Lancaſter* Biſhop of *Kildare*, who was at the ſame time put from his Biſhoprick, with ſeveral others of the Clergy, being all expulſed upon Queen *Mary*'s coming to the Crown.

When theſe Paſſages had paſſed, Sir *Anthony* was in a ſhort time after recall'd for *England*, and Sir *James Crofts* of *Herefordſhire* Knight, placed Chief in his ſtead; who began his Government from the 29th of *April* 1551.

Sir *James Crofts*, upon his coming over, endeavour'd much for the perſuading of *George Dowdall* to adhere to the Order aforeſaid; but *Dowdall* being obſtinate, his Majeſty and the Learned Privy-Council then of *England*, (for his perverſeneſs) upon the 20th of *October* following, took away the Title of *Primate* of all *Ireland* from him, and conferred the ſame on *George Browne* then Archbiſhop of *Dublin*, and to his Succeſſors, by by reason that he was the first of the *Irish* Bishops who embraced the Order for Establishing of the *English* Liturgy and Reformation in *Ireland*: which Place he enjoy'd during the remainder of King *Edward*'s Reign, and for a certain time after; as you shall know further in its due course and place.

Alterations following one after another, (even upon this Reformation of the Church of *England*) and the Title of Primacy being dispos'd of, as we have already mention'd, unto *George Browne* aforesaid; some Writers saying that *George Dowdall* was banish'd, others that he was not, but went voluntarily of his own Will; yet, not to dispute the Case, another Archbishop was consecrated in lieu of him, tho then living; by which it was then held lawful: As also, that constituting of Archbishops and Bishops was in the Power of Kings, and not in the Power of Popes, or of the Bishop of *Rome*, which would be much to the Abasement of the Powers of the Crown of *England* ever to resign, or to acknowledg to the contrary.

Hugh Goodacre, Batchelor of Divinity, was consecrated Archbishop of *Armagh* by the said *George Browne*, together with *John Bale* Bishop of *Ossory* (already mention'd) in *Christ-Church* in *Dublin*, on the second of *February*, *Anno* 1552. *Thomas* Bishop of *Kildare*, and *Eugenius* Bishop of *Down* and *Conner* assisting him; yet notwithstanding *Hugh Goodacre*'s Consecration, *George Browne* then held the Title of Primacy of all *Ireland*.

This Reformation and Alteration having not time to settle, or to take root, it was soon quash'd and pull'd down by that lamentable Loss of that hopeful Prince King *Edward* the Sixth, who died at *Greenwich* the 6th of *June*, 1553.

Upon King *Edward*'s Decease, the Council having met to consult together upon the Affairs of these Dominions, as also how they might confirm and establish what they had already ordered and enacted, as well in Ecclesiastical Matters as Temporal, a Division soon sprung up; some being for the Choice of the Lady *Jane Gray*, others for Queen *Mary*. At last, upon conclusion, *Mary* the King's Sister was voted Queen, upon the Proposals and Promises which she made to the Council, to confirm all that had been perfected by her Father King *Henry* the Eighth, and her Brother King *Edward* and his Honoured Council.

After she had been crown'd and enthron'd, she, for the space of three or four Months, seem'd moderate to the Protestant Reformers, yet all that while combining with *Rome* and her Emissaries; but having accomplish'd her Designs, she revok'd her fair Promises, (which with Papists is a Rule) esteeming it no Sin to break Contracts or Covenants with Hereticks and

Proteſtants, numbred with ſuch ſort of People, eſpecially with Papiſts, theſe Promiſes vaniſh'd: and then began the *Romiſh* Church not only to undo what King *Henry*, and his Son King *Edward*, had reform'd, but to proſecute the Reformers and Reformed with Fire and Faggot.

But, to our purpoſe, upon the 11th of *November*, *Anno* 1553. ſhe recall'd Sir *James Crofts*, and ſent over Sir *Anthony St. Leger*, Lord Deputy into *Ireland*. This Sir *Anthony* had not been half a year Chief Governour of *Ireland*, before Queen *Mary* revok'd the Title of Primacy from *George Browne*, expulſing *Hugh Goodacre* out of the Archbiſhoprick of *Armagh*, and recalling *George Dowdall* to his See, and reſtoring him to the Primacy of all *Ireland*, as formerly; which Title hath ever ſince ſtood firm in *Armagh*, without any Revocation, either by Queen *Elizabeth*, or by any of her Succeſſors.

George Browne, upon this Revocation, was by *George Dowdall* expulſed, and not thought fit to continue in his See of *Dublin*, as being a married Man; and it is thought, had he not been married, he had been expulſed, having appear'd ſo much for the Reformation, in both theſe former King's days. Upon the expulſing of this *George Browne*, all the Temporalities belonging to the Archbiſhoprick were diſpoſed of unto *Thomas Lockwood*, then Dean of *Chriſt-Church* in *Dublin*. It having been an antient Cuſtom ever upon the Tranſlation or Death of any of thoſe Archbiſhops, to depoſit the Temporalities into the hands of the Priors, formerly of that Cathedral, when it was a Priory, and call'd by the name of the Cathedral of the *Bleſſed Trinity*. And it is obſervable, the laſt Prior became the firſt Dean upon the alteration, as aforeſaid.

The See of *Dublin*, after this Expulſion, lay vacant for two years or thereabouts, until *Hugh Corrin*, alias *Corwine*, was placed therein: This *Hugh* was born in *Weſtmoreland*, a Doctor of the Law, being formerly Archdeacon of *Oxford*, and Dean of *Hereford*; he was conſecrated Archbiſhop of *Dublin* in the Cathedral of St. *Paul's* in *London*, on the 8th of *September*, *Anno* 1555. He after, upon the 13th of the ſame Month, was by Queen *Mary* made Chancellor of *Ireland*; and upon the 25th of the ſaid *September*, he receiv'd this Letter from the Queen, directed to *Thomas Lockwood*, the Dean of *Chriſt-Church*; it being an antient Cuſtom formerly to recommend the Archbiſhop, whenſoever conſtituted for that See, to the Prior of that ſaid Cathedral.

Queen Mary's *Letter to the Dean and Chapter of* Christ-Church *in* Dublin, *to receive the Archbishop of* Dublin *honourably, and with due respect.* Copia vera, ex Libro nigro Sanctæ Trinitatis Dublinii.

MARY the Queen.

Trusty and Well-beloved, We greet you well; and forasmuch as the Right Reverend Father in God, our Right Trusty and Well-beloved Counsellor the Archbishop of Dublin, *being lately chosen for that See, repaireth speedily to that our Realm of* Ireland, *as well to reside upon the Cure of his Bishoprick, which now of long time hath been destitute of a Catholick Bishop, as also to occupy the Office of our High Chancellor of that our Realm; albeit we have good hopes ye will in all things of your selves carry your selves towards him as becometh you, yet to the intent he might the better govern the Charge committed unto him, to the Honour of Almighty God, and for the remain of our Service, We have thought fit to require and charge you, that for your part ye do reverently receive him, honour and humbly obey him in all things, as appertaineth to your Duties, tending to God's Glory, our Honour, and the Common Weal of that our Realm; whereby ye shall please God, and do us acceptable Service.*

Given under our Signet at our Mannor of *Greenwich*, the 25th of *September*, in the second and third Years of our Reign.

To our Trusty and Well-beloved the Dean and Chapter of the Cathedral of Christ-Church, *within our Realm of* Ireland.

I have here inserted this Letter upon two Accounts: First, as being a Record remaining in the Cathedral; Secondly, because there hath been some discourse of late, whether the Archbishop of *Dublin* had power herein, or whether it was upon King *Henry*'s Mutation made a Deanery, as *Whitehall* Chappel is, and no Cathedral; but by this Letter it shews it is both still a Cathedral, and subject to the Archbishop of *Dublin*.

George Browne liv'd not long after the Consecration of this *Hugh Corwine*; yet I have, among my Manuscripts, a Writing of a Papist, who would fain have persuaded the World, that this *George Browne* died through Joy, having had a Bull from the Pope to be restor'd to his See of *Dublin*: which must needs be falſe, upon this account of Sir *James Ware*'s, who writeth theſe very words of him, in his Book entituled *De Præſulibus Hiberniæ*, pag. 120. 1554. *Circa tempus Georgius Browneus (quod conjugatus eſſet) per Dowdallum Archiepiſcopum Armachanum & alios Delegatos exauthoritatus eſt*; otherwiſe the Pope, if he had granted ſuch a Bull, muſt likewiſe have diſpenſed with his Marriage, it being contrary to the *Romiſh* Tenents for Biſhops to marry. Having related thus much of *George Browne*, and of Eccleſiaſtical Matters during his Life, we ſhall proceed a little further concerning a ſhort Sermon of his, preached unto the People in *Chriſt-Church*, upon the firſt *Sunday* after *Eaſter*, *Anno* 1551. being a Copy of the ſame given to Sir *James Ware* Knight, by *Anthony Martin* late Biſhop of *Meath*, who formerly was Tutor to the ſaid Sir *James Ware*, when he was a Student in *Trinity-College*, *Dublin*.

The Text, Pſal. 119. Ver. 18.

Open mine eyes, that I may ſee the wonders of thy Law.

'THE Wonders of the Lord God have for a long time 'been hid from the Children of Men, which hath hap-'ned by *Rome*'s not permitting the Common People to read 'the Holy Scriptures; for to prevent you, that you might 'not know the comfort of your Salvation, but to depend 'wholly on the Church of *Rome*, they will not permit it to 'be in any Tongue but in the Latin, ſaying, That Latin was 'the *Roman* Tongue: But the wonderful God inſpir'd the 'Holy Apoſtles with the Knowledg of all Languages, that 'they might teach all People in their proper Tongue and 'Language, which caus'd our wiſe King *Henry*, before his 'Death, to have the Holy Scriptures tranſlated into the 'Engliſh Tongue, for the good of his Subjects, that their '*Eyes may be opened to behold the wondrous things out of the Law of 'the Lord*. But there are falſe Prophets at this inſtant, and 'will be to the end of the World, that ſhall deceive you with 'falſe Doctrines, expounding this Text, or that, purpoſely 'to confound your Underſtandings, and to lead you captive 'into a Wilderneſs of Confuſion, whom you ſhall take as 'your Friends, but they ſhall be your greateſt Enemies, ſpeak-'ing againſt the Tenents of *Rome*, and yet be ſet on by *Rome*; 'theſe ſhall be a rigid People, full of Fury and Envy.

'But, to prevent theſe things that are to come, obſerve 'Chriſt and his Apoſtles: *Let all things be done with decency, with 'mildneſs, and in order*; fervently crying unto God, *Open thou 'mine eyes, that I may behold the wondrous things out of thy Law*.

'then

'then should you rightly keep the Law and the Prophets. 'It is the part of a Prince to be wise, for he hath a great 'Charge to Rule and Govern a Nation: Your late King 'foreseeing *Rome* and her Pope's Intentions, how that he in-'tended to inslave his Subjects, and to keep them in the state 'of Ignorance, consulted with the Learned of his Realm, 'knowing that Youth might quickly be wrought on; there-'fore he prepar'd before his Death a wise and learned sort 'of Counsellors for his Son's Overseers; not trusting to one 'or two, but to several, that he might the better rule his 'People, whose Eyes the Lord God Almighty hath opened 'betimes, to behold his *wondrous Works*.

'Tho the Words of my Text be plainly thus (*Open thou 'mine eyes*) the meanest of you that hear me have Eyes; 'but the true meaning of the Words is, Endue us with Un-'derstanding: for a Fool hath Eyes, and sees Men, Women, 'Beasts, Birds, and other things, but yet wants Understand-'ing: So when we say, *Open thou our Eyes*, we desire the Lord 'God to instruct and teach us the Knowledg of his Laws.

'When you were lately led in Blindness, your Eyes beheld 'the Images that then stood in several of the Monasteries 'and Churches until they were remov'd; yet all this while 'were your Understandings blinded, because ye believ'd in 'them, and plac'd your Trust in them.

'Suppose an Artist or Workman make an Image either of 'Man or Woman, and at last a Clergy-man of *Rome* give it 'such a name, calling it St. *Peter*, or St. *Paul*, or St. *Mary*, 'or St. *Anne*; must not that Man, tho he behold his own 'handy-work and knows in his heart that it was his own 'work, be blind, and void of Reason, and Understanding of 'the Law of God, and of the *wondrous things that are contain'd 'in the Law of the Lord?* Yes surely, he must be blind, and 'void of Reason, and of the true Faith, that would worship 'the same.

'The Workman carv'd the Eyes, but these Eyes see not; 'he likewise carv'd the Ears, but they hear not; the Nose, 'and it smells not; the Mouth, and it neither breathes nor 'speaks; the Hands, they feel not; the Feet, but they stand 'stock still.

'How therefore can your Prayers be acceptable unto this 'Image, that sees you not approaching towards it, that hears 'you not when you pray to it, that smells not the sweet Smells, 'be they of *Myrrhe* or *Frankincense*, burning before it? How can 'it absolve you, when the Mouth is not able to say, *Thy sins 'are forgiven thee?* And if you place a certain Sum of Mony 'in the Palm of the Hand of that Image; come you again 'to morrow, the Mony, it is true, ſhall find a cuſtomer, but 'the Image never the wiſer, who took it; and if you deſire 'to have it come unto you, it cannot without help: There-'fore the Workman that made this Image is as blind, as 'deaf, as dumb, and as void of ſenſe as the Image it ſelf; and 'ſo be ye all that put your Truſt in them.

'Therefore of late, new Artificers, by Springs, have made 'artificial ones, which for a certain time ſhall move, and ye 'ſhall believe it to be real and certain: But beware, good 'people, for they be but lying Wonders, purpoſely that ye 'may break the Law of God. And thus hath the Devil de-'viſed a lying Wonder, that ye may be deluded to break the 'Law of the Lord; which is, *Thou ſhalt not make unto thy ſelf 'any Graven Image.* O Lord, *open thou our Eyes, our Ears, and 'our Underſtanding, that we may behold the wondrous things that are 'in thy Law. The Law of God is an undefiled Law.* Oh! why 'ſhould we be ſo wicked then as to defile that Law, which 'the Almighty God hath made ſo pure without blemiſh. '*Jeſus came to fulfil the Law, and not to aboliſh the Law.* But 'there are a new Fraternity of late ſprung up, who call 'themſelves *Jeſuits*, which will deceive many, who are much 'after the Scribes and Phariſees manner amongſt the *Jews*: 'They ſhall ſtrive to aboliſh the Truth, and ſhall come very 'near to do it; for theſe ſorts will turn themſelves into ſe-'veral Forms; with the Heathen, an Heatheniſt; with Athe-'iſts, an Atheiſt; with the Jews, a Jew; and with the Re-'formers, a Reformade, purpoſely to know your Intentions, 'your Minds, your Hearts, and your Inclinations; and there-'by bring you at laſt to be like the Fool, that *ſaid in his heart, 'There was no God.* Theſe ſhall ſpread over the whole World, 'ſhall be admitted into the Council of Princes, and they ne-'ver the wiſer; charming of them, yea, making your Prin-'ces reveal their hearts, and the ſecrets therein unto them, 'and yet they not perceive it: which will happen from fal-'ling from the Law of God, by neglect of fulfilling of the 'Law of God, and by winking at their Sins. Yet in the end, 'God to juſtify his Law, ſhall ſuddenly cut off this Society, 'even by the hands of thoſe who have moſt ſuccour'd them, 'and made uſe of them; ſo that at the end they ſhall become 'odious to all Nations: They ſhall be worſe than Jews, ha-'ving no reſting-place upon the Earth, and then ſhall a Jew 'have more favour than a Jeſuit. Now, to arm you all, good 'Chriſtians, againſt theſe things that are to come, leſt 'ye be led into temptation; cry unto the Lord your God, 'and heartily pray that he would be ſo merciful unto you, 'as *to open the eyes of your underſtanding, that you may behold the*

'*wonders*

'*wonders and pleaſantneſs that is in his Law.* Which God of his 'Mercy grant that you may all do.

Thus concluding with the Acts and Deeds of this Reverend Father, we ſhall end with Queen *Mary*'s Deſigns, how ſhe intended to have perſecuted the Proteſtants in *Ireland*, but was by Providence prevented; as you ſhall further know by this following Relation, being averred by ſeveral ſufficient Perſons, as well Eccleſiaſtical as Civil.

Queen *Mary* having dealt ſeverely with the Proteſtants in *England*, about the latter end of her Reign, ſigned a Commiſſion for to take the ſame courſe with them in *Ireland:* and to execute the ſame with greater force, ſhe nominates Dr. *Cole* one of the Commiſſioners, ſending the Commiſſion by this Doctor, who in his Journey coming to *Cheſter*, the Mayor of that City hearing her Majeſty was ſending a Meſſenger into *Ireland*, and he being a Churchman, waited on the Doctor, who, in diſcourſe with the Mayor, taketh out of a Cloak-bag a Leather Box, ſaying unto him, *Here is a Commiſſion that ſhall laſh the Hereticks of* Ireland, calling the Proteſtants by that Title. The good Woman of the Houſe being well affected to the Proteſtant Religion, and alſo having a Brother named *John Edmonds* of the ſame, then a Citizen in *Dublin*, was much troubled at the Doctor's words; but watching her convenient time, whilſt the Mayor took his leave, and the Doctor complementing him down the Stairs, ſhe opens the Box and takes the Commiſſion out, placing in lieu thereof a Sheet of Paper with a Pack of Cards, the Knave of Clubs faced uppermoſt, wrapt up. The Doctor coming up to his Chamber, ſuſpecting nothing of what had been done, put up the Box as formerly. The next day, going to the Water-ſide, Wind and Weather ſerving him, he ſails towards *Ireland*, and landed on the 7th of *October*, 1558. at *Dublin*; then coming to the Caſtle, the Lord *Fitz-Walters* being Lord Deputy, ſent for him to come before him and the Privy Council; who coming in, after he had made a Speech, relating upon what account he came over, he preſents the Box unto the Lord Deputy; who cauſing it to be opened, that the Secretary might read the Commiſſion, there was nothing ſave a Pack of Cards, with the Knave of Clubs uppermoſt; which not only ſtartled the Lord Deputy and Council, but the Doctor, who aſſured them he had a Commiſſion, but knew not how it was gone: Then the Lord Deputy made anſwer, *Let us have another Commiſſion, and we will ſhuffle the Cards in the mean while.* The Doctor being troubled in his Mind, went away, and returned into *England*;

land; and coming to the Court, obtain'd another Commission; but staying for a Wind at the Water-side, News came unto him, that the Queen was dead: and thus God preserv'd the Protestants in *Ireland*.

This is a Copy of *Richard* Earl of *Cork*'s Memorials, as also of *Henry Usher*, sometime Lord Primate of *Armagh*, being also entred amongst Sir *James Ware*'s Manuscripts, who hath often heard the late *James Usher*, Nephew to the said *Henry*, and also Primate of *Armagh*, aver the same, and wondred that Mr. [illegible] had not inserted it in his *Acts* and *Monuments*; there is yet living a Reverend Father of the Church, *Henry* now Lord Bishop of *Meath*, who can affirm this Relation from the said *James Usher*, late Lord Primate of all *Ireland*.

Upon the recalling of the Lord *Fitz-Walters* into *England*, Queen *Elizabeth*, who succeeded her Sister, discoursing with the said Lord concerning several Passages in *Ireland*; amongst other Discourses, he related the aforesaid passage that had hapned in *Ireland*: which so delighted the Queen, that her Majesty sent for the good Woman, named *Elizabeth Edmonds*, but by her Husband named *Mattershad*, and gave her a Pension of Forty pound *durante vita*, for saving her Protestant Subjects of *Ireland*.

Phenix

Phenix VI.

The Sum and Substance of the Conference, which it pleas'd his Excellent Majesty to have with the Lords Bishops, and others of his Clergy (at which most of the Lords of the Council were present) in his Majesty's Privy Chamber at Hampton Court, *Jan.* 14. 1603.

Contracted by WILLIAM BARLOW, *Doctor of Divinity, and Dean of* Chester.

To the READER.

THIS *Copy of the Conference in* January *last hath been long expected, and long since it was finish'd, Impeachments of the divulging were many; two main above the rest: One, his untimely Death, who first impos'd it upon me, with whom is buried the most famous Glory of our* English *Church, and the most kind Encouragement to Pains and Study:* A Man happy in his Life, and Death; loved of the best while he liv'd, and heard of God for

Archiepisc. Cantuar.

for his Deceaſe; moſt earneſtly deſiring, not many days before he was ſtricken, that he might not yet live to ſee this Parliament, as near as it was.

The other, an Expectation of this late Comitial Conference, *much threatned before, and triumph'd in by many; as if that Regal and moſt honourable Proceeding ſhould thereby have receiv'd his Counterblaſt for being too forward. But his Majeſty's Conſtancy having by the laſt added Comfort and Strength to this former, which now at length comes abroad; therein, Good Reader, thou mayſt both ſee thoſe huge pretended Scandals (for which our flouriſhing Church hath been ſo long diſturb'd) objected and removed; and withal behold the expreſs and vive Image of a moſt learned and judicious King, whoſe manifold Gifts of Grace and Nature, my ſcant meaſure of Gift is not able to delineate, nor am I willing to enumerate, becauſe I have ever accounted the perſonal Commendation of* living Princes, *in men of our ſort, a verbal Symony. Such Flies there are too many, which puff the Skin, but taint the Fleſh. His Majeſty's humble Deportment in thoſe Sublimitys, will be the eternizing of his Memory; the rather, becauſe* καταπέψαι τὸν ὄλβον, to digeſt ſo great Felicity without Surfeit of *Surquedry, is a* Virtue *rare in great Perſonages; and that which the King of Heaven fear'd, even the King of his own choice would want. The more eminent he is in all Princely Qualities, the happier ſhall we be: Our Duty, as we are Chriſtians, is* Prayer *for him; as we are Subjects,* Obedience to him; *as we are Men,* Acknowledgment of our ſettled State in him. *Our Unthankfulneſs may remove him, as it did the Mirror of Princes, our late Famous* Elizabeth. *She reſts with God; the* Phenix *of her Aſhes reigns over us, and long may he ſo do to God's Glory, and the Church's Good; which his excellent Knowledg beautifies, and Government adjoin'd will beatify it. A Hope of this laſt we conceive by his writen* Βασίλικον; *a Specimen of the other in this* Interlocutory Conference; *whereof take this, which is printed, but as an Extract, wherein is the Subſtance of the whole.* Intercourſe *of Speeches, there occaſion'd, would cauſe Prolixity without Profit. What every Man ſaid,* point device, *I neither could, nor cared to obſerve. The Vigor of every* Objection, *with the Sum of each* Anſwer, *I gueſs, I miſs not: For the firſt day, I had no help beyond mine own; yet ſome of good place and underſtanding have ſeen it, and not control'd it, except for the Brevity: for the two laſt, out of divers * Copies, I have ſelected and order'd what you here ſee. In them all, next unto God, the King's Majeſty alone muſt have the Glory: Yet to ſay, that the preſent State of our Church is very much oblig'd to the Reverend Fathers, my Lords of* London *and* Winton, *their Pains and Dexterity in this buſineſs; were neither* Detraction *from other, nor* Flattery *of them. His*

* *Ep. Londi.* Deans of Chr. Church, Wincheſt. Windſor, Archdeacon of Nottingham, and mine own.

His Highness purposed to compose all Quarrels of this kind; whereby, and supposing he had settled all matters of the Church, it pleas'd him so to signify by Proclamation *after it was done; but there is a* Triple Generation *in the world, of whom the* Wise Man *speaketh*, Prov. 30. 12,13,14. *Marry, I say nothing (for even private Speeches cannot now pass without the smear of a* Black Cole) *in one rank whereof you may place our* Hercules Limbomastix, *whom it might have pleas'd, without this* Gnathonical *Appeal, to have rested in his Majesty's* Determination; *and being a* Synoptical Theologue, ἐν πλάτει; *and angry that he was not; so,* κατ' ἐπιτομὴν, *have learn'd the difference in Divinity between* viam Regis *and* viam Gregis.

Many Copies of divers sorts have been scatter'd and sent abroad, some partial, some untrue, some slanderous. What is here set down, for the Truth thereof shall be justify'd: the only wrong therein is to his Excellent Majesty, a Syllable of whose admirable Speeches it was pity to lose; his words, as they were utter'd by him, being as Solomon *speaks*, like Apples of Gold with Pictures of Silver. *And therefore I request thee, good Reader, when thou comest to any of his Highness's Speeches, to turn* Martial's *Apostrophe upon me*,

Tu male jam recitas, incipit esse tuus.

And I will take it kindly. If thou be honest and courteous, thou wilt rest satisfy'd, and that is my Content. To lay a Pillow for a Dog, sutes neither with my Leisure nor Purpose. Farewel.

Thine in Christ Jesus,

W. BARLOW.

The First Day's CONFERENCE.

THE Day appointed was, as by his Majesty's Proclamation we all know, Thursday the 12*th* of *January*; on which there met at *Hampton-Court* by nine of the clock, all the Bishops and Deans summon'd by Letters, namely, the Archbishop of *Canterbury*, the Bishops of *London*, *Durham*, *Winchester*, *Worcester*, *St. Davids*, *Chichester*, *Carlisle*, and *Peterborow*; the Deans of the Chappel, *Christ-Church*, *Worcester*, *Westminster*, *Pauls*, *Chester*, *Windsor*, with Dr. *Field*, and Dr. *King* Archdeacon of *Nottingham:* Who, tho the night before they heard a rumor that it was defer'd till the fourteenth day, yet according to the first Summons, thought it their Duty

to

to offer themselves to the King's Presence, which they did. At which time it pleas'd his Highness to signify to the Bishops, That the Day having prevented or deceiv'd him, he would have them return on Saturday next following. On which day all the Deans and Doctors attending my Lords the Bishops into the Presence Chamber, there we found sitting upon a Form, Dr. *Reinolds*, Dr. *Sparks*, Mr. *Knewstubs*, and Mr. *Chaderton*, Agents for the Millenary Plaintiffs. The Bishops entring the Privy Chamber, staid there, till Commandment came from his Majesty, that none of any sort should be present, but only the Lords of the Privy Council, and the Bishops, with five Deans, *viz.* of the Chappel, *Westminster*, *Pauls*, *Westchester*, *Salisbury*; who being call'd in, the Door was close shut by my Lord Chamberlain.

After a while his excellent Majesty came in, and having pass'd a few pleasant Gratulations with some of the Lords, he sat down in his Chair, remov'd forward from the Cloth of State a pretty distance; where beginning with a most grave and princely Declaration of his general drift in calling this Assembly, 'no noval Device, but according to the Example 'of all Christian Princes, who in the Commencement of their 'Reign usually take the first course for the establishing of 'the Church, both for Doctrine and Policy, to which the 'very Heathens themselves had relation in their Proverb, '*A Jove principium*; and particularly in this Land, King '*Henry* VIII. toward the end of his Reign: after him, King '*Edward* VI. who alter'd more; after him, Queen *Mary*, 'who revers'd all; and last the Queen of famous Memory; 'so his Highness added (for it is worth noting, that his Majesty never remember'd her, but with some honourable Addition) 'who settled it as it now standeth: Wherein he said 'that he was happier than they, in this, because they were 'fain to alter all things they found establish'd, but he saw 'yet no cause so much to alter and change any thing, as 'to confirm that which he found well settled already: Which 'State, as it seem'd, so affected his Royal Heart, that it 'pleas'd him both to enter into a Gratulation to Almighty 'God (at which words he put off his Hat) for bringing him 'into the Promised Land, where Religion was purely profess'd, where he sat among grave, learned, and reverend 'Men; not, as before elsewhere, a King without State, without Honour, without Order, where beardless Boys would 'brave him to his face. And to assure us, that he call'd not 'this Assembly for any Innovation, acknowledging the Government Ecclesiastical, as now it is, to have been approv'd 'by manifold Blessings from God himself, both for the Increase

'of

'of the Gospel, and with a most happy and glorious Peace; 'yet because nothing could be so absolutely order'd, but something might be added afterward thereunto; and in any 'State, as in the Body of Man, Corruptions might insensibly 'grow, either thro Time or Persons; and in that he had 'receiv'd many Complaints since his first entrance into the 'Kingdom, especially thro the Dissensions in the Church, of 'many Disorders, as he heard, and much Disobedience to the 'Laws, with a great falling away to Popery; his purpose 'therefore was, like a good Physician, to examine and try 'the Complaints, and fully to remove the occasions thereof, 'if they prove scandalous, or to cure them if they were dangerous; or if but frivolous, yet to take knowledg of them, 'thereby to cast a sop into *Cerberus*'s mouth, that he may never bark again: his meaning being, as he pleas'd to profess, 'to give factious Spirits no occasion hereby of boasting or glory, 'for which cause he had call'd the Bishops in severally by themselves, not to be confronted by the contrary Opponents, 'that if any thing should be found meet to be redress'd, it 'might be done (which his Majesty twice or thrice reiterated, 'as occasion serv'd) without any visible Alteration.

And this was the Sum, so far as my dull Head could conceive and carry it, of his Majesty's general Speech. In particular he signify'd unto them, 'the principal matters, why 'he call'd them alone, with whom he would consult about 'some special Points, wherein himself desir'd to be satisfy'd. 'These he reduc'd to three Heads: First, concerning the 'Book of Common Prayer, and Divine Service used in this 'Church. Secondly, Excommunication in the Ecclesiastical 'Courts. Thirdly, the providing of fit and able Ministers 'for *Ireland*.

'In the Book he requir'd Satisfaction about three things. 'First, about Confirmation: (1.) For the Name, if arguing 'a confirming of Baptism, as if this Sacrament without it 'were of no validity, then were it blasphemous. (2.) For 'the Use, first brought upon this occasion; Infants being 'baptiz'd, and answering by their *Patrini*, it was necessary 'they should be examin'd, when they came to years of Discretion, and after their Profession made by themselves, to be 'confirm'd with a Blessing or Prayer of the Bishop, laying his 'hands upon their Heads; abhorring the Abuse in Popery, 'where it was made a Sacrament and Corroboration to Baptism.

'The second was for Absolution, which how we us'd it in 'our Church, he knew not: He had heard it liken'd to the 'Pope's Pardons, but his Majesty's Opinion was, that there 'being only two kinds thereof from God, the one gene-

'ral,

'ral, the other particular; for the firſt, all Prayers and Preachings do import an Abſolution; for the ſecond, it is to be apply'd to ſpecial Parties, who having committed a Scandal, and repenting, are abſolv'd: otherwiſe, where there precedes not either Excommunication or Penance, there needs no Abſolution.

'The third was private Baptiſm; if private for place, his Majeſty thought it agreed with the Uſe of the primitive Church; if for Perſons, that any but a lawful Miniſter might baptize any where, he utterly diſlik'd: and in this point his Highneſs grew ſomewhat earneſt againſt the baptizing by Women and Laicks.

'The ſecond Head was Excommunication, wherein he offer'd two things to be conſider'd of; firſt the Matter, ſecondly the Perſon. In the Matter; firſt, whether it were executed (as it is complain'd) in light cauſes: ſecondly, whether it were not uſed too often. In the Perſons; firſt, why Laymen, as Chancellors and Commiſſaries, ſhould do it? Secondly, why the Biſhops themſelves, for the more Dignity to ſo high and weighty a Cenſure, ſhould not take unto them, for their Aſſiſtants, the Dean and Chapter, or other Miniſters and Chaplains of gravity and account; and ſo likewiſe in other Cenſures, and giving of Orders, *&c*?

The laſt for *Ireland*, his Majeſty referred, as you ſhall in the laſt day's Conference hear, to a Conſultation. His Highneſs (to whom I offer great wrong, in being as *Phocion* to *Demoſthenes*, κόπτις ῶν λόγων, the Hatchet to cut ſhort ſo amiable a Speech) having ended, the Lord Arch-Biſhop, after that on his Knee he had ſignified how much this whole Land was bound to God, for ſetting over us a King, ſo wiſe, learned and judicious, addreſſed himſelf to inform his Majeſty of all theſe points in their ſeveral order.

And firſt, as touching Confirmation, he ſhewed at large the Antiquity of it, as being uſed in the Catholick Church ever ſince the Apoſtles time, till that of late ſome particular Churches had unadviſedly rejected it. Then he declared the lawful uſe of it, agreeable to his Majeſties former Speech, affirming it to be a mere Calumniation, and a very untrue Suggeſtion, if any had inform'd his Highneſs, that the Church of *England* did hold or teach, that without Confirmation, Baptiſm was imperfect, or that it did add any thing to the Virtue and Strength thereof. And this he made manifeſt by the Rubricks in the Communion-Book ſet before Confirmation, which were there read.

My Lord of *London* ſucceeded, ſaying, That the Authority of Confirmation did not depend only upon the Antiquity and

Practice

Practice of the primitive Church, which out of *Cyprian*, Ep.73. and *Hieron. adversus Luciferian.* he ſhew'd, but that it was an Inſtitution Apoſtolical, and one of the particular Points of the Apoſtles Catechiſm, ſet down and named in expreſs words, *Heb.* 6. 2. and ſo did Mr. *Calvin* expound that very place, who wiſh'd earneſtly the Reſtitution thereof in thoſe Reformed Churches, where it had been aboliſh'd. Upon which place the Biſhop of *Carliſle* alſo inſiſted, and urg'd it both gravely and learnedly. His Majeſty call'd for the Bible, read the place of the *Hebrews*, and approv'd the Expoſition.

Something alſo the Biſhop of *Durham* noted, out of the Goſpel of St. *Matthew*, for the Impoſition of Hands upon Children. The Concluſion was, for the fuller Explanation (that we make it not a Sacrament, or a Corroboration to a former Sacrament) that it ſhould be conſider'd of by their Lordſhips, whether it might not without alteration (whereof his Majeſty was ſtill very wary) be intitled an Examination with a Confirmation.

Next in order was the point of Abſolution, which the Lord Archbiſhop clear'd from all Abuſe or Superſtition, as it is uſed in our Church of *England*; reading unto his Majeſty both the Confeſſion in the beginning of the Communion Book, and the Abſolution following it, wherein, ſaith he, the Miniſter doth nothing elſe but pronounce an Abſolution in general. His Highneſs peruſed them both in the Book it ſelf, liking and approving them, finding it to be very true, which my Lord Archbiſhop ſaid. But the Biſhop of *London* ſtepping forward, added, it becometh us to deal plainly with your Majeſty; there is alſo in the Communion Book another more particular and perſonal Form of Abſolution, preſcribed to be uſed in the Order for the Viſitation of the Sick. This the King requir'd to ſee, and whilſt Maſter Dean of the Chappel was turning to it, the ſaid Biſhop alledg'd, that not only the Confeſſions of *Auguſta*, *Bohemia*, *Saxony*, which he there cited, do retain and allow it; but that Mr. *Calvin* did alſo approve ſuch a general kind of Confeſſion and Abſolution, as the Church of *England* uſeth; and withal did very well like of thoſe which are private, for ſo he terms them. The ſaid particular Abſolution in the Common Prayer Book being read, his Majeſty exceedingly well approv'd it: adding, 'That it was 'Apoſtolical, and a very good Ordinance, in that it was given 'in the name of Chriſt to one that deſir'd it, and upon the 'clearing of his Conſcience.

The concluſion was, that it ſhould be conſulted of by the Biſhops, whether unto the Rubrick of the general Abſolution, theſe words, *Remiſſion of Sins*, might not be added for explanation ſake.

In the third place, the Lord Archbishop proceeded to speak of private Baptism; shewing his Majesty, that the Administration of Baptism by Women and Lay-persons was not allow'd in the Practice of the Church, but enquir'd of by Bishops in their Visitation, and censur'd; neither do the words in the Book infer any such meaning. Whereunto the King excepted, 'urging and pressing the words of the Book, 'that they could not but intend a Permission, and suffering of 'Women and private Persons to baptize. Here the Bishop of *Worcester* said, that indeed the words were doubtful, and might be press'd to that meaning; but yet it seem'd by the contrary Practice of our Church (censuring Women in this case) that the Compilers of the Book did not so intend them, and yet propounded them ambiguously, because otherwise perhaps the Book would not have then pass'd in the Parliament (and for this conjecture, as I remember, he cited the Testimony of my Lord ABp of *York*.) whereunto the Bp of *London* reply'd, that those Learned and Reverend Men, who framed the Book of Common Prayer, intended not by ambiguous terms to deceive any, but did indeed by those words intend a Permission of private Persons, to baptize in case of necessity, whereof their Letters were Witnesses: some parts whereof he then read, and withal declar'd that the same was agreeable to the Practice of the antient Church; urging to that purpose, both *Acts* 2. where 3000 were baptiz'd in one day, which for the Apostles alone to do, was impossible, at least improbable; and besides the Apostles, there were then no Bishops or Priests: and also the Authority of *Tertullian*, and St. *Ambrose* in the fourth to the *Ephesians*, plain in that point; laying also open the Absurdities and Impieties of their Opinion, who think there is no necessity of Baptism. Which word *Necessity*, he so press'd not, as if God without Baptism could not save the Child: but the case put, that the State of the Infant dying unbaptiz'd being uncertain, and to God only known; but if it die baptiz'd, there is an evident assurance that it is sav'd; Who is he that having any Religion in him, would not speedily, by any means, procure his Child to be baptiz'd, and rather ground his Action upon Christ's Promise, than his Omission thereof upon God's secret Judgment?

His Majesty reply'd, first to that place of the *Acts*, 'That 'it was an Act extraordinary, neither is it sound Reasoning 'from things done before a Church be settled and grounded, 'unto those which are to be perform'd in a Church stablish'd 'and flourishing. That he also maintain'd the Necessity of 'Baptism, and always thought, that the place of St. *John*, *Nisi quis renatus fuerit ex aqua, &c.* was meant of the Sacrament

'ment of Baptism, and that he had so defended it against 'some Ministers in *Scotland*. And it may seem strange to you 'my Lords, said his Majesty, that I, who now think you in '*England* give too much to Baptism, did fourteen months ago 'in *Scotland* argue with my Divines there for ascribing too 'little to that Holy Sacrament. Insomuch that a pert Mi-'nister ask'd me, if I thought Baptism so necessary, that if it 'were omitted, the Child should be damn'd: I answer'd him, 'No; but if you, being call'd to baptize the Child, tho pri-'vately, should refuse to come, I think you shall be damned. 'But this Necessity of Baptism his Majesty so expounded 'that it was necessary to be had where it might be lawfully 'had, *id est*, minister'd by lawful Ministers, by whom alone 'and by no private Person, he thought it might not in any 'case be administer'd; and yet utterly dislik'd all Rebap-'tization, altho either Women or Laicks had baptized.

Here the Bishop of *Winchester* spake very learnedly and ear-nestly in that point, affirming, that the denying of private Per-sons, in cases of necessity, to baptize, were to cross all Anti-quity; seeing that it had been the antient and common Prac-tice of the Church, when Ministers at such times could not be got, and that it was also a Rule agreed upon among Divines, that the Minister is not of the Essence of th Sacrament. His Majesty answer'd, 'Tho he be not of the Essence of the Sa-'crament, yet is he of the Essence of the right and lawful 'Ministry of the Sacrament, taking for his ground the Com-'mission of Christ to his Disciples, Mat. 28. 20. *Go preach and* '*baptize*.

The issue was a consultation, whether into the Rubrick of private Baptism, which leaves it indifferently to all Laicks or Clergy, the words, *Curate or lawful Minister*, might not be in serted; which was not so much stuck at by the Bishops. And so his Majesty proceeded to the next point, about Excommu-nication in causes of lesser moment: first, whether the Name might not be alter'd, and yet the same Censure be retain'd: or secondly, whether in place of it, another Coercion equi-valent thereunto might not be invented and thought of. A thing very easily yielded unto of all sides, because it had been long and often desir'd, but could not be obtain'd from her Majesty, who resolv'd to be still *semper eadem*, and to alter nothing which she had once settled.

And thus the Wednesday succeeding being appointed for the exhibiting of their Determinations in these points, and the Monday next immediately following this present day, for the Opponents to bring in their Complaints, we were dismiss'd after three hours and more spent. Which were soon gone, ſo admirably both for Underſtanding, Speech, and Judgment did his Majeſty handle all thoſe Points, ſending us away, not with Contentment only, but Aſtoniſhment; and, which is pitiful you will ſay, with ſhame to us all, that a King brought up among Puritans, not the learnedſt men in the world, and ſchool'd by them; ſwaying a Kingdom full of buſineſs and troubles, naturally given to much Exerciſe and Repaſt, ſhould in points of Divinity ſhew himſelf ſo expedite and perfect, that the greateſt Scholars, and moſt induſtrious Students there preſent might not outſtrip him. But this one thing I might not omit, 'that his Majeſty ſhould profeſs, howſoever he liv'd 'among Puritans, and was kept for the moſt part as a Ward 'under them, yet ſince he was of the age of his Son, ten years 'old, he ever diſlik'd their Opinions; as the Saviour of the World ſaid, *Tho he lived among them, he was not of them.*

Finis primæ diei.

The Second Day's CONFERENCE.

ON Monday, *January* 16. between eleven and twelve of the clock, were the four Plaintiffs call'd into the Privy Chamber (the two Biſhops of *London* and *Wincheſter* being there before) and after them all the Deans and Doctors preſent, which had been ſummon'd, *Patr. Galloway*, ſometime Miniſter of *Perth* in *Scotland*, admitted alſo to be there; the King's Majeſty entring the Chamber, preſently took his Chair, placed as the day before (the noble young Prince ſitting by upon a Stool) where making a ſhort, but a pithy and ſweet Speech, to the ſame purpoſe which the firſt day he made, *viz.* 'of 'the end of the Conference, meet to be had, he ſaid, by 'every King at his firſt entrance to the Crown; not to in-'novate the Government preſently eſtabliſh'd, which by long 'Experience he had found accompany'd with ſo ſingular Bleſ-'ſings of God forty five years, as that no Church upon the 'face of the Earth more flouriſh'd than this of *England.* But 'firſt to ſettle an uniform Order thro the whole Church: 'Secondly, to plant Unity for the ſuppreſſing of Papiſts and 'Enemies to Religion: Thirdly, to amend Abuſes, as natural 'to Bodys Politick and corrupt Man, as the Shadow to the 'Body, which once being enter'd, hold on as a wheel, his 'motion once ſet going. And becauſe many grievous Com-'plaints had been made to him, ſince his firſt entrance into

* 'the

'the Land, he thought it beſt to ſend for ſome, whom his 'Majeſty underſtood to be the moſt grave, learned, and modeſt of the aggrieved ſort, whom being there preſent, he 'was now ready to hear at large what they could object or 'ſay; and ſo will'd them to begin. Whereupon they four kneeling down, Dr. *Reynolds* the Foreman, after a ſhort Preamble gratulary, and ſignifying his Majeſty's Summons, by virtue whereof they then and there appear'd, reduced all matters diſlik'd or queſtion'd into theſe four Heads:

1. That the Doctrine of the Church might be preſerv'd in Purity according to God's Word.

2. That good Paſtors might be planted in all Churches to preach the ſame.

3. That the Church-Government might be ſincerely miniſtred, according to God's Word.

4. That the Book of Common Prayer might be fitted to more increaſe of Piety.

1. For the firſt, he moved his Majeſty, that the Book of Articles of Religion, concluded 1562. might be explain'd in places obſcure, and enlarg'd where ſome things were defective. For Example; whereas *Acts* 16. the words are theſe; *After we have receiv'd the Holy Ghoſt, we may depart from Grace:* Notwithſtanding the meaning be ſound, yet he deſir'd that, becauſe they may ſeem to be contrary to the Doctrine of God's Predeſtination and Election in the 17th Article, both thoſe words might be explain'd with this or the like addition, *Yet neither totally, nor finally*; and alſo that the nine Aſſertions Orthodoxal, as he term'd them, concluded upon at *Lambeth*, might be inſerted into that Book of Articles.

2. Secondly, Where it is ſaid in the 23d Article, 'That it is 'not lawful for any Man to take upon him the Office of 'Preaching or Adminiſtring the Sacraments, in the Congre- 'gation, before he be lawfully call'd; Dr. *Reynolds* took exception to theſe words, *In the Congregation*; as implying a Lawfulneſs for any Man whatſoever, out of the Congregation, to Preach and Adminiſter the Sacraments, tho he had no lawful Calling thereunto.

Thirdly, In the 25th Article, theſe Words touching Confirmation, grown partly of the corrupt following the Apoſtles, being oppoſite to thoſe in the Collect of Confirmation in the Communion-Book; upon whom, after the Example of the Apoſtles, argue, ſaith he, a Contrariety each to other: The firſt, confeſſing Confirmation, to be a deprav'd Imitation of the Apoſtles: The ſecond, grounding it upon their Example,

ple, *Act.* 8. and 9. as if the Bishop, in Confirming of Children, did by his Imposing of Hands, as the Apostles in those places, give the visible Graces of the Holy Ghost; and therefore he desir'd that both the Contradiction might be consider'd, and this ground of Confirmation examin'd.

Thus far Dr. *Reynolds* went on without any interruption: But here, as he was proceeding, the Bishop of *London*, much moved to hear these Men, who some of them the Evening before, and the same Morning, had made semblance of joining with the Bishops, and that they sought for nothing but Unity, now strive to overthrow (if they could) all at once, cut him off; and kneeling down, most humbly desir'd his Majesty, first, That the antient Canon might be remember'd which saith, that *Schismatici contra Episcopos non sunt audiendi.* Secondly, That if any of these Parties were in the Number of the Thousand Ministers, who had once subscrib'd to the Communion-Book, and yet had lately exhibited a Petition to his Majesty against it, they might be remov'd, and not heard, according to the Decree of a very antient Council; providing, that no Man should be admitted to speak against that, whereto he had formerly subscrib'd. Thirdly, He put Dr. *Reynolds* and his Associates in mind, how much they were bound to his Majesty's exceeding great Clemency, in that they were permitted, contrary to the Statute, 1 *Eliz.* to speak so freely against the Liturgy and Discipline establish'd. Lastly, Forasmuch as that he perceiv'd they took a course, tending to the utter overthrow of the Orders of the Church, thus long continu'd, he desir'd to know the End which they aim'd at, alledging a place out of Mr. *Cartwright*; affirming, that we ought rather to conform our selves in Orders and Ceremonies to the fashion of the *Turks*, than to the *Papists*: which Position, he doubted, they approv'd; because, contrary to the Orders of the Universities, they appear'd before his Majesty in Turky-Gowns, not in their Scholastical Habits, sorting to their Degrees.

His Majesty perceiving my Lord of *London* to speak in some Passion, said, 'That there was in it something which he 'might excuse, something that he did mislike: Excuse his 'Passion he might, thinking he had just Cause to be so mov'd, 'both in respect that they did thus traduce the present well-'setled Church-Government; and also, did proceed in so in-'direct a course, contrary to their own pretence, and the in-'tent of that meeting also. Yet he mislik'd his sudden in-'terruption of Dr. *Reynolds*, whom he should have suffer'd to 'have taken his course and liberty; concluding, that there is

no

'no Order, nor can be any effectual Issue of Disputation, if
'each Party might not be suffer'd, without chopping, to speak
'at large what he would. And therefore willed, that either
'the Doctor should proceed, or that the Bishop would frame
'his Answer to these Motions already made; altho, saith his
'Majesty, some of them are very needless. It was thought fitter to answer, lest the Number of Objections increasing, the Answers would prove confus'd.

Upon the first Motion, concerning falling from Grace: The Bishop of *London* took occasion to signify to his Majesty, how very many in these days, neglecting Holiness of Life, presum'd too much of persisting in Grace, laying all their Religion upon Predestination, If I shall be sav'd, I shall be sav'd; which he term'd a desperate Doctrine, shewing it to be contrary to good Divinity, and the true Doctrine of Predestination; wherein we should reason rather *ascendendo*, than *descendendo*, thus: I live in Obedience to God, in Love with my Neighbour; I follow my Vocation, *&c.* therefore I trust that God hath elected me, and predestinated me to Salvation: Not thus, which is the usual course of Argument, God hath predestinated and chosen me to Life; therefore tho I sin never so grievously, yet I shall not be damn'd: *For whom he once loveth, he loveth to the end.* Whereupon he shew'd his Majesty out of the next Article, what was the Doctrine of the Church of *England*, touching Predestination, in the very last Paragraph; *scil.* We must receive God's Promises, in such wise, as they be generally set forth to us in Holy Scripture, and in our doings, that the Will of God is to be follow'd, which we have expresly declar'd unto us in the Word of God: which
'part of the Article his Majesty very well approv'd; and after he had, after his manner, very singularly discours'd on
'that place of St. *Paul*, *Work out your Salvation with fear and trembling*; he left it to be consider'd, whether any thing
'were meet to be added, for the clearing of the Doctor's
'Doubt, by putting in the word *Often*, or the like; as thus:
'We may often depart from Grace; but in the mean time
'wish'd, that the Doctrine of Predestination might be very
'tenderly handled, and with great discretion; lest on the one
'side, God's Omnipotency might be call'd in question, by impeaching the Doctrine of his eternal Predestination; or, on
'the other, a desperate presumption might be arrear'd, by
'inferring the necessary Certainty of standing and persisting
'in Grace.

To the second it was answer'd, that it was a vain Objection, because, by the Doctrine and Practice of the Church of *England*, none but a licensed Minister might preach, nor either publickly or privately administer the Eucharist, or the Lord's Supper. 'And as for private Baptism, his Majesty answer'd, 'That he had taken Order for that with the Bishops already.

In the third Point (which was about Confirmation) was observ'd either Curiosity or Malice; because the Article which was there presently read, in those words; 'These five, 'commonly call'd *Sacraments*; that is to say, *Confirmation, Penance, Orders*, &c. are not to be accounted for Sacraments of 'the Gospel: being such as have grown partly of the cor-'rupt following the Apostles, *&c.* insinuateth, that the making of *Confirmation* to be a Sacrament, is a corrupt Imitation; but the Communion-Book aiming at the right use, and proper course thereof, makes it to be according to the Apostles Example: which his Majesty observing, and reading both the places, concluded the Objection to be a meer Cavil. And this was for the pretended contradiction.

Now, for the ground thereof, the Bishop of *London* added, That it was not so much founded upon the places in the *Acts* of the Apostles, which some of the Fathers had often shew'd; but upon *Heb.* 6. 2. where it is made, as the first day he had said, a part of the Apostles Catechism; which was the Opinion, besides the Judgment of the Holy Fathers, of Mr. *Calvin* and Dr. *Fulk*; the one upon *Heb.* 6. 2. as upon *Saturday* he had declar'd: the other upon *Acts* 8. verse 27. where, with St. *Augustine*, he saith, that we do not in any wise mislike that antient Ceremony (of Imposition of Hands, for strengthning and confirming such as had been Baptiz'd) but use it in our selves, being nothing else but, as St. *Austin* affirmeth, Prayer over a Man to be strengthned and confirm'd by the Holy Ghost; or to receive increase of the Gifts of the Holy Ghost, as St. *Ambrose* saith: and a little after alludeth unto *Heb.* 6. 2, &c. Neither need there any great proof of this (saith my Lord) for Confirmation to be unlawful, it was not their Opinion who objected this, as he suppos'd: This was it that vex'd them, that they had not the use thereof in their own hands, every Pastor in his Parish to confirm, for then it would be accounted an Apostolical Institution; and willed Dr. *Reynolds* to speak herein what he thought: who seem'd to yield thereunto, replying, That some Diocess of a Bishop, having therein Six hundred Parish-Churches (which Number caus'd the Bishop of *London* to think himself personally touch'd, because in his Diocess there are 609, or thereabouts) it was a thing very inconvenient to commit Confirmation unto the Bishop alone, supposing it impossible that he could take due Examination of

them

them all which came to be confirm'd. To the Fact, my Lord of *London* answer'd, for his Majesty's Information, That the Bishops, in their Visitations, give out notice to them, who are desirous either to be themselves, or to have their Children confirm'd, of the place where they will be; and appoint either their Chaplains, or some other Ministers, to examine them which are to be confirm'd, and lightly confirm none, but either by the Testimony or Report of the Parsons or Curates where the Children are bred, and brought up. To the Opinion he reply'd, That none of all the Fathers ever admitted any to confirm but Bishops alone; yea, even St. *Jerom* himself, tho otherwise no friend to Bishops, by reason of a quarrel between the Bishop of *Jerusalem* and him; yet confesseth, that the execution thereof was restrain'd to Bishops only, *Ad honorem potius Sacerdotii, quam ad legis necessitatem.* Whereof, namely of this Prerogative of Bishops, he giveth this reason; *Ecclesiæ salus in summi Sacerdotis dignitate pendit; cui si non exors quædam & ab omnibus eminens detur potestas, tot in Ecclesiis efficerentur schismata, quot Sacerdotes.* My Lord Bishop of *Winchester* challeng'd Dr. *Reynolds*, willing him, of his Learning, to shew wherever he had read, that Confirmation was at all us'd in antient Times by any other but Bishops; and added withal, that it was us'd, partly to examine Children, and after Examination, by Imposition of Hands (which was a Ceremony of Blessing among the *Jews*) to bless them and pray over them: and partly to try whether they had been baptiz'd in the right Form or no. For, in former Ages, Baptism was administred in divers sorts: some gave it, *In nomine Patris & Filii, &c.* Others, *In nomine Patris majoris, & Filii minoris*, as the *Arians* did: Some, *In nomine Patris per Filium, in Spiritu sancto*; Others, not in the Name of the Trinity, but in the Death of Christ, *&c.* Whereupon Catholick Bishops were constrain'd to examine them who were Baptiz'd *in remotis*, far from them, how they were taught to believe concerning Baptism: If it were right, to confirm them; if amiss, to instruct them.

His Majesty concluded this Point, first by taxing St. *Jerom* for his Assertion, that a Bishop was not *Divinæ Ordinationis*; (the Bishop of *London* thereupon inferring, That unless he could prove his Ordination lawful out of the Scriptures, he would not be a Bishop four Hours) which Opinion his Ma-
'jesty much distasted, approving their Calling and Use in the
'Church, and clos'd it up with this short Aphorism, *No Bi-*
'*shop, no King.* Secondly, For Confirmation, his Highness
'thought, that it sorted neither with the Authority, nor De-
'cency of the same, that every ordinary Pastor should do it:
'and therefore said, That for his part, he meant not to take

'that

'that from the Bishops, which they had so long retain'd and
'enjoy'd; seeing, as it pleased him to add, as great reason,
'that none should confirm without the Bishop's License, as
'none should preach without his License: and so referring,
'as the day before, the word *Examination* to be added to the
'Rubrick, in the Title of Confirmation in the Communion-
'Book, if it were thought good so to do, He willed Dr. *Rey-*
nolds to proceed.

Who after that he had deprecated the Imputation of Schism, with a Protestation, That he meant not to gall any Man, goeth on to the 37th Article, 'wherein he said these words,
'The Bishop of *Rome* hath no Authority in this Land, not to
'be sufficient, unless it were added, nor ought to have.
Whereat his Majesty heartily laugh'd, and so did the Lords: the King adding an Answer, which the Rhetoricians call ἐγώ-τημα ἐλέγχικον. 'What speak you of the Pope's Authority here?
'*Habemus jure quod habemus*; and therefore, in as much as it is
'said, he hath not; it is plain enough, that he ought not to
'have.

This, and some other Motions, seeming both to the King and Lords very idle and frivolous, occasion was taken, in some by-talk, to remember a certain description, which Mr. *Butler* of *Cambridge* made of a Puritan; *viz.* A Puritan is a Protestant frayed out of his Wits. But my Lord of *London* there seriously put his Majesty in mind of the Speeches, which the *French* Embassador Mr. *Rogne* gave out concerning our Church of *England*, both at *Canterbury* after his Arrival; and after, at the Court, upon the view of our solemn Service and Ceremonies; namely, that if the Reformed Churches in *France* had kept the same Orders among them which we have, he was assured that there would have been many Thousands of Protestants more there, than now there are: And yet our Men stumble and strain at these petty Quillets, thereby to disturb and disgrace the whole Church.

After this the Doctor mov'd that this Proposition, *The Intention of the Minister is not of the Essence of the Sacrament*, might be added unto the Book of Articles; the rather, because that some in *England* had preach'd it to be Essential. And here again he remembred the nine Orthodoxal Assertions concluded at *Lambeth*. 'His Majesty utterly dislik'd that first
'part of the Motion, for two Reasons: First, thinking it un-
'fit to thrust into the Book every Position negative, which
'would both make the Book swell into a Volume as big as
'the Bible, and also confound the Reader; bringing, for
'Example, the Course of one Mr. *Craig*, in the like case, in
'*Scotland*, who with his, *I renounce and abhor his Detestations and*

'*Abrenun-*

'*Abrenunciations*, did so amaze the simple People, that they, 'not able to conceive all those things, utterly gave over all, 'falling back to Popery, or remaining still in their former 'Ignorance. Yea, if I, said his Majesty, should have been 'bound to his Form, the Confession of my Faith must have 'been in my Table-book, not in my Head. But because you 'speak of *Intention*, saith his Highness, I will apply it thus: 'If you come hither with a good Intention, to be inform'd 'and satisfy'd where you shall find just Cause, the whole Work 'will sort to the better effect: but if your Intention be to 'go as you came (whatsoever shall be said) it will prove 'that the Intention is very material and essential to the end 'of this present Action. To the other part, for the nine Assertions, his Majesty could not suddenly answer, because he understood not what the Doctor meant by those Assertions or Propositions at *Lambeth*; but when it was inform'd his Majesty, that by reason of some Controversies arising in *Cambridge* about certain Points of Divinity, my Lord's Grace assembled some Divines of especial Note, to set down their Opinions, which they drew into nine Assertions, and so sent them to the University, for the appeasing of those Quarrels: Then his Majesty answer'd, First, That when such Questions arise among Scholars, the quietest Proceeding were, to determine them in the Universities, and not to stuff the Book with all conclusions Theological. Secondly, The better course would be to punish the Broachers of false Doctrine, as occasion should be offer'd: For were the Articles never so many and sound, who can prevent the contrary Opinions of Men till they be heard?

Upon this the Dean of St. *Paul*'s kneeling down, humbly desir'd leave to speak, signifying unto his Majesty, that this matter somewhat more nearly concern'd him, by reason of Controversy between him and some other in *Cambridge*, upon a Proposition which he had deliver'd there; Namely, that whosoever (altho before justified) did commit any grievous Sin, as Adultery, Murder, Treason, or the like, did become, *ipso facto*, subject to God's Wrath, and guilty of Damnation, or were in a state of Damnation (*quoad præsentem statum*) until they repented; adding hereto, that those which were called and justified according to the purpose of God's Election, however they might, and did, sometime fall into grievous Sins, and thereby into the present state of Wrath and Damnation; yet did never fall, either totally from all the Graces of God, to be utterly destitute of all the Parts and Seed thereof, nor finally from Justification, but were in time renew'd, by God's Spirit, unto a lively Faith and Repentance; and so justified from those Sins, and the

Wrath,

Wrath, Curse, and Guilt annex'd thereunto, whereinto they are fallen, and wherein they lay, so long as they were without true Repentance for the same. Against which Doctrine, he said, that some had opposed; teaching, that all such persons as were once truly justified, tho after they fell into never so grievous Sins; yet remain'd still just, or in the state of Justification, before they actually repented of those Sins; yea, and tho they never repented of them, through forgetfulness or sudden death, yet they should be justified and saved without Repentance. 'In utter dislike of this Doctrine, his Majesty entred into a longer Speech of Predestination and Reprobation than before, and of the necessary conjoyning Repentance and Holiness of Life with true Faith; concluding, that it was Hypocrisy, and not true justifying Faith, which was severed from them: For altho Predestination and Election depend not upon any Qualities, Actions, or Works of Man, which be mutable, but upon God's eternal and immutable Decree and Purpose; yet such is the Necessity of Repentance, after known Sins committed, as that, without it, there could not be, either Reconciliation with God, or Remission of those Sins.

Next to this, Dr. *Reynolds* complain'd, that the Catechism in the Common-Prayer-Book was too brief; for which one by Mr. *Nowell*, late Dean of St. *Paul's*, was added, and that too long for young Novices to learn by heart: Requested therefore, that one uniform Catechism might be made, which, and none other, might be generally receiv'd. It was demanded of him, Whether if, to the short Catechism in the Communion-Book, something were added for the Doctrine of the Sacrament, it would not serve? His Majesty thought the Doctor's Request very reasonable; but yet so, that he would 'have a Catechism in the fewest and plainest Affirmative terms that may be; taxing withal, the Number of ignorant Catechisms set out in *Scotland*, by every one that was the Son of a Good Man: Insomuch as, that which was Catechism-Doctrine in one Congregation, was in another scarcely accepted as Sound and Orthodox; wished therefore, one to be made and agreed upon, adding this Excellent, Gnomical and Canon-like Conclusion, That in Reforming of a Church, he would have two Rules observ'd: First, that old, curious, deep and intricate Questions might be avoided in the fundamental Instruction of a People. Secondly, That there should not be any such departure from the Papists in all things, as that, because we in some Points agree with them; therefore we should be accounted to be in an Error.

To

To the former, Dr. *Reynolds* did add the Prophanation of the Sabbath-day, and Contempt of his Majesty's Proclamation, made for the Reforming of that Abuse, of which he earnestly desir'd a straighter course for Reformation thereof; and unto this he found a general and unanimous Assent.

After that, he mov'd his Majesty, that there might be a New Translation of the Bible; because, those which were allow'd in the Reign of King *Henry* the Eighth, and *Edward* the Sixth, were corrupt, and not answerable to the Truth of the Original. For Example; First, *Galat.* 4. 25. the Greek word συστοιχεῖ is not well translated, as now it is; *Bordereth*, neither expressing the force of the word, nor the Apostle's sense, nor the Situation of the place.

Secondly, *Psalm* 105. 28. They were not *obedient*; The Original being, They were not *disobedient.*

Thirdly, *Psalm* 106. verse 30. *Then stood up Phinehas, and prayed*; the Hebrew hath it, *Executed judgment.* To which motion there was, at the present, no gainsaying, the Objections being trivial and old, and already in Print, often answer'd: Only my Lord of *London* well added, That if every Man's humour should be follow'd, there would be no end of Translating. 'Whereupon his Highness wish'd, that some especial pains 'should be taken in that behalf for one uniform Translation '(professing that he could never yet see a Bible well translated 'into *English*; but the worst of all his Majesty thought the '*Geneva* to be) and this to be done by the Best Learned in 'both Universities; after them to be review'd by the Bishops, 'and the chief Learned of the Church; from them to be pre-'sented to the Privy Council; and lastly, to be ratify'd by his 'Royal Authority; and so this whole Church to be bound un-'to it, and none other. Marry, withal he gave this Caveat, '(upon a word cast out by my Lord of *London*) that no margi-'nal Notes should be added, having found in them which are 'annex'd to the *Geneva* Translation (which he saw in a Bible 'given him by an *English* Lady) some Notes very partial, un-'true, seditious, and favouring too much of dangerous and trai-'torous Conceits. As for example, the first Chapter of *Exodus* 'and the nineteenth Verse, where the marginal Note alloweth 'Disobedience unto Kings. And 2 *Chron.* 15. 16. the Note 'taxeth *Asa* for deposing his Mother only, and not killing her. 'And so concludeth this point as all the rest, with a grave and 'judicious Advice. First, that Errors in matters of Faith 'might be rectify'd and amended. Secondly, that matters 'indifferent might rather be interrupted, and a gloss added; 'alledging from *Bartolus de Regno*, that as better a King with 'some weakness than still a Change; so rather a Church with

'some

'some faults than an Innovation. And surely, saith his Ma-
'jesty, if these be the greatest matters you be griev'd with,
'I need not have been troubled with such Importunities and
'Complaints, as have been made unto me; some other more
'private course might have been taken for your Satisfaction:
'and withal looking upon the Lords, he shook his Head,
'smiling.

The last Point (noted by Dr. *Reynolds*) in this first Head, for Doctrine, was, That unlawful and seditious Books might be suppress'd, at least restrain'd, and imparted to a few: for by the liberty of publishing such Books so commonly, many young Scholars, and unsettled Minds in both Universities, and thro the whole Realm, were corrupted and perverted; naming for one instance that Book entitled, *De jure Magistratus in Subditos*, publish'd of late by *Ficlerus* a Papist, and apply'd against the Queen's Majesty that last was, for the Pope. The Bishop of *London* supposing, as it seem'd, himself to be principally aim'd at, answer'd first to the general, that there was no such licentious divulging of those Books, as he imagin'd or complain'd of; and that none, except it were such as Dr. *Reynolds*, who were suppos'd would consume them, had liberty by Authority to buy them. Again, such Books came into the Realm by many secret Conveyances; so that there could not be a perfect notice had of their Importation. Secondly, to the particular Instance of *Ficlerus*, he said that the Author *De Jure, &c.* was a great Disciplinarian; whereby it did appear what advantage that sort gave unto the Papists, who *mutatis personis*, could apply their own Arguments against Princes of the Religion: but for his own part he said, he detested both the Author and the Applier alike. My Lord *Cecil* here taxing also the unlimited Liberty of the dispersing and divulging these Popish and seditious Pamphlets, both in *Paul's* Churchyard and the Universities, instanc'd one lately set forth and publish'd, namely, *Speculum Tragicum*; which both his Majesty and the Lord *H. Howard*, now Earl of *Northampton*, term'd a dangerous Book, both for Matter and Intention. And the Lord Chancellor also dividing all such Book into *Latin* and *English*, concluded, that these last dispers'd, did most harm. Yet the Lord Secretary affirm'd, that my Lord of *London* had done therein what might be for the suppressing of them; and that he knew no man else had done any thing in that kind but he. At length it pleas'd his excellent Majesty to tell Dr. *Reynolds*, 'That he was a better Collegeman than a States-
'man; for if his meaning were, to tax the Bishop of *London*
'for suffering those Books, between the Secular Priests and
'Jesuits, lately publish'd, so freely to pass abroad; his Ma-
'jesty

'jesty would have him and his Associates to know, and willed 'them also to acquaint their Adherents and Friends abroad 'therewith, that the said Bishop was much injur'd and slander'd in that behalf, who did nothing therein but by warrant from the Lords of the Council; whereby both a Schism 'between them was nourish'd, and also his Majesty's own 'Cause and Title handled. The Lord *Cecil* affirming thereunto, that therefore they were tolerated, because in them was the Title of *Spain* confuted. The Lord Treasurer added, That Dr. *Reynolds* might have observ'd another use of those Books, *viz.* that now by the Testimony of those Priests themselves, her late Majesty and the State were clear'd of that Imputation, of putting Papists to death for their Consciences only, and for their Religion, seeing in those Books they themselves confess, that they were executed for Treason. Dr. *Reynolds* excus'd himself, expounding his Complaint, not meant of such Books as had been printed in *England*, but such as came from beyond the Seas, as Commentaries both in Philosophy and Divinity. And these were the parts of the first Head, concerning Purity of Doctrine.

Touching Pastors { *Resident,* *Learned.* }

To the second general Point concerning the planting of Ministers learned in every Parish; it pleas'd his Majesty to answer, 'That he had consulted with his Bishops about that, 'whom he found willing and ready to second him in it; inveighing herein against the Negligence and Carelessness 'which he heard of many in this Land: but as *subita Evacuatio* was *periculosa*, so *subita mutatio.* Therefore this matter 'was not for a present Resolution, because to appoint to every Parish a sufficient Minister, were impossible; the Universities would not afford them. Again, he had found already that he had more learned Men in this Realm, than he 'had sufficient Maintenance for; so that Maintenance must 'first be provided, and then the other to be required. 'In the mean time, ignorant Ministers, if young, to be remov'd, if there were no hope of their Amendment; if old, 'their Death must be expected, that the next course may be 'better supply'd: and so concluded this Point with a most 'religious and zealous Protestation, of doing something daily 'in this case, because *Jerusalem* could not be built up in a day. The Bishop of *Winchester* made known to the King, that this Insufficiency of the Clergy, be it as it is, comes not by the Bishops Defaults, but partly by Lay-Patrons, who present very mean

mean Men to their Cures; whereof in himſelf he ſhew'd an Inſtance, how that ſince his being Biſhop of *Wincheſter*, very few Maſters of Arts were preſented to good Benefices: partly, by the Law of the Land, which admitteth of a very mean and tolerable Sufficiency in any Clerk; ſo that if the Biſhop ſhould not admit them, then preſently a *Quare impedit* is ſent out againſt him.

Here my Lord of *London* kneeling, humbly deſir'd his Majeſty (becauſe he ſaw, as he ſaid, it was a time of moving Petitions) that he might have leave to make two or three. Firſt, that there might be amongſt us a Praying Miniſtry another while: for whereas there are in the Miniſtry many excellent Duties to be perform'd, as the abſolving of the Penitent, praying for and bleſſing of the People, adminiſtring of the Sacraments, and the like; it is come to that paſs now, that ſome ſort of Men thought it the only Duty requir'd of a Miniſter, to ſpend the time in ſpeaking out of a Pulpit; ſometimes, God wot, very indiſcreetly and unlearnedly: and this with ſo great injury and prejudice to the Celebration of Divine Service, that ſome Miniſters would be content to walk in the Churchyard till Sermon time, rather than to be preſent at publick Prayer. He confeſs'd, that in a Church new to be planted, Preaching was moſt neceſſary; but among us, now long eſtabliſh'd in the Faith, he thought it not the only neceſſary Duty to be perform'd, and the other to be ſo profanely neglected and contemn'd. Which Motion his Majeſty liked exceeding well, 'very acutely taxing the Hypocriſy of 'our times, which placeth all Religion in the Ear, thro which 'there is an eaſy Paſſage; but Prayer, which expreſſeth the 'Heart's Affection, and is the true Devotion of the Mind, as 'a matter putting us to overmuch trouble (wherein there 'concur, if Prayer be as it ought, an impartial Conſideration 'of our own Eſtates, a due Examination to whom we pray, an 'humble Confeſſion of our Sins, with an hearty Sorrow 'for them, and Repentance not ſever'd from Faith) is ac'counted and uſed as the leaſt part of Religion.

The ſecond was, That till ſuch time as learned and ſufficient Men might be planted in every Congregation, that godly Homilies might be read, and the number of them increas'd; and that the Opponents would labour to bring them into credit again, as formerly they brought them into contempt. Every man, ſaith he, that can pronounce well, cannot indite well.

'The King's Majeſty approv'd this Motion, eſpecially where 'the Living is not ſufficient for Maintenance of a learned 'Preacher; as alſo in places where plenty of Sermons are, as 'in

' in the City and great Towns. In the Country Villages, ' where Preachers are not near together, he could wish ' Preaching; but where there are a multitude of Sermons, ' there he would have *Homilies* to be read divers times; and ' therein he ask'd the Assent of the Plaintiffs, and they con- ' fess it. A preaching Ministry, saith his Majesty, was best; ' but where it might not be had, godly Prayers and Exhor- ' tations did much good. That that may be done, let it, and ' let the rest that cannot, be tolerated. Somewhat was here spoken by the Lord Chancellor, of Livings rather wanting Learned Men, than Learned Men Livings. Many in the Uni- versities pining, Masters, Batchelors, and upwards; wishing therefore, that some might have single Coats, before others had Doublets: And here his Lordship shewed the Course, that he had ever taken, in bestowing the King's Benefices. My Lord of *London* commending his Honourable Care that way; withal excepted, that a Doublet was necessary in cold Weather: The Lord Chancellor reply'd, That he did it not for dislike of the Liberty of our Church, in granting one Man two Benefices, but out of his own private purpose and practice, grounded upon the foresaid Reason,

The last Motion by my Lord of *London* was, That Pulpits might not be made Pasquils, wherein every humorous or dis- contented Fellow might traduce his Superiors. ' Which the ' King very graciously accepted, exceedingly reproving that ' as a lewd Custom; threatning, that if he should but hear ' of such a one in a Pulpit, he would make him an Example; ' concluding with a sage Admonition to the Opponents, that ' every Man should sollicit and draw his Friends to make ' Peace; and if any thing were amiss in the Church-Officers, ' not to make the Pulpit the place of personal Reproof, but ' to let his Majesty hear of it; yet by degrees.

' First, let complaint be to the Ordinary of the place, from ' him to go to the Archbishop; from him, to the Lords of his ' Majesty's Council; and from them, if in all these places no ' remedy is found, to his own self. Which Caveat his Majesty put in, for that the Bishop of *London* had told him, that if he left himself open to admit of all Complaints, neither his Ma- jesty should ever be quiet, nor his Under-Officers regarded; seeing that now already no fault can be censured, but presently the Delinquent threatneth a Complaint to the King: and for an instance, he added, how a Printer, whom he had taken faulty, very lately answer'd him in that very kind.

Dr. *Reynolds* cometh now to *Subscription* (which concerneth the fourth General Head, as he first propounded it, namely, *The Communion Book*) taking occasion to leap into it here, as

 making

making the urging of it to be a great Impeachment to a learned Ministry; and therefore intreated it might not be exacted as heretofore, for which many good Men were kept out, others remov'd, and many disquieted. To subscribe according to the Statutes of the Realm, namely, to the Articles of Religion, and the King's Supremacy, they were not unwilling. The reason of their Backwardness to subscribe otherwise was, first the Book *Apocryphal*, which the *Common Prayer Book* enjoin'd to be read in the Church, albeit there are in some of those Chapters appointed, manifest Errors, directly repugnant to the Scriptures: the particular instance, which he then infer'd, was *Ecclus.* 48. 10. where he charg'd the Author of that Book, to have held the same Opinion with the *Jews* at this day, namely, that *Elias* in person was to come before Christ; and therefore as yet Christ, by that reason, not come in the flesh: and so consequently it imply'd a Denial of the chief Article of our Redemption. His reason of thus charging the Author was, because that *Ecclus.* used the very word of *Elias in person*, which the Prophet *Malachi*, chap. 4. doth apply to an *Elias* in resemblance; which both an Angel, *Luke* 17. and our Saviour Christ, *Mat.* 11. did interpret to be *John Baptist*. The Answer was, as the Objection, twofold. First, General, for *Apocryphal Books*; the Bishop of *London* shewing, first, for the Antiquity of them, that the most of the Objections made against those Books, were the old Cavils of the *Jews*, renew'd by St. *Jerom* in his time, who was the first that gave them the name of *Apocrypha*; which Opinion, upon *Ruffinus*'s Challenge, he after a sort disclaim'd; the rather, because a general Offence was taken at his Speeches in that kind: first for the continuance of them in the Church, out of *Kimedoncius* and *Chemnitius*, two modern Writers.

The Bishop of *Winton* remember'd the Distinction of St. *Jerom*; *Canonici sunt ad informandos mores, non ad confirmandam fidem*: which Distinction, he said, must be held for the justifying of sundry Councils. His Majesty in the end said, 'he would 'take an even order between both; affirming, that he would 'not wish all *Canonical Books* to be read in the Church, unless 'there were one to interpret, nor any *Apocrypha* at all, wherein there was any Error; but for the other, which were clear 'and correspondent to the Scriptures, he would have them 'read: for else, saith his Majesty, why were they printed? 'and therein shew'd the use of the Books of *Maccabees*, very 'good to make up the Story of the Persecution of the *Jews*; 'but not to teach a Man either to sacrifice for the Dead, or 'to kill himself.

And

And here his Highness arose from his Chair, and withdrew himself into his inner Chamber a little space. In the mean time a great questioning was amongst the Lords, about that place of *Ecclus.* with which, as if it had been their rest and upshot, they began afresh, at his Majesty's return; who seeing 'them so to urge it, and stand upon it, calling for a Bible, 'first shew'd the Author of that Book, who he was, then the 'cause why he wrote that Book; next analiz'd the Chapter 'it self, shewing the Precedents and Consequents thereof; 'lastly, so exactly and Divine-like unfolded the Sum of that 'place, arguing and demonstrating, that whatsoever *Ben Sirach* had said there of *Elias*, *Elias* had in his own person, 'while he liv'd, perform'd and accomplish'd. So that the *Susurrus* at the first mention was not so great, as the Astonishment was now at the King's sudden and sound, and indeed so admirable an Interpretation: Concluding first with a serious Check to Dr. *Reynolds*, That it was not good to impose upon a man that was dead, a Sense never meant by him. Secondly, with a pleasant *Apostrophe* to the Lords; *What, trow ye, make these men so angry with* Ecclesiasticus? *By my Soul I think he was a Bishop, or else they would never use him so.* But for the general, it was appointed by his Majesty, that Dr. *Reynolds* should note those Chapters in the *Apocrypha* Book, where those offensive places were, and should bring them unto the Lord Archbishop of *Canterbury* against Wednesday next; and so he was willed to go on.

The next Scruple against *Subscription* was: That old *Crambe bis posita*, that in the Common Prayer Book it is twice set down, *Jesus said to his Disciples*; when as by the next Original it is plain, that he spake to the *Pharisees*. To which it was answer'd, that for ought that could appear by the places, he might speak as well to his *Disciples*, they being present, as to the *Pharisees*. But his Majesty keeping an even hand, willed that the word *Disciples* should be omitted, and the words *Jesus said*, to be printed in a different Letter, that might appear not to be a part of the Text.

The third Objection against *Subscription*, were *Interrogatories in Baptism*, propounded to Infants, which being a profound Point, was put upon Mr. *Knewstubs* to pursue; who in a long and perplex'd Speech said something out of *Austin*, that *Baptizare* was *Credere*; but what it was, his Majesty plainly confess'd, *Ego non intelligo*; and asked the Lords, what they thought he meant. It seem'd that one present conceiv'd him; for he standing at his back, bad him urge that Punct, *Urge that Punct; that is a good Point.* My Lord of *Winton* aiming at his meaning, shew'd him the use thereof out of St. *Austin*, and added the

Father's reaſon for it, *Qui peccavit in altero, credat in altero*; which was ſeconded by his Majeſty (whom it pleas'd, for the reſt of the matters which follow'd, himſelf alone to anſwer; and juſtly might he appropriate it to himſelf, for none preſent were able with quicker Conceit to underſtand, with a more ſingular Dexterity to refute, with a more judicious Reſolution to determine, than his Majeſty: herein being more admirable, that theſe Points, wherein ſome thought him prejudicial to the contrary, all of us ſuppos'd him to have been but a Stranger to them, he could ſo intelligently apprehend, and ſo readily argue about them) it was, I ſay, ſeconded by his Majeſty: 'Firſt, by reaſon that the Queſtion ſhould be propounded to 'the Party whom it principally concern'd. Secondly, by 'example of himſelf, to whom Interrogatories were pro-'pounded when he was crown'd in his Infancy, King of '*Scotland*.

And here his Majeſty (as hereafter at the end of every Objection he did) asked them, whether they had any more to ſay.

Mr. *Knewſtubs* took exceptions at the Croſs in Baptiſm, being in number two. 1*ſt*, The Offence of weak Brethren, grounded upon the words of St. *Paul*, *Rom.* 14. and 1 *Cor.* 8. *viz.* the Conſciences of the Weak not to be offended. Which places his excellent Majeſty anſwer'd moſt acutely, beginning with that general Rule of the Fathers: '*Diſtingue tempora, & 'concordabunt Scripturæ*; ſhewing here the difference of thoſe 'times and ours, then a Church not fully planted nor ſettled, 'but ours long ſtabliſh'd and flouriſhing; then Chriſtians new-'ly call'd from Paganiſm, and not thoroly grounded; which is 'not the caſe of this Church, ſeeing that Heatheniſh Doctrine 'for many years has been hence abandon'd. 2*ly*, With a Queſtion 'unanſwerable, asking them how long they would be Weak? 'Whether 45 years were not ſufficient for them to grow ſtrong? '3*dly*, Who they were pretended this Weakneſs: For we, ſaith 'the King, require not now Subſcription of Laicks and Idiots, 'but Preachers and Miniſters, who are not ſtill, I trow, to be 'fed with milk, but are enabled to feed others. 4*thly*, That 'it was to be doubted ſome of them were ſtrong enough, 'if not headſtrong; and howſoever they in this caſe pretended 'Weakneſs, yet ſome, in whoſe behalf they now ſpake, 'thought themſelves able to teach him, and all the Biſhops 'of the Land.

His Objection againſt the Croſs conſiſted of three Interrogatories: Firſt, Whether the Church had power to inſtitute an external ſignificant Sign? To which was reply'd, 1*ſt*, That he miſtook the Uſe of the Croſs with us, which was not uſed in in Baptiſm, any otherwiſe than only as a Ceremony. *2dly*, By their own example, who make Impoſition of Hands, in their Ordination of Paſtors, to be a Sign ſignificant.

Thirdly, in Prayer, ſaith the Biſhop of *Winton*, the kneeling on the ground, the lifting up of our Hands, the knocking of our Breaſts, are Ceremonies ſignificant ; the firſt, of our Humility coming before the mighty God ; the ſecond, of our Confidence and Hope ; the other of our Sorrow and Deteſtation of our Sins : and theſe are and may lawfully be uſed. Laſtly, Mr. Dean of the Chappel remember'd the Practice of the *Jews*, who unto the Inſtitution of the Paſſover, preſcribed unto them by *Moſes*, had, as the Rabbins witneſs, added both Signs and Words, eating four Herbs, and drinking Wine, with theſe words to both, *Take and eat theſe in remembrance*, &c. *Drink this in remembrance*, &c. Upon which Addition and Tradition of theirs, our Saviour inſtituted the Sacrament of his laſt Supper, in celebrating it with the ſame words, and after the ſame manner ; thereby approving that Fact of theirs in particular, and generally, that a Church may inſtitute and retain a Sign ſignificant : which ſatisfy'd his Majeſty exceeding well.

And here the King deſir'd to have himſelf made acquainted about the Antiquity of the Uſe of the Croſs, which Dr. *Reynolds* confeſs'd to have been ever ſince the Apoſtles times ; but this was the difficulty, to prove it of that antient uſe in Baptiſm. For that at their going abroad, or entering into the Church, or at their Prayers and Benedictions, it was uſed by the Antients, requir'd no great proof. But whether in Baptiſm, Antiquity approv'd it, was the doubt caſt in by Mr. Dean of *Sarum*, whom his Majeſty ſingled out, with a ſpecial Encomium, that he was a man well vers'd in the Antients : Which doubt was anſwer'd, *obſignatis tabulis*, by the Dean of *Weſtminſter* (whom the King's Majeſty, upon my Lord of *London*'s motion, willed to ſpeak to that point) out of *Tertullian*, *Cyprian*, *Origen*, and others, that it was uſed in *Immortali lavacro* ; which words being a little deſcanted, it fell from one, I think it was my Lord of *Wincheſter*, *obiter*, to ſay, that in *Conſtantine*'s time it was uſed in Baptiſm. ‘ What, quoth the King, and ‘ is it now come to that paſs, that we ſhall appeach *Conſtantine* ‘ of Popery and Superſtition ? If then it were uſed, ſaith his ‘ Majeſty, I ſee no reaſon but that ſtill we may continue it.

Mr. *Knewſtubs*'s ſecond Queſtion was, That put caſe the Church had ſuch power to add ſignificant Signs, whether it might there add them, where Chriſt had already ordain'd one ; which he ſaid was no leſs derogatory to Chriſt's Inſtitution, as he thought, than if any Potentate of this Land ſhould preſume fume to add his Seal to the Great Seal of *England*. To which his Majesty answer'd, 'that the case was not alike; for that 'no sign or thing was added to the Sacrament, which was 'fully and perfectly finish'd, before any mention of the Cross 'is made; for Confirmation whereof, he willed the place 'to be read.

Lastly, if the Church had that Power also, yet the greatest Scruple to their Conscience was, how far such an Ordinance of the Church was to bind them, without impeaching their Christian Liberty? Whereat the King, as it seem'd, was much moved, and told him, 'he would not argue that Point 'with him, but answer therein, as Kings are wont to speak 'in Parliament, *Le Roy s'avisera*; adding withal, that it smell'd 'very rankly of Anabaptism: comparing it to the Usage 'of a beardless Boy (one Mr. *John Black*) who the last Con-'ference his Majesty had with the Ministers of *Scotland*, in '*December* 1602. told him, That he would hold Conformity 'with his Majesty's Ordinances, for matters of Doctrine; but 'for matters of Ceremony, they were to be left in Christian 'Liberty to every man, as he receiv'd more and more Light 'from the Illumination of God's Spirit: Even till they go mad, 'quoth the King, with their own Light. But I will none of 'that; I will have one Doctrine, and one Discipline, one 'Religion in Substance and in Ceremony: and therefore I 'charge you never to speak more to that point (how far you 'are bound to obey) when the Church hath ordain'd it. And so asked them again, if they had any thing else to say.

Dr. *Reynolds* objected the Example of the Brazen Serpent, demolish'd and stampt to pouder by *Hezechiah*, because the People abus'd it to Idolatry, wishing that in like sort the Cross should be abandon'd, because in the time of Popery it had been superstitiously abus'd. Whereunto the King's Majesty answer'd divers ways: First, quoth he, tho I be suffi-'ciently persuaded of the Cross in Baptism, and the com-'mendable Use thereof in the Church so long; yet if there 'were nothing else to move me, this very Argument were 'an Inducement to me for the retaining of it, as it is 'now by Order establish'd. For inasmuch as it was abu-'sed, so you say, to Superstition in time of Popery, it doth 'plainly imply, that it was well used before Popery. I will 'tell you, I have lived among this sort of men (speaking to 'the Lords and Bishops) ever since I was ten years old; but 'I may say of my self, as Christ did of himself, Tho I lived 'among them, yet since I had Ability to judg, I was never 'of them: neither did any thing make me more to condemn 'and detest their courses, than that they did so peremptorily

'disallow

'disallow of all things, which at all had been used in Popery. 'For my part, I know not how to answer the Objection of the 'Papists, when they charge us with Novelties; but truly to 'tell them, that their Abuses are new, but the things which 'they abused, we retain in their primitive Use, and forsake 'only the novel Corruption. By this Argument we might 'renounce the Trinity, and all that is Holy, because it was 'abused in Popery: and (speaking to Dr. *Reynolds* merrily) 'they used to wear Hose and Shoos in Popery, therefore 'you shall now go barefoot.

'Secondly, quoth his Majesty, what resemblance is there 'between the Brazen Serpent, a material visible thing, and 'the Sign of the Cross made in the Air?

'Thirdly, I am given to understand by the Bishops, and I 'find it true, that the Papists themselves did never ascribe 'any Power or spiritual Grace to the Sign of the Cross in 'Baptism.

'Fourthly, you see that the material Crosses, which in 'time of Popery were made, for men to fall down before 'them, as they pass'd by them to worship them (as the Idolatrous *Jews* did the Brazen Serpent) are demolish'd, as 'you desire.

The next thing which was objected, was the wearing of the Surplice, a kind of Garment, which the Priests of *Isis* used to wear. 'Surely, saith his Majesty, till of late I did 'not think that it had been borrow'd from the Heathen, because it is commonly term'd, *a Rag of Popery*, in scorn; but 'were it so, yet neither did we border upon Heathenish Nations, neither are any of them conversant with us, or commorant amongst us, who thereby might take just occasion 'to be strengthned, or confirm'd in Paganism; for then there 'were just cause to suppress the wearing it: but seeing it 'appear'd out of Antiquity, that in the Celebration of Divine 'Service, a different Habit appertaineth to the Ministry, 'and principally of white Linen; he saw no reason, but that 'in this Church, as it had been for comeliness and for order 'sake, it might still be continued. This being his constant 'and resolute Opinion, That no Church ought further to 'separate it self from the Church of *Rome*, either in Doctrine 'or Ceremony, than she had departed from herself, when she 'was in her flourishing and best Estate, and from Christ her 'Lord and Head. And here again he ask'd what more they 'had to say.

Dr. *Reynolds* took exceptions at those words in the Common Prayer Book, of Matrimony. *With my Body I thee worship.* His Majesty looking upon the place; 'I was made believe, saith

' he, that the Phrase did import no lefs than Divine Worfhip
' and Adoration: But by the Examination I find, that it is
' an ufual Englifh term, as a *Gentleman of Worfhip*, &c. and
' the fenfe agreeable unto the Scripture's *Giving honour to the*
' *Wife*, &c. But turning to Dr. *Reynolds* (with fmiling, faith
' his Majefty) Many a Man fpeaks of *Robin Hood*, who never
' fhot in his Bow: If you had a good Wife your felf, you would
' think all the Honour and Worfhip you could do to her, were
' well beftow'd.

' The Dean of *Sarum* mention'd the Ring in Marriage;
' which Dr. *Reynolds* approv'd, and the King confefs'd that he
' was Married withal; and added, that he thought they would
' prove to be fcarce well Married, who are not Married with
' a Ring.

' He likewife fpake of the Churching of Women, by the
' name of *Purification*; which being read out of the Book, his
' Majefty very well allow'd it, and pleafantly faid, That Wo-
' men were loth enough of themfelves to come to Church;
' and therefore he would have this, or any other occafion, to
' draw them thither.

And this was the Subftance and Sum of that Third general Point. At which paufe, it growing toward night, his Majefty ask'd again, if they had any more to fay? If they had, becaufe it was late, they fhould have another day: but M. Dr. *Reynolds* told him, That they had but one Point more, which was the laft General Head. But it pleas'd his Majefty, firft to ask, what they could fay to the Corner'd Cap? They all approv'd it: ' Well then, faid his Majefty, turning him-
' felf to the Bifhops, you may now fafely wear your Caps:
' But I fhall tell you, if you fhould walk in one Street in *Scot-*
' *land*, with fuch a Cap on your Head, if I were not with you,
' you fhould be ftoned to Death with your Cap.

In the fourth General Head, touching Difcipline, Dr. *Reynolds* firft took exception to the committing of Ecclefiaftical Cenfures unto Lay-Chancellors: His Reafon was, That in the Statute made in King *Henry*'s time for their Authority, ' that was Abrogated in Queen *Mary*'s time, and not revived in the late Queen's days; and Abridg'd by Bifhops themfelves 1571. ordering, that the faid Lay-Chancellors fhould not Excommunicate in Matters of Correction; and *Anno* 1584, and 1589. not in Matters of Inftance, but to be done only by them, who had Power of the Keys. His Majefty anfwer'd,
' He had already conferred with his Bifhops about that Point,
' and that fuch order fhould be taken therein, as was conve-
' nient; willing him in the mean time, to go to fome other
' matter, if he had any. Then he defireth, that according to certain

certain Provincial Constitutions, they of the Clergy might have Meetings once every three Weeks: First, in Rural Deanries, and therein to have Prophecying, according as the Reverend Father Archbishop *Grindall*, and other Bishops desir'd of her late Majesty. Secondly, That such things as could not be resolv'd upon there, might be referred to the Archdeacon's Visitation: And so, Thirdly, from thence to the Episcopal Synod, where the Bishop, with his Presbytery, should determine all such Points, as before could not be decided.

1 *Cor.* 14.

Acts 21.

At which Speech, his Majesty was somewhat stirred; yet, which is admirable in him, without Passion, or shew thereof; thinking that they aimed at a Scotish Presbytery, which, saith he, as well agreeth with a Monarchy, as God and the Devil. 'Then *Jack*, and *Tom*, and *Will*, and '*Dick* shall meet, and at their pleasures censure me and my 'Council, and all our Proceedings: Then *Will.* shall stand up 'and say, It must be thus: Then *Dick* shall reply, and say, 'Nay, marry, but we will have it thus. And therefore, here 'I must once reiterate my former Speech, *Le Roy s' avisera*: 'Stay, I pray you, for one seven years, before you demand 'that of me; and if then you find me pursy and fat, and my 'Wind-pipes stuff'd, I will perhaps hearken to you: For let 'that Government be once up, I am sure I shall be kept in 'breath; then shall we all of us have work enough, both our 'hands full. But, Dr. *Reynolds*, till you find that I grow lazy, 'let that alone.

And here, because that Dr. *Reynolds* had twice before obtruded the King's Supremacy; First, in the Article concerning the Pope; Secondly, in the Point of Subscription; his 'Majesty at those times said nothing: But now growing to 'an end, he said, I shall speak of one Matter more; yet some-'what out of order: but it skilleth not. Dr. *Reynolds*, quoth 'the King, you have often spoken for my Supremacy; and it 'is well: But know you any here, or any elsewhere, who like 'of the present Government Ecclesiastical, that find fault, 'or dislike my Supremacy? Dr. *Reynolds* said, No. Why then, 'said his Majesty, I will tell you a Tale. After that the Re-'ligion restor'd by King *Edward* the Sixth was soon over-'thrown by the Succession of Queen *Mary* here in *England*, we 'in *Scotland* felt the effect of it. Whereupon Mr. *Knox* writes 'to the Queen Regent, (of whom, without Flattery, I may 'say, that she was a vertuous and moderate Lady) telling her, 'that she was Supreme Head of the Church; and charg'd her 'as she would answer it before God's Tribunal, to take care of 'of Chrift's Evangil, and of fuppreffing the Popifh Prelates, 'who withftood the fame. But how long, trow ye, did this 'continue? Even fo long, till by her Authority, the Popifh 'Bifhops were reprefs'd, he himfelf, and his Adherents, were 'brought in, and well fetled, and by thefe means made ftrong 'enough to undertake the Matters of Reformation them-'felves. Then lo, they began to make fmall account of her 'Supremacy, nor would longer reft on her Authority, but 'took the Caufe into their own hand, and according to that 'more light, wherewith they were illuminated, made a fur-'ther Reformation of Religion. How they us'd that poor 'Lady, my Mother, is not unknown, and with grief I may 'remember it: Who, becaufe fhe had not been otherwife in-'ftructed, did defire only a private Chappel, wherein to ferve 'God after her manner, with fome few felected Perfons; but 'her Supremacy was not fufficient to obtain it at their hands: 'And how they dealt with me in my Minority, you all know; 'it was not done fecretly; and tho I would, I cannot conceal 'it. I will apply it thus: And then putting his Hand to 'his Hat, his Majefty faid, My Lords the Bifhops, I may 'thank you, that thefe Men do thus plead for my Supremacy. 'They think they cannot make their Party good againft you, 'but by appealing unto it, as if you, or fome that adhere un-'to you, were not well affected towards it. But if once you 'were out, and they in place, I know what would become of 'my Supremacy. No Bifhop, no King, as before I faid. Nei-'ther do I thus fpeak at random, without ground; for I have 'obferv'd, fince my coming into *England*, that fome Preachers 'before me, can be content to pray for *James* King of *Eng-'land*, *Scotland*, *France* and *Ireland*, Defender of the Faith; 'but as for fupreme Governor, in all Caufes, and over all Per-'fons (as well Ecclefiaftical as Civil) they pafs that over with 'filence; and what Cut they have been of, I after learned. After this, asking them, If they had any more to object? and Dr. *Reynolds* anfwering, No; his Majefty appointed the next Wednefday for both Parties to meet before him; and rifing from his Chair, as he was going to his inner Chamber, 'If 'this be all, quoth he, that they have to fay, I fhall make 'them conform themfelves, or I will harry them out of this 'Land, or elfe do worfe. And this was the Sum of the Second Day's Conference; which raifed fuch an admiration in the Lords, in refpect of the King's fingular Readinefs, and exact Knowledg, that one of them faid, He was fully perfuaded his Majefty fpake by the Inftinct of the Spirit of God. My Lord *Cecill* acknowledg'd, that very much we are bound

to

to God, who had given us a King of an underſtanding Heart. My Lord Chancellor paſſing out of the Privy Chamber, ſaid unto the Dean of *Cheſter*, ſtanding by the Door, I have often heard and read, that *Rex eſt mixta perſona cum Sacerdote*; but I never ſaw the Truth thereof till this day.

Surely, Whoſoever heard his Majeſty, might juſtly think, that Title did more properly fit him, which *Eunapius* gave to that famous Rhetorician, in ſaying, that he was, βιβλιοθήκη τις ἔμψυχος, καὶ περιπατοῦν μουσεῖον, A Living Library, and a Walking Study.

Finis ſecundæ Diei.

The Third Day's Conference.

Upon Wedneſday, *January* 18. all the Biſhops aforenam'd, attended at the Court, and the Deans: who were all call'd into the Privy Chamber; and whoſo elſe my Lord Archbiſhop appointed, (for ſuch was his Majeſty's pleaſure) whereupon the Knights and Doctors of the Arches, *viz.* Sir *Daniel Dunne*, Sir *Thomas Crumpton*, Sir *Richard Swale*, Sir *John Bennet*, and Dr. *Drury* entred in. As ſoon as the King was ſet, the Lord Archbiſhop preſented unto him a Note of thoſe Points, which his Majeſty had referred to their Conſideration upon the firſt Day, and the Alteration, or rather Explanation of them in our Liturgy.

1. Abſolution or Remiſſion of Sins, in the Rubrick of Abſolution.
2. In private Baptiſm, the lawful Miniſter preſent.
3. Examination, with Confirmation of Children.
4. *Jeſus* ſaid to them, twice to be put into the Dominical Goſpels, inſtead of *Jeſus* ſaid to his Diſciples.

'His Majeſty here taking the Common-Prayer-book, and 'turning to private Baptiſm, willed, that where the Words 'were (in the Rubrick, the ſecond Paragraph) *They Baptize* '*not Children*, now it ſhould be thus read; *They cauſe not Chil-* '*dren to be Baptized*. And again, in the ſame Paragraph, for 'thoſe words, *Then they Miniſter it*; it ſhould be, *The Curate, or* '*lawful Miniſter preſent, ſhall do it on this faſhion*. Concluding 'very gravely, that in this Conference, he aim'd at three 'Things principally. Firſt, The ſetting down of Words fit 'and convenient. Secondly, Contriving how Things might 'be

'be best done, without appearance of alteration. Thirdly,
'Practised, that each Man may do his Duty in his place.

'After this, his Majesty fell into discourse about the High 'Commission; wherein he said, that he understood how the 'Parties named therein, were too many and too mean; that 'the Matters they dealt in were base, and such as Ordinaries 'at home, in their Courts, might censure; that the Branches 'granted out to the Bishops, in their several Dioceses, were 'too frequent and large. To which my Lord's Grace answer'd severally. First, For the Number, it was requisite it should be great; for otherwise, he must be forc'd, as oft-times now it fell out, to sit alone; because, that albeit all the Lords of the Privy-Council were in, all the Bishops, many of the Judges at Law, and some of the Clerks of the Council, yet very few, or none of them, sitting with him at ordinary times, some of meaner place, as Deans, and Doctors of Divinity, and Law, must needs be put in; whose Attendance his Grace might with more Authority command and expect. Secondly, For the Matters handled therein, he said, That he oftentimes had complained thereof, but saw that it could not be remedied; because, that the fault may be of that nature, as that the ordinary Jurisdiction might censure it: But eftsoons it falls out, that the Party delinquent is too great, and so the Ordinary dare not proceed against him; or so mighty in his State, or so wilful in his Contumacy, that he will not obey the Summons or Censure; and so the Ordinary is forc'd to crave help at the High Commission. To the third, his Grace said, that it concern'd not him to make answer thereunto, for such Commissions have been granted against his Will oftentimes, and without his Knowledg for the most part. My Lord Chancellor therefore offer'd it to his Majesty's Wisdom to consider, if such Commissions should not be granted to any Bi'shop, but such as have the largest Dioceses, which his Ma'jesty well approv'd; and added withal, that those Bishops 'who have in their Dioceses the most troublesome and re'fractory persons, either Papists, or Puritans: But of this, as 'also of the other things found fault with herein, he willed 'those to consult, to whom should be appointed the Review 'of the Commission. And here that Point had ended, but that one of the Lords (I think verily rather upon misinformation, than set-purpose) pleased to say, That the proceeding thereby, was like unto the *Spanish* Inquisition, wherein Men were urg'd to subscribe more than Law requir'd; that by the Oath *Ex Officio*, they were inforc'd to accuse themselves; that they were examin'd upon 20, or 24 Articles, upon the sudden,

without

without deliberation, and for the most part against themselves: For the Evidence thereof, a Letter was shewed of an antient Honourable Counsellor, written to the Lord Archbishop, *Anno* 1584. of two Ministers of *Cambridgeshire*, then or thereabouts, examin'd upon many Articles, and in the end depriv'd. The Lord Archbishop answer'd, first, to the matter; that in the manner of proceeding, and examining, his Lordship was deceiv'd: For if any Article did touch the Party any way, either for Life, Liberty, or Scandal, he might refuse to answer, neither was he urg'd thereunto. Secondly, To the Letter, being in a Cause twenty years since determin'd, he could not answer the particulars; but if his Answer to that Letter were found out, he doubted not, but as it did satisfy that Honourable Counsellor when he lived, so it would also sufficiently clear this Complaint before his Majesty.

My Lord of *London*, for the matter of Subscription, shewed his Highness the three Articles, which the Churchmen of *England* are to approve by Subscribing; namely, the King's Supremacy; the Articles of Religion; and the Book of Common-Prayer. All which it pleas'd his Majesty himself to read, and (after a little glance given, that the mention of the Oath *Ex Officio*, came in before his due time) he dilated, First, how necessary Subscription was, in every well-govern'd Church; that it was to be urg'd for the keeping of Peace: For as Laws to prevent Killing, did provide there should be no Quarrelling; so, to prevent greater Tumults in the Church, Subscription was requisite. Secondly, Because the Bishop is to answer for every Minister, whom he admitteth into his Diocess, it were fittest for him to know the Affection of the Party before his admittance; the best way to know him, and to prevent future Factions, was to urge his Subscription at his first Entrance: For, *Turpius ejicitur, quàm non admittitur hospes.* Thirdly, As Subscription was a good means to discern the Affection of Per-
' sons, whether quiet or turbulent; withal, it was the princi-
' pal way to avoid Confusion: concluding, that if any, after
' Things were well order'd, would not be quiet, and shew his
' Obedience, the Church were better without him, he were
' worthy to be hang'd. *Præstat ut pereat unus, quam unitas.*

Touching the Oath, *Ex Officio*, the Lord Chancellor, and after him the Lord Treasurer, spake both for the Necessity and Use thereof in divers Courts and Cases. ' But his Ex-
' cellent Majesty preventing that old Allegation, *Nemo cogitur*
' *detegere suam turpitudinem*, said, That the Civil Proceedings
' only punish'd Facts; but in Courts Ecclesiastical, it was re-
' quisite, that Fame and Scandals should be look'd unto. That
' here was necessary, the Oath *Compurgatory*, and the Oath *Ex*

' *Officio*

' *Officio* too; and yet great Moderation should be us'd, First, ' In *gravioribus criminibus:* And Secondly, in such, whereof ' there is a publick Fame. Thirdly, In distinguishing of pub- ' lick Fame, either caused by the inordinate Demeanor of ' the Offendor, or raised by the undiscreet proceeding in trial ' of the Fact: As, namely in *Scotland*, where the lying with ' a Wench (tho done privately, and known, or scarce sus- ' pected by two or three persons before) was made openly ' known to the King, to the Queen, to the Prince, to many ' hundreds in the Court, by bringing the Parties to the Stool ' of Repentance, and yet perhaps be but a suspicion only.' ' And here his Majesty so soundly describ'd the Oath *Ex Offi- ' cio:* First, For the Ground thereof. Secondly, The Wis- ' dom of the Law therein. Thirdly, The Manner of pro- ' ceeding thereby, and the necessary and profitable Effect ' thereof, in such a compendious, but absolute Order; that ' all the Lords, and the rest of the present Auditors, stood ' amaz'd at it. The Archbishop of *Canterbury* said, that undoubtedly his Majesty spake by the special Assistance of God's Spirit: The Bishop of *London* upon his Knee protested, that his Heart melted within him, (as so, he doubted not, did the Hearts of the whole Company) with joy, and made haste to acknowledg unto Almighty God, the singular Mercy we have receiv'd at his hands, in giving us such a King, as, since Christ's time, the like, he thought, had not been; whereunto the Lords, with one Voice, did yield a very affectionate Acclamation. The Civilians present confessed, that they could not in many Hours warning, have so judicially, plainly, and accurately, and in such a Brief describ'd it.

' After this, his Majesty committed some weighty Matters ' to be consulted of, by the Lords and Bishops: First, For ' Excommunication, in Causes of less moment; the Name ' or Censure to be altered. Secondly, For the High Com- ' mission, the Quality of the Persons to be nam'd, and the ' Nature of the Causes to be handled therein. Thirdly, For ' Recusant Communicants: For there are three sorts, saith ' his Majesty, of the Papists: Some, First, which come to ' Sermons, but not to Service and Prayer: Secondly, Some ' which come to both of them, but not to the Communion. ' Thirdly, A Number which abstain from all. That Inquiry ' might be made of all those, who were of the first, second, ' or third Rank; concluding therein, That the Weak were ' to be inform'd, the Wilful to be punish'd.

Here my Lord Chancellor mention'd the Writ, *De Excommunicato capiendo*, which his Honour said did most affright the Papists, of all other Punishments; because, by reason of that, they

they were many ways disabled in Law: Therefore he would take Order, if his Majesty so pleas'd, to send that Writ out against them freely, without charge; and if they were not executed, his Lordship would lay the Under-Sheriffs in Prison; and to this the King assented.

'The fourth Thing to be consulted of, was for the sending and appointing of Preachers into *Ireland*; whereof, saith 'his Majesty, I am but half a King, being Lord over their 'Bodies; but their Souls seduced by Popery, he much pitied; 'affirming, that where there is not true Religion, there can 'be no continued Obedience: Nor for *Ireland* only, but for 'some part of *Wales*, and the Northern Borders, so once 'call'd, tho now no Borders: The Men to be sent, not to 'be factious, or scandalous; for Weeds will be Weeds, wheresoever they be, and are good for nothing, but to be pick'd 'over the Wall; therefore they should single out Men of Sincerity, of Knowledg, of Courage.

'The last was, for Provision of sufficient Maintenance for 'the Clergy; and withal, for the planting of a learned and 'painful Minister in every Parish, as time shall serve.

To every of those, his Majesty willed, that several Commissioners of his Council and Bishops should be appointed 'by the Lords, upon the dissolving the Assembly present.

And thus having conferred of these Points with the Bishops, and referred other-some of them, as you heard, to Special Committees; his Majesty willed, that Dr. *Reynolds*, and his Associates, should be call'd in; to whom he presently signified what was done, and caused the Alterations, or Explications, before named, to be read unto them. A little disputing there was about the Words in Marriage, *With my Body I thee Worship*; and arguing no other thing to be meant by the word *Worship*, than that which St. *Paul* willeth, 1 *Cor*. 7. 4. the Man thereby ackowledging, that hereby he worshippeth his Wife, in that he appropriateth his Body unto her alone; nor any more than that which St. *Peter* counselleth, 1 *Pet*. 3. 7. That the Man should give honour to his Wife, as the weaker Vessel; yet for their satisfaction, should be put in, *With my Body I thee worship and honour*, if it were thought fit: and so his Majesty shut up 'all with a most pithy Exhortation to both sides for Unity, 'persuading Diligence in each man's place, without Violence 'on the one Party, or Disobedience on the other; and willed them to deal with their Friends abroad to that purpose: For his Majesty feared, and had some experience, 'that many of them were ticklish and humorous; nor that 'only, but Labourers to pervert others to their fancies. He 'now saw, that the Exceptions against the Communion-Book,

'were

'were matters of Weakneſs: Therefore, if the Perſons re-
'luctant be diſcreet, they will be won betimes, and by good
'perſuaſions; if undiſcreet, better they were remov'd; for
'many, by their factious Behaviour, were driven to be Pa-
'piſts. Now then of their Fruits he ſhall judg them; Obe-
'dience and Humility being marks of honeſt and good Men.
'Thoſe he expected of them, and by their Example and
'Perſuaſion of all their ſort abroad; for if hereafter, things
'being thus well order'd, they ſhould be unquiet, neither his
'Majeſty nor the State had any cauſe to think well of them.
To which they gave all their unanimous Aſſent, taking exception againſt nothing that was ſaid or done, but promiſed to perform all Duty to the Biſhops, as their Reverend Fathers, and to join with them againſt the common Adverſaries, and for the Quiet of the Church.

Only, Mr. *Chatterton* of *Emanuel* College, kneeling, requeſted, that the Wearing of the Surplice, and the Uſe of the Croſs in Baptiſm, might not be urg'd upon ſome honeſt, godly, and painful Miniſters in ſome Parts of *Lancaſhire*; who feared, that if they ſhould be forced unto them, many whom they had won to the Goſpel, would ſlide back, and revolt unto Popery again; and particularly, inſtanced the Vicar of *Rateſdale*, (he could not have light upon a worſe) for not many years before, he was prov'd before my Lord Archbiſhop, as his Grace there teſtified, and my Lord Chancellor, by his unſeemly and unreverent Uſage of the Euchariſt, dealing the Bread out of a Basket, every Man putting in his hand, and taking out a piece, to have made many loath the Holy Communion, and wholly refuſe to come to Church. His Majeſty anſwer'd,
'That it was not to his purpoſe, and he durſt anſwer for the
'Biſhops, that it was not their intent, preſently, and out of
'hand, to inforce thoſe things, without fatherly Admonitions,
'Conferences and Perſuaſions premiſed; but wiſhed, that it
'ſhould be examined, if thoſe Men by their Pains and Preach-
'ing had converted any from Popery, and were withal Men
'quiet of diſpoſition, honeſt of life, and diligent in their
'calling; if ſo, Letters ſhould be written to the Biſhop of
'*Cheſter* (of whom his Majeſty gave a very good Teſtimony)
'to that purpoſe: If not, but that they were of a turbulent
'and oppoſite ſpirit, both they and other of that unquiet
'humor ſhould preſently be enforced to a Conformity. And
'ſo for that Point, it was concluded, that my Lord Arch-
'biſhop ſhould write to the Biſhop of *Cheſter*, his Letters for
'that matter.

My Lord of *London* replieth, That if this were granted, the Copy of theſe Letters (eſpecially if his Majeſty had written, as as at firſt it was propoſed) would fly over all *England*, and then other, for their Confines, would make the ſame requeſt; and ſo no fruit ſhould follow of this Conference, but things would be worſe than they were before. Therefore he humbly deſir'd his Majeſty, that a time ſhould be limited, within which compaſs they ſhould conform themſelves. 'To which 'his Majeſty readily aſſented, and willed, that the Biſhop of 'the Dioceſs ſhould ſet them down the time, and in the mean 'while confer with them; and if they would not yield, what-'ſoever they were, to remove them, after their time expired.

No ſooner was that Motion ended, but down falls Mr. *Knew-ſtubs*; and he requeſts the like favour of Forbearance, for ſome honeſt Miniſters in *Suffolk*; telling the King, it would make much againſt their Credits in the Country, to be now forc'd to the Surplice, and the Croſs in Baptiſm. My Lord's Grace was anſwering; 'Nay, ſaith his Majeſty, let me alone with him. 'Sir, ſaith the King, you ſhew your ſelf an uncharitable Man; 'we have here taken pains, and in the end have concluded 'of an Unity, and Uniformity; and you, forſooth, muſt pre-'fer the Credits of a few private Men, before the general 'Peace of the Church. This is juſt the *Scotiſh* Argument: 'For when any thing was there concluded, which diſliked 'ſome humors, the only reaſon why they would not obey, was, 'it ſtood not with their credits to yield, having ſo long time 'been of the contrary Opinion. I will none of that, ſaith 'the King; and therefore, either let them conform them-'ſelves, and that ſhortly, or they ſhall hear of it. My Lord *Cecill* put his Majeſty in mind, of a word his Highneſs had us'd the day before; namely, of Ambling-Communions; ſay-ing, That the Indecency thereof was very offenſive, and had driven many from the Church. And here Mr. *Chatterton* was told of Sitting-Communions in *Emanuel* College; which he ſaid was ſo, by reaſon of the Seats, ſo placed as they be; yet, that they had ſome Kneeling alſo.

Finally, They jointly promis'd to be quiet and obedient, now they knew it to be the King's mind to have it ſo. His Ma-jeſty's gracious Concluſion was ſo piercing, as that it fetch'd Tears from ſome on both ſides. My Lord of *London* ended all, in the Name of the whole Company, with a Thankſgiving unto God for his Majeſty, and a Prayer for the Health and Proſperity of his Highneſs, our gracious Queen, the young Prince, and all their Royal Iſſue.

His Majeſty departed into the Inner Chamber: All the Lords went preſently to the Council-Chamber, to appoint Commiſſioners, for the ſeveral matters before referred.

The PREFACE.

Many Copies were sent me, whereof some were so shamelesly untrue, and I assure you so obscene, that I think his Majesty would have been as much offended with me for Printing, *as with the Authors for* Dispersing *them. I have chosen thereof the best and cleanliest, which do here-under follow.*

I give no Censure, neither know I the Dispersers; let the Reader confer and judg. Rectum est judex sui & obliqui.

The First COPY.

January 15. 1603.

SIR,

I Cannot conceal from you the good Success, which it hath pleas'd God to send us, by the *Conference* which his Majesty had with the Bishops at the Court. There appear'd none but the Bishops, which were with the King above three Hours. *Cant. Lond. Win.* fell down on their Knees, and desir'd, that all things might remain, lest the Papists should think we have been in an Error. The King reply'd, that in 42 years Corruptions might creep in. He spake of Confirmation, private Baptism, the Cross, Dumb Ministry, Non-residence, the Courts, which he promised to amend; especially he spake bitterly against private Baptism, saying, He had as lieve an Ape as a Woman should Baptize his Child; and against Courts, which, he said, he would put down. The Lord Chief Justice, and the Lord Keeper, spake much against them, and the Lord *Cecill* against Excommunications by Lay-men. Mr. Dean of the Chappel, speaking something to the King in his Ear, the Bishop of *London* insolently said unto him, Dr. *Montague*, speak out, that we may hear you, and seek not to cross us. At their departure they said, That if the King should use the Ministers in such sort as they were used, they would be too insolent. The King said, they were his Subjects; and if he would not hear them, then they had just Cause to complain. The Bishops brought forth many Popish Arguments, which the King very earnestly answer'd, and learnedly, more than ten times calling them Papish Arguments, and said, by those Reasons they might prove Popery. The Bishop of *Winchester* said, That

That if he took away private Baptiſm, he overthrew all Antiquity. The Biſhop of *Peterborow* brought forth a fooliſh Argument, with much diſgrace to himſelf. The Biſhops having taken Wedneſday to conſider of the King's Speech, the Miniſters came to the King on Monday at Nine of the Clock. Honeſt Men about the Court are comforted. Conformitans hang down their heads, and the Biſhop's Men curſe the Puritans.

Sic explicit prima dies.

Another Copy.

I Have ſent you the Declaration of the Conference; the which was in this manner. The firſt day the Biſhops of *Canterbury*, *London*, and *Wincheſter*, making earneſt ſuit, that all things might ſtand as they did, leſt the Papiſts ſhould take offence, who might ſay, We would perſuade them to come to a Church, having Errors in it; and the Puritans will ſay, they have been perſecuted long. The King anſwer'd, That the beſt State would gather Corruptions; and that it was no Argument for them to ſay, They would not be cured of the Pox, becauſe they had had it 30 years. He concluded againſt Abſolution, Confirmation, and private Baptiſm, the dumb and ſcandalous Miniſters, Pluralities, the Courts, and the Authority of the Biſhops by the High Commiſſioners, *&c.* The ſecond Day the Miniſters were convented before the King, who anſwer'd fearfully and modeſtly: The Biſhop of *London* behav'd himſelf inſolently, ſaying, Theſe are *Cartwright*'s Scholars, Schiſmaticks, Breakers of your Majeſty's Laws; you may know them by their Turky-Gowns, and ſilk Turky Grogoram. The third Day they met all, where the King ſpake much to Unity, that they might join againſt the Papiſts. All the three Days the King behav'd himſelf admirable to the Beholders, granting to the Miniſters their earneſt requeſt, that the Ceremonies of the Croſs in Baptiſm, and the Surplices reverent for Antiquity, ſhould not be urg'd upon the Conſciences of the Miniſters; ſo that they were peaceable Men, and that they ſhould have time to conſider of them; many hundreds being reſolv'd rather to have loſt their Places, than to have yielded to thoſe Superſtitions againſt which they had preached. The laſt Day the Biſhop of *Canterbury* was intreated, to be a means that the Ceremonies might not be preſſed: But he anſwer'd, They had been urg'd as neceſſary, and ſhould be ſo ſtill. But it pleas'd God to move his his Majeſty to a more peaceable Courſe. The Biſhop of *Peterborow* came in with his Argument about Baptiſm, which the King made void to his great Reproach. The King ſaid many times, that the Biſhop's Reaſons were Popiſh, and that they might eſtabliſh Popery by them. It is thought that the King will be ſhortly in *Huntingtonſhire*. The Lord Chancellor, the Lord *Cecill*, the Lord Chief Juſtice, and the Attorney-General, muſt ſet down ſome Courſe for the High Commiſſion, and the Spiritual Courts.

A Third Copy.

Some of the Speeches that are bruted upon M. Doctor Reynolds's *Return to* Oxon, *concerning the late Conference before his Majeſty.*

1. THat the King's Majeſty did gratify Maſter Dr. *Reynolds* in every thing which he propos'd; or that Dr. *Reynolds* obtain'd and prevail'd in every thing he did deſire.

2. That if any Man report the contrary, he doth lye, or that they ſhould give him the Lye, from Mr. Doctor *Reynolds*.

3. That theſe things, now obtain'd by the Reformers, were but the beginning of Reformation: the greater Matters are yet to come.

4. That my Lord of *Winton* ſtood mute, and ſaid little or nothing.

5. That my Lord of *London* call'd Dr. *Reynolds* Schiſmatick indeed (he thanks him for it) but otherwiſe ſaid little to purpoſe.

6. That the King's Majeſty us'd the Biſhops with very hard words, but imbraced Maſter Dr. *Reynolds*, and us'd moſt kind Speeches to him.

7. That my Lord of *Canterbury*, or my Lord of *London*, falling on his Knees, beſought his Majeſty to take their Cauſe into his own hands, and to make ſome good End of it, ſuch as might ſtand with their Credit.

Phenix VII.

FRAGMENTA REGALIA:

OR,

Observations on the Late Queen ELIZABETH, *Her Times and Favourites.*

Written by Sir ROBERT NAUNTON, *Master of the Court of Wards.*

TO take herein the Original, ſhe was Daughter to *Henry* VIII. by *Anne Bullen*, the ſecond of ſix Wives, which he had, and one of the Maids of Honour to the divorced Queen *Katherine* of *Auſtria*, or (as they now ſtile it) *Infanta* of *Spain*, and from thence taken into the Royal Bed.

That ſhe was not of a moſt Noble and Royal Extract by her Father, will not fall into queſtion; for on that ſide there was diſimbogued into her Veins, by a Confluence of Blood, the very Abſtract of all the greateſt Houſes in *Chriſtendom*. And remarkable it is (concerning that violent Deſertion of the Royal

Royal House of the *Britans*, by the Invasion of the *Saxons*, and afterwards by the Conquest of the *Normans*) that by their Vicissitude of Times, and thro a discontinuance (almost a thousand years) the Royal Scepter should fall back into the Current of the old *British* Blood, in the person of her renown'd Grandfather, *Henry* VII. together with whatsoever the *German*, *Norman*, *Burgundian*, *Castilian*, and *French* Atchievements, with the Intermarriages which eight hundred years had acquir'd, incorporated, and brought back into the old Royal Line.

By her Mother she was of no Sovereign Descent, yet Noble, and very antient in the Name and Family of *Bullen*; tho some erroneously brand it with a Citizen's Rise or Original, which was yet but of a second Brother, who as it were divining the Greatness and Lustre to come to his House, was sent into the City to acquire Wealth, *ad ædificandum antiquam domum*; unto whose Atchievements (for he was Lord Mayor of *London*) fell in, as it was aver'd, both the Blood and Inheritance of the eldest Brother, for want of Issue Male; by which Accumulation the House within a few Descents mounted *in culmen honoris*, and was suddenly related to the best Families of *England* and *Ireland*, as *Howard*, *Ormond*, *Sackvile*, and divers others. Having thus touch'd, and now leaving her Strip, I come to her Person, and as she came to the Crown by the Decease of her Brother and Sister. Under *Edward*, she was his, and one of the Darlings of Fortune; for besides the consideration of Blood, there was between these two Princes a Concurrency and Sympathy in their Natures and Affections together, with the celestial Bond (Conformity in Religion) which made them one and Friends; for the King ever call'd her his sweetest and dearest Sister, and was scarce his own man, she being absent; which was not so between him and the Lady *Mary*.

Under her Sister she found her condition much alter'd: for it was resolv'd, and her Destiny had decreed to set her an Apprentice in the School of Affliction, and to draw her thro the Ordeal fire of trial, the better to mould and fashion her to Rule and Sovereignty: which finish'd, and Fortune calling to mind, that the time of her Servitude was expir'd, gave up her Indentures, and therewith deliver'd up into her custody a Scepter, as a Reward for her Patience: Which was about the 26*th* year of her Age; a time in which, as for Externals, she was full blown, so was she for her Internals grown ripe, and season'd with Adversity, and in the exercise of her Virtue: For it seems Fortune meant no more, than to shew her a piece of her Variety, and Changeableness of her Nature, and so to conduct her to her destin'd Felicity.

She

She was of Personage tall, of Hair and Complexion fair, and therewith well-favour'd, but high-nos'd, of Limbs and Feature neat; and, which added to the Lustre of those exterior Graces, of Stately and Majestick Comportment; participating in this more of her Father than Mother, who was of an inferior allay, plausible, or as the *French* hath it, more debonair and affable; Virtues which might well sute with Majesty, and which descending as hereditary to the Daughter, did render her of a more sweet Temper, and endear'd her more to the love and liking of the People, who gave her the Name and Fame of a most gracious and popular Prince; the Atrocity of her Father's Nature being rebated in hers, by the Mother's sweeter Inclinations: for to take, and that no more than the Character out of his own mouth, *He never spared Man in his Anger, nor Woman in his Lust.*

If we search further into her Intellectuals and Abilities, the whole course of her Government deciphers them to the Admiration of Posterity; for it was full of Magnanimity temper'd with Justice and Piety; and to speak truly, noted but with one Act or Taint, all her Deprivations either of Life or Liberty, being legal and necessitated. She was learned (her Sex and the time consider'd) beyond common belief; for Letters about this time, and somewhat before, began to be of esteem and in fashion, the former Ages being overcast with the mists and Fogs of the *Roman* Ignorance: and it was the maxim that over-ruled the foregoing times, *That Ignorance was the Mother of Devotion.*

Her Wars were a long time more in the auxiliary part, in assistance of foreign Princes and States, than by Invasion of any; till common Policy advis'd it for a safer way to strike first abroad, than at home to expect the War, in all which she was felicitous and victorious.

The Change and Alteration of Religion, upon the instant of her Accession (the Smoke and Fire of her Sister's Martyrdoms scarcely quench'd) was none of her least remarkable Accounts. But the Support and Establishment thereof, with the means of her Subsistance amidst so powerful Enemies abroad, and those many domestick Practices, were (methinks) Works of Inspiration, and of no human Providence; which on her Sister's departure, she most religiously acknowledg'd, ascribing the Glory of her Deliverance to God alone; for she receiv'd the News both of the Queen's Death, and her Proclamation by the general Consent of the House, and the publick Suffrage of the People; whereat falling on her knees (after a good time of Respiration) she utter'd this Verse of the Psalms, *A Domino factum est istud, & est mirabile in oculis*

 nostris:

nostris: which we find to this day on the Stamp of her Gold, with this on her Silver, *Posui Deum adjutorem meum.*

Her Ministers and Instruments of State, such as were *Participes Curarum*, and bare a great part of the Burden, were many, and those memorable: but they were only Favourites, not Minions; such as acted more by her own Princely Rules and Judgments, than by their own Wills and Appetites, which she observ'd to the last. For we find no *Gaveston*, *Vere*, or *Spencer*, to have sway'd alone, during 44 years, which was a well-settled and advis'd Maxim; for it valu'd her the more, it aw'd the most secure, and it took best with the People, and it starv'd all Emulations, which are apt to rise and vent in obloquious Acrimony (even against the Prince) where there is only a *Major Palatii.*

The principal Note of her Reign will be, that she ruled much by Faction and Parties, which her self both made, upheld, and weaken'd, as her own great Judgment advis'd; for I dissent from the common receiv'd Opinion, that my Lord of *Leicester* was absolute and above all in her Grace. And tho I come somewhat short of the knowledg of those Times, yet (that I might not rove, and shoot at random) I know from assur'd Intelligence that it was not so. For proof whereof (among many that I could present) I will both relate a short, and therein a known Truth. And it was thus: *Bowyer*, a Gentleman of the Black Rod, being charg'd by her express Command to look precisely to all Admissions into the Privy Chamber, one day staid a very gay Captain, and a Follower of my Lord of *Leicester*, from entrance, for that he was neither well known, nor a sworn Servant to the Queen. At which repulse the Gentleman bearing high on my Lord's Favour, told him, he might perchance procure him a Discharge. *Leicester* coming into the contestation, said publickly, (which was none of his wont) That he was a Knave, and should not continue long in his Office. And so turning about to go into the Queen, *Bowyer* (who was a bold Gentleman, and well belov'd) stept before him, and fell at her Majesty's feet, related the Story, and humbly crav'd her Grace's pleasure, and whether my Lord of *Leicester* was King, or her Majesty Queen: whereunto she reply'd, with her wonted Oath (*God's Death*) *my Lord, I have wish'd you well, but my Favour is not so lockt up for you, that others shall not partake thereof; for I have many Servants, unto whom I have, and will at my pleasure bequeath my Favour, and likewise resume the same; and if you think to rule here, I will take a course to see you forth-coming; I will have here but one Mistress, and no Master: and look that no ill happen to him, lest it be severely required at your hands.* Which so quell'd my Lord of *Leicester*, that his feign'd Humility was long after one of his best Virtues.

tues. Moreover, the Earl of *Sussex*, then Lord Chamberlain, was his profess'd Antagonist to his dying day: And for my Lord of *Hunsdon*, and Sir *Thomas Sackvile*, after Lord Treasurer (who were all Contemporaries) he was wont to say of them, That they were of the Tribe of *Dan*, and were *noli me tangere's*; implying, that they were not to be contested with, for they were indeed of the Queen's near Kindred. From whence, and in more Instances, I conclude that she was absolute and sovereign Mistress of her Graces; and that all those to whom she distributed her Favours, were never more than Tenants at Will, and stood on no better ground than her Princely Pleasure, and their own good Behaviour. And this also I present as a known Observation, that she was (tho very capable of Counsel) absolute enough in her own Resolutions; which was ever apparent even to her last, in that her Aversion to grant *Tyrone* the least drop of her mercy, tho earnestly and frequently advis'd, yea wrought on by the whole Council of State, with very many pressing Reasons, and as the State of her Kingdom then stood (I may speak it with assurance) necessitated Arguments.

If we look into her Inclination, as it is dispos'd either to Magnificence or Frugality, we shall find in them many notable Considerations: for all her Dispensations were so pois'd, as tho Discretion and Justice had both agreed to stand at the Beam, and see them weigh'd out in due proportion; the Maturity of her Years and Judgment meeting in a concurrency, and at such an Age as seldom lapseth into Excess.

To consider them apart, we have not many Precedents of her Liberality, or of any large Donatives to particular men, my Lord of *Essex* Book of *Parkes* only excepted, which was a Princely Gift: and some few more of a lesser size to my Lord of *Leicester*, *Hatton*, and others. Her Reward consisted chiefly in Grants of Leases, of Offices, and Places of Judicature; but for ready Mony, and in any great Sums, she was very sparing: which we partly conceive was a Vertue rather drawn out by necessity, than her nature; for she had many layings out, and to her last period. And I am of opinion with Sir *Walter Rawleigh*, that those many brave men of our times, and of the *Militia*, tasted little more of her Bounty, than in her Grace and good Word with their due Entertainment; for she ever paid the Soldiers well, which was the Honour of her times, and more than her great Adversary of *Spain* could perform. So that when we come to the consideration of her Frugality, the Observation will be little more, than that her Bounty and It were so woven together, that the one was suted by an honourable way of spending, the other limited by a necessitated way of sparing.

The

The *Irish* Action we may call a Malady, and a Consumption of her times; for it accompany'd her to her end, and it was of so profuse and vast an Expence, that it drew near a Distemperature of State, and of Passion in her self; for toward her last, she grew somewhat hard to please. Her Arms being accustom'd to Prosperity, and the *Irish* Persecution not answering her Expectation, and wonted Success for a good while, it was an unthrifty and inauspicious War, which did much disturb, and mislead her Judgment: and the more, for that it was a Precedent which was taken out of her own Pattern. For as the Queen (by way of diversion) had at the coming to the Crown, supported the revolted States of *Holland*; so did the King of *Spain* turn the trick on her self towards her going out, by cherishing the *Irish* Rebellion: Where it falls under consideration, what the State of the Kingdom, and the Crown Revenues were then able to embrace and endure. If we look into the Establishment of those times, with the List of the *Irish* Army, considering the Defeatments of *Blackwater*, with all precedent Expences, as it stood from my Lord of *Essex*'s Undertaking to the Surrender of *Kingsale* under the General *Mountjoy*, and somewhat after, we shall find the Horse and Foot Troops, were for three or four years together much about 20000. Which, besides the Naval Charge that was a Dependent on the same War, in that the Queen was then forc'd to keep in continual pay a strong Fleet at Sea, to attend the *Spanish* Coasts and Ports, both to alarm the *Spaniard*, and to interrupt his Forces design'd for the *Irish* Assistance: so that the Charge of that War alone did cost the Queen 300000*l*. *per annum* at least; which was not the Moity of her other Disbursements. An Expence which (without the publick Aid) the State and the Royal Receipts could not have much longer endur'd; which out of her own frequent Letters and Complaints to the Deputy *Mountjoy*, for cashiering part of that List as soon as he could, may be collected; for the Queen was then driven into a strait.

We are naturally prone to applaud the Times behind us, and to vilify the present; for the current of her Fame carries it to this day, how royally and victoriously she liv'd and dy'd, without the grievance and grudge of the People. Yet that Truth may appear without Retraction from the Honour of so great a Princess, it is manifest she left more Debts unpay'd, taken upon the Credit of her Privy Seals, than her Progenitors did, or could have taken up that way in a hundred years before her: Which was an inforc'd piece of State, to lay the burden on that Horse that was best able to bear it, at the dead lift, when neither her Receipts could yield her Re-

lief

lief at the pinch, nor the Urgency of her Affairs endure the Delays of Parliamentary Assistance; and for such Aids it is likewise apparent, that she receiv'd more, and with the Love of the People, than any two of her Predecessors that took most. Which was a Fortune strain'd out of the Subject, thro the plausibility of her Comportment, and as I would say without offence, the prodigal Distribution of her Graces to all sorts of Subjects; for I believe no Prince living that was so tender of Honour, and so exactly stood for the Preservation of Sovereignty, was so great a Courtier of her People, yea of the Commons, and that stoopt and descended lower in presenting her Person to the publick view, as she past in her Progresses and Perambulations, and in the Ejaculation of her Prayers on her People. And truly tho much may be given in praise of her Magnanimity, and therewith comply with her Parliaments, and for all that come off at last with Honour and Profit; yet must we ascribe some part of the Commendation to the Wisdom of the times, and the Choice of Parliament-men: For I find not that they were at any time given to any violent or pertinacious Dispute, Elections being made of grave and discreet Persons, not factious and ambitious of Fame, such as came not to the House with a malevolent Spirit of Contention, but with a Preparation to consult on the publick Good, rather to comply than contest with her Majesty. Neither do I find that the House was at any time weaken'd and pester'd with the Admission of too many young Heads, as it hath been of later times. Which remembers me of Recorder *Martin*'s Speech, about the tenth of our late Sovereign Lord King *James*, when there were accounts taken of forty Gentlemen, not above twenty, and some not exceeding sixteen: which mov'd him to say, That it was the antient Custom for old Men to make Laws for young ones; but that then he saw the case alter'd, and that there were Children elected into the great Council of the Kingdom, which came to invade and invert Nature, and to enact Laws to govern their Fathers. Sure we are, the House always took the common Cause into their consideration, and they saw the Queen had just occasion and need enough to use their Assistance. Neither do I remember that the House did ever capitulate, or prefer their private Affairs to the publick, *&c.* The Queen's Necessities but waited their times, and in the first place gave their Supply, and according to the Exigency of her Affairs; yet fail'd not at last to obtain what they desir'd. So that the Queen and her Parliaments had ever the good fortune to depart in love, and on reciprocal terms: Which are Considerations that have not been so exactly observ'd in our last Assem-

blies,

blies, as they might, and I would to God they had been. For considering the great Debt left on the King, and in what Incumbrances the House it self had then drawn him, his Majesty was not well us'd; tho I lay not the blame on the whole Suffrage of the House, where he had many good Friends. For I dare avouch, had the House been freed of half a dozen of popular and discontented Persons, such as (with the Fellow that burnt the Temple at *Ephesus*) would be talk'd of, tho but for doing of mischief; I am confident the King had obtain'd that which in reason, and at his first Accession, he ought to have receiv'd freely and without any condition. But pardon the Digression, which is here remember'd, not in the way of Aggravation, but in true Zeal to the publick Good, and presented as a Caveat to future times; for I am not ignorant how the Spirit of the Kingdom now moves to make his Majesty amends on any occasion, and how desirous the Subject is to expiate that Offence at any rate; may it please his Majesty graciously to make trial of his Subjects Affection, and at what price they now value his Goodness and Magnanimity. But to our purpose: The Queen was not to learn, that as the Strength of her Kingdom consisted in the multitude of her Subjects, so the Security of her Person rested in the Love and Fidelity of her People, which she politickly affected (as it hath been thought) somewhat beneath the height of her Spirit and natural Magnanimity. Moreover, it will be a true Note of her Providence, that she would always listen to her Profit; for she would not refuse the Informations of mean Persons, with purpos'd Improvement, and had learn'd the Philosophy of *Hoc agere*, to look into her own Work: of the which there is a notable Example of one *Carwarden*, an Under-Officer of the Custom-house, who observing his time, presented her with a Paper, shewing how she was abus'd in the under-renting of her Customs; and therewithal humbly desir'd her Majesty to conceal him, for that it did concern two or three of her great Counsellors, whom Customer *Smith* had bribed with 200 *l.* a man, so to lose the Queen 2000 *l. per ann.* Which being made known to the Lords, they gave strict order, that *Carwarden* should not have access to the Back-stairs, till at last her Majesty smelling the craft, and missing *Carwarden*, she sent for him back, and encourag'd him to stand to his Information; which the poor man did so handsomly, that within the space of ten years he brought *Smith* to double his Rent, or to leave the Customs to new Farmers. So that we may take this also into Observation, that there were of the Queen's Council that were not in the Catalogue of Saints.

Now

Now as we have taken a view of ſome particular Notions of her Times, her Nature, and Neceſſities, it is not without the Text to give a ſhort touch on the Helps and Advantages of her Reign, which were without parallel; for ſhe had neither Huſband, Brother, Siſter, nor Children to provide for, who as they are Dependents of the Crown, ſo do they neceſſarily draw maintenance from thence, and do oftentimes exhauſt and draw deep, eſpecially when there is an ample Fraternity of the Blood Royal, and of the Princes of the Blood, as it was in the time of *Edward* the Third, and *Henry* the Fourth. For then when the Crown cannot, the Publick ought to give them honourable Allowance; for they are the Honour and Hopes of the Kingdom, and the Publick which enjoys them, hath alike Intereſt in them, with the Father that begot them: And our Common Law, which is the Heritance of the Kingdom, did ever of old provide Aids for the *Primogenitures*, and the eldeſt Daughter. So that the multiplicity of Courts, and the great Charge which neceſſarily follow a King and Queen, a Prince, and the Royal Iſſue, was a thing which was not *in rerum natura* during the ſpace of forty years; and which by time was worn out of memory, and without the conſideration of the preſent times. Inſomuch that the Aids given to the late and right Noble Prince *Henry*, and to his Siſter the Lady *Elizabeth*, were at firſt generally receiv'd for Impoſitions of a new Coinage. Yea the late Impoſitions for Knighthood (tho an antient Law) fell alſo into the imputation of a Tax of novelty; for that it lay long cover'd in the Embers of Diviſion, between the Houſes of *York* and *Lancaſter*, and forgotten or conniv'd at by the ſucceeding Princes. So that the ſtrangeneſs of the Obſervation, and the difference of thoſe latter Reigns, is; That the Queen took up beyond the Power of the Law, which fell not into the murmur of the People; and her Succeſſors nothing but by Warrant of the Law, which nevertheleſs was conceiv'd (thro diſuſe) to be injurious to the Liberty of the Kingdom.

Now before I come to any further mention of her Favourites, (for hitherto I have deliver'd but ſome obvious Paſſages, thereby to prepare and ſmooth a way for the reſt that follows) it is requiſite that I touch on the Reliques of the other Reign; I mean the Body of her Siſter's Council of State, which ſhe retain'd intire, neither removing nor diſcontenting any, altho ſhe knew them averſe to her Religion (and in her Siſter's time perverſe towards her Perſon) and private to her Troubles and Impriſonment: A Prudence which was incompatible with her Siſter's nature; for ſhe both diſſipated and perſecuted the major part of her Brother's Council. But this will be of certainty,

tainty, that how compliable ſoever and obſequious ſhe found them, yet for a good ſpace ſhe made little uſe of their Counſels, more than in the ordinary courſe of the Board; for ſhe held a dormant Table in her own Princely Breaſt, yet ſhe kept them together, and their places without any ſudden change. So that we may ſay of them, that they were of the Court, not of the Council; for whilſt ſhe amuz'd them with a kind of permiſſive Diſputation concerning the Points controverted by both Churches, ſhe did ſet down her own Reſervations, without their privity, and made all her Progreſſions Gradations; but ſo that the Tenents of her Secrecy, with intent of her Eſtabliſhment, were pitcht before it was known where the Court would ſet down. Neither do I find that any of her Siſter's Council of State were either repugnant to her Religion, or oppos'd her Doings (*Englefield*, Maſter of the Horſe, excepted) who withdrew himſelf from the Board, and ſhortly after from out of her Dominions; ſo pliable and obedient they were to change with the times, and their Princes: and of this there will fall in here a Relation both of Recreation and known Truth.

Pawlet Marquiſs of *Wincheſter*, and Lord Treaſurer, having ſerv'd then four Princes in as various and changeable ſeaſon, that I may well ſay, Time nor any Age hath yielded the like Precedent: This Man being noted to grow high in her Favour (as his Place and Experience requir'd) was queſtion'd by an intimate Friend of his, how he ſtood up for thirty years together amidſt the Changes and Reigns of ſo many Chancellors and great Perſonages. Why, quoth the Marquiſs, *Ortus ſum ex ſalice, non ex quercu*; *I was made of the pliable Willow, not of the ſtubborn Oak*. And truly the old man hath taught them all, eſpecially *William* Earl of *Pembroke*; for they two were always of the King's Religion, and over-zealous Profeſſors. Of this it is ſaid, That being both younger Brothers (yet of Noble Houſes) they ſpent what was left them, and came on truſt to the Court; where, upon the bare ſtock of their Wits, they began to traffick for themſelves, and proſper'd ſo well, that they got, ſpent, and left more than any Subjects from the *Norman* Conqueſt to their own times. Whereunto it hath been prettily reply'd, That they liv'd in a time of Diſſolution. To conclude then; of any of the former Reign, it is ſaid, that theſe two liv'd and dy'd chiefly in her favour. The latter, upon his Son's Marriage with the Lady *Katherine Grey*, was like utterly to have loſt himſelf; but at the inſtant of the Conſummation, apprehending the Inſafety and Danger of an Intermarriage with the Blood Royal, he fell at the Queen's feet, where he both acknowledg'd his Preſumption with tears,

and

and projected the Cause and the Divorce together; and so quick he was at his work (for it stood him upon) that upon Repudiation of the Lady, he clapt up a Marriage for his Son, the Lord *Herbert*, with *Mary Sidney* Daughter to Sir *Henry Sidney*, then Lord Deputy of *Ireland:* The Blow falling on *Edward* late Earl of *Hereford*, who (to his cost) took up the divorc'd Lady, of whom the Lord *Beauchampe* was born, and *William* Earl of *Hereford* is descended.

I come now to present those of her own Election, which she either admitted to her Secrets of State, or took into her Grace and Favour; of whom, in their order, I crave leave to give unto Posterity a cautious Description, with a short Character or Draught of the Persons themselves: For without offence to others, I would be true to my self; their Memories and Merits distinguishing them of the *Militia*, from the *Togati*; and of these she had as many, and those as able Ministers, as any of her Progenitors.

LEICESTER.

IT will be out of doubt, that my Lord of *Leicester* was one of the first whom she made Master of the Horse: He was the youngest Son (then living) of the Duke of *Northumberland*, beheaded *primo Mariæ*; and his Father was that *Dudley*, which our Histories couple with *Empson*, and both so much infam'd for the Caterpillars of the Commonwealth, during the Reign of *Henry* the Seventh. Who being of Noble Extract, was executed the first year of *Henry* the Eighth; but not thereby so extinct, but that he left a plentiful Estate, and such a Son, who (as the Vulgar speaks it) could live without the Teat: For out of the Ashes of his Father's Infamy, he rose to be a Duke, and as high as Subjection could permit, or Sovereignty endure. And tho he could not find out any Appellation to assume the Crown in his own Person, yet he projected, and very nearly effected it for his Son *Gilbert*, by Intermarriage with the Lady *Jane Grey*, and so by that way to bring it about into his Loins. Observations, which tho they lie behind us, and seem impertinent to the Text, yet are they not much extravagant; for they must lead and shew us how the After-Passages were brought about with the Dependences, and on the Hinges of a collateral Workmanship. And truly it may amaze a well-settled Judgment to look back into those times, and to consider how this Duke could attain to such a pitch of Greatness, his Father dying in ignominy, and at the Gallows, his Estate confiscate, and that for peeling and polling, by the Clamour

Clamour and *Crucifige* of the People. But when we better think upon it, we find that he was given up, but as a Sacrifice to pleaſe the People, not for any Offence committed againſt the Perſon of the King; ſo that upon the matter he was a Martyr of the Prerogative, and the King in honour could do no leſs than give back to his Son the Privilege of his Blood, with the Acquirings of his Father's Profeſſion; for he was a Lawyer, and of the King's Counſel at Law, before he came to be *ex interioribus Conſiliis*: where beſides the lickings of his own fingers, he got the King a Maſs of Riches; and that not with the hazard, but the loſs of his Fame and Life, for the King's Father's ſake. Certain it is, that his Son was left rich in Purſe and Brain, which are good Foundations, and full to Ambition; and it may be ſuppos'd, he was on all occaſions well heard of the King, as a Perſon of mark and compaſſion in his eye: but I find not that he did put up for Advancement, during *Henry* the Eighth's time, tho a vaſt Aſpirer and provident Storier. It ſeems he thought the King's Reign was much given to the Falling Sickneſs; but eſpying his time fitting, and the Sovereignty in the hands of a pupil Prince, he thought he might as well then put up for it as the beſt. For having then poſſeſſion of Blood, and a Purſe, with a Head-piece of a vaſt extent, he ſoon got Honour; and no ſooner there, but he began to ſide it with the beſt, even with the Protector: and in concluſion got his and his Brother's Heads; ſtill aſpiring, till he expir'd in the loſs of his own. So that Poſterity may, by reading the Father and Grandfather, make judgment of the Son: For we ſhall find that this *Robert* (whoſe Original we have now trac'd, the better to preſent him) was Inheritor of the Genius and Craft of his Father; and *Ambroſe*, of the Eſtate; of whom, hereafter we ſhall make ſome ſhort mention.

We take him now as he was admitted into the Court, and the Queen's Favour, where he was not to ſeek to play his part well and dexterouſly. But his play was chiefly at the Foregame, not that he was a Learner at the latter, but he lov'd not the After-wit. For they report (and I think not untruly) that he was ſeldom behind-hand with his Gameſters, and that they always went away with the loſs.

He was a very goodly Perſon, and ſingular well-featur'd, and all his Youth well-favour'd, and of a ſweet aſpect, but high-foreheaded, which, as I ſhould take it, was of no diſcommendation: but towards his latter end (which with old Men was but a middle Age) he grew high-colour'd and red-fac'd. So that the Queen in this had much of her Father; for (excepting ſome of her Kindred, and ſome few that had handſom

Wits

Wits in crooked Bodies) ſhe always took Perſonage in the way of her Election; for the People have it to this day in proverb, *King* Harry *loved a Man.* Being thus in her Grace, ſhe call'd to mind the Sufferings of his Anceſtors, both in her Father's and Siſter's Reigns, and reſtor'd his and his Brother's Blood; creating *Ambroſe*, the elder, Earl of *Warwick*, and himſelf Earl of *Leiceſter*, &c. And he was *ex primitiis*, or of her firſt choice; for he reſted not there, but long enjoy'd her Favour, and therewith much what he liſted, till Time and Emulation (the Companions of Great ones) had reſolv'd on his period; and to cover him at the ſetting in a cloud at *Cornbury*, not by ſo violent a Death, and by the fatal Sentence of Judicature, as that of his Father's and Grandfather's was, but as it is ſuggeſted, by that Poiſon which he had prepar'd for others: wherein they report him a rare Artiſt. I am not bound to give credit to all vulgar Relations, or to the Libels of the Times, which are commonly forc'd, and falſify'd ſutable to the Moods and Humours of Men in paſſion and diſcontent; but that which leads me to think him no good Man, is (amongſt others of known Truth) that of my Lord of *Eſſex*'s Death in *Ireland*, and the Marriage of his Lady yet living; which I forbear to preſs, in regard that he is long ſince dead, and others living, whom it may concern.

To take him in the Obſervations of his Letters and Writings (which ſhould beſt ſet him off) for ſuch as fell into my hands, I never yet ſaw a Stile or Phraſe more ſeemingly Religious, and fuller of the Strains of Devotion; and were they not ſincere, I doubt much of his Well-being: And I may fear he was too well ſeen in the Aphoriſms and Principles of *Nicholas* the *Florentine*, and in the Reaches of *Cæſar Borgia.* And hitherto I have only touch'd him in his Courtſhip.

I conclude him in his Lance: He was ſent Governour by the Queen to the United States of *Holland*, where we read not of his Wonders; for they ſay that he had more of *Mercury* than *Mars*, and that his Device might have been, without prejudice to the Great *Cæſar*; *Veni, Vidi, Redii.*

SUSSEX.

HIS Corrival before mention'd, was *Thomas Radcliff* Earl of *Suſſex*; who (in his Conſtellation) was his direct Oppoſite, for he was indeed one of the Queen's Martialiſts, and did very good ſervice in *Ireland* at her firſt Acceſſion; till ſhe recall'd him to the Court, where ſhe made him Lord Chamberlain: But he play'd not his game with that Cunning and

 Dexterity

Dexterity as *Leicester* did, who was much more the facete Courtier, tho *Sussex* was thought much the honester Man, and far the better Soldier; but he lay too open on his guard.

He was a goodly Gentleman, and of a brave noble nature, true and constant to his Friends and Servants; he was also of a very noble and antient Lineage, honour'd thro many Descents by the Title of Viscounts *Fitzwalters*. Moreover, there was such an Antipathy in his Nature to that of *Leicester*'s, that being together in Court, and both in high Imployments, they grew to a direct Frowardness, and were in continual opposition; the one setting the Watch, the other the Centinel, each on the other's Actions and Motions. For my Lord of *Sussex* was of a great Spirit; which, backt with the Queen's special Favour, and supported by a great and antient Inheritance, could not brook the other's Empire: Insomuch as the Queen upon sundry occasions had somewhat to do to appease and attain them, till Death parted the Competition, and left the place of *Leicester*, who was not long alone without his Rival, in Grace and Command. And to conclude this Favourite, it is confidently affirm'd, That lying in his last Sickness, he gave this Caveat to his Friends: *I am now passing into another World, and I must now leave you to your Fortunes, and to the Queen's Grace and Goodness; but beware of the Gipsy* (meaning *Leicester*) *for he will be too hard for you all: You know not the Beast so well as I do.*

Lord BURLEIGH.

I Now come to the next, which was Secretary *William Cecil*: For on the death of the old Marquiss of *Winchester*, he came up in his room. A Person of a most subtil and active Spirit; who stood not altogether by the way of Constellation, and making up of a Part and Faction; for he was wholly intentive to the Service of his Mistress, and his Dexterity, Experience, and Merit, challeng'd a room in the Queen's Favour; which eclips'd the others over-seeming Greatness, and made it appear that there were others that steer'd and stood at the Helm besides himself; and more Stars in the Firmament of her Grace than *Ursa major*, or the Bear with the ragged Staff.

He was born (as they say) in *Lincolnshire*; but as some upon knowledg aver, of a younger Brother of the *Cecils* of *Hertfordshire*; a Family (of my own knowledg) tho now private, yet of no mean Antiquity: who being expos'd, and sent to the City, as poor Gentlemen use to do their younger Sons, he came

came to be a rich man on *London* Bridg, and purchasing in *Lincolnshire*, where this man was born, he was sent to *Cambridge*, then to the Inns of Court, and so he came to serve the Duke of *Somerset*, in the time of his Protectorship, as Secretary. And having a pregnancy to great Inclinations, he came by degrees to a higher Conversation with the chiefest Affairs of State and Councils. But on the Fall of the Duke he stood some years in umbrage, and without Employment, till the State found and needed his Abilities. And tho we find not that he was taken into any place during *Mary*'s Reign, unless (as some have said) towards the last; yet the Council on several occasions made use of him: And at the Queen's entrance he was admitted Secretary of State; afterwards he was made Master of the Court of Wards, then Lord Treasurer; a Person of most requisite Abilities: and indeed the Queen began then to need, and to seek out for Men of both Garbs. And so I conclude, and rank this great Instrument of State among the *Togati*; for he had not to do with the Sword, more than as the great Paymaster and Contriver of the War, which shortly follow'd, wherein he accomplish'd much thro his Theoretical Knowledg at home, and his Intelligence abroad, by unlocking the Counsels of the Queen's Enemies.

We must now take (and that of Truth) into observation, That until the Tenth of her Reign, her Times were calm and serene, tho sometimes a little overcast, as the most glorious Sunrisings are subject to shadowings and droppings in; for the Clouds of *Spain*, and Vapors of the Holy League, began then to disperse and threaten her Serenity. Moreover, she was then to provide against some intestine Storms, which began to gather in the very Heart of her Kingdom, all which had a relation and corrrespondency each with the other to dethrone her, and to disturb the publick Tranquillity, and therewithal (as a principal Work) the Establish'd Religion; for the name of *Recusant* began then, and first to be known in the World, and till then the Catholicks were no more than Church-Papists, but were commanded by the Pope's express Letters to appear, and forbear Church going, as they tender their Holy Father, and the Holy Catholick Church their Mother. So that it seems the Pope had then his aims to take a true muster of his Children; but the Queen had the greater advantage, for she likewise took tale of her Apostate Subjects, their Strength, and how many they were that had given up their Names unto *Baal*; who then, by the hands of some of his Proselytes, fix'd his Bulls on the Gates of *Paul's*, which discharg'd her Subjects of all Fidelity, and laid siege to the receiv'd Faith, and so under the Veil of the next Successor, to replant the Catholick

Religion. So that the Queen had then a new Task and Work in hand, that might well awake her beſt Providence, and requir'd a muſter of Men of Arms, as well as Courtſhips and Counſels; for the Times began then to be quick and active, fitter for ſtronger Motions than thoſe of the Carpet and Meaſure. And it will be a true Note of her Magnanimity, That ſhe lov'd a Soldier, and had a propenſion in her Nature to regard, and always to grace them; which the Courtiers taking into obſervation, took it as an Invitation to win Honour, together with her Majeſty's Favour, by expoſing themſelves to the Wars, eſpecially when the Queen's and the Affairs of the Kingdom ſtood in ſome neceſſity of a Soldier. For we have many Inſtances of the Sallies of the Nobility and Gentry, yea and out of the Court, and her Privy Favourites (that had any Touch or Tincture of *Mars* in their Inclinations) and to ſteal away without licence, or the Queen's privity; which had like to have coſt ſome of them dear: ſo predominant were their Thoughts and Hopes of Honour growing in them; as we may truly obſerve in the Expeditions of Sir *Philip Sidney*, my Lord of *Eſſex*, *Mountjoy*, and divers others, whoſe Abſence, and the manner of their Eruptions, was very diſtaſtful to her. Whereof I can here add a true, and no impertinent Story, and that of the laſt *Mountjoy*; who having twice or thrice ſtoln away into *Britany* (where under Sir *John Norris* he had then a Company) without the Queen's leave and privity, ſhe ſent a Meſſenger unto him, with a ſtrict Charge to the General to ſee him ſent home. When he came into the Queen's preſence, ſhe fell into a kind of Reviling, demanding how he durſt go over without her leave: *Serve me ſo*, quoth ſhe, *once more, and I will lay you faſt enough for running. You will never leave till you are knockt on the head, as that inconſiderate Fellow* Sydney *was. You ſhall go when I ſend you: In the mean time ſee that you lodg in the Court* (which was then at *Whitehall*) *where you may follow your Book, read and diſcourſe of the Wars.*

But to our purpoſe: It fell out happily to thoſe, and (as I may ſay) to thoſe Times, that the Queen, during the calm of her Reign, was not idle, nor rockt aſleep with Security; for ſhe had been very provident in the Reparation and Augmentation of her Shipping and Ammunition. And I know not, whether by a Foreſight of Policy, or an Inſtinct, it came about, or whether it was an Act of her Compaſſion: But it is moſt certain, that ſhe ſent Levies, and no ſmall Troops to the Aſſiſtance of the Revolted States of *Holland*, before ſhe had receiv'd any Affront from the King of *Spain*, that might deſerve or tend to a Breach in Hoſtility; which the Papiſts to this day maintain, was the Provocation, and

* Cauſe

Cause of the after Wars. But omitting what might be said to this Point, those *Netherland* Wars were the Queen's Seminaries, and the Nurseries of very many brave Soldiers; and so were likewise the Civil Wars of *France* (whither she sent five several Armies) the Fencing-Schools that inur'd the Youth and Gallantry of the Kingdom: And it was a *Militia*, where they were daily in acquaintance with the Discipline of the *Spaniards*, who were then turn'd the Queen's inveterate Enemies.

And thus have I taken into observation, her *Dies Halcionii*, those years of hers which were more serene and quiet than those that follow'd; which tho they were not less propitious, as being touch'd more with the point of Honour and Victory; yet were they troubled, and ever clouded over, both with domestick and foreign Machinations: and it is already quoted, they were such as awaken'd her Spirits, and made her cast about how to defend, rather by offending, and by the way of diversion to prevent all Invasions, than to expect them; which was a piece of Policy of the Times. And with this I have noted the Causes or *Principia* of the Wars following, and likewise pointed to the Seed-plots, from whence she took up those Brave Men and Plants of Honour, which acted on the Theatre of *Mars*, and on whom she dispers'd the Rays of her Grace; which were Persons in their kinds of rare Virtues, and such as might, out of height of merit, pretend Interest to her Favour: of which Rank, the number will equal, if not exceed that of the Gownmen; in recount of whom I proceed with Sir *Philip Sydney*.

Sir PHILIP SYDNEY.

HE was Son to Sir *Henry Sydney*, Lord Deputy of *Ireland*, and President of *Wales*, a Person of great Parts, and in no mean Grace with the Queen. His Mother was Sister to my Lord of *Leicester*, from whence we may conjecture, how the Father stood up in the place of Honour and Employment; so that his Descent was apparently noble on both sides. For his Education, it was such as Travel and the University could afford, or his Tutors infuse: for after an incredible Proficiency in all the Species of Learning, he left the Academical Life for that of the Court; whither he came by his Uncle's Invitation, fam'd aforehand by a noble Report of his Accomplishments, by which, together with the state of his Person, fram'd by a natural propension to Arms, he soon attracted the good Opinion of all men, and was so highly priz'd in the good Opinion of the Queen, that ſhe thought the Court deficient without him. And whereas, thro the Fame of his Deſerts, he was in the Election for the Kingdom of *Poland*, ſhe refus'd to further his Advancement, not out of emulation, but out of fear to loſe the Jewel of her Times. He marry'd the Daughter and ſole Heir of Sir *Francis Walſingham*, then Secretary of State; a Lady deſtinated to the Bed of Honour, who (after his deplorable Death at *Zutphen* in the *Netherlands*, where he was Governour of *Fluſhing*, and at the time of his Uncle's being there) was marry'd to my Lord of *Eſſex*, and ſince his death to my Lord of *St. Albans*; all Perſons of the Sword, and otherwiſe of great Honour and Vertue.

They have a very quaint and factious Figment of him; That *Mars* and *Mercury* fell at variance, whoſe Servant he ſhould be. And there is an Epigrammatiſt who ſaith, That Art and Nature had ſpent their Excellencies in his faſhioning, and fearing they ſhould not end what they begun, they beſtow'd him on Fortune; and Nature ſtood muzing, and amaz'd to behold her own work. But theſe are the Petulancies of Poets.

Certain it is, he was a noble and matchleſs Gentleman; and it may be juſtly ſaid without Hyperboles of Fiction, as is was of *Cato Uticenſis*, that he ſeem'd to be born to that only which he went about, *verſatilis ingenii*, as *Plutarch* has it. But to ſpeak more of him, were to make him leſs.

Sir FRANCIS WALSINGHAM.

SIR *Francis Walſigham*, as we have ſaid, had the honour to be Sir *Philip Sydney*'s Father in Law: He was a Gentleman at firſt of a good Houſe, but of a better Education, and from the Univerſity travel'd for the reſt of his Learning. He was doubtleſs the beſt Linguiſt of his times, but knew beſt how to uſe his own Tongue, whereby he came to be imploy'd in the chiefeſt Affairs of State. He was ſent Ambaſſador into *France*, and ſtaid there Leiger long, in the heat of the Civil Wars, and at the ſame time that *Monſieur* was here a Suiter to the Queen; and, if I be not miſtaken, he play'd the very ſame part there, as ſince *Gundamore* did here. At his return, he was taken principal Secretary, and was one of the great Engines of State, and of the Times, high in the Queen's Favour, and a watchful Servant over the Safety of his Miſtreſs.

They note him to have had certain Curioſities, and ſecret ways of Intelligence above the reſt: but I muſt confeſs I am

to

to seek wherefore he suffer'd *Parry* to play so long on the Hook, before he hoised him up; and I have been a little curious in the search thereof, tho I have not to do with the *Arcana Imperii.*

For to know is sometimes a Burthen; and I remember, that it was *Ovid*'s *Crimen aut Error*, that he saw too much. But I hope these are Collaterals of no danger: But that *Parry* having an intent to kill the Queen, made the way of his Access, by betraying of others, and impeaching of the Priests of his own Correspondency, and thereby had Access and Conference with the Queen, and also oftentimes familiar and private Conference with *Walsingham*, will not be the Query of the Mystery; for the Secretary might have had end of discovery on a further maturity of the Treason: but that after the Queen knew *Parry*'s intent, why she should then admit him to private Discourse, and *Walsingham* to suffer it, considering the condition of all Assailings, and to permit him to go where, and whither he listed, and only on the Security of a dark Sentinel set over him, was a piece of reach and hazard, beyond my apprehension.

I must again profess, that having read many of his Letters (for they are commonly sent to my Lord of *Leicester* and *Burleigh* out of *France*) containing many fine Passages and Secrets; yet if I might have been beholden to his Cyphers (whereof they are full) they would have told pretty Tales of the Times. But I must now close up, and rank him amongst the *Togati*, yet chief of those that laid the Foundation of the *French* and *Dutch* Wars; which was another piece of his Fineness, and of the Times, with one Observation more: That he was one of the great Allays of the Austerian Embracements; for both himself, and *Stafford* that preceded him, might well have been compar'd to the Fiend in the Gospel, that sowed his Tares in the night; so did they their Seeds of Division in the dark: and it is a likely Report that they father on him, at his return, that he said to the Queen, who had some sensibility of the *Spanish* Designs on *France*: Madam, I beseech you be content not to fear, the *Spaniard* hath a great Appetite, and an excellent Digestion; but I have fitted him with a Bone for this Twenty years, that your Majesty shall have no cause to doubt him, provided that if the Fire chance to slack, which I have kindled, you will be ruled by me, and now and then cast in some *English* Fewel, which will revive the Flame.

WILLOUGHBY.

MY Lord *Willoughby* was one of the Queen's firſt Swordmen; he was of the antient Extract of the *Bartues*, but more ennobled by his Mother, who was Dutcheſs of *Suffolk*.

He was a great Maſter of the Art Military, and was ſent General into *France*, and commanded the Second of five Armies, that the Queen ſent thither in Aid of the *French*. I have heard it ſpoken, that had he not ſlighted the Court, but applied himſelf to the Queen, he might have enjoy'd a plentiful Portion of her Grace; and it was his Saying (and it did him no good) That he was none of the *Reptilia*; intimating, that he could not creep on the ground; and that the Court was not his Element: For indeed, as he was a great Soldier, ſo was he of a ſuitable Magnanimity, and could not brook the Obſequiouſneſs and Aſſiduity of the Court; and as he then was ſomewhat deſcending from Youth, happily he had an *Animam reverendi*, and to make a ſafe Retreat.

Sir NICHOLAS BACON.

I Come to another of the *Togati*, Sir *Nicholas Bacon*, an arch piece of Wit and Wiſdom; he was a Gentleman, and a Man of Law, and of great Knowledg therein; whereby, together with his other Parts of Learning and Dexterity, he was promoted to be Keeper of the Great Seal; and being of Kin to the Treaſurer *Burleigh*, had alſo the help of his hand to bring him into the Queen's favour; for he was abundantly Factious, which took much with the Queen, when it was ſuited with the ſeaſon, as he was well able to judg of his Times. He had a very quaint Saying, and he us'd it often to good purpoſe, That he lov'd the Jeſt well, but not the Loſs of his Friend: He would ſay, and that tho he knew it, *Unuſquiſque ſuæ fortunæ faber*, was a true and good Principle; yet the moſt in number were thoſe that marred themſelves: but I will never forgive that Man that loſeth himſelf, to be rid of his Jeſt.

He was Father to that refined Wit, which ſince hath acted a diſaſterous Part on the publick Stage, and of late ſate in his Father's room as Lord Chancellor. Thoſe that lived in his Age, and from whence I have taken this little Model of him, give him a lively Character, and they decipher him for another *Solon*, and the *Symon* of thoſe Times; ſuch a one as *Oedipus* was

was in diſſolving of Riddles; doubtleſs he was as able an Inſtrument, and it was his Commendation, that his Head was the Mawl (for it was a great one) and therein he kept the Wedg, that entred the knotty pieces which came to the Table: And now I muſt again fall back, to ſmooth and plain a way to the reſt that is behind, but not from the purpoſe.

There were, about theſe Times, two Rivals in the Queen's favour, old Sir *Francis Knowles*, Comptroller of the Houſe, and Sir *Henry Norris*, whom ſhe call'd up at a Parliament, to ſit with the Peers in the higher Houſe, as Lord *Norris* of *Rycott*, who had married the Daughter and Heir of the old Lord *Williams* of *Tame*; a noble Perſon, and to whom in the Queen's adverſity, ſhe had been committed to ſafe Cuſtody, and from him had receiv'd more than ordinary Obſervances. Now ſuch was the Goodneſs of the Queen's Nature, that ſhe neither forgot the good Turns receiv'd from the Lord *Williams*, neither was ſhe unmindful of this Lord *Norris*, whoſe Father, in her Father's time, and in the buſineſs of her Mother, died in a noble Cauſe, and in the Juſtification of her Innocency.

Lord Norris.

MY Lord *Norris* had by this Lady an ample Iſſue, which the Queen highly reſpected; for he had ſix Sons, and all Martial brave Men: The firſt was *William*, his eldeſt, and Father to the late Earl of *Barkſhire*; Sir *John*, Vulgarly call'd General *Norris*; Sir *Edward*, Sir *Thomas*, Sir *Henry*, and *Maximilian*; Men of an haughty Courage, and of great Experience in the Conduct of Military Affairs: and to ſpeak in the Character of their Merit, they were ſuch Perſons of ſuch Renown and Worth, as future Times muſt, out of Duty, owe them the debt of an honourable Memory.

Knowles.

SIR *Francis Knowles* was ſomewhat of the Queen's Affinity, and had likewiſe no incompetent Iſſue; for he had alſo *William* his eldeſt, and ſince Earl of *Banbury*, Sir *Thomas*, Sir *Robert*, and Sir *Francis*, if I be not a little miſtaken in their Names, and Marſhalling; and there was alſo the Lady *Lettice*, a Siſter of theſe, who was firſt Counteſs of *Eſſex*, and after of *Leiceſter*: and theſe were alſo brave Men in their Times and Places; but they were of the Court and Carpet, not led by the Genius of the Camp.

Be-

Between these two Families, there was (as it falleth out amongst great Ones, and Competitors for favour) no great Correspondency; and there were some Seeds, either of Emulation, or Distrust, cast between them; which had they not been disjoyn'd in the Residence of their Persons, (as it was the Fortune of their Employments) the one side attending the Court, the other the Pavillion, surely they would have broken out into some kind of Hostility, or at least they would have wrestled one in the other, like Trees, incircled with Ivy; for there was a time when (both these Fraternities being met at Court) there passed a Challenge between them at certain Exercises (the Queen and the Old Men being Spectators) which ended in a flat quarrel amongst them all: and I am persuaded (tho I ought not to judg) that there were some Relicks of this Feud, that were long after the Causes of the one Family's (almost utter) Extirpation, and of the other's Improsperity: For it was a known Truth, that so long as my Lord of *Leicester* lived, who was the main Pillar of the one side, as having married the Sister, none of the other side took any deep rooting in the Court; tho otherwise they made their ways to Honour by their Swords; and that which is of more note (considering my Lord of *Leicester*'s use of Men of Arms, being shortly after sent Governour to the Revolted States, and no Soldier himself) is that, he made no more account of Sir *John Norris*, a Soldier then deservedly famoused, and trained from a Page, under the Discipline of the great Captain of Christendom, the Admiral *Castillon*, and of Command in the *French* and *Dutch* Wars almost Twenty years. It is of further Observation, That my Lord of *Essex* (after *Leicester*'s decease) tho initiated to Arms, and honoured by the General in the *Portugal* Expedition, whether out of Instigation (as it hath been thought) or out of Ambition and Jealousy, to be eclipsed and over-shadowed by the Fame and Splendor of this great Commander, loved him not in Sincerity. Moreover, certain it is, he not only crusht, and (upon all occasions) quell'd the Growth of this brave Man, and his famous Brethren, but therewith drew on his own fatal End, by undertaking the *Irish* Action, in a time when he left the Court empty of Friends, and full fraught with his profess'd Enemies. But I forbear to extend my self in any further Relation upon this Subject, as having left some Notes of Truth in these two noble Families, which I would present, and therewith touch'd somewhat, which I would not, if the Equity of the Narration would have admitted an intermission.

Sir

Sir JOHN PERROT.

SIR *John Perrot* was a goodly Gentleman, and of the Sword: and as he was of a very antient Descent, as an Heir to many Abstracts of Gentry, especially from *Guy de Bryan* of *Lawhern*; so was he of a vast Estate, and came not to the Court for want. And to these Adjuncts, he had the Endowments of Courage, and height of Spirit, had it lighted on the Allay of Temper, and Discretion; the Defect whereof, with a native Freedom, and boldness of Speech, drew him on to a clouded setting, and laid him open to the Spleen and Advantage of his Enemies; amongst whom Sir *Christopher Hatton* was profest. He was yet a Wise man, and a brave Courtier, but rough, and participating more of active than sedentary Motions, as being in his Constellation destinated for Arms. There is a Query of some Denotations, how he came to receive his Foil, and that in the Catastrophe; for he was strengthned with honourable Alliances, and the privy Friendships of the Court.

My Lord of *Leicester* and *Burleigh* were both his Cotemporaries and Familiars, but that there might be (as the Adage hath it) Falsity in Friendship; and we may rest satisfied, that there is no dispute against Fate.

They quote him for a Person that loved to stand too much alone, and on his own Legs, of too often Recesses, and discontinuance from the Queen's Presence; a fault which is incompatible with the ways of Court and Favour.

He was sent Lord Deputy into *Ireland*, (as it was thought) for a kind of Haughtiness of Spirit, and Repugnancy in Counsels: or, as others have thought, the fittest Person then to bridle the Insolency of the *Irish*; and probable it is, that both these (considering the sway that he would have at the Board, and Head in the Queen's) concurred, and did a little conspire his Remove, and his Ruin. But into *Ireland* he went, where he did the Queen very great and many Services, if the surplusage of the Measure did not abate the value of the Merit, as after-times found that to be no Paradox; for to save the Queen's Purse (which both her self and my Lord Treasurer *Burleigh* ever took for good Services) he imposed on the *Irish* the Charge of bearing their own Arms; which both gave them the Possession, and taught them the use of Weapons, which prov'd in the end a most fatal Work, both in the profusion of Blood and Treasure.

But at his return, and on some account sent home before touching the State of the Kingdom, the assiduous Testimonies of of her Grace towards him, till by his Retreat to his Castle at *Cary*, where he was then building, and out of desire to be in Command at home (as he had been abroad) together with the hatred and practice of *Hatton*, then in high favour, whom not long before he had too bitterly taunted for his Dancing; he was accused of High-Treason, and for high Words, and a forged Letter, condemn'd; tho the Queen, on the news of his Condemnation. swore by her wonted Oath, That they were all Knaves. And they deliver with assurance, that on his Return to the Tower, after his Trial, he said in Oaths, and in Fury, to the Lieutenant Sir *Owen Hopton*, What, will the Queen suffer her Brother to be offer'd up as a Sacrifice to the Envy of my frisking Adversaries? Which being made known to the Queen, and the Warrant for his Execution tender'd, and somewhat enforc'd, she refus'd to sign it, and swore he should not dye, for he was an honest, and a faithful Man. And surely, tho not altogether to set up our Rest and Faith upon Tradition, and upon old Reports, as that Sir *Thomas Perrot* his Father was a Gentleman of the Privy-Chamber to *Henry* the Eighth, and in the Court married to a Lady of great Honour, of the King's familiarity, which are presumptions of some implication: But if we go a little further, and compare his Picture, his Qualities, Gesture, and Voice, with that of the King's, which Memory retains yet amongst us, they will plead strongly, that he was a subreptitious Child of the Blood-Royal.

Certain it is, that he liv'd not long in the Tower; and that after his decease, Sir *Thomas Perrot* his Son (then of no mean Esteem with the Queen) having before married my Lord of *Essex*'s Sister, since Countess of *Northumberland*, had restitution of all his Lands, tho after his decease also (which immediately followed) the Crown resumed his Estate, and took advantage of the former Attainder. And to say the Truth, the Priest's forged Letter was, at his Arraignment, thought but as a Fiction of Envy, and was soon after exploded by the Priest's own confession. But that which most exasperated the Queen, and gave advantage to his Enemies, was (as Sir *Walter Rawleigh* takes into his Observation) Words of Disdain; for the Queen by sharp and reprehensive Letters had nettled him, and shortly after sending others of Approbation, commending his Service, and intimating an Invasion from *Spain*; which he no sooner perus'd, but he said publickly in the great Chamber at *Dublin*: Lo, now she is ready to piss her self for fear of the *Spaniard*, I am again one of her white Boys.

Words which are subject to a various construction, and tended to some disreputation of his Soveraign, and such as may serve for Instruction to Persons in place of Honour and Command,

Command, to beware of the Violences of Nature, but especially of the Exorbitances of the Tongue. And so I conclude him with this double Observation; the one of the Innocency of his Intentions (exempt and clear from the guilt of Treason) and Disloyalty; the other of the Greatness of his Heart; for at his Arraignment he was so little dejected, by what might be alledg'd and prov'd against him, that he rather grew troubled with Choler, and in a kind of exasperation despised his Jury, tho of the Order of Knighthood, and of the Special Gentry, claiming the Privilege of Trial by the Peers, and Baronage of the Realm. So prevalent was that of his native Genius, and the Haughtiness of his Spirit, which accompanied him to his last, and (till any diminution of Courage) it brake in pieces the Cords of his Magnanimity, for he died suddenly in the Tower; and when it was thought the Queen did intend his Inlargement, with the restitution of his Possessions, which were then very great, and comparable to most of the Nobility.

HATTON.

SIR *Christopher Hatton* came into the Court as his Opposite; Sir *John Perrot* was wont to say, by the Galliard, for he came thither as a private Gentleman of the Inns of Court in a Mask; and for his Activity and Person, which was tall and proportionable, taken into her favour. He was first made Vice-Chamberlain, and shortly afterward advanc'd to the Place of Lord Chancellor: A Gentleman, that besides the Graces of his Person and Dancing, had also the Adjuncts of a strong and subtil Capacity, one that could soon learn the Discipline and Garb both of the Times and Court. The Truth is, he had a large proportion of Gifts and Endowments, but too much of the season of Envy; and he was a mere Vegetable of the Court, that sprung up at Night, and sunk again at his Noon.

Lord EFFINGHAM.

MY Lord of *Effingham*, tho a Courtier betimes; yet I find not, that the Sunshine of her favour broke out upon him, until she took him into the Ship, and made him High Admiral of *England*. For his Extract, it may suffice that he was the Son of a *Howard*, and of a Duke of *Norfolk*.

And for his Person, as goodly a Gentleman as the Times had any, if Nature had not been more intentive to compleat his Person,

Person, than Fortune to make him Rich; for the Times considered which were then active, and a long time after lucrative, he died not Wealthy, yet the honester Man: tho it seems the Queen's purpose was to tender the occasion of his Advancement, and to make him capable of more Honour, which at his return from *Cadiz* Action she conferred upon him, creating him Earl of *Nottingham*, to the great discontent of his Colleague, my Lord of *Essex*, who then grew accessive in the Appetite of her favour; and the Truth was, so exorbitant in the limitation of the Soveraign Aspect, that it much alienated the Queen's Grace from him, and drew others, together with the Admiral, to a Combination, and to conspire his Ruin. And tho I have heard it from that Party (I mean of the Admiral's Faction) that it lay not in his proper Power to hurt my Lord of *Essex*; yet he had more Followers, and such as were well skill'd in setting of the Gin: But I leave this to these of another Age.

It is out of doubt, that the Admiral was a good, honest, and a brave Man, and a faithful Servant to his Mistriss; and such a one as the Queen, out of her own Princely Judgment, knew to be a fit Instrument for that Service: for she was no ill Proficient in the Reading of Men, as well as Books, and his sundry Expeditions, as that afore-mention'd, and 88, do both express his Worth, and manifest the Queen's Trust, and the Opinion she had of his Fidelity and Conduct.

Moreover, the *Howards* were of the Queen's Alliance and Consanguinity by her Mother, which swayed her Affection, and bent it toward this great House; and it was a part of her natural Propension to grace and support antient Nobility, where it did not intrench, neither invade her Interest: for on such Trespasses she was quick and tender, and would not spare any whatsoever, as we may observe in the Case of the Duke, and my Lord of *Hereford*, whom she much favour'd and countenanc'd, till they attempted the forbidden Fruit: the fault of the last, being in the severest Interpretation, but a Trespass of Incroachment; but in the first it was taken for a Riot against the Crown, and her own Soveraign Power; and, as I have ever thought, the cause of her Aversion against the rest of the House, and the Duke's great Father-in-law *Fitz-Allen*, Earl of *Arundel*, a Person of the first Rank in her Affections before these and some other Jealousies made a separation between them, this noble Lord, and the Lord *Thomas Howard*, since Earl of *Suffolk*, standing alone in her Grace, the rest in Umbrage.

Sir

Sir JOHN PACKINGTON.

SIR *John Packington* was a Gentleman of no mean Family, and of Form and Feature no way despisable; for he was a brave Gentleman, and a very fine Courtier; and for the time which he staid there (which was not lasting) very high in her Grace: but he came in, and went out, and through disassiduity drew the Curtain between himself, and the Light of her Grace: and then Death overwhelm'd the Remnant, and utterly depriv'd him of recovery. And they say of him, that had he brought less to the Court than he did, he might have carried away more than he brought, for he had a time on it, but an ill husband of opportunity.

Lord HUNSDON.

MY Lord of *Hunsdon* was of the Queen's nearest Kindred, and on the decease of *Sussex*, both he and his Son took the place of Lord Chamberlain: he was a fast Man to his Prince, and firm in his Friends and Servants; and tho he might speak big, and therein would be born out, yet was he not the more dreadful, but less harmful, and far from the practice of my Lord of *Leicester*'s Instructions, for he was downright. And I have heard those that both knew him well, and had interest in him, say merrily of him, That his Latin, and his Dissimulation, were both alike; and that his custom of Swearing, and obscenity in Speaking, made him seem a worse Christian than he was, and a better Knight of the Carpet than he should be. As he lived in a ruffling-time, so he loved Sword and Buckler-men, and such as our Fathers were wont to call Men of their hands; of which sort, he had many brave Gentlemen that followed him, yet not taken for a popular and dangerous Person: and this is one that stood amongst the *Togati*, of an honest stout Heart, and such a one as (upon occasion) would have fought for his Prince, and his Country; for he had the Charge of the Queen's Person, both in the Court, and in the Camp at *Tilbury*.

RAW-

RAWLEIGH.

SIR *Walter Rawleigh* was one that (it ſeems) Fortune had pickt out of purpoſe, of whom to make an Example, or to uſe as her Tennis-Ball, thereby to ſhew what ſhe could do, for ſhe toſs'd him up of nothing, and to and fro to Greatneſs; and from thence down to little more, than to that wherein ſhe found him (a bare Gentleman) not that he was leſs, for he was well deſcended, and of good Alliance, but poor in his beginnings. And for my Lord of *Oxford*'s Jeſt of him (the Jack, and an Upſtart) we all know, it ſavours more of Emulation, and his Humor, than of Truth; and it is a certain Note of the Times, that the Queen in her choice never took into her favour a mere new Man, or a Mechanick, as *Comines* obſerves of *Lewis* the Eleventh of *France*, who did ſerve himſelf with Perſons of unknown Parents, ſuch as was *Oliver* the Barber, whom he created Earl of *Dunoyes*, and made him *Ex ſecretis Conſiliis*, and alone in his favour and familiarity. His Approaches to the Univerſity, and Inns of Court, were the Grounds of his Improvement; but they were rather Excurſions, than Sieges, or Settings down, for he ſtaid not long in a Place; and being the youngeſt Brother, and the Houſe diminiſh'd in Patrimony, he foreſaw his own deſtiny, that he was firſt to rowl (through want and diſability to ſubſiſt otherways) before he could come to a repoſe, and as the Stone doth, by long lying, gather Moſs: He firſt expos'd himſelf to the Land-ſervice of *Ireland*, (a *Militia*) which then did not yield him Food and Rayment, (for it was ever very poor) nor had he patience to ſtay there, (tho ſhortly after he came thither again) under the Command of my Lord *Grey*, but with his own Colours flying in the Field, having in the interim caſt a new Chance, both in the Low-Countries, and in a Voyage to Sea; and if ever Man drew Vertue out of Neceſſity, it was he; therewith was he the great Example of Induſtry. And tho he might then have taken that of the Merchant to himſelf, *Per mare, per terras, currit mercator ad Indos*; he might alſo have ſaid, and truly with the Philoſopher, *Omnia mea mecum porto*: For it was a long time before he could brag of more than he carried at his Back; and when he got on the winning-ſide, it was his Commendation that he took pains for it, and underwent many various Adventures for his After-perfection, and before he came into the publick Note of the World. And that it may appear how he came up (*per ardua*) *per varios caſus, per tot diſcrimina rerum*, not pulled up by Chance, or by any gentle admittance of Fortune,

I

I will briefly deſcribe his native Parts, and thoſe of his own acquiring, which were the hopes of his riſing.

He had in the outward Man, a good Preſence, in a handſome and well-compacted Perſon; a ſtrong natural Wit, and a better Judgment, with a bold and plauſible Tongue, whereby he could ſet out his Parts to the beſt advantage: and to theſe he had the Adjuncts of ſome general Learning, which by diligence he enforc'd to a great Augmentation and Perfection; for he was an indefatigable Reader, whether by Sea or Land, and none of the leaſt Obſervers both of Men, and the Times: and I am confident, that among the ſecond Cauſes of his Growth, that Variance between him and my Lord *Grey*, in his Deſcent into *Ireland*, was a Principal; for it drew them both over to the Council-Table, there to plead their Cauſe, where (what advantage he had in the Cauſe, I know not, but) he had much the better in the telling of his Tale; and ſo much, that the Queen and the Lords took no ſlight Mark of the Man, and his Parts: for from thence he came to be known, and to have acceſs to the Queen, and the Lords. And then we are not to doubt how ſuch a Man would comply, and learn the way of Progreſſion; and whether or no my Lord of *Leiceſter* had then caſt in a good word for him to the Queen, which would have done no harm, I do not determine: But true it is, he had gotten the Queen's Ear at a trice, and ſhe began to be taken with his Elocution, and loved to hear his Reaſons to her Demands; and the Truth is, ſhe took him for a kind of Oracle, which nettled them all: yea, thoſe that he relied on, began to take this his ſudden Favour for an Alarm, and to be ſenſible of their own ſupplantation, and to project his, which made him ſhortly after ſing, *Fortune my Foe*, &c. So that finding his Favour declining, and falling into a Receſs, he undertook a new Peregrination, to leave that *Terra infirma* of the Court for that of the Wars, and by declining himſelf, and by abſence to expel his and the Paſſion of his Enemies: which, in Court, was a ſtrange device of recovery, but that he knew there was ſome ill Office done him, that he durſt not attempt to mind any other ways than by going aſide, thereby to teach Envy a new way of Forgetfulneſs, and not ſo much as to think of him, howſoever he had it always in mind never to forget himſelf. And his device took ſo well, that at his return he came in (as Rams do, by going backward) with the greater ſtrength, and ſo continued to her laſt, great in her Grace, and Captain of the Guard, where I muſt leave him; but with this Obſervation, That tho he gained much at the Court, yet he took it not out of the Exchequer, or merely out of the Queen's Purſe, but by his Wit, and the

P help

help of the Prerogative; for the Queen was never profuse in the delivering out of her Treasure, but paid many, and most of her Servants part in Mony, and the rest with Grace; which, as the Case stood, was taken for good Payment, leaving the Arrear of Recompence due to their Merit, to her great Successor, who paid them all with Advantage.

GREVILL.

SIR *Fulk Grevill*, since Lord *Brook*, had no mean Place in her Favour; neither did he hold it for any short Term: For if I be not deceiv'd, he had the longest Lease, and the smoothest Time, without Rub of any of her Favourites. He came to the Court in his Youth and Prime, or that is the time or never; he was a brave Gentleman, and honourably descended from *Willoughby* Lord *Brook*, and Admiral to *Henry* the Seventh; neither illiterate, for he was, as he would often profess, a Friend to Sir *Philip Sydney*; and there are of his, now extant, some Fragments of his Poems, and of those Times, which do interest him in the Muses, and which shew, the Queen's Election had ever a noble Conduct; and it motions more of Vertue and Judgment, than of Fancy. I find that he neither sought for, or obtain'd any great Place or Preferment in Court, during all the time of his Attendance; neither did he need it, for he came thither backt with a plentiful Fortune, which, as himself was wont to say, was the better held together by a single Life; wherein he liv'd and dy'd a constant Courtier of the Ladies.

ESSEX.

MY Lord of *Essex* (as Sir *Henry Wotton*, a Gentleman of great Parts, and partly of his Times and Retinue, observes) had his Introduction by my Lord of *Leicester*, who had married his Mother; a Tye of Affinity, which, besides a more urgent Obligation, might have invited his Care to advance him, his Fortune being then (and through his Father's infelicity) grown low: but that the Son of a Lord *Ferrers* of *Charley*, Viscount *Hertford*, and Earl of *Essex* (who was of the antient Nobility) and formerly in the Queen's good Grace, could not have a Room in her Favour, without the Assistance of *Leicester*, was beyond the Rule of her Nature; which, as I have elsewhere taken into Observation, was ever inclinable to favour the Nobility. Sure it is, that he no sooner appear'd in Court, but

but he took with the Queen and Courtiers; and I believe they all could not chuse but look thro the Sacrifice of the Father on his living Son, whose Image, by the remembrance of former Passages, was afresh (like the bleeding of men murder'd) represented to the Court, and offer'd up as a Subject of Compassion to all the Kingdom. There was in this young Lord, together with a most goodly Person, a kind of Urbanity or innate Curtesy, which both won the Queen, and too much took upon the People, to gaze upon the new adopted Son of her Favour. And as I go along, it were not amiss to take into observation two notable Quotations: The first was a violent Indulgency of the Queen (which is incident to old Age, where it encounters with a pleasing and sutable Object) towards this Lord; all which argu'd a Non-perpetuity: The second was a Fault in the Object of her Grace, my Lord himself, who drew in too fast, like a Child sucking an over-uberous Nurse. And had there been a more decent Decorum observ'd in both, or either of those, without doubt the Unity of their Affections had been more permanent, and not so in and out as they were, like an Instrument ill-tun'd, and lapsing to Discord.

The greater Error of the two (tho unwillingly) I am constrain'd to impose on my Lord of *Essex*, or rather on his Youth; and none of the least of his Blame, on those that stood Centinels about him, who might have advis'd him better; but that like men intoxicated with hopes, they likewise had suckt in with the most, and of their Lord's receit, and so like *Cæsar* would have all or none: a Rule quite contrary to Nature, and the most indulgent Parents, who tho they may express more Affection to one in the abundance of Bequests, yet cannot forget some Legacys, just Distributives, and Dividends to others of their begetting. And how hateful Partiality proves, every day's Experience tells us; out of which, common Consideration might have fram'd to their hands a Maxim of more discretion for the Conduct and Management of their now graced Lord and Master.

But to omit that of Infusion, and to do right to Truth, my Lord of *Essex* (even of those that truly lov'd and honour'd him) was noted for too bold an Ingrosser both of Fame and Favour; and of this, without offence to the Living, or treading on the sacred Urn of the Dead, I shall present a Truth, and a Passage yet in memory.

My Lord *Mountjoy*, who was another Child of her Favour, being newly come to Court, and then but Sir *Charles Blunt* (for my Lord *William*, his elder Brother, was then living) had the good fortune one day to run very well a Tilt, and the Queen therewith was so well pleas'd, that she sent him, in token of her Favour, a Queen at *Chesse* of Gold richly enamel'd, which his Servants had the next day fasten'd on his Arm with a Crimson Ribband; which my Lord of *Essex*, as he pass'd thro the Privy Chamber, espying, with his Cloke cast under his Arm, the better to commend it to the view, inquir'd what it was, and for what cause there fix'd. Sir *Fulk Grevill* told him, That it was the Queen's Favour, which the day before, and after the Tilting, she had sent him. Whereat my Lord of *Essex*, in a kind of Emulation, and as tho he would have limited her Favour, said, *Now I perceive every Fool must have a Favour*. This bitter and publick Affront came to Sir *Charles Blunt's* Ear, who sent him a Challenge, which was accepted by my Lord; and they met near *Maribone-Park*, where my Lord was hurt in the Thigh, and disarm'd. The Queen missing the Men, was very curious to learn the Truth; and when at last it was whisper'd out, she swore by God's Death it was fit that some one or other should take him down, and teach him better manners, otherwise there would be no Rule with him. And here I note the Inition of my Lord's Friendship with *Mountjoy*, which the Queen her self did then conjure.

Now for Fame we need not go far: for my Lord of *Essex* having born a grudg to General *Norris*, who had unwittingly offer'd to undertake the Action of *Britany* with fewer men than my Lord had before demanded; on his return with Victory, and a glorious Report of his Valour, he was then thought the only man for the *Irish* War: wherein my Lord of *Essex* so wrought, by despising the number and quality of Rebels, that *Norris* was sent over with a scanted Force, join'd with the Relicks of the veteran Troops of *Britany*, of set purpose (as it fell out) to ruin *Norris*; and the Lord *Burrows*, by my Lord's procurement, sent at his heels, and to command in chief, and to confine *Norris* only to his Government at *Munster*: which brake the great Heart of the General, to see himself undervalu'd and undermin'd by my Lord and *Burrows*; which was, as the Proverb speaks it, *Imberbes docere Senes*.

My Lord *Burrows* in the beginning of his Persecution dy'd; whereupon the Queen was fully bent to have sent over *Mountjoy*, which my Lord *Essex* utterly dislik'd, and oppos'd with many Reasons, and by Arguments of Contempt against *Mountjoy*, his then profess'd Friend and Familiar; so predominant were his Words, to reap the Honour of closing up that War, and all other.

Now the way being open'd and plain'd by his own Workmanship, and so handled that none durst appear to stand for the place; at last with much ado he obtain'd his own ends, and

withal

withal his fatal Destruction, leaving the Queen and the Court (where he stood firm and impregnable in her Grace) to men that long had sought and watcht their times to give him the trip, and could never find any opportunity, but this of his Absence, and of his own creation. And these are the true Observations of his Appetite and Inclinations, which were not of any true proportion, but carry'd and transported with an Over-desire and Thirstiness after Fame, that deceitful Fame of Popularity, and to help on his Catastrophe. I observe likewise two sorts of People that had a hand in his Fall; the first was the Soldiery, which all flockt unto him, as foretelling a Mortality, and are commonly of blunt and too rough Counsels, and many times dissonant from the tune of the Court and the State: the other sort were of his Family, his Servants, and his own Creatures; such as were bound by the Rules of Safety, and Obligations of Fidelity, to have look'd better to the steering of that Boat wherein they themselves were carry'd, and not have suffer'd it to float and run on ground, with those empty Sails of Fame and Tumor of popular Applause. Methinks one honest man or other, that had but the Office of brushing his Clothes, might have whisper'd in his ear: *My Lord, look to it, this Multitude that follows you, will either devour you, or undo you; strive not to rule, and over-rule all, for it will cost hot water, and it will procure Envy: and if needs your Genius must have it so, let the Court, and the Queen's Presence be your Station.* But, as I have said, they had suckt too much of their Lord's milk, and instead of withdrawing, they blew the Coals of his Ambition, and infus'd into him too much of the Spirit of Glory; yea, and mix'd the Goodness of his Nature with a Touch of Revenge, which is ever accompany'd with a Destiny of the same fate. And of this number there were some of insufferable Natures about him, that towards his last gave desperate Advice, such as his Integrity abhor'd, and his Fidelity forbad; amongst whom Sir *Henry Wotton* notes (without injury) his Secretary *Cuffe*, a vile man, and of a perverse nature. I could also name others, who when he was in the right course of Recovery, and setling to Moderation, would not suffer a recess in him, but stir'd up the Dregs of those rude Humours, which by time and his affliction, out of his own judgment, he sought to repose, or to give them all a vomit. And thus I conclude this noble Lord, as a mixture between Prosperity and Adversity; once the Child of his great Mistriss's Favour, but the Son of *Bellona*.

BUCKHURST.

MY Lord of *Buckhurst* was of the Noble House of the *Sackvills*, and of the Queen's Consanguinity. His Father was Sir *Richard Sackvill*, or, as the People then call'd him, *Fill-Sack*, by reason of his great Wealth, and the vast Patrimony which he left to this his Son; whereof he spent in his Youth the best part, until the Queen by her frequent Admonitions diverted the Torrent of his Profusion. He was a very fine Gentleman of Person, and Endowments both of Art and Nature, both without measure magnificent, till on the turn of his Humour, and the Allay that his Years and good Counsels had wrought upon those immoderate Courses of his Youth, and that height of Spirit inherent to his House: And then did the Queen, as a most judicious and indulgent Prince, when she saw the man grow stay'd and settled, give him her Assistance, and advanc'd him to the Treasureship; where he made amends to his House for his mispent time, both in the Increasement of Estate and Honour, which the Queen confer'd on him, together with the opportunity to remake himself, and thereby to shew that this was a Child, that should have a share in her Grace, and a taste of her Bounty.

They much commend his Elocution, but more the Excellency of his Pen; for he was a Scholar, and a Person of a quick Dispatch (Faculties that yet run in the Blood) and they say of him, that his Secretaries did little for him, by way of Indictment, wherein they could seldom please him, he was so facete and choice in his Phrase and Stile; and for his Dispatches, and the content he gave to Suiters, he had a Decorum seldom since put in practice: for he had of his Attendants that took into Roll the Names of all Suiters, with the date of their first Addresses, and these in their order had hearing; so that a fresh man could not leap over his head, that was of a more antient edition, except in the urgent Affairs of State. I find not that he was any ways insnar'd in the Factions of the Court, which were all his times strong, and in every man's note; the *Howards* and the *Cecills* of the one part, my Lord of *Essex*, &c. on the other part: for he held the Staff of the Treasury fast in his hand, which once in the year made them all beholden to him. And the truth is (as he was a wise man and a stout) he had no reason to be a Partaker; for he stood sure in Blood, and in Grace, and was wholly intentive to the Queen's Service. And such were his Abilities, that she receiv'd assiduous Proofs of his

Suffi-

Sufficiency; and it hath been thought, that ſhe might have more cunning Inſtruments, but none of a more ſtrong Judgment and Confidence in his ways; which are Symptoms of Magnanimity and Fidelity, whereunto methinks this Motto hath ſome kind of reference, *Aut nunquam tentes, aut perfice:* As tho he would have character'd in a word the Genius of his Houſe, or expreſs'd ſomewhat of an higher Inclination, than lay within his compaſs. That he was a Courtier, is apparent; for he ſtood always in her eye and favour.

Lord MOUNTJOY.

MY Lord *Mountjoy* was of the antient Nobility, but utterly deceiv'd in the Support thereof, Patrimony, thro his Grandfather's Exceſs in the Action of *Bullen*, his Father's Vanity in the ſearch of the Philoſopher's Stone, and his Brother's untimely Prodigalities; all which ſeem'd by a joint Conſpiracy to ruin the Houſe, and altogether to annihilate it. As he came from *Oxford*, he took the Inner Temple in his way to Court; whither no ſooner came, but (without asking) he had a pretty ſtrange kind of Admiſſion, which I have heard from a diſcreet man, of his own, and much more of the Secrets of thoſe Times. He was then much about twenty years of age, of a brown Hair, a ſweet Face, a moſt neat Compoſure, and tall in his perſon. The Queen was then at *Whitehall*, and at dinner, whither he came to ſee the faſhion of the Court. The Queen had ſoon found him out, and with a kind of an affected Frown, ask'd the Lady Carver what he was. She anſwer'd, ſhe knew him not. Inſomuch as an Inquiry was made from one to another, who he might be; till at length it was told the Queen, he was Brother to the Lord *William Mountjoy*. This Inquiſition, with the Eye of Majeſty fix'd upon him (as ſhe was wont to do, and to daunt men ſhe knew not) ſtir'd the Blood of this young Gentleman, inſomuch as his Colour came and went: Which the Queen obſerving, call'd him unto her, and gave him her Hand to kiſs, incouraging him with gracious Words, and new Looks; and ſo diverting her Speech to the Lords and Ladies, ſhe ſaid, That ſhe no ſooner obſerv'd him, but that ſhe knew there was in him ſome noble Blood; with ſome other Expreſſions of Pity towards his Houſe. And then again demanding his Name, ſhe ſaid, *Fail you not to come to the Court, and I will bethink my ſelf how to do you good.* And this was his Inlet, and the Beginnings of his Grace; where it falls into conſideration, that tho he wanted not Wit and Courage, for he had very fine Attractions, and being a good piece of a Scholar, yet were they accompany'd with the Retractives of Bashfulness, and a natural Modesty, which (as the Tone of his House, and the Ebb of his Fortune then stood) might have hinder'd his Progression, had they not been reinforc'd by the Infusion of Sovereign Favour, and the Queen's gracious Invitation. And that it may appear how low he was, and how much that heretick Necessity will work in the Dejection of good Spirits, I can deliver it with assurance, that his Exhibition was very scant until his Brother dy'd, which was shortly after his Admission to the Court; and then was it no more than a thousand Marks *per ann.* wherewith he liv'd plentifully in a fine way and garb, and without any great Sustentation, during all her times. And as there was in his nature a kind of Backwardness, which did not befriend him, nor suit with the Motion of the Court; so there was in him an Inclination to Arms, with a humour of travelling, and gadding abroad; which had not some wise Men about him labour'd to remove, and the Queen her self laid in her Commands, he would (out of his natural Propension) have marr'd his own market. For as he was grown by reading (whereunto he was much addicted) to the Theory of a Soldier, so was he strongly invited by his Genius to the Acquaintance of the Practice of the War, which were the causes of his Excursions. For he had a Company in the *Low Countries*, from whence he came over with a noble Acceptance of the Queen, but somewhat restless; and in honourable Thought he exposed himself again and again, and would press the Queen with the Pretences of visiting his Company so often, that at length he had a flat Denial; yet he stole over with Sir *John Norris* into the Action of *Britany* (which was then a hot and active War) whom he would always call his Father, honouring him above all men, and ever bewailing his end; so contrary he was in his Esteem and Valuation of this great Commander, to that of his Friend, my Lord of *Essex*: till at last the Queen began to take his Decessions for Contempts, and confin'd his Residence to the Court, and her own Presence. And upon my Lord of *Essex*'s Fall (so confident she was in her own Princely Judgment, and Opinion she had conceiv'd of his Worth and Conduct) she would have this noble Gentleman, and none other, to finish and bring the *Irish* War to a propitious end: for it was a Prophetical Speech of her own, That it would be his Fortune and his Honour to cut the Thred of that fatal Rebellion, and to bring her in Peace to the Grave. Where she was not deceiv'd; for he atchieved it, but with much pains and carefulness, and not without the Fears and many Jealousies of the Court and Times,

Times, wherewith the Queen's Age, and the Malignity of her ſetting Times were replete. And ſo I come to his dear Friend in Court, Mr. Secretary *Cecill*, whom in his long Abſence from Court he ador'd as his Saint, and courted for his only *Mœcenas*, both before and after his Departure from Court, and during all the times of his Command in *Ireland*; well knowing that it lay in his power, and by a word of his mouth, to make or mar him.

CECILL.

SIR *Robert Cecill*, ſince Earl of *Saliſbury*, was the Son of the Lord *Burleigh*, and the Inheritor of his Wiſdom, and by degrees Succeſſor of his Places and Favours, tho not of his Lands; for he had Sir *Thomas Cecill* his elder Brother, ſince created Earl of *Exeter*. He was firſt Secretary of State, then Maſter of the Wards, and in the laſt of her Reign came to be Lord Treaſurer: all which were the Steps of his Father's Greatneſs, and of the Honour he left to his Houſe. For his Perſon he was not much beholden to Nature, tho ſomewhat for his Face, which was the beſt part of his Outſide; but for his Inſide, it may be ſaid, and that without a Solœciſm, that he was his Father's own Son, and a pregnant Proficient in all Diſcipline of State. He was a Courtier from his Cradle, which might have made him betimes; yet at the Age of Twenty and upwards he was much ſhort of his After-proof, but expoſed; and by change of Climate he ſoon made ſhow what he was, and would be. He lived in thoſe times wherein the Queen had moſt need and uſe of Men of weight; and amongſt able ones, this was a Chief, as having his Sufficiency from his Inſtructions that begat him, the Tutorſhip of the Times and Court, which were then the Academies of Art and Cunning. For ſuch was the Queen's condition from the tenth or twelfth of her Reign, that ſhe had the Happineſs to ſtand up (whereof there is a former Intimation) tho inviron'd with more Enemies, and aſſaulted with more dangerous Practices, than any Prince of her Times, and of many Ages before. Neither muſt we in this her Preſervation attribute too much to human Policy, for that God in his omnipotent Providence had not only ordain'd thoſe ſecundary means, as Inſtruments of the Work; but by an evident Manifeſtation, that the ſame Work which ſhe acted, was a well-pleaſing Service of his own, out of a peculiar Care had decreed the Protection of the Work-Miſtriſs, and thereunto added his abundant Bleſſing upon all, and whatſoever ſhe undertook. Which is an Obſervation of Satisfaction to my ſelf, that ſhe was in the

the right, tho to others now breathing under the same Form and Frame of her Government, it may not seem an Animadversion of any worth; but I leave them to the peril of their own Folly. And so again to this great Master of State, and the Staff of the Queen's declining Age; who tho his little crooked Person could not promise any great Supportation, yet it carry'd thereon a Head, and a Headpiece of a vast content. And therein it seems Nature was so diligent to compleat one, and the best part about him, as that to the Perfection of his Memory and Intellectuals, she took care also of his Senses, and to put into him *Linceos oculos*, or to pleasure him the more, borrow'd of *Argus* so to give unto him a prospective sight; and for the rest of his sensitive Vertues, his Predecessor *Walsingham* had left him a Receipt, to smell out what was done in the Conclave. And his good old Father was so well seen in the Mathematicks, as that he could tell you throughout all *Spain*, every Part, every Ship, with their Burdens, whither bound with Preparation, what Impediments for Diversion of Enterprises, Counsels, and Resolutions. And that we may see, as in a little Map, how docible this little man was, I will present a taste of his Abilities.

My Lord of *Devonshire*, upon the certainty the *Spaniard* would invade *Ireland* with a strong Army, had written very earnestly to the Queen and the Council, for such Supplies to be timely sent over, that might enable him to march up to the *Spaniard*, if he did land, and follow on his Prosecution against the Rebels. Sir *Robert Cecill*, besides the general Dispatch of the Council, as he often did, wrote this in private; for these two began then to love dearly.

My Lord,

OUT of the abundance of my Affection, and the Care I have of your well-doing, I must in private put you out of doubt (for I fear, I know you cannot be otherwise sensible than in the way of Honour) that the Spaniard *will not come unto you this year; for I have it from my own, what Preparations are in all his parts, and what he can do: for be confident, he beareth up a Reputation by seeming to embrace more than he can gripe. But the next year be assured he will cast over unto you some forlorn Hopes, which how they may be reinforc'd beyond his present Ability, and his first Intention, I cannot as yet make any certain Judgment. But I believe out of my Intelligence, that you may expect their landing in* Munster; *and the more to distract you, in several places, as at* Kingsale, Beerhaven, Baltimore; *where you may be sure (coming from Sea) they will first fortify, and learn the Strength of the Rebels, before they dare take the field. Howsoever (as I know) you will not lessen your Care, neither your Defences;*

fences; and whatsoever lies within my power, to do You and the Publick service, rest thereof assured.

And to this I would add much more, but it may as it is suffice to present much, as his Abilities in the Pen, that he was his Crafts-master in foreign Intelligence; and for domestick Affairs, as he was one of those that sat at the Stern to the last of the Queen, so was he none of the least in Skill, and in the true use of the Compass. And so I shall only vindicate the Scandal of his Death, and conclude him; for he departed at *St. Margarets* near *Marlborough*, in his return from the *Bath*, as my Lord Viscount *Cranborne*, my Lord *Clifford* his Son, and Son in Law, my self, and many more can witness: but that the day before he founded in the way, was taken out of the Litter, and laid into his Coach, was a Truth, out of which that Falshood concerning the manner of his Death had its derivation, tho nothing to the purpose, or to the prejudice of his Worth.

VERE.

SIR *Francis Vere* was of the antient and the most noble Extract of the Earls of *Oxford*; and it may be a question, whether the Nobility of his House, or the Honour of his Atchievements, might most commend him; but that we have an authentick Rule to decide the Doubt:

> *Nam genus & proavos, & quæ non fecimus ipsi,*
> *Vix ea nostra voco.*

For tho he were an honourable Slip of that antient Tree of Nobility (which was no disadvantage to his Vertue) yet he brought more Glory to the Name of *Vere*, than he took of Blood from the Family. He was amongst the Queen's Sword-men inferior to none, but superior to many; of whom it may be said, To speak much of him were the way to leave out something that might add to his Praise, and to forget more that could add to his Honour. I find not, that he came much to the Court, for he lived almost perpetually in the Camp; but when he did, no man had more of the Queen's Favour, and none less envy'd, for he seldom troubled it with the Jealousy and Alarms of Supplantation: his way was another sort of undermining. They report that the Queen, as she loved Martial Men, would court this Gentleman, as soon as he appear'd in her presence; and surely he was a Soldier of great worth, and commanded thirty years in the Service of the

the States, and twenty years over the *English* in chief, as the Queen's General: And he that had seen the Battel of *Newport*, might there best have taken him, and his Noble Brother my Lord of *Tilbury*, to the life.

WORCESTER.

MY Lord of *Worcester* I have here put last, but not least in the Queen's Favour. He was of the antient and noble Blood of the *Beauforts*, and of her Grandfather's Line by the Mother, which the Queen could never forget, especially where there was a concurrency of old Blood with Fidelity, a Mixture which ever sorted with the Queen's Nature. And tho there might appear something in this House which might avert her Grace (tho not to speak of my Lord himself, but with due Reverence and Honour) I mean Contrariety or Suspicion of Religion, yet the Queen ever respected this House, and principally this Noble Lord, whom she first made Master of the Horse, and then admitted of her Council of State. In his Youth (part whereof he spent before he came to reside at Court) he was a very fine Gentleman, and the best Horseman and Tilter of the Times, which were then the manlike and noble Recreations of the Court, and such as took up the Applause of Men, as well as the Praise and Commendation of the Ladies. And when years had abated these Exercises of Honour, he grew then to be a faithful and profound Counsellor; and as I have plac'd him last, so was he the last Liver of all the Servants of her Favour, and had the Honour to see his renown'd Mistress, and all of them laid in the places of their rest; and for himself, after a Life of a very noble and remarkable Reputation, he dy'd rich, and in a peaceable old Age: A Fate (that I make the last, and none of the slightest Observations) which besel not many of the rest; for they expir'd like unto Lights blown out, with the Snuff stinking, not commendably extinguish'd, and with offence to the Standers by.

And thus have I deliver'd up this my poor Essay; a little Draught of this great Princess, and her Times, with the Servants of her State and Favour. I cannot say, I have finish'd it; for I know how defective and imperfect it is, as limbed only in the original Nature, not without the active Blemishes, and so left it as a Task fitter for remote times, and the Sallies of some bolder Pencil to correct that which is amiss, and draw the rest up to the life, as for me to have endeavour'd it.

I

I took it to conſideration how eaſily I might have daſht in too much of the ſtrain of Pollution, and thereby have defac'd that little which is done: For I profeſs I have taken care ſo to maſter my Pen, that I might not (*ex animo*, or of ſet purpoſe) diſcolour Truth, or any of the parts thereof, otherwiſe than in concealment. Haply there are ſome who will not approve of this Modeſty, but will cenſure me for Puſillanimity, and with great cunning Artiſts attempt to draw their Line further out at large, and upon this of mine, which may with ſomewhat more eaſe be effected, for that the Frame is ready made to their hands; and then haply I could draw one in the midſt of theirs, but that Modeſty in me forbids the Defacements of men departed, whoſe Poſterity yet remaining, enjoys the Merit of their Virtues, and do ſtill live in their Honour. And I had rather incur the Cenſure of Abruption, than to be conſcious, and taken in the manner of ſinning by eruption, and of trampling on the Graves of Perſons at reſt, which living we durſt not look in the face, nor make our Addreſſes to them, otherwiſe than with due Regards to their Honours, and Renown to their Vertues.

Phenix

Phenix VIII.

JOHN KEYMOR'S *Observation made upon the* Dutch *Fishing, about the Year* 1601.

Demonstrating that there is more Wealth rais'd out of Herrings and other Fish in his Majesty's Seas, by the Neighbouring Nations, in one Year, than the King of Spain *hath from the* Indies *in four:*

And that there were Twenty Thousand Ships and other Vessels, and about Four Hundred Thousand People then set on work both by Sea and Land; and maintain'd only by Fishing upon the Coasts of England, Scotland, ***and*** Ireland.

BEING desirous to look into the World, to get knowledg for my Country's good, I travel'd *France*, *Germany*, and divers other places and Free States. I found in *Lubeck* 700 great Ships, in *Hamborough* about 600: *Embden* lately a Fisher-Town, within the memory of Man not known to have 60 Ships, hath 1400, almost as many as belongs to all *England*.

England. *Holland*, not so big as one of your Majesty's Shires, eighteen *Dutch* miles long, and five broad, hath about it 39 walled Towns, 400 Villages, and 20000 Sail of Ships and Hoys; which is more than *England*, *France*, *Spain*, *Portugal*, *Italy*, *Scotland*, *Denmark*, *Poland*, *Sweden*, and *Russia* have, all put together: and builds every year 1000 new Ships, having in their Soil neither Matter to build them, nor Merchandizes to set them forth. Standing in admiration how this might be, I trac'd the Countries twice over from Town to Town, and from thence along his Majesty's Sea-Coast of *England*, *Scotland*, and *Ireland*; where I found not only an *Indian* Fleet of 40 or 50 Sail, with 5 or 6000 People yearly employ'd in this your Fishing, one of the greatest Sea-businesses of the World; but at the least 20000 Sail, and above 400000 Persons of all Nations set on work in his Majesty's Seas, about taking those innumerable Riches of Herrings and other Fish, which offer themselves to his Majesty's Kingdoms above all Nations.

The *Hollanders* have above 4100 fishing Ships and Vessels; whereof 100 Dogger-boats, 700 Pinks and Well-boats, 700 Strand-boats, 400 Evers, and 400 Galliots, Drivers, and Tod-boats, and 1200 Busses. Since I sollicited this, to have 200 Busses built for *England*, the *Hollanders* have made 800 new Busses more; in all belonging to *Holland* 4100 Busses, and other fishing Ships.

The 1500 Strand-boats, Evers, Galliots, Drivers, and Tod-boats fish upon their own Coasts; and every of them sets on work one other Vessel to fetch Salt and transport Fish into other Countries; so are there 3000 Vessels, and 40000 Persons employ'd and maintain'd by fishing upon their own Coasts.

The 700 Pinks and Well-boats from 60 to 100 Tuns a-piece, Dogger-boats of about 150 Tuns a-piece, do fish altogether upon the Coasts of *England* and *Scotland* for Cod and Ling only; and every of these do set on work one other Vessel, to fetch Salt and transport Fish into other Countries, after they are brought into their own Countries, out of his Majesty's Seas.

The 2000 Busses from 60 to 100 and 200 Tuns a-piece, are employ'd only to take Herrings about *Baughamness* in *Scotland*, all along the Coasts of *England* to the *Thames* mouth, from *June* to *November* 26 weeks; and one of their great Busses do take 8, 12, or 20 Last of Herrings at a Draught in one night, and carries into their own Country 40, 50, or 100 Last in a Buss. And our Fishing continueth but seven weeks with small Crayers and Cobles, from 5 to 10, 20 Tuns, when the Herrings come home to our own Road stead, and we take 1, 2, or 3 Lasts in a night; and when we bring home seven, it is a great wonder.

Besides

Besides the number taken by their 2000 Busses, the *Hollanders* have above 400 other Vesses, call'd Gaynes and Evers, which do take Herrings at *Yarmouth*, and there sell them, and carry away ready mony; they have yet 500 other Ships usually trading every year to *London* with Cod and Ling taken in his Majesty's Seas, as also other parts of *England*, and here sell them, and carry away most fine Gold, which is made into base Gold beyond Seas; a great hurt to the Wealth and Strength of our Land, and hinderance to Navigation and Mariners, and Employment of the Poor of this Nation.

The *Hollanders* have made a Law in their own Country, that we shall sell no White Herrings nor other Fish there (upon penalty of Confiscation) because they will have no other Nation to serve their Country with Fish, but what they take themselves; as well for the Increase as Maintenance of Navigation, and setting their People on work. *Hamborough* likewise hath made an Order that we shall sell no Herrings there, before their Busses be come from fishing, and have sold all theirs. Thus they take Herrings in his Majesty's Seas, make Laws to cross and hinder us in our own Sales, for the inriching and strengthning themselves, and the increasing their Ships and Mariners.

The *Hollanders* do take in the time of 26 weeks with 2000 Busses, about 300000 Lasts (12 Barrels to the Last) which are sold to the Merchants at 10 or 12 *l.* the Last, the Fisherman's price, which amounteth to three Millions and 600000 *l.* The Merchants transport and sell them into *Pomerland*, *Spruceland*, *Poland*, *Denmark*, *Liefland*, *Russia*, *Sweden*, *Germany*, *Brabant*, *Flanders*, *France*, *Lukeland*, some into *England*, and other parts; and so sell them from 16, to 18, 20, 30, and 36 *l.* the Last, and more, which I cannot esteem to be sold for less than five millions of pounds. All this Benefit they make yearly of Herrings taken out of his Majesty's Seas.

Besides the Busses of *France*, *Hamborough*, and *Embden*, the *Hollanders* with their 2000 Busses do get the start of us for the Herring-fishing nineteen weeks, and every Buss doth take her self twice or thrice full; and they do serve near twenty Kingdoms, Dukedoms, and Free States in the East and North-East Regions, before our great Fishing begins at *Yarmouth*. And before our Fishing be ended, the *Sound* and the Rivers that way are frozen, so we cannot pass, nor vent into those places.

For Cod and Ling they send forth about 1000 Sail from 50 to 100 Tun a-piece, every Ship making four or five, and some six Voyages in a year, where our small Crayets seldom make two Voyages. Which huge quantity of Fish and Herrings taken in his Majesty's Seas, they carry into their own Country,

and

and afterwards by their own Shipping transport them into foreign Kingdoms, so much to their exceeding advantage, that in short time they will be able to eat all our Shipping out at Sea, as may be conjectur'd by their former Increase in so few years.

Besides the principal Adventurers, I noted that thousands of Men, their Sons, Daughters, and Maid-servants, which take 40 *s.* or 3 *l.* wages in a year, some of them have 5 *l.* 10 *l.* and 20 *l.* Adventure, and more, in the Busses; whereby they grow to great Wealth before they come to be married; besides the Men-Servants.

The Return of Merchandize, Wares, and Coin, for Herrings and other Fish (out of other Countries) is so great, that it maketh the Bank for Coin, and Staple for all kind of Merchandize in *Holland*, where nothing groweth but a few Hops, Mader, and Cheese; so they make the Commodities of other Kingdoms serve their turns, to set their Ships and People on work, wherewith they enrich and strengthen themselves, to the admiration of all Nations. The States of *Holland* receive more Duties and Customs for Lasts of Herrings, Fish, and other Profits inwards and outwards in one year, than all the Customs of *England* come unto in two years. There was paid above 300000 *l.* fourteen years past, besides the Custom of all other Merchandize, for Excises, Licences, Wastage, and Lastage.

It is most evidently true, that his Majesty's Seas are far richer than the King of *Spain*'s *Indies*; and there is more made of Fish taken by the *French*, *Biscainers*, *Portuguese*, *Spaniards*, *Hollanders*, *Hamburghers*, *Bremers*, *Embdeners*, *Scotish*, *Irish*, and *English*, in one year, than the King of *Spain* hath in four years out of the *Indies*. For there are about 20000 Ships and Vessels, and above 400000 Persons set on work, and maintain'd only by the Fishing upon the Coasts of *England*, *Scotland*, and *Ireland*; such an excellent Jewel have neighbouring Princes and States upon his Majesty's Seas.

There were in *Holland* 126000 Mariners twenty years past, since which time their Shipping and Mariners are mightily increased; every Town is grown as great again as they were before the Wars, and beautify'd with an infinite number of sumptuous Buildings, enrich'd with all kind of Merchandizes and Coin; and where they had but one Haven in a Town before the Wars, they have now two or three, and yet not able to hold their Ships, if they were all at home at one time. And they employ'd daily much of their studies to open the Gap of Traffick, and to make fulness of Trade, because it maketh a rich Commonwealth; and they spare for no Cost, nor deny any

any Privileges that may advance Trade, and defend them from their Enemies, whereby they prevail greatly.

These Herrings are sent Southward, by 20, 30, or 40 Last in a Ship, and make rich Return for Herrings, with Oil, Wine, Prunes, Hony, Wool, and such-like Commodites, as *France*, *Spain*, and *Portugal* yield, with much Coin.

For the *Straits* they load 60 or 70 Last of Red Herrings in a Ship, returning for Herrings, Velvets, Sattens, and all manner of Silks, Allums, Currants, and such Wares as those parts yield, with much Coin.

Into the East Countries they load 50 or 60 Last of Herrings in a Ship, making up their Lading with *French* and *Italian* Merchandize, which they brought home for Herrings; and return for Herrings from the East Countries, Corn, Wax, Flax, Hemp, Pitch, Tar, Soap-ashes, Iron, Copper, Deal, Clapboard, Wainscot, Masts, Timber for Houses, Shipping, Waterworks, *Polish* Dollars, and *Hungary* Guilders.

Upon the River of *Rhine* towards *Weesel*, and *Cologn*, and *Frankfort*, other Vessels call'd Lurdains, drawn up with Horses, containing 3, 400, and some 5 and 600 Tuns a-piece. The Skippers have no other Houses with their Wives and Children to dwell in, and are born in them, and go always with them. These Vessels carry up 50 or 60 Last of Herrings a-piece, and Barrel'd Fish, and store of Salt upon Salt, returning for the same Commodities, Iron, Steel, Glass, Milstones, Rhenish Wines, Battery, Plate for Harness, with other Munition; Silks, Velvets, Buratoes, Rash, Fustians, and other Commodities, from *Frankfort* Mart, and other places of *Germany*; as those Parts yield store of Cassiars, Guilders and rich Dollars. The same kind of Vessels pass up to *Lukeland* in like sort, and these do make but one Voyage in a year, but very rich.

To *Brabant* and *Flanders* they load 20 and 30 Last of Herrings in a Ship, returning for the same most part Coin, some quantity of Tapistry, Says, and *Hulst* Hops.

Besides, of those Herrings and Fish taken in his Majesty's Seas (and none other) are vented in great abundance into *Grecia*, *Alexandria*, *Venice*, *Leghorn*, and all over the *Mediterranean Seas*, and other parts even as far as *Brazil*.

Into the East Kingdoms and Dukedoms, the *Hollanders* vent above 100000 Last in a year, and we not 80 Last. At *Roan* this last year we had not 80 Last, and the *Hollanders* had and sold there 3000 Last, and so in other parts accordingly.

Thus are we eaten out of Trade, and the Bread taken out of our mouths in our own Seas, and the great Customs carry'd from his Majesty's Coffers to foreign Princes and States, by the

the greatneſs of their Buſſes, and the multitudes they take 19 Weeks before our great Fiſhing begins at *Yarmouth*, and our Fiſhing laſteth but 7 Weeks with ſmall Crayets and Gobles, where their great Buſſes continue the Herring-Fiſhing 26 Weeks together.

So it appears how they make the Commodities of other Nations ſerve their turns to enrich themſelves, and increaſe their Shipping and Mariners, and to ſet their People on work to good benefit, to enlarge their Cities and Towns, and to ſtrengthen and fortify themſelves exceedingly; and what an infinite ſtore of Wealth they bring into that ſmall Country, having ſo ſlender a foundation as Fiſhermen, is admirable to behold.

Thus they make their Landmen Seamen, their Seamen Fiſhermen, their Fiſhermen Mariners, Mariners Merchants, and of their Merchants Stateſmen, to govern and make their Country proſper by long experience.

It followeth, that one Buſs of 100 or 80 Tuns imployeth three Ships, ſets on work and maintaineth both at Sea and Land above 400 Perſons, and 30 ſeveral Trades and Occupations; that it may evidently appear how the 1000 Sail of Pinks, Welboats, and Doggerboats, and their 2000 great Buſſes, do ſet on work 200000 Perſons, and 7200 Sail of Ships of the *Hollanders*, by Fiſhing upon his Majeſty's Coaſts.

Firſt, She ſets on work in her own Hull, within her ſelf, of Mariners and Fiſhermen 40.

Secondly, She imployeth three Ships beſides her ſelf, one to fetch home Salt into their own Country, another to carry forth Barrels and Salt into her at Sea, and to bring her Herrings back into her own Country; and the third, to tranſport her Herrings beyond the Seas: and in three Ships and Buſſes 100 Mariners are imploy'd. Thus are three Ships and 100 Perſons buſied at Sea by one Buſs.

Thirdly, At Land of Spinners and Hemp-winders to make Cables and Cordage, likewiſe Yarn Twine, and Thred for the making of Nets and Lines, Weavers to make Sail-cloth, Viewers, Packers, Tellers, Dreſſers, Couchers to make the Herrings lawful Merchandizes; Tanners to tan their Nets and Sails, Saltmen to make Salt upon Salt, Coopers in great abundance to make Barrels, Block and Bowl-Makers for Ships, Porters, Keelmen, Lightermen, and Labourers to be imploy'd in carrying and removing; as alſo Hewers and Squarers of Timber, Sawyers of Planks, Carpenters, Shipwrights, Smiths, Sledgmen, Carmen, Boatmen, Brewers, Bakers, and a number of other perſons, too tedious to repeat.

The Sailsmen and the Mariners, with divers others, depending upon this unsearchable business, there cannot be less than 200; so that with the former, there are 300 Persons, and three Ships set on work by one Buss.

And yet besides all these that work, they have their Wives, Children, and Families hardly to be numbred, that neither do nor can work, and yet are maintain'd, and live wealthily out of this one Buss; the Merchants, Sailsmen, Owners of Ships, Masters, Mariners and Fishermen cannot deny this.

I have seen of *English*, *Scotish*, *French*, *Hollanders*, *Embdeners*, *Bremers*, *Hamburghers*, and others, near 3000 Sail fishing at one time, upon the Coast of *Scotland*, *Shotland*, *Orkney*, *Cattney*, *North-farrel*, *Fowl-Isle*, and divers other places.

All the Busses of *Holland*, *France*, *Embden* and *Hamborough* have their first Lading of Herrings near *Baughawanes*; and above 1000 Sail of Pinks, Welboats, Doggerboats take Cod, Ling, and other Fish there. Furthermore, All the great Staple-Ling, called *Holland* Ling, taken only by the *Hollanders*, are gotten about these Isles, wherewith they serve all Christendom.

From the Staple near *Berwick*, all along the Coast of *England* to the *Thames* Mouth, are innumerable shoals, and variety of Fish; besides the multitude of Cods, Lings and Herrings, as Mackerels, Whitings, Haddock, Soals, Thornback, Floith, Scate, Brett, Gurnet, Turbutt, Plaice, Congers, Butts, and others innumerable.

From the *Thames* Mouth, all over the Coasts of *Kent*, *Sussex*, *Hampshire*, *Wiltshire*, and *Dorsetshire*, not such store of Cod, Ling, and Herrings; yet the like variety of other Fish (and more) as the eyes of the Fishmongers of *London*, the Country, and their Fishermen, can testify.

All over the Coasts of *Devonshire* and *Cornwall*, exceeding great shoals and variety of Fish, with Pilchards and Herrings; the last year in *June*, such multitudes of Herrings came so near the Shoar of *Claverly-Key*, and all over those places, that the People went with that small provision of Nets they had, and took and drew them up the Land in such plenty, that they were sold for 4 *s.* the Thousand, the number of a Barrel; and were such store, that they gave them to their Hogs to eat, and buried the rest in the ground, for lack of Salt and Barrels to preserve them.

Also about 20 Miles from thence, there was abundance of Herrings spread the Seas; but the People took no more than they could spend presently, for lack of provision to take and preserve them; of which there is great want about *England*.

From

From the Mouth of *Severn*, round about the Coaſt of *Wales*, *Hollihead*, *Weſtcheſter*, *Leverpool*, and ſo along the Coaſts of *England* to *Scotland*, there is ſtore and variety of Fiſh.

All over the Coaſt of *Ireland*, *Galloway*, *Slego*, and the Coaſts of *Connaught* to *Balliſhannon*, the *Band*, and the North of *Ireland*, *Longford*, *Karickfergus*, and *Strengford*, there is ſtore and variety of Fiſh; beſides the multitude of Cods, Lings, Herrings, Salmons, Seals, Porpoſes, Wherpool, and Dogfiſh.

In the Mouth of *Ireland*, not far from *Dunegal*, there are ſuch multitudes of Herrings, that it is hardly to be believed, ſo big and large, that three Herrings make a Yard in length. From *Carlingford* to *Dundalk*, the *Bay* of *Dublin*, and *Warford*, *Waterford*, *Bear-haven*, *Crook-haven*, and ſo round about the Coaſt of *Ireland*, the like variety, and Fiſh in abundance.

The *French*, *Hollanders*, *Embdeners*, *Bremeners*, *Hamburgers*, and others, fiſh upon the Coaſt of *England*, *Scotland*, and *Ireland*: and this is the difference between them and us, they go forth in *June* to ſeek the Shoals of Herrings; and having found them, do dwell amongſt them, coming along with them until *November*, taking them in great abundance; and we ſtay till the Herrings come home to our own Coaſt, and ſome time ſuffer them to paſs by us before we look out, and ſo loſe God's Bleſſing.

All theſe Nations do beat upon all his Majeſty's Coaſts for Fiſh, with great Ships take and carry away innumerable Riches, when our little Boats, Crayers, and Cobles, dare not look out at Sea but in fair Weather (for in foul Weather the Sea ſwalloweth them up) neither dare they fiſh far from the Shore in fair Weather, their Boats are ſo ſlender and ſlight.

The People of *Ireland*, and round about the Coaſts of *England*, after they have been at Sea, and brought home their Veſſels full of Fiſh, will not go to Sea again for more till thoſe be ſpent, and they in debt, till Neceſſity compels them, unleſs it be ſome few, and they proſper; yet they are loth to take too much, leſt it ſhould be too cheap, for they never ſeek other Markets but their own: and our Fiſhermen go to Sea over-night to take Fiſh to ſerve the Markets the next day, and ſome at three a Clock in the morning go to fetch Fiſh, and yet return home at nine a Clock in the ſame morning, to ſerve their Market with their Boats full, laden with Cod and Ling, and other Fiſh, and then to the Alehouſe, drinking day and night, till all be ſpent, and they in debt, and can be no longer truſted, and then to Sea again for more. This is the life of theſe people, where great Riches are to be gotten.

 Such

Such an excellent Benefit hath God sent his Majesty and his Kingdoms; as, let all the Kingdoms in Christendom be put together, they are not able to compare with the Fishing upon these Coasts, nor yet the *Spanish Indies*: I speak it knowingly.

And further, Let all the Mines of these Kingdoms, as Lead, Tin, Iron, Copper, Allum, yea, Cloth and Wool, be put together; yet, the Fishing will do more good to his Majesty's Kingdoms than all these, in these four Points.

First, For the Augmentation, Maintenance, and Increase of Navigation and Mariners, which hath ever been held a special Jewel for *England*.

Secondly, In bringing in to his Majesty and Kingdoms, great Riches of all kinds, and making such strength of Ships and Mariners, as will make all Nations of the World to vail the Bonnet to *England*.

Thirdly, For the bringing in, and making Imployment for all People, both young and old; for the keeping of them from begging and stealing, and other disorders: And hereby his Majesty shall make exceeding great Trade and Traffick within this Land, upon the Seas, as the like hath never been effected by any King of *England* for the general Good.

Fourthly, For the bringing in, and making all things plenty, and causing many Store-houses in *England* to be erected and filled full of Fish, to serve our selves, and transport into other Kingdoms; like as *Blackwell-Hall* in *London*, and other places in *England* are with Cloth, which continually are emptied, and yet are always filled.

It is most evident true (God be thanked) that there is Fish and Herrings enough, and Vent enough for us all, if we had as many Busses as they; for the 20 hundred great Busses belonging to *Holland*, *France*, *Embden*, and *Hamborough*, and above 200 new Busses which they build and increase yearly, (all not able to serve Christendom with Fish and Herrings) they are scarce and dear in most Foreign Kingdoms in *Lent*; and afterwards few or none to be had until *August*. For in the East and North-East Regions, and so in most Foreign Kingdoms and Dukedoms, the Herrings are every day's meat Winter and Summer, as well to make them drink as to suffice their Appetites; in such exceeding request are the Herrings, that there is great Utterance for them in all Parts through Christendom, and in the Heathen Countries: So that if we had 20 Score Busses, and increase them to 20 Hundred; yet is there Vent enough, and Herrings enough for us all to take upon his Majesty's Coasts, God continue it.

And

And for as much as God hath sent this excellent Blessing to his Majesty above all other Kings; and that this huge quantity of Fish and Herrings do offer themselves to his Majesty's Kingdoms beyond all Nations; and that it is manifest that the Trade of Fishing is Work-master to all other Trades, and by that means the *Dutch* increase their Farthings to Pounds, and their Pounds to Thousands; and what fruitfulness is in their Country? And not a Beggar there, every one getting his own Living, is admirable to behold; that the Poor man, tho he be Blind, and have but one Hand, will get his own Living by turning the Wheel for making Cables and Cordage; and another that has not one Leg, will get his own Living, sitting on a Seat, with Knitting, and making of Nets and Hooks; every Boy and Wench, from 10 and 12 years, and upwards, will get their own Living by Winding Hemp, Spinning Yarn, making Twine and Thread for Nets. So Idleness, Beggary, and Penury, will be driven out of this Land, by commodious Constitutions, as in other places they do; which never any Statute heretofore made could bring to pass, to the great Glory of God, and Comfort of his Majesty's Subjects.

Phenix IX.

The Form and Order of the Coronation of CHARLES the Second, King of Scotland, England, France and Ireland; as it was acted and done at Scoon, the first Day of January, 1651.

The Coronation of CHARLES the Second, &c.

FIrst the King's Majesty, in a Prince's Robe, was conducted from his Bed-chamber, by the Constable on his Right hand, and the Marshal on his Left, to the Chamber of Presence; and there was placed in a Chair, under a Cloth of State, by the Lord of *Angus*, Chamberlain appointed by the King for that day: and there, after a little Repose, the Noblemen, with the Commissioners of Barons and Burroughs, enter'd the Hall, and presented themselves before his Majesty.

Thereafter the Lord Chancellor spoke to the King to this purpose: *Sir, Your good Subjects desire You may be Crowned, as the Righteous and Lawful Heir of the Crown of this Kingdom; That You would maintain Religion, as it is presently professed, and established; Conform to the National Covenant, League and Covenant, and according to Your Declaration at* Dumferling, *in* August *last; Also, that You would be graciously pleas'd to receive them under Your Highness's Pro-*

Protection, to govern them by the Laws of the Kingdom, and to defend them in their Rights and Liberties, by Your Royal Power: offering themselves in most humble manner to Your Majesty, with their Vows, to bestow Land, Life, and what else is in their power for the Maintenance of Religion, for the Safety of Your Majesty's Sacred Person, and Maintenance of Your Crown, which they intreat Your Majesty to accept, and pray Almighty God, that for many years You may happily enjoy the same.

The King made this Answer: *I do esteem the Affections of my good People, more than the Crowns of many Kingdoms; and shall be ready, by God's Assistance, to bestow my Life in their Defence; Wishing to live no longer than I may see Religion, and this Kingdom flourish in all Happiness.*

Thereafter, the Commissioners of Burroughs and Barons, and the Noblemen accompanied his Majesty to the Kirk of *Scoon*, in Order and Rank according to their Quality, two and two. The Spurs being carried by the Earl of *Eglington*. Next, the Sword by the Earl of *Rothes*. Then the Scepter, by the Earl of *Crauford* and *Lindesay*. And the Crown by Marquis of *Argile*, immediately before the King. Then came the King, with the great Constable on his Right hand, and the great Marshal on his Left, his Train being carried by the Lord *Ereskine*, the Lord *Montgomery*, the Lord *Newbottle*, and the Lord *Machlene*, four Earl's eldest Sons, under a Canopy of crimson Velvet, supported by six Earl's Sons; to wit, the Lord *Drummond*, the Lord *Carnegie*, the Lord *Ramsey*, the Lord *Johnstoun*, the Lord *Brechin*, the Lord *Yester*; and the six Carriers supported by six Noblemen's Sons. Thus the King's Majesty enter'd the Kirk.

The Kirk being fitted, and prepared with a Table, whereupon the Honours were laid, and a Chair set in a fitting place for his Majesty's hearing of Sermon, over against the Minister; and another Chair on the other side, where he receiv'd the Crown; before which there was a Bench decently cover'd, as also for Seats about for Noblemen, Barons, and Burgesses. And there being also a Stage in a fit place, erected of 24 Foot square, about four Foot high from the ground, cover'd with Carpets, with two Stairs, one from the West, another to the East: upon which great Stage, there was another little Stage erected, some two Foot high, ascending by two Steps; on which the Throne or Chair of State was set.

The Kirk thus fittingly prepar'd, the King's Majesty entereth the same, accompanied as aforesaid, and first setteth himself in his Chair, for hearing of Sermon.

All being quietly compos'd unto Attention, Mr. *Robert Dowglas*, Moderator of the Commission of the General Assembly, after incalling upon God by Prayer, preach'd the following Sermon.

A SERMON preach'd at *Scoon*, *Jan.* 1. 1651. at the Coronation of CHARLES the Second.

By *Robert Dowglas*, Minister at *Edinburgh*, Moderator of the Commission of the General Assembly.

2 KINGS XI. Verf. 12, 17.

And he brought forth the King's Son, and put the Crown upon him, and gave him the Teſtimony; and they made him King, and anointed him, and they clapt their hands and ſaid, God ſave the King.

And Jehoiada made a Covenant between the Lord, and the King, and the People, that they ſhould be the Lord's people, between the King alſo and the People.

IN this Text of Scripture, you have the Solemn Enthroning of *Joaſh*, a young King, and that in a very troubleſome time; for *Athaliah*, the Mother of *Ahaziah*, had cruelly murder'd the Royal Seed, and uſurp'd the Kingdom by the ſpace of ſix years. Only this young Prince was preſerv'd by *Jehoſheba*, the Siſter of *Ahaziah*, and Wife to *Jehoiada* the High-Prieſt, being hid with her in the Houſe of the Lord all that time.

Good Interpreters do conjecture, tho *Joaſh* be call'd the Son of *Ahaziah*, that he was not his Son by Nature, but by Succeſſion to the Crown. They ſay, that the Race of *Solomon* ceaſed here, and the Kingdom came to the Poſterity of *Nathan*, the Son of *David*. Becauſe, 2 *Chron.* 12. 9. it is ſaid, *The houſe of Ahaziah had no power to keep the Kingdom*, which they conceive to be for the want of Children in that Houſe; and becauſe of the abſurdity and unnaturalneſs of the fact, that *Athaliah* the Grandmother ſhould have cut off her Son's Children. I ſhall not ſtand upon the matter; Only I may ſay, if they were

were *Ahaziah*'s own Children, it was a moſt unnatural and cruel Fact of *Athaliah* to cut off her own Poſterity.

For the Uſurpation, there might have been two Motives. 1. It ſeemeth, that when *Ahaziah* went to Battel, *Athaliah* was left to govern the Kingdom; and her Son *Ahaziah* being ſlain before his return, ſhe thought the Government ſweet, and could not part with it; and becauſe the Royal Seed ſtood in her way, ſhe cruelly deſtroy'd them, that ſhe might reign with the greater freedom. 2. She was earneſt to ſet up a falſe Worſhip, even the Worſhip of *Baal*, which ſhe thought could not be ſo well done, as by cutting off the Royal Race, and getting the ſole Power in her Hand, that ſhe might do what ſhe pleas'd.

The Buſineſs you are about this day is not unlike. You are to inveſt a young King in the Throne in a very troubleſome time; and wicked Men have riſen up, and uſurp'd the Kingdom, and put to Death the late King moſt unnaturally. The like Motives ſeem to have prevail'd with them. 1. Theſe Men by Falſhood and Diſſimulation have gotten Power in their hands, which to them is ſo ſweet, that they are unwilling to part with it: And becauſe the King and his Seed ſtood in their way, they have made away the King, and diſinherited his Children, that the ſole Power might be in their hand. 2. They have a Number of damnable Errors, and a falſe Worſhip to ſet up; and intend to take away the Ordinances of Chriſt, and Government of his Kirk. All this cannot be done, unleſs they have the ſole Power in their hands; and this they cannot have, till the King and his Poſterity be cut off. But I leave this, and come to the preſent Solemnity. There is a Prince to be inthron'd, good *Jehoiada* will have the Crown put upon his Head.

It may be queſtion'd, why they went about this Coronation in a time of ſo great hazard, when *Athaliah* had reign'd ſix years? Had it not been better to have defeated *Athaliah*, and then to have crowned the King? Two Reaſons may be render'd, why they delay not the Coronation. 1. To crown the King, was a Duty they were bound to; Hazard ſhould not make them leave their Duty. They did their Duty, and left the ſucceſs to God. 2. They crowned the young King, to endear the People's Affections to their own native Prince, and to alienate their Hearts from her that had uſurp'd the Kingdom. If they had delay'd, the King being known to be preſerv'd, it might have brought on, not only Compliance with her, but alſo Subjection to her Government, by reſting in it, and being content to lay aſide the righteous Heir of the Crown.

The

The ſame is obſerv'd in our Caſe, and many wonder that you ſhould Crown the King in a dangerous time, when the Uſurpers have ſuch Power in the Land; the ſame Reaſons may ſerve to anſwer for your doing. 1. It is our neceſſary Duty to Crown the King upon all hazards, and to leave the ſucceſs to God. 2. It appeareth now, it hath been too long delay'd. Delay is dangerous, becauſe of the Compliance of ſome, and Treachery of others. If it ſhall be delay'd longer, it is to be fear'd, that the moſt part ſhall ſit down under the ſhadow of the *Bramble*, the deſtroying Uſurpers.

I come to the particular handling of this preſent Text, and to ſpeak from it to the preſent Time: I have read the 12th and 17th Verſes; becauſe of theſe two which meet together, the Crowning of a King, and his renewing the Covenant. Amongſt many particulars which may be handled from the Text, I ſhall confine my ſelf to theſe Five. 1. The Crown; *He put the Crown upon his Head*. 2. The Teſtimony; *He gave him the Teſtimony*. 3. The Anointing; *They Anointed him*. Theſe three are in the 12th Verſe. As for that which is ſpoken of the People's Joy, we ſhall give it a touch when we come to the People's Duty. 4. The Covenant between God, and the King, and the People: *Jehoiada made a Covenant between God and the King, and the People; that they ſhould be the Lord's People*. 5. The Covenant between the King and the People; *Between the King alſo and the People:* both in the 17th Verſe.

Firſt, The Crown is put upon his Head. A Crown is the moſt excellent Badg of Royal Majeſty. To diſcourſe on Crowns in a State-way, I ſhall leave unto States-men, and lay only theſe Three before you of the Crown.

I. In putting on of the Crown, it would be well faſtned. For Kings Crowns are oftentimes tottering; and this is a time wherein they totter. There are two Things which make King's Crowns to totter, Great Sins, and great Commotions and Troubles: take heed of both.

1. There are many Sins upon our King and his Family. Sin will make the ſureſt Crown, that ever Men ſet on, to totter. The Sins of former Kings have made this a tottering Crown. I ſhall not inſiſt here, ſeeing there hath been a ſolemn Day of Humiliation through the Land, on *Thurſday* laſt, for the Sins of the Royal Family. I wiſh the Lord may bleſs it; and deſire the King be truly humbled for his own Sins, and the Sins of his Father's Houſe, which have been great. Beware of putting on theſe Sins with the Crown; for if you put them on, all the Well-wiſhers to a King, in the Three Kingdoms, will not be able to hold on the Crown, and keep

it

it from tottering; yea, from falling. Lord, take away the Controversy with the Royal Family, that the Crown may be fastned sure upon the King's Head, without falling or tottering.

2. Troubles and Commotions in a Kingdom, make Crowns to totter. A Crown at the best, and in the most calm Times, is full of Trouble; which if it were well weigh'd by Men, there would not be such hunting after Crowns. I read of a great Man who, considering the Trouble and Care that accompanied a Crown, said, He would not take it up at his Foot, tho he might have it for taking. Now if a Crown at the best be so full of Troubles, what shall one think of a Crown at the worst, when there are so great Commotions, wherein the Crown is directly aim'd at? Surely it must be a tottering Crown at the least, especially when former Sins have brought on these Troubles. As the remedy of the former is true Humiliation, and turning unto God; so the remedy of the latter, is *Psal.* 21. 3. (speaking of *David's* Crown) *Thou settest a Crown of pure Gold upon his Head.* God set on *David's* Crown; and therefore it was setled, notwithstanding of many Troubles. Men may set on Crowns, and they may be thrown off again: But when God setteth them on, they will be fast. Enemies have touched the Crown of our King, and casten it off in the other Kingdom, and have made it totter in this Kingdom. Both the King who is to be crown'd, and you who are to crown him, should deal earnestly with God, to set the Crown on the King's Head, and to keep it on against all the Commotions of this Generation. 2. A King should esteem more of the People he reigneth over, than of his Crown: Kings use to be so taken up with their Crowns, that they despise their People. I would have a King following Christ, the King of his People, who saith of them, *Isa.* 62. 3. *Thou shalt be a Crown of Glory in the hand of the Lord, and ā Royal Diadem in the hand of thy God.* Christ counteth his People his Crown and Diadem; so should a King esteem the People of the Lord, over whom he ruleth, to be as his Crown and Diadem; take away the People, and a Crown is but an empty Symbol. 3. A King, when he getteth his Crown on his Head, should think at the best, it is but a fading Crown. All the Crowns of Kings are but fading Crowns; therefore they should have an eye upon that *Crown of Glory that fadeth not away*, 1 *Pet.* 5. 4. and upon a *Kingdom that cannot be shaken*, *Heb.* 12. 28. That Crown and Kingdom belongeth not to Kings as Kings, but unto Believers; and a believing King hath this comfort, that *when he hath endured a while, and been tried, he shall receive the Crown of Life, which the Lord hath promised to them that love him.*

II. The

II. The ſecond Thing in this Solemnity, is the *Teſtimony*; by this is meant the Law of God, ſo call'd, becauſe it teſtifieth of the Mind and Will of God. It was commanded, *Deut.* 17. 18, 19. *When the King ſhall ſit upon the Throne of his Kingdom, he ſhall write a Copy of the Book of the Law, and it ſhall be with him, that he may read therein all the days of his life.* The King ſhould have the *Teſtimony* for theſe three main Uſes.

1. For his Information in the Way of God, *Deut.* 17. 19. This Uſe of the King's having the Book of the Law is expreſſed, *That he may learn to fear the Lord his God:* The Reading of other Books may do a King good for Government, but no Book will teach him the Way of Salvation, but the Book of God. Chriſt biddeth *ſearch the Scriptures, for in them ye think to have eternal life, and they teſtify of me*, Joh. 5. 39. He is *a bleſſed Man who meditateth in the Law of the Lord day and night*, Pſal. 1. 1. King *David* was well acquainted herewith, as appeareth, *Pſal.* 119. Kings ſhould be well exerciſed in Scripture. It is reported of *Alphonſus*, King of *Aragon*, that he read the Bible fourteen times, with Gloſſes thereupon. I recommend to the King, to take ſome Hours for reading Holy Scripture: It will be a good means to make him acquainted with God's Mind, and with Chriſt a Saviour.

2. For his direction in Government. Kings read Books that they may learn to govern well, which I condemn not; but all the Books a King can read, will not make him govern to pleaſe God, as this Book; I know nothing that is good in Government, but a King may learn it out of the Book of God. For this Cauſe *Joſhua* is commanded, *Joſh.* 1. 8. *That the Book of the Law ſhall not depart out of his mouth*; and he is commanded *to do according to that which is written therein.* He ſhould not only do himſelf that which is written in it, but do and govern his People according to that is written in it. King *David* knew this Uſe of the Teſtimony, who ſaid, *Pſal.* 119. 24. *Thy Teſtimonies are my delight, and my Counſellors.* The beſt Counſels that ever a King getteth, are in the Book of God; yea, the Teſtimonies are the beſt and ſureſt Counſellors: becauſe, altho King's Counſellors be never ſo wiſe and truſty, yet they uſe not to be ſo free with a King as they ought: But the Scripture will tell Kings very freely both their Sin and their Duty.

3. For Preſervation and Cuſtody. The King is *Cuſtos utriuſque Tabulæ*; the Keeper of both Tables: Not that he ſhould take upon him the Power to diſpenſe the Word of God, or to diſpenſe with it: But that he ſhould preſerve the Word of God, and the true Religion according to the Word of God, pure, intire, and uncorrupted, within his Dominions, and tranſmit them ſo to Poſterity; and alſo be careful to ſee his Subjects

Subjects observe both Tables, and to punish the Transgressors of the same.

III. The third Thing in this Solemnity is, the Anointing of the King. The Anointing of Kings was not absolutely necessary under the Old Testament; for we read not that all the Kings of *Judah* and *Israel* were Anointed. The *Hebrews* observe, that Anointing of Kings was used in three Cases.

1. When the first of a Family was made King, as *Saul, David*. 2. When there was a Question for the Crown, as in the Case of *Solomon* and *Adonijah*. 3. When there was an Interruption of the Lawful Succession by Usurpation, as in the Case of *Joash*, there is an Interruption by the Usurpation of *Athaliah*; therefore he is Anointed. If this Observation hold, as it is probable, then it was not absolutely necessary under the Old Testament; and therefore far less under the New.

Because it may be said, That in our Case there is an Interruption by Usurpation, let it be consider'd, That the Anointing under the Old Testament was Typical; altho all Kings were not Types of Christ, yet the Anointing of Kings, Priests, and Prophets, was Typical of Christ, and his Offices: But Christ being now come, all these Ceremonies cease; and therefore the Anointing of Kings ought not to be us'd in the New Testament.

If it be said, Anointing of Kings hath been in use among Christians, not only Papists, but Protestants; as in the Kingdom of *England*, and our late King was Anointed with Oyl. It may be reply'd, They who us'd it under the New Testament, took it from the *Jews*, without warrant. It was most in use with the Bishops of *Rome*, who, to keep Kings and Emperors subject to themselves, did swear them to the Pope, when they were Anointed, (and yet the *Jewish* Priests did never swear Kings to themselves) As for *England*, altho the Pope was casten off, yet the Subjection of Kings to Bishops was still retain'd; for they Anointed the King, and sware him to the Maintenance of their Prelatical Dignity. They are here who were Witnesses at the Coronation of the late King. The Bishops behoved to perform that Rite, and the King behoved to be sworn to them. But now, by the Blessing of God, Popery and Prelacy are remov'd: The Bishops, as Limbs of Antichrist, are put to the Door; let the Anointing of Kings with Oyl go to the Door with them, and let them never come in again.

The Anointing with material Oyl, maketh not a King the Anointed of the Lord, for he is so without it. He is the Anointed of the Lord, who by the Divine Ordinance and Appointment is a King, *Isa.* 45. 1. God called *Cyrus* his Anointed; yet

yet we read not that he was Anointed with Oyl. Kings are the Anointed of the Lord, becauſe by the Ordinance of the Lord, their Authority is ſacred and inviolable. It is enough for us to have the Thing, tho we want the Ceremony; which being laid aſide, I will give ſome Obſervations of the Thing.

1. A King being the Lord's Anointed, ſhould be thinking upon a better Unction, even that Spiritual Unction wherewith Believers are Anointed, which you have 1 *John* 2. 27. *The Anointing ye have received of him, abideth in you.* And 2 *Cor.* 1. 21. *He that hath anointed us, is God, who hath alſo ſealed us.* This Anointing is not proper to Kings, but common to Believers. Few Kings are ſo Anointed. A King ſhould ſtrive to be a good Chriſtian, and then a good King: The Anointing with Grace, is better than the Anointing with Oyl. It is of more Worth for a King to be the Anointed of the Lord with Grace, than to be the greateſt Monarch of the World without it.

2. This Anointing may put a King in mind of the Gifts, wherewith Kings ſhould be indu'd, for diſcharge of the Royal Calling. For Anointing did ſignify the Gifts of Office. It is ſaid of *Saul*, when he was anointed King, as 1 *Sam.* 10. 9. *God gave him another heart.* And Chap. 11. 6. *The Spirit of God came upon him.* It is meant, of a heart for his Calling, and a ſpirit of Ability for Government. It ſhould be our deſire this day, that our King may have a Spirit for his Calling, as the Spirit of Wiſdom, Fortitude, Juſtice, and other Princely Endowments.

3. This Anointing may put Subjects in mind of the Sacred Due of the Authority of a King. He ſhould be reſpected as the Lord's Anointed. There are divers ſorts of Perſons that are Enemies to the Authority of Kings: As, 1. *Anabaptiſts*, who deny there ſhould be Kings in the New Teſtament. They will have no Kings, nor Civil Magiſtrate. 2. The late *Photinians*, who ſpeak reſpectfully of Kings and Magiſtrates, but they take away from them their Power, and the Exerciſe of it in the Adminiſtration of Juſtice. 3. Theſe who riſe againſt Kings in open Rebellion, as *Abſalom* and *Sheba*, who ſaid, *What have we to do with* David, *the Son of* Jeſſe? *To your Tents, O* Iſrael. 4. They who do not rebel openly, yet they deſpiſe a King in their heart, like the Sons of *Belial*, 1 *Sam.* 10. laſt, who ſaid of *Saul*, after he was anointed King, *Shall this Man ſave us? And they deſpiſed him, and brought him no Preſents.*

All theſe meet in our preſent Age. 1. *Anabaptiſts*, who are againſt the Being of Kings, are very riſe: You may find, to your great Grief, a great Number of them in that Army, that have unjuſtly invaded the Land, who have trampled upon the

the Authority of Kings. 2. There are also of the second sort, who are secretly *Photinians* in this Point; they allow of Kings in Profession, but they are against the Exercise of their Power in the Administration of Justice. 3. A third sort are in open Rebellion, even all that Generation which are risen up, not only against the Person of the King, but Kingly Government. 4. There is a fourth who profess they acknowledg a King, but despise him in their heart, saying, *Shall this Man save us?* I wish all had *David's* Tenderness, whose *heart smote him when he did but cut off the lap of Saul's garment*; that we may be far from cutting off a lap of that just Power and Greatness which God hath allowed to the King, and we have bound our selves by Covenant not to diminish.

I have gone through the three Particulars contain'd in *ver.* 12. I come to the other two in *ver.* 17. which appertain also to this day's Work: For our King is not only to be crowned, but to renew a Covenant with God and his People, and to make a Covenant with the People. Answerable hereto, there is a twofold Covenant in the Words; one between God, and the King and the People; God being the one Party, the King and the People the other. Another between the King, and the People; the King being the one Party, the People the other. The Covenant with God is the fourth Particular propounded to be spoken of. The Sum of the Covenant ye may find 2 *Kings* 23. 3. in *Josiah* his renewing the Covenant, *To walk after the Lord, and keep his Commandments and Testimonies with all thy heart, and to perform the words of the Covenant.* The renewing of the Covenant was after a great Defection from God, and the setting up of false Worship. The King and the People of God bound themselves before the Lord, to set up the true Worship, and to abolish the false. *Scotland* hath a preference in this before other Nations. In time of Defection they have renew'd a Covenant with God to reform all: And because the King, after a great Defection in that Family, is to renew the Covenant, I shall mention some Particulars from the League and Covenant.

1. We are bound to maintain the *True Reform'd Religion* in Doctrine, Worship, Discipline and Government establish'd in this Kingdom, and to endeavour the Reformation of Religion in the other two Kingdoms, according to the Word of God, and the Example of the best Reformed Kirks. By this Article the King is oblig'd, not only to maintain Religion as it is establish'd in *Scotland*, but also to endeavour the Reformation of Religion in his other Kingdoms: The King should consider well, when it shall please God to restore him to his

 Govern-

Government there, that he is bound to endeavour the Establishment of the Work of Reformation there, as well as to maintain it here.

2. According to the second Article, the King is bound, without respect of persons, to extirpate *Popery*, *Prelacy*, *Superstition*, *Heresy*, *Schism* and *Prophaneness*, and whatsoever shall be found contrary to Sound Doctrine, and the Power of Godliness; and therefore *Popery* is not to be suffer'd in the Royal Family, nor within his Dominions: *Prelacy*, once pluckt up by the root, is not to be permitted to take root again; all *Heresy* and *Error* whatsoever must be opposed by him to the utmost of his power; and by the Covenant the King must be far from Toleration of any false Religion within his Dominions.

3. As the People are bound to maintain the King's Person and Authority in the Maintenance of the True Religion and Liberties of the Kingdom: So the King is bound with them to maintain the Rights and Privileges of the Parliament, and Liberties of the Subjects, according to the third Article.

4. We are bound to discover, and to bring unto condign Punishment all such as have been, or shall be, *Incendiaries*, *Malignants*, or *evil Instruments*, in hindering the Reformation of Religion, dividing the King from the People, or one of the Kingdoms from another, or making any Faction or Parties amongst the People. Hereby the King is bound to have an eye upon such, and neither allow of them, nor comply with them, but to concur according to his power to have them censured and punished, as is express'd in the fourth Article. I shall sum up all this, That a King entring in Covenant with God should do as Kings did of old, when they entred into Covenant; they and their People went on in the Work of Reformation, as appeareth here, verse 8. *And all the people of the Land went into the house of Baal, and brake it down*, &c. And Godly *Josiah*, when he entred in Covenant, made a thorow Reformation. There is a fourfold Reformation in Scripture, and contain'd in the League and Covenant. 1. A Personal Reformation. 2. A Family-Reformation. 3. A Reformation of Judicatories. 4. A Reformation of the whole Land. Kings have had their hand in all the four, and therefore I recommend them to our King.

1. A Personal Reformation. A King should reform his own Life, that he may be a Pattern of Godliness to others; and to this he is tied by the Covenants. The Godly Reformers of *Judah* were Pious and Religious Men. A King should not follow *Machiavel* his Counsel, who requireth not that a Prince should be truly Religious, but saith, that a shadow of it, and external Simulation are sufficient: A devilish Counsel, and it

it is just with God to bring a King to the shadow of a Kingdom, who hath but the shadow of Religion. We know that dissembling Kings have been punish'd of God; and let our King know, that no King but a Religious King can please God. *David* is highly commended for Godliness. *Hezekiah*, a Man eminent for Piety. *Josiah*, a young King, commended for the Tenderness of his Heart, when he heard the Law of the Lord read: He was much troubled before the Lord, when he heard the Judgments threatned against his Father's House and his People. It is earnestly wish'd, that our King's Heart may be tender, and he truly humbled before the Lord for the Sins of his Father's House, and of the Land; and for the many Evils that are upon that Family, and upon the Kingdom.

2. A Family-Reformation. The King should reform his Family after the Example of Godly Kings. *Asa*, when he entred in Covenant, spared not his Mother's Idolatry. The House of our King hath been much defiled by Idolatry. The King is now in Covenant, and to renew the Covenant, let the Royal Family be reform'd; and that it may be a Religious Family, wherein God will have pleasure, let it be purged, not only of Idolatry, but of Prophaneness and Looseness, which hath abounded in it. Much hath been spoken of this matter, but little hath been done in it. Let the King and others, who have charge in that Family, think it lieth upon them as a duty to purge it. And if you would have a Family well purg'd and constitute, take *David* for a Pattern, in the purgation and constitution of his, Psalm 10. *The froward heart, wicked persons and slanderers he will have far from him, but his eyes are upon the faithful of the Land, that they may dwell with him.* If there be a Man better than the other in the Land, he shall be for the King and his Family: Ye may extend this Reformation to the Court. A prophane Court is dangerous for a King; it hath been observ'd as a provoking Sin in *England*, which hath drawn down Judgment upon King and Court, as appeareth this day. It is to be wish'd that such were in the Court, as *David* speaketh of in that *Psalm*. Let the King see to it, and resolve with *David*, Psal. 101. 7. That *he who worketh deceit, shall not dwell within his house: and he who telleth lies, shall not tarry in his sight.*

3. Reformation in Judicatories. It should be carefully seen to, that Judicatories be reformed; and that Men fearing God, and hating Covetousness, may be placed in them. A King in Covenant should do as *Jehoshaphat* did, 2 *Chron.* 19. 5, 6, 7. *He set Judges in the Land, and said, Take heed what you do: Ye judg not for Men, but for the Lord, who is with you in judgment. Wherefore now let the fear of the Lord be before you*, &c.

4. The Reformation of the whole Land. The King's Eye ſhould be upon it, 2 *Chron.* 19. 4. *Jehoſhaphat went out through the people, from Beerſheba to mount Ephraim, and brought them back to the Lord God of their Fathers.* Our Land hath great need of Reformation; for there is a part of it, that hath ſcarce ever yet found the benefit of it; they are lying without the Goſpel. It will be a good Work for a covenanted King to have a care, that the Goſpel may be preached through the whole Land: Care alſo would be taken, that they who have the Goſpel, may live ſuitably thereto.

If a King would be a thorow Reformer, he muſt be reform'd himſelf, otherways he will never lay Reformation to heart. To make a King a good Reformer, I wiſh him theſe qualifications according to the Truth, and in Sincerity, wherewith they report *Trajan* the Emperor to have been indued. He was, 1. Devote at home. 2. Courageous in War. 3. Juſt in his Judicatories. 4. Prudent in all his Affairs. True Piety, Fortitude, Juſtice, and Prudence, are notable Qualifications in a Prince, who would reform a Kingdom, and reform well.

V. I come now to the fifth and laſt Particular; and that is the Covenant made between the King and the People. When a King is crowned, and received by the People, there is a Covenant or mutual Contract between him and them, containing Conditions mutually to be obſerv'd. Time will not ſuffer to inſiſt upon many Particulars, I ſhall only lay before you three. Firſt, It is clear from this Covenant, That a King hath not abſolute Power to do what he pleaſeth; he is tied to Conditions by virtue of a Covenant. Secondly, It is clear from this Covenant, That a People are bound to obey their King in the Lord. Thirdly, I ſhall preſent the King with directions, for the right Government of the People, who are bound to obey.

I. It is clear, That the King's Power is not abſolute, as Kings and flattering Courtiers apprehend; a King's Power is a limited Power by this Covenant. And there is a threefold Limitation of the King's Power.

1. In regard of Subordination. There is a Power above his, even God's Power, whom he is oblig'd to obey; and to whom he muſt give an account of his Adminiſtration. Ye heard yeſterday that Text, *By me Kings reign*, Prov. 8. 15. Kings have not only their Crowns from God, but they muſt reign according to his Will, which is clear from *Rom.* 13. 4. He is call'd the Miniſter of God: He is but God's Servant. I need not ſtay upon this, Kings and all others will acknowledg this Limitation.

2. In regard of Laws. A King is ſworn at his Coronation, to rule according to the ſtanding receiv'd Laws of the Kingdom. The Laws he is ſworn to, limit him, that he cannot do againſt them, without a ſinful Breach of this Covenant between the King and the People.

3. In regard of Government. The total Government is not upon a King. He hath Counſellors, a Parliament, or Eſtates in the Land, who ſhare in the burden of Government. No King ſhould have the ſole Government. It was never the mind of theſe, who receiv'd a King to rule them, to lay all their Government upon him, to do what he pleaſeth, without controulment. There is no Man able alone to govern all. The Kingdom ſhould not lay that upon one Man, who may eaſily miſcarry. The Eſtates of the Land are bound in this Contract, to bear a burden with him.

Theſe Men who have flatter'd Kings, to take unto them an abſolute Power to do what they pleaſe, have wronged Kings and Kingdoms. It had been good, that Kings of late had carried themſelves ſo, as this Queſtion of King's Power might never have come in debate; for they have been great loſers thereby: Kings are very deſirous to have things ſpoken and written to hold up their arbitrary and unlimited Power; but that way doth exceedingly wrong them. There is one, a learned Man, I confeſs, who hath written a Book for the Maintenance of the abſolute Power of Kings, call'd *Defenſio Regia*, whereby he hath wrong'd himſelf in his Reputation, and the King in his Government. As for the Fact in taking away the Life of the late King (whatever was God's Juſtice in it) I do agree with him to condemn it, as a moſt unjuſt and horrid Fact, upon their part who did: But when he cometh to ſpeak to the Power of Kings, in giving unto them an abſolute and illimited Power, urging the damnable Maxim, *Quod libet licet*, he will have a King to do what he pleaſeth *impune*, and without controulment; in this I cannot but diſſent from him.

In regard of Subordination, ſome ſay, That a King is countable to none but God: Do what he will, let God take order with it. This leadeth Kings to Atheiſm, let them do what they pleaſe, and take God in their own hand. In regard of Laws, they teach nothing to Kings but Tyranny: And in regard of Government, they teach a King to take an arbitrary Power to himſelf, to do what he pleaſeth without controulment. How dangerous this hath been to Kings, is clear by ſad experience. Abuſe of Power, and Arbitrary Government, hath been one of God's great Controverſies with our Kings and Predeceſſors; God in his Juſtice, becauſe Power hath been abuſed,

abused it hath thrown it out of their hands: And I may confidently ſay, That God's Controverſy with the Kings of the Earth, is for their Arbitrary and Tyrannical Government.

It is good for our King to learn to be wiſe in time, and know, that he receiveth this day a Power to govern, but a Power limited by Contract; and theſe Conditions he is bound by Oath to ſtand to. Kings are deceiv'd, who think that the People are ordain'd for the King, and not the King for the People. The Scripture ſheweth the contrary, *Rom.* 13. 4. *The King is the Miniſter of God for the People's good.* God will not have a King in an arbitrary way to encroach upon the Poſſeſſions of Subjects, *Ezek.* 45. 7, 8. *A portion is appointed for the Prince.* And it is ſaid, *My Princes ſhall no more oppreſs my People; and the reſt of the Land ſhall he give unto the Houſe of* Iſrael, *according to their Tribes.* The King hath his diſtinct Poſſeſſions and Revenues from the People's: He muſt not oppreſs and do what he pleaſeth, there muſt be no Tyranny upon the Throne.

I deſire not to ſpeak much of this Subject. Men have been very tender in meddling with the Power of Kings; yet ſeeing theſe days have brought forth Debates concerning the Power of Kings, it will be neceſſary to be clear in the matter. Extremities would be ſhun'd. A King ſhould keep within the bounds of the Covenant made with the People, in the Exerciſe of his Power. Concerning the laſt, I ſhall propound theſe three to your conſideration.

1. A King abuſing his Power, to the Overthrow of Religion, Laws, and Liberties, which are the very Fundamentals of this Contract and Covenant, may be control'd and oppoſ'd: And if he ſet himſelf to overthrow all theſe by Arms, then they who have power, as the Eſtates of a Land, may and ought to reſiſt by Arms; becauſe he doth, by that Oppoſition, break the very Bonds, and overthroweth all the Eſſentials of this Contract and Covenant. This may ſerve to juſtify the Proceedings of this Kingdom againſt the late King, who in a hoſtile way ſet himſelf to overthrow Religion, Parliaments, Laws, and Liberties.

2. Every Breach of Covenant, wherein a King faileth, after he hath enter'd in Covenant, doth not diſſolve the Bond of the Covenant. Neither ſhould Subjects lay aſide a King for every Breach, except the Breaches be ſuch as overthrow the Fundamentals of the Covenant with the People. Many Examples of this may be brought from Scripture. I ſhall give but one: King *Aſa* enter'd ſolemnly in Covenant with God and his People, 2 *Chron.* 15. After that he falleth in groſs

Tranſ-

Transgressions and Breaches, 2 *Chron.* 16. He associates himself and enter'd in League with *Benhadad* King of *Syria*, an Idolater; he imprison'd *Hanani* the Lord's Prophet, who reprov'd him, and threaten'd Judgment against that Association; and at the same time he oppress'd some of the People: And yet, for all this, they neither lay aside, nor count him an Hypocrite.

3. Private Persons should be very circumspect about that which they do in relation to the Authority of Kings. It is very dangerous for private Men to meddle with the Power of Kings, and the suspending of them from the Exercise thereof. I do ingenuously confess, that I find no Example of it. The Prophets taught not such Doctrine to their People, nor the Apostles, nor the Reformed Kirks. Have ever private Men, Pastors, or Professors, given into the Estates of a Land as their Judgment, unto which they resolv'd to adhere, That a King should be suspended from the Exercise of his Power? And if we look upon those godly Pastors who liv'd in King *James*'s time, of whom one may truly say, more faithful men liv'd not in these last times; for they spar'd not to tell the King his faults to his face; yea, some of them suffer'd Persecution for their Honesty and Freedom: yet we never read nor have heard, that any of those godly Pastors join'd with other private men, did ever remonstrate to Parliament or Estate, as their Judgment, That the King should be suspended from the Exercise of his Royal Power.

II. It is clear from this Covenant, that People should obey their King in the Lord: For as the King is bound by Covenant to make use of his Power to their Good, so are they bound to obey him in the Lord, in the Exercise of that Power. About the People's Duty to the King, take these four Observations.

1. That the Obedience of the People is in subordination to God: for the Covenant is first with God, and then with the King. If a King command any thing contrary to the Will of God, in this case *Peter* saith, *It is better to obey God than Man.* There is a Line drawn from God to the People; they are lowest in the Line, and have Magistrates superior and supreme above them, and God above all. When the King commandeth the People that which is lawful and commanded by God, then he should be obey'd, because he standeth in the right Line under God, who hath put him in his place. But if he command that which is unlawful, and forbidden of God, in that he shall not be obey'd to do it, because he is out of his line. That a King is to be obey'd with this Subordination, is evident from Scripture: Take one place for all, *Rom.* 13. At the

beginning ye have both Obedience urg'd to Superior Power as the Ordinance of God, and Damnation threaten'd against those who resist the lawful Powers.

It is said by some, that many Ministers in *Scotland* will not have King *Jesus*, but King *Charles* to reign. Faithful men are wrong'd by such Speeches. I do not understand these men. For if they think that a *King* and *Jesus* are inconsistent, then they will have no King. But I shall be far from entertaining such Thoughts of them. If they think the doing of a necessary Duty for King *Charles*, is to prefer his Interest to Christ's, this also is an Error. Honest Ministers can very well discern between the Interest of Christ and of the King. I know no Ministers that set up King *Charles* with prejudice to Christ's Interest.

There are three sorts of Persons who are not to be allow'd in relation to the King's Interest. (1.) Such as have not been content to oppose a King in an evil course (as they might lawfully do) but contrary to Covenant, Vows, many Declarations, have cast off Kings and Kingly Government. These are the Sectaries. (2.) They who are so taken up with a King, as they prefer a King's Interest to Christ's Interest; which was the Sin of our Engagers. (3.) They who will have no Duty done to a King, for fear of prejudging Christ's Interest. Those are to be allow'd, who urge Duty to a King in subordination to Christ.

I shall desire that men be real, when they make mention of Christ's Interest: For these three mention'd, profess and pretend the Interest of Christ. The *Sectaries* cover their destroying of Kings with Christ's Interest; whereunto indeed they have had no respect, being Enemies to his Kingdom, and Experience hath made it undeniable. The *Engagers* alledg'd they were for Christ's Interest, but they misplac'd it: Christ's Interest should have gone before, but they drew it after the Interest of a King; which evidenc'd their want of due Respect to Christ's Interest. As for the third, who delay Duty for fear of preferring the King's Interests to Christ, I shall not take upon me to judg their Intentions; I wish they have charity to those who think they may do Duty to a King in subordination to Christ, yea that they ought and should do Duty, whatever mens fear of the prejudice may follow.

If to be against the suspending of the King from the Exercise of his Power, and to be for the crowning of the King according to the publick Faith of the Kingdom, he first performing all that Kirk and State requir'd of him, in relation to Religion and Civil Liberties: If this be, I say, to prefer a *KING* to *CHRIST*, let all men that are unbiass'd be Judges

Judges in the caſe. We ſhall well avow, that we crown a King in ſubordination to God, and his Intereſt in ſubordination to Chriſt's; which we judg not only agreeable to the Word of God, but alſo that we are bound expreſly in the Covenant to maintain the King, in the Preſervation and Defence of the True Religion and Liberties of the Kingdom, and not to diminiſh his juſt Power and Greatneſs.

2. That the Covenant between God, and the King and the People, goeth before the Covenant between the King and the People; which ſheweth that a People's entring Covenant with God, doth not leſſen their Obedience and Allegiance to the King, but increaſeth it, and maketh Obedience firmer: becauſe we are in covenant with God, we ſhould the more obey a covenanted King. It is a great error to think that a Covenant diminiſheth Obedience; it was ever thought cumulative. And indeed true Religion layeth ſtrict Ties upon Men, in doing of their Duty: Rom. 13. 5. *We muſt needs be ſubject, not only for Wrath, but alſo for Conſcience ſake.* A Neceſſity to obey is laid upon all. Many Subjects obey for Wrath, but the Godly obey for Conſcience ſake.

3. That a King covenanted with God, ſhould be much reſpected by his Subjects; they ſhould love him: There is an inbred Affection in the Hearts of the People to their King. In the 12th Verſe it is ſaid, That *the People clap'd their hands for Joy, and ſaid, God ſave the King.* They had no ſooner ſeen their native King inſtall'd in his Kingdom, but they rejoic'd exceedingly, and ſaluted him with Wiſhes of Safety. Whatever be mens Affections or Reſpects this day to our King, certainly it is a Duty lying on us, both to pray for and rejoice in his Safety. The very end that God hath in giving us Kings, maketh this clear, 1 Tim. 2. 1, 2. *That we may live under them in Godlineſs and Honeſty.* And therefore Prayers and Supplications are to be made for all Kings, even for thoſe that are not in covenant, much more for thoſe that are in covenant. You are receiving this day a crowned covenanted King; pray for ſaving Grace to him, and that God would deliver him and us out of the hand of *theſe cruel Enemies*, and bleſs his Government, and cauſe us to live a quiet and peaceable life under him in all Godlineſs and Honeſty.

4. That as the King is ſolemnly ſworn to maintain the Rights of the Subjects againſt Enemies, and is bound to hazard his Life, and all that he hath, for their defence; ſo the People are alſo bound to maintain his Perſon and Authority, and to hazard Life, and all that they have, in defending him.

I ſhall not take the Queſtion in its full latitude, taking in what a People are bound to, in purſuing a King's Right in another

ther Nation; which is not our preſent Queſtion. Our Queſtion is, what a People ſhould do, when a Kingdom is unjuſtly invaded by a foreign Enemy, which ſeeks the Overthrow of Religion, King, and Kingdom? Surely, if Men be ty'd to any Duty to a King and Kingdom, they are ty'd in this caſe. I have two ſorts of Men to meet with here, who are deficient in doing this covenanted Duty: 1. Thoſe who do not act againſt the Enemy. 2. Thoſe who do act for the Enemy.

1. The firſt I meet with, are they who act not, but lie by to behold what will become of all. Three ſorts of men act not for the Defence of an invaded Kingdom: 1*ſt*, Thoſe who withdraw themſelves from publick Counſels, as from Parliament or Committee of Eſtates. This withdrawing is not to act. 2*dly*, Theſe act not, who upon an apprehenſion of the deſperate ſtate of things, do think that all is in ſuch a condition by the prevailing of the Enemy, that there is no Remedy; and therefore that it is beſt, to ſit ſtill and ſee how things go. 3*dly*, They who do not act, upon ſcruple of Conſcience. I ſhall ever reſpect Tenderneſs of Conſcience, and wiſh there be no more but Tenderneſs. If there be no more, men will ſtrive to have their Conſciences well inform'd.

They may be ſuppoſed to ſcruple upon one of theſe grounds. 1. To act in ſuch a Cauſe, for the King's Intereſt: Sure I am, this was a doubt before, but all ſeem'd to agree to act for the King's Intereſt in ſubordination to Chriſt, and this day there is no more ſought. We own the King's Intereſt, only in ſubordination to Chriſt. Or 2. To join to him with ſuch Inſtruments as are Enemies to the work of God. Our Anſwer to the Eſtates Query reſolves, that ſuch ſhould not be truſted: But we do not count theſe Enemies, who profeſs Repentance, and declare themſelves ſolemnly to be for the Cauſe and the Covenant; and do evidence it by their willingneſs to fight for them. If it be ſaid their Repentance is but counterfeit, we are bound to think otherwiſe in Charity, till the contrary be ſeen. No man can judg of the Reality of Hearts; for we have now found by Experience, that men, who have been accounted above all exception, have betray'd their Truſt. If any who have not yet repented of their former courſe ſhould be intruſted, we ſhall be ſorry for it; and plainly ſay, that it ought not to be.

But I think there muſt be more in this, that men ſay they cannot act: For my ſelf, I love not that word in our caſe. It is too frequent, *He cannot act*, and *He cannot act*. I fear there be three ſorts of Perſons lurking under this cover: 1*ſt*, Such as are *Puſillanimous*, who have no courage to act againſt the Enemy. The word is true of them, *They cannot act*, becauſe

the

they dare not act. 2*dly*, Such as are selfish men, serving their *Idol Credit.* He hath been a man of Honour, and now he feareth here will be no credit to fight against the prevailing Enemy; therefore he cannot act, and save his credit. Be who thou wilt that hath this before thee, God shall blast thy Reputation. Thou shalt neither have Honour nor Credit, to do a right turn in God's Cause. 3*dly*, Such as are *Compliers*, who cannot act, because they have a purpose to comply. There are that cannot act in an Army, but they can betray an Army by not acting. There are that cannot act for Safety of a Kingdom, but they do betray it by not acting. In a word, there are those who cannot join to act with those whom they account *Malignants* (I speak not of declar'd and known *Malignants*) but they can join with *Sectaries, open and declared Enemies to Kirk and Kingdom.* I wish Subjects, who are bound to fight for the Kingdom, would lay by that Phrase of not acting, which is so frequent in the mouth of Compliers, and offensive to them who would approve themselves in doing Duty for endanger'd Religion, King, and Kingdom.

That Men may be more clear to act, I shall offer to your Consideration some Passages of Scripture about those who do act against a *common Enemy.*

1. *Judges* 5. There are many reprov'd for lying still, while an Enemy had invaded the Land; as *Reuben* with his Divisions, *Gilead*, *Dan*, and *Asher*, seeking themselves; all are reproved for not joining with the People of God, who were willing to jeopard their Lives against a *mighty oppressing Enemy.* But there is one Passage concerning *Meroz*, ver. 23. which fitteth our purpose; *The Angel of the Lord said, Curse ye* Meroz, *Curse ye bitterly the Inhabitants thereof; they came not to the help of the Lord, to help the Lord against the Mighty.* What this *Meroz* was, is not clear; yet all Interpreters agree, that they had opportunity and power to have join'd with and help'd the People of God, and it is probable they were near the place of the Fight. They are cursed for not coming to the help of the Lord's People. This may be apply'd to these in the Land, who will not help the Lord against the Mighty.

2. Another Passage you have, *Numb.* 23. *Reuben* and *Gad* having a multitude of Cattel, and having seen the Land of *Gilead*, that it was a place for Cattel, they desire of *Moses* and the Princes, that that Land be given them, and they may not pass over *Jordan*, ver. 6, 7. *Moses* reprov'd them in these words; *Shall your Brethren go to War, and shall ye sit still? Wherefore discourage ye the Hearts of the Children of* Israel? *Verse* 16, 17, 18. *Reuben* and *Gad* make their Apology, shewing that they have no such Intention to sit still, only they desire their

their Wives and little ones may ſtay there; they themſelves promiſe to go over *Jordan* armed before *Iſrael*, and not return before they were poſſeſs'd in the Land. Then *Moſes* ſaid unto them, ver. 20, 21, 22. *If you do ſo, then this ſhall be your Poſſeſſion:* but ver. 23. *If you do not ſo, behold ye have ſinned againſt the Lord, and be ſure your Sin ſhall find you out.*

I may apply this to them that cannot act; Will ye ſit ſtill when the reſt of your Brethren are to hazard their Lives againſt the Enemy? We have reaſon to reprove you. If *Moſes*, that faithful Servant of God, was ſtill jealous of *Reuben* and *Gad*, even after their Apology and Promiſe to act (for he ſaith, *if you do not ſo*) have not honeſt and faithful Servants of God ground to be jealous of their Brethren who refuſe to act? Let them apologize what they will for their not acting, I ſay they ſin againſt the Lord, and their Sin ſhall find them out. It will be clearly ſeen upon what intention they do not act.

3. A third Paſſage is in 1 *Sam.* 23. 26. *Saul* hath *David* incloſ'd that he can hardly eſcape; in that very inſtant there cometh a Meſſenger to *Saul*, ſaying, verſe 27. *Haſte thee and come, for the Philiſtines have invaded the Land.* At the hearing of this Meſſage, *verſe* 28. Saul *return'd from purſuing after* David, *and went againſt the Philiſtines.* It is true, the Lord did provide for his Servant *David*'s Eſcape by this means; but if you conſider *Saul*, he took it not ſo. Nothing moved him to leave this Purſuit, but the Condition of the Land, by the invading of an Enemy.

Three things might have mov'd *Saul* to ſtay and purſue *David*.

1. He hath him now in a ſtrait, and hath ſuch advantage, that he might have thought not to come readily by the like.

2. That altho the *Philiſtines* be Enemies, yet *David* is the moſt dangerous Enemy; for he aimeth at no leſs than the Crown. It were better to take Conditions of the Enemy, than to ſuffer *David* to live, and take the Crown.

3. He might have ſaid, If I leave *David* at this time, and fight with the *Philiſtines*, and be beaten, he will get a power in his hand to undo me and my Poſterity. Theſe may ſeem ſtrong Motives, but *Saul* is not moved with any of theſe. The preſent Danger is the *Philiſtines* invading the Land: and this Danger is to be oppoſed, come of the Danger from *David* what will. As if *Saul* had ſaid, I will let *David* alone, I will meet with him another time, and reckon with him; now there is no time for it, the *Philiſtines* are in the Land, let us make haſt againſt them. I wiſh that many of our Countrymen had as great Love to their Country, and as publick a Spirit for it, as this profane King had; then there would not be ſo many Queſtions for acting, as men make this day.

The Objections I have been touching are in men's Thoughts and Heads. First, some say now the Malignants are under, for this Enemy is their Rod, it is best to put them out of having any power. Yea, there are some who would more willingly go to undo those, whom they account Malignants, than against the common Enemy who are wasting the Land. If they had *Saul*'s Resolution, they would say, the *Philistines* are in the Land, let them alone, we will reckon with them at another time; we will now go against the common Enemy.

They have also the second Objection: The Malignants are more dangerous Enemies than the Sectaries. I shall not now compare them at equal distance, and abstract from the present Danger: But I shall compare them in the present posture of Affairs. I am sure the Sectaries having power in their hands, and a great part of the Land in their possession, are far more dangerous than Malignants, who have no power for the present; and therefore the Resolution should be, The Sectaries have invaded the Land, and are destroying it, let us go against them.

The third Objection weigheth much with many; The Malignants being employ'd to fight for their Country, may get such power in their hands, as may hurt the Cause. For answer, 1*st*, The Resolution given to the Query of the Estates, provideth against that; for therein is a Desire that no such Power should be put into their hands. 2*dly*, This Fear goeth upon a supposition that they do not repent their former course. This is an uncharitable Judgment. We are bound to be more charitable of men professing Repentance; for with such we have to do only. And to speak a word by the way, to you who have been upon a malignant course; Little good is expected from you, I pray you be honest and disappoint them. I wish you true Repentance, which will both disappoint them, and be profitable to your selves. 3*dly*, I desire it may be consider'd, whether or not fear of a Danger to come from Men, if they prevail against the common Enemy, being only clothed with a capacity to fight for their Country, be an Argument of rising to oppose a seen and certain Danger coming from an Enemy clothed with Power, and still prevailing. I conceive it ought to be far from any, to hinder Men to defend their Country in such a case. I confess indeed, the Cause which we maintain hath met with many Enemies which have been against it, which require much tenderness. Therefore Men are to be admitted to Trust, with such Exceptions as may keep them out who are still Enemies to the Cause of God, have not profess'd Repentance, renounc'd their former Courses, and declar'd themselves for *Cause and Covenant.* I doubt

doubt not but it shall be found, that the admitting of such to fight in our case, as it standeth, is agreeable to the Word of God, and is not against the former publick Resolutions of Kirk and State.

The second sort of Persons we are to meet with, are such as act for the Enemy against the Kingdom. If they be curs'd who will not come out to help the Lord against the Mighty, what a Curse shall be upon them, who help the Mighty against the Lord, as they do who act for the Enemy? Three ways is the Enemy help'd against the Cause and People of God.

1. By keeping Correspondence with them, and giving them Intelligence: There is nothing done in Kirk or State, but they have Intelligence of it: A baser way hath never been used in any Nation. Your Counsels and Purposes are made known to them. If there be any such here (as I fear there be) let them take this to them, they are of those *who help the Mighty against the Lord*, and the Curse shall stick to them.

2. By strengthening the Enemies hands with Questions, Debates, and Determinations, in Papers tending to the justifying of their unjust Invasion. Whatever hath been mens Intentions in taking that way, yet the thing done by them hath tended to the advantage of the Enemy, and hath divided those who should have been join'd in the Cause, to the great weakning of the Kingdom; and this interpretatively is to act for the Mighty against the Lord.

3. By gross Compliance with the Enemy, and going in to them; doing all the evil Offices they can against their native Kingdom. If *Meroz* was curs'd for not helping, shall not these perfidious Covenant-Breakers, and treacherous Dealers against a distressed Land, be much more accursed for helping and assisting a destroying Enemy, so far as lieth in their power? *Isa.* 31. 3. may be truly apply'd to them who are helping Strangers, Enemies to God, his Kirk and Religion; *Both he that helpeth shall fall, and he that is holpen shall fall down, and they all shall fall together.*

III. The third particular about this Covenant resteth to be spoken of; to wit, some Directions to the King, for the right performing his Duty: whereof I shall give seven.

1. A King meeting with many difficulties in doing of Duty, by reason of strong Corruption within, and many Tentations without, he should be careful to seek God by Prayer for Grace to overcome these Impediments, and for an understanding Heart to govern his People. *Solomon* having in his Option to ask what he would, he ask'd an understanding Heart, to go in and out before his People; knowing that the Government of

of a People was a very difficult work, and needed more than ordinary Understanding. A King a Foe hath many Enemies (as our King hath this day) and a Praying King is a Prevailing King. *Asa* when he had to do with a mighty Enemy, 2 *Chron.* 14. pray'd fervently, and prevail'd. *Jehoshaphat* was invaded with a mighty Enemy, 2 *Chron.* 20. he pray'd and did prevail. *Hezekiah* pray'd against *Senacherib*'s huge Army, and prevail'd, 2 *Chron.* 32.

Sir, you have many Difficulties and Oppositions to meet with: Acquaint your self with Prayer: Be instant with God and he will fight for you. Prayers are not in much request at Court; but a covenanted King must bring them in request. I know a King is burden'd with a multiplicity of Affairs, and will meet with many Diversions: But, Sir, you must not be diverted; take hours and set them apart for that Exercise: Men being once acquainted with your way, will not dare to divert you. Prayer to God will make your Affairs easy all the day. I read of a King of whom his Courtiers said, He spoke oftner with God, than with Men. If you be frequent in Prayer, you may expect the Blessing of the most High upon your self and upon your Government.

2. A King must be careful of the Kingdom which he hath sworn to maintain. We have had many of too private a Spirit, by whom Self-interest hath been prefer'd to the publick. It becometh a King well to be of a publick Spirit, to care more for the Publick than his own Interest. Senates and States have had Motto's written over the doors of the Meeting-places: Over the Senate-House of *Rome* was written, *Ne quid Respublica detrimenti capiat:* I shall wish this may be written over your Assembly-Houses; but there is another which I would have written with it, *Ne quid Ecclesia detrimenti capiat.* Be careful of both; let not Kirk nor State suffer hurt; let them go together. The best way for standing of a Kingdom, is a well-constitute Kirk. They deceive Kings, who make them believe that the Government of the Kirk, I mean Presbyterian Government, cannot sute with Monarchy. They sute well, it being the Ordinance of Christ, rendring to God what is God's, and to *Cæsar* what is *Cæsar*'s.

Sir, Kings who have a tender Care of the Kirk, *Isa.* 41. 3. are call'd *Nursing Fathers.* You would be careful that the Gospel may have free Passage thro the Kingdom, and that the Government of the Kirk may be preserv'd intire, according to your solemn Engagement. The Kirk hath met with many Enemies, as *Papists*, *Prelatists*, *Malignants*, which I pass as known Enemies. But there are two sorts more, who at this time would be carefully look'd on.

1st. *Sectaries*,

1st, *Sectaries*, great Enemies to the Kirk, and to all the Ordinances of Christ, and more particularly to Presbyterian Government, which they have and would have altogether destroy'd. A King should set himself against these, because they are Enemies as well to the King as to the Kirk, and strive to make both fall together.

2dly, *Erastians*, more dangerous Snares to Kings, than *Sectaries*; because Kings can look well enough to these, who are against themselves and their Power, as *Sectaries*, who will have no King; but *Erastians* give more Power to Kings than they should have, and are great Enemies to Presbyterian Government: For they would make Kings believe, that there is no Government but the Civil, and deriv'd from thence; which is a great wrong to the Son of God, who hath the Government of the Kirk distinct from the Civil, yet no ways prejudicial to it, being spiritual, and of another nature. Christ did put the Magistrate out of suspicion, that his Kingdom was prejudicial to Civil Government, affirming, *My Kingdom is not of this world*. This Government Christ hath not committed to Kings, but to the Office-bearers of his House; who in regard of Civil Subjection are under the Civil Power as well as others, but in their Spiritual Administration they are under Christ, who hath not given to any King upon earth the Dispensation of Spiritual things to his People.

Sir, you are in Covenant with God and his People, and are oblig'd to maintain *Presbyterian Government*, as well against *Erastians* as *Sectaries*. I know this *Erastian* Humour aboundeth at Court. It may be some endeavour to make your Reproach upon that, for which God hath punish'd your Predecessors. Be who he will that meddleth with this Government to overturn it, it shall be as heavy to him as the burdensom Stone to the Enemies of the Kirk; *They are cut in pieces, who burden themselves with it*, Zach. 12.

3. A King in Covenant with the People of God, should make much of those who are in Covenant with him; having in high estimation the faithful Servants of Christ, and the godly People of the Land. It is rare to find Kings Lovers of faithful Ministers and pious People. It hath been the fault of our own Kings to persecute the Godly.

(1.) Let the King love the Servants of Christ, who speak the Truth. Evil Kings are branded with this, that they contemn'd the Prophets: 2 *Chron.* 25. when *Amaziah* had taken the Gods of *Seir*, and set them up for his Gods, a Prophet came to him, and reprov'd him, unto whom the King said, *Who made thee of the King's Council? Forbear, lest thou be smitten.* This Contempt of the Prophet's Warning, is a Fore-runner of of following Destruction. Be a careful Hearer of God's Word; take with Reproof, esteem of it, as *David* did, *Psal.* 141. 5. *An excellent Oil, which shall not break the Head.* To make much of the faithful Servants of Christ, will be an Evidence of Reality

(2.) Let the King esteem well of godly Professors. Let Piety be in account. It is a fault very common, that pious Men, because of their conscientious and strict walking, are hated by the Profane, who love to live loosly. It is usual with Profane Men, to labour to bring Kings unto a distaste of the Godly; especially when Men who have profess'd Piety, become scandalous: whereupon they are ready to judg all pious Men to be like them, and take occasion to speak evil of Piety. I fear at this time, when Men who have been commended for Piety, have faln foully, and betray'd their Trust; that men will take advantage to speak against the Godly of the Land. Beware of this, for it's Satan's Policy to put Piety out of request. Let not this move any: Fall who will, Piety is still the same, and pious men will make Conscience both of their ways and trust. Remember they are precious in God's eyes, who will not suffer men to despise them, without their Reward. Sir, let not your Heart be from the Godly in the Land. Whatever hath faln out at this time, I dare affirm, there are very many really Godly Men, who by their Prayers are supporting your Throne.

4. A King should be careful whom he putteth in Places of Trust, as a main thing for the Good of the Kingdom. It is a Maxim, That Trust should not be put in their hands who have oppress'd the People, or have betray'd their Trust. There is a Passage in Story meet for this purpose: One *Septimius Arabinus*, a Man famous, or rather infamous, for Oppression, was put out of the Senate, but re-admitted. About this time *Alexander Severus* being chosen to the Empire, the Senators did entertain him with publick Salutations and Congratulations. *Severus* espying *Arabinus* amongst the Senators, cry'd out, *O Numina! Arabinus non solum vivit, sed in Senatum venit. Ah!* Arabinus *not only liveth, but he is in the Senate.* Out of just Indignation he could not endure to see him As all are not meet for Places of Trust in Judicatories, so all are not meet for Places of Trust in Armies. Men would be chosen, who are godly and able for the Charge.

But there are some who are not meet for Trust: 1. They who are godly, but have no Skill or Ability for the Place. A man may be a truly godly man, who is not fit for such a Place; and no wrong is done to him, nor to Godliness, when the Place is deny'd to him. I wonder how a godly Man can take upon him a Place, whereof he hath no Skill. 2. They who have neither Skill nor Courage, are very unmeet; for if it be a Place of ever so great moment, Faint-heartedness will make them quit it. 3. They who are both skilful and stout, yet are not honest, but perfidious and treacherous, should have no Trust at all.

Of all these we have sad Experience, which should not move you to make choice of profane and godless men, by whom a Blessing is not to be expected; but it should move you to be wary in your Choice. I am confident such may be had, who will be faithful for Religion, King, and Kingdom.

5. There hath been much Debate about the Exercise of the King's Power, yet he is put in the Exercise of his Power, and this day put in a better capacity to exercise it by his Coronation. Many are afraid that the Exercise of his Power shall prove dangerous to the Cause; and indeed I confess there is a ground of fear, when we consider how this Power hath been abus'd by former Kings. Therefore, Sir, make good use of this Power, and see that you rather keep within bounds, than exceed in the Exercise of it. I may very well give such a Counsel, as an old Counsellor gave to a King of *France*. He having spent many years at Court, desir'd to retire into the Country for enjoying privacy fit for his Age; and having obtain'd leave, the King his Master requir'd him to set down and write some Advice of Government, to leave behind him; which he out of modesty declined. The King would not be deny'd, but left with him Pen and Ink, and a Sheet of Paper. He being alone, after some Thoughts wrote with fair and legible Characters in the head of the Sheet, *Modus*; in the middle of the sheet, *Modus*; and in the foot of the sheet, *Modus*; and wrote no more in all the Paper, which he wrap'd up and deliver'd to the King: meaning that the best Counsel he could give him, was, That he should keep temper in all things. Nothing more fit for a young King, than to keep temper in all. Take this Counsel, Sir, and be moderate in the use of your Power. The best way to keep Power, is Moderation in the use of it.

6. The King hath many Enemies, even such as are Enemies to his Family, and to all Kingly Government, and are now in the Bowels of this Kingdom, wasting and destroying. Bestir your self according to Vows and Oaths that are upon you, to be active for the Relief of Christ's Kingdom, born down by them in all the three Kingdoms; and for the Relief of this Kingdom grievously oppress'd by them. We shall earnestly desire, that God would put that Spirit upon our King, now enter'd upon publick Government, which he hath put

upon

upon the Deliverers of his People from their cruel Oppressors.

In ſpeaking of the King's Behaviour to Enemies, one thing I cannot paſs. There is much ſpoken of a Treaty with his Enemy. I am not of the judgment of ſome, who diſtinguiſh a Treaty before Invaſion, and after Invaſion; and ſay, Treating is very lawful before Invaſion, becauſe it is ſuppoſed there is little wrong done; but after Invaſion, when a Kingdom is wrong'd, and put to infinite Loſſes, they ſay a Treaty is to be ſhun'd: But in my judgment a Treaty may be lawful after Invaſion, and Wrongs ſuſtain'd. The end of War is Peace, neither ſhould Deſire of Revenge obſtruct it, providing it be ſuch a Treaty and Peace, as is not prejudicial to Religion, nor to the Safety of the Kingdom, nor to the undoubted Right of the King, nor the League and Covenant whereunto we are ſolemnly engaged.

But I muſt break off this Treaty with a Story related in *Plutarch*. The City of *Athens* was in a great ſtrait, wherein they knew not what to do. *Themiſtocles* in this ſtrait ſaid, he had ſomething wherein to give his Opinion, for the behoof of the State; but he thought it not fit to deliver himſelf publickly. *Ariſtides*, a man of great Truſt, is appointed to hear him privately, and to make an account as he thought meet. When *Ariſtides* came to make his Report to the Senate, he told them, That *Themiſtocles*'s Advice was indeed profitable, but not honeſt; whereupon the People would not ſo much as hear it. There is much whiſpering of a Treaty, they are not willing to ſpeak publickly of it. Hear them in private, and it may be the beſt Advice ſhall be profitable, but not honeſt. If a Treaty ſhould be, let it be both profitable and honeſt, and no Lover of Peace will be againſt it.

7. Seeing the King is now upon renewing of the Covenants, it would be remember'd, that we enter into Covenant, according to our Profeſſion therein, with Reality, Sincerity, and Conſtancy; which are the Qualifications of good Covenanters. Many doubt of your Reality in the Covenant: Let your Sincerity and Reality be evidenc'd by your Stedfaſtneſs and Conſtancy; for many have begun well, but have not been conſtant.

In the Sacred Hiſtory of *Kings*, we find a Note put upon Kings according to their Carriages. One of three Sentences written upon them: 1. Some Kings have this written on them, *He did evil in the ſight of the Lord.* They neither begin well, nor end well. Such a one was *Ahaz* King of *Judah*, and divers others in that Hiſtory. 2*dly*, Others have this written on them, *He did that which was right in the ſight of the Lord, but not with a perfect Heart.* Such a one was *Amaziah* King of *Judah*, 2 Chron. 25. 2. he was neither ſincere nor conſtant: When God bleſs'd him with Victory againſt the *Edomites*, he fell foully from the true Worſhip of God, and ſet up the Gods of *Edom.* 3*dly*, A third Sentence is written upon the godly Kings of *Judah*; *He did right in the ſight of the Lord, with a perfect Heart*, as *Aſa*, *Hezekiah*, *Jehoſhaphat*, and *Joſiah*. They were both ſincere and conſtant. Let us neither have the firſt nor the ſecond, but the third written upon our King; *He did right in the ſight of the Lord, with a perfect Heart.* Begin well, and continue conſtant.

Before I cloſe, I ſhall take leave to lay before our young King two Examples to beware of, and one to follow: The two warning Examples, one of them is in my Text, another in our own Hiſtory.

The firſt Example of *Joaſh*; he began well, and went on in godly Reformation all the days of *Jehoiada:* But it is obſerv'd, 2 *Chron.* 2. 17. after the days of *Jehoiada*, the Princes of *Judah* came and did obeiſance to the King, and he hearkned unto them, *ver.* 18. It appeared they had been at wait till the Death of *Jehoiada*, and took that opportunity to deſtroy the true Worſhip of God, and ſet up falſe Worſhip, flattering the King for that effect: for it is ſaid, *They left the Houſe of the Lord, and ſerved Groves and Idols*; and were ſo far from being reclaim'd by the Prophet of the Lord that was ſent unto them, that they conſpir'd againſt *Zechariah* the Son of *Jehoiada*, who reprov'd them mildly for their Idolatry, and ſtoned him with Stones, and ſlew him at the King's Commandment. And *ver.* 22. it is ſaid, Joaſh *remember'd not the Kindneſs that* Jehoiada *his Father had done to him, but ſlew his Son.*

Sir, take this example for a Warning. You are oblig'd by the Covenant to go on in the Work of Reformation. It may be ſome Great ones are waiting their time, not having opportunity to work for the preſent, till afterward they may make obeiſance, and perſuade you to deſtroy all that hath been done in the Work of God theſe divers years. Beware of it, let no Allurement of Perſuaſion prevail with you to fall from that, which this day you bind your ſelf to maintain.

Another Example I give you, yet in recent memory, of your Grandfather King *James.* He happen'd to be very young, in a time full of Difficulties; yet there was a godly Party in the Land, who did put the Crown upon his Head. And when he came to ſome years, he and his People enter'd in a Covenant with God: He was much commended by godly and faithful Men, comparing him to young *Joſiah* ſtanding at

the

the Altar, renewing a Covenant with God. And he himſelf did thank God, that he was born in a Reformed Kirk, better reform'd than *England*, for they retain'd many Popiſh Ceremonies; yea, better reform'd than *Geneva*, for they keep ſome Holy-days: Charging his People to be conſtant, and promiſing himſelf to continue in that Reformation, and to maintain the ſame. Notwithſtanding of all this, he made a foul Defection: He remember'd not the Kindneſs of them who had held the Crown upon his Head; yea, he perſecuted faithful Miniſters, for oppoſing that courſe of Defection. He never reſted till he had undone Presbyterian Government and Kirk-Aſſemblies, ſetting up Biſhops, and bringing in Ceremonies, againſt which he had formerly given large Teſtimony. In a word, he laid the Foundation, whereupon his Son, our late King, did build much miſchief to Religion all the days of his Life.

Sir, I lay this Example before you the rather, becauſe it is ſo near you, that the Guiltineſs of the Tranſgreſſion lieth upon the Throne and Family, and it is one of the Sins for which you have profeſs'd Humiliation very lately. Let it be laid to heart, take warning, requite not faithful mens Kindneſs with Perſecution; yea, requite not the Lord ſo, who hath preſerv'd you to this time, and is ſetting a Crown upon your Head. Requite not the Lord with Apoſtacy and Defection from a ſworn Covenant, but be ſtedfaſt in the Covenant, as you would give Teſtimony of your true Humiliation for the Defection of thoſe that went before you.

I have ſet up theſe two Examples before you, as Beacons to warn you to keep off ſuch dangerous Courſes, and ſhall add one for Imitation; which, if follow'd, may happily bring with it the Bleſſing of that godly man's adherence to God. The Example is of *Hezekiah, who did that which was right in the ſight of the Lord*; 2 Kings 18. 5, 6. It is ſaid of him, *He truſted in the Lord God of* Iſrael, *and he clave unto the Lord, and departed not from following him, but kept his Commandments.* And *verſe* 7. *The Lord was with him, and he proſper'd whitherſoever he went forth.*

Sir, follow this Example, cleave unto the Lord, and depart not from following him, and the Lord will be with you, and proſper you whitherſoever you go.

To this Lord, from whom we expect a Bleſſing on this day's Work, be Glory and Praiſe for ever. *Amen.*

SERMON being ended, Prayer was made for a Bleſſing upon the Doctrine deliver'd.

The King being to renew the Covenants, firſt the National Covenant, then the ſolemn League and Covenant were diſtinctly read.

After the reading of theſe Covenants, the Miniſter pray'd for Grace to perform the Contents of the Covenants, and for faithful Stedfaſtneſs in the Oath of God; and then (the Miniſters and Commiſſioners of the General Aſſembly, deſir'd to be preſent, ſtanding before the Pulpit) he miniſtred the Oath unto the King; who kneeling, and lifting up his right Hand, did ſwear in the words following:

I Charles *King of* Great Britain, France, *and* Ireland, *do aſſure and declare, by my ſolemn Oath, in the Preſence of Almighty God, the Searcher of Hearts, my Allowance and Approbation of the National Covenant, and of the Solemn League and Covenant above-written, and faithfully oblige my Self to proſecute the Ends thereof in my Station and Calling; and that I for my ſelf and Succeſſors, ſhall conſent and agree to all Acts of Parliament enjoining the National Covenant, and of the Solemn League and Covenant, and fully eſtabliſh Presbyterian Government, the Directory of Worſhip, Confeſſion of Faith, and Catechiſms in the Kingdom of* Scotland, *as they are approv'd by the General Aſſemblies of this Kirk and Parliament of this Kingdom: And that I ſhall give my Royal Aſſent to Acts and Ordinances of Parliament, paſſed or to be paſſed, enjoining the ſame in my other Dominions: And that I ſhall obſerve theſe in my own Practice and Family, and ſhall never make oppoſition to any of theſe, or endeavour any Change thereof.*

After the King had thus ſolemnly ſworn the National Covenant, the League and Covenant, and the King's Oath ſubjoin'd unto both, being drawn up in a fair Parchment, the King did ſubſcribe the ſame in preſence of all.

Thereafter the King aſcendeth the Stage, and ſitteth down in the Chair of State.

Then the Lords, Great Conſtable, and Marſhal, went to the four corners of the Stage, with the Lyon going before them; who ſpoke to the People theſe words: *Sirs, I do preſent unto you the King,* Charles, *the rightful and undoubted Heir of the Crown and Dignity of this Realm: This day is by the Parliament of this Kingdom appointed for his Coronation; and are you not willing to have him for your King, and become Subjects to his Commandments?*

In which Action the King's Majeſty ſtood up, ſhowing himſelf to the People in each corner; And the People expreſs'd their Willingneſs by chearful Acclamations, in theſe words, *God ſave the King,* Charles *the Second.*

There-

Thereafter the King's Majesty, supported by the Constable and Marshal, cometh down from the Stage, and sitteth down in the Chair, where he heard the Sermon.

The Minister, accompany'd with the Ministers before mention'd, cometh from the Pulpit toward the King, and requireth, if he was willing to take the Oath, appointed to be taken at the Coronation.

The King answer'd, He was most willing.

Then the Oath of Coronation, as it is contain'd in the eighth Act of the first Parliament of K. *James*, being read by the Lyon, the Tenour whereof followeth:

Because that the Increase of Vertue, and suppressing of Idolatry, craveth, That the Prince and the People be of one perfect Religion, which of God's mercy is now presently profess'd within this Realm: Therefore it is statuted and ordain'd, by our Sovereign Lord, my Lord Regent, and three Estates of this present Parliament, That all Kings, Princes, and Magistrates whatsoever, holding their place, which hereafter at any time shall happen to reign, and bear rule over this Realm, at the time of their Coronation, and receit of their Princel Authority, make their faithful Promise in the presence of the Eternal God; That enduring the whole course of their Lives, they shall serve the same Eternal God to the uttermost of their power, according as he hath requir'd in his most Holy Word, reveal'd and contain'd in the New and Old Testaments: And according to the same Word, shall maintain the true Religion of Christ Jesus, the Preaching of his Holy Word, and due and right Ministration of the Sacraments now receiv'd, and preach'd within this Realm. And shall abolish and gain-stand all false Religions, contrary to the same: and shall rule the People committed to their charge, according to the Will and Command of God reveal'd in his foresaid Word, and according to the loveable Laws, and Constitutions receiv'd in this Realm, no ways repugnant to the said Word of the Eternal God; and shall procure to the uttermost of their Power, to the Kirk of God, and whole Christian People, true and perfect Peace, in time coming. The Right and Rents, with all just Privileges of the Crown of Scotland, *to preserve and keep inviolated; neither shall they transfer, nor alienate the same. They shall forbid and repress in all Estates and Degrees, Reaf, Oppression, and all kind of Wrong. In all Judgments they shall command and procure that Justice and Equity be kept to all Creatures, without exception, as the Lord and Father of Mercies be merciful unto them: And out of their Lands and Empire they shall be careful to root out all Hereticks, and Enemies to the true Worship of God, that shall be convict by the True Kirk of God of the aforesaid Crimes: And that they shall faithfully affirm the things above-written by their solemn Oath.*

The Minifter tender'd the Oath unto the King, who kneeling, and holding up his Right hand, fwore in thefe words: *By the Eternal and Almighty God, who liveth and reigneth for ever, I fhall obferve and keep all that is contain'd in this Oath.*

This done, the King's Majefty fitteth down in his Chair, and repofeth himfelf a little.

Then the King arifeth from his Chair, and is difrobed by the Lord Great Chamberlain of the Princely Robe, wherewith he entred the Kirk, and is invefted by the faid Chamberlain in his Royal Robes.

Thereafter, the King being brought to the Chair on the North-fide of the Kirk, fupported as formerly, the Sword was brought by Sir *William Cockburn* of *Langtown* Gentleman-Ufher, from the Table, and deliver'd to Lion King of Arms, who giveth it to the Lord Great Conftable, who putteth the fame in the King's hand, faying, Sir, *Receive this Kingly Sword, for the defence of the Faith of Chrift, and Protection of his Kirk, and of the true Religion, as it is prefently profeffed within this Kingdom, and according to the National Covenant, and League and Covenant, and for executing Equity and Juftice, and for punifhment of all iniquity and injuftice.*

This done, the Great Conftable receiveth the Sword from the King, and girdeth the fame about his fide.

Thereafter the King fitteth down in his Chair; and then the Spurs were put on him by the Earl-Marfhal.

Thereafter, *Archibald* Marquis of *Argyle*, having taken the Crown in his hands, the Minifter prayed to this purpofe:

That the Lord would purge the Crown from the fins and tranfgreffions of them that did reign before him: That it might be a pure Crown; That God would fettle the Crown upon the King's Head: And fince Men that fet it on, were not able to fettle it; that the Lord would put it on, and preferve it. And then the faid Marquis put the Crown on the King's Head.

Which done, Lion King of Arms, the Great Conftable ftanding by him, caufeth an Herauld to call the whole Noblemen one by one, according to their Ranks; who coming before the King kneeling, and with their Hand touching the Crown on the King's Head, fwore thefe words: *By the Eternal and Almighty God, who liveth and reigneth for ever, I fhall fupport thee to my utmoft.* And when they had done, then all the Nobility held up their hands, and *fware to be loyal and true Subjects, and faithful to the Crown.*

The Earl-Marfhal, with the Lion, going to the four Corners of the Stage, the Lion proclaimeth the Obligatory Oath of the People. And the People holding up their hands all the time, did fwear, *By the Eternal and Almighty God, who liveth*

and

and reigneth for ever, we become your Liege-men, and Truth and Faith shall bear unto you, and live and die with you against all manner of folks whatsoever, in your service, according to the National Covenant, and solemn League and Covenant.

Then did the Earls and Vicounts put on their Crowns: and the Lion likewise put on his.

Then did the Lord Chamberlain loose the Sword wherewith the King was girded; and drew it, and deliver'd it drawn into the King's hands, and the King put it into the hands of the great Constable to carry it naked before him.

Then *John* Earl of *Crawford* and *Lindsay* took the Scepter, and put it in the King's Right hand, saying, *Sir, receive this Scepter, the sign of Royal Power of the Kingdom, that you may govern your self right, and defend all the Christian People committed by God to your charge, punishing the wicked, and protecting the just.*

Then did the King ascend the Stage, attended by the Officers of the Crown and Nobility, and was installed in the Royal Throne by *Archibald* Marquis of *Argyle*, saying, *Stand and hold fast from henceforth, the place whereof you are the Lawful and Righteous Heir, by a long and lineal Succession of your Fathers, which is now delivered unto you by authority of Almighty God.*

When the King was set down upon the Throne, the Minister spoke to him a word of Exhortation, as followeth.

Sir, *You are set down upon the Throne in a very difficult time: I shall therefore put you in mind of a Scriptural expression of a Throne,* 1 Chron. 29. 23. *It is said,* Solomon sate on the Throne of the Lord. *Sir, you are a King, and a King in Covenant with the Lord; if You would have the Lord to own you to be his King, and his Throne to be your Throne, I desire you may have some thoughts of this expression.*

1. *It is the Lord's Throne; Remember you have a King above you, the King of Kings, and Lord of Lords, who commandeth Thrones: He setteth Kings and Thrones, and dethroneth them at his pleasure: Therefore take a word of advice: Be thankful to him, who hath brought you through many wanderings to set you on this Throne: Kiss the Son, lest he be angry; and learn to serve him with fear, who is terrible to the Kings of the Earth.* 2. *Your Throne is the Lord's Throne, and your People the Lord's People: Let not your heart be lifted up above your brethren,* Deut. 17. 20. *They are your brethren, not only flesh of your flesh, but brethren by Covenant with God; let your Government be refreshing unto them, as the rain on the mown grass.* 3. *Your Throne is the Lord's Throne; beware of making his Throne a Throne of Iniquity: There is such a Throne,* Psal. 94. 20. which frameth mischief by a Law: *God will not own such a Throne, it hath no fellowship with him. Sir, there is too much iniquity upon the Throne by your Predecessors, who framed mischief by a Law; such Laws as have been destructive*

to

to Religion, and grievous to the Lord's People: You are on the Throne, and have the Scepter; beware of touching mischievous Laws therewith. But as the Throne is the Lord's Throne, let the Laws be the Lord's Laws, agreeable to his Word; such as are terrible to evil doers, and comfortable to the godly, and a relief to the poor and oppressed in the Land. 4. *The Lord's Throne putteth you in mind whom you shall have about the Throne; wicked Counsellors are not for a King upon the Lord's Throne:* Solomon *knew this, who said,* Prov. 25. 5. Take away the wicked from before the King, and his Throne shall be establish'd in Righteousness. *And* Prov. 20. 8. A King upon the Throne scattereth away all evil with his eyes. 5. *The Lord's Throne putteth you in mind, that the Judgment on the Throne should be the Lord's; take the Exhortation,* Jer. 22. *from the beginning; the Prophet hath a Command to go to the House of the King of Judah, and say, Hear the Word of the Lord, O King of Judah, that sitteth upon the Throne, and thy servants, and thy people; Execute ye Judgment and Righteousness, and deliver the Spoil out of the hand of the Oppressor: and do no wrong, do no violence to the Stranger, the Fatherless, nor the Widow, neither shed innocent blood in this place. If ye do this thing indeed, then shall there enter by the gates of this House, Kings sitting upon the Throne of* David. *But if ye will not hear these words, I swear by my self, saith the Lord, This house shall become a desolation. And* ver. 7. *I will prepare Destroyers against thee.*

Sir, Destroyers are prepar'd for the Injustice of the Throne; I intreat you, execute righteous Judgment; if you do it not, your House will be a Desolation: But if you do that which is right, God shall remove the Destroyers, and you shall be establish'd on your Throne: and there shall yet be Dignity in your House, for your Servants, and for your People.

Lastly, If your Throne be the Throne of the Lord, take a word of Encouragement against Throne-Adversaries. Your Enemies are the Enemies of the Lord's Throne: Make your Peace with God in Christ, and the Lord shall scatter your Enemies from the Throne, and he shall magnify you yet in the sight of these Nations, and make the misled People submit themselves willingly to your Government. Sir, If you use well the Lord's Throne, on which you are set, then the two words in the place cited, 1 *Chron.* 29. 23. spoken of *Solomon* sitting on the Throne of the Lord, *He prospered,* and all *Israel* obey'd him, shall belong unto you; your People shall obey you in the Lord, and you shall prosper in the sight of the Nations round about.

Then the Lord Chancellor went to the four Corners of the Stage, the Lion King of Arms going before him; and proclaim'd his Majesty's free Pardon to all Breakers of Penal Statutes, and made offer thereof. Whereupon the People cried, *God save the King.*

Then

Then the King, supported by the great Constable, Marshal, and accompanied with the Chancellor, arose from the Throne, and went out at door prepared for that purpose, to a Stage, and showeth himself to the People without, who clapped their hands, and cried with a loud Voice, a long time, *God save the King*.

Then the King returning, and sitting down upon the Throne, deliver'd the Scepter to the Earl of *Crawford* and *Lindsay*, to be carried before him. Thereafter the Lion King of Arms rehearsed the Royal Line of the Kings upward, to *Fergus* the first.

Then the Lion called the Lords one by one, who kneeling, and holding their hands betwixt the King's hands, did swear these words; *By the Eternal and Almighty God, who liveth and reigneth for ever, I become your Liegeman, and Truth and Faith shall bear unto you, and live and dye with you, against all manner of folks whatsoever, in your service, according to the National Covenant, and solemn League and Covenant.*

And every one of them kissed the King's left Cheek.

When these Solemnities were ended, the Minister standing before the King on his Throne, pronounced this Blessing.

The Lord bless thee, and save thee; the Lord hear thee in the day of trouble; the Name of the God of Jacob defend thee: the Lord send thee help from the Sanctuary, and strengthen thee out of Sion. *Amen.*

After the Blessing pronounc'd, the Minister went to the Pulpit, and had the following Exhortation, the King sitting still upon the Throne. Ye have this day a King Crowned, and entred into Covenant with God, and his People; look, both King and People, that ye keep this Covenant, and beware of the breach of it. That you may be the more careful to keep it, I will lay a few things before you.

I remember when the Solemn League and Covenant was entred by both Nations, the Commissioners from *England* being present in the East Kirk of *Edinburgh*, a passage was cited out of *Nehem.* 6. 13. which I shall now again cite. *Nehemiah* required an Oath of the Nobles and People, to restore the mortgaged Lands, which they promised to do: after the Oath was tendred, in the 13th Verse he did shake his Lap, and said, *So God shake out every man from his house, and from his labour, that performeth not his promise; even thus be he shaken out and emptied, and all the Congregations said, Amen.* Since that time many of those who were in Covenant are shaken out of it, yea, they have shaken off the Covenant, and laid it aside. It is true, they are prospering this Day, and think that they prosper by laying aside the Covenant: but they will be deceiv'd; that word spoken then, shall not fall to the ground; God shall shake them

them out of their possession, and empty them for their perfidious Breach of the Covenant.

The same I say to King and Nobles, and all that are in Covenant. If you break that Covenant, being so solemnly sworn, all these who have touch'd your Crown, and sworn to support it, shall not be able to hold it on; but God will shake it off, and turn you from the Throne: And ye Noblemen, who are assistant to the putting on of the Crown, and setting the King upon the Throne; if ye shall either assist, or advise the King to break the Covenant, and overturn the Work of God, he shall shake you out of your Possessions, and empty you of all your Glory.

Another passage I offer to your Consideration, *Jer.* 34. 8. After that *Zedekiah* had promised to proclaim Liberty to all the Lord's People, who were Servants, and entred in a Covenant, he and his Princes, to let them go free, and according to the Oath had let them go; afterwards they caused the Servants to return, and brought them in subjection, *ver.* 11. What followeth upon this Breach? *Ver.* 15, 16. *Ye were now turned, and had done right in my sight in proclaiming liberty: but ye turned, and made them servants again.* And therefore, *ver.* 18, 19, 20, 21. *I will give the men who have transgressed my Covenant, who have not performed the words of the Covenant which they made before me, when they cut the Calf in twain, and passed between the parts thereof, I will even give them into the hands of their enemies, into the hand of them that seek their life, even* Zedekiah *and his Princes.* If the Breach of a Covenant, made for the Liberty of Servants, was so punish'd, what shall be the Punishment of the Breach of a Covenant for Religion, and Liberty of the People of God? There is nothing more terrible to Kings and Princes, than to be given into the hands of Enemies, that seek their life. If ye would escape this Judgment, let King and Princes keep their Covenant made with God: Your Enemies, who seek your Life, are in the Land; if you break the Covenant, it may be fear'd, God will give you over unto them as a Prey: But if ye yet keep Covenant, it may be expected, God will keep you out of their hands.

Let not the place ye heard opened be forgotten; for in it ye have an Example of Divine Justice against *Joash* and the Princes, for breaking that Covenant, 2 *Chron.* 24. 23. The Princes, who inticed that Breach, are destroy'd. And in the 24th Verse it is said, *The Army of the Syrians came with a small company of men, and the Lord deliver'd a very great Host into their hands; because they had forsaken the Lord God of their Fathers: so they executed judgment against* Joash. And verse 25. *His own servants conspired against him, and slew him on his bed,* &c. The Conspiracy

ſpiracy of Servants or Subjects againſt their King, is a wicked courſe: But God in his righteous Judgments ſuffereth Subjects to conſpire and rebel againſt their Princes, becauſe they rebel againſt God: And he ſuffereth Subjects to break the Covenant made with a King, becauſe he breaketh the Covenant made with God. I may ſay freely, that a chief cauſe of the Judgment upon the King's Houſe, hath been the Grandfather's Breach of Covenant with God, and the Father's following his ſteps, in oppoſing the Work of God, and his Kirk within theſe Kingdoms: They broke Covenant with God, and Men have broken Covenant with them; yea, moſt cruelly and perfidiouſly have invaded the Royal Family, and trodden upon all Princely Dignity.

Be wiſe by their Example. You are now ſitting upon the Throne of the Kingdom, and your Nobles about you; there is one above you, even *Jeſus* the King of *Sion*; and I, as his Servant, dare not but be free with you. I charge you Sir, in His Name, that you keep this Covenant in all Points; if you break this Covenant, and come againſt this Cauſe, I aſſure you the Controverſy is not ended between God and your Family, but will be carried on to further weakning, if not the overthrow of it: But if you ſhall keep this Covenant, and befriend the Kingdom of Chriſt, it may be from this day God ſhall begin to do you good; altho your Eſtate be very weak, God is able to raiſe you, and make you to reign, maugre the oppoſition of all your Enemies: And howſoever it ſhall pleaſe the Lord to diſpoſe, you ſhall have peace toward God, through Chriſt the Mediator.

As for you who are Nobles and Peers of the Land, your ſhare is great in this Day of Coronation; ye have come and touched the Crown, and ſworn to ſupport it; ye have handled the Sword and Scepter, and have ſet down the King upon his Throne.

1. I charge you keep your Covenant with God; and ſee that ye never be moved your ſelves to come againſt it in any Head or Article thereof; and that ye give no Counſel to the King to come againſt that Doctrine, Worſhip, Government and Diſcipline of the Kirk, eſtabliſh'd in this Land, as you would eſchew the Judgment of Covenant-breakers. If the King and ye, who are engag'd to ſupport the Crown, conſpire together againſt the Kingdom of Chriſt; both ye that do ſupport, and he that is ſupported, will fall together. I preſs this the more, becauſe it is a rare thing to ſee a King and Great Men for Chriſt; in the long Catalogue of Kings, which ye have heard recited this Day, there will be found few who have been for Chriſt.

2. I

2. I charge you alſo, becauſe of your many Oaths to the King, that you keep them inviolably. Be faithful to him according to your Covenant, the Oaths of God are upon you; if directly or indirectly you do any thing againſt his ſtanding, God, by whom ye have ſworn, will be avenged upon you for the Breach of his Oath.

And now I will cloſe up all in one word more to You, Sir: You are the only Covenanted King with God and his People in the World: Many have obſtructed your Entry in it; now ſeeing the Lord hath brought you in over all theſe Obſtructions, only obſerve to do what is contained therein; and it ſhall prove a happy Time for You and Your Houſe. And becauſe you are entered in Times of great difficulty, wherein ſmall ſtrength ſeems to remain with you in the eyes of the World, for recovering your juſt Power and Greatneſs; therefore take the Counſel which *David*, when he was dying, gave to his Son *Solomon*, 1 Kings 2. 2, 3. *Be ſtrong, and ſhow thy ſelf a Man, and keep the Charge of the Lord thy God, to walk in his ways, and keep his Commandments, that thou may'ſt proſper in all that thou do'ſt, and whitherſoever thou turneſt thy ſelf.*

After this Exhortation, the Miniſter cloſed the whole Action with Prayer; and the 20th Pſalm being ſung, he diſmiſſed the People with the Bleſſing.

Then did the King's Majeſty deſcend from the Stage, with the Crown upon his Head; and receiving again the Scepter in his Hand, returned with the whole Train in ſolemn manner to his Palace, the Sword being carried before him.

Phenix

Phenix X.

The ANSWER *of the States-General of the United Provinces of the* Low-Countries, *to the Declaration of War of the King of* Great Britain. *Printed in* 1674.

Publish'd by Their Lordship's Order.

THE *States-General of the United Provinces of the* Low-Countries; *To all to whom these shall come, Greeting.* The Hopes we had hitherto, that Our continual seeking of Peace would, in time, prove more successful; and that the reiterated Instances of the Prince of *Orange* should at last carry it above the Arts which have been us'd against us, have kept us from publishing sooner an Answer to the *Declaration* of War of his Majesty of *Great Britain*; Being unwilling to encrease the Feud, or to let the whole World see at what rate so great a King hath been abus'd, by the publishing in his Name of a *Manifest*, wherein Truth is what hath been least aim'd at, and which is all full of things that deserve so little to bear in the Front so Illustrious a Name.

But since all our Endeavours, as well as those of the Prince of *Orange*, have prov'd fruitless; and that our most earnest Suits are not only rejected with Scorn, but are also look'd upon as Injuries, as it appears by the Exceptions that have been taken

taken at the reſpectful Letter we had written to his ſaid Majeſty, the care we are bound to have of our Honour, and what we owe to our Subjects, doth not give us leave to defer any longer the laying of our Innocence open, and to make known to all *Europe* the Juſtice of our Arms, which we'll be always ready to lay down as ſoon as the Violence of our Enemies ſhall ceaſe; as we did not take them up, but out of an unavoidable neceſſity.

Howbeit, before we go further, we think it neceſſary to deſire his Majeſty of *Great Britain* to be perſuaded, that our intention is not to offend his Royal Perſon, for which we have ever had, and will ſtill have, all imaginable Reſpect, altho the ſtrength of Truth doth conſtrain us to diſown moſt of what his Miniſters have perſuaded him to aver.

We do alſo deſire all thoſe of the *Engliſh* Nation, into whoſe hands theſe may come, to read them with an impartial Mind, and to ſeek only the Truth in them, without conſidering it comes from Enemies, ſince we bear that Title with much regret; and that we deſire nothing more earneſtly, than to ſee our ſelves united again with a Nation, to which we are link'd by the ſacred Bond of the ſame Religion, beſides a joint Intereſt in ſeveral other reſpects.

Engliſh Declaration.

WE have been always ſo zealous for the Quiet of Chriſtendom, and ſo careful not to Invade any other Kingdom or State, that We hope the World will do Us the Juſtice to believe, that it is nothing but inevitable Neceſſity forceth Us to the Reſolution of taking up Arms.

Immediately upon Our Reſtauration to Our Crowns, the firſt work We undertook, was the eſtabliſhing of Peace, and the ſetling a good Correſpondence between Us and Our Neighbours; and in particular, Our care was, to conclude a ſtrict League with the States-General of the United Provinces, upon

ANSWER.

WE never intended to call in queſtion the peaceable and generous Intentions of the King of *Great Britain*; and we are enough perſuaded, that all the miſunderſtanding that hath been between us ſince his Reſtoration, hath proceeded only from the Counſels of ill-affected Perſons. But by reaſon that to what concerns the Perſon of his Majeſty, (which we do not gainſay) they add ſeveral groundleſs Accuſations relating to our ſelves, a ſhort and faithful Account of what hath paſs'd moſt conſiderable before the

upon such equal Terms, as would certainly not have been broken, if any Obligations could have kept them within the bounds of Friendship or Justice.

This League was maintain'd inviolable on Our part. But in the Year 1664. we were stirred up by the Complaints of Our People, and the unanimous Vote of Both Our Houses of Parliament; finding it a vain Attempt to endeavour the Prosperity of Our Kingdoms by peaceable ways at home, whilst Our Subjects were still expos'd to the Injuries and Oppressions of those States abroad.

That whole Summer was spent in Negotiations and Endeavours on Our side, to bring them to reasonable Terms, which notwithstanding all We could do, proved at length ineffectual; for the more we pursued them with friendly Propositions, the more obstinately they kept off from agreeing with us.

Upon this ensued the War in the Year 1665. and continued to the Year 1667. in all which time Our Victories and their Losses were memorable enough, to put them in mind of being more faithful to their Leagues for the future. But instead of that, the Peace was no sooner made, but they returned to their usual custom of breaking Articles, and supplanting our Trade.

the Treaty of *Breda*, will sufficiently demonstrate which of both Parties hath most endeavour'd to preserve a fair Correspondence, and who have fought Peace with the greatest reality and zeal.

When his Majesty of *Great Britain* was miraculously called again by his Subjects to the Government of his Kingdoms, he was pleased to make choice of one of our Towns to receive the Deputies that were sent to him, and stay'd with us till all things were ready for his Transportation. During the said time, we endeavour'd to give him all possible Demonstrations of Our respect to his Person, and of the fervent desire we had to purchase his Friendship, and to preserve the same inviolable. And what we did in that respect, prov'd so acceptable to his Majesty, and did so far persuade him of the sincerity of our intentions, that he was pleased to acknowledg it much beyond what we expected; and assured us, with the most obliging Expressions, that he was resolved, and did earnestly desire to enter with our State into a stricter Alliance than any of his Predecessors had done, and that he did hope his Restoration would be of no less advantage to the Inhabitants of our Provinces than to his own Subjects, and that they should all taste the fruits of it with an equal satisfaction: Adding to this, that he should not without jealousy see us prefer the Friendship or Alliance of any other Prince before his. Several general Proposals and Projects of Treaties were made even at that time; after which we sent a solemn Embassy to put an end to what had been already propos'd, and to offer on our part all that was both reasonable and feasable. But our Embassadors were no sooner arriv'd, but they perceiv'd a great Alteration in the Mind and Inclinations of his said Majesty, and found that some ill-affected Persons had possess'd him against us since he had left the *Hague:* So that instead of concluding the Alliance which he had propos'd to us Himself, he began to side with other Princes against us. And in particular, tho the War we had with *Portugal* was most just and most warrantable, yet he openly threatned to break with us, if we did seek any longer, by way of Arms, a reparation of the Wrongs we had receiv'd from that Crown.

In the mean time, our Embassadors did not intermit their Instances, and press'd with all possible Zeal for the concluding of a stricter Alliance with the Crown of *England:* But after several Objections and Difficulties rais'd by that Court, upon the Articles which our Embassadors had propos'd, in conformity to the Project that had been made, whilst his Majesty was still at the *Hague*; the Commissioners with whom they treated, offer'd them at last, after above a Year's delay, the Treaty which was concluded in the Year 1654 with *Cromwell:* And this Treaty could not be confirm'd neither, but with much difficulty and trouble, and with the addition of several Points, that made it more disadvantagious to us than the very Treaty of 1654.

At last, having overcome all those Difficulties, and given to the King of *Great Britain* so clear Proofs of the singular Esteem we had of his Friendship, we thought thereby to have laid the Foundation of a firm and durable Peace, and did hope the *English* Ministers would have contributed on their part, as we did on ours, to extinguish the least Sparks of Discord: But the Treaty was no sooner concluded, than they begun to renew and set on foot certain Pretensions, that were regulated in general by the Treaty, but not perfectly ended. And whilst the Embassador *Downing* made a great Noise in the *Hague*, of a few groundless Demands of some private Merchants, they sent a Fleet to possess themselves of several Places belonging to us upon the Coast of *Guiney*, and of all the *New Netherlands*; and that in the midst of a setled Peace, without a previous Declaration of War, and without any denial on our part, to give them satisfaction upon any Complaint they had made: and afterwards they seiz'd all our Merchant Ships that sail'd along their Coast.

These Excesses were follow'd by a Declaration of War; during which, we may truly say, we never refus'd to hearken to any Overture of Peace that was made to us, either by Princes and States, or by any other unconcern'd Persons: But, to the

the contrary: we let no opportunity slip of making Overtures of Peace our selves, upon the least glimpse of hopes it might be done with success. Having in order to that kept our Embassador in *England*, during the best part of the War; and having still, since his coming away, offer'd from time to time to his Majesty of *Great Britain*, the very Alternative upon which Peace was at last concluded (which was either to keep what had been conquer'd on either side, or to restore all reciprocally) without seeking to make any advantage of the Conjunction of *France*, which had then declar'd in our behalf.

All this doth sufficiently shew how zealous we have always been for Peace; and even without any other proof, one may easily imagine we'll ever be desirous of what is the true Foundation of the Happiness of our Country, as it is the Support of our Trade.

All those that are in any measure acquainted with the state of our Affairs, can't but know that a War by Sea, such as this we are engag'd in now, is of all Rocks, that which at all times we'll avoid with the greatest Care; and that nothing but an inevitable Necessity can bring us to the Taking up of Arms: in case they will but grant us ever so little Prudence and Wisdom, altho they would not own we keep our Treaties (as we may truly say we have ever done) out of a Principle of Conscience and Honour. And therefore the Proofs which *England* doth instance in, of our aversenes to Peace, and of the perpetual Infraction of our Treaties, must needs carry a strong Demonstration with them, to make good a Paradox that is so much against all Sense and Reason. Let us then examine in order those pretended *Infractions*, and see how far the Compilers of the *Manifesto* do make it appear we have violated the Peace of *Breda*.

FOR Instance; The States were particularly engag'd in an Article of the Treaty at Breda, *to send Commissioners to Us at* London, *about the Regulation of our Trade in the* East-Indies: *But they were so far from doing it upon that Obligation, that when we sent over Our Ambassador to put them in mind of it, he could not in three years time get from them any satisfaction in the material Points, nor a forbearance of the Wrongs which Our Subjects receiv'd in those Parts*

THE first Infraction they complain of, and which in all likelihood ought to be very considerable, since it leads the Van, hath four several Branches: 1. That we were bound by the aforesaid Treaty of *Breda*, to send Commissioners to *London*, to regulate the *East-India* Trade; which we have not done. 2. That this forc'd the King of *Great Britain* to send us an Embassador, to put us in mind of what we had promis'd. 3. That the said Embassador could not in three years time get from us any satisfaction in the material Points; nor, 4. A forbearance of the Wrongs which the Subjects of his said Majesty receiv'd in those Parts.

Whereupon we can't but take notice, that this, in all probability, is the first *Manifesto* in the World that ever began with an Article, whereof every part is a mere Supposition; and wherein, of all the Matter of Fact that is alledg'd, there is not the least Point agreeable to Truth. For, 1. Let the whole Treaty of *Breda* be read and examin'd with Care, no Clause will be found whereby either in express or equivalent Terms, we were bound to send Commissioners to *London*; much less to send any thither for the Regulation of the *East-India* Trade, which is not so much as mention'd in all the Treaty. Which makes us wonder at the surprizing Boldness of those who dare publish and aver, in the sight of all *Europe*, a thing which doth confute it self; and the Falshood whereof may be evinc'd, by producing only the very Treaty they do quote and ground themselves upon. 2. How is it possible the King of *Great Britain* should send us an Ambassador, to put us in mind of that which never was, and which we could not have promised, since it had not been so much as spoken of? 3. What Essential Points could have been mov'd upon an imaginary Clause and Engagement? and there being nothing in that respect agreed upon by the Treaty of *Breda*, what satisfaction could they demand from us? 4. We may with Sincerity and Truth affirm, that hitherto we have not heard that our *East-India* Company, since the last Peace, hath done any wrong to, or committed any Violence against the Subjects of the King of *Great Britain*; and withal, that his Embassador never complain'd to us of it in the least; which undoubtedly he would have done, if there had been any ground for it. But to demonstrate further the Injustice of this Complaint, and how ill grounded it is, we are assured from good hands, that the Committee of the *English East-India* Company, having been desir'd by the Court to bring in their Grievances, with a List of the Injuries they had receiv'd in the *Indies* since the Treaty of *Breda*; they answer'd in writing, They had receiv'd none.

But what is little less surprizing than all the rest, is, that they lay to our charge to have violated the Treaty of *Breda* in relation to the *East-India* Trade, which is not mention'd in it, instead of returning us Thanks for what we have done in that respect, without being bound to't by any Treaty; and merely to let the King and all the *English* Nation see at what rate we were willing to purchase and to preserve their Friendship. In few words, the thing was thus.

The

The Peace which was treated of at *Breda* being much deſir'd by the greateſt part of *Europe*, and the time being too ſhort to enter into a particular Negotiation for a Treaty of Marine between *England* and us, it was agreed to make uſe proviſionally of that which we had concluded with *France* in the Year 1662, beginning from the 26th Article, to the 42d incluſively; it being reſolv'd at the ſame time that, after the Peace concluded, Commiſſioners ſhould be choſen on both ſides to agree upon a more particular Regulation of Marine, for the reciprocal Eaſe and Convenience of the Merchants of both Nations: Which kind of Treaties being only to determine the *Countraband* Goods, and to prevent the Interruption, which War commonly cauſeth in the Trade of Neutral Nations, is altogether different from a Regulation of Trade in the *Eaſt-Indies*. Moreover, the Winter following *England* having deſign'd the Preſervation of the *Spaniſh Netherlands*, and having ſent us Sir *William Temple* to enter into a Negotiation with us in order to it, we concluded in a little time three ſeveral Treaties with him; *viz*. The one a *Defenſive League* between Us; The other for the Defence of the *Low-Countries*, which afterwards was call'd the *Triple Alliance*; and the third an abſolute Treaty of *Marine*, which was concluded on the $\frac{7}{17}$ of *February* 1668, and which left no room for the Nomination of the Commiſſioners that had been ſpoken of at *Breda*, ſince this Treaty had ſettled what they ſhould have treated about, and that there was nothing to be added to a formal and abſolute Regulation.

After the Concluſion of this Treaty, ſome *Engliſh* Merchants did repreſent to the Court, that ſome Articles of it were doubtful and impracticable; whereupon Sir *William Temple* deliver'd us a Memorial, dated the 26th of *November* 1668, without mentioning therein the *Eaſt-India* Trade: and on the firſt of *December* following he gave our Commiſſioners two Articles of the Treaty of *Marine*, which were complain'd of, and added to them four Articles more, to be as a Rule between the two Companies in their *Eaſt-India* Trade; but which, in truth, were mere Demands the *Engliſh* Company made for their private advantage. Whereupon we muſt not omit, that neither in the Memorials which the ſaid Embaſſador gave us, nor in all the Conferences he had with our Deputies, he never mention'd in the leaſt the Treaty of *Breda*, and did never ground his Demands either upon the ſaid Treaty, or upon any other Engagement or Obligation on our part.

The whole was imparted to our Aſſembly on the very ſame day; where after a ſerious Debate, altho we might have refus'd to make any Alteration in a Treaty which had been Concluded and Ratified in the usual Forms: That withal, as to what related to the Articles which the *English East-India* Company had procur'd to be deliver'd to us, we were not bound by any Treaty, or other Engagement, to enter with them into a Regulation of the *East-India* Trade, much less to grant them several Points, which were all for their private advantage, without any possibility for us to reap reciprocally the least benefit of the said Regulation; which was also directly contrary to the Laws generally receiv'd in, and to the common use of the *Indies*. And lastly, that they complain'd of no wrong (as indeed they could not have done it with any Justice) done to them by our Company: And thus had so much the less cause to urge for a more particular Regulation, whilst there was no necessity for it. Yet we thought fit to pass by all those Considerations, and to give to his Majesty of *Great Britain*, and to all the *English* Nation, this new Proof of the singular Esteem we had of their Friendship, and of our desire to tie the Knot of our Union yet faster, and to make it, if it were possible, indissoluble. Upon which ground we order'd our Commissioners to prepare an Answer to the Proposals of the aforesaid Embassador, and to confer with him in order to a speedy conclusion of that Work. And all we can say in general of the said Negotiation, the Particulars whereof would be too tedious for those that are not vers'd in those matters, is, That of four principal Points which were propos'd by the said Embassador, we granted and agreed upon three; and without rejecting the fourth, we only desir'd a further clearing of some ambiguous Clauses one of the Articles contain'd; which, instead of settling a good Correspondence between the two Companies, might have occasion'd new Debates, and have prov'd of dangerous consequence.

And the better to evidence how desirous we were to give all possible satisfaction to *England*, being sensible that the Letters which were written on both sides, did not sufficiently clear all Doubts, we sent the Sieur *Van Beuningen* chiefly to put an end to the said Treaty between the two Companies. But whether the *English* Ministers, who were appointed to treat with him as Commissioners, were unwilling to explain themselves more particularly upon the ambiguous Clauses, whereof a further clearing was demanded, lest they should discover the unjust Sense wherein they intended to take them afterwards; Or that they were afraid lest the conclusion of that Treaty should have united more strictly both Nations, and so might have prov'd a new Obstacle to the War they already design'd at that time; the said *Van Beuningen* could obtain no positive Answer upon what he desir'd, and came back without any

any progress made in his Negotiation; which could not be renew'd since, by reason of the misunderstanding, which still encreas'd from that time, unto the breaking out of the War.

IN *the* West-Indies *they went a little farther: For by an Article in the same Treaty, we were to restore* Surinam *into their hands; and by Articles upon the place confirm'd by that Treaty, they were to give Liberty to all Our Subjects in that Colony, to transport themselves and their Estates into any other of Our Plantations. In pursuance of this Agreement, We deliver'd up the Place, and yet they detain'd all Our Men in it; only Major* Banister *they sent away Prisoner, for but desiring to remove according to the Articles. Our Ambassador complaining of this behaviour, after two years sollicitation, obtain'd an Order for the performance of those Articles: But when We sent Commissioners, and two Ships to bring Our Men away, the* Hollanders *(according to their former practice in the business of* Poleroon *for above forty years together) sent private Orders contradictory to those they had own'd to Us in publick; and so the only effect of Our Commissioners journey thither, was to bring away some few of the poorest of Our Subjects, and the Prayers and Cries of the most considerable and wealthiest of them, for relief out of that Captivity. After this, We made Our Complaints by Our Letter in* August *last to the* States General, *wherein We desir'd an Order to their Governours there, for the full observance of those Articles; yet to this time We could never receive one word of answer or satisfaction.*

SUrinam is a Colony upon the Coast of *Guiana* in *America*, which did belong to the *English*, and which some Ships we had sent thither, master'd during the late War, on the 6th of *March* 1667. N. S.

At the taking of it, our Officers granted to the Inhabitants a Capitulation; wherein, amongst other things, it was express'd, that whenever any of the said Inhabitants should have a mind to remove out of the Colony, they should have leave to sell their Estates; and that in such case the Governour should take care for their Transportation, together with their Effects, at a reasonable Rate.

After we had had the said Colony some Months in our possession, the *English* Forces conquer'd it again. But as by the Treaty of *Breda* it was agreed to surrender reciprocally, and transfer to each other all Right of Soveraignty to the Places which were possess'd on either side on the $\frac{10}{20}$ *May* 1667, and that we were then yet in possession of *Surinam*, the said Colony did belong to us, and was to be restor'd us by the Treaty aforesaid; as it was at last (after long delays, and many reiterated Instances from us) by virtue of an Order of the King of *Great Britain*, dated the 8th of *July* 1668.

Being thus possess'd again of the said Place, one *Banister*, who commanded there at the time our Officers brought the last Order of the King of *England* for the restitution of it, declar'd to our Governour, that he intended to leave the Colony, and enjoy the benefit of the aforesaid Capitulation; which indeed he might lawfully do. But not being satisfied with demanding for himself what would not have been denied him, he acted as if he had been still Governour of the Colony, and demanded in a very high manner the same permission, in the name of several Planters, as their Deputy, and thereunto by them authoriz'd. Whereupon the Governour aforesaid being inform'd, that the said *Banister* did Night and Day cabal in the Colony, and us'd in a seditious manner both Promises and Threats to associate to him as many as he could, and engage them to go away with him; and looking upon such a carriage as directly contrary to the Soveraignty which had been transfer'd to us by the Treaty of *Breda*, by virtue whereof all the Inhabitants of the said Colony were become our Subjects, and consequently could not meet together, nor act as a Body without our leave, much less to make themselves Heads of Parties, and to cabal against our Interest, as the said *Banister* had done; our said Governour not thinking fit to punish him himself, sent him to us to inflict upon him what Punishment we should think convenient. Upon his Arrival, Sir *William Temple* having spoken to us in his behalf, we granted him his liberty: And altho the Inhabitants of *Surinam*, by their being become our Subjects, had lost all Right of applying themselves to any other Authority but our own, and so, that no Foreign Prince could with any Justice make himself Judg of any former Capitulation; Our Subjects having no lawful way to go out of our Territories but by asking our leave, which also we may affirm, never to have denied to any of the Inhabitants of that Colony that have apply'd themselves to us, or to our Officers; Yet to let his Majesty of *Great Britain* see how ready we were to comply with him, and how far we were from designing to use our new Subjects with any rigour, or to deny to them the least of the Privileges which were promised them in our name, we consented to enter with his Majesty's Embassador into a Negotiation upon the said matter, and to regulate with him the manner how the aforesaid Capitulation should be executed. Upon this several Difficulties did arise; The Court of *England* endeavouring to strain the words of the Capitulation beyond their true sense, thereby to destroy as much as they could our said Colony, and asking every day somewhat new; whilst the Intention of those that govern'd was not to compose Differences in an amicable way, but rather to leave still, with

with much Art, ſome Seed of Diſſenſion, thereby to have an opportunity of making a noiſe, and by their falſe Complaints to perſuade the *Engliſh* Nation, we were ſtrange Tyrants who kept their Countrymen in a barbarous Captivity, without being moved by their Prayers and Crys. Whereas we may truly ſay, that excepting *Baniſter*, we have heard of no *Engliſh*-man at *Surinam* that deſir'd to remove, without being thereunto induc'd either thro the Promiſes or Threats of ſome of the Agents from *England*.

The firſt Difficulty was concerning the Slaves, which *Baniſter*, with his Aſſociates, did pretend they might carry off, and take along with them, by virtue of the Capitulation; altho it be plain both by the Words of the Capitulation aforeſaid, and by the Teſtimony of our Officers that ſign'd it, that no ſuch Privilege had been granted to them. But at laſt, to oblige as much as we were able his Majeſty of *Great Britain*, we yielded that Point, and conſented to what his ſaid Majeſty deſir'd of us, how prejudicial ſoever the thing was to us.

But as the Intention of the Court of *England*, was only either to deſtroy our Colony, or to force us to deny them ſomewhat that might give them a pretence of complaining of us, tho never ſo unjuſtly; they did not think to have done their work by carrying away from us a very great number of Slaves. And foreſeeing we would not be long without buying new ones in ſtead of them, they thought upon a new way to deſtroy our Sugar-Works, which they were forc'd to leave behind, and deſir'd afterwards they might carry away the Coppers and other neceſſary Utenſils for the making of Sugar; altho in the common Acceptation, thro all the Colonies of *America*, and by the manner they were faſten'd and fix'd, they were properly a part of the Sugarworks, and therefore not tranſportable in their nature. This Demand was ſo unreaſonable, and ſo foreign to all that was ſpecify'd in the Capitulation, that we had but too much cauſe wholly to reject it. But ſtill to demonſtrate what value we did ſet upon the Friendſhip of the King of *Great Britain*, and how far we were willing to condeſcend even to all his Deſires, we did likewiſe give way to it.

Beſides this, they deſir'd they might ſend *Engliſh* Ships, for the Tranſportation of ſuch as ſhould be minded to leave the Colony; in hopes that this ſending might engage thoſe to go off, that had not deſign'd it: not to reject the Invitation of ſo Great a King, by ſuffering the Ships he ſent them at his own charge, to return empty. Theſe little Arts were not unknown to us. And altho this Demand was directly contrary to the Laws and to the Practice of all Colonies in *America*,

rica, where no Prince or State do ſuffer any Ships but their own to come to any Plantation they do reſpectively poſſeſs; and that withal it was expreſly agreed by the Capitulation, that our Governour ſhould furniſh with Ships (at a moderate rate) ſuch Inhabitants as would remove out of the ſaid Colony: Yet we once more paſs'd by all thoſe Conſiderations, and granted it, as we had done all the reſt.

But by reaſon they fear'd ſtill, the ſending of the Ships might not have the Succeſs they expected, unleſs they did ſend at the ſame time ſome truſty Agents, to give the ſame a greater Reputation, and to endeavour underhand to perſuade the *Engliſh* Inhabitants to go away with them; they preſs'd that they might name Commiſſioners to carry the Orders we ſent to our Governour (in conformity to what we had granted to his Majeſty of *Great Britain*) and to be preſent at the executing of them. This we granted them alſo, and deſired only they would make choice of ſuch Perſons as were unconcern'd and well-meaning, to the end all things might be fairly ended, and with mutual Satisfaction. But how rational and how juſt ſoever this our Requeſt was, the *Engliſh* Court inſiſted upon the often-mention'd *Baniſter* to be the chief Perſon of this Embaſſy: And being reſolv'd on our part to give the higheſt Proofs of our Condeſcenſion, we oppos'd it no longer; altho we had ſo much cauſe to ſuſpect him.

A final end was put to this Negotiation by our Miniſters in *England*; and the laſt Orders we ſent to our Governour were agreed upon between the late Secretary *Trevor* and them, much againſt the Expectation of the other *Engliſh* Miniſters, who did not think we could have been brought to part with ſo much of our Right, nor grant ſo many things we were not bound to, and which were ſo prejudicial to us. But as the ſecret Reaſons and Motives which kept the ſaid Miniſters from perfecting the private Treaty between the *Eaſt-India* Companies, which was ſo far advanc'd, made them fear likewiſe leſt the buſineſs of *Surinam* ſhould be amicably ended, neither of them agreeing with the meaſures they had lately taken at *Dover*, where the Court had gone to receive the Dutcheſs of *Orleans*; they were not in the leaſt pleas'd with what the ſaid Secretary *Trevor* had done, and began to think of means to ſtop the Execution of it; without remembring then the Prayers and the Crys of thoſe poor Subjects, who (ſay they in their *Manifeſto*) long for Relief out of their Captivity.

In order to that, not daring to fall openly upon the ſaid Secretary, nor to impeach him themſelves, they refer'd the Agreement he had made to the Scrutiny of the Council of Plantations, to ſee whether they could not find ſomewhat elſe to to demand, beyond what he had obtain'd from us. And in truth their Policy was so successful, that if *Banister* himself, as partial as he was, had not declar'd to the said Council that he was satisfy'd with what we had granted, and had not express'd with some heat his Impatience of going away, our Orders would not have been accepted of, and they would have made new Demands to us before they had dispatch'd the said *Banister*.

Yet to perplex the thing with new Difficulties, they gave *Banister* as ample a Commission, as if the Colony of *Surinam* had not belong'd to us with Right of Sovereignty; with several Clauses, which shew'd plainly that their Intention and Design was to force a Denial from us; having even (by an unheard of proceeding) named, at the recommendation and choice of *Banister*, five of our Subjects in *Surinam*, to be Commissioners from and by order of the King of *Great Britain.* Our Ministers in *England* having had notice of it, were infinitely surpris'd, and express'd highly their Resentment: Whereupon the abovenam'd Secretary *Trevor*, who, as it hath appear'd since, had no share in their Counsels, being sensible that the overthrowing of all that had been done, was what the other Ministers did most desire, made several Instances to our said Ministers to pass by the just Considerations they might have, and even to grant to *Banister* a Letter of Recommendation, wherein they should persuade our Governor to execute his Orders *bona fide*, without taking exception at such Circumstances as might be irregular. Which at last they granted him by a kind of implicit Faith, and out of the strong persuasion they had of his Integrity. Which is very far from sending private Orders contradictory to those we had own'd in publick, as is here laid to our charge against all Truth, and with as little ground as what they add concerning *Poleroon*.

After all those Delays, whereof we were not the cause, the *English* Ships at last went away, and arriv'd at *Surinam* on the 19*th* of *January* 1671. where the Commissioners were receiv'd with all imaginable Civility. And all we can say in few words, concerning what pass'd between them and our Governour, is, that on his part there was nothing forgotten that might oblige the *English* Nation; he having gone much beyond what might have been expected of him, and what the Orders that were agreed upon with *England* requir'd. But as to the Commissioners, their whole Carriage was a perpetual Mixture of unreasonable Passion, groundless Complaints, and unjust Demands, as if they had had no other Design than to breed a Misunderstanding between the two Nations. They having

having withal endeavour'd by all possible means to destroy our Colony, against the Allegiance of those amongst them that were our Subjects; against the Promises which *Banister* had in particular made to our Ministers in *England*; and lastly, against the Engagement of the King of *England* himself, and his Royal Word, which he had often given to us of the contrary. But by reason the proof of all this would take too much time, we have order'd the publishing of the Journal of our Governour, with his Answer to the Protest the aforesaid Commissioners left with him when they went away; to let the whole World in general, and in particular the *English* Nation, see the notorious Falshood of what is laid to our charge, and the Uprightness of the Carriage of our Officers, as well as the Sincerity of our Intentions.

BUT it is no wonder that they venture at these Outrages upon our Subjects in remote parts, when they dare be so bold with our Royal Person, and the Honour of this Nation so near us, as in their own Country, there being scarce a Town within their Territories, that is not fill'd with abusive Pictures, and false Historical Medals and Pillars: some of which have been exposed to the publick view by command of the States *themselves, and in the very time when we were join'd with them in united Counsels for the Support of the Triple League, and the Peace of* Christendom. *This alone were cause sufficient for our Displeasure, and the Resentment of all our Subjects.*

FROM the pretended Outrages committed against the King of *Great Britain*'s Subjects, in remote parts; they come now to our affronting here (as they groundlesly affirm) his Royal Person, and the *English* Nation; which alone had been cause sufficient for his said Majesty's Displeasure, and the Resentment of all his Subjects. Which in other words is as much as if the *English* Ministers had said, that to punish the Ambition of a Burguemaster of a private Town, who had caus'd himself to be drawn somewhat too vainly, *Europe* was at least to be set in a flame; and that so horrid a Sin could not be wash'd away but by a Deluge of Christian Blood.

But to answer this Accusation more exactly, we cannot sufficiently wonder at the carriage of the Court of *England*, who think to justify to the full a War, wherein so much innocent Blood is shed, and which causeth so general a Desolation, by telling little Tales that have no ground in Truth, and which are so much beneath the Gravity of a *Manifesto*; and by their talking of abusive Pictures, and false Medals, and Pillars, wherewith they say all our Towns are fill'd. For first, as to their

their false Pillars (which by the way is an Expression somewhat singular) if they mean by it that we have erected Pillars to the dishonour of the King of *Great Britain*, or the *English* Nation, it will never be found we had so much as the Thoughts of doing any thing like it. And in that sense only those Pillars may with truth be call'd *False*.

And as to the Medals (which they also do call false) we never knew but of a true one, wherein under the known and usual Emblems, with both Poets and Painters, on the one side *War* was represented, and on the other *Plenty*, and *Peace* that produceth it; having under her feet *Discord* in the shape of a Fury, that was vanquish'd, and should no longer desolate States that were become Friends.

And this Medal, tho it was not done by our Order, being look'd upon as very inoffensive, one of our Provinces gave the Engraver leave to sell it publickly; as it is usual to permit the Printing, and the Sale of Books, which are not thought dangerous; or out of a particular Kindness, to grant a special Privilege to some private Bookseller, and thus to prefer him before his Neighbours. Not to insist now upon the Right we had, as well as any other Sovereigns, to make use of either Medals, or any other usual means, to preserve the Memory of any Action, or Event, we might have thought considerable; and whereof especially there are so many Instances in *England*.

But tho we did not think the said Medal could have given the least offence, yet there were those who did maliciously make use of it, to exasperate the King of *Great Britain*: and howbeit there was nothing more false, nor more groundless than what was suggested by these weak Informers; yet to take off all pretence, and to demonstrate, even in the least Circumstances, the Sincerity of our Intentions, the Privilege granted to the Engraver was call'd in, all the Medals that could be found were suppress'd, and the Stamp was order'd to be broken, to prevent the coining of any more of them in private.

As to the abusive Pictures, whereof they pretend all our Towns are full, the great noise they make hath no other ground but a Picture, which the *Schepen* (or Sheriffs) of *Dort* caus'd to be made of the Sieur *Cornelius de Witt*, one of their Burguemasters; and which, by a Civility somewhat excessive, they order'd to be hung in the Chamber where the Council of their Town used to meet. In this Picture he was drawn with a Staff of Command, because in the preceding War he had been upon the Fleet as our Deputy; and the Painter had added to it on the one hand a River with several Ships, whereof

whereof some were on fire; and on the other a Horn of *Plenty*, out of which flow'd all sorts of Goods and Commodities; to signify that War had made room for Peace, and that Trading and Commerce had succeeded to Battels and Fights. Whereupon it is observable, 1. That the State had no share in the erecting of the said Picture. 2. That it was not the whole Body of the Town of *Dort* neither, but the aforesaid *Schepen* only, that were his particular Friends. 3. That this Picture (of what nature soever it might have been) was in a private Room, where none but those of the Council of the Town had right to come in. 4. And lastly, that there was nothing abusive in the whole Picture; and all that could be censur'd in it was the Vanity of him, who had either sought or accepted of an Honour, which a more prudent Man would have refus'd.

Excepting this only Picture, we may truly say we never heard of any other that was excepted against, or complain'd of; and in case any abusive ones had been to be found, the King of *England*'s Ministers that have resided here with us, would undoubtedly have spoken of it, and desir'd that the Authors or Publishers of them might have been punish'd. Which is a clear proof there was never any such thing publickly known. And in case any have been sold or dispers'd secretly (which yet we do not believe) how can we be answerable for, or be suppos'd to have a hand in what never so much as came to our knowledg?

Would his Majesty of *Great Britain*, on pain of making war upon us, expect more from us within our Dominions, than he can do himself within his own Kingdoms, where it is sufficiently known how many bitter Libels, against both his Person and his Government, have been dispers'd notwithstanding the strictest Searches? And it may be his own Court hath not been freer from it than the rest of the Kingdom. And the Liberty his Subjects do take hath been so universal, that they have not spar'd even his most retir'd Apartments. His Ministers have been used worse yet, since the Chancellor doth confess in the Speech he made at the opening of the former Session of Parliament, that they were accus'd openly of *Treachery* and *Folly*, and were call'd, even in the Coffee-houses, both *Fools* and *Villains*. These are his own words.

After all this, with what Justice can they complain of us, who in the very heat of all our Wars, have been guilty of no Excesses that came near unto these; and who in this last have suppress'd of our own accord, under very severe penaltys, two Pamphlets that spoke with too little respect of the

Person

Person of his Majesty of *Great Britain*, altho the Author seem'd to have been very affectionate to the Welfare of our State?

BUT We are urged to it by Considerations yet nearer to Us, than what only relates to our Self; the Safety of our Trade, upon which the Wealth and Prosperity of our People depends, the Preservation of them abroad from Violence and Oppression, and the Hollanders *daring to affront us almost within our very Ports, are the things which move our just Indignation against them.*

AS this Article is hardly to be understood, and is back'd by no manner of proof, we suppose they intended it for an Introduction to what followeth; and therefore we can confute it no better, than by answering in order to the Matters of Fact they do alledg.

THE Right of the Flag is so antient, that it was one of the first Prerogatives of our Royal Predecessors, and ought to be the last from which this Kingdom should ever depart. It was never question'd, and it was expresly acknowledg'd in the Treaty at Breda; *and yet this last Summer it was not only violated by their Commanders at Sea, and that Violation afterwards justify'd at the* Hague, *but it was also represented by them in most Courts of* Christendom, *as ridiculous for Us to demand. An ungrateful Insolence! That they should contend with Us about the Dominion of these Seas, who even in the Reign of Our Royal Father, thought it an Obligation to fish in them, by taking of Licences, and for a Tribute; and who owe their being now in a condition of making this Dispute, to the Protection of our Ancestors, and the Valour and Blood of their Subjects.*

THIS is the Grand Battery of the *English* Ministers: 'Tis what they think we cannot withstand; and which they do with the greatest confidence rely upon. Before they had this Pretence, they knew not how to overcome all the Difficultys, which still hinder'd their Design. They were resolv'd to make War upon us: They had promis'd it to *France*; and withal they flatter'd themselves, it would much advance their private Designs at home: But they still wanted Arguments that were popular enough to incense the Nation against us. They had need of somewhat more than their Pictures and their Medals. And in order to that, they contriv'd the sending of a Yacht to seek our Fleet, which lay at anchor not far from our Coasts, to require Striking from our Admirals; in hopes that the Novelty of the thing would occasion some Accident that

that might further their Deſigns. Which Plot of theirs, as we have ſince found, having too well anſwer'd their Deſires; and excepting this ſingle point, there being nothing in all their *Manifeſto*, wherein the *Engliſh* Nation may concern themſelves in the leaſt; we think it neceſſary, before we anſwer it more fully, to declare both unto the King, and to the ſaid Nation, that as on our part, we ſhould be ſorry to deny them the leaſt Prerogative that of right may belong to them, or ſo much as to enter into any debate concerning what they may claim as their due, when the thing doth not relate to us, or is not made uſe of againſt us: We do hope likewiſe they'l have ſo much Equity, as to hear us in our juſt Defence; and that the great noiſe the Contrivers of this War do make, ſhall not drown the Strength and the Solidity of our Anſwer.

For the clearing of this point, it is to be obſerv'd that till the Year 1653. as there had never been any Diſpute about the *Flag*, between the *Engliſh* Nation and Us, ſo it was never ſo much as propos'd to mention it in any Treaty. Which is a clear and certain proof, that till then the Sea-Commanders on both ſides, were ſufficiently acquainted with what was to be done in thoſe caſes; and that nothing had been demanded in that reſpect by the *Engliſh*, but what we had been ſtill ready to grant.

It is likewiſe very obſervable, that *England* had never no thoughts of ſecuring this Right of the *Flag* by a formal Treaty, till they began to ſuſpect ſome difficulty might be made of paying to them, as a Commonwealth, the ſame Honour that had been paid to their Kings. Which induc'd them to have an Article about it in the Treaty of Peace, which was concluded between us in the Year 1654.

The third thing which is to be obſerv'd, is, That whereas the Court of *England*, inſtead of entering with us into the ſtrict Alliance which his Majeſty himſelf had propos'd to us whilſt he was here, did only renew the Treaty we had made with *Cromwel*, with ſome addition as we have ſaid before; the Article of the *Flag* being part of the ſame was concluded with the reſt, *Ann.* 1662. without any conference upon the Contents of the ſaid Article, or the leaſt Explanation of its true Senſe, further than what the Words did bear. And afterwards, in the Treaty of *Breda*, the nineteenth Article, which is ſo much ſpoken of, was tranſcrib'd out of the Treaty of 1662. as that of the Treaty of 1662. had been taken out of the Treaty of 1654. So that to underſtand rightly the true Senſe of the ſaid Article, we muſt go back to the Original, and examine what hath paſs'd in *London* in the Conferences and Debates between the *Engliſh* Commiſſioners

(whereof

(whereof *Cromwel* himself was one) and our Extraordinary Deputys, in relation to the Article aforesaid.

And it doth appear by the Journal of our Deputys, which we have ready to produce to justify what we do alledg (not doubting but that in case the *English* Commissioners have follow'd the same method, and have likewise register'd what pass'd, the same Particulars will be found therein) That on the $\frac{8}{18}$ of *November* 1653. the *English* Commissioners deliver'd to our said Deputys twenty seven Articles, which they propos'd to be agreed upon, and to make up the Treaty that was to be concluded. And that in the fifteenth of those Articles, it was amongst other things expresly said, That all our Ships, as well Men of War as others, whether single or in Fleets, meeting with any of the Ships of War of *England*, should strike their *Flag*, and lower their Topsail.

Whereupon our Deputies did declare, that they had order from us, to assure the Commonwealth, our Intention was not to make any Innovation, and that we were very ready to pay to the Commonwealth all the same Respects, as we had paid to *England* under the former Government: And that therefore since they would have a particular Article about it, it was necessary, in order to that, to inquire of the oldest, and most experienc'd Sea-Officers on both sides, in what manner the thing had been constantly practis'd, to settle it accordingly for the future: And the rather, because it was never mention'd in any former Treaty.

The Conferences, both upon that Point and several others, did continue for several days: But in all that time the *English* Commissioners could not be brought to enter into the Examination which was propos'd, nor to refer it (notwithstanding the reiterated Instances of our Deputys) to the decision of Seamen, as well in respect of the Coasts and Places, where *Striking* had till then been us'd, as for the Number of Ships; Which certainly they would not have refus'd, if they could have prov'd that any Fleet of ours had ever struck to a single Ship of *England*, as they had pretended at first. And on the *26th* of *Decemb.* V. S. following, they gave our Deputys this Article, instead of the former they could not agree upon:

That the Ships and Vessels of the United Provinces, *as well Men of War as others, meeting at Sea with any of the Ships of War of the State of* England, *shall strike their Flag and lower their Topsail, and perform all the other Respects due to this State, until they be pass'd by.*

In this new Article, the *English* Commissioners not being able to instance in any Fleet that had struck to a single Ship,

 nor

nor consequently to justify their Pretension, they left out the word *Fleets*, which was in the former Article, and left the thing undecided in this, *That the Ships and Vessels*, without saying more. And at last, after several Conferences upon the whole Article, it was agreed on both sides to make no Innovation, and to keep to the Practice, without determining the same more particularly. The said Article having accordingly been worded thus:

Quod Naves & Navigia dictarum Fœderatarum Provinciarum, tam bellica & ad hostium vim propulsandam instructa, quam alia, quæ alicui è Navibus bellicis hujus Reipublicæ in Maribus Britannicis obviam dederint, vexillum suum è mali vertice detrahent, & supremum velum demittent, eo modo quo ullis retro temporibus sub quocunque anteriori Regimine observatum fuit.

That the Ships and Vessels of the said United Provinces, *as well Men of War as others, meeting in the* British Seas *with any of the Ships of War of this Commonwealth, shall strike their Flag, and lower their Topsail, in the same manner as hath been heretofore done, under any former Government.*

This Point having been thus ended, and the whole Treaty concluded and ratify'd on both sides, we gave still our general Instructions to our Admirals and other Sea-Commanders, in the very same words as before, not seeing any ground to make the least Alteration in them, since the said Article left things in the same condition and state as before; adding only to them the Treaty that had been concluded, to be a Rule to our said Officers. And being there had never been any Clause in the said Instructions, that order'd the Commanders of our Fleets to strike their *Flag* to any of the *English* Ships of War they should meet with, we did not add it neither; it being plain by all that hath been said now, that we were no ways bound to it, and that the *English* Commissioners had waved that point, and insisted upon it no longer, for no other cause but that they wanted Proofs to back their Assertion.

In the mean time several years pass'd without any Dispute or Difference upon that matter, between the Commonwealth of *England* and Us. His Majesty now reigning was afterwards restor'd to his Crowns; and in the Treaty which was concluded with him in 1662, the same Article was inserted with the rest, but without any more particular Explanation, either by Word of mouth or in Writing. In 1667. it was transcrib'd *verbatim* out of the Treaty of 1662. to have it the nineteenth Article of that of *Breda:* And in all these Revolutions there had never been yet any difference upon the executing of it, till

till the Month of *August* 1671. at which time the Court of *England* was pleas'd to send a Yacht into our Fleet, that lay at anchor (as we said before) not far from our Coast; which sailing by one of our Admirals, shot twice sharp upon him, because he did not strike his Flag, and lower his Topsail. Whereupon the said Admiral, who had no other Order concerning the Flag, but to observe the 19th Article of the Treaty of *Breda*, considering that the said Article did not mention whole Fleets, but spoke only of Ships in general, and that for the above-mention'd Reasons; besides several other Circumstances our Fleet lay then under, to which the Article could not be apply'd: And being desirous withal to pay to his Majesty of *Great Britain* all the Respect he possibly could, he went himself on board the Yacht (which was a thing almost without precedent, for an Admiral in actual Command) and told the Captain with all imaginable Civility, that without a particular Order he could not take upon him a thing of that importance: And that in case his Majesty of *Great Britain* did think it was his due, the Difference was to be decided with Us, who were the Masters of him the said Admiral.

This is the grand Crime of our Admiral; 'tis what we are accus'd of our selves with so much Heat and Passion; and this is the unpardonable Affront we are guilty of, towards the King and all the *English* Nation. As for what they add of our Carriage upon this Accident, we shall have a fitter opportunity to speak of it in another place. And as to the Dominion of the Seas, and a pretended Tribute for Fishing (which no man can tell how they come to mention in this place) we'll only answer in few Words, That both the one and the other is altogether foreign to this War: And that as in all that relateth to the Ceremony of the Flag, we never intended to make the least Innovation, and would have no other Judges to regulate and decide it, than the oldest and most experienc'd Sea-Commanders; so we desire no new Privilege for the Liberty of Fishing, and claim nothing in that respect, but to keep close to what hath been hitherto the constant Practice; and to preserve what hath been regulated by solemn Treaties, near two hundred years since; and which the Inhabitants of our Provinces, under all Changes and Forms of Government, have constantly enjoy'd without interruption.

Notwithstanding all these Provocations, We patiently expected Satisfaction, not being willing to expose the Peace of Christendom

IT is hard to apprehend what Provocations are meant here, for which Satisfaction had been so patiently ex-

ſtendom *for our particular Reſentments ; whilſt they ceas'd not on their parts to endeavour to provoke the moſt Chriſtian King againſt Us ; of which they thought themſelves ſo ſecure, that for above theſe twelve months their Miniſters here have threaten'd us with it.*

expected by the King of *Great Britain*, whilſt he was unwilling to expoſe the Peace of *Chriſtendom* for his particular Reſentments, and which made him ſend us another Embaſſador, as it is ſaid a little after. For if they mean by it the Buſineſſes of the *Eaſt-Indies* and of *Surinam*, with our pretended abuſing his Majeſty's Perſon, which they lay to our charge ; We have already made it appear, that in all theſe reſpects the *Engliſh* Court had much cauſe to thank us for our Condeſcenſion, far from complaining of us. And this ſecond Embaſſador they ſpeak of, did never make the leaſt mention of it ; which yet, in caſe their Complaints had been well grounded, was altogether neceſſary, to the end our Denial might have juſtify'd their War.

But on the contrary it is plain, it was not without Myſtery they call'd back Sir *William Temple*, who had always been zealous to prevent, or to ſtop the progreſs of all that might breed the leaſt Miſunderſtanding between both Nations, and who had ſtill endeavour'd, by all poſſible means, to preſerve an Alliance (whereof he had been an happy Inſtrument) entire ; to ſend us a great while after an Embaſſador, who neither in the Memorials he deliver'd us, nor in his private Diſcourſes, did ſo much as mention what they have ſince made ſo much noiſe about. And if this *Patient Expectation* relates only to the Buſineſs of the Flag, we'll demonſtrate in the two following Articles the Injuſtice of this Complaint.

In the mean time, what they do add concerning our Endeavours to provoke the *French* King againſt his Majeſty of *Great Britain*, is as far from Truth as all the reſt of their Accuſations : And we do not doubt but that all the *Engliſh* Nation will give more credit to the ſincere Proteſtation we do make here, in the preſence of God and Men, that we had not ſo much as the Thoughts of what they lay to our charge, than to what ſome *French* Emiſſarys do ſurmiſe, as much againſt all Likelihood as againſt Truth.

We were then ſo far from having any ſecret Underſtanding with *France*, that we have drawn their Arms upon us merely by our being enter'd into too ſtrict an Alliance with the King of *Great Britain*. And 'tis too well known to all *Europe*, whether the *Engliſh* Court, or We, have beſt kept the ſaid Alliance, and which of us hath leaſt ſought the Friendſhip of the *French* King to each other's prejudice. Since the Embaſ-

ſador

ſador *Mountague* was ſent into *France* (which was in the beginning of the Year 1669) the leaſt clear-ſighted could eaſily perceive who have been the boſom Friends. And after reiterated Embaſſys of their grand Miniſters, as well as what had paſs'd at *Dover*, together with the great Levys they had given leave to the *French* to make againſt us in *England*, *Scotland*, and *Ireland*; We muſt needs have been of a very eaſy belief, to have fancy'd, we had a greater ſhare in the Friendſhip of the *French*, than the Court of *England* had: We, who at the ſame time had ſet out a conſiderable Fleet, to protect the *Spaniſh Netherlands*, in caſe of a ſecond Invaſion, and who were very earneſt with *England* to ſet out another for the ſame end, that we might act jointly, and keep up the Reputation of the Alliance we were enter'd into; the *French* King being then advanc'd as far as *Dunkirk*.

But to demonſtrate further the Injuſtice of this Accuſation, our Embaſſador in *England* having ſent us word, that notwithſtanding all the convincing Proofs we had given of the contrary, yet there were ſome ill-affected Perſons who endeavour'd to perſuade both the King and all the Nation, we treated underhand with *France*, contrary to our Engagements. We immediately order'd him to declare in our name to his Majeſty of *Great Britain*, That to evidence the Falſhood of thoſe Reports which were ſpread abroad to our diſadvantage, and to give his ſaid Majeſty eſſential and undeniable Proofs of the Sincerity of our Intentions, we were ready to enter into ſuch an Alliance with him as he ſhould think fit, how ſtrict ſoever the ſame might be, and to go far beyond any thing we had already done, for ſecuring the Peace of *Europe*.

It is true, the reiterated Proffers of our Embaſſador were rejected with ſcorn: But we could hardly have imagin'd, that after this Proceeding of ours, the Court of *England* could ſince have laid to our charge Threats, which they knew full well to be imaginary, and which we could not be guilty of, at a time wherein we ſought to unite us more ſtrictly; and whilſt we were too well acquainted with their ſecret Intrigues with the *French*, to expect the Aſſiſtance of theſe againſt *England*.

AT length, hearing nothing from them, We ſent another Embaſſador to them, who after ſeveral preſſing Memorials in our Name, could receive no Anſwer, till after he had declar'd his Revocation. Then they offer'd a Paper

THEIR manner of ſpeaking here, of the ſending of their ſecond Embaſſador, doth ſeem to imply that either this complain'd in the uſual Form, of all they are pleas'd to accuſe us of in their *Manifeſto*;

Paper to this effect, That in this Conjuncture they would condescend to strike to Us, if We would assist them against the French: *But upon condition, that it should never be taken for a Precedent hereafter to their prejudice.*

festo; or that Sir *William Temple* had already made his Complaints upon the business of the Flag, without receiving any answer to't. As to the first we have already made it appear how far the same is from being true. And as to Sir *William Temple*, it would have been hard for him to complain to us of what did not happen, but very near a year after he had left us. But to insist no longer upon the Contradictions, which will be found in more than one place in this *Manifesto*, and to give an answer to what they do alledg; it is true we did not send first into *England* upon the Dispute of the Flag. And as we were not satisfy'd our Admiral had violated the 19th Article of the Treaty of *Breda*, we thought it fit to stay for the Complaint of the King of *Great Britain*, in case he did conceive we had not paid him what respect was due to him: The rather because the Proposal which the Sieur *Boreel*, our Embassador, had made to his Majesty and to his Ministers, (very little after the Accident of the Flag) to enter into Conference with them upon the same, was rejected, under pretence that an Embassador should be sent to us. And when at last Sir *George Downing* came from his said Majesty, we declar'd, in answer to the Memorial he deliver'd us the of *January*, that all our Admirals and other Sea-Commanders had a strict Order from us, to observe punctually and regulate themselves by the 19th Article of the Treaty concluded at *Breda*, with his Majesty of *Great Britain*; and that our Intention was to have it as a standing Rule to us, in all its Circumstances: But that since the matter in question related to the Execution of an Article, upon which the Complaints made were grounded, it was to be observ'd, 1. That it did not appear to us, that general Fleets were comprehended in it, and that nothing else was mention'd therein but *Ships* and *Vessels* indefinitely. And 2. that it was to be done *eo modo quo ultis retro temporibus unquam observatum fuit*, in the same manner it had ever been practis'd.

Upon the first Point, to shew the true Sense of the said Article, we used part of the Arguments above-mention'd. And as to the second, we offer'd again to the said Embassador to enter with him, if the King his Master pleas'd, into a strict Inquiry of the usual Practice concerning the Flag; and that in case it were found that our Fleets had ever struck to a single *English* Ship, we should acknowledg the thing to be due, and would dispute it no further: our

Intention

Intention being not to recede from what had been formerly practis'd.

Thus far our Anſwer related to the matter in debate, and evidenced with how little reaſon we were accuſed of having violated the Treaty of *Breda.* But we went further than this: And tho we knew very well that in the Examination which we did propoſe, it would never be found that our general Fleets had ſtruck to a ſingle Ship; yet inſiſting no further upon the ſaid Inquiry (which could not but have prov'd much to our advantage) we declar'd that upon the Confidence we had in the true and ſolid Friendſhip of the King of *Great Britain,* and in hopes he would perform what he was bound to, by the fifth Article of the *Triple Alliance,* in caſe *France* made war upon us; we readily conſented that our whole *Fleets,* as well as our particular *Ships,* ſhould ſtrike to any ſingle Man of War, that carry'd the Flag of his Majeſty of *Great Britain:* thereby to give his ſaid Majeſty the higheſt proof of the Reſpect and Honour we would at all times endeavour to pay ſo great a Monarch: Proffering withal to his Majeſty, to agree with him upon a certain Regulation concerning the ſame, to prevent all future Diſputes and Controverſies.

This, in ſhort, is the Subſtance of the Anſwer we gave to the Memorial of Sir *George Downing*; which the Compilers of the *Manifeſto* are pleas'd to turn into *Ridicule,* whilſt they knew they were not able to object any thing rational againſt it: As tho to juſtify their War, they had nothing to do but to introduce us ſpeaking impertinently, and to make us ſay what we never ſo much as thought on.

But theſe Gentlemen do not tell us that, leſt the thing ſhould be throughly examin'd, and to avoid ſerious Debates, which undoubtedly would have taken off the pretence they did ſeek, and which they had need of, to keep their word to the *French,* the ſaid Embaſſador *Downing* was order'd to receive nothing from us after a certain number of Days that were preſcrib'd to him, and which they knew to be too ſhort a time to have an Anſwer of ſo high an importance ready, under ſuch a Form of Government as ours, where the Remoteneſs of the Members that have a deciſive Voice, doth much retard the Reſolutions that are taken. So that when our Anſwer was brought to him, he would not receive it, under pretence it came too late: And whilſt they extol ſo much in this *Manifeſto* their great Patience, we could not ſo much as be heard, merely becauſe we had not ſpoken ſome few hours ſooner. And therefore upon the denial of the Embaſſador, we were forc'd to ſend our ſaid Anſwer directly to the King his Maſter; tho with little better ſucceſs.

SINCE the return of our said Embassador, they have sent an Extraordinary one to Us, who in a most extraordinary manner has given Us to understand, That he can offer us no Satisfaction till he hath sent back to his Masters.

THEY still make themselves merry, and do fancy a cold Allusion to the Character of our Embassador, will justify their Carriage, and their invincible Obstinacy, in refusing to enter with him into regular Conferences upon what he was to offer them from us; as will best appear by what followeth.

Our Answer to the Memorial of Sir *George Downing* (which he refus'd to receive) having been deliver'd to his Majesty of *Great Britain* by our Embassador, he receiv'd a Reply from the Court of *England*, wherein they complain'd, our said Answer was nothing less than satisfactory, and was full of dark and ambiguous words; with some other Objections of the like nature. Whereupon we thought fit to send an Extraordinary Embassador into *England*, with full power to clear what might be doubtful or dark, and to add (in order to it) what would be necessary to express our true Intention and Meaning; which was to go much beyond what had till then been agreed upon, in relation to the Flag. In the first Conference, which the said Extraordinary Embassador, together with our Legier, had with the *English* Ministers, they acquainted them with the Orders they had receiv'd from Us; and having assur'd them they were ready to clear in our Name what might be *dark* or *ambiguous* in our Answer (without being able to bring the said Ministers to instance in what they found amiss therein) they offer'd them a Project of an Article, or Declaration more ample in writing, upon the business of the Flag; wherein it was expresly said, That our Fleets in a Body, as well as our single Ships, meeting with any of the Ships of War that had the Flag of his Majesty of *Great Britain*, should strike their Flag and lower their Topsail (which one would think was the fullest and strongest explanatory Clause, that could be added to the 19th Article of *Breda*) without annexing the same, or making it depend upon any Condition or Demand whatsoever from *England*. Whereupon our said Embassadors desir'd to know of the *English* Commissioners, whether such a Declaration would satisfy his Majesty? and if so, they were ready to sign it. But the *English* Commissioners answer'd, they expected an Answer to the King's above-mention'd Memorial (or Reply) dated the $\frac{3}{13}$ of *February*, and could receive no Papers that were not sign'd. And our Embassadors refusing then to sign it, before they

they knew whether the same should be satisfactory, the Conference thus broke off without any further discourse. But afterwards our said Embassadors reflecting upon the strictness of the Orders they had from us, to omit nothing of what might demonstrate the Sincerity of our Intentions, and the respect we did bear to the Person of his Majesty of *Great Britain*, resolved to pass by all other Considerations; and having drawn up and signed a Memorial (wherein the aforesaid Declaration was comprehended, with a Promise of clearing it yet further, in case they should think it still ambiguous or dark) they demanded a new Conference to deliver it to the Commissioners: But these foreseeing that such a Condescension in our Embassadors might be a great Obstacle to their Designs, and prevent the Breach, if it came to be publickly known, and they had free Conferences upon it; They had the Skill to cause their *Declaration* of War to be read and approv'd in the King's Council, which was extraordinarily call'd for that End, and with great Precipitation, an hour before the time they had appointed to our Embassadors, for the Conference which was granted them. So that when our said Embassadors came to the place of the Conference, they were told they came too late, and that the War had been just then resolv'd upon, and decreed in his Majesty's Council. Upon which ground, the *English* Commissioners refused to receive the Paper our Embassadors had written, and which they still were willing to deliver, tho they were told the War was declared.

It is easy to imagine how great the surprizal of our Embassadors was, when they receiv'd this Answer; and we are no less astonish'd to see the Court of *England*, after all the Endeavours of our Extraordinary Embassador to prevent the Breach, to accuse him now so groundlesly to have declar'd to them, he could offer no satisfaction to his Majesty of *Great Britain*, till he had sent back to us.

WHerefore, despairing now of any good Effect of a further Treaty, We are compell'd to take up Arms in Defence of the Antient Prerogative of Our Crowns, and the Glory and Safety of Our Kingdoms; And We put Our trust in God, that He will give Us His Assistance in this Our just Undertaking, since We had no way left to defend Our People from the Artifice

ALL we have said hitherto in general, and in particular the faithful Account of what pass'd in *London*, between our Embassadors and the *English* Ministers, doth sufficiently evidence with what Justice they accuse us here, to have compell'd the King of *Great Britain* to take up Arms, by taking from him (as they pretend)

tifice of that Nation in Peace, but by the Valour of Our Subjects in War.

We have therefore thought fit to Declare, and do hereby Declare, That We will prosecute War both by Sea and Land against the States General *of the* United Provinces, *and all their Subjects and Inhabitants. Hereby enjoyning Our most dear and most beloved Brother the Duke of* York *Our High Admiral, Our Lieutenants of Our several Counties, Governors of Our Forts and Garisons, and all other Officers and Soldiers under them by Sea and Land, to oppose all the Attempts of the* States General of the United Provinces, *or their Subjects, and to do and execute all Acts of Hostility in the prosecution of this War against the said* States General of the United Provinces, *their Vassals, Subjects, and Inhabitants; Willing and Requiring all Our Subjects to take notice of the same, Whom We henceforth straightly forbid, on pain of Death, to hold any Correspondence or Communication with the said* States General, *or their Subjects, (those only excepted who are necessitated thereunto for the withdrawing their Persons and Estates out of the* United Provinces.) *And because there are remaining in our Kingdoms many Subjects of the* States General of all the United Provinces, *We do Declare, and give Our Royal Word, that all such of the* Dutch *Nation, as shall demean themselves dutifully towards Us, and not correspond with Our Enemies, shall be safe in their Persons and Estates, and free from all Molestation and Trouble of any kind.*

tend) all hopes of receiving any satisfaction by a Treaty. After that, it is not to be wonder'd at if they do think themselves so secure of the Divine Assistance in their just Undertakings. So *Godly* a War could not want a happy Success.

Yet we must not forget that (as we have said it already) in the very moment they call God to witness of our Obstinacy, and at the time this *Manifesto* was read and approv'd in the Council, they expected an hour after our Embassadors, from whom they knew beforehand they should receive all the satisfaction they could reasonably expect: And even, that this Council was call'd with so much precipitation, to no other end, but to make the Endeavours of our Ministers fruitless, and to leave no further room to Negotiation.

Besides, if the War, which the Court of *England* is enter'd into against us, be such as they could not avoid, and which they had not design'd themselves; to what end did they (several Months before the Breach) send Ministers to the Court of *Sueden*, and that of *Brandenburgh?* Was it to persuade those Princes to stand faster to us? And do they think we are altogether Strangers to what they negotiated? Would they have us and the World believe, by an implicit Faith, their secret Understanding with *France* began with this War; and that they

they were not bent upon our deſtruction long before that time? All *Europe* is ſufficiently acquainted with what hath been done in that reſpect. And without going back to leſs publick Engagements, and of an antienter date (as might be that of *Dover*) in the very additional Articles which were agreed upon in the *French* Camp, and whereof the *Engliſh* Plenipotentiaries themſelves ſent a Copy to the Prince of *Orange*, they do own they had already concluded a Treaty ag inſt us, on the $\frac{2}{12}$ of *February* 1672; that is, near two Months before the Breach, as well as before they knew how far we might comply with them.

Laſtly, To evidence that their Declaring War was nothing leſs than grounded upon the Neceſſity they ſpeak of; it is obſervable, they made War upon us, before they declar'd it; and by an unheard-of Proceeding had already fallen upon our Merchant Ships that came from the *Straits*; at the ſame time we had ſent them an Extraordinary Embaſſador, to offer them ſatisfaction upon what they did chiefly complain of, and to let his Majeſty of *Great Britain* know, how far we were deſirous of preſerving his Friendſhip.

AND further We do Declare, That if any of the Low-Country *Subjects, either out of Affection to Us or Our Government, or becauſe of the Oppreſſion they meet with at home, ſhall come into Our Kingdoms, they ſhall be by Us protected in their Perſons and Eſtates.*

AS to the Protection which is promis'd here to ſuch of our Subjects as ſhall tranſport themſelves into the Kingdoms of his Majeſty of *Great Britain*, 'tis what we do not oppoſe: And all we can ſay, is, That we have not been as yet ſenſible of any great Depopulation in our Provinces, through the removal of our Inhabitants, nor that they have hitherto prefer'd the Domination of our Neighbours before Ours.

AND whereas We are engag'd by a Treaty to ſupport the Peace made at Aix la Chapelle, *We do finally Declare, That notwithſtanding the proſecution of this War, We will maintain the true Intent and Scope of the ſaid Treaty; and that in all the Alliances, which We have or ſhall make in the progreſs of this War, We have and will take care, to preſerve the Ends thereof inviolable, unleſs provok'd to the contrary.*

THE Concluſion of this *Manifeſto* is no leſs ſurprizing than all the reſt. And if the Compilers of it had had never ſo little care of their Reputation, they ought much rather to have ſtifled (if it had been poſſible) the Memory of the *Triple Alliance*, and of the Treaty of *Aix*, than to have ſo untimely put us in mind of the little value they have ſet upon

upon their Promises, and the solemn Engagements they were entred into, both with the Crown of *Spain* and with us. And indeed, it is hard to imagine they are in earnest, when they tell us they will maintain the true Intent and Scope of the Peace of *Aix la Chapelle*, and preserve the Ends thereof inviolable, whilst they have enter'd into a League with *France* to invade our Provinces, and have kindled a War much more dangerous than that which was compos'd at *Aix*.

But the better to judg of the Sincerity of this Declaration; and to the end it may appear how far the Court of *England* hath preserv'd the Ends of the said Treaty, we desire the Reader to reflect upon the following Hints, which we dare not enlarge upon, for fear of being too tedious. This single Head, to clear it fully, requiring a *Manifesto* by it self.

The first Thing to be observ'd, is, That the Treaty of *Aix la Chapelle* was only the Complement, and perfecting of the *Triple Alliance*; wherein what was executed at *Aix*, had been already design'd and agreed upon: And that consequently those two Treaties cannot be divided, and ought to be look'd upon as one single Treaty, tho concluded in several places, and at some months distance of one another. So that the Court of *England* cannot pretend to have kept the Treaty of *Aix*, unless at the same time they can make it appear they have not violated the *Triple Alliance*, and that they have on their part answer'd its true end.

2. It is further to be observ'd, it was his Majesty of *Great Britain* who propos'd the said *Alliance*, having sent us in order to it Sir *William Temple*, who did earnestly press us to join with the King his Master, to stop the progress of the *French* Arms; and by re-establishing the Quiet of Christendom, to set bounds to a Power, which gave so much jealousy to all its Neighbours.

3. That being overcome by the powerful Arguments of the aforesaid Sir *William Temple*, we consented to what he desir'd of us. But as we could not but foresee, that such an Alliance would exasperate *France*, and might be attended with evil Consequences, we desir'd at the same time, for our greater security, to unite us more strictly with *England*, and concluded with them a *Defensive League*, which till then we could never obtain since the King's Restoration: not thinking that after that there could be any danger in acting jointly with his said Majesty, and complying with his desires.

4. That upon the same grounds, when *Sueden* was admitted into the same *Alliance*, which from thence was called *Triple*, it was stipulated in express words in the second and third Articles,

cles, That to establish this Alliance upon a surer Foundation, there should be for ever, between the contracting Parties, a firm and sincere Friendship; and that to cultivate it, and preserve it really and sincerely, each of the said Confederates should heartily endeavour to procure all Good and Advantage to the others, and to preserve them, as far as they were able, from all damage and peril: For which end also, all the Treaties and reciprocal Engagements, that were respectively between them, should be preserv'd entire, and kept inviolable. And in the fifth Article it was added, That in case the aforesaid good Intentions of the Confederates should be ill resented by any other State or Prince, and that by reason of the same any injury were done to, or War made upon any of the Confederates, the other two should be bound to assist him with all possible vigour both by Sea and Land, and not to call back their Succors before they had procur'd him a reparation, and until the Danger was over.

Now we ask the Compilers of the *Manifesto*, whether it was by their giving leave to the *French*, to make so great Levies in *England*, *Scotland*, and *Ireland* (whilst they knew they were intended against us) they began to promote our Good and our Advantage, as they were bound? Whether their secret Intrigues with the *French*, and the Engagements they had with the said Crown, be what they call to cultivate the sincere Friendship they had promis'd us? How far their Carriage in the Courts of *Sueden* and *Brandenburgh* hath been agreeable to the Obligation they lay under, to preserve us, as far as they were able, from the Danger that did threaten us? And lastly, whether they do persuade themselves, they have honestly perform'd the *Defensive League* they had concluded with us, by their breaking with us, the very first, without any provocation from us?

But it is not only in relation to us, the Court of *England* did not observe the *Triple Alliance*: They have valued it as little both in other respects, and upon other occasions. Thus, altho by the seventh Article of the Treaty of *Aix*, all *Kings*, *Potentates* and *Princes* had a right to give their Guaranty for the performance of the said Treaty, that is, in other words, to come into the *Triple Alliance*, wherein the same thing had already been covenanted; And that pursuant to the said Treaty, the King of *Great Britain* (whilst his Ministers had other thoughts) had sollicited several *German* Princes to come into the same *Alliance*: Yet when the Emperor desir'd, a while after, to be admitted into it, the Persuasions of the *French* were so powerful, that it was denied in *England*, after they had promis'd it at first; and the said Court began to fear to see the

Peace

Peace too well ſettled, far from continuing in their firſt Zeal, and keeping up the reputation of a League, which ow'd its Being to them.

Laſtly, Seeing the chief End of the *Triple Alliance* was to ſettle the Peace of Chriſtendom; and that the Jealouſy, which the Greatneſs of *France* rais'd in ſeveral Princes, had been the occaſion of their uniting themſelves, and which in particular had mov'd the Court of *England* to make the firſt Overtures of it: The ſaid Court could not overthrow more openly all that they had done before, nor violate the *Triple Alliance* more directly, than by ſetting, as they have done, all Chriſtendom in a flame; and by countenancing with ſo much Zeal, the Arms of a Prince whom they had, for ſome years, made it their Glory to depreſs.

And now upon all that has been ſaid (wherein we hope it will appear to every impartial Eye, that we have not us'd the diſingenuous Licence of our Adverſaries, in aſſerting whatſoever may be for their purpoſe, without the leaſt colour of Truth to ſupport it; but have ſtrictly confin'd our ſelves to matter of Fact, juſtified by Authentick Originals, and carrying undeniable Self-demonſtration along with it) We appeal to all the World, whether or no there has been any thing done on our part, which may truly be ſaid to be an Infraction of the late Treaty at *Breda*, and of the Sacred *Triple League*, ſo religiouſly entred into, for the Common Preſervation of the Peace and Safety of all *Europe*. And altho through the Goodneſs of God, who has miraculouſly put a ſtop to the Deſigns of our Enemies, we are at preſent in a Condition to deſend our ſelves, (jointly with our Allies, to whom we are ſtrictly united) and have no cauſe to deſpair, but that our Arms will ſtill be attended with that ſucceſs, which the righteous God do's uſually give to ſo juſt a Cauſe: yet being always ready to apply our ſelves to the moſt hopeful ways of procuring Peace with all our Neighbours; and having more particular Inclinations to do any thing which may be leading to a right Underſtanding with the Kingdom of *England* (whoſe Friendſhip we moſt earneſtly deſire, and ever ſhall eſteem as the greateſt worldly Bleſſing) We do here, in the ſimplicity of our Hearts, and in the confidence of our own Integrity, ſubmit the Sincerity of this our Defence to the Judgment of the *Engliſh* Nation in general, and more particularly of the High and Honourable Court of Parliament, as repreſenting the whole Body of the Nation; whom we are not only willing to make the ſole Arbitrators of all the unhappy Differences betwixt the Court of *England* and us; but ſhould account it the

the most prosperous Step to an happy Accommodation, if they (who must be allow'd to be the best Judges of this Controversy) would take the pains rightly to discriminate betwixt the true Interest of the Nation (which they represent) and the Artificial Pretences of some few Evil-minded Men, who (for some sinister Purposes of their own, very little agreeable to the Duty they owe both to God and their Country) have contriv'd this War, in order to Ends equally destructive to *England*, as to this State.

Phenix

Phenix XI.

The Peoples Antient and Just Liberties asserted, in the Tryal of William Penn *and* William Mead, *at the Sessions held at the* Old-Baily *in* London, *the first, third, fourth and fifth of* Sept. 1670. *against the most Arbitrary Procedure of that Court.*

To the English Reader.

If ever it were time to speak, or write, 'tis now, so many strange Occurrences requiring both.

How much thou art concern'd in this ensuing Tryal *(where not only the Prisoners, but the Fundamental Laws of* England, *have been most Arbitrarily Arraigned) read, and thou may'st plainly judg.*

Liberty of Conscience *is counted a Pretence for Rebellion, and* Religious Assemblies, Routs *and* Riots; *and the* Defenders *of both, are by them, reputed* Factious *and* Disaffected.

Magna Charta *is Magnaf——with the* Recorder *of* London; *and to demand* Right, *an Affront to the Court.*

Will *and* Power *are their great* Charter; *but to call for* England's, *is a Crime, incurring the Penalty of their* Bale-Dock, *and* Nasty-hole; *nay, the Menace of a* Gag, *and* Iron Shackles *too.*

The

The Jury (tho proper Judges of Law and Fact) they would have over-ruled in both, as if their Verdict signified no more, than to eccho back the illegal Charge of the Bench; and because their Courage and Honesty did more than hold pace with the Threat and Abuse of those who sate as Judges, (after two days and two nights Restraint for a Verdict) in the end were Fined and Imprisoned for giving it.

O! what monstrous and illegal Proceedings are these? Who reasonably can call his Coat his own, when Property is made subservient to the Will and Interest of his Judges? *Or, who can truly esteem himself a Free-man,* when all Pleas for Liberty are esteem'd Sedition, *and the Laws that give, and maintain them, so many insignificant pieces of Formality?*

And what do they less than plainly tell us so, who at Will and Pleasure break open our Locks, rob our Houses, raze their Foundations, imprison our Persons, and finally deny us Justice *to our Relief? as if they then acted most like Christian Men, when they were most barbarous in ruining such as really are so; and that no Sacrifice could be so acceptable to God, as the destruction of those that most fear him.*

In short; That the Conscientious should only be obnoxious, and the just Demand of our Religious Liberty, the Reason why we should be denied our civil Freedom (as if to be a Christian and an English-man were inconsistent) and that so much solicitude and deep contrivance should be imploy'd only to ensnare and ruin so many Ten thousand conscientious Families, so eminently industrious, serviceable *and* exemplary; *whilst Murders can so easily obtain Pardons, Rapes be remitted, publick Uncleanness pass unpunish'd, and all manner of* Levity, Prodigality, Excess, Prophaneness *and* Atheism *universally conniv'd at, if not in some respect manifestly encourag'd, cannot but be detestably abhorrent to every serious and honest Mind.*

Yet that this lamentable State is true, and the present Project in hand, let London'*s Recorder, and* Canterbury'*s Chaplain be heard.*

The first in his publick Panegyrick upon the Spanish Inquisition, highly admiring the Prudence of the Romish Church, in the erection of it, as an excellent way to prevent Schism; *which unhappy Expression, at once passeth Sentence, both against our Fundamental Laws, and Protestant Reformation.*

The second, in his printed Mercenary Discourse against Toleration, *asserting for a main Principle,* That it would be less injurious to the Government, to dispense with prophane and loose Persons, than to allow a Toleration to Religious Dissenters. *It were to over-do the business, to say any more, where there is so much said already.*

And therefore, to conclude, we cannot chuse but admonish all, as well Persecutors, *to relinquish their Heady, Partial and Inhumane Prosecutions (as what will certainly issue in disgrace here, and inevitable condign Punishment hereafter) as those who yet dare express their Moderation (however out of fashion, or made the Brand of Phanaticism) not to be huff'd or menaced out of that excellent Temper, to make their Parts and Persons subservient to the base Humors, and sinister Designs, of the biggest Mortal upon Earth: But to reverence and obey the Eternal just God,* before whose great Tribunal all must render their accounts, and where he will recompense to every Person according to his Works.

The TRYAL *of* William Penn *and* William Mead.

AS there can be no Observation, where there is no Action; so it's impossible, there should be a judicious Intelligence, without due Observation.

And since there can be nothing more seasonable than a right Information, especially of *Publick Acts*; and well knowing, how industrious some will be, to misrepresent this Tryal to the disadvantage of the Cause and Prisoners, it was thought requisite, in defence of both, and for the satisfaction of the People, to make it more publick; nor can there be any business wherein the People of *England* are more concern'd, than in that which relates to their Civil and Religious Liberties, question'd in the Persons above-named, at the *Old-Baily*, the first, third, fourth and fifth of *Septemb.* 1670.

There being present,

Sam. Starling, Mayor.
Tho. Howel, Recorder.
Tho. Bludworth, Alderm.
William Peak, Alderm.

Richard Ford, Alderman.
Joseph Shelden, Alderman.
John Smith, } Sheriffs.
James Edwards, } Sheriffs.

Cryer. O Yes, *Thomas Veer*, ——— *Bushel, John Hammond, Charles Milson, Gregory Walklet, John Brightman, William Plumsted, Henry Henley, Thomas Damask, Henry Michel, William Lever, John Baily.*

The Form of the Oath.

You shall well and truly try, and true Deliverance make, betwixt our Sovereign Lord the King, and the Prisoners at the Bar, according to your Evidence: So help you God.

That

That *William Penn* Gent. and *William Mead*, late of *London*, Linen-Draper, with divers other Persons, to the Jurors unknown, to the number of Three hundred, the 14th Day of *August*, in the 22d Year of the King, about Eleven of the Clock in the Forenoon, the same Day, with Force and Arms, *&c.* in the Parish of St. *Bennet Grace-Church* in *Bridg-ward*, *London*, in the Street called *Grace-Church-Street*, Unlawfully and Tumultuously did Assemble and Congregate themselves together, to the Disturbance of the Peace of the said Lord the King: And the aforesaid *William Penn*, and *William Mead*, together with other Persons, to the Jurors aforesaid unknown, then and there so assembled and congregated together; the aforesaid *William Penn*, by agreement between him and *William Mead*, before made; and by Abetment of the aforesaid *William Mead*, then and there, in the open Street, did take upon himself to Preach and Speak, and then and there did Preach and Speak unto the aforesaid *William Mead*, and other Persons there, in the Street aforesaid, being assembled and congregated together; by reason whereof, a great Concourse and Tumult of People in the Street aforesaid, then and there a long time did remain and continue, in contempt of the said Lord the King, and of his Law, to the great Disturbance of his Peace, to the great Terror and Disturbance of many of his Liege People and Subjects, to the ill Example of all others, in the like case Offenders, and against the Peace of the said Lord the King, his Crown and Dignity.

What say you, *William Penn* and *William Mead*? are you guilty as you stand indicted, in manner and form, as aforesaid, or not guilty?

Penn. It is impossible that we should be able to remember the Indictment *verbatim*; and therefore we desire a Copy of it, as is customary in the like occasions.

Rec. You must first plead to the Indictment, before you can have a Copy of it.

Penn. I am unacquainted with the Formality of the Law; and therefore, before I shall answer directly, I request two Things of the Court. First, That no Advantage may be taken against me, nor I deprived of any Benefit, which I might otherwise have received. Secondly, That you will promise me a fair Hearing, and Liberty of making my Defence.

Court. No Advantage shall be taken against you; you shall have liberty; you shall be heard.

Penn. Then I plead Not guilty in manner and form.

Cler. What sayest thou, *William Mead*? art thou guilty in manner and form, as thou standest indicted, or not guilty?

Mead. I shall desire the same Liberty as is promised *William Penn.*

Court. You shall have it.

Mead. Then I plead Not guilty in manner and form.

The Court adjourned until the Afternoon.

Cryer. O Yes, *&c.*

Cler. Bring *William Penn* and *William Mead* to the Bar.

Observ. The said Prisoners were brought, but were set aside, and other business prosecuted. Where we cannot chuse but observe, that it was the constant and unkind Practice of the Court to the Prisoners, to make them wait upon the Tryals of Felons and Murderers, thereby designing, in all probability, both to affront and tire them.

After five hours attendance, the Court broke up, and adjourned to the third instant.

The third of *September*, 1670. the Court sate.

Cryer. O yes, *&c.*

Cler. Bring *William Penn* and *William Mead* before the Bar.

Mayor. Sirrah, who bid you put off their Hats? put on their Hats again.

Observ. Whereupon one of the Officers putting the Prisoners Hats upon their Heads (pursuant to the Order of the Court) brought them to the Bar.

Record. Do you know where you are?

Penn. Yes.

Record. Do not you know it is the King's Court?

Penn. I know it to be a Court, and I suppose it to be the King's Court.

Record. Do you not know there is Respect due to the Court?

Penn. Yes.

Record. Why do you not pay it then?

Penn. I do so.

Record. Why do you not pull off your Hat then?

Penn. Because I do not believe that to be any Respect.

Record. Well, the Court sets forty Marks a piece upon your Heads, as a Fine for your Contempt of the Court.

Penn. I desire it might be observ'd, that we came into the Court with our Hats off, (that is, taken off) and if they have been put on since, it was by Order from the Bench; and therefore not we, but the Bench should be fined.

Mead. I have a Question to ask the *Recorder*; Am I fined also?

Recor. Yes.

Mead.

Mead. I desire the Jury, and all people, to take notice of this Injustice of the *Recorder*; who spake to me to pull off my Hat; and yet hath he put a Fine upon my Head. O fear the Lord, and dread his Power, and yield to the guidance of his holy Spirit, for he is not far from every one of you.

The Jury Sworn again.

Obser. *J. Robinson*, Lieutenant of the *Tower*, disingenuously objected against —— *Bushell*, as if he had not kiss'd the Book, and therefore would have him Sworn again; tho indeed, it was on purpose, to have made use of his Tenderness of Conscience in avoiding reiterated Oaths, to have put him by his being a Jury-man, apprehending him to be a person not fit to answer their arbitrary Ends.

The Clerk read the Indictment, as aforesaid.

Cler. Cryer, call *James Cook* into the Court; give him his Oath.

Cler. James Cook, *lay your Hand upon the Book; the Evidence you shall give to the Court betwixt our Sovereign the King, and the Prisoners at the Bar, shall be the Truth, and the whole Truth, and nothing but the Truth: So help you God*, &c.

Cook. I was sent for from the Exchange, to go and disperse a Meeting in *Gratious-street*, where I saw Mr. *Penn* speaking to the People; but I could not hear what he said, because of the noise: I endeavour'd to make way to take him, but I could not get to him for the Croud of People: upon which Captain *Mead* came to me, about the Kennel of the Street, and desired me to let him go on; for when he had done, he would bring Mr. *Penn* to me.

Cour. What number do you think might be there?

Cook. About three or four hundred People.

Cour. Call *Richard Read*: Give him his Oath.

Read being sworn, was ask'd, What do you know concerning the Prisoners at the Bar?

Read. My Lord, I went to *Gratious-street*, where I found a great Croud of People, and I heard Mr. *Penn* preach to them; and I saw Captain *Mead* speaking to Lieutenant *Cook*, but what he said, I could not tell.

Mead. What did *William Penn* say?

Read. There was such a great noise, that I could not tell what he said.

Mead. Jury, observe this Evidence; He saith he heard him preach, and yet saith, he doth not know what he said.

Jury, take notice; he swears now a clean contrary thing to what he swore before the Mayor, when we were committed: For now he swears that he saw me in *Gratious-street*, and yet swore

ſwore before the Mayor, when I was committed, that he did not ſee me there. I appeal to the Mayor himſelf, if this be not true; but no Anſwer was given.

Cour. What number do you think might be there?

Read. About four or five hundred.

Penn. I deſire to know of him what day it was?

Read. Anſw. the 14th day of *Auguſt*.

Penn. Did he ſpeak to me, or let me know he was there? for I am very ſure I never ſaw him.

Cler. Cryer, call ——— ——— into the Court.

Cour. Give him his Oath.

My Lord, I ſaw a great number of People, and Mr. *Penn* I ſuppoſe was Speaking; I ſee him make a motion with his hands, and heard ſome noiſe, but could not underſtand what he ſaid: but for Captain *Mead*, I did not ſee him there.

Rec. What ſay you, Mr. *Mead?* were you there?

Mead. It is a Maxim in your own Law, *Nemo tenetur accuſare ſeipſum*; which if it be not true Latin, I am ſure it is true Engliſh, *That no man is bound to accuſe himſelf:* And why doſt thou offer to enſnare me with ſuch a Queſtion? Doth not this ſhew thy Malice? Is this like unto a Judg, that ought to be Counſel for the Priſoner at the Bar?

Record. Sir, Hold your Tongue, I did not go about to enſnare you.

Penn. I deſire we may come more cloſe to the Point, and that Silence be commanded in the Court.

Cry. O yes; All manner of Perſons keep Silence, upon pain of Impriſonment ——— Silence in the Court.

Penn. We confeſs our ſelves to be ſo far from recanting, or declining to vindicate the Aſſembling of our ſelves to Preach, Pray, or Worſhip the Eternal, Holy, Juſt God; that we declare to all the World, that we do believe it to be our indiſpenſable duty, to meet inceſſantly upon ſo good an account; nor ſhall all the Powers upon Earth be able to divert us from reverencing and adoring our God, who made us.

Brown. You are not here for worſhipping God, but for breaking the Law; you do your ſelves a great deal of wrong in going on in that diſcourſe.

Penn. I affirm I have broken no Law, nor am I guilty of the Indictment that is laid to my charge; and to the end, the Bench, the Jury, and my ſelf, with theſe that hear us, may have a more direct underſtanding of this procedure, I deſire you would let me know by what Law it is you proſecute me, and upon what Law you ground my Indictment.

Rec. Upon the Common Law.

Penn. Where is that Common Law?

Rec.

Rec. You must not think that I am able to run up so many years, and over so many adjudged Cases, which we call Common Law, to answer your curiosity.

Penn. This Answer, I am sure, is very short of my Question; for if it be Common, it should not be so hard to produce.

Rec. Sir, will you plead to your Indictment?

Penn. Shall I plead to an Indictment that hath no Foundation in Law? If it contain that Law you say I have broken, why should you decline to produce that Law, since it will be impossible for the Jury to determine, or agree to bring in their Verdict, who have not the Law produc'd, by which they should measure the Truth of this Indictment, and the Guilt, or contrary of my Fact?

Rec. You are a sawcy Fellow, speak to the Indictment.

Penn. I say, it is my place to speak to Matter of Law; I am arraigned a Prisoner, my Liberty, which is next to Life it self, is now concerned; you are many Mouths and Ears against me, and if I must not be allowed to make the best of my Case, it is hard: I say again, unless you shew me, and the People, the Law you ground your Indictment upon; I shall take it for granted, your Proceedings are merely Arbitrary.

Obser. *At this time several upon the Bench urged hard upon the Prisoner to bear him down.*

Rec. The Question is, Whether you are guilty of this Indictment?

Penn. The Question is not, Whether I am guilty of this Indictment, but whether this Indictment be legal; it is too general and imperfect an Answer, to say it is the Common Law, unless we knew both where, and what it is: For where there is no Law, there is no Transgression; and that Law which is not in being, is so far from being Common, that it is no Law at all.

Rec. You are an impertinent Fellow; will you teach the Court what Law is? It's *Lex non scripta*, that which many have studied thirty or forty years to know; and would you have me to tell you in a moment?

Penn. Certainly; If the Common Law be so hard to be understood, it's far from being very Common: But if the Lord *Cook*, in his Institutes, be of any consideration, he tells us, That Common Law is Common Right, and that Common Right is the great Charter-Privileges, confirm'd 9 *Hen.* 3. 29. 25 *Edw.* 1. 1. 2 *Edw.* 3. 8. *Cook Instit.* 2. p. 56.

Rec. Sir, you are a troublesome Fellow, and it is not for the Honour of the Court to suffer you to go on.

Penn. I have ask'd but one Queſtion, and you have not anſwer'd me; tho the Rights and Privileges of every Engliſhman be concern'd in it.

Rec. If I ſhould ſuffer you to ask Queſtions till to morrow morning, you would be never the wiſer.

Penn. That is according as the Anſwers are.

Rec. Sir, We muſt not ſtand to hear you talk all night.

Penn. I deſign no Affront to the Court, but to be heard in my juſt Plea; and I muſt plainly tell you, that if you will deny me *Oyer* of that Law, which you ſuggeſt I have broken, you do at once deny me an acknowledged Right, and evidence to the whole World your reſolution to ſacrifice the Privileges of Engliſh-men to your ſiniſter and arbitrary Deſigns.

Rec. Take him away: My Lord, if you take not ſome courſe with this peſtilent Fellow, to ſtop his mouth, we ſhall not be able to do any thing to Night.

May. Take him away, Take him away; turn him into the Bale-dock.

Penn. Theſe are but ſo many vain Exclamations: Is this Juſtice or true Judgment? Muſt I therefore be taken away, becauſe I plead for the Fundamental Laws of *England*? However, this I leave upon your Conſciences, who are of the Jury (and my ſole Judges) that if theſe Antient Fundamental Laws, which relate to Liberty and Property, (and are not limited to particular Perſuaſions in Matters of Religion) muſt not be indiſpenſibly maintain'd and obſerv'd; Who can ſay he hath right to the Coat upon his Back? Certainly our Liberties are openly to be invaded, our Wives to be raviſhed, our Children ſlaved, our Families ruined, and our Eſtates led away in Triumph, by every ſturdy Beggar and malicious Informer, as their Trophies, but our (pretended) Forfeits for Conſcience ſake; the Lord of Heaven and Earth will be Judge between us in this matter.

Rec. Be ſilent there.

Penn. I am not to be ſilent in a Caſe wherein I am ſo much concerned; and not only my ſelf, but many Ten thouſand Families beſides.

Obſer. They having rudely hal'd him into the Bale-dock, *William Mead* they left in Court, who ſpake as followeth.

Mead. You Men of the Jury, here I do now ſtand, to anſwer to an Indictment againſt me, which is a bundle of Stuff, full of Lies and Falſhoods; for therein I am accuſed, that I met *Vi & armis, illicite & tumultuoſe:* Time was, when I had freedom to uſe a carnal Weapon, and then I thought I feared no Man: but now I fear the Living God, and dare not make uſe thereof, nor hurt any Man; nor do I know I demeaned

my

my ſelf as a tumultuous perſon: I ſay, I am a peaceable Man, therefore it is a very proper Queſtion what *William Penn* demanded in this Caſe, An *Oyer* of the Law, on which our Indictment is grounded.

Recor. I have made Anſwer to that already.

Mead, turning his Face to the Jury, ſaith, You Men of the Jury, who are my Judges, if the *Recorder* will not tell you what makes a Riot a Rout, or an unlawful Aſſembly, *Cook*, he that once they called the Lord *Cook*, tells us what makes a Riot, a Rout, and an unlawful Aſſembly——— A Riot is when three, or more, are met together to beat a Man, or to enter forcibly into another Man's Land, to cut down his Graſs, his Wood, or break down his Pales.

Obſer. Here the *Recorder* interrupted him, and ſaid, I thank you Sir, that you will tell me what the Law is, ſcornfully pulling off his Hat.

Mead. Thou may'ſt put on thy Hat, I have never a Fee for thee now.

Brown. He talks at random, one while an *Independent*, another while ſome other Religion, and now a *Quaker*, and next a *Papiſt.*

Mead. Turpe eſt doctori cum culpa redarguit ad ipſum.

May. You deſerve to have your Tongue cut out.

Rec. If you diſcourſe on this manner, I ſhall take occaſion againſt you.

Mead. Thou didſt promiſe me I ſhould have fair liberty to be heard; Why may I not have the privilege of an Engliſh-man? I am an Engliſh-man, and you might be aſham'd of this dealing.

Rec. I look upon you to be an Enemy to the Laws of *England*, which ought to be obſerv'd and kept; nor are you worthy of ſuch Privileges as others have.

Mead. The Lord is Judg between me and thee in this matter.

Obſer. Upon which they took him away into the Bale-dock, and the Recorder proceeded to give the Jury their Charge, as followeth.

Rec. You have heard what the Indictment is; It is for preaching to the People, and drawing a tumultuous Company after them, and Mr. *Penn* was ſpeaking; if they ſhould not be diſturbed, you ſee they will go on; there are three or four Witneſſes that have proved this, that he did preach there, that Mr. *Mead* did allow of it; after this, you have heard by ſubſtantial Witneſſes what is ſaid againſt them. Now we are upon the Matter of Fact, which you are to keep to, and obſerve, as what hath been fully ſworn, at your peril.

Obſer.

Obser. The Prisoners were put out of the Court, into the Bale-dock, and the Charge given to the Jury in their absence; at which *W. P.* with a very raised Voice, it being a considerable distance from the Bench, spake:

Penn. I appeal to the Jury, who are my Judges, and this great Assembly, whether the Proceedings of the Court are not most arbitrary, and void of all Law, in offering to give the Jury their Charge in the absence of the Prisoners; I say, it is directly opposite to, and destructive of, the undoubted Right of every English Prisoner, as *Cook* in the 2 *Instit.* 29. on the Chap. of *Magna Charta* speaks.

Obser. The Recorder being thus unexpectedly lasht for his extra-judicial procedure, said with an inraged Smile,

Rec. Why, ye are present, you do hear, do you not?

Penn. No Thanks to the Court, that commanded me into the Bale-dock; and you of the Jury take notice, that I have not been heard, neither can you legally depart the Court before I have been fully heard, having at least ten or twelve Material Points to offer, in order to invalid their Indictment.

Rec. Pull that Fellow down, pull him down.

Mead. Are these according to the Rights and Privileges of English-men, that we should not be heard, but turned into the Bale-dock for making our Defence, and the Jury to have their Charge given them in our absence? I say, these are Barbarous and Unjust Proceedings.

Rec. Take them away into the Hole; to hear them talk all night, as they would, that I think doth not become the Honour of the Court; and I think you (*i. e.* the Jury) your selves wonld be tired out, and not have patience to hear them.

Obser. The Jury were commanded up to agree upon their Verdict, the Prisoners remaining in the stinking Hole; after an hour and half's time eight came down agreed, but four remain'd above, the Court sent an Officer for them, and they accordingly came down: The Bench used many unworthy Threats to the four that dissented; and the Recorder, addressing himself to *Bushell*, said, 'Sir, You are the cause of this 'disturbance, and manifestly shew your self an Abettor of 'Faction; I shall set a Mark upon you, Sir.

J. Robinson, 'Mr. *Bushell*, I have known you near this four-'teen years; you have thrust your self upon this Jury, because 'you think there is some service for you; I tell you, you de-'serve to be indicted more than any Man that hath been 'brought to the Bar this day.

Bush. No, Sir *John*; there were threescore before me, and I would willingly have got off, but could not.

Bloodw.

Bloodw. I said when I saw Mr. *Bushell*, What I see is come to pass, for I knew he would never yield. Mr. *Bushell*, we know what you are.

May. Sirrah, you are an impudent Fellow, I will put a mark upon you.

Obser. They used much menacing Language, and behaved themselves very imperiously to the Jury, as persons not more void of Justice than sober Education. After this Barbarous Usage, they sent them to consider of bringing in their Verdict, and after some considerable time they returned to the Court. Silence was called for, and the Jury called by their Names.

Cler. Are you agreed upon your Verdict?

Jury. Yes.

Cler. Who shall speak for you?

Jury. Our Fore-man.

Cler. Look upon the Prisoners at the Bar; How say you? Is *William Penn* guilty of the Matter wherefore he stands indicted in Manner and Form, or Not guilty?

Fore-m. Guilty of speaking in *Gracious-street.*

Court. Is that all?

Fore-m. That is all I have in Commission.

Recor. You had as good say nothing.

May. Was it not an unlawful Assembly? you mean he was speaking to a Tumult of People there?

Fore-m. My Lord, this was all I had in Commission.

Obser. Here some of the Jury seem'd to buckle to the Questions of the Court; upon which *Bushell*, *Hammond*, and some others opposed themselves, and said, They allowed of no such word as an unlawful Assembly in their Verdict: At which the *Recorder*, *Mayor*, *Robinson* and *Bloodworth* took great occasion to vilify them with most opprobrious Language; and this Verdict not serving their turns, the *Recorder* expressed himself thus.

Recor. The Law of *England* will not allow you to part till you have given in your Verdict.

Jury. We have given in our Verdict, and we can give in no other.

Recor. Gentlemen, you have not given in your Verdict, and you had as good say nothing; therefore go and consider it once more, that we may make an end of this troublesom business.

Jury. We desire we may have Pen, Ink and Paper.

Obser. The Court adjourned for half an hour; which being expired, the Court returns, and the Jury not long after.

The Prisoners were brought to the Bar, and the Juries Names called over.

Clar.

Cler. Are you agreed of your Verdict?

Jury. Yes.

Cler. Who ſhall ſpeak for you?

Jury. Our Fore-man.

Cler. What ſay you; look upon the Priſoners; Is *William Penn* guilty in Manner and Form, as he ſtands indicted, or not guilty?

Fore-m. Here is our Verdict, (holding forth a piece of Paper to the Clerk of the Peace) which follows.

WE the *Jurors*, hereafter named, do find *William Penn* to be guilty of Speaking or Preaching to an Aſſembly, met together in *Gracious-ſtreet*, the 14th of *Auguſt* laſt, 1670. And that *William Mead* is Not guilty of the ſaid Indictment.

Fore-m.	*Thomas Veer,*	*Charles Milſon,*
	Edward Buſhell,	*Gregory Walklet,*
	John Hammond,	*John Baily,*
	Henry Henley.	*William Lever,*
	Henry Michel,	*James Damask,*
	John Brightman,	*Will. Plumſted.*

Obſer. This both *Mayor* and *Recorder* reſented at ſo high a rate, that they exceeded the bounds of all Reaſon and Civility.

May. What, will you be led by ſuch a ſilly Fellow as *Buſhell?* an impudent canting Fellow; I warrant you, you ſhall come no more upon Juries in haſte: You are a Fore-man indeed, addreſſing himſelf to the Fore-man, I thought you had underſtood your place better.

Recor. Gentlemen, you ſhall not be diſmiſs'd till we have a Verdict that the Court will accept; and you ſhall be lockt up, without Meat, Drink, Fire, and Tobacco; you ſhall not think thus to abuſe the Court; we will have a Verdict, by the help of God, or you ſhall ſtarve for it.

Penn. My Jury, who are my Judges, ought not to be thus menaced; their Verdict ſhould be free, and not compelled; the Bench ought to wait upon them, but not foreſtall them. I do deſire that Juſtice may be done me, and that the arbitrary Reſolves of the Bench may not be made the meaſure of my Jury's Verdict.

Recor. Stop that prating Fellow's mouth, or put him out of the Court.

May. You have heard that he preach'd, that he gather'd a Company of tumultuous People, and that they do not only diſobey the Martial Power, but Civil alſo.

Penn.

Pen. It is a great mistake, we did not make the Tumult, but they that interrupted us; the Jury cannot be so ignorant, as to think that we met there with a design to disturb the Civil Peace; since first we were by Force of Arms kept out of our lawful House, and met as near it in the Street, as their Soldiers would give us leave: And secondly, because it was no new thing (nor with the Circumstances express'd in the Indictment) but what was usual and customary with us. 'Tis very well known that we are a peaceable People, and cannot offer violence to any man.

Obser. The Court being ready to break up, and willing to huddle the Prisoners to their Goal, and the Jury to their Chamber, *Penn* spoke as follows.

Pen. The Agreement of twelve men is a Verdict in Law; and such a one being given by the Jury, I require the Clerk of the Peace to record it, as he will answer it at his peril. And if the Jury bring in another Verdict, contradictory to this, I affirm they are perjur'd Men in Law. And looking upon the Jury, said, *You are* Englishmen, *mind your Privilege, give not away your Right.*

Bush. &c. Nor will we ever do it.

Obser. One of the Jury-men pleaded Indisposition of Body, and therefore desir'd to be dismiss'd.

May. You are as strong as any of them; Starve them; and hold your Principles.

Rec. Gentlemen, you must be contented with your hard fate; let your Patience overcome it; for the Court is resolv'd to have a Verdict, and that before you can be dismiss'd.

Jury. We are agreed, we are agreed, we are agreed.

Obser. The Court swore several Persons, to keep the Jury all night without Meat, Drink, Fire, or any other Accommodation: They had not so much as a Chamber-pot, tho desired.

Cry. O yes, *&c.*

Obser. The Court adjourns till seven of the clock next morning (being the fourth instant, vulgarly call'd *Sunday*) at which time the Prisoners were brought to the Bar; the Court sate, and the Jury call'd to bring in their Verdict.

Cry. O yes, &c.——Silence in the Court, upon pain of Imprisonment.

The Juries Names call'd over.

Clerk. Are you agreed upon your Verdict?

Jury. Yes.

Clerk. Who shall speak for you?

Jury. Our Foreman.

Clerk.

Clerk. What say you? Look upon the Prisoner at the Bar; Is he guilty of the matter whereof he stands indicted, in manner and form as aforesaid, or not guilty?

Foreman. William Penn is guilty of speaking in *Grace-Church-street.*

May. To an unlawful Assembly?

Bush. No, my Lord, we give no other Verdict, than what we gave last night; we have no other Verdict to give.

May. You are a factious Fellow, I'll take a course with you.

Blood. I knew Mr. *Bushel* would not yield.

Bush. Sir *Tho.* I have done according to my Conscience.

May. That Conscience of yours would cut my throat.

Bush. No, my Lord, it never shall.

May. But I will cut yours so soon as I can.

Rec. He has inspir'd the Jury, he has the Spirit of Divination, methinks I feel him: I will have a positive Verdict, or you shall starve for it.

Pen. I desire to ask the Recorder one question; Do you allow of the Verdict given of *William Mead?*

Rec. It cannot be a Verdict, because you were indicted for a Conspiracy; and one being found not guilty, and not the other, it could not be a Verdict.

Pen. If *Not Guilty* be not a Verdict, then you make of the Jury and *Magna Charta* but a mere Nose of Wax.

Mead. How! Is *not guilty* no Verdict?

Rec. No, 'tis no Verdict.

Pen. I affirm, that the Consent of a Jury is a Verdict in Law; and if *W. M.* be not guilty, it consequently follows that I am clear; since you have indicted us of a Conspiracy, and I could not possibly conspire alone.

Obser. There were many Passages that could not be taken, which past between the Jury and the Court. The Jury went up again, having receiv'd a fresh Charge from the Bench, if possible, to extort an unjust Verdict.

Cry. O yes, *&c.* Silence in the Court.

Court. Call over the Jury. Which was done.

Clerk. What say you? Is *William Penn* guilty of the matter whereof he stands indicted, in manner and form aforesaid, or not guilty?

Foreman. Guilty of speaking in *Grace-Church Street.*

Rec. What is this to the purpose? I say, I will have a Verdict. And speaking to *Edw. Bushel*, said, You are a factious Fellow; I will set a mark upon you; and whilst I have any thing to do in the City, I will have an eye upon you.

May. Have you no more wit than to be led by such a pitiful Fellow? I will cut his Nose.

Pen.

Pen. It is intolerable that my Jury should be thus menaced; Is this according to the fundamental Laws? Are not they my proper Judges by the Great Charter of *England*? What hope is there of ever having Justice done, when Juries are threaten'd, and their Verdicts rejected? I am concern'd to speak, and grieved to see such arbitrary Proceedings. Did not the Lieutenant of the Tower render one of them worse than a Felon? And do you not plainly seem to condemn such for factious Fellows, who answer not your ends? Unhappy are those Juries, who are threaten'd to be fin'd, and starv'd, and ruin'd, if they give not in Verdicts contrary to their Consciences.

Rec. My Lord, you must take a course with that same Fellow.

May. Stop his mouth; Goaler bring Fetters, and stake him to the ground.

Pen. Do your pleasure, I matter not your Fetters.

Rec. Till now I never understood the reason of the Policy and Prudence of the *Spaniards*, in suffering the Inquisition among them: And certainly it will never be well with us, till something like unto the *Spanish* Inquisition be in *England*.

Obser. The Jury being requir'd to go together to find another Verdict, and stedfastly refusing it (saying they could give no other Verdict, than what was already given) the Recorder in great passion was running off the Bench, with these words in his mouth; *I protest I will sit here no longer to hear these things*: At which the Mayor calling, *Stay, Stay*, he return'd, and directed himself unto the Jury, and spoke as followeth:

Rec. Gentlemen, we shall not be at this trade always with you; you will find the next Sessions of Parliament there will be a Law made, that those that will not conform, shall not have the Protection of the Law. Mr. *Lee* draw up another Verdict, that they may bring it in special.

Lee. I cannot tell how to do it.

Jury. We ought not to be return'd, having all agreed, and set our hands to the Verdict.

Rec. Your Verdict is nothing, you play upon the Court; I say you shall go together, and bring in another Verdict, or you shall starve; and I will have you carted about the City, as in *Edward* III's time.

Foreman. We have given in our Verdict, and all agreed to it; and if we give in another, it will be a force upon us to save our Lives.

May. Take them up.

Offic. My Lord, they will not go up.

Obser.

Obſer. The Mayor ſpoke to the Sheriff, and he came off of his Seat, and ſaid,

Sheriff. Come, Gentlemen, you muſt go up; you ſee I am commanded to make you go.

Obſer. Upon which the Jury went up; and ſeveral ſworn, to keep them without any Accommodation as aforeſaid, till they brought in their Verdict.

Cry. O yes, *&c.* The Court adjourns till to morrow morning, at ſeven of the clock.

Obſer. The Priſoners were remanded to *Newgate*; where they remain'd till next morning, and then were brought unto the Court; which being ſate, they proceeded as followeth.

Cry. O yes, *&c.* Silence in the Court upon pain of Impriſonment.

Clerk. Set *William Pen* and *William Mead* at the Bar. Gentlemen of the Jury, anſwer to your Names; *Tho. Veer*, *Edward Buſhel*, *John Hammond*, *Henry Henly*, *Henry Michell*, *John Brightman*, *Charles Milſon*, *Gregory Walklet*, *John Baily*, *William Lever*, *James Damask*, *William Plumſtead*: Are you all agreed of your Verdict?

Jury. Yes.

Clerk. Who ſhall ſpeak for you?

Jury. Our Foreman.

Clerk. Look upon the Priſoners. What ſay you, is *William Penn* guilty of the matter whereof he ſtands indicted, in manner and form, *&c.* or not guilty?

Foreman. Here is our Verdict in writing, and our Hands ſubſcrib'd.

Obſer. The Clerk took the Paper, but was ſtopt by the Recorder from reading of it; and he commanded to ask for a poſitive Verdict.

Foreman. That is our Verdict; we have ſubſcrib'd it.

Clerk. How ſay you, is *William Penn* guilty, *&c.* or not guilty?

Foreman. Not guilty.

Clerk. How ſay you, is *William Mead* guilty, *&c.* or not guilty?

Foreman. Not guilty.

Clerk. Then hearken to your Verdict, you ſay that *William Penn* is not guilty in manner and form as he ſtands indicted; you ſay that *William Mead* is not guilty in manner and form as he ſtands indicted, and ſo you ſay all.

Jury. Yes, we do ſo.

Obſer. The Bench being unſatisfy'd with the Verdict, commanded that every Perſon ſhould diſtinctly anſwer to their Names,

Names, and give in their Verdict, which they unanimously did, in saying, *Not Guilty*; to the great satisfaction of the Assembly.

Rec. I am sorry, Gentlemen, you have follow'd your own Judgments and Opinions, rather than the good and wholsom Advice, which was given you; God keep my Life out of your hands; but for this the Court fines you forty mark a man, and Imprisonment, till paid. At which *Penn* stept up towards the Bench, and said,

Pen. I demand my Liberty, being freed by the Jury.

May. No, you are in for your Fines.

Pen. Fines, for what?

May. For contempt of the Court.

Pen. I ask, if it be according to the fundamental Laws of *England*, that any *English*-man should be fined or amerced, but by the Judgment of his Peers or Jury; since it expresly contradicts the fourteenth and twenty ninth Chapter of the great Charter of *England*, which say, No Freeman ought to be amerced but by the Oath of good and lawful Men of the Vicinage.

Rec. Take him away, take him away, take him out of the Court.

Pen. I can never urge the fundamental Laws of *England*, but you cry, Take him away, take him away. But it is no wonder, since the *Spanish* Inquisition hath so great a place in the Recorder's Heart. God Almighty, who is just, will judg you all for these things.

Obser. They haled the Prisoners into the Bale-dock, and from thence sent them to *Newgate*, for Non-payment of their Fines; and so were their Jury.

An APPENDIX, *by way of Defence for the Prisoners, as what might have been offer'd against the Indictment, and illegal Proceedings of the Court thereon, had they not violently over-rul'd and stop'd them.*

UPON a sober Disquisition into the several parts of the Indictment, we find it so wretchedly defective, as if it were nothing else but a mere Composition of Error, rather calculated to the malicious Designs of the Judges, than to the least Verity of Fact committed by the Prisoners.

To prove this, what we say will be a main help to discover the Arbitrary Proceedings of the Bench in their frequent Menaces to the Jury; as if it were not so much their Business to try, as to condemn the Prisoners; and that not so much for any Fact they had committed, as what the Court would have suggested to the Jury to have been their Fact.

Sect. 1. It is the constant Common Law of *England*, that no man should be taken, imprison'd, amerced, disseiz'd of his Freehold, of his Liberties or free Customs, but by the Judgment of his Peers, which are vulgarly call'd a Jury from *Jurare*, because they are sworn to do right.

Sect. 2. The only Assistance that is given the Jury, in order to a Verdict, is;

First, the Evidence given of the Fact committed by the Person indicted.

Secondly, the Knowledg of that Law, Act, or Statute the Indictment is grounded upon, and which the Prisoners are said to have transgress'd.

Sect. 3. We shall neglect to mention here, how much they were depriv'd of that just advantage the antient equal Laws of *England* do allow; designing it for a Conclusion of the whole, and shall only speak here to matter of Fact and Law.

Sect. 4. The Evidence you have read in the Trial, the utmost Import of which is no more than this; That *William Penn* was speaking in *Grace-Church-street* to an Assembly of People, but knew not what he said; which is so great a Contradiction, as he that runs may read it. For no man can say another man preaches, and yet understand not what he saith: He

He may conjecture it, but that is a lame Evidence in Law: It might as well have been ſworn, That he was ſpeaking of Law, Phyſick, Trade, or any other matter of Civil Concernment. Beſides, There is no Law againſt Preaching what is Truth, whether it be in the Street, or in any other place: Nor is it poſſible, that any man can truly ſwear, That he preach'd Sedition, Hereſy, *&c.* unleſs he ſo heard him, that he could tell what he ſaid.

Sect. 5. The Evidence further ſaith, That *W. Mead* was there; but till being in *Gracechurch-ſtreet* be a Fault, and hearing a Man ſpeak the Witneſs knows not what, be contrary to Law, the whole Evidence is uſeleſs and impertinent: but what they want of that, they endeavour to ſupply with Indictment; whoſe parts we proceed to conſider.

Exceptions againſt the Indictment.

Sect. 6. It ſaith, That the Priſoners [*were met upon the 15th Day of* Auguſt, 1670.] whereas their own Evidence affirms it to be upon the 14th Day of *Auguſt*, 70.

Sect. 7. [*That they met with Force and Arms*] which is ſo great a Lye, that the Court had no better cover for it, than to tell the Jury, it was only a piece of Form, urging that the man tried for clipping of Mony this preſent Seſſions had the ſame words uſed in his Indictment.

But that this Anſwer is too ſcanty, as well as it was too weak to prevail with the Jury; we deſire it may be conſider'd, that the ſame words may be uſed more of courſe, and out of form at one time, than at another. And tho we grant they can have little force with any Jury in a Clipper's caſe, for mere Clipping; yet they are words that give ſo juſt a ground of Jealouſy, nay that carry ſo clear an Evidence of Illegality, where they are truly prov'd and affirm'd of any Meeting, as that they are the proper Roots from whence do ſpring thoſe Branches which render an Indictment terrible, and an Aſſembly truly the Terror of the People.

Sect. 8. [*Unlawfully and tumultuouſly to diſturb the Peace*] which is as true as what is ſaid before, that is as falſe. This will evidently appear to all that conſider how lawful it is to aſſemble with no other deſign than to worſhip God: and their calling a lawful Aſſembly an unlawful one, no more makes it ſo, than to ſay Light is Darkneſs, Black is White, concludes ſo impudent a Falſity true.

In ſhort, becauſe to worſhip God can never be a Crime, no Meeting or Aſſembly deſigning to worſhip God, can be unlawful. Such as go about to prove an unlawful Aſſembly, must prove the Assemblers intent not to worship God; bu that no man can do, because no man can know another man's Intentions; and therefore it's impossible that any should prove such an Assembly unlawful. That is properly an unlawful Assembly, according to the Definition of the Law, when several Persons are met together, with design to use violence, and to do mischief; but that Dissenters meet with no such Intention, is manifest to the whole World, therefore their Assemblies are not unlawful. He that hath only Right to be worship'd, which is God, hath only Right to institute how he will be worship'd; and such as worship him in that way they apprehend him to have instituted, are so far from being unlawful Assemblers, that therein they do but express the Duty they owe to God.

[*Tumultuously*] imports as much as Disorderly, or an Assembly full of Noise, Bustle, and Confusion, using Force and Violence, to the injury of Persons, Houses, or Grounds. But whether Religious Dissenters, in their peaceable Meetings, therein desiring, and seeking nothing more than to express that Duty they owe to God Almighty, be a tumultuous Action, or Meeting in the Sense exprest (and which is the very Definition of the Law) will be the question. Certainly such as call these Meetings tumultuous, as to break the Peace, offer the greatest violence to common words, that can be well imagin'd; for they may as rightly say, such Persons meet adulterously, thievishly, *&c.* as to affirm they meet tumultuously, because they are as truly applicable. In short, such Particulars as are required to prove them such Meetings in Law, are wholly wanting.

Sect. 9. [*To the Disturbance of the Peace.*]

If the Disturbance of the Peace be but matter of form with the rest, as is usually pleaded, leave out this matter of form, and then see what great matter will be left.

Certainly such Assemblies, as are not to the breach and disturbance of the Peace, are far from being unlawful or tumultuary: But if the Peace be broken by them, how comes it the Evidence was so short? We cannot believe it was in favour of the Prisoners. This may shew to all the reasonable World how forward some are, to brand Innocency with hateful Names, to bring a Suspicion, where there was none deserved.

Sect. 10. [*That the said* Penn *and* Mead *met by agreement beforehand made.*]

But if Persons that never saw each other, nor converse together, neither had Correspondence by any other hand, cannot be said to be agreed to any Action, before it be done; then

then the Prisoners were far from an Agreement, for they had never seen, convers'd, nor corresponded, directly nor indirectly, before the Officers came to disturb the Assembly. We well know how far they would have stretch'd the word *Agreement* or *Conspiracy*; but God, who brings to nought the Counsels of the Wicked, prevented their cruel Designs.

Sect. 11. [*That* William Mead *did abet the said* William Penn *in Preaching.*]

No man can be said to abet another, whilst they are both unknown to each other, especially in this case, where abetting follows agreeing, and agreeing supposes Foreknowledg. Nay the word *abet* in Law signifies to *command*, *procure*, or *counsel* a Person, which *W. Mead* could not be said to do, in reference to *W. Penn*, they being so great Strangers one to another, and at so great a distance: for the Evidence proves that he was with Lieutenant *Cook*; and Lieutenant *Cook* swears he could not make his way to *W. Penn*, for the Croud.

Sect. 12. [*That* W. Penn's *Preaching and Speaking caused a great Concourse and Tumult of People, to remain and continue a long time in the Street.*]

But this is so improbable to believe, that the very nature of a Tumult admits of no such thing as Preaching; but implies a disorderly Multitude, where all may be said to speak, rather than any to hear.

Sect. 1. [*In contempt of the King and his Laws.*]

They are so far from contemning the King and his Laws, that they are oblig'd and constrain'd by their own Principles, to obey every Ordinance of Man for the Lord's sake, *but not against the Lord for Man's sake*; which is the question in hand. Besides, their continuance there, was not in contempt, but by the permission of the chief Officer present, that came there by the King's Authority; nor is it for the Honour of the King, that such Persons should be said to act in contempt of his Laws, as only meet to honour God and his Laws.

Sect. 2. [*And to the great disturbance of the King's Peace.*]

It is far from disturbing and breaking the King's Peace, for men peaceably to meet to worship God; for it is then properly broken and invaded, when Force and Violence are used, to the hurt and prejudice of Persons and Estates; or when any thing is done that tends to the stirring up of Sedition, and begetting in People a dislike of the Civil Government: But that such things are not practis'd by us in our Assemblies, either to offer violence to mens Persons and Estates, or to stir up People to Sedition, or dislike to the Civil Government, is obvious to all that visit our Assemblies.

Sect. 3. [*To the great terror and disturbance of the King's liege People and Subjects, and to the evil Example of all others in the like case offending, against the King's Peace, his Crown, and Dignity.*]

Were these black Criminations as true as they are wretchedly false, we should give as just an occasion to lose our Liberties, as our cruel Adversaries are ready to take any to deprive us unjustly of them. O how notorious is it to all sober People, that our manner of Life is far from terrifying any; and how absurd to think that naked Men (in the generality of their Conversation known to be harmless and quiet) should prove a terror or disturbance to the People? Certainly, if any such thing should be in the time of our Meetings, it is brought with the Cruelty and barbarous Actions of your own Soldiers; they never learnt by our example to beat, hale before Magistrates, fine, and imprison for matters relating to God's Worship; neither can they say, we are their Precedents for all those Adulterous, Prodigal, Lascivious, Drunken, Swearing, and Profane Acts they daily commit, and esteem rather occasion of Brag and Boast, than Sorrow and Repentance: No, they need not go so far, they have too many (God Almighty knows) of their own Superiors for their example.

Sect. 4. But we can never pass over with silence, nor enough observe the detestable juggle of such Indictments, which we require all *English* and conscientious Men to mind, as they value themselves in the like occasions. How little a grain of fact was prov'd, yet how specious an Indictment was made? Had it related to the Evidence, the bulk had been excusable; but when it only swell'd with malicious scaring Phrases, to suggest to the People that they were the merest Villains, the most dangerous Persons, and designing mutually the Subversion of the Laws, and Breach of the Peace, to the terrifying of the People, *&c.*

Who can chuse but tell them of their Romance-Indictment, that is so forg'd, as it truly merits another against it self, This they childishly call *Form*; but had an *Italian*, or other Stranger been in Court, he would have judg'd it matter of fact, as thinking it unworthy of a King's Court, to accuse men in terms, not legally, truly, or probably due to the Fact they really had committed; as well as that no Court would practise it, but that which lov'd to deprive Men of their Liberties and Lives, rather than to save them; *Nolens Volens.*

Sect. 5. Had their Cruelty and Juggle ended here it self, they would have spar'd us the pains of any further Observation. But that which we have to add, on the Prisoners behalf, renders their Actions so abominable in the sight of Justice,

Juſtice, that all honeſt and ingenuous Hearts muſt needs abhor their baſe Snares.

They tell the Jury, *That being but Judges of Fact only, they were to bring the Priſoners in guilty* (that is, of the fact) *at their peril; and it was the part of the Bench, to judg what was Law.* So that if the Jury had brought them in *Guilty*, without any further additional Explanation (tho intentionally they meant only of the Fact proved by Evidence) yet the Bench would have extended it to every part of the Indictment; and by this impious Deluſion to have perjur'd a well-meaning Jury, and have had their barbarous ends upon the innocent Priſoners. But the Jury better underſtanding themſelves, brought in *Will. Penn* guilty of the Fact proved, namely, *That he was ſpeaking to ſome People met in* Grace-Church-ſtreet, *but not of an unlawful Aſſembly, ſo circumſtantiated* (the mention of which ſtab'd their Deſign of moulding the general Anſwer of *Guilty*, to their own ends, to the heart) nor indeed could they do otherwiſe; for as well the Jury as Priſoners, were deny'd to have any Law produced, by which they might meaſure the Truth of the Indictment, and Guilt of the Fact. But becauſe the Recorder would or could not (perhaps 'tis ſo long ſince he read Law that he may have forgotten it) we ſhall perform his part, in ſhewing what is that *Common Law of the Land*, which in general, he ſaid, they were indicted for the Breach of, and which indeed, if rightly underſtood, is the undoubted Birthright of every *Engliſhman*; yea, the Inheritance of Inheritances: *Major Hæreditas venit unicuique noſtrum a Jure & Legibus, quam a Parentibus.* Coke Inſtit. 2. 56.

Sect. 6. All the various kinds or models of Government that are in the world, ſtand either upon *Will* and *Power*, or *Condition* and *Contract*: The firſt rule by Men, the ſecond by Laws. It is our happineſs to be born under ſuch a Conſtitution, as is moſt abhorrent in it ſelf of all arbitrary Government, and which is, and ever has been moſt choice and careful of her Laws, by which all Right is preſerv'd.

Sect. 7. All Laws are either Fundamental, and ſo immutable; or Superficial, and ſo alterable. By the firſt we underſtand ſuch Laws, as injoin men to be juſt, honeſt, vertuous; to do no wrong, to kill, rob, deceive, prejudice none; but to do as one would be done unto; to cheriſh good, and to terrify wicked Men: In ſhort, univerſal Reaſon, *which are not ſubject to any Revolutions, becauſe no Emergency, Time, or Occaſion can ever juſtify a Suſpenſion of their Execution, much leſs their utter Abrogation.*

Sect. 8. By Superficial Laws, we underſtand ſuch Acts, Laws, or Statutes, as are ſuted to preſent Occurrences; and which may as well be abrogated, for the good of the Kingdom, as they were first made for it. For instance, those Statutes that relate to Victuals, Clothes, and Places of Trade, *&c.* which have ever stood whilst the Reason of them was in force; but when that Benefit, which once redounded, fell by cross Occurrences, they ended; according to that old Maxim, *Cessante ratione Legis, cessat Lex.* But this cannot be said of Fundamental Laws, *till Houses stand without their Foundations, and* English *Mankind wholly cease to be*; which brings close upon the point.

Sect. 9. There is not any Country, that has more constantly express'd her Care and deep Sollicitude, to the preservation of her fundamental Laws, than the *English* Nation. And tho the Evil of some particular Times and Persons have endeavour'd an utter Abolition of those excellent Fundamentals, which we have before defined and defended from any just reason of Revolution; yet God Almighty, who is always concern'd to avenge the Cause of Justice, and those excellent good Laws by which it is upheld, has by his Providence befool'd their Contrivances, and baffled their Attempts, by bringing their Designs to nought, and their Persons frequently to condign Punishment and Disgrace. Their Age no Antiquary living can assure us unless they say, as old as Reason it self; but our own Authors are not lacking to inform us, that the Liberties, Properties, and Privileges of the *English* Nation are very antient.

Sect. 10. For *Horn*, in his *Mirror of Justice*, (writ in *Edward* the First's time) *fol.* 1. tells us, " That after God had abated " the Nobility of the *Britons*, he did deliver the Realm to men " more humble and simple, of the Countries adjoining; to " wit, the *Saxons*, who came from the parts of *Almaign* to " conquer this Land; of which Men there were forty Sove-" reigns, which did rule as Companions; and those Princes " did call this Realm *England*, which before was named the " *Greater Britain*. These, after great Wars, Tribulations, " and Pains, by long time suffer'd, did chuse a King to " reign over them, to govern the People of God, and to " maintain and defend their Persons, and their Good in " quiet, by the Rules of Right. And at the beginning they " did cause him to swear to maintain the Holy Christian " Faith, and to guide his People by Right, with all his " Power, without respect of Persons, and to observe the " Laws. And after, when the Kingdom was turn'd into an " Heritage, King *Alfred* that govern'd this Kingdom about " an hundred seventy one years before the Conquest, did " cause the Great Men of the Kingdom to assemble at

" *London*

" *London*, and there did ordain for a perpetual Usage, That " twice in the Year, or oftner, if need should be, in time of " Peace, they should assemble at *London* in Parliament, for " the Government of God's People, that men might live " in quiet, and receive Right by certain Usages and Holy " Judgments.

" In which Parliament (saith our Author) the Rights and " Prerogatives of the Kings and of the Subjects are distin- " guish'd and set apart; and particularly by him express'd, too tedious here to insert: amongst which Ordinances we find, " That no man should be imprison'd, but for a capital " Offence. And if a man should detain another in Prison, " by colour of Right (where there was none) till the Party " imprison'd dy'd; he that kept him in Prison should be " held guilty of Murder, as you may read *page* 33. And *pag.* 36. " He is declar'd guilty of Homicide, by whom a " Man shall die in prison, whether it be the Judges, that shall " too long delay to do a Man right, or by Cruelty of Goalers, or " suffering him to die of Famine; or when a Man is adjudg'd " to do penance, and shall be surcharg'd by his Goaler with " Irons, or other pain, whereby he is depriv'd of his life. And *p.* 149. " That by the antient Law of *England*, it was " Felony to detain a man in prison, after sufficient Bail of- " fer'd, where the Party was plevisable; every Person was " plevisable, but he that was appeal'd of Treason, Murder, " Robbery, or Burglary, *pag.* 35. None ought to be put in " common Prisons, but only such as were *Attainted*, or prin- " cipally *Appealed* or *Indicted* of some capital Offence, or *At-* " *tainted* of false or wrongful Imprisonment. So tender have " the antient Laws and Constitutions of this Realm been of " the Liberty of their Subjects Persons, that no man ought to " be imprison'd, but for a Capital Offence, as *Treason*, *Murder*, " *Robbery*, or *Burglary*.

Sect. 11. Nor is *Lambard* short, in his excellent Translation of the *Saxon* Laws, from King *Ina*'s time 712. to *Henry* III. 1100. in describing to us the great Obligation, and strong Condition the People were wont to put upon their Kings, *to observe the antient fundamental Laws, and free Customs of this Land*; which were handed down from one Age to another. And in the 17th Chapter of *Edward* the Confessor's Laws, the mention there made of a King's Duty is very remarkable, That if he break his Oath, or perform'd not his Obligation, *nec nomen Regis in eo constabit*. The same *Lambard* further tells us, That however any may affirm *William* of *Normandy* to be a Conqueror, he was receiv'd by the People as *Edward*'s Successor, and by solemn Oath taken, to maintain unto them the

same

ſame Laws, that his Kinſman *Edward* the Confeſſor did. This Doctrine remain'd in the general unqueſtion'd, to the Reign of King *John*, who imperiouſly thought that *Voluntas Regis*, and not *Salus Populi*, was *Suprema Lex*; or the King's Will was the Supreme Law, and not the People's Preſervation: till the incens'd Barons of that time betook themſelves to a vigorous Defence of their antient Rights and Liberties, and learnt him to keep thoſe Laws by a due Reſtraint and timely Compulſion, which his former Invaſion of them evidenc'd to the World he would never have done willingly.

Sect. 12. The Propoſals and Articles of Agreement, with the Pledges given to the Barons, on the behalf of the People by the King, were confirm'd in *Henry* III's time, his Son and Succeſſor; *when the abuſed, ſlighted, and diſregarded Laws by his Father*, were thought fit to be reduc'd to Record, *that the People of* England *might not for ever after be to ſeek for a written recorded Law to their Defence and Security*: for, *Miſera Servitus eſt ubi Jus eſt vagum aut incognitum.* And ſo we enter upon that *Grand Charter of Liberty and Privilege*, in the Cauſe, Reaſon, and End of it.

Sect. 1. We ſhall firſt rehearſe it, ſo far as we are concern'd, (with the Formalities of *Grant* and *Curſe*) and ſhall then ſay ſomething as to the Cauſe, Reaſon, and End of it.

A Rehearſal of the Material Parts of the Great Charter of England.

HENRY, by the Grace of God, King of *England*, &c. To all Archbiſhops, or Earls, Barons, Sheriffs, Provoſts, Officers, and to all Bailiffs, and our faithful Subjects, who ſhall ſee this preſent Charter, Greeting. Know ye that we, unto the Honour of Almighty God, and for the Salvation of the Souls of our Progenitors, and our Succeſſors, Kings of *England*, to the Advancement of Holy Church, and Amendment of our Realm, of our mere and free Will have given and granted to all Archbiſhops, &c. and to all Freemen of this our Realm, theſe Liberties under-written, to be holden and kept in this our Realm of *England* for evermore.

9 H. 3. *confirm'd* 28 E. 3.

Chap. 1. The Form of antient Acts, &c. Coke 2. Inſt. fol. 2.

We have granted and given to all Freemen of our Realm, for us and our Heirs for evermore, theſe Liberties underwritten, to have and to hold, to them and to their Heirs, of us and our Heirs forenam'd.

A

A Freeman ſhall not be amerced for a ſmall Fault, but after the quantity of the Fault. Chap. 14.
And for a great Fault, after the manner thereof, ſaving to him his Contenements or Free-hold. And a Merchant likewiſe ſhall be amerced, ſaving to him his Merchandize; and none of the ſaid Amercements ſhall be aſſeſs'd, but by the Oath of good and honeſt men of the Vicinage.

No Freeman ſhall be taken or impriſoned, nor be diſſeized of his Freehold, or Liberties, or Chap. 29.
free Cuſtoms, or be outlaw'd, or exil'd, or any other ways deſtroy'd; nor we ſhall not paſs upon him, nor condemn him, but by lawful Judgment of his Peers, or by the Law of the Land. We ſhall ſell to no man, we ſhall deny nor defer to no Man either Juſtice or Right.

And to all theſe Cuſtoms, Liberties aforeſaid, which we have granted to be holden within this our Realm, as much as appertaineth to us and our Heirs, we ſhall obſerve; and all Men of this our Realm, as well Spiritual as Temporal (as much as in them is) ſhall obſerve the ſame againſt all Perſons in likewiſe. And for this our Gift, and Grant of theſe Liberties, and for other contain'd in our Charter of Liberties of our *Foreſt*, the Archbiſhops, Biſhops, Abbots, Priors, Earls, Barons, Knights, Freeholders, and other our Subjects, have given unto us the fifteenth parts of all their Movables: And we have granted unto them on the other part, That neither We, nor our Heirs ſhall procure or do any thing whereby the Liberties in this Charter contain'd ſhall be infring'd or broken; and if any thing be procur'd by any Perſon contrary to the Premiſes, ſhall be had of no force or effect. Theſe being Witneſſes, *Boniface* Archbiſhop of *Canterbury*, &c. We ratifying and approving thoſe Gifts and Grants aforeſaid, confirm and make ſtrong all the ſame, for us and our Heirs perpetually, and by the Tenor of theſe Preſents do renew the ſame willingly; and granting for us and our Heirs, that this Charter, in all and ſingular its Articles, for evermore ſhall be ſtedfaſtly, firmly, and inviolably obſerv'd. And if any Article in the ſame Charter contain'd, yet hitherto peradventure hath not been obſerv'd nor kept, we will, and by our Authority Royal command, from henceforth firmly they be obſerv'd. Witneſs, *&c.*

The

The Sentence of Curse given by the Bishops, with the King's Consent, against the Breakers of the Great Charter.

IN the Year of our Lord 1253. the third day of *May*, in the great Hall of the King at *Westminster*, in the presence, and by the Consent of the Lord *Henry*, by the Grace of God, King of *England*, and the Lord *Richard*, Earl of *Cornwal*, his Brother; *Roger Bigot* Earl of *Norfolk*, Marshal of *England*; *Humphry* Earl of *Hereford*; *Henry* Earl of *Oxford*; *John* Earl Warren; and other Estates of the Realm of *England*: We *Boniface*, by the mercy of God, Archbishop of *Canterbury*, Primate of *England*, *F.* of *London*, *H.* of *Ely*, *S.* of *Worcester*, *E.* of *Lincoln*, *W.* of *Norwich*, *P.* of *Hereford*, *W.* of *Salisbury*, *W.* of *Durham*, *R.* of *Excester*, *M.* of *Carlisle*, *W.* of *Bath*, *E.* of *Rochester*, *T.* of *St. Davids*; Bishops, apparel'd in Pontificals, with Tapers burning, against the Breakers of the Church's Liberties, and of the Liberties and other Customs of this Realm of *England*; and namely these which are contain'd in the Charter of the common Liberties of *England*, and Charter of the *Forest*, have denounc'd Sentence of Excommunication in this form, by the Authority of Almighty God, the Father, the Son, and the Holy Ghost, *&c.* of the blessed Apostles *Peter* and *Paul*, and of all Apostles, and of all Martyrs, of blessed Edward *King of* England, and of all the Saints of Heaven; We excommunicate and accurse, and from the Benefits of our holy Mother the Church we sequester all those that hereafter willingly and maliciously deprive or spoil the Church of her Right; and all those that by any craft or willingness, do violate, break, diminish, or change the Church's Liberties, and free Customs contain'd in the Charters of the common Liberties, and of the *Forest*, granted by our Lord the King to Archbishops, Bishops, and other Prelates of *England*, and likewise to the Earls, Barons, Knights, and other Freeholders of the Realm. And all that secretly and openly, by deed, word, or counsel do make Statutes, or observe them being made, and that bring in Customs to keep them, when they be brought in, against the said Liberties, or any of them, and all those that shall presume to judg against them; and all and every such Person, beforemention'd, that wittingly shall commit any thing of the

Premises

Premiſes, let them well know that they incur the aforeſaid Sentence *ipſo facto*.

A Confirmation of the Charters and Liberties of England, *and of the* Foreſt, *made the twenty fifth Year of* Edward *the Firſt*.

E*Dward*, by Grace of God, King of *England*, Lord of *Ireland*, Duke of *Guyen*; To all thoſe that theſe preſent Letters ſhall hear or ſee, greeting. Know ye that we, to the Honour of God, and to the Profit of our Realm, have granted for us, and our Heirs, and the Charter of Liberties, and the Charter of Foreſt, which were made by common Aſſent of all the Realm, in the time of King *Henry* our Father, ſhall be kept in every point without breach. And we will that the ſame Charters ſhall be ſent under our Seal, as well to our Juſtices of the Forreſt, as to others, and to all Sheriffs of Shires, and to all our other Officers, and to all our Cities throughout the Realm, together with our Writs; in the which it ſhall be contain'd, that they cauſe the aforeſaid Charters to be publiſh'd, and to declare to the People, that we have confirm'd them in all points: And that our Juſtices, Sheriffs, Mayors, and other Miniſters, which under us have the Laws of our Land to guide, ſhall allow the ſame Charters pleaded before them in Judgment, in all their points; that is, to wit, the Great Charter, as the Common Law; and the Charter of our Foreſt, for the *Welch* of our Realm.

And we will, that if any Judgment be given from henceforth contrary to the Points of the Charter aforeſaid, by the Juſtices, or by any other of our Miniſters that hold Plea before them, againſt the Points of the Charters, it ſhall be undone, and holden for nought.

And we will that the ſame Charters ſhall be ſent under our Seal to Cathedral Churches throughout our Realm, there to remain; and ſhall be read before the People two times by the year.

And that all Archbiſhops and Biſhops ſhall pronounce the Sentence of Excommunication againſt all thoſe that by word, deed, or counſel do contrary to the foreſaid Charters, or that in any point do break or undo them; and that the ſaid Curſes be twice a year denounc'd and publiſh'd by the Prelates

lates aforesaid; and if the same Prelates, or any of them be remiss in the Denunciation of the said Sentences, the Archbishops of *Canterbury* and *York*, for the time being, shall compel and distrain them to the Execution of their Duties in form aforesaid.

The Sentence of the Clergy against the Breakers of the Articles above-mentioned.

IN the Name of the Father, the Son, and the Holy Ghost, Amen. Whereas our Sovereign Lord the King, to the honour of God, and of Holy Church, and for the common profit of the Realm, hath granted for him, and his Heirs for ever, these Articles above-written: Robert *Archbishop of* Canterbury, *Primate of all* England, *admonish'd all his Province once, twice and thrice, because that shortness will not suffer so much delay, as to give knowledg to all the People of* England *of these Presents in writing: We therefore enjoin all Persons, of what estate soever they be, that they and every of them, as much as in them is, shall uphold and maintain these Articles granted by our Sovereign Lord the King in all points: And all those that in any point do resist, or break, or in any manner hereafter procure, counsel, or in any wise assent to, testify, or break those Ordinances, or go about it by word or deed, openly or privily, by any manner of pretence or colour; we, the aforesaid Archbishop, by our Authority in this writing expressed, do excommunicate and accurse, and from the Body of our Lord Jesus Christ, and from all the Company of Heaven, and from all the Sacraments of Holy Church do sequester and exclude.*

We may here see, that in the obscurest times of sottish Popery, they were not left without a sense of Justice, and the necessity of *Liberty* and *Property* to be inviolably enjoy'd; which brings us to the Cause of it.

First, The Cause of this famous Charter was, as we have already said, the Incroachments that were made by several Ministers of precedent Kings, that almost became customary, and which had near extinguish'd the free Customs due to *English*-men: How great care it cost our Ancestors, it unbecomes us to ignore, or by our silence to neglect. It was that *Yoke* and *Muzzle*, which fail'd not to disable many raging Bears from entring *the pleasant Vineyard of* English *Freedoms*, that otherwise would not have left a fruitful Vine in being. Anon we may give the Reader an account of some, with their Wages as well as Works.

Secondly,

Secondly, The Reason of it is so great, that it seems to be its own. It is the very *Image* and *Expression* of *Justice*, *Liberty*, and *Property*; Points of such eminent Importance, as without which no Government can be said to be Reasonable, but Arbitrary and Tyrannical. It allows every Man that Liberty God and Nature have given him, and the secure Possession of his Property, from the In-road or Invasion of his Neighbour, or any else of that Constitution. It justifies no Man in a fault, only it provides equal and just Ways to have the Offender try'd; considering the Malice of many Prosecutors, and the great Value of Liberty and Life.

Thirdly, The End of it was the most noble of any Earthly projection; to wit, *The refixing of those shaken Laws*, held for many hundred years, by constant Claim, that they living might be re-instated in their primitive Liberty, and their Posterity secured in the possession of so great a happiness.

Amongst those many rich Advantages, that accrew to the free People of *England*, from this great Charter; and those many confirmatory Statutes of the same, we shall present the Reader with the sight of some few, that may most properly fall under the Consideration and Inquiry of these present Times, as found in our Common Law-Books.

First, *That every English-man is born free.*

Secondly, *That no such Free-man shall be taken, attached, assessed, or imprisoned, by any Petition or Suggestion to the King or his Council, unless by the Indictment or Presentment of good and lawful Men where such Deeds be done.* 5 Edw.3. Chap.9. 25 Edw. 3. Chap.4. 17 R. 2. Chap. 6. Rot. Parl. 42 Edw. 3. Cook 2 Inst. 46.

Thirdly, *That no Free-man shall be disseiz'd of his Free-hold or Liberties, or free Customs*, &c. Hereby is intended, saith *Cook*, That *Lands*, *Tenements*, *Goods and Chattels*, shall not be seiz'd into the King's hands contrary to this great Charter, *&c.* 43 Ass. pag. 12. 43 *Edw.* 3. *Cook* 2. *Inst.* 32. Neither shall any such Free-man be put from his Livelihood without answer, *Cook* 2. *Inst.* 47.

Fourthly, *That no Free-man shall be Out-law'd, unless he shroud and hide himself voluntarily from the Justice of the Law.* 2 *&* 3 Phil. *&* Mar. Dier. 114. 145.

Fifthly, *No Free-man shall be exil'd.* *Cook* says there are but two Grounds upon which any Man may be exil'd. One by Act of Parliament (supposing it not contrary to the great Charter.) —— The other in case of Abjuration, for Felony by the Common Law, &c. *Cook* 2. *Inst.* 47.

Sixthly, *No Free-man shall be destroy'd*; that is, he shall not be *fore-judg'd of Life, Limb, Disinherited, or put to Torture, or Death.* Every Oppression against Law, by colour of any usurp'd Authority,

thority, is a kind of Destruction, and 'tis the worst Oppression that is done by colour of Justice. *Cook Instit.* 2. 48.

Seventhly, *That no Free-man shall be thus taken, or imprison'd, disseiz'd, Out-law'd, exil'd, or destroy'd of his Liberties, Free-holds, and free Customs, but BY THE LAWFUL JUDGMENT OF HIS PEERS, (vulgarly call'd Jury.)* So that the Judgment of any Fact or Person is, by this Fundamental Law, refer'd to the Breasts and Consciences of the Jury: it's rendred in Latin *PER LEGALE JUDICIUM*; that is, Lawful Judgment. From whence it is to be observ'd, that the Judgment must have Law in it, and be according to Law, which cannot be where they are not Judges, how far the Fact is legal, or the contrary; *Judicium quasi Juris Dictum, The Voice of Law and Right.* And therefore is their Verdict not to be rejected, because it is suppos'd to be the Truth, according to their Consciences: For *Verdictis* from *vere dictum* is, *quasi dictum veritatis*, or a true Saying or Judgment, 9 *Hen.* 3. 29. *Cook Inst.* 1. 39. *Inst.* 4. 207. *Cook* says, that by the word *LEGALE*, three Things are imply'd.

First, *That this was by Law before the Statute; and therefore this Statute but Declaratory of the antient Law.*

2dly, That their Verdict must be legally given. Wherein is to be observ'd, (1st.) *The Jury ought to hear no Evidence, but in the hearing and presence of the Prisoner.* (2dly.) *That they cannot send to ask any Question in Law of the Judges, but in the presence of the Prisoner: for,* de facto Jus oritur.

3dly, The Evidence produc'd by the King's Counsel, being given, *the Judges cannot collect the Evidence, nor urge it by way of Charge to the Jury; nor yet confer with the Jury about the Evidence, but in the presence of the Prisoner.* Cook Inst. 2. 49.

Eighthly, *Or by the Law of the Land.* It is a *Synonimous* Expression, importing no more *than by a Tryal of Peers, or a Jury.* For it is sometimes rendred not (*or*) disjunctively, but (*and*) which is connectively; however, it can never signify any thing contrary to the Old way of Trying by Peers, for then it would be connected to a contradiction.

Besides, *Cook* well observes, that in the 4th Chapter of the 25th *Edw.* 3. *Per Legem Terræ*, imports no more than a Tryal by due Process, and Writ Original at Common Law, which cannot be without a Jury; therefore, *Per Judicium Parum, & per Legem Terræ*, signify the same Privilege unto the People. *Cook. Inst.* 2. pag. 50.

Thus

Thus have we presented you with ſome of thoſe Maxims of Law, dearer to our Anceſtors than Life; *Becauſe they are the Defence of the Lives and Liberties of the People of* England: It is from this 29th Chapter of the Great Charter, (*Great*, not for its Bulk, but the Privileges in it) as from a ſpacious Root, that ſo many fruitful Branches of the Law of *England* ſprings, if *Cook* may be credited. But how *ſacred* ſoever they have been eſteem'd, and ſtill are by noble and juſt Minds; yet ſo degenerate are ſome in their Proceedings, that conſcious to themſelves of their baſeneſs, they will not dare ſtand the Touch of this Great Charter, and thoſe juſt Laws grounded upon it; of which number we may truly rank the Mayor and Recorder of *London*, with the reſt of their wiſe Companions, in their late Seſſions at the *Old-Baily*, upon the occaſion of the Priſoners.

Firſt, The Priſoners were taken, and impriſon'd without Preſentment of good and lawful Men of the Vicinage, or the Neighbourhood, *but after a military and tumultuous manner, contrary to the Grand Charter.*

2dly, *They refuſed to produce the Law upon which they proceeded*; leaving thereby the Priſoners, Jury, and whole Aſſembly in the dark.

3dly, *They refuſed the Priſoners to plead*, and directly withſtood that great Privilege, mention'd in the firſt Chapter, 25 *Edw.* 1. *Where all Juſtices, Mayors, Sheriffs, and other Miniſters, that have the Laws of the Land to guide them, are required to allow the ſaid Charter to be pleaded in all its Points, and in all Cauſes that ſhall come before them in Judgment.* For no ſooner did *William Penn*, or his Fellow Priſoner, urge upon them the great Charter, and other good Laws, but the Recorder cry'd, Take him away, take him away, put him into the Bale-dock or Hole: From which the Recorder can never deliver himſelf, unleſs it be by avowing, *the Laws are not his Guide, and therefore does not ſuffer them to be pleaded before him in Judgment.*

4thly, *They gave the Jury their Charge in the Priſoner's abſence, endeavouring highly to incenſe the Jury againſt them.*

5thly, The Verdict being given, which is in Law *DICTUM VERITATIS, The Voice of Truth her ſelf*, (becauſe not ſutable to their humour) *They did five times reject it, with many abuſive, imperious and menacing Expreſſions to the Jury*, (ſuch as no Precedent can afford us) as if they were not the only conſtituted Judges by the Fundamental Laws of the Land, *but mere Cyphers only, to ſignify ſomething behind their Figures.*

6thly, Tho the Priſoners were clear'd by their Jury, yet were they continued for the non-payment of their Fines laid upon them, for not pulling off their Hats; in which the Law is notoriouſly broken.

(1ft.) *In that no Man ſhall be amerced, but according to the Offence; and they have fined each forty Marks.*

(2.) *They were not merced by any Jury, but at the Will of an incens'd Bench.*

Beſides, there is no Law againſt the Hat; and where there is no Law, there can be no Tranſgreſſion, and conſequently no legal Amercement or Fine, 9 *H.* 3. Chap. 14. But how the Priſoners were trapanned into it, is moſt ridiculous on the ſide of the Contrivers, that finding their Hats off, would have them put on again by their Officers, to fool the Priſoners, with a trial of putting them off again; which childiſh Conceit not being gratified, they Fined them the Forty Marks apiece.

7thly, Inſtead of accepting their Verdict as good in Law, and for the true deciſion of the matter, according to the Great Charter (that conſtitutes them proper Judges, and which bears them out, with many other good Laws, in what they agreed to, as a Verdict) the Court did moſt illegally and tyrannically Fine and Impriſon them, as in the Tryal was expreſs'd: And that notwithſtanding the late juſt Reſentment of the Houſe of Commons, in Judg *Keeling*'s Caſe, where they reſolv'd, that the precedent and practice of Fining and Impriſoning *of Juries, for their Verdicts, were illegal.* And here we muſt needs obſerve two Things.

Firſt, That the Fundamental Laws of *England* cannot be more ſlighted and contradicted in any thing (next Engliſhmen's being quite deſtroy'd) than in not ſuffering them to have that equal *medium*, or juſt way of tryal, that the ſame Law has provided, *which is by a Jury.*

Secondly, That the late Proceeding of the Court at the *Old-Baily*, is an evident Demonſtration, that Juries are now but *mere Formality*, and that the partial Charge of the Bench muſt be the Verdict of the Jury; *for if ever a Rape were attempted on the Conſciences of any Jury, it was there.* And indeed the Ignorance of Jurors of their Authority by Law, is the only Reaſon of their unhappy cringing to the Court, and being ſcared into an *Anti-Conſcience Verdict*, by their lawleſs Threats.

But we have lived to an Age, ſo devoid of all Humanity and Reaſon, as well as Faith and Religion, that ſome ſtick not to turn *Butchers to their own Privileges, and Conſpirators againſt their own Liberties.* For however, *Magna Charta* had once the Reputation of a ſacred unalterable Law, and few hardned enough to incur and bear the long Curſe that attended the Violaters of it; yet it is frequently objected now, that the Benefits there deſign'd *are but Temporary*, and therefore liable to alteration, as other Statutes are. *What Game ſuch Perſons play at, may be lively*

* *read,*

read, in the attempts of Dionysius, Phalaris, *&c. which would have Will and Power be the People's Law.*

But that the Privileges due to *English-men* by the Great Charter of *England*, have their Foundation in Reason and Law; and that those new *Cassandrian* ways, to introduce *Will* and *Power*, deserve to be detested by all Persons professing Sense and Honesty, and the least Allegiance to our *English* Government; we shall make appear from a sober Consideration of the Nature of those Privileges contain'd in that *Charter*.

1. The Ground of Alteration of any Law in Government (where there is no Invasion) should arise from the universal *discommodity of its continuance*; but there can be no disprofit in the discontinuance of *Liberty* and *Property*, *therefore there can be no just ground of alteration.*

2. No one *English-man* is born Slave to another, neither has the one a right to inherit the sweat and benefit of the other's labour (without consent;) *therefore the Liberty and Property of an* English-man *cannot reasonably be at the Will and Beck of another, let his Quality and Rank be never so great.*

3. *There can be nothing more unreasonable than that which is partial*; but to take away the LIBERTY and PROPERTY of any (which are natural Rights) without breaking the Law of *Nature* (and not of Will and Power) is manifestly partial, *and therefore unreasonable.*

4. If it be just and reasonable *for Men to do as they would be done by*, then no sort of Men should invade the Liberties and Properties of other Men, because they would not be serv'd so themselves.

5. Where Liberty and Property are destroy'd, there must always be a State of Force and War; which however pleasing it may be unto the *Invaders*, it will be esteem'd intolerable by the *Invaded*; who will no longer remain subject in all humane Probability, than while they want as much Power to free themselves, as their Adversaries had to enslave them: *The troubles, hazards, ill-consequences, and illegality of such Attempts, as they have declined by the most prudent in all Ages; so have they proved most uneasy to the most savage of all Nations, who first or last have by a mighty Torrent freed themselves, to the due punishment and great infamy of their Oppressors:* Such being the advantage, such the disadvantage which necessarily do attend the fixation and removal of Liberty and Property.

We shall proceed to make it appear, that *Magna Charta* (as recited by us) imports nothing less than their preservation.

No Free-man shall be taken, or imprisoned, or be disseized of his Freehold, or Liberties, or free Customs, or be Out-law'd, or Exil'd, or any other

other ways destroy'd; nor we will not pass upon him, nor condemn him, but by lawful judgment of his Peers, &c.

A Free-man shall not be amerced for a small fault, but after the manner of the fault; and for a great fault, after the greatness thereof; and none of the said Amercement shall be assessed, but by the Oath of good and lawful Men of the Vicinage.

First, It asserts *English-men* to be free; *that's Liberty.*

Secondly, That they have Free-holds; *that's Property.*

Thirdly, That Amercement, or Penalties, should be proportioned to the faults committed; *which is Equity.*

Fourthly, That they shall lose neither, but when they are adjudged to have forfeited them, in the judgment of their honest Neighbours, according to the Law of the Land; *which is lawful Judgment.*

It is easy to discern to what pass the Enemies of the *Great Charter* would bring the People.

First, They are now Free-men; *but they would have them Slaves.*

Secondly, They have now Right unto their *Wives*, *Children*, and *Estates*, as their undoubted Property; *but such would rob them of all.*

Thirdly, Now no Man is to be amerc'd, or punish'd, but sutably to his fault; *whilst they would make it sutable to their revengeful minds.*

Fourthly, Whereas the Power of Judgment lies in the Breasts and Consciences of twelve honest Neighbours; *they would have it at the discretion of mercenary Judges.* To which we cannot chuse but add, *That such Discourses manifestly strike at this present Constitution of Government*; for it being founded upon the *Great Charter*, (which is the Antient Common Law of the Land) as upon its best Foundation, none can design the cancelling of the *Charter*, but they must necessarily intend the extirpation *of the English Government:* For where the Cause is taken away, the Effect must consequently cease. *And as the Restoration of our antient English Laws, by the* Great Charter, *was the soveraign Balsam which cured our former Breaches, so doubtless will the continuation of it prove an excellent prevention to any future disturbances.*

But some are ready to object, *That the Great Charter consisting as well of Religious as Civil Rights; the former having receiv'd an Alteration, there is the same reason why the latter may have the like.*

To which we answer, That the reason of Alteration cannot be the same; therefore the Consequence is false: The one being Matter of Opinion, about Faith and Religious Worship, which is as various as the unconstant Apprehensions of Men: but

but the other is Matter of ſo immutable Right and Juſtice, that all Generations (however differing in their Religious Opinion) have concenter'd and agreed to the *certainty*, *equity*, and *indiſpenſable neceſſity of preſerving theſe Fundamental Laws*; ſo that *Magna Charta* hath not riſen and fallen with the differing religious Opinions that have been in this Land, but have ever remain'd as *the ſtable Right of every individual Engliſh-man, purely as an Engliſh-man.* Otherwiſe, if the *Civil Privileges* of the People had fallen with the pretended Religious Privileges of the *Popiſh Tyranny*, at the firſt Reformation (as muſt needs be ſuggeſted by this Objection) our Caſe had ended here, *That we had obtain'd a Spiritual Freedom at the coſt of a Civil Bondage*; which certainly was far from the intention of the firſt Reformers, and probably an unſeen Conſequence, by the Objectors, to their idle Opinion.

In ſhort, there is no time in which any Man may plead the Neceſſity of ſuch an Action, as is unjuſt in its own Nature, which he muſt unavoidably be guilty of, *that doth deface or cancel that Law by which the Juſtice of Liberty and Property is confirm'd and maintain'd to the People.* And conſequently, that no perſon may legally attempt the Subverſion, or Extenuation of the force of the *Great Charter*, we ſhall proceed to prove from Inſtances out of both.

1ſt. *Any Judgment given contrary to the ſaid Charter, is to be undone, and holden for nought.* 25 Edw. 1. *Chap.* 2.

2dly. *Any that by Word, Deed, or Counſel, go contrary to the ſaid* Charter, *are to be Excommunicated by the Biſhops: And the Archbiſhops of* Canterbury *and* York, *are bound to compel the other Biſhops to denounce Sentence accordingly, in caſe of their remiſneſs, or neglect*; which certainly hath relation to the State, rather than the Church; *Since there was never any neceſſity of compelling the Biſhops to denounce Sentence in their own Caſe, tho frequently in the Peoples.* 25 Edw. 1. *Chap.* 4.

3dly, *That the Great* Charter, *and* Charter *of Foreſt, be holden and kept in all Points; and if any Statute be made to the contrary, that it ſhall be holden for nought.* 42 Edw. 3. 1. Upon which *Cook*, that famous Engliſh Lawyer, ſaid, *That albeit Judgments in the King's Court are of high regard in Law, and* Judicia *are accounted as* Juris Dicta: *Yet it is provided by Act of Parliament, That if any Judgment be given contrary to any of the Points of the Great* Charter, *it ſhall be holden for nought.*

He further ſaith, *That upon the Statute of the 25th* Edw. 1. Chap. 1. *That this Great* Charter, *and the* Charter *of Foreſt, are properly the Common Law of this Land, or the Law is Common to all the People thereof.*

4thly, Another Statute runs thus; *If any force come to disturb the Execution of the Common Law, ye shall cause their Bodies to be arrested, and put in Prison: Ye shall deny no Man right by the King's Letters, nor counsel the King any thing that may turn to his damage, or disherison,* 18 Edw. 3. Chap. 7. *Neither to delay Right by the great and little Seal.* This is the Judg's Charge and Oath. 2 *Edw.* 3. Chap. 8. 14 *Edw.* 3. 14. 11 *R.* 2. Chap. 10.

5thly, Such care hath been taken, for the preservation of this Great Charter, that in the 25th of *Edw.* 1. it was enacted, *That Commissioners should issue forth, that there should be chosen in every Shire-Court, by the Commonalty of the same Shire, three substantial Men, Knights, or other lawful, wise, and well-dispos'd Persons, to be Justices; which shall be assigned by the King's Letters Patents, under the Great Seal, to hear and determine (without any other Writ, but only their Commission) such Plaints as shall be made upon all those that commit, or offend against any Point, contain'd in the aforesaid* Charters. 28 *Edw.* 1. Chap. 1.

6thly, The Necessity of preserving these *Charters* hath appear'd in nothing more, than in the care they have taken to confirm them; which, as *Cook* observes, hath been by Thirty-two *Parliaments confirm'd, establish'd, and commanded to be put in execution,* with the condign Punishment they had inflicted upon the Offenders. *Cook's Proem* to the second Book of his Institut.

7thly, That in the notable *Petition* of *Right*, many of these great Privileges, and free Customs, contain'd in the aforesaid Charters, and other good Laws, *are recited and confirmed,* 3 Car. 1.

8thly, The late King, in his Declaration at *New-Market*, 1641. acknowledged *the Law to be the Rule of his Power:* By which he doubtless intended *Fundamental Laws*, since it may be the great Advantage of Countries, sometimes to suspend the execution of *Temporary Laws.*

Having so manifestly evidenc'd that *venerable Esteem* our Ancestors had of that *Golden Rule* (the Great Charter) with their deep Solicitude to preserve it from the defacing of Usurpation and Faction; we shall proceed to give an account of their just Resentment and earnest Prosecution against some of those, who in any Age have adventured to undermine that antient Foundation, by introducing an Arbitrary way of Government.

First, As Judicious *Lambard* reports in his *Saxon* Translation; *That the Kings, in those days, were by their Coronation-Oaths obliged to keep the antient Fundamental Laws and Customs of this Land,* (of which this Great Charter is but declaratory) *so did King* Alfred (reputed the most famous Compiler of Laws amongst them)

them) *give this discovery of his Indignation against his own Judges, for Actions contrary to those Fundamental Laws, that he commanded the execution of forty of them*; which may be a seasonable *Caveat* to Judges of our Times.

Secondly, *Hubert de Burgo*, once Chief Justice of *England*, (having advised *Edw.* 1. in the 11th Year of his Reign, in his Council holden at *Oxford, to cancel this Great Charter, and that of the Forest*) *was justly sentenced according to Law, by his Peers, in open Parliament.* When the Statute call'd *CONFIRMATIONES CHARTARUM* was made; in the first Chapter whereof, *Magna Charta* is peculiarly call'd the *Common Law*, 25 Edw. 1. Chap. 2.

Thirdly, The *Spencers* (both Father and Son) for their arbitrary Domination, and rash and evil Counsel to *Edward* the Second (by which he was seduced to break the Great *Charter*) were banish'd for their pains, as *Cook* relates.

Fourthly, The same Fate attended *Tresilian* and *Belknap* for their illegal Proceedings.

Fifthly, The Breach of this Great Charter was the ground of that exemplary Justice, done upon *Empson* and *Dudley*, whose Case is very memorable in this Point: *For tho they gratified* Henry *the Seventh in what they did, and had an Act of Parliament for their Warrant, made the* 11*th of his Reign; yet met they with their due Reward from the hands of Justice, that Act being against Equity and Common Reason, and so no justifiable Ground or Apology for those frequent Abuses and Oppressions of the People they were found guilty of.* Hear what the Lord *Cook* further saith concerning the Matter: "There was an Act of Parliament made in the 11th Year of "King *Henry* the Seventh, which had a *fair flattering Preamble*, "pretending to avoid divers mischiefs, which were (1st) *The* "*high Displeasure of Almighty God.* (2d) *The great Let of the Com*"*mon Law.* And (3d) *The great Let of the Wealth of this Land.* "And the Purvien of that *Act*, tended in the Execution con"trary, *EX DIAMETRO*, viz. *To the high Displeasure of Al*"*mighty God, and the great Let, nay the utter Subversion of the Com*"*mon Law, and the great Let of the Wealth of this Land, as here*"*after shall appear:* The substance of which *Act*, follows in these words:

That from thenceforth, as well Justices of Assize, as Justices of the Peace, in every County, upon Information for the King before them made, without any Finding or Presentment by Twelve Men, *shall have full Power and Authority, by their discretion, to hear and determine all Offences, as Riots, unlawful Assemblies*, &c. *committed and done against any Act or Statute made, and not repeal'd*, &c. (a Case that very much resembles this of our own Times.)

" By pretext of this Law, *Empson* and *Dudley* did commit " upon the Subjects unsufferable Pressure and Oppressions; " and therefore this Statute *was justly, soon after the decease of* " Hen. 7. *repealed*, at the next Parliament after his decease, by " the Statute of 1 *Hen.* 8. Chap. 6.

" *A good Caveat to Parliaments, to leave all Causes to be measur'd* " *by the Golden and Streight Metwand of the Law*, and not to the " uncertain and crooked Cord of Discretion.

" It is almost incredible to foresee, when any *Maxim or Fun-* " *damental Law of this Realm is alter'd* (as elsewhere hath been " observ'd) *what dangerous inconveniences do follow*; which most " expresly appeareth by this most unjust and strange Act of " the 11th of *Hen.* 7. For hereby, not only *Empson* and *Dudley* " themselves, but such Justices of Peace (corrupt Men) as " they caused to be authoriz'd, committed most grievous and " heavy Oppressions and Exactions; grinding the Faces of the " poor Subjects by Penal Laws (be they never so obsolete, or " unfit for the time) by Information only, without any Pre- " sentment or Tryal by Jury, being the antient Birth-right " of the Subject; but to hear and determine the same, by their " discretions; inflicting such Penalty, as the Statute not re- " pealed, impos'd. These and other like Oppressions and Ex- " actions by, or by the means of *Empson* and *Dudley*, and their " Instruments, brought infinite Treasure to the King's Cof- " fers; whereof the King himself, at the end, with great " grief and compunction, repented, as in another place we " have observ'd.

" This Statute of the 11th of *Hen.* 7. we have recited, and " shewed the just inconveniences thereof; to the end, that the " like should never hereafter be attempted in any Court of " Parliament; and that others might avoid the fearful End of " those two Time-servers, *Empson* and *Dudley*, *Qui eorum nequitiis* " *insistunt, eorum exitus perhorrescant.*

" See the Statute of 8 *Edw.* 4. Chap. 2. A Statute of Live- " ries, an Information, *&c.* By the discretion of the Judges, " to stand as an Original, *&c.* This Act is deservedly repeal'd, " *vide* 12 *R.* 2. Chap. 13. Punishment by Discretion, *&c.* " *vide* 5th of *Hen.* 4. Chap. 6, 8. See the Commission of " Sewers: Discretion ought to be thus describ'd; *Discretio est* " *discernere per Legem, quid sit justum.* From whence three Things " seem most remarkable.

First, The great Equity and Justice of the Great Charter, with the high Value our Ancestors have most deservedly set upon it.

Secondly, The dreadful Maledictions, or Curse, they have denounc'd upon the Breakers of it; with those exemplary Punish-

Punishments they have not spared to inflict upon such notorious Offenders.

Thirdly, So hainous a thing was it esteem'd of old, to endeavour an Enervation or Subversion of these antient Rights and Privileges, that Acts of Parliaments themselves (otherwise the most sacred with the People) have not been of force enough to secure or defend such persons from condign Punishment, who, in pursuance of them, have acted inconsistent with our Great Charter. Therefore it is that great Lawyer, the Lord *Cook*, doth once more aggravate the Example of *Empson* and *Dudley* (with persons of the same Rank) into a just Caution, as well to Parliaments as Judges, Justices and inferior Magistrates, to decline making or executing any Act that may in the least seem to restringe or confirm this so often avowed and confirmed *Great Charter* of the Liberties of *England*, since Parliaments are said to err when they cross it; the Obeyers of their Acts punish'd as Time-serving Transgressors; and that Kings themselves (tho enrich'd by those courses) have, with great Compunction and Repentance, left among their dying Words their Recantations.

Therefore most notable and true it was, with which we shall conclude this present Subject, what the King pleased to observe in a Speech to the Parliament, about 1662. (*viz.*) *The good old Rules of Law are our best Security.*

The manner of the *Court*'s Behaviour towards the Prisoners and Jury, with their many extravagant Expressions, must not altogether slip our Observation.

First, Their Carriage to the *Jury* out-do's all Precedents; they entertain'd them more like a *Pack of Felons*, than a *Jury of honest Men*; as being fitter to be try'd themselves, than to acquit others. In short; no *Jury*, for many Ages, receiv'd so many Instances of Displeasure and Affront; *because they prefer'd not the humour of the Court, before the quiet of their own Consciences, even to be esteem'd as perjur'd; tho they had really been so, had they not done what they did.*

Secondly, Their Treatment of the Prisoners was not more unchristian than inhumane. History can scarce tell us of one *Heathen Roman* that ever was so ignoble to his *Captive:* What! *to accuse, and not hear them; to threaten to Bore their Tongues, Gag and Stop their Mouths, Fetter their Legs, merely for defending themselves, and that by the antient Fundamental Laws of* England *too.* O Barbarous! had they been *Turks* and *Infidels*, that Carriage would have ill become a Christian Court; *such Actions proving much stronger Dissuasives, than Arguments to convince them, how much the Christian Religion inclines Men to Justice and Moderation above their dark Idolatry.* It is truly lamentable that such occasion should

be

be given *for Intelligence to Foreign Parts*, where *England* hath had the Reputation of a Christian Country, *by the ill treating of its sober and religious Inhabitants for their conscientious Meetings to worship God.* But above all, *Dissenters* had little reason to have expected this boarish fierceness from the *Mayor* of *London*, when they consider his eager prosecution of the King's Party under *Cromwell*'s Government, as thinking he could never give too great a Testimony of his Loyalty to that new Instrument; which makes the old Saying true, *That one Runagade is worse than three Turks.*

Alderman *Bludworth*, being conscious to himself of his partial kindness to the *Popish Firers*, hopes to make amends by his zealous Prosecution of the poor *Dissenters*; for at the same Sessions he moved to have an Evidence (*of no small quality*) against *Harrison* the Friar, sent to *Bridewell* and Whipt; That he was earnest to have the Jury fined and imprisoned, because they brought not the Prisoners guilty for only worshipping their God. Whence it may be easy to observe, *That Popish Friars, and Prelatical Persecutors, are mere Confederates.*

But what others have only adventured to stammer at, the Recorder of *London* has been so ingenuous as to speak most plainly; or else what mean those two fatal Expressions, *which are become the talk and terror both of City and Country?*

First, In assuring the Jury, *That there would be a Law next Session of Parliament, That no Man should have the protection of the Law, but such as conformed to the Church?* Which, should it be as true, as we hope it is false (and a dishonourable *Prophecy* of that great Assembly) the *Papists* may live to see their *Marian* days outdone by profess'd *Protestants.*

But surely no *English-man* can be so sottish, as to conceive that his Right to *Liberty* and *Property* came in with his Profession of the *Protestant Religion*; or that his *natural and humane Rights are dependant on certain religious Apprehensions*; and consequently he must esteem it a Cruelty in the Abstract, that Persons should be deny'd the benefit of those Laws which relate to civil Concerns, who by their deportment in civil Affairs have no ways transgress'd them, but merely upon an Opinion of Faith, and Matter of Conscience.

It is well known, that *Liberty* and *Property*, *Trade* and *Commerce*, were in the World long before the Points in difference betwixt *Protestants* and *Dissenters*, as the common Privileges of Mankind; and therefore not to be measured out by a conforming to this, or the other religious Persuasion, but purely as *English-men.*

Secondly,

Secondly, But we ſhould rather chuſe to eſteem this an Expreſſion of *Heat* in the *Recorder*, than that we could believe a *London*'s Recorder ſhould ſay, an *Engliſh Parliament* ſhould impoſe ſo much Slavery on the preſent Age, and entail it upon their own Poſterity (who, for ought they know, may be reckon'd among the Diſſenters of the next Age) did he not encourage us to believe, it was both his Deſire and his Judgment, from that deliberate *Elogy* he made on the *Spaniſh Inquiſition*, expreſſing himſelf much to this purpoſe: *Viz.* "Till now I never underſtood the Reaſon of the Policy and "Prudence of the *Spaniards*, in ſuffering the *Inquiſition* amongſt "them: And certainly it will never be well with us, till "ſomething like unto the *Spaniſh Inquiſition* be in *England*. The groſs Malignity of which Saying, is almoſt inexpreſſable. What does this but juſtify that helliſh Deſign of the Papiſts, to have prevented the firſt Reformation? If this be good Doctrine, then *Hoggeſtrant*, the grand *Inquiſitor*, was a more venerable Perſon than *Luther* the Reformer. It was an expreſſion that had better become *Cajetan*, the Pope's Legate, than *Howel*, a Proteſtant City's Recorder. This is ſo far from helping to convert the *Spaniard*, that it is the way to harden him in his Idolatry; when his abominable Cruelty ſhall be eſteem'd Prudence, and his moſt barbarous and exquiſite torturing of Truth, an excellent way to prevent Faction.

If the *Recorder* has ſpoke for no more than himſelf, it is well; but certainly he little deſerves to be thought a *Proteſtant, and a Lawyer, that put both Reformation and Law into the Inquiſition:* There being nothing more deſtructive of the Fundamental Laws and Liberties of *England*, and that noble Deſign of Primitive Reformation, than the Arbitrary Power and Terrifying Racks of the *Spaniſh* Inquiſition. And doubtleſs the ſupreme Governors of the Land are highly oblig'd in Honour and Conſcience (in diſcharge of their Truſt to God and the People) to take theſe things into their ſerious Conſideration, as what is expected from them by thoſe who earneſtly wiſh Theirs and the Kingdom's Safety and Proſperity.

A Poſt-

A Postscript.

The Copy of Judg Keeling's *Case, taken out of the Parliament-Journal.*

Die Mercurii, 11. Decembris, 1667.

THE *House resumed the Hearing of the rest of the Report touching the Matter of Restraints upon Juries; and that upon the Examination of divers Witnesses, in several Clauses of Restraints put upon Juries, by the Lord Chief Justice* Keeling: *Whereupon the Committee made their Resolutions, which are as followeth.*

First, *That the Proceedings of the Lord Chief Justice, in the Cases now reported, are Innovations, in the Tryal of Men for their Lives and Liberties; and that he hath used an Arbitrary and Illegal Power, which is of dangerous Consequence to the Lives and Liberties of the People of* England, *and tends to the introducing of an Arbitrary Government.*

Secondly, *That in the place of Judicature, the Lord Chief Justice hath undervalued, vilified and contemned* Magna Charta, *the great Preserver of our Lives, Freedom and Property.*

Thirdly, *That he be brought to Tryal, in order to condign Punishment, in such manner as the House should judg most fit and requisite.*

Die Veneris, 13. Decembris, 1667.

Resolved, *&c.*

That the Precedents and Practice of Fining or Imprisoning Jurors for Verdicts, is Illegal.

Now whether the Justices of this Court, in their Proceedings (both towards the Prisoners and Jury) have acted according to Law, to their Oaths and Duty, and to do Justice without partiality; whereby Right might be preserv'd, the Peace of the Land secur'd, and our antient Laws establish'd: Or, whether such Actions tend not to deprive us of our Lives and Liberties, to rob us of our Birth-right, the Fundamental Laws of *England:* And finally, to bring in an Arbitrary and Illegal Power to usurp the Benches of all our Courts of Justice, we leave the *English* Reader to judg.

Certainly there can be no higher Affront offer'd to King and Parliament, than the bringing their Reputations into suspi-
cion

cion with their People, by the irregular Actions of ſubordinate Judges: And no Age can parallel the Carriage of this *Recorder*, *Mayor*, &c. Nor can we think ſo ignobly of the Parliament, as that they ſhould do leſs than call theſe Perſons to account, who fail'd not to do it to one leſs guilty, and of more repute, (to wit) Judg *Keeling:* For if his Behaviour gave juſt ground of Jealouſy, that he intended an Innovation, and the introducing an Arbitrary Government, This *Recorder* much more. Did Chief Juſtice *Keeling* ſay, *Magna Charta* was *Magna farta?* ſo did this *Recorder* too. And did Juſtice *Keeling* Fine and Impriſon Juries contrary to all Law? ſo did this *Recorder* alſo. In ſhort, there is no difference, unleſs it be, that the one was queſtion'd, and the other deſerves it: But we deſire in this, they may be ſaid to differ; That tho the former eſcap'd Puniſhment, the latter may not; who having a Precedent before, did notwithſtanding notoriouſly tranſgreſs.

To conclude: The Law ſuppoſes the King can't err, becauſe it is willing to ſuppoſe he always acts by Law (*Et Voluntas Legis eſt Voluntas Regis*, or the King's Will is regulated by the Law) but it ſays no ſuch thing of his Judges. And ſince they are oblig'd by Oath to diſregard the King's Letters (tho under the Broad and Privy-Seal) if they any wiſe oppugn or contradict the Laws of the Land; and conſidering that every ſingular Action of an inferior Miniſter, has an ugly Reference to the Supreme Magiſtrate, where not rebúked; we can't but conclude, that both Judges are anſwerable for their Irregularities, eſpecially where they had not a Limitation of a King's Letter, or Command; and that the Supreme Magiſtrate is oblig'd, as in Honour and Safety to himſelf, *Alfred*-like, to bring ſuch to condign Puniſhment, leſt every Seſſions produce the like Tragical Scenes of Uſurpation over the Conſciences of Juries, to the vilifying and contemning of Juſtice, and great Detriment and Prejudice of the good and honeſt Men of this Famous and Free City.

FIAT JUSTITIA.

Phenix

Phenix XII.

The Second Part of the People's Antient and Just Liberties asserted, in the Proceedings against, and Tryals of Thomas Rudyard, Francis Moor, Richard Mew, Richard Mayfield, Richard Knowlman, Gilbert Hutton, Job Boulton, Richard Thornton, Charles Banister, John Boulton, *and* William Bayly.

At the Sessions begun and held at the Old-Baily *in* London *the last Day of the 6th Month, and there continued till the 7th Day of the 7th Month next following, in the Year 1670. against the Arbitrary Procedure of that Court, and Justices there.*

The PREFACE to the READER.

THAT State which would preserve it self from Ruin and Destruction is ever to keep its Inhabitants pure and clean from Vice and Debauchery, and their Laws from Violation and Corruption; as the first is a way or means to engage a con-

conscientious Obedience and Observation of the just and upright Law of God; so the second, by reason of their due execution, are the Sinews or Sanctuaries that bind the Inhabitants of such State in a perpetual Bond of Safety and Tranquillity: And it's certainly true, where either of these are violated or neglected, the Ruin of that State is near at hand. There's no better way to incline the Subjects of any State to Morality and Vertue, than that those that sit at the Helm, or have the Government thereof, should hold forth clear Examples and Patterns of Piety and Justice in their Lives and Actions.

Regis ad exemplum totus componitur Orbis,

Saith the Poet, The whole World imitate the Example of their King. *And the Divine Historian,* Josephus, *observes in his Ecclesiastical History,* fol. 209. But *(saith he)* mortal men most usually are corrupted by the untoward Flatteries of wavering Fortune, as appeareth by King *Rehoboam:* seeing his Kingdom thus increas'd, he bent himself to all unjust and impious Actions, and contemn'd the Service of God; the People also conform'd themselves to his Impieties; for the Life of the Subjects is oftentimes perverted by reason of the corrupt and dissolute Life of their Princes: And those that are Inferiors beholding the Riot of their Superiors, will easily be withdrawn from all Modesty, and follow those Vices they profess, as if they had been their profess'd Vertues: For should they do the contrary, they should seem to disannul and misslike the Actions of their Princes——The Subjects addicted themselves to Impiety, and all Errors; for they would not make profession of Honesty, for fear they should seem to study the means to be offensive unto the King.

2 *Chron* 13. 18, 19, 20.

From this lively Pattern, or Representative of our present Times or State, we must wish that Princes in this Age would consider, and put in practice that Golden Rule of Demosthenes, Bene gubernare, recte judicare, juste facere; *to govern well, judg rightly, and do justly; so should their Kingdoms flourish, and they themselves be in high estimation in the eyes of their People.*

W.H's Epistle in his Translation of *Mirror of Justice.*

And next the Prince's curious eye over his own personal Actions, a due heed, care and regard is to be had to his Representatives in his Courts of Justice; viz. *those Justices whom he constitutes by his Commission to hear and determine betwixt him and his People, that they be such who by their due Administration and faithful dispensing of the Laws, Justice and Right may be done to all men without respect of Persons.*

But

But as Vice and Debauchery have devour'd and eaten up the Nation's Practice of Religion, ſcarce leaving us the outſide ſhell of Profeſſion: So hath the Corruption of our Laws, and the Violation thereof, turn'd back thoſe wholeſom Streams of Juſtice which ſhould naturally flow from the uſe of them.

And that thou, Reader, *mayſt ſee that thy ſelf art one, who is in danger of being buried in the Ruins of Religion and Piety, as well as thy Civil Rights and Liberties; which are the two Baſes, or Foundations, on which thy temporary here, and future well-being hereafter, conſiſts and ſtands: Caſt thy eye upon the Magiſtrates of the City of* London *(antiently ſtiled* Caput Regni & Legum*) in their Court of Judicature at the* Old Baily, *and behold on the one hand Vertue term'd Vice, Sobriety Debauchery, Religion Faction, Pious and Peaceable Aſſemblies Riots and Routs, and puniſh'd as ſuch; on the other hand, the antient written Laws denied, and their not written ones the Court's Authority: Juſtice turn'd into Gaul, Right and Equity by Will and Power over-ruled. So that it's now become a Proverb,* Tell me thy Judg, and I'll tell thee thy Law.

Quod non lego non credo. *Auguſt.*

Said the Learned Coke, Qui non libere veritatem pronunciat, proditor veritas eſt; *He who conceals Truth, is a Betrayer thereof. Therefore for the ſake of Truth, and the Reader's Benefit, were theſe Proceedings made publick, and according to that due Obſervation and impartial Account, which could be taken and collected of the manner of that Bench's Arraigning and Condemning as well Religion, Piety, Vertue and Sobriety, as Right, Equity, Liberty and Property, with due Comments upon their Procedures from the antient and fundamental Laws of this Land, are laid to thy view.*

And had not the Mayor and Recorder, with the reſt of the Bench, prohibited many, by ſevere Threats, from writing down the Court's partial Dealings both towards the Priſoners and Jurors; and alſo by violence took away what others had adventur'd to collect (commanding ſome to their Bale-dock) in all probability this enſuing Piece might have been much more enlarg'd to thy ſatisfaction.

But what has been faithfully collected and obſerved, and whereof there were ſome hundreds of Witneſſes, is preſented to the World; the Author (deſiring rather to ſpare their Injuſtice, than wrong their Judicature) has contracted this Relation to what comes within the limits of his own knowledg and undeniable proofs; but impartially laid Judgment to the Line, and diſcover'd that which may tend to the Good of his Countrymen, in the Vindication of the Laws, Truth, Innocency, Equity, and Juſtice.

The

The Second Part of the People's Antient and Just Liberties asserted, &c.

THE Laws of *England*, by just and upright Ministers and Officers faithfully dispens'd, and impartially administer'd, have ever been the Upholders and Preservers of Right and Liberty, the high esteem'd and precious Jewels of its free-born Inhabitants. But when unlimited Prerogatives have sprung up, like Mushrooms, out of the sappy Apprehensions, aspiring Brains, and heady Humours of inferior Officers and Ministers; then Tyranny and Oppression have, under disguise of Justice and colour of Law, depriv'd the Commonalty of these things, which they have held most precious and dear to them.

The pretended Crimes or Offences laid to the charge of *Thomas Rudyard*, are far different in their kind and nature from those other Persons, who have undergone with him the severe Judgments, or as some call them, the Inquisitory-like Censures of that Court; which were so far from *Juris Dicta*, the Law of Right, or impartial dispensing of Justice, that they are clear contrary and directly opposite unto them. The Justices of that Court, Judge *Coke*, that famous *English* Lawyer, doth well describe in his *2d Inst. Fol.* 55. in a Poetical Simile of an unjust Judg:

Grosius hic Rhadamanthus habet durissima Regna,
Castigatque auditque dolos, subigitque fateri.

And in another place:

Leges fixit pretio atque refixit.

They punish, then hear, compel to confess, make and mar Laws at pleasure.

The Occasion of *T. R*'s being envy'd and prosecuted by these Adversaries of Peace, was because of his faithful defending and constant appearing (when call'd thereto) for his Clients and Retainders, in such Matters and Causes as Will and Power had forged, and daily did put in execution against them. So that the third of the fourth Month, call'd *June*, the Magistrates of the City of *London*, in the name or colour of a Lieutenancy or Militia, issued out a Warrant, to break open his House in the dead of the Night, to apprehend him (when they might have had him at Noon-day, upon the Exchange, about his occasions) and did take and carry away him, and also what Arms they there could find. Which Warrant was executed by the Soldiers of one Captain *Holford*; and the next day he was sent to the Goal of *Newgate*, as a Person suspected and disaffected to the Peace of the Kingdom, as was alledg'd in his Mittimus, under the Hands and Seals of *Samuel Starling* Mayor, *W. Peak*, *R. Hanson*, *A. King*, *J. Dawes*, *John Cutler*, *W. Rouswel*, *A. Stanyon*, *J. Tivell*, *W. Allott*, *J. Sheldon*, and *T. Davis*.

The seventh of the fourth Month, the Lieutenancy (so call'd) order'd *T. R.* to be again brought before them, who without alledging any Crime, or certain Matter that was prov'd against him, tho earnestly requested by him that he might hear his Accusation, or see his Accusers face to face, did demand 2000 *l.* Security for his Good Behaviour: which unreasonable Demand being not comply'd withal, *T. R.* was remanded to Goal, with a Mittimus under *S. Starling* and *J. Robinson*'s Hand and Seal, pretending therein, That *T. R.* did stir up Persons to the Disobedience of Laws, and abetted and encourag'd such as met in unlawful and seditious Conventicles, contrary to the late Act in the 22 *Car.* 2. of which things, they alledg'd, that they found cause to suspect *T. R.* to be guilty.

Trin. 22. *C.* 2.

Which Case being brought before the Justices of the Court of *Common-Pleas* at *Westminster*, by *Habeas Corpus*; that Court, after solemn debate, gave their Judgment, *That* T. R. *was unjustly imprison'd, and unlawfully detain'd.* And so by them was set at liberty.

His Adversary, *viz.* *S. Starling* the Mayor, being incens'd at his Deliverance and Discharge, finds out new Stratagems to encompass his ends upon him. So that at a Sessions of the Peace, at the *Old Baily*, the 29*th* of the fourth Month, an Indictment is fram'd and prefer'd against *T. R.* the Tenor whereof was, " That whereas at a Sessions of the Peace held " at *Guildhall* for the City of *London*, the 30th of *May*, the 22d " year of the King, before *S. Starling*, &c. and other Justices " of the Peace of the said City, assign'd, &c. a certain Bill " of Indictment was exhibited and prefer'd against one *Samuel* " *Allingbridge*, late of *London*, Stationer, written in Parchment, " for speaking these seditious and menacing Words, viz. *The* " *first man that shall disturb Mr.* Vincent, *will never go out of the* " *House alive.* And whereas one *N. Grove* and *J. Tillot* were " sworn to give Evidence (in behalf of the King) to the " grand Inquest, that *T. R.* intending to hinder and pervert

" Justice

" Justice and due course of Law against *S. A.* for speaking " the seditious and menacing words aforesaid, the 30th of " *May*, with Force and Arms, *&c.* the said Bill of Indictment, " before it came to the Grand Inquest, unlawfully, secretly, " and subtilly, did get, take, and had in his hands, and un- " lawfully did conceal and detain from the Jury, in contempt " of the King and his Laws, to the hindrance of Justice and " due course of Law against *Allingbridge*, unto the evil example " of others, and against the King's Peace, Crown and Dig- " nity.

To which Indictment *T. R.* appearing in Court, and pleading not guilty, *John Lee* told the Bench that there was no cause for that Indictment, by reason that *S. A.* was try'd, convicted, and acquitted the same Sessions that the pretended Indictment miscarry'd. Whereupon the Mayor pulling an Affidavit out of his pocket, that bore date the 29th then instant, alledg'd, That the Indictment was not drawn to the Case, and according to the Instructions that he gave to *John Lee*, and shew'd that Affidavit to ——— *Archer*, one of the Justices of the *Common-Pleas*; who when he had perus'd and read it over, acquainted the Mayor, that the matter therein contain'd *was no cause for an Indictment*. To which the Mayor answer'd, That it is cause, and shall be cause, and he would stand to it; withal affirming, That he had ask'd Chief Justice *Keeling*'s Judgment, and he advis'd him to prosecute it. So the Instructions were deliver'd to *John Lee* to draw up another Indictment.

This piece of Practice was in open Court; which manifests their Partiality and unequal Dealings to such whom they convened before them, to receive Justice at their hands. And how little they (who sat there as Judges) regarded their Oaths, and the Duty of that place of so great a Trust, is easily resolved, weighing them in the Ballance of Law and Justice. Said the Learned *Coke* in his 3 *Inst.* *fol.* 29. " The Judges ought not to deliver " their Opinion before-hand upon a Case put, " and Proofs urg'd on one side in absence of " the Party accus'd: For how (saith he) can they be indif- " ferent who have deliver'd their Opinions before-hand, " without hearing of the Party accus'd, when a small addi- " tion or substraction may alter the Case? And how doth " it stand with their Oaths, that are sworn, That they shall " well and lawfully serve our Lord the King, and his People " in the Office of a Justice? And they should do equal Law, " and execution of Right to all his Subjects. Yea, he saith further, " That the King's Council shall not so much as put

1 Hen. 7. Fol. 27.

" the Case in absence of the Prisoner, to the Judges. As may be seen at large in 3 *Inst. fol.* 30. And the third Statute of 18 *Edward* 3. in the Judges Oath it's said, " And that ye give " no Advice nor Counsel to no man great nor small, in no " case where the King is Party.

Now if the Mayor's Prosecution, and Justice *Keeling's* Advice, be according to the Law, Justice, their Oaths and Duty, in their respective places, let the World judg.

The Clerk of the Peace drew up another Indictment, by the Mayor's Directions, which contain'd the Substance of the former; and further, " That the said *T. R.* the said 30th of " *May*, coming to the aforesaid *Nicholas Grove*, said to him, " That the Bill against *S. A.* was lost, and that *N. S.* should " attend next Saturday; and that *T. R.* unlawfully and " craftily did say to *N. G.* these words, *viz. I will come to you* " *some time this week, and we will go and drink a Pint of Wine* " *with Mr.* Tanner, *and contrive to draw up a slight Bill, that* " *may not be found, and so make an end of the business:* In con" tempt of the King and his Laws, to the hindrance of Justice, " and perverting of due course of Law against *S. A.* for his " Offence; to the evil Example of others, and against the " Peace of the said King, his Crown and Dignity.

To this Indictment also *T. R.* pleaded, *Not guilty*, and gave security by Recognizance to try them both the next Sessions.

This Prosecution falling short still of the Mayor's purpose, which was to clap *T. R.* up in a Goal, demands of him to give Security, or at least his own Recognizance for his good Behaviour; being the same thing that the Judges lately had given their Opinion against.

Therefore he refus'd that piece of Bondage (yet offering the Court, in case of Health, to appear once every day at the Mayor's House, there to answer any matter that should be justly charg'd against him.) Whereupon he was committed to Prison, and by the Mayor's special Order and Direction kept close Prisoner in *Newgate*.

During the time of this unequal Prosecution of *T. R.* many others felt the weight of the Mayor's Injustice, and were made witnesses of various Stratagems used and practised by him and his Brethren, upon several Citizens of *London*; and likewise upon several other innocent peaceable men.

Upon the 19th of the 4th Month, *Francis Moor*, *Richard Mew*, *Richard Mayfield*, *Richard Knowlman*, and *Gilbert Hutton*, with divers others of their Friends, being (as at other times) met together (to wait upon and worship the living God in Spirit and in Truth) at *Whitehart-Court* in *Grace-Church-Street*, *London*

London (being forcibly kept out of their own House by Watchmen and Constables) after they had there peaceably continued together, about the space of one hour, the two Sheriffs of *London*, with their Guard of Officers and Soldiers, came in and made a Proclamation by one of their Servants, That all Persons there present should depart. Which being not regarded by those who peaceably came there, to give to God the things that were Gods; they continu'd in peaceable manner together without distraction, not fearing what man's Violence could do unto them, knowing that against the Innocent there was no Law. Yet the Sheriffs singled out of the Assembly the abovesaid Persons, and delivering them into the custody of one *Whiting*, Beadle to the Bridg-Ward (who was a Person very diligent in such Services) and his Watchmen, who carried them by the Sheriffs order to *Bishopsgate* Goal; a Place, who ever has had the experience thereof, can witness its filthy Noisomness: And a horrid shame it is, that the Magistrates of this City should make no better Provision, than to incarcerate peaceable Men, and their Fellow-Creatures, in places as it were on purpose to stifle or poison them, that they might be incapacitated to make a due Defence against their intolerable and arbitrary Oppression.

The day following they were call'd before the Lieutenancy, or Council of War, at *Guildhall*, who wanting proof and witness of some hostile Action done by them, they were remanded back to Prison.

The 21st of the 4th Month, they being brought before the Mayor, and the Officers swearing that they saw them in *Whitehart-Court* in *Grace-Church-street*, tho peaceable and quiet (as the Sheriffs being then present acknowledg'd) yet because the Sheriffs of *London* had taken up and apprehended them, as Persons present after their Proclamation made, as may appear by their Commitment; the Mayor made their Mittimus to *Newgate*, as Rioters: The Tenor whereof was thus.

Lond. ss. *Receive into your custody the Bodies of* Francis Moor, Richard Mew, *&c. herewith sent you; being apprehended and brought before me, and charged to have made, and to have been present on the last Lord's Day at an unlawful Assembly, Riot and Rout in* Whitehart-yard *in* Grace-Church-street, London; *and for want of Sureties for their Good Behaviour, and personal Appearance at the next Sessions of Goal-Delivery, to be held for the said City and Liberties: And them safely keep in your custody, until they shall be thence legally discharg'd. And this shall be your Warrant, dated the* 21st *of* June, 1670. Samuel Starling *Mayor, To the Keepers of his Majesty's Goal of* Newgate.

 Where

Where they were kept till the Sessions following, with several others of their Friends, which were sent to them as like Offenders.

The Court order'd these, with *Richard Thornton*, *Charles Banister*, *Job Boulton*, *Ezekiel Archer*, *Margery Fann*, and *Samuel Slaughter*, whom the Sheriffs had taken up from their Meeting in *Bishopsgate-street*, to be indicted; the Tenor of which Inditement was, " That they together with others were met at *London*, &c. with Force and Arms in a riotous manner, *&c.* " to the disturbance of the Peace of our Lord the King; and " that they, together with about 200 more unknown, did " assemble in an unlawful manner, riotously, routously, and tumultuously, under colour and pretence of Religious Worship, " in other manner than was practis'd in the Church of *England*; and that after three Proclamations then and there, " in the name of the King, by *John Smith* Esquire, and *James* " *Edwards* Esquire, then and yet Sheriffs of the City of *London*, were made, That all Persons there present should from " thence depart forthwith, upon their peril; the said *F. M.* " *&c.* together with the other 200 unknown, then and there, " by the space of half a quarter of an hour, did remain and " continue together, riotously, routously, and unlawfully, in " contempt of the King and his Laws, to the disturbance of " his Peace, to the evil example of all others in the like case " Offenders, and against the Peace of the said King, his " Crown and Dignity, *&c.*

Justice *Moreton* sitting on the Bench, the Prisoners were call'd to the Bar; and as they pass'd along, the Goalers would have taken off their Hats, but Justice *Moreton* commanded they should be let alone, and said he would fine them five Marks a-piece for their Contempt to the Court, and so urg'd them to plead, *Guilty*, or *Not Guilty*; to which they generally answer'd, That they were not Guilty of the breach of any Just Law. So the Court took that for a Plea, as not guilty, and ask'd them whether they would be try'd presently or traverse; to which they answer'd, That if they might have a Copy of their Inditement, they would be try'd next day. The Court reply'd, That they must either try it presently, without a Copy of the Inditement, or traverse till next Sessions, and then they should have a Copy thereof, and Justice done them. To which they agreed, and pass'd their words to appear the next Sessions.

Soon after that Sessions, the Military Forces (who were every First Day order'd by the Lieutenancy to guard as well the publick Meeting House in *Grace-Church-street*, as their Mercenary

cenary Priests, whom the Bishops sent thither, to read their Church-Homilies and Prayers) apprehended and took into custody *William Bayly*, whom they carry'd before the Mayor; and upon Information of the Priest (who on that day was to have officiated in that place, had he had courage to have perform'd what he had undertook) the Mayor committed *W. B.* to *Newgate*, for opposing the Priest in officiating his Function, as was alledg'd in his Mittimus; whenas the said *W. B.* had not at any time either seen or spoke with the said Priest.

Not long after, *John Boulton* an antient Citizen of *London*, of seventy Years of Age, and very well known to be a quiet and peaceable Person, was sent by the Mayor to *Newgate*, as a riotous Person. And soon after him, *William Penn* and *William Mead*; all which were taken up by arm'd Forces, from their publick and peaceable Assemblies, and committed to the Prison of *Newgate*.

The last of the 6th Month, the Sessions of *Oyer* and *Terminer* beginning at the *Old Baily*, not only such, who the former Sessions had been indicted, but those newly committed, attended the Court; where constantly waiting three days in expectation of being call'd to their Tryals, and according to the Laws of this Land to be condemn'd or acquitted, were never once call'd until the 3d of the 7th Month; at which time the Bench of Justices consisted of *Samuel Starling* Mayor, *John Robinson*, *Richard Ford*, *Joseph Sheldon*, *George Waterman*, *William Peak*, *Thomas Bloodworth*, Aldermen of *London*; *John Howel* the City Recorder; together with *Richard Brown*, who pretending himself to be something learned in the Law, came there to second the Recorder, and with much confidence took upon him to examine Persons according to his Will and Pleasure, as if he had been a Justice in Commission for *London*. *John Smith* and *James Edwards* were Sheriffs. O yes being made, and Silence commanded, *William Penn*, *William Mead*, *John Boulton*, *William Bayly*, *Francis Moor*, *Richard Mew*, *Richard Mayfield*, *Richard Knowlman*, *Gilbert Hutton*, *Richard Thornton*, *Charles Banister*, *Job Boulton*, *Ezekiel Archer*, and *Thomas Rudyard*, were all call'd into the Court; and not giving that *Cap-Reverence* and *Hat Honour* to the Place, which the *Haman-like-spirited* there upon the Bench expected, and look'd for, the Mayor with great Indignation, openly amongst his Brethren, first express'd himself against them (calling out to the Officers who attended the Court) saying, *Pox on them, knock them all down.*

Surely such Language as this was very ill becoming that Court of Justice, and especially to proceed from the chief Magistrate of this Imperial City. It's said, *He bears the Sword in vain, that's not a Terror to Evil-doers, and a Praise to them that do well.* If in this the Mayor of *London* has manifested his Christian Behaviour, let him have the Praise thereof. A time has been when such an Expression, for its Prophaneness, should have merited a pair of Stocks, or a Whip; and for its Rashness and Violence to be bound to the Good Behaviour.

But the Misery of our Age is such, That *Judgment is turned back, and Justice standeth afar off: And he alone who turneth himself from Evil, maketh himself a Prey.*

But the Under-Marshals and Goalers manifesting more of Humanity, than to obey the inhumane and unchristian Command of the Mayor, exercis'd no other Violence upon the Prisoners than pulling off their Hats; for which the Recorder rebuk'd them, and bid the Officers put on the Prisoner's Hats upon their Heads again; which was no sooner done, in Obedience to the Court's Command, but presently the Clerk of the Peace requires every of the Prisoners, in Obedience and Reverence to the Court, to pull off their own Hats: the Prisoners not complying with these whimsical Humors, ridiculous Precepts, and antick Acts of Justice, the Recorder gives Order to the Officers a second time to pull off all their Hats, and set Fines upon their Heads, some twenty Marks, some twenty Nobles, using variety of airy Expressions against, and taunting those Prisoners, whom he so illegally fined.

Which piece of ridiculous Pageantry being over, O yes being made, and Silence commanded, (as truly there was need of it) the Cryer call'd over the Jury; who, when they had answer'd to their Names, and taken their Places, were commanded to look upon the Prisoners at the Bar; the Prisoners were also requir'd to look upon the Jurors, and make their Challenge before they were sworn: The Names of the Jury-men were, *Thomas Veer, Edward Bushell, John Hammond, Henry Henley, Henry Michel, Charles Milson, Gregory Walklet, John Brightman, William Plumsted, James Damask, William Lever, John Bailey.* Who all took an Oath, Well and truly to try, and true deliverance make, betwixt the King and the Prisoners at the Bar, according to their Evidence; and so that God should them help. The Prisoners, without objecting against any one Man of the whole Pannel, accepted freely of them, tho they had Liberty by the Law, to have made their Challenge against whom they pleas'd. So now their Country being thus solemnly sworn to Try and Deliver, *&c.* they were the true and proper Judges, to acquit or condemn, to deliver or judg guilty, the persons that were given them in charge.

In this of the Jury, it's acknowledg'd, the Prisoners had Right and Justice done them. and the Court acted under their Com-

Commission, according to that Clause, *Facturi quod ad Justitiam pertinet secundum Legem & Consuetudinem Angliæ*; To do Justice according to the Law and Custom of *England*, contain'd in the Charter of the *English-man's* Liberties; which declares, *Quod Dominus Rex non capiet, imprisonabit, nec super eum ibit, nec mittet nisi per legale judicium parium suorum*; That the King shall not take, imprison, or pass upon any Free-man, without Tryal by his Equals. *Co.* 2 Inst. Fol. 51.

And these are call'd the Good and Lawful Men of the *Vicinage*, whom the Prisoners had freely accepted and given up Themselves and Causes unto, as to their Judges, to be by them condemned or acquitted, as in their Consciences they should judg Equal, Just and Righteous, according to the Establish'd and Fundamental Laws of *England*. The Court proceeded to Try *William Penn* and *William Mead*; the manner whereof is more largely set forth in a Book call'd, *The Peoples Antient and Just Liberties asserted, in the Tryal of* William Penn *and* William Mead, *at the Sessions held at the* Old-Baily *in* London, *the first, third, fourth and fifth of the 7th Month*, 1670. *against the most Arbitrary Procedure of that Court*. *Mag. Char.* chap. 14.

Which was but an Introduction to their after Illegal and Tyrannical Proceedings against the other Prisoners: For when the Court found that all their severe Menaces, scurrilous Invectives, and hard Usage towards the Jury, could nowise avail, to make them alter that Verdict; which, according to their Oaths, they brought in for *William Penn* and *William Mead*, they presently consult how they might separate this Jury and the rest of the Prisoners, whom they had sworn to try and deliver, according to Evidence: Thereupon most *Arbitrarily* and *Illegally* against our Fundamental Law, *Magna Charta*, the great Preserver of our Lives, Freedom and Property, this Court impos'd Fines of forty Marks apiece upon every of the Jury-men, and committed them to the Goal of *Newgate*, until they should pay the same: "Which Proceedings "are Innovations, in the Tryal of Men for their Lives and "Liberties; and the Usage of such arbitrary and illegal Power, is of dangerous "consequence to the Lives and Liberties "of the People of *England*, and tends to "the introducing of an Arbitrary Govern-"ment; as was Resolv'd by the High Court of Parliament of *England*, *Decemb*. 11. 1667. in the Case of Justice *Keeling*. Vide *Postscript to the People's Antient and Just Liberties asserted*.

Observe,

Observe, All Ages have had a venerable Esteem of Juries; and this Tryal of the Fact, *Per duodecim liberos & legales Homines*, by Twelve good and lawful Men, is very antient, saith *Cook*, 1 Inst. Fol. 155. For (saith he) hear what the Law was before the Conquest; *In singulis Centuriis comitia sunto, atque liberæ conditionis viri duodecim ætate superiores, una cum præposito sacra tenentes juranto, &c.* Twelve just and honest grave Men were to be in every Hundred, to judg their Neighbours. And thereupon in affirmance of this upright Way of Tryals by Twelve Men, were the Charter of our Liberties made, and from time to time confirm'd; and how this Tryal excels others, and wherefore other Countries have them not, see *Fortescue*, cap. 25. and 29. And, as one observes, our *English* Laws have taken so great care to find out the true Matter of Fact in issue, That every one of the Jurors agree together in the Matter in issue, before they give their Verdict, which is the Foundation on which the Judgment of the Court is grounded: for, *Ex facto jus oritur*, as saith *Cook*, 2 Inst. 49.

Lambert verb. Centura.

Artic. super Cart. cap. 9.

29 *Assize*, *pre.* 27.

And in the 29th Chapter of our Great Charter, it's said, *No Man shall be taken, imprisoned, &c. but* per legale Judicium—*by lawful Judgment of his Equals*; shewing, that antiently the Jurors were sole Judges, to pronounce and give Judgment against their Neighbours, and such whom they had in charge, according unto that *Mirror of Justice*, written by *Andrew Horn*, in the time of *Edw.* 1. Chap. 1. Sect. 3. "It was assented unto, that "free Tenants should meet together in the Counties, Hun-"dreds, and the Lord's Courts, if they were not especially "exempted, to do such Suits, and there judg their Neigh-"bours. Hence we may observe, and impartially conclude,

1. That a Jury of Twelve Men are (and antiently were) the proper Judges of their Neighbour's Actions, Misdeeds, or Miscarriages; which is founded on Reason and Equity, because the Neighbourhood is best acquainted with, and has the most certain knowledg both of the Persons and Actions there done and acted.

2. The Law requiring, that Twelve good and honest Men should agree as One, before they determine their Neighbour to be guilty, or not guilty of the Fact or Matter charg'd against him, shews us, not only that the *Fundamental Laws* of this Land have appointed its Inhabitants, merciful Judges; but also such who should be the proper, sole and ultimate Judges (in the Matters charg'd against any Man) to acquit or condemn

demn according to the Laws, as in their Consciences they should find Equitable, Just and Righteous.

3. The high Esteem our Ancestors have ever had of these twelve Righteous Judges in former Ages, bespeaks the little regard and honour that the *Recorder* of *London*, the *Mayor* and his *Brethren*, have shew'd to their *Predecessors* and *Antiquity*; as also their low Esteem of the *English-man's Liberties*; which, in all Ages and Generations, have been mostly preserv'd and secur'd by weighing mens Actions in the equal Ballance of their *Good* and *Honest Neighbours* Judgments.

4. We may observe how little regard this Court has had to the performance of such *Oaths*, which they impose upon Men at pleasure: for, notwithstanding they had sworn Twelve good and lawful Men of the City of *London*, *Well and truly to try, and true deliverance make, between the King and the Prisoners at the Bar*; yet they refuse and deny these Jurors to perform that Oath, which they had so solemnly taken; manifesting to the World, that the Bench assumes a Power and Jurisdiction equal with the Church of *Rome*, to enforce and absolve from Oaths and Covenants at their Wills and Pleasures.

5. It's most apparent how little this Court minded or regarded their own Duty, Oaths and Commission, to do Equal Law, and Execution of Right, without respect to Persons, according to the Laws of this Land: For when the Prisoners had given their consent to be try'd, and the Jury had sworn to try; without, and against the consent of both, or either of them (or any Act done whereby Common Right should be denied the Prisoners, or Justice to the Jurors) to separate them each from other, is such a piece of *Tortious Justice*, which there is no Law or Custom of *England* can or will justify or maintain.

20 *Edw.* 3. chap. 1.

6. We cannot but own and acknowledg the *Parliament* of the Commons of *England*, their industrious Care and Prudence to preserve our Lives and Liberties from the Violence of Usurpation, and Practice of Arbitrary and Illegal Powers over Juries, who are sworn to try and deliver their Neighbours, according to Evidence of Fact committed. And since once in their Prudence they thought meet, just and righteous, to check the Author of such *Arbitrary Innovations*, as Fining of Jurors for their Verdicts, we hope they will take occasion, at this time, to manifest their Care and Tenderness of the People of *England* (whose Representatives they are) in bringing these latter Malefactors to condign Punishment, that for the future Justice may run down its proper Channels, and be faithfully executed and equally dispensed according to our *Antient* and *Fundamental Laws*, and the Laudable Customs of this our Land.

Whilst

Whilst the Recorder thus treated this Jury of the Citizens of *London*, the Sheriffs had summon'd a new Pannel, to appear at *Justice-Hall* the 5th of the 7th Month; the Prisoners, on whom the former *Jury* had sworn to pass their Verdicts upon, *viz.* *John Boulton*, *William Bailey*, *Francis Moor*, *Thomas Rudyard*, &c. were call'd again into Court in the Afternoon, and each of them fined as formerly, twenty Nobles apiece for their Hats. A Precedent or Foundation for such Judgments, Fines and Amercements, we challenge the City's Recorder, and the conceitedly-learned Mayor, to shew or make out to the World by the Laws of *England*.

So soon as the Recorder had finish'd or pass'd these new sort of *Judgments*, or rather *Inquisitory Censures* upon or against the Prisoners, he perus'd the Pannel of the last summon'd *Jury*, and gave directions to the Clerk to call them over; who, as it was observ'd, *pickt* here and there such persons that were judg'd the most likely to answer the malicious Ends and horrid Designs of that Bench, calling not the Jury-men in order and direct course, as is usual in all Courts of *Justice*, where Right is impartially administred; and withal, bidding the Prisoners to look upon the Jurors, and before they were Sworn to make their Challenges.

So now a second *Jury* was going to be sworn upon them for the Tryal of one single Fact, which was a further manifestation of the Court's evil Intentions against them; having now neither Equity, Justice nor Law, for their Boundaries or Guides, it being such a piece of practice that no Age can parallel.

Saith the Learned *Cook* in his 2 Inst. 56. *Lex est tutissima Cassis*; The Law is the safest Guard to defend the Innocent from Tort and Wrong; which declares, *That Justice and Right shall be denied to none.* Neither shall any Man be destroy'd by any manner of wise; on which *Cook* observes, *That every Oppression against Law by colour of any usurp'd Authority, is a kind of Destruction:* For, saith he, *Quando aliquod prohibetur, prohibetur & omne per quod devenitur ad illud.* The Law admits not of the least Wrong to be done to any Man. Therefore, saith the same Author, *That it's the worst Oppression which is done by colour of Justice.*

Mag. Char. Chap. 29.

Cook 2. Inst. 48.

Observe then, First, The Court to swear two several Juries upon one person, to Try one and the same Cause or Fact, upon one and the same Indictment; What is it but under disguise of Justice to commit such Absurdities, that our Laws allow not, or Lawyers ever before heard of?

Secondly,

Secondly, If such Practices as these be allowable, what person shall know when that Jury, whom the Court will permit to try him, is or shall be sworn upon him, to acquit or condemn him, according to his Fact, and the Law of the Land?

Thirdly, What Right and Justice can a Prisoner expect, when his Adversary shall not only summon what Jurors they please, but also in the Court pack together such, whom they judg will answer their *Malicious Designs*, upon those who shall be committed to their charge?

The Prisoners taking notice of the Court's partial *Prosecution, and unequal distribution of Justice*, and bold Attempts to commit such *horrid Rapes* upon their Liberties, made an unanimous *Protestation* against the 2d Jury. First, Desiring to know by what Law or just Precedent they practised such sort of Justice upon them; and how the Recorder could Swear two Juries to try one and the same Fact, *&c.* The Recorder answer'd, *That the first Jury was imprisoned for their* Misdemeanor, (meaning the not finding *William Penn* and *William Mead* guilty) *and the Prisoners must take that for an Answer:* Which being far short of the Question, the Prisoners still persisted to know what Law or Custom justified their Proceedings. The Recorder reply'd, *That the Court had over-ruled them:* The *Prisoners* told him, That the Law should be, and ought to be, the *Rule* and *Guide* of all Courts of Justice, and that such Answers as (*The Court over-ruled you*) was not sufficient to satisfy their reasonable and just Demands.

Whereupon the Recorder, with great Indignation and Rage, told one of the Prisoners, *That he should be Gagg'd, and deserv'd to have his* Tongue *bored through with a Hot Iron, and his* Mouth *Nail'd to the Dust*; with many other inveterate, opprobrious, and taunting Expressions; telling him, That he was not bound to produce Precedents, but it should satisfy, *That the Court was of another Opinion against them, and had over-ruled them.* To which the Mayor joyn'd his consent, saying also, *We will over-rule you.*

By the Statute 25 *Edw.* 1. chap. 1. it was accorded, "That "the King's Justices, Sheriffs, Mayors, *&c.* that had the Laws "to guide them, *&c. This is a Clause* (saith *Cook*) *worthy to be written in Letters of GOLD, That the Laws are to be the Judges Guides: And therefore not Judges by their Arbitrary Glosses, to be Guides of the Laws, which never yet misguided any that truly followed them. Sub clipeo Legis nemo dicipitur*, as saith the same Author. *Common Right* in 2 *Edw.*3. is call'd *Common Law* in 14 *Edw.* 3, &c. and in this sense it is taken, where it is said, *Ita quod stet recto in curia*, i. e. *Legis in curia*; The Law is called *rectum*, (that is, *Right*, or a *Rule*) because

Cook 2. Inst. 56.

cause it discovereth that which is tort, crooked, or wrong; so as *Right* signifieth *Law*, so *Tort*, *Crooked* or *Wrong*, signifieth *Injury*; and *Injuria est contra jus*, against Right. *Hereby* (saith *Cook*) *the crooked Cord of that which is called Discretion appeareth to be unlawful.*

So that (First) it's plain, The Law rules and guides, but Discretion, Force and Violence, over-rule.

Secondly, The Just Judg makes the Law his Rule and Guide, but the Unjust over-rules the Law: So that it's apparent, that this Over-ruling is no other than by Discretion (which is tort, crooked and rough) to oppose with Violence that Justice and Right, which the Laws allow and afford every Free-man of *England*; then there's no Defence to be made against the *Recorder*'s Over-ruling, that is gone beyond the Law's Rule, to his own Over-ruling Will and Discretion.

The Clerk of the Peace, in obedience to the Court's Command, proceeds to swear the second Jury upon the Prisoners; upon which some of the Prisoners objected against several of them, as one *Steed* the Fore-man, and several others: The Recorder denied them their Challenges, telling them still, that *the Court over-rul'd them*. And altho Judg *Cook* in his 3 Inst. fol. 27. saith, *That the end of Challenge is to have an indifferent Tryal, and which is required by Law; and to bar the Party indicted of his lawful Challenge, is to bar him of a principal concern in his Tryal*: Yet this *Recorder*, who doth, or should know the Law, and those Rights and Privileges which it affords the Prisoners (both in the Challenge of the Array of the Pannel, and also of the Poles) admitted their *Challenges* to neither, but cried out still, *The Court over-rules you*; that as well the Spectators, as Prisoners, were fully satisfied, that the Purpose and Resolution of the *Bench* was, to make them subject and slaves to their Injustice, and most Tyrannical Will and Pleasure, in despight of the Laws, and that undoubted Right and Liberty, which is the best Birth-right the Free-men of *England* have.

The Names of the Jury were, *Henry Steed*, Fore-man; *Edward Dermer*, *Thomas Mosse*, *John Ashborne*, *Edward Langton*, *Henry Offley*, *Edward Hanney*, *Walter Hungerford*, *Thomas Pendleton*, *Robert Twiford*, *Robert Cooper*, and *Daniel Walton*.

As it's most certainly true, that every Free-man of *England* may, and doth challenge the benefit of *Antient Fundamental Laws* to protect and defend his *Life* and *Liberty* against Violence and Oppression, most especially that which is contain'd in the 29th Chapter of the *Charter of Liberties*, viz. *Not to be taken, imprisoned*, &c. *but by Judgment of his Equals*, (which *Cook* calls in his Expo-

Expoſition, Twelve of his good and honeſt Neighbours) and to have equal *Juſtice* and *Right* done him, according to that Charter, as by the firſt Statute of 20 *Edw.* 1. So it's as true, that by the *Recorder* of *London*, the *Mayor* and his *Brethren*, thoſe Rights and Privileges have been denied; thoſe *Laws*, and ſuch who claim a benefit from them, have been contemned and over-ruled by the Cenſures and Judgments which they paſſed upon, and Carriages and Uſages which they practiſed toward both Priſoners and Jurors; ſo that this Conſequence will follow.

Firſt, Altho a Jury of good and honeſt Men ſhall be ſworn well and truly to Try, and true Deliverance make between, *&c.* according to their Evidence; yet if the Verdict that is confirm'd by the Oaths of Twelve Men (agreed together as one) be not congruous to the Will and Humour of one Perſon ſitting on the Bench (as the *Recorder*) theſe Twelve Judges ſhall be Fined and Impriſoned as *perjur'd Perſons*, and as ſuch who are guilty of as high *Miſdemeanors* as any they came to Judg and Try.

Secondly, When Twelve good and lawful Men ſhall be ſo impannel'd and ſworn to try, *&c.* and the Priſoners ſhall accept of them without Challenge (except after this the Court alſo approves of them) theſe firſt ſworn ſhall be impriſoned, and another Jury ſummoned, and packed together, to ſerve and anſwer the Ends of the *Informers* and *Proſecutors* upon the *Priſoners*, contrary to Law, any Uſage or Cuſtom whatſoever.

And now we dare put thoſe *Queſtions* to be reſolv'd by the very Enemies of theſe Priſoners that were ſo try'd by that Court, Whether this Bench (and the Sheriffs of *London*, who from the beginning were either Proſecutors or Informers againſt theſe Priſoners) Firſt, ſo Menacing and Threatning, and afterwards Fining and Impriſoning one Jury; Secondly, Summoning, Packing and Enforcing another Jury upon Priſoners, (to try that Fact which a former Jury were ſworn to determine) againſt the Law, Uſages and Practices of all Courts of Judicature; have not with *Violence oppreſſed* the *Free-men* of this Land, and denied them that *Juſtice* and *Right*, which by the *Fundamental Laws* they ought freely to have and enjoy, and which alſo theſe Juſtices (by their Commiſſions, Oaths and Duty of their Places) ought to allow, *yea or nay?*

The ſecond Jury being thus ſworn, the Clerk of the Peace read over the Indictment againſt *Francis Moor*, *Richard Mew*, *Richard Mayfeild*, *Richard Knowlman*, and *Gilbert Hutton*; as alſo that againſt *Richard Thornton*, *Charles Baniſter*, and *Job Boulton*, (the ſubſtance whereof is before ſet down) and their *Indictment ments* for Form and Matter being alike, they were try'd together.

The Cryer calling the Witneſſes, the Court proceeded to Tryal. The Proſecutors and Witneſſes were one *Whiting*, the Beadle of *Bridg-Ward*; and the reſt were the Sheriff's Officers, whom the Mayor had bound over to proſecute the Priſoners. Whence it may be obſerv'd, That either the Sheriffs themſelves, or their Servants, were the Informers in this Work; from which ſo many large Perquiſites have fallen to them, as hereafter ſhall be mention'd.

The Subſtance of the Witneſſes Evidence was, *That they ſaw the Priſoners in* Grace-Church-ſtreet, *in* Whitehart-Court, *amongſt the Aſſembly of People there met together*; *and that they ſtay'd there till after Proclamation was made, That all perſons there preſent ſhould depart.*

The Priſoners being ask'd what they could ſay for themſelves? they anſwer'd, That they *owned* that they were at *Gracious-ſtreet*, met together to worſhip the true and living God in Spirit and in Truth, againſt which there is no Law: And further ſaid, That the *Indictment* conſiſted of much Matter, as meeting with Force and Arms to diſturb the Peace, and continuing there Riotouſly, Routouſly and Tumultuouſly, in contempt of the King and his Laws, and againſt the King's Crown and Dignity, which none of the Witneſſes had ſworn; therefore they deſir'd to know upon what Law they were Indicted, and that the Law might be produc'd, and read to the Jury, that thereby they might know whether they had made a Breach of any juſt Law. The Recorder anſwer'd, That he was not bound to produce the Law, for it was *Lex non ſcripta.* Then, reply'd the Priſoners, How ſhall the Jury know whether we are guilty of the Breach thereof? Said the Recorder, It is the *Common Law*, which you have broken in your tumultuous Aſſemblies, and ſtaying there after Proclamations were made to depart. The *Priſoners* objected, That the Indictment alledgeth three ſeveral Proclamations were made, whenas but one was made that day. Whereupon the Witneſſes were again examin'd, Whether there were not three Proclamations made? Who anſwer'd, That there was but one made. Upon which the Mayor demanded of one of the Witneſſes, whether *O Yes* was not ſaid thrice? Who anſwer'd, That the Officer who made Proclamation ſaid *O Yes* three times, before he commanded the People in the King's Name to depart: Then, ſaid the Mayor, that was three Proclamations. Such a piece of Violence in the explanation of a Word, that has not been known in a Court of Juſtice.

The

The *Prisoners* further urg'd, That they were always quiet and peaceable in their Assemblies; That the Law against *Riots* was never intended against them, but *Popish*, or such like Disturbers of the Peace. To which the *Recorder* answer'd, That the *Papists* were better Subjects to the King than they were, and that they were a stubborn and a dangerous People, *and must either be brought under, or there were no safe living by them.*

The Prisoners offer'd to vindicate themselves from those foul Aspersions laid upon them by the Recorder; telling him, That they had broken no just Law to their knowledg, and that they never had been guilty of being Rioters and Routers, as was pretended; which they desir'd the Jury to take notice of, and that there had not any such Proof been offer'd by the Witnesses.

Whereupon the *Mayor* and *Recorder* commanded the Goalers to thrust them into the Bale-dock, and in their absence the Recorder gave his Charge to the Jury, not so much as summing up the Evidence (which truly prov'd not the tenth part of the Indictment) as giving in Matter of his own, of foul *Criminations*, telling the Jury, that they were a Refractory People, such who delighted in Deeds of Darkness, and that they must be crush'd, or there would be no living by them; so that upon the *Indictment* they must find them Guilty.

Now surely there never was greater Oppression and Violence manifested in a Court of Justice, either upon the just and righteous Law, or a quiet and peaceable People, as has been acted by the Lieutenancy (it's pity to say Magistrates) of the famous City of *London*. Had there been colour for their Proceedings by any Statute-Law of the Land, pointing out the Offenders and their Punishment, these several Actings of theirs might have been in some measure tolerable. But when Men dare at once, against the very face of *Law, Justice, Equity, Reason, Right* and *Liberty*, commit such Oppressions upon their Fellow-Creatures, yea, on a People too, who never yet could be justly charg'd for using Violence, Force or Arms against any Man; no, not so much as to defend themselves against such, who have violently and inhumanly abused and tortured their Bodies, without the least colour of Warrant or Authority from the Civil Magistrate: we cannot but stand in admiration of this Court of Judicature. Let us a little see the Judgments of our Sages of the Law, touching the matter of Riots, in former and latter Times; not only Statute-Law, but also the Opinion of the Learned.

First see the Statute of 17 *R.* 2. chap. 8. (1393.) It was Enacted, " That the Sheriffs, and all other the King's Offi-

" cers, ſhould ſuppreſs Rioters, and impriſon them. 13 *H.* 4. " chap. 7. (*An.* 1411.) If any Aſſembly or Rout of People " againſt the Law be made, that three or two Juſtices of the " Peace and Sheriff, or Under-Sheriffs, ſhall come with the " Power of the County (if need be) to Arreſt them, and ſhall " record what is done againſt the Law; and that the perſons " by that Record ſhall be convict in manner, as inforceable " Entries. 2 *H.* 5. 8. The King's Liege People, that were " Travellers, ſhould be aſſiſtant to the Juſtices, *&c.* when " warned to ride with them in Aid to reſiſt *Riots*, *Routs*, &c. " upon pain of Impriſonment.

The *Riotors* and *Routers*, mention'd in theſe Statutes, were certainly ſuch perſons, who did really meet with *Force* and *Arms*; elſe, what need was there of the Power of the County, as is directed, to quiet, appeaſe, and arreſt them? or elſe, what need of engaging Travellers to aſſiſt them, notwithſtanding they may have the Power of the County to apprehend them?

2dly, Read the *Judgment* of the Oracle of our Laws: *Cook* in his 3 Inſt. c. 79. title Riots, Routs, and unlawful Aſſemblies, Forces, *&c.* ſaith thus: Riotum *cometh of the French Word* Rioter, *i. e.* Rixari; *and in the Common Law ſignifieth, When three, or more, do any unlawful Act, as to beat any Man, or hunt in his Park, Chaſe, or Warren, or to enter or take poſſeſſion of another man's Land, or to cut or deſtroy his Corn, Graſs, or other profit,* &c.

Lamb. intr. Legib. Inſt. ch.13, 14,15. vide *Abu.* chap. 26.

Routa *is deriv'd of the French Word* Rout, *and properly in Law ſignifieth, When three, or more, do any unlawful Act, for their own, or the common quarrel,* &c. *As when Commoners break down Hedges, or Pales, or caſt down Ditches, or Inhabitants, for a way claimed by them, or the like.*

An unlawful Aſſembly is, When three, or more, aſſemble themſelves together, to commit a Riot or Rout, and do it not.

So that it's moſt plain and evident, That a Quiet, Religious, and Peaceable Aſſembly of People, were never intended by our Predeceſſors, to be puniſh'd as Rioters, Routers, and unlawful Aſſemblies, as our Law-Executioners now-a-days would have it.

The Lord *Cook* ſaid, *Intereſt regi habere ſubditos pacatos*, That the King's Intereſt was to have his Subjects peaceable. And what, muſt it be the inferior Officer's Intereſt to have them accounted otherwiſe, and that for filthy Lucre-ſake?

A new Contrivance to advance the Sheriff's Perquiſites, which our Fore-fathers were ignorant of, (*viz.*) The Sheriffs to ride to an Aſſembly of People, whom they, or their Confederates, againſt all Law, had forceably kept out of their Houſe

and

and Free-hold; and because (upon *Proclamation* by them made, for which they have no Ground or Authority by the Law) the People presently departed not from their *own Ground*, and before the Door of their *own House*, they shall be committed to Goal as Rioters, condemned as such, and the Sheriffs shall have 400, or 500 *l.* for their day's work out of these Innocent persons Fines.

This new construction of Religious Assemblies seems the more strange, by reason there cannot be one Precedent produced, to back this upstart Opinion, that Religious Meetings deserve of late years that ignominious term of Riots or Routs.

So that this seemly piece of Law, or Wit, must be owned to have had its Rise, Spring, and Original, from the Prerogative Brain of *S. S.* Mayor of *London*, and confirm'd by the City-Recorder, who doubtless will not be the last that may repent of his day's work.

The next whom the Court call'd to their Tryal, was *Ezekiel Archer*, and *Margery Fann*; who being indicted for Rioters the Sessions before, and the Evidence being deficient, the Court coveting to come off with credit in all such *Indictments* as were of the new Stamp, order'd an *Indictment* for *Felony* to be read against them, which they had forg'd and fram'd for that purpose, and piece of Iniquity, which well deserves the search, and *condign Punishment* for the Contrivers: so these two were found *Not guilty*.

The same day this Bench call'd *T. Rudyard* into Court. When the Clerk had read over the first *Indictment*, which the Mayor the former Sessions declar'd was not drawn up according to Instructions and Evidence; and also the second, which the Mayor said he would stand by, and prosecute: The Informer's Witnesses were sworn, *viz. N. Grove* and *J. Tillot*; *Grove* being first to give in his Testimony, declar'd, *That there was an Indictment drawn against* S. Allingbridge, *for saying, The first Man that disturb'd Mr.* Vincent *should never go out of the House alive; and that he saw* T. R. *take it out of Mr.* Lee's *hand, and told him that it was lost, and* T. R. *would go with him to Mr.* Tanner, *and drink a Pint of Wine with him, and draw up a slight Bill that might not be found.* So (said the Mayor) here's both the Indictments prov'd already; which Evidence *Grove* deliver'd, as being one entire Action and Discourse. And being ask'd what time this Discourse was, whether when *T. R.* took the Bill? he answer'd, He did not well know; and *T. R.* asking him some further Questions, the Mayor interrupted him, saying, He was not to examine the King's Witnesses. *J. Tillot* was next call'd, who swore that *T. R.* acknowledg'd to him, that he had the Indictment. *T. R.* acquainted the Court, that he own'd that he was at the Sessions

 at

at *Guildhall*; where *S. Allingbridge* attending, requested him to enquire and know from the Clerk, whether his *Adversaries* had drawn any Bill of Indictment against him, and what the Indictment might be: Thereupon *T. R.* enquir'd of the Clerk, whether he had drawn such a Bill: *Jo. Forman*, an Officer, standing by him, with several Bills in his hand, gave this Bill into *T. R*'s hand to read; which when he had done, in open Court, return'd the Bill to *Forman*, and immediately went out of Court, ordering *S. A.* to send for his Witness to try the Indictment, in case the Grand Inquest should find it *Billa vera.* The Evidence, as it was much contrary to Truth, so it was as far short of proving the Indictments, as by the ensuing Exceptions may appear. But what was deficient in that respect, the Recorder made up in his Charge to the Jury.

Exceptions to the Indictment.

First, It appears not by the Indictment, that the Bill of Indictment against *S. Allingbridge* was cognizable to the Court, it being against the Justices Oath to take notice of it before the Grand Inquest had found it.

Secondly, It appears not, that the Words charg'd against *Allingbridge* were punishable by Law; for the House mention'd in the Indictment might be *Vincent*'s Dwelling-house, so Burglary to break into it without lawful Warrant.

Then, as to the Evidence to the first Indictment: 1. No proof that *Grove* ever read the Indictment (which indeed he could not) against *S. A.* so he swore peremptorily upon the Clerk's Information, which was a false Oath.

2. That *T. R.* took the Bill out of *Lee*'s hand, could not be, for the Officer keeps the Bills of Indictments when the Witnesses are sworn, and not the Clerk of the Peace.

3. Improbable that *Grove* should know that Bill amongst so many more; but impossible that he should see the Bill taken away (knowing it) and not mention one word of it all that day, no, not when the Bill was pretended to be wanting.

4. Not sworn he took it out of Court.

5. Not sworn that Justice, or that any course of Law was hindred against *S. A.*

6. As to the *acknowledging* the Indictment to *Tillot*, it was not three hours before the Tryal; who asking *T. R.* whether he ever read the Indictment, *T. R.* answer'd, he did, and left it in *Forman*'s hand; Why that's enough, said *Tillot*, the Mayor sent for me to swear it, which I could not do before.

7. If *T. R.* had taken the Bill, it could not benefit *S. A.* or hinder the Prosecutor.

8. That

8. That *T. R.* ſhould hazard his Reputation in a thing of no value, wherein he could neither advantage his Friend, nor prejudice his Enemy, could not ſtop the Proceedings half an hour, yea in a quarter another might have been written and prefer'd, is very improbable.

9. It's moſt apparent, that if *Grove* did not perjure himſelf, in ſwearing ſuch a Bill was drawn againſt *S. A.* (he having neither read it, or had a Copy of it) he or the Mayor, or ſome of the Confederates muſt themſelves have conceal'd the Bill, and kept it in their own Cuſtody, elſe *N. Grove* could not ſwear to it; one of which muſt neceſſarily be.

As to the ſecond Indictment, the Words there pretended to be ſpoken, 1. If true, were not adviſing *Grove* to do an Action, but telling him that we would go, *&c.* ſo nothing being done in proſecution of the words, it was only diſcourſe.

2. Not ſworn that the Advice was taken.

3. Improbable that *T. R.* ſhould thus diſcourſe to a Stranger, whom before he had never ſeen.

4. That he ſhould undertake to go to *Tanner*, that was as much a Stranger to him.

5. *T. R.* never came afterward to *Grove*, nor ſpoke with *Tanner*; but *S. Allingbridge* was try'd and convicted the very ſame Week, in an Adjournment of the ſame Seſſions.

Now whether there was either ſufficient Cauſe for an Indictment, or apparent Proofs to evidence the Truth of theſe upon which *T. R.* was try'd; or whether all theſe pretended Crimes and Miſdemeanors, were not the product of the Mayor's malicious, envious, and inveterate Spirit, cauſleſly carried on againſt him, (who not only appears to be the firſt Informer, but the Maintainer and Proſecutor of the Quarrel, as alſo Evidence and Judg upon) let every unprejudic'd perſon (ſeriouſly conſidering) give his Judgment.

The Jury was commanded to withdraw, which, for the Formality's ſake, they did, and not longer ſtaying than about a quarter of an hour, return'd again, and brought in the nine perſons that were try'd, guilty in manner and form as they ſtood indicted; which ſome of theſe Jurors had over their Cups ſworn they would do, if ever they came to try the *Quakers*.

John Boulton and *William Bayly* were the laſt call'd to their Tryal, who were indicted ſeveral; For that *they ſuch a day, and year, and place, with Force and Arms,* &c. *with Two hundred more Perſons, were aſſembled together, to diſturb the King's Peace; and being*

ing ſo aſſembled, they unlawfully took upon themſelves to Preach and Teach to the People, then and there aſſembled and congregated; by reaſon whereof, a great concourſe of People did remain together in contempt of the King and his Laws, to the diſturbance of his Peace, to the terror and diſturbance of his Subjects, unto the evil Example of others, and againſt the King's Crown and Dignity, &c.

Not guilty being pleaded, the Informer's Evidence being produc'd, ſwore, That they ſaw or heard them ſpeak or preach to the People, which was ſufficient for the Court to make out the whole Indictments: for the *Recorder* ſaid, the Jury were only Judges of Matter of Fact; ſo that if the Jury have Evidence they *ſpoke* or *preach'd*, the Court ſays that muſt be with *Force and Arms, unlawfully and tumultuouſly to diſturb the King's Peace, and that Tumults of People were occaſion'd thereby, and continued together, in contempt of the King and his Laws, to the diſturbance of his Peace, terror of his People, evil Example of others, and againſt the King's Crown and Dignity:* A ready way to perjure Jurors, and oppreſs the Innocent.

Theſe are the Concomitants of Speaking in the Name of the Living God, and worſhipping him in the Ways of his own Appointment. And altho the Priſoners deſir'd to ſee the Law that their Adverſaries pretend they have broken, they ſhall have neither that, nor Reaſon produc'd that might give ſatisfaction either to the Priſoners or Spectators. The Lord *Cook* gave this as a Rule, viz. *Incivile eſt, parte una perſpecta, tota re non cognita, de ea judicare*; That it was uncivil, ſeeing only one part, to give Judgment on the whole matter. Yet how little regarded theſe Jury-men, or the Court, to know the whole Matter before they gave Judgment upon the whole Charge? Surely this Jury was pack'd to be Cut-throats to their own Liberties, and Reputations alſo, or elſe they would have better regarded what they undertook; to find guilty every one in manner and form, and yet not the tenth part of any Indictment prov'd; to be ſworn truly to try according to Evidence, and yet to find that for which no Evidence was given. Is it poſſible that they ſhould commit this horrid Perjury out of a ſlaviſh Fear, debauch'd Principle, and horrid Partiality, and yet be quiet from the Terrors of Conſcience; nay, for which we are ſure they cannot free themſelves without ſerious Repentance?

At the cloſe of the *Seſſions*, all the Priſoners (who had been found guilty by this Jury of the Benches) were call'd down t the Seſſions-houſe, where all day they expected to be call'd in to Court to receive *Judgment*, being prepar'd alſo to give in their *Exceptions* in Arreſt of Judgment, purpoſed to be deliver'd

to

to the *Recorder* in writing: but of this expected Defence they were all prevented, the Bench giving their Judgments or Cenſures without calling any of the Priſoners to hear them; the *Tenor* of which, as appears by the *Newgate*-Book, are in this manner: *John Boulton* fined forty Mark, *William Bayly* fined thirty one pound thirteen ſhillings four pence, *William Penn* forty Mark, *Francis Moor* fined twenty Mark, *Richard Mew*, *Richard Mayfeild*, *Richard Knowlman*, *Gilbert Hutton*, *Richard Thornton*, *Charles Baniſter*, *Job Boulton*, *Thomas Rudyard*, every of them fined twenty Mark a-piece; *Ezekiel Archer* fined forty Mark, for divers evil Carriages and Contempts in Words and Deeds by them ſeverally, openly, voluntarily and obſtinately committed in and towards the Court. And the *Court* gave further Judgments or Cenſures, viz. *Francis Moor*, *R. M. R. M. R. K. G. H. R. T. C. B. J. B. Katherine Everett*, *J. Boulton*, and *W. Bayly*, fined every of them twenty Marks a-piece, and *T. R.* fined a hundred pound, being convicted of ſeveral Treſpaſſes and Contempts, and to be committed to Priſon until every of them pay their ſeveral reſpective Fines.

The Court underſtanding that their Goal of *Newgate* was ſo full of Priſoners, that there could be no tolerable Entertainment for theſe new Convicts, diſcours'd with the Keepers where to impriſon them: ſo the Bench having an account, that out of the *Dog*, by *Newgate*, that very Seſſions there died two perſons of the *Spotted-Fever*, or *Plague*, (one, the Maſter of the Houſe, the other a Priſoner, whom *Jo. Robinſon*, Alderman, had there ſent for refuſing to take an Oath, preſcrib'd in the 3d of *Ja.*) whereupon they were commanded to be impriſon'd there, and a Keeper ſet upon them to prevent their going abroad upon the moſt urgent occaſion. Where through the Goodneſs of the Almighty, they were preſerv'd in Health, beyond the expectation of their Friends, or hopes of their Enemies, who doubtleſs out of an evil End and Purpoſe ſent them thither, into an infected Houſe.

But that Goalers, of what degree or ſtate ſoever, may in ſome meaſure know the Duties of their reſpective places, and not through Ignorance abuſe ſuch who are committed to their Charge, we have thought it meet at this time to inſtance and give an account what their duty is to their Priſoners, according to the Laws of this Land, which all Goalers are oblig'd under great Penalties to obſerve, and the People of this Land to preſerve, as their Liberties, leſt by ſuch neglect Slavery be inſenſibly drawn upon them.

By the Common Law we find, *Quod cura ad continendos non ad puniendos haberi debet*, as *Bracton* lib. 3. fol. 105. *Goalers are ordain'd to hold Priſoners, not to puniſh them.* For Impriſonment by the Law is is (neither ought to be) no more than a bare Restraint of Liberty, without those illegal and unjust Destructions of close and open Prison (as is usual.) See *Stamf.* Ple. Cro. fol. 70.

Therefore *Cook* in his 3 Inst. 91. saith, *That if the* Britton *Goaler keep the Prisoners more streightly than he ought of* *fol.* 18. *right, whereof the Prisoner dieth, this is Felony in the Goaler by the Common Law. And this is the Cause, That* Flet. *lib.* 1. *if a Prisoner die in Prison, the Coroner ought to sit upon* *chap.* 26. *him.* See also the said *Cook*, Fol. 34. *Cap. Petty-Treason*, how Prisoners are to be us'd; wherein is also an Account of an Indictment of a Goaler for evil Usage of his Prisoner, *Fol.* 35. *in Trin. Term*, 7 *E.* 3. *cor, Rege rot.* 44.—*Præsentat, quod ubi quidam* Robertus Bayhens, *de* Tavesly *captus fuit, & in prisona Castri Lincoln detentus per quodam debito Statut. mercatorii in Custodia* Tho. Boteler, *Constabularii Castri de* Lincoln *ibid. prædict.* Tho. Boteler *posuit ipsum* Robertum *in profundo Gaole inter Felones, ubi Prisona, contra formam Sta-* 1 E. 3. *tuti, &c. Et eadem profundo detinuit, quousque idem* Ro- *cap.* 7. bertus *fecit finem cum eo de* 40 s. *quos ei solvit per Extortionem.* That whereas one *R. B.* of *T.* was taken and detain'd in the Prison of *Lincoln* Castle, for a certain Debt of Statute-Merchant, in the Custody of *T. B.* Constable of the Castle of *L.* aforesaid; That the said *T. B.* put the said *R.* into the Common-Goal amongst Thieves, in a filthy Prison, contrary to the Form of the Statute, *&c.* and there detain'd him, till he had paid him a Fine of 40 *s.* Whereupon *Cook* makes this Observation, *So as hereby it appeareth, where the Law requireth that a Prisoner should be kept* (in salva & arcta custodia) *that is, In safe and sure Custody; yet that must be without any pain or torment to the Prisoner.*

So *Co.* 3 Inst. 52. saith, *If a Prisoner by the Duress, that is, Hard-usage of the Goaler, cometh to untimely Death, this is Murder in the Goaler:* And in the Law implieth Malice, in respect of the Cruelty.

Horn, in the Mirror of Justice, pag. 288. saith, *That it is an Abusion of the Law, that Prisoners are put into Irons, or other pain, before they are Attainted.*

See also *Cook* 3 Inst. 34, 35.

And *Horn* also, pag. 34, 36. reckons the star- *Vox plebis*, par. ving of Prisoners by Famine, to be among the 1. fol. 55, 56. Crimes of *Homicide* in a Goaler.

Which also *Cook* in his 3 Inst. chap. 29. Title of *Felony* in *Goalers* by *Duress* of Imprisonment, *&c.* by Statute and by the Common Law. *Fol.* 91.

And next, let us see what the Law saith for the Fees due to Goalers. The Mirror of *Justice*, pag. 288. tells us, That it's it's an Abusion of the Law, that Prisoners, or others for them, pay any thing for their Entries into the Goal, or for their going out. This is the Common Law, there is no Fee due to them by the Common Law. See what the Statutes say; The Statute of *Westm.* 1. chap. 26. saith, "That no Sheriff, "or other Minister of the King, shall take Reward for doing "their Offices, but what they take of the King; if they "do, they shall suffer double to the Party aggriev'd, and be "punish'd at the Will of the King. Under this word *Minister of the King*, are included all *Escheators*, *Coroners*, *Goalers*, and the like. See *Coke* 2 *Inst. fol.* 209. affirms. And agreeable is *Stamf. pl. Coron.* 49. Nay by the Statute of 4 *E.* 3. chap. 10. Goalers are to receive Thieves and Felons, taking nothing by way of Fees for the receipt of them. So odious is this Extortion of Goalers, that very Thieves and Felons are exempt from payment of Fees.

And we find in our Law-Books, That no Fees are due to any Officer, Goaler, or Minister of Justice, but only those which are given by Act of Parliament. For if a Goaler will prescribe for any Fees, the Prescription is void, because against this Act of Parliament, made 3 *E.* 1. being an Act made within time of memory, and takes away all manner of pretended Fees before: and we are sure none can be rais'd by colour of Prescription since. And therefore we find by the Books of 8 *E.* 4. fol. 18. *That a Marshal or Goaler cannot detain any Prisoner after his Discharge from the Court, but only for the Fees of the Court* (the Court being not barred by this Statute of *Westm.* 1. aforemention'd) *and if he do, he may be indicted for Extortion.* And agreeable to this is the Book of 21 *E.* 7. *fol.* 16. where, amongst other things, it's held for Law, *That if a Goaler or Guardian of a Prison takes his Prisoner's proper Garment, Cloke, or Mony from him, it is a Trespass, and the Goaler shall be answerable for it.* So that we may undeniably conclude, That there is no Fee at all due to any Goaler or Guardian of a Prison from the Prisoner, but what is due unto him by special Act of Parliament.

And if a Goaler or Guardian of a Prisoner, shall take any thing as a Fee of his Prisoner, he may and ought to be indicted of Extortion, and upon conviction to be remov'd from his Office; and if his Prisoner by Constraint, Menace, or Duress be enforc'd to give him Mony, he may recover that Mony against the Goaler again, in an Action of the Case at Common Law.

Item, The King considering the great Perjury, Extortion, and Oppression, which be and have been in this Realm by his Sheriffs, Un- *Stat.* 23 H. 6. *chap.* 10.

der-

der-Sheriffs, and their Clerks, Bailiffs, and

*Stat.*4H.4,5. Keepers of Prisons, *&c.* hath ordain'd by Authority aforesaid, in eschewing all such Extor-

Rast. predict. fol. 318. tion, Perjury, and Oppression, that no Sheriff shall let to Farm in any manner his County, nor any of his Bailiwicks. Nor that any of

Co. pred.365. the said Officers and Ministers, by occasion, or under colour of their Office, shall take any

21 H. 7. f.16. other thing by them, nor by any other Person to their use, profit, or avail; if any person by them or any of them to be arrested or attached, for the omitting of any Arrest or Attachment to be made by their Body, or of any Person by them, or any of them (by force or colour of their Office arrested or attached) for Fine, Fee, Suit of Prison, Mainprise, letting to Bail, or shewing any Ease or Favour (to any such Person so arrested or to be attached) for their Reward or Prefit, but such as follow; that is to say, for the Sheriff 20 *d.* the Bailiff which maketh the Arrest or Attachment, 4 *d.* and the Goaler of the Pri-

Rast. predict. fol. 371. son, if he be committed to ward, 4 *d.*——— And that all Sheriffs, Bailiffs, Goalers, or any other Officer or Ministers, which do con-

Stat. 21 E. o. trary to this Ordinance, in any point of the same, shall lose to the Party in this behalf indamag'd or griev'd, his treble Damages, and shall forfeit the Sum of 40 *l.* for every such Offence, the one Moiety to the King, the other to the Prosecutor, to be recover'd at Common Law, in either of the Courts of *King's-Bench*, or *Common-Pleas* at *Westminster*.

This is a perfect Account of the Goalers Fees in all cases, where Persons are laid in Prison upon Civil Matters and Causes; which Fee of 4 *d.* is more than any other Statute or Law allows them to take from their Prisoners: But in such Cases where the King is Party, it's stablish'd, "That the "Prisoners in all the King's Prisons should be maintain'd at "the King's Charge and out of the King's Revenues, according to the old Law of the Land; much less to have Mony extorted from him by the Goaler. But look into the Prisons in and about the City of *London*, what horrible Oppressions, Extortions, and Cruelties, are exercised upon the Free-born People of *England*, yea in most Prisons throughout this Kingdom.

Which excessive Amercements and Fines (after all their other partial Dealings, lawless Proceedings, and arbitrary Carriages towards the Prisoners from first to last) do manifest and evidence to the World, their Malice and Envy against an Inno-

Innocent, Upright, Quiet, and Peaceable People. What proportion is there here betwixt the pretended Fault, and the assessed Fine? Provides not the fourteenth Chapter of the Great Charter against such unjust Judgments and partial Censures, which declares, ' A Freeman shall not be amerced " for a small Fault, but after the quantity of the Fault; for " a great Fault after the manner thereof? And the Amerce- " ment shall be assess'd by the Oath of honest Men of the " Vicinage.

Here's Justice and Equity, Righteousness in Judgment, which affords every man common Right, declares, That all Offenders ought to be amerced by their Neighbourhood, according to the quantity of the Trespass. Wherein have these Judges (who are commanded by the Statute of 25 *E.* 1. confirm'd by *Pet. Right*, 3 *Car.* 1.) allow'd the Charter before them in Judgment, in all its Points, *&c.*

It may truly be said, that our antient, just, and fundamental Laws, which *Coke* on the 14th Chapter of *Magna Charta* calls a Law of Mercy, are (as the same Author there writes) now turn'd into a shadow. For by the Wisdom of the Law, these Amercements were instituted to deter both Demandants and Plaintiffs from unjust Suits, and Tenants and Defendants from unjust Defences; which was the Canse in antient time of fewer Suits: but now we have but a shadow of them. *Habemus quidem senatusconsultum, sed in tabulis reconditum & tanquam gladium in vagina repositum.* Cicero. Yea, our antient Charters are as a Sword in its Sheath, which if drawn, are and will be sufficient to defend us against all Injustice, Tyranny, or Oppression whatsoever. 2 *Inst.f.*28.

But it's often objected by many of their Adversaries, That the Publick Meeting-Houses, wherein the People call'd *Quakers* are, and have been of late accustom'd to meet, and assemble themselves together, and out of which the Military Forces do from time to time hale and expel them, and by force keep and restrain them from entrance, are by Orders of the King and Council, invested and stablish'd in the now King, and that he has right to dispose of them, as his own Inheritance; yea, to pull them down, sell and burn the Materials of them, as his inferior Officers have lately done by some about *London*: And thereupon such who come there to assemble together, are Trespassers, Rioters, Routers, and unlawful Assemblers, and as such are rightly and duly punish'd according to the Laws.

To which is anſwer'd, That by the Antient and Fundamental Laws, which have been already recited, as the 29th of *Magna Charta*, there is no man's Right, Property or Free-hold ſhall be taken away from him, but by trial of a Jury, and the Law of the Land. Read *Stat.* 2 E. 3. 8. 5 E. 3. 9. 14 E. 3. 14. 28 E. 3. 3. *Regiſt. fol.* 186. *Coke pla. fol.* 456. *Coke* 2 *Inſt.* 45. 3 *Inſt.* 136.

And ſee a Statute of latter date, 17 *Car.* 1. *cap.* 10. entitled, *An Act for Regulating the Privy Council*, &c. which ſpeaks in this wiſe: *Be it likewiſe declar'd and enacted by the Authority of this preſent Parliament, That neither his Majeſty, nor his Privy Council, have or ought to have any Juriſdiction, Power, or Authority, by* Engliſh *Bill, Petition, Articles, Libel, or any other Arbitrary way whatſoever, to examine or draw into queſtion, determine or diſpoſe of the Lands, Tenements, Hereditaments, Goods or Chattels of any of the Subjects of this Kingdom; but that the ſame ought to be tried and determin'd in the Courts of Juſtice, and by the ordinary courſe of Law.*

Alſo Learned *Coke* in his 2 *Inſt. fol.* 36. ſaith, *The Common Law* (of which the Great Charter is declaratory) *hath ſo admeaſured the Prerogative of a King, as he cannot take or prejudice the Inheritance of any.*

So that by the Law of the Land theſe pretended Offenders are ſtill rightfully poſſeſs'd of their own Houſes and Places of publick Aſſemblies; and their cruel Adverſaries have no more Property, Right, Intereſt, or due Claim therein or thereto, than a Pirate has to the peaceable Merchantman's Ship, a Robber has to the innocent Traveller's Purſe, or the Wolf to the Blood of the harmleſs Lamb. And in caſe ſuch Laws as theſe will not preſerve that Intereſt which thoſe People have to their Inheritances and Properties, we can none of us expect to have our Rights or Liberties, Wives or Children, yea, or our Lives ſecured unto us longer than pleaſeth or liketh the Will and Pleaſure of cruel and ravenous Adverſaries.

It's worthy taking notice of, that after the Jury had, on ſo ſlight ground, brought in *T. R.* amongſt others guilty in manner and form, how palpably the Court manifeſted their Envy and Malice, in the Fines impoſed upon him. And tho, as is declar'd by the Statute of 20 *E.* 3. *cap.* 1. *That Juſtices ſhall do even Right to all People, without ſhewing favour more to one than to another*; according to that juſt Law, *Lev.* 19. 15. *Ye ſhall do no Unrighteouſneſs in Judgment; thou ſhalt not reſpect the Perſon of the Poor, nor honour the Perſon of the Mighty, but in Righteouſneſs ſhalt thou judg thy Neighbour:* Yet for a piece of writen Parchment, the Value whereof was not 1 *d.* a thing whereof a Court of Juſtice could not take cognizance, according to the juſt Laws of this Land, or Damages in caſe it had been

taken

taken away, or Profit to any man that could have it, not appearing to be any, neither indeed could there be to any Person living; no course of Law obstructed, admitting all to be true of that Fact, which the Mayor gave in, or his Witnesses swore falsly to the Jury; the Cause of Justice against an Offender not a moment prevented; these painted Sepulchers or partial Inquisitors fined or censur'd him an hundred pounds, altho they had before convicted *S. Allingbridge*, and fined him but five marks for being Principal (yet too much for such an offence) and *T. Rudyard* being as an Accessary must be a hundred pounds. Whether this be just and equal, let the World be judg; and to proceed from a Person (I mean the Recorder) who has had for many years the Reputation of Honesty and Justice, which it's fear'd he carry'd about with him, only as that aspiring Clergyman did his Fishing-Net, which he caus'd to be laid aside, so soon as he had procured a Cardinal's Cap, saying, *The Fish is caught*. And truly so may the City of *London* say of its Recorder, who has not since he came to be Recorder, manifested that candid and equal Justice towards this City, or Citizens in their publick Concerns, as was expected; yea, little but what first passes the Stamp of our Sword-Aldermen, and Classis of the City Lieutenancy: And since he by experience has found, that sowing and dedicating his Law and Endeavours to their Designs, is that which procures him the best, and most fruitful Harvest, he ever has been sedulous to plead and study that cause: whose Actions may be the more clearly manifested to this City and Nation, if weigh'd in the Ballance of Justice and Righteousness.

As God's Indignation rested on the Children of *Israel*, till one *Achan*'s Theft was discover'd and punish'd; so this City suffers sore Judgments, till it has purged it self of these many *Achans* that lodg in her Bosom, not only robbing her Inhabitants of their Rights, Liberties, and Properties, but also her Chamber of her Treasure, the poor Orphans Security.

Our Predecessors, out of their prudence and care that equal Justice and Right should be done to all men, by a Statute in the 18 *E*. 3. 3. appointed Judges an Oath, wherein is this Charge; " And that you take not by your self, or any other " privily nor apertly, Gift, nor Reward of Gold, nor Silver, " nor of any other thing that may turn to your profit, unless " it be Meat or Drink, and of small value, of any man that shall " have any Plea or Process hanging before you, as long as the " Process shall be so hanging, nor after the same Cause.

If the City Recorder hath forgotten this Oath, his Crime's not the less in breaking it; the Justice of it remains, and all Persons

Persons in Judicature are to do justice to all, and sell or deny it to none. And Bribery is such a Crime, that it's punishable wherever it's found: And it's hoped Justice may reach this Recorder, if it appear that his Fingers have touch'd this forbidden *Babylonish* Garment.

Magna Charta c. 29.

But in order to discourse of this so foul a Crime, first see the mark which such an Action leaves behind it: *Fortescue cap.* 51. " Bribery (saith he) is a great Misprision, when any " man in judicial place takes any Fee, or Pension, Roll, or " Livery, Gift, Reward, or Brocage of any Person, that " hath to do before him any way, for doing his Office, " or by colour of his Office, but of the King only, unless it " be of Meat and Drink, and that of small value, upon di- " vers and grievous Punishments. Saith *Coke*, " This word *Bribery* cometh of the *French* word " *Briber*, which signifieth to *Devour* or *Eat gree-* " *dily*, applied to the devouring of a corrupt Judg; of whom the " Psalmist, speaking in the Person of God, saith, *Qui devorat plebem meam sicut escam panis: Qui cog-* " *noscit faciem in judicio, non bene facit, iste pro* " *buccella panis deserit veritatem.* In the 23d " Year of *E.* 3. Sir *William Thorpe*, Chief Justice " of the King's Bench, for taking of four Per- " sons 50 *l.* against his Oath, was tried and judg'd upon his " acknowledging the Fact, to be hang'd, *&c.* *Coke* further sets forth, " That this Offence of Bribery may be committed by any that hath " any Judicial Place (or Ministerial Office) either Ecclesiasti- " cal or Temporal. *Non accipies personam nec* " *munera* (and the reason is express'd by the " Holy Ghost) *quia munera excæcant oculos sapi-* " *entum, & mutant verba justorum.* If Bribery hath so great " force, as to blind the Eyes of the wise Judg, and to change " the words of the Just: *Beatus ille qui exuit manus suas ab* " *omni munere, Judex debet habere duos Sales; salem sapientiæ, ne* " *sit insipidus, & salem conscientiæ, ne sit diabolus.*

3 *Inst.* 145.

Psalm 13. 4. Prov. 28. 21. *Coke* 3. *Inst.* 145.

Fol. 147.

Deut. 16. 19.

" Tho the Bribe be small, yet the Fault is great; and this " appeareth by a Record in the Reign of " E. 3. *Quia diversi justiciarii ad audiendum &* " *terminandum assignat, ceperant de Johanne Ber-* " *ners, qui indictatus fuit,* 4 l. *pro favore habendo* " *die deliberationis suæ, finem fecerant domino Regi* " *per* IV. M. *Marcas*: So as they paid for every " Pound a thousand Marks. See before Sir " *William Thorp*'s Case, *Rot. Par.* 7 *R.* 2. The " Chan-

Pasc. 17 E. 3. *Coram Rege. Rot.* 139. *Esse Jo. Berner's* Case, *Rot. Pa.* 7 *R.* 2. *num.* 12, 13.

" Chancellor was accused of a Bribe of ten pounds, and " his Man four pounds and certain Fish; which tho the " things are small, yet it had been punish'd, if it had been " proved.

But now to the Fact of the City Recorder, it was observed, That when he gave Judgment against the several Convicts before related, and assess'd the several Fines and Amercements upon the Convicts and others, both for their Hats and pretended Crimes for which they were indicted; that *John Smith*, one of the Sheriffs of *London*, being, as was supposed, overjoy'd to hear the Court's Gratitude in rewarding his pains, for making Proclamations in the Streets, *&c.* but being somewhat in doubt whether many of the Fines might not fall short, or prove bad Debts, hastily steps out of his Chair, and going to the Recorder, said, *But how shall we come by these Fines?* To which the Recorder answer'd, *Give me one of them, and I will secure you all the rest.* At which answer, with a seeming Joy and Alacrity, *J. Smith* return'd to his Chair, and spoke to some who were supposed his Friends, there present in Court, and audibly declar'd to them, that the Recorder told him, *That if we* (meaning the Sheriffs) *would give him one of the Fines, he would secure us all the rest of them.*

Surely this was too open and publick a place to make such Bargains as these: But what wonder, when scarce any Passage or Action of theirs, that Sessions, was in Law and Righteousness any more justifiable? What Ratification or Confirmation of this piece of contracted Bribery has been since betwixt them in their private Chambers, we know not; but what's done and acted in publick Courts, we may and can assert, and declare to the world.

Some may conjecture, That the Mony which *J. Howel* the Recorder afterwards receiv'd, was upon the first proposed and offered Contract, made in open Court with *J. Smith* the Sheriff.

Others may imagine, That it was the Mayor's Benevolence, for justifying his dirty and filthy Actions and Prosecutions before the People at the Sessions. But the case is this, That the Mayor, Sheriffs, *J. Robinson*, &c. and other the Justices for that Sessions, being met together at *Guildhall* in a Court of Aldermen, proposed to pay the Recorder for his extraordinary pains, and reward him for his execution of Justice, or sitting in Judgment at the *Old Baily* upon the Quakers. *J. Robinson*, the chief of that Flock, and not the backwardest to give what's not his own, told the Court, *That the Recorder deserved an hundred pounds for his Service done at the* Old Baily *the last Sessions.* Whereupon the Court consented to pay him

him for that ſervice an hundred Pounds, by the Chamberlain of *London*. Who doubts of the truth hereof, are deſir'd to repair to the Chamberlain's Office, and they may there find the Order, bearing date the 8th of *October*, 1670. beſides other Orders for 200 *l.* more to him, within eight months laſt paſt. An excellent way to eaſe that Treaſury of being overburden'd with Orphans Mony! By which ſiniſter Ends and curſed Diſpoſitions of its Caſh, the Chamber is run ſo deeply in debt, that it's almoſt incredible: And here Modeſty engages to conceal, being in hopes that e'er long ſome more faithful Stewards and Guardians may be appointed to have the Charge and Wardſhip of it, *&c.*

So that notwithſtanding that large Proviſion which *England*'s Laws have made for the Safety of its Inhabitants (as in Chapter 29. of its Charter of Liberties, *Nulli vendimus*, &c. on which *Coke* obſerves, That all the King's People, Eccleſiaſtical and Temporal, Free or Bond, Old or Young, yea, altho he be outlaw'd or excommunicated, or any other without exception, *is to have Juſtice freely without ſale, and fully without denial*) yet thoſe Priſoners at the hand of this Recorder and Bench, inſtead of having Juſtice freely, have been apparently ſold into the hands of their cruel Adverſaries; and inſtead of having it fully, they have been unjuſtly over-ruled by their Arbitrary and Illegal Sentences and Cenſures againſt them.

Thus are we forced to caſt the blame of the Priſoners Sufferings upon the Authors thereof, which we muſt attribute either ſprung from their Falſneſs to their Truſt, or their Incapacity to execute that weight of Authority committed to them: And ſurely this Nation throughout is made ſenſible of nothing more, than the daily Breach of their Liberties, and of Violence to the Freedom of their Perſons and Eſtates, by ſuch *hoſtes humani generis*, as theſe oppreſſed Priſoners have had juſt occaſion to complain of.

The Actions of that Seſſions were a Riddle to the *Engliſh*-man, beyond all that this latter monſtrous Age hath brought forth. It's needleſs to repeat how much the publick Liberty (in denying the Commonalty that Freedom of Jurors the Law allows, fining and impriſoning Jurors for doing their Duty, impoſing Fines arbitrarily without Inqueſt upon the freeborn men of *England*, denying to produce that Law which is pretended to have been tranſgreſs'd) is wounded, and how much the Injuries are doubled and trebled upon their Fellow-members, and the evil Conſequence thereof, which if drawn into precedent, who can count himſelf free either in Perſon or Eſtate? The Conſequence of a wicked Sentence (ſaid Chancellor

cellor *Bacon*) was infinitely worse than a wicked Fact, as being held a precedent and pattern whereby Oppression beginning upon one, is extended as warrantable upon all.

And this conclusion he draweth out of this place of Scripture, *Fons turbatus & urina corrupta est justus cadens coram impio:* A just man falling into the hands of the wicked, is like a Fountain troubled with the foot, or the Urine corrupted in the Body.

To the honour of which arbitrary Sentences, Censures and severe *Judgments* have stricken the Commonalty with Amazement, that the Courts of Justice, ordain'd for publick Preservation and Safety, should be wrested to enslave, oppress, ruin and destroy us. How much that Mayor and Recorder have usurp'd upon the Rights and Liberties of these Prisoners, is too apparent in their waving the Rules of Law, and measuring out Justice by their fantastical Discretions and Arbitrary Wills and Power; the consequence of which cannot but be inevitably mischievous and inconvenient to both those that there were censur'd and judg'd evil, and to the People of *England*. Hence was deriv'd that excellent Maxim; *Melius sub iniquissima lege quam sub æquissimo arbitrio vivere:* That is, *It's better to live under a hard and harsh known written Law, where every man may read his Duty, and know his Offence and Punishment, than under the mildest Arbitrary Government, where the Subject is condemn'd at the Will of every Bench of Justice before which he shall appear, without any certain or known Rules and Measures for the Offence and Punishment.* And how specious soever the pretence for these Proceedings may be, we know that the pretence of Necessity to act contrary to the known written Laws, in the Mayor, Recorder, &c. or any others, is but to usher in Tyranny and Oppression.

There appears no other end that this Bench had in this tortious sort of proceeding, than to fill their Sheriffs Pockets with extorted Gain, or arbitrarily to punish a most innocent and peaceable People, to gratify their Lusts and Malice.

And how many flourishing States have been ruin'd by the Avarices, Cruelty, and Non-observance of the Laws, by the Governours and Magistrates, were tedious to insert. Only take notice what *Coke* in his 2 *Inst.* 388. declares, *That three things overthrew the flourishing State of the* Roman *Empire: Latens odium, juvenile consilium, & privatum lucrum.* And observes there, *That it's the greatest Injustice, when the Innocent, under colour of Justice, whereby he ought to be protected, is oppress'd.*

But good Government consisting principally in the execution of their just and known Laws, procures Love from the Subject. It's only their Love which supports a State in adverſity: And our deſire that ſuch as *London*'s Mayor and Recorder, *&c.* may not by their Actions ſow a jealouſy among the Freeborn People of *England*, that it's the intent of our Supreme Magiſtrates to hold up that common Maxim of all oppreſſing States, *That their Intereſt is to maintain the Publick wealthy, and the Particular poor.*

Therefore permit not theſe Perſons in their Courts to create the Precedents of Oppreſſion to enſlave our Poſterity in future times: to that end hath this been made publick, that the Supreme Magiſtrate and Legiſlators of this Nation, for the Dignity and Honour of their Rule and Government, and for the Safety of the free-born People of this Land, not only take care to purge the Benches of Juſtice from that Partiality and Corruption, which hath uſurp'd thoſe Places of great Truſt, and puniſh the Offenders who have been guilty of ſuch enormous Crimes with condign Puniſhment, anſwerable to their reſpective Offences and horrid Oppreſſion; but alſo command the keeping, obſerving, and executing in all their Courts the known, written, promulg'd, antient, and fundamental Laws of this Land: And that they may, as they have often avow'd, maintain the Liberties of the Freeborn People of *England*, in aſſuring to them, that *Salus Populi eſt ſuprema Lex.* Can it be reaſonably thought, that the Impunity of theſe that have been ſo faithleſs to their Oaths and Truſts repos'd in them, ſhall ever be ſerviceable to this State or Magiſtrates under whom they act? No, they'll rather take courage to betray them, when they find the firſt opportunity. Therefore like our old Proverb, *Tho we love the Treaſon, yet we hate the Traitor:* So it hath been the prudence of the wiſeſt and beſt-govern'd States, *Never to pardon any man for a notorious Crime committed againſt the Commonwealth, for any good Service before done to it.* To which *Clement Edmonds*, upon *Cæſar*'s Commentaries, well agrees, fol. 174. *It more importeth a Commonwealth to puniſh an ill Member, than to reward a good Act.* So that State or Commonwealth that will keep it ſelf in good order, and free from ruin, muſt cheriſh Impeachments and Accuſations of the People againſt thoſe that thro Ambition, Avarice, Pride, Cruelty, or Oppreſſion, ſeek to deſtroy the Liberty and Property of the People; ſo ſhall they keep their State free from Envy, and ſecure from Supplantation. And the Free-born People of this Nation being thus preſerv'd and ſecur'd againſt Tyranny and Oppreſſion, will never ſeek after other Liberty, but rejoice under their own Governours. For as it never turn'd to any State's advantage to gain the People's Hatred, ſo it's the moſt ſtable laſting Government, under which the People rejoice and live cheerfully; according to that Maxim of *Camillus* the *Roman*, *Firmissimum Imperium quo obedientes gaudent.*

An APPENDIX, *by way of Dialogue, in a Plain and Friendly Discourse between a Student in the Laws and Liberties of* England, *and a true Citizen of* London: *Whereby is shew'd, That a Jury of twelve Men are the only proper Judges of their Neighbours Actions, and may by the establish'd Laws of* England *give a Verdict of such Facts, according to their Consciences, without incurring Fine and Imprisonment*, &c.

Student. WHither are you hasting out so fast this morning, my Friend?

Cit. Truly, about some earnest Business, that will not admit of delay.

Stud. I know you to be a Man of business; but in my apprehension you seem more than usually in haste, now I am come to give you a visit.

Cit. I acknowledg your kindness; and since you are so opportunely come, I would request your Advice in what I am going about.

Stud. Yea, most freely: But what's the Case?

Cit. I am summon'd to appear to morrow, as a Juryman, at the *Old Baily*, but would willingly get my self excus'd, and was but now going out to one of the Sheriffs, my old Acquaintance, to intreat his Favour, to do me that kindness; but it's probable you know a nearer way to effect such a matter, and may direct me.

Stud. It's very like, did it much concern you, I might get your discharge: But why should not you rather serve your Country in these publick concerns? If all men were of your mind, how should Right be done in Courts of Justice?

Cit. There's many others that are better skill'd in such matters, who are more fit to perform that Office; as for my part, I have ever so loved Peace that I have forborn going to Law, tho it has been much to my loss.

Stud. That's no Excuſe; for the more peaceable man you have been, the more fit you are for ſuch Services. The Office of a Jury-man is conſcientiouſly to judg his Neighbour, who needs no more Law than is eaſily learned to direct him therein.

Cit. I ſhould willingly appear according to this Summon, but that the Mayor's and Recorder's carriage to Juries was ſuch the laſt Seſſions, that I queſtion whether I could undergo ſo much hardſhip, and not endanger my Life; ſo I find that all my Neighbours, as well as I, are endeavouring to get themſelves excus'd.

Stud. Then it's a Reſtraint from your Trade that deters you?

Cit. No truly, that's not all; but to be kept without Meat and Drink two days and nights together, and not to be allow'd the privilege of Nature's eaſement, and after all, to be caſt into *Newgate*, is hard ſervice.

Stud. I muſt confeſs this was very hard, yet it ſhould not deter you from doing your Duty: and if thoſe Jurors ſuffer'd unjuſtly (which I queſtion not) their Service was the eaſier to them.

Cit. I am of opinion they were unjuſtly dealt withal; many of them I know, who had the Repute of Honeſty, eſpecially thoſe four, who yet lie in Durance: but I may ſuffer by reaſon of my Ignorance of the Duty and Office of a Jury-man; therefore on that account principally I deſire to be excus'd my appearance, which if I underſtood as well as many do, with all my heart I would do my ſervice.

Stud. Now you ſpeak honeſtly like an *Engliſh*-man; and in caſe that be all your cauſe of ſcruple, it may ſoon be remov'd if you will take my Advice.

Cit. Yes, with all my heart: Then pray let me have your Anſwer to ſome Queſtions, which often of late I have had upon my thoughts to propound to you, or ſome Practitioner of the Law, that would be plain with me.

Stud. Offer what you think meet, and I will endeavour to give you that Satisfaction you deſire.

Cit. Since Jurors are thus of late menaced, threatned, fined, and impriſon'd by our Recorder at the *Old Baily*; pray wherein lies their Privilege and Safety? What ſay the Fundamental Laws of *England* to ſuch Practices?

Stud. The Jurors Privileges, and every *Engliſh*-man's by them, as they are very conſiderable, ſo the Laws have very well guarded them againſt Uſurpation, as I ſhall ſhew you.

Cit. But pray firſt let me know their Antiquity. I have heard it ſaid, That Tryals by Juries have been of long ſtanding in this Nation.

Stud.

Stud. Their Antiquity no one knows, but all Authors agree that they have been very antient. *Coke*, the Oracle of our *English* Laws, writes, That long before the Conquest it was order'd, that in every Century there should be twelve good and honest men to judg, *&c.* And *Camden* in his *Britannia* correcteth *Polidore Virgil*, for saying *William* the Conqueror first brought in this way of Tryal; affirming that it was most certain and apparent by the Laws of *Etheldred*, that such Tryals were in use many years before: Which *Horn* in his *Mirror of Justice*, written in the time of *E.* 1. doth well confirm and assure us. Co. 1 *Inst.* 155.

Cit. But what say the Law-Books of later date, and our Predecessors in later years about them?

Stud. When the great Charter of our *English* Liberties, in the 9th year of *H.* 3. was made, and put under the Great Seal of *England*, then were these Tryals by Juries confirm'd down to us; and therein it was stablish'd, That no Amercements should be assess'd upon any man, but by the Oaths of good and lawful Men of the Vicinage: And also that no Freeman of *England* should be imprison'd in his Person, or destroy'd in his Estate and Liberties, without the lawful Judgment of his Equals. Which Charter has been confirm'd by thirty two Parliaments, and now stands firm to justify and maintain the Freedom of this sort of Tryals, which *Coke* calls the Subjects Birthright; and which I must say is the only Preserver of our Lives, Freedom and Property; as you may read in the Book of the Tryal of *W. P.* and *W. M.* last Sessions. 9 *H.* 3. 14.29. Co. 2 *Inst.* 41.

Cit. I am very well satisfy'd in this point; but pray, what says the Law about menacing, threatning, fining and imprisoning of Jurors, as before I mention'd to you?

Stud. As to the menacing and threatning Language which that Bench gave the Jurors, it only evidenced and manifested to the world their Envy and Malice against the Prisoners that the Jury had in charge, and so may be said also of their fining and imprisoning of the Jury afterwards.

Cit. Hath a Court then no power by the Law to fine and imprison a Jury?

Stud. We find in our Law-Books, or Books of Cases, that Jurors have been fined by a Court, for these following matters.

1. If a Jury-man take mony (from the Party to be try'd) before or after he be sworn. 39 *Ass.* 19. *Fitz. Exam.*

2. If they receive any Writings from the Persons they have in tryal. 17. 14 *H.* 7. 30.

36 H. 6. 27. per Cur. C.B. & B.R. 3. If a Jury-man appear, and then depart before he be ſworn, it is a contempt of the Court.

34 E. 3. Fitz. Office de Court 12. *40 Aſſ. pl. 10.* 4. If a Juror, after he ſhall be ſworn, depart from his Fellows before they deliver in their Verdict.

5. If Eleven Jurors ſhall give in their Verdict without, or againſt the Conſent of the Twelfth.

Dyer 37. b. 218. a. b. Old Entries 251. 6. If a Jury eat or drink after they are gone from the Bar, and before they bring in their Verdict (This, I ſuppoſe, is meant where the Court will accept of the Verdict, when the Jurors tender it.) And for ſuch like Miſdemeanors as theſe, they have been Fined and Impriſoned, but how warrantable, is a *Query*.

Cit. As for theſe Miſcarriages you have inſtanc'd, it ſeems reaſonable they ſhould be puniſh'd, which no honeſt Man will be found guilty of; neither do I fear to ſuffer for ſuch like Miſdemeanors. But what ſay you to the Fining a Jury for giving in a Verdict according to their Conſciences, yet pretended by the Court to be contrary to Evidence?

Stud. To Fine them at all is an Abuſe, tho it has been long practiſed; but to Fine them for giving their Verdict according to their Conſcience, ſuch Practices are very much againſt Law and Reaſon too: For a Jury of twelve Men are by the Laws the only proper Judges of matter in iſſue before them: As for inſtance, *Co. 4. Inſt. 84.*

Firſt, That Evidence which is deliver'd to induce a Jury to believe, or not to believe the Matter of Fact in iſſue, is call'd Evidence, becauſe the Jury may out of many Matters of Fact (*videre veritatem*) that is, ſee clearly the Truth, of which they are proper Judges.

Secondly, When any Matter is ſworn, Deed read, or offer'd, whether it ſhall be believ'd, or not; or whether it be true or falſe in point of Fact, the Jurors are the proper Judges.

Thirdly, Whether ſuch Men met together intentionally to do ſuch an Act or not, the Jurors are Judges; for the Court is not Judg of theſe Matters, which are Evidence to prove or diſprove the thing in iſſue.

Cit. What then is the Court to take cognizance of in the Tryals of mens Liberties and Properties?

Stud. The Court, as their Duty is, are to do equal Juſtice and Right: ſo they in ſuch Tryals do direct, whether ſuch Matter ſhall be admitted to be given in Evidence, or not; ſuch a Writing read, or not; or ſuch a Man to be admitted a Witneſs,

ness, or not: And this belongs to the Judgment of the Court, as they are upon their Oaths to see Justice done 'twixt Party and Party. Therefore has the Common Law ordain'd, That Matters of Fact (which are drawn to an Issue) shall be try'd by Jurors, and Matters of Law (upon a Demurrer and special Verdict, *&c.*) by the Justices, according to that Rule or Maxim of Sir *Edw. Cook*; *Ad Questionem facti non respondent Judices, ita ad questionem Legis non respondent Juratores:* The Justices meddle not with Matter of Fact, nor Jurors wih Matter of Law. So it's the Juror's Office to find (*veritatem Facti*) the Truth of the Fact in issue, and the Court's to give Judgment accordingly. By which we may see the Wisdom of the Law, in referring Things to Persons, in which they have cognizance, and are most expert, according to that Maxim, *Quod quisque norit, in hoc se exerceat.*

11 *Co.* 10. *b.* 4 Inst. 84. 4 Inst. 207. 9 *Cook* 13.

Cit. According to this Account you have given me of the Duty and Office, as well of the Court, as the Jurors; the Law seems to have dealt justly and equally betwixt them both. But one Question further, Pray whence is it that Jurors are summon'd of the Neighbourhood, where the Fact is suppos'd to be done or acted?

Stud. As the Common Law of this Land is nothing else than Common Right, pure and try'd Reason; so it never fails to render a Reason of its own Actions: A *Jury* is therefore summon'd of the Vicinage, because it's always presum'd that the Neighbourhood are best acquainted with the Persons inhabiting, or the Actions and Facts done or acted within their own Limits and Jurisdiction; and that they themselves may know something of the matter in controversy, being (*de Vicineto*) of the Vicinage where such matter was in action. Therefore the *Jury* must be return'd, *de Vicineto*, of the place where the Fact was done, and of Men (*per quos rei veritas melius scire poterit*) by whom the Truth of the matter may be better known: So the *Jury* having some Self-knowledg of the Matters afore-hand, besides hearing the Evidence, may the better pronounce (*veritatis dictum*) or a just Verdict of the Fact.

Cit. But wherein do you conceive a Jury-man may have Self-knowledg of Matter, that may not as fully be evidenc'd by Witness?

Stud. It's probable, First, That they may know the Witness on the one side, or the other, to be Persons of no Credit; or,

Secondly, They may know the Party accus'd to be a Man otherwise qualify'd or principl'd, than to do ſuch an act or thing that is charg'd againſt him. As for inſtance; They may know a Man to be,

1. A quiet peaceable *Quaker*; therefore no Fighter or Rioter, or Routous Perſon.

2. A *Proteſtant* of the *Epiſcopal* Church of *England*; therefore no Houſe-Preacher.

3. An honeſt ſober Man amongſt his Neighbours; therefore probably no Thief or Robber. And many other Inſtances might be offer'd to this purpoſe.

Cit. To Fine a Jury then for things, which probably they may know of their own knowledg to be true or falſe, ſeems very hard; and ſurely our Jurors of *London* have met with hard uſage, to be fin'd and impriſon'd for doing their Duty, in what the Laws of this Land have made them ſole and proper Judges.

Stud. Their hard uſage and ſeverity to the Jurors is not ſo much as the ill conſequence that ſuch practices will be to every Engliſh-man, and their Poſterity, if not timely remedied.

Cit. Truly the Citizens of *London*, in general, have much dreaded the late Procedure at the *Old-Baily*, and fear it's a Fore-runner of much Miſchief that may be acted in the Country, who generally take *London* for a Precedent in their Courts of Juſtice. But pray what's your Thoughts about theſe things?

Stud. The Conſequence of ſuch Practices, the Parliament have very well ſet forth in Chief Juſtice *Keeling*'s Caſe, 11 *Dec.* 1667. when they Voted, That Fining *Juries* were not only Innovations, in the Tryals of Men for their Lives and Liberties, but that it was of Dangerous Conſequence to the Lives and Liberties of the People of *England*; and tended to the introducing of an Arbitrary Government: And their Reaſon was very good; for the King ſits not in Judgment upon his Subjects, but by his Juſtices in his Courts: And if the Juſtices, who are commanded to be guided by the Law, ſhall, contrary to the Law, fine and impriſon Juries, for giving Verdicts in ſuch Matters which the Laws allow and appoint them to be proper Judges of, where then is the Engliſh-man try'd by his Peers, and by the Law of the Land? To deny us this free Tryal, is to rifle us of our Birth-right, and moſt arbitrarily and tyrannically to deny us Equal Law, Juſtice and Right.

Stat.3. 13 *E*.3.

Cit.

Cit. Surely when the Parliament meets again, they will call these illegal Proceedings of that Bench to Question before them, as well as they did *Keeling*'s.

Stud. It as much concerns them, in behalf of themselves and Posterity, as any of us, to curb these subordinate Judges, who have broken both their Oaths and the Law, to run into those Arbitrary and Illegal Practices; the consequence of which, if suffer'd, in a short time will be, *Sic volo, sic jubeo, stat pro ratione voluntas.* And it will necessarily follow, That,

First, Every Justice of Peace, Mayor, Bailiffs of Corporations, Stewards of Leets, *&c.* whatever Matters are try'd before them, shall have Verdicts to their minds, or Fine and Imprison the Jurors till they have; so that such must be either pleas'd, humour'd, or gratify'd, else no Justice or Right to be had before them in their Courts.

Secondly, A further ill consequence will be, That altho a person may challenge a Jury-man, or Sheriffs, if they be of Kin to this Adversary, yet he cannot challenge a Justice, Mayor, *&c.* who will have a Verdict for their Kinsman, or Fine and Imprison them till they have. So that by this means our Lives, Liberties and Properties shall be solely try'd, and wholly at the Will, and in the power of every mercenary or corrupted Justice, Mayor, Recorder, Bailiff, *&c.*

Cit. But has it been practicable in former times to fine and imprison Juries, for finding contrary to Evidence, as the Recorder pretends our Jurors have done?

Stud. No surely, we find not one Precedent in all our Books, till *Keeling*'s; and he 'scaping that condign Punishment which the Parliament promis'd him, your Recorder and Mayor has trod in his Steps. And pray see how such Judgments on Jurors leave them remediless of relief, which is sufficient ground to conclude such practices to be against the Law.

First, It can never be try'd, whether they found with or against their Evidence, by reason no Writ of Error lies in the Case.

Secondly, They are in worse condition than the Criminals that are try'd by them; for in all civil Actions, Informations, and Indictments, Appeals and Writs of Error, do lie into superior Courts, to try their regular Proceedings of the Inferior: but here can be none.

Thirdly, In the way of an Attaint, the Truth or Falshood of a Juror's Verdict, in Matters of Fact, may be try'd by another Jury: but in this case the Jurors are concluded, by reason that whether they have found with or against their Evidence, can never be try'd. *Litt. Sect.* 108.

And

And further, Reason (which is Law) tells us,
F. N. B. 21. That as the King's Justices of the Law have given out, that they ought not to have any Action
Par. Max. 62. brought against them, if they shall in any thing
Co. 2 Inst.422. err or mistake the Law: So much the more twelve Jurors, who are Judges of all Matters in issue before them, agreeing together in one, ought not to be fined, where they find a Verdict according to their Consciences; albeit, the Evidence may seem strong and clear to another person, to the contrary of which the Jury have found: For they may (being *de Vicineto* where the Fact was done) know something of their own knowledg of the Matter of Fact before them, which the Judg or Standers-by are probably Strangers unto, and ignorant of it. Therefore the Knowledg of twelve Men, agreeing together, ought to be prefer'd before the single Apprehension of any one Person whatsoever. All which does manifest, not only the Illegal and Arbitrary Proceedings of your Mayor and Recorder, against those twelve Men, but the Ill and Dangerous Consequence of such Practices to all the People of *England*.

Cit. But it's pretended, That one of the Crimes charg'd upon the Jurors (by the Recorder) was for finding their Verdict against Law. How can the Jury justify such an Action? Sure they are not (as it is said) Judges of Law, but Fact.

Stud. Admitting they are so, which will not be granted, yet that a Jury can find against Law, is to me a Paradox: For as we say, Where there is no Law, there is no Transgression; so where there is no Transgression, there is no place for Law, the Law being made for the Transgressor. And, said Learned *Cook (Ex facto jus oritur)* upon stating the
4 *C.* 42. *b.* 53. *b.* Fact or Transgression, Law doth arise; yea,
11 *Coo.* 10. *b. in* the Law doth grow out of the Root of the
Pinddle & Nap- Fact: Therefore it's one of their adjudg'd
per's Case. Cases, That if a Jury find a Matter of Fact, but conclude against the Law, the Conclusion is void, and the Court ought to give Judgment according to Law.

Now the Jury being the sole Judges of Fact, and Matter in Issue before them, not finding the Fact on which the Law should arise, cannot be said to find against the Law, which is no other than a Superstructure of Fact. Then to say they have found against the Law, when no Fact is found, is most impossible.

Cit. You have given me very good satisfaction as to the Unreasonableness and Illegality of that Court's Procedure; and since I see the Law has made so good provision for our

safety,

ſafety, I purpoſe to appear upon the Jury, according to my Summons, but deſire withal a little of your Direction about my Office of a Jury-man.

Stud. I am very confident, that you would not willingly violate an Oath, which you take; but that there are ſuch, who as frequently break them as take them, is too too much apparent, through their careleſs Cuſtom on the one hand, or ſlaviſh Fear on the other; againſt which I would fully caution you, that you may defend your ſelf againſt thoſe Enemies of your Country's Peace, and keep a good Conſcience towards God and Man.

Firſt, The Oath that's adminiſtred to you at the Seſſions, is, That you ſhall well and truly Try, and true Deliverance make, between our Soveraign Lord the King, and the Priſoners at the Bar, according to your Evidence. Then is the Indictment read againſt the Priſoner, either for his Life or Liberties, which probably takes up a large time in debate, and in examining Witneſſes on both ſides, according as the Caſe may be. And when the Jurors are commanded to withdraw, that they may conſult of their Verdict; they ſoon forget that ſolemn Oath they took, or that great Charge of the Life and Liberty of Men, whereof they are made Judges; and without one ſerious Thought, or conſulted Reaſon offer'd, *pro* or *con*, preſently go to holding up of hands, or ſome other way voting, whether to find for Proſecutor or Priſoner; ſo the major Votes of ſuch ſhall diſpoſe of men's Lives, Liberties and Properties, which the Law counts ſo dear to every Man. This practice is too cuſtomary among Jurors, as I'm credibly inform'd, which occaſions their diſpatch of that buſineſs in a quarter of an hour, which held the Court full ſix hours Debate: Witneſs that ſecond Jury, that were ſworn on the Priſoners laſt Seſſions, and try'd *T. R. F. M. &c.* Therefore have a care of ſuch Fellow-Jurors.

Secondly, Such a ſlaviſh Fear attends many Jurors, that let the Court direct to find Guilty, or not Guilty, accordingly they bring in their Verdict; and therefore many of them never regard what the Evidence was, more or leſs, to prove the Indictment, but as the Court ſums it up, they bring in; as if Jurors were appointed for no other purpoſe, but to eccho back to the Court (as one obſerv'd) what the Bench would have moſt Illegally and Arbitrarily acted upon ſuch perſons, againſt whom they themſelves Proſecute and Inform. Now againſt thoſe Companions I caution you to beware.

Cit. I am very well ſatisfy'd that theſe Practices are too frequent amongſt Jurors, of which I have been witneſs. But pray what

what is the Reaſon that the Mayor turns Informer, and forceth his Officers and Servants to proſecute?

Stud. You Citizens ſhould beſt know the reaſon of your Magiſtrate's Actions: But it's moſt probable, that your Mayor turns Informer to get Money into the Sheriff's Pockets, who have purchas'd all the Fines from the King, which the laſt Seſſions amounted to no leſs than 500 *l.*

Cit. It's too apparent they are Confederated; I have heard a muttering, that they together have lick'd their Fingers of 500 *l.* and more of *Cripplegate*-Ward Money. I can give no certain account of the buſineſs; but the Hue-and-Cry is gone out, and it's like, in a little time, the Malefactors may be apprehended: And ſince *London* was incorporated, I believe it never had ſuch a pack of Knights to govern it. But to our buſineſs; Let me have ſome farther direction.

Stud. My Advice to you is, That thoſe things in iſſue, whereof you are proper Judges, you ſtill remember, as I inſtanc'd before, (*Ad queſtionem facti non reſpondent Judices*) If any injuſtice be done by the Court to a Priſoner, by reaſon of their negligence or careleſneſs, that injuſtice will lie at your door: *Qui non malum prohibet cum poteſt, facit:* He that prevents not an Evil when it is in his power, does it. Therefore remember, as you of the Jury are Judges of the Matters of Fact in Iſſue, (that is) Whether a thing ſworn is to be believ'd, or not? Whether any thing offer'd be true, or falſe? Whether Men met together to do ſuch an Act againſt the Law, or not, in Manner and Form as the perſon is indicted? You are conſcientiouſly to look to. Therefore,

Firſt, Obſerve well the Indictment that is read, and the ſeveral Parts thereof, both as to the Matter, Manner and Form.

Secondly, Take due notice and regard to the Evidence offer'd for Proof of the Indictment, and each part of it; as well to Manner and Form, as Matter: which endeavour to write down, or ſo much thereof as you are able; and weighing them ſeriouſly together, you may give a Verdict upon that joyn'd Iſſue, according to Truth, which is call'd by *Cook* (*Veritatis dictum*) The Saying of Truth.

And obſerve, That as you are ſworn to try and deliver according to Evidence; ſo alſo you deliver in your Verdict, That the perſon, you have had in Tryal, is guilty in Manner and Form, as the Party ſtands indicted; which thing you ſhould very well weigh: and tho a perſon be prov'd to be guilty of ſome Fact or Miſdemeanor, yet if it be not alſo prov'd to be done in ſuch Manner and Form as the Party ſtands indicted, he is not Guilty, and ought to be acquitted by you.

Cit.

Cit. But is not there both Law and Fact in an Indictment, as those against *W. P.* and *W. M.* and the rest of the *Quakers* last Sessions? And how shall a Jury deal in such Cases?

Stud. If Matter of Law do or shall arise, and mingle it self with the Fact, the Jury are not compellable to find the Law, but only the Fact, if they will, according to the Statute of *Westm.* cap. 30. the second, which declareth, That, *Justiciarii ad Assisas capiendas assignati non compellant Juratores dicere precise si sit disseisina vel non, &c.* Justices of Assize shall not compel Jurors to say precisely; that is, to determine a Matter in Law. And *Cook* commenting upon this Statute, puts a Question, Whether in all Actions a Jury might give a special Verdict. "In the end "(saith he) it hath been resolv'd, that in all Actions, real, "personal and mixt, and upon all Issues joyn'd, general and "special, the Jury might find the special Matter of Fact per-"tinent, and tending only to the Issue joyn'd, and thereupon "pray the discretion of the Court for the Law: and this the Jurors may do at the Common Law, not only in Cases between Party and Party, but also in Pleas of the Crown at the King's Suit. And if Jurors be not Judges of Law, but Fact, as our Sophisters in Law would have it; then the Jury may give in the Matter of Fact, and leave the Matters of Law to the Court: Which special Verdict (*Cook* says the Court cannot refuse, it being pertinent to the Matter in Issue. So according to their distinction of Law and Fact, the Jury is not bound to give in upon their Oaths, that Men did meet or assemble themselves together unlawlawfully, but only to find that they did meet and assemble themselves together, and let the Court judg of the Lawfulness or Unlawfulness of it; for, *Ex facto* (says *Cook*) *jus oritur*. Therefore upon an Indictment for Murder (*Quod felonice percussit*) that he feloniously struck him, the Jury finding (*percussit tantum*) only that he struck him, the Verdict was adjudg'd good, *&c.*

Cook 2. *Inst.* 425.

Cook 1 *Inst.* 92.

Pla. Cau. 92.

Lib. 9. 12.

Lib. 9. 69.

Cit. What's the Reason then, that the Court will not accept of such special Verdicts, but frequently turn the Jury back, till they bring in general?

Stud. Because then they have your Oaths as well for Law as Fact; and if the Judgments be severe, it shall lie at your door.

Cit. But we are not Judges of Law, as they say: Wherefore then should they have our Oaths for the Law?

Stud. This is an Artifice, whereby they cheat the Jury into frequent Perjury, as I shall at large plainly shew you. As,

First,

First, Obſerve the Form wherein they draw up their Indictments; that is, ſubtilly to place a ſmall Matter of Fact, as they call it, in the midſt of a whole Sea of their Decriminating and Obnoxious Terms, which they call Law, that deſerve ſevere Puniſhments wherever they are found, viz. *To do an Act with Force and Arms, Riotouſly, Routouſly, Tumultuouſly, Seditiouſly, Illegally, Deceitfully, Subtilly, Fallaciouſly, in contempt of the King and his Laws, to the Diſturbance and Affrighting the King's Liege People, to the evil Example of others, againſt the King's Peace, his Crown and Dignity*, and ſuch like.

Secondly, The Fact in iſſue, pretended to be committed, altho it be never ſo Innocent or Lawful, (as ſtanding in the Street, or High-way, in peaceable Manner, or Aſſembling in their own Houſe, there perſuading the People to turn from the Evil of their ways, as *Drunkenneſs, Whoredom, Swearing*, &c.) they environ with many of thoſe foul Criminations, thereby to miſrepreſent the Fact, or Matter in Iſſue, to the Jury; like as the Inquiſitors in *Spain* (ſo much applauded by *J. H.* your Recorder) do cloath thoſe Innocent Chriſtian *Proteſtants* (whom they have cenſur'd to the Faggot) with their * *Sambenitoes*, that the People beholding them in ſo Diſmal and Helliſh a Dreſs, may be ſo far from pitying them, that they may rather condemn them in their very Thoughts as Miſcreants, not worthy to live.

* *Garments on which are painted the ſhapes of Devils, and infernal Spirits*, &c.

Againſt any of which criminal Terms, if the Jurors object, by reaſon the Evidence did not reach them; the Court preſently ſtops their mouths with ſaying, *You have nothing to do with that, it's only matter of Form or matter of Law, you are only to examine the Fact.* Which the ignorant Jurors taking for Anſwer, bring in the Priſoners Guilty (as they ſuppoſe) of the Fact or Treſpaſs only; but the Clerk of the Peace recording it, demands a further Confirmation, ſaying thus, *Well then, you ſay* A. B. *is guilty of the Fact or Treſpaſs, in manner and Form as he ſtands indicted, and ſo you ſay all?* To which the Fore-man anſwers for himſelf and Fellows, *Yes.*

Whereupon the Verdict is drawn up (*Juratores ſuper Sacramentum ſuum dicunt*) that the Jurors do ſay upon their Oaths, *That* A. B. *did, or committed ſuch a Fact, with Force and Arms—did ſuch a ſeditious Action——did meet ſuch Perſons in a riotous, routous manner——did ſuch an Act deceitfully, ſubtilly, illegally, fallaciouſly, in contempt of the King and his Laws, to diſturb or affright the King's Liege People, againſt the King's Peace, his Crown, and Dignity.* So the Jurors are ignorantly and fallaciouſly perjur'd upon Record, and Oppreſſion thereby is acted upon the Innocent.

cent. So by reason of the Court's Subtilty on the one hand, and the Juries Ignorance on the other, they upon their Oaths having clothed the innocent Matter or Fact in issue with the *Sambenitish* Garment, the Court with safety passes most severe Judgments and Censures upon such Prisoners; and all because the Jury have upon their Oaths (as was said before) made that innocent Action, or pretended Fact, criminal, which the Law or Court never could have done, had not they in such manner given a Verdict, so many degrees worse than the Fact in issue was evidenc'd unto them.

Cit. Then I perceive those subtil Fellows make use of our Oaths (as it's fabled the Monky did by the Cat's Foot, to claw the Chessnuts out of the Fire) and so thereby cover their cursed Ends and Designs upon the Innocent, whom they daily prosecute; as for my part, I never heard of so much of their Knavery before, neither did I think that it was possible that so much Villany should have been acted under colour of Justice.

Stud. Sir *John Howel* your Recorder, and your City Magistrates, have a further Artifice; that is, to indict all Men by the Common Law, and wave intermeddling with any of the Statutes in force against such Misdemeanours, as they pretend the Persons indicted are guilty of.

Cit. Pray what do you suppose their drift is in that?

Stud. No other than that they may as well make the Law, as proportion the Punishmment; for when an Indictment is grounded on the Common Law, and the Prisoner desires to have the Law read to the Jury (who are his Judges, whether he be guilty or not guilty *Modo & Forma* of the matter in issue) on which such Indictment is grounded, the Court answers, *It's* Lex non scripta, *a Law not written, therefore not to be produced.* By this means the Prisoner is incapacitated to make his Defence, and the Jury kept ignorant, whether the Offence charg'd to be done by the Prisoner be Innocency or Guilt: And so the Bench at the *Old Baily* acted last Sessions, in the Case of Riots, Routs, and unlawful Assemblies. And altho there be several Statutes in force, which point out the Persons that ought to be apprehended and punish'd, as Rioters and Routers, as the Statute of 17 *R.* 2. 8. 13 *H.* 4. 7. 2 *H.* 5. 8. with others; yet your Recorder and Magistrates pretending to proceed by the Common Law (*non scripta*) apprehended quiet and peaceable Religious Assemblies, as Riots and Routs, and punish'd them as such: the greatest Abuse to the Common Law, as has been done in any Age, by such who pretend to sit upon a Bench of Justice.

And

And after the rate of their Proceedings, by their abuſe of the Law, they might have fram'd an Indictment againſt a man, for *(vi & armis)* eating Meat at his own Table with his Wife and Children, and at laſt uſhering in the Fact committed with theſe obnoxious Terms, as, *Againſt the King and his Laws, illegally, and in contempt of his Crown and Dignity,* &c. And a Jury of their packing would have found them guilty *Modo & Forma.* Therefore it concerns you to have great care and regard to the Charge you undertake; which is, well and truly to try, and true deliverance make, according to what is evidenc'd to your Conſcience.

Cit. But what's the reaſon that Indictments, and all the Proceedings of the Seſſions, be drawn and enter'd in *Latin*; Language which few, either Jurors or Priſoners, underſtand?

Stud. It's ſuch a practice, that no reaſon can be given for it, except to keep the People ignorant, eſpecially the Grand Inqueſts who firſt paſs the Bills of Indictment; who being generally unknowing in ſuch Language, may perjure themſelves blindfold, being only inform'd or made to underſtand ſo much of what they ſwear to, as a mercenary Clerk will read to them, or let them know, which beſure ſhall be no more than what's for the intereſt of the Proſecutors, and the Priſoners diſadvantage. And if theſe twelve Men (who by the Law are uncontrolable Judges) ſhall not bring in, or return *Billa Vera*, to ſuch Indictments as the Bench ſhall favour, your Mayor and Recorder, after Juſtice *Keeling*'s Example, do frequently command them back, till they find thoſe Bills according to their direction; which great abuſe of the Law, as *Horn* calls it, is not only one of the greateſt Violences that is offer'd to our Lives and Liberties, but alſo expreſly againſt the very Oath that thoſe Juſtices take for the Execution of that place of Truſt, which ſaith, *Ye ſhall do even Law and Execution of Right to all, Rich and Poor, without having regard to any Perſon; and that ye give none Advice, nor Counſel to no man, great nor ſmall, in no caſe where the King is Party.*

Mir. Juſtice cap. 5. Sect. 1. 134.

18 *Edw.* 3. 3.

Cit. How comes it to paſs, that theſe Judges (who ſo violate their Oaths, oppreſs the People, ſo illegally cenſure the Innocent, and condemn the Juſt) eſcape condign Puniſhment in all Ages, which is a due Reward for their Oppreſſion and Injuſtice?

Stud. To call them Judges, is a Title beyond their Place or Commiſſion; they are ſtil'd Juſtices, according to their Office, which is to

Coke 2 Inſt. 26.

to see Justice done betwixt Party and Party, not to Fine and Imprison persons at their will and pleasure without a Jury; which practice of theirs is no more legal than evil Custom can make it; and which practice *A. Horn*, in his *Mirror of Justice*, reckons amongst the Abuses of the Law, they having no other Law, Ground or Authority for it, than some former Uses, or rather Abuses, acted by their Predecessors. And by the same Rule, in case the Jurors bring their *Habeas Corpus* for relief, the Recorder or his Council may offer *Keeling*'s Fining of the Jury, altho condemn'd in Parliament, to justify this latter piece of Injustice. After which rate, a Thief or a Robber may legally justify his Actions, because of his long Use, Custom, and frequent Practice: which Abuses the Justices at *Westminster* rarely dare or will punish, by reason (such Crimes advancing Prerogative) it may occasion a Frown or Rebuke from one or other Superior; forgetting, or else neglecting that Obligation that lies upon them, *To deny no man Common Right by the King's Letters, nor none other man's, nor for none other cause: Nor delay Justice or Right to any Man, according to the Charter of Liberties.* And altho many corrupt and faithless Executioners of Justice have escap'd their due Reward in all Ages, yet there are some who have receiv'd their Portion; as *Lambert*, in the Translation of his *Saxon* Laws, reports, *That King* Alfred, *the famous Compiler of our English Laws, executed many such.* Of which *Andrew Horn*, a worthy Author (in his *Mirror of Justice*, written in the time of *Edw.* 1. cap. 5. sect. 1. among the many Violences and Abuses offer'd to the Common Law, i. e. *The Common Right of the People of* England) gives a punctual account, saying, *It was an Abuse that Justices and their Officers (who kill People by false Judgment) were not destroy'd as other Murderers, which King* Alfred *caused to be done, who caused Forty Four Justices, in one Year, to be Hang'd as Murderers, for their false Judgments.* Amongst which, says the Author,

5 *Chap.* 1. *Sect. numb.* 32. *&* 33.

Stat. 18. *E.* 3. 3. 9 *H.* 3. 29.

He Hang'd Cadwine, *because that he Judg'd* Hackwy *to death without the consent of all the Jurors: And whereas he stood upon his Jury of Twelve Men, because part of them would have sav'd him*; Cadwine (like your Recorder) *remov'd those, and put others on the Jury, against* Hackwy's *consent.*

So observe, It's said without the Consent of his Jurors, tho Twelve Men had given a Verdict against him; for those who were put upon him against his Consent, were not his Jurors, by reason all, or any of those who were first sworn to try him, could not (by the Law) be remov'd, and others put in their places. This is a Case (save only in the Punishment of the

Justices) parallel to that of your Mayor and Recorder at the *Old-Baily, London*, 5 *Septemb.* 1670. who when one Jury of Twelve Men were ſworn to try ſeveral perſons call'd *Quakers*, and the Priſoners had accepted of them; they (*Cadwine* like) remov'd the firſt Jury, and forc'd other Jurors upon them againſt their conſent, and by that means condemn'd them (like *Hackwy*) without the conſent of their Jurors.

He Hang'd Seafoul, *becauſe he judg'd* Ording *to Death for not Anſwering.*

So it was Murder in a Juſtice to condemn a Perſon, before a Jury had try'd the Fact; which in this Caſe they could not do, the Priſoner not pleading to the Indictment.

He Hang'd Freburn, *becauſe he judg'd* Harpyn *to die; whenas the Jury were in doubt of their Verdict*, (and the reaſon is given) *becauſe in doubtful Caſes one ought rather to ſave than condemn.*

Here's not only a Maxim for Jurors and Juſtices, *rather* (in doubtful Caſes) *to ſave than condemn*, but a ſeaſonable Caution to Juſtices of Aſſize and Seſſions; who, not only when a Jury are doubtful, but when they are agreed to acquit, will menace and threaten them with Fines and Impriſonment, until they bring in a Verdict againſt a Priſoner, upon whom they purpoſe to paſs a *Freburn's Judgment.*

He Hang'd Hale, *becauſe he ſav'd* Triſtram *the Sheriff from Death, who took to the King's uſe from another, Goods againſt his will, for as much as any ſuch Taking or Robbery hath no difference.*

He Hang'd Arnold, *becauſe he ſav'd* Boyliffe, *who rob'd the People by colour of Diſtreſſes; whereof ſome were by ſelling Diſtreſſes, and ſome by Extortion of Fines: as if in Extortion of Fines, releaſing of tortious Diſtreſſes (as under-ſelling ſuch Diſtreſſes) and Robbery, there were difference.*

How many *Burglaries, Thefts* and *Robberies* are daily committed by the Miſcreants of our Age, under the Names of Informers, and other the King's Officers (like *Triſtram* the Sheriff) by taking away Goods againſt the Will of the Owner, to the King's uſe (as they pretended) and by colour of Diſtreſſes, and ſelling and releaſing Diſtreſſes, and Extortion of illegal impos'd Fines, againſt the Fundamental Laws, upon *England's* quiet, peaceable and religious, yet oppreſſed and abuſed Inhabitants; and the Juſtices of the Peace, not only like *Hale* and *Arnold*, ſave and ſecure them from condign Puniſhment, but abet and encourage them to ſuch ſore and grievous Oppreſſions: yet no relief upon the Oppreſſor's complaint, nor redreſs for theſe publick Grievances.

He Hang'd Oskitell, *becauſe he judg'd* Cathing *to Death by Record of a Coroner, without tryal of the Truth of the Fact by the Jury.* So zealous was this King for the Execution of Juſtice, and tender

der of the Lives of his Subjects, *That* (as says the same Author) *he hang'd all the Judges, who had falsly sav'd a Man guilty of Death, or had falsly hang'd any Man against Law, or any reasonable Exception.*

And in lesser Offences, where they wrongfully griev'd any Man, or passed the Bounds of their Commission, or the Law, he disinherited and remov'd them, to the satisfaction of the People, establishing of sure upright Laws, maintenance of the honour of his Courts of Justice, and his perpetual Renown and Fame to future Ages and Generations.

Besides, *Hubert de Burgo*, in the 17th Year of *E.* 3. ——*Spencers*, Father and Son; *Tresilian* and *Belknap*; Sir *William Thorpe* in 23 *E.* 3. *Empson* and *Dudley*, persons most famous for Tyranny and Oppression, left upon Record, that our Justices of later date, beholding their Ends, should avoid their Foot-steps. So altho some of your Fellow-Citizens, by reason of this Injustice and Oppression of your City-Recorder, Mayor, *&c.* have undergone the hardship of Imprisonment, yet they standing in the Gap against the introducing of an Arbitrary Government, they may live to see a due Reward rendred to their Oppressions, and enjoy the fruit of their Faithfulness to the Trust reposed in them; that is, Liberty and Freedom from Tyranny and Oppression: then, as says the Wise-man, *Prov.* 21. 18. *The Wicked shall be a Ransom for the Righteous, and the Transgressor for the Upright.*

Co. 3 *Inst.* 145.

Votes Parl. 11. *Decemb.* 1667.

Cit. Well, I acknowledg you have given me ample Satisfaction as to what is the Juror's Duty; and since I see that the *English*-man's Life, Freedom and Property, principally depends on the Faithfulness and Honesty of his Jurors, I shall endeavour to perform my Duty in that Office: and what my Assistance may avail to defend us against that Torrent of Violence, Usurpation and Oppression (which is overflowing all our Liberties) shall be freely tendred and given up for the good of this City and my Native Country.

Stud. Now (my Friend) you speak like an *English*-man, and as one that would faithfully serve your Country; and if you will take my advice, at leasure hours read your *Charter of Liberties*, and the *Fundamental Laws, by which* (as *Cook* says) *you have a better Inheritance than by your natural Parents.* Some of the most impartial Writers have been the said Sir *Edw. Cook* in his 2d, 3d and 4th Institutes; *Horn*'s *Mirror of Justice*; *Lambert*'s *Translation of the* Saxon *Laws*; as also, *The Tryal of* W. P. *and* W. M. lately printed: they are Books without difficulty to be had, and very worthy your perusal; wherein you may not only see the *English*-man's Rights and Liberties asserted, but

Tyranny and Oppression in all Ages (endeavouring to extirpate and violate our Laws, the equal Distributer of every man's Property) detected and laid open. These I would not have one true *English*-man want in his House ; the consulting with which at vacant hours, will so accommodate and furnish him with the Knowledg and Understanding of his own inherent Rights and Liberties, that he may be able to defend, not only himself from Violence and Oppression, but also his Neighbours from Tort and Wrong.

Prov. 29. 7. *Cognoscit justus causam tenuium, improbus non animadvertit ut cognoscat.*

A Postscript.

THIS Impartial Account of these persons Tryals, with the Appendix of the Jury-man's Duty and Rights, had been earlier presented to thy view, but that the difficulty of a Printing-Press is such (by reason of their frequent Searching and Examination) that it's no easy matter to bring forth Truth to Light without Hazard. As the Author hath, on the one hand, avoided the Censure of a flattering Hypocrite (that with his Mouth destroyeth his Neighbour) so, on the other hand, the *Lash* of the Wise Man, *Prov.*24. 24. *He that saith unto the Wicked, Thou art Righteous, him shall the People curse, Nations shall abhor him.*

What Violences and Oppressions may, at the rate of that Court's proceedings (against these Prisoners) be committed, not only upon the Citizens of *London*, but upon every Freeman of *England*, are apparent to the Judicious.

Have not such Arbitrary and Illegal Proceedings upon Jurors (the Staff of the *English*-man's Liberty) been condemn'd by the Commons of *England* in Parliament ; and declar'd, *That they were of evil Consequence to the Lives and Liberties of the People*, (which thing these Prisoners have sadly experienc'd) *and that they tended to the Introducing of an Arbitrary Government ?* Which no sober Man questions, yet no sufficient Caution to that Court.

O Wicked Times! O Miserable Age! What! Injustice avow'd, Oppression become familiar, yea Legal; Oaths of Jurors in publick Courts, solemnly made and taken in the Presence of God and Man, by a Bench of Justice absolv'd, or denying them to perform what they had enforc'd them to Swear? Must we by our Laws, under grievous Penalties, abjure the See

of

of *Rome*, and our Magiſtrates tread its ſteps in aſſuming the like Prerogative? And not only ſo, but commending their Idolatrous, Cruel, Tyrannical and Inquiſitory Practices, upon ſober and religious People; as *John Howel* the Recorder, frequently did that Seſſions.

What's the end theſe perſons aim at in their Judicature? It's too apparent, not (*ſalus Populi*) the Commonalties Good: What Religious Perſuaſion do they defend or ſtand for? In puniſhing Diſſenters from the National Church, we know they commend the *Papiſts*, and ſpare the *Atheiſts*. Never were there any ſo wicked or curſed Betrayers of Right, Liberty, Juſtice or Religion in any Age, but they would pretend to be Patronizers of them: Yea, it's recorded, That the Thieves and Vagabond *Jews* getting power into their hands (a Preſage and Fore-runner of the ſore and lamentable Calamities that befel that People) choſe themſelves a High-Prieſt, and uſurp'd Power in *Jeruſalem*, to give Laws and oppreſs at pleaſure: of whom *Joſephus* thus writes, pag. 637. *D.* "But they us'd the "Temple as a Caſtle and Defence for themſelves againſt the "People, and made the Sanctuary a place for them to exer- "ciſe Tyranny in.

Conſider well, and weigh the Actions of *S. Starling*, *London*'s Mayor; *John Edwards* and *John Smith* its Sheriffs, the Head and Chieftains of the People's Oppreſſors, in enforcing their Officers, Serjeants and Servants, to be Informers and Proſecutors againſt the Innocent, by their Proclamations making peaceable people Rioters; and thereby not only to forfeit their Rights and Liberties, but theſe their Adverſaries aſſuming Authority to demand what part of their Eſtate they ſhall think meet. And judg if theſe practices run not parallel to thoſe of *Albinus*, Preſident of *Judea*: which *Joſephus* thus impartially relates; "Who was over all as a Tyrant, and a Prince of Thieves; and "he us'd the help of his Guard to rob the meaner ſort—Nay, "he was not aſham'd to proclaim it throughout the whole "Country, Lawful for any one that would, to Rob and Steal, "ſo that they would bring him a part of their Booty. Fol. 623. *E. & F.*

And altho he had (like theſe late Oppreſſors) Power for his Law, and Authority to enforce what he willed upon the People; yet the Divine Hiſtorian terms *Albinus* but a Tyrant, and his Actions Theft and Robbery.

Thus are poor *England*'s quiet, peaceable and religious Inhabitants torn in pieces by thoſe Sons of *Belial*; their Lives, Liberties and Eſtates made preys, to gratify their Luſts, Avarice, and Wills and Pleaſures. And where do theſe Violences and Oppreſſions ariſe, but from the undervaluing and vilifying of our Good,

 Antient,

Votes Parl. 11 Dec. 1667. Antient, Wholesom and Fundamental Laws, our great Charter of Liberties, the Preserver of our Lives, Freedom and Property?

However too many of the Minds and Spirits of our Countrymen are besotted, through that Deluge of Vice and Debauchery, that has over-spread and cover'd the Face of our Land; sure we are, that the right Noble and Virtuous will ever have a high Esteem of those Laws, that were not only dear to our Ancestors, but famous throughout the World, for an equal Balance of Justice, whereby every man's Right and Liberty might be weigh'd.

It's observable what that *Roman* Senator, *C. S. Saturninus* (a Lover of Vertue, Liberty, and wholesom Laws) declaims in the Senate: (saith he) "For to them that know what Vertue is, it "is no small Felicity to live one Hour in Freedom of Mind, and "in a free Country, govern'd by such Laws, which in times past "have made our Commonwealth to flourish——For in regard "of the present time, there is not any thing that we ought "more earnestly to effect, than to live vertuously; for only Vertue is the thing that confirmeth Men in their Liberty.——I "know how great Mischiefs Tyranny do ordinarily breed in "a publick State; for they utterly extinguish all Vertue, and "deprive Free-men of that perfect Magnanimity that may be "in them, and teach both to Flatter and to Fear; for that "the Commonwealth is abandon'd, not to the Wisdom of the "Laws, but to the Fury of the intemperate Governors.

And complaining of *Julius Cæsar*'s Violation of that course of Law whereby the State was polliced: (says he) "In subverting the Laws to his good liking, and himself to his particular desires, there is not any kind of Misery and Mischief "that hath not overthrown our City.

Whence we may observe and conclude, that all these horrid Oppressions and Violences, that have been in Ages past inflicted upon, and offer'd to any People, State or Commonwealth, they have naturally flown from the want of Vertue, or from the debauch'd Practice of the Magistrates, governing and judging the People by Will and Power, and not by establish'd Laws: which is the Case of these Prisoners, who yet lie in Durance at the Will of their cruel Adversaries; because, as one saith,

Sepultum est jus in Regno, prava Voluntas,
Vis & Violentia magis regnat quam Judicium.

[The following Report of Mr. *Bushell*'s Case, by that Great Man the Lord Chief Justice *VAUGHAN*, having a near Relation to the first (especially) of the foregoing Tryals, the Reader is here presented with it, on the Desire of some Gentlemen, who wish well to this Collection.]

Bushell's

Bushell's CASE.

THE King's Writ of *Habeas Corpus*, Dat. 9 *die Novembris* 22 *Car*. 2. Issued out of this Court, directed to the then Sheriffs of *London*, to have the Body of *Edward Bushell*, by them detain'd in Prison, together with the Day and Cause of his Caption and Detention, on *Friday* then next following, before this Court, to do and receive as the Court shall consider; as also to have then the said Writ in Court.

Of which Writ, *Patient Ward* and *Dannet Foorth*, then Sheriffs of *London*, made the Return following, annex'd to the said Writ.

That at the King's Court, of a Session of *Oyer* and *Terminer*, held for the City of *London* at *Justice-Hall* in the *Old-Baily*, *London*, in the Parish of St. *Sepulchres*, in *Farringdon*-Ward without, *London*, on *Wednesday* 31 *die August* 22 *Car*. 2. before Sir *Samuel Starling*, then Mayor of *London*, and divers other his Majesty's Justices, by virtue of his Majesty's Letters Patents under the Great Seal of *England*, to them, any Four or more of them, directed to enquire, hear and determine according to the Tenor of the said Letters Patents, the Offences therein specified: and, amongst others, the Offences of unlawful Congregating, and Assemblies within the Limits appointed by the said Commission within the said City, as well within Liberties as without. *Edward Bushell*, the Prisoner at the Bar, was committed to the Goal of *Newgate*, to be there safely kept under the Custody of *John Smith* Knight, and *James Edwards*, then Sheriffs of the said City, by virtue of a certain Order then and there made by the said Court of Sessions, as followeth.

Ordinatum est per Curiam hic quod Finis 40 *Marcarum separatim ponatur super* Edwardum Bushell, and other Eleven persons particularly nam'd, and upon every of them, being the Twelve Jurors then and there sworn, and charg'd to Try several Issues then and there joyn'd between our Lord the King and *William Penn* and *William Mead*, for certain Trespasses, Contempts, unlawful Assemblies and Tumults, made and perpetrated by the said *Penn* and *Mead*, together with divers other unknown persons, to the Number of Three hundred, Unlawfully and Tumultuously assembled in *Grace-Church-street* in *London*, to the Disturbance of the Peace whereof, the said *Penn* and

and *Mead* were then indicted before the ſaid Juſtices. Upon which Indictment the ſaid *Penn* and *Mead* pleaded they were not Guilty, for that they the ſaid Jurors, then and there the ſaid *William Penn* and *William Mead* of the ſaid Treſpaſſes, Contempts, unlawful Aſſemblies and Tumults, *contra Legem hujus Regni Angliæ, & contra plenam & manifeſtam Evidentiam, & contra directionem Curiæ in materia Legis hic de & ſuper præmiſſis eiſdem Juratoribus verſus præfatos* Will. Penn *&* Will. Mead *in Curia hic aperte datam & declaratam, de præmiſſis iis impoſitis in Indictamento prædicto acquietaverunt in Contemptum Domini Regis nunc legumque ſuarum & ad magnum Impedimentum & obſtructionem Juſtitiæ, necnon ad malum exemplum omnium aliorum Juratorum in conſimili caſu delinquentium. Ac ſuper inde modo ulterius ordinatum eſt per Curiam hic quod præfatus* Edw. Buſhell *capiatur & committatur Gaolæ dicti Domini Regis de* Newgate, *ibidem remanſurus quouſque ſolvat dicto Domino Regi 40 Marcas, pro fine ſuo prædicto, vel deliberatus fuerit per debitum Legis curſum. Ac eodem* Edwardo Buſhell, *ad tunc & ibidem capto & commiſſo exiſtente ad dictam Gaolam de* Newgate, *ſub Cuſtodia præfat.* Johannis Smith *&* Jacobi Edwards *ad tunc Vic. Civitatis* Lond. *prædict. & in eorum Cuſtodia in Gaola prædict. exiſtente & remanente virtute Ordinis prædict. iidem* Johannis Smith *&* Jacobus Edwards, *poſtea in eorum exitu ab Officio Vic. Civitatis* Lond. *prædict. ſcilicet 28 die Septembris Anno 22. ſupra dicto eundem* Edwardum Buſhell, *in dicta Gaola dicti Domini Regis adtunc exiſtentem, deliberaverunt nobis præfatis nunc Vicecomitibus Civitatis prædict. in eadem Gaola ſalvo cuſtodiendum ſecundum tenorem & effectum Ordinis prædictæ. Et quia prædictus* Edwardus *nondum ſolvit dicto Domino Regi prædictum finem 40 Marcarum, nos iidem Vicecomites Corpus ejuſdem* Edwardi *in Gaola prædicta hucuſque detinuimus ; & hæc eſt Cauſa Captionis & Detentionis præfati* Edwardi, *cujus quidem Corpus coram præfatis Juſtitiariis paratum habemus.*

The Writ of *Habeas Corpus* is now the moſt uſual Remedy by which a Man is reſtor'd again to his Liberty, if he have been againſt Law depriv'd of it.

Therefore the Writ commands the Day, and the Cauſe of the Caption and Detaining of the Priſoner, to be certify'd upon the Return ; which if not done, the Court cannot poſſibly judg whether the Cauſe of the Commitment and Detainer be according to Law, or againſt it.

Therefore the Cauſe of Impriſonment ought by the Return to appear as *ſpecifically* and *certainly* to the Judges of the Return, as it did appear to the *Court*, or perſon authoriz'd to commit ; elſe the Return is inſufficient, and the Conſequence muſt be,

That either the Priſoner, becauſe the Cauſe return'd of his Impriſonment is *too General*, muſt be diſcharg'd : whenas if the

Cauſe

Cause had been more particularly return'd, he ought to have been remanded; or else he must be remanded, when if the Cause had been particularly return'd, he ought to have been discharg'd: Both which are Inconveniences not agreeing with the Dignity of the Law. (There is a specious Exception to this Rule, but doth not materially vary it, as shall appear.)

In the present Case it is return'd, That the Prisoner being a Juryman among others, charg'd at the Sessions-Court of the *Old Baily*, to try the Issue between the King and *Penn* and *Mead*, upon an Indictment for assembling unlawfully and tumultuously, did *contra plenam & manifestam evidentiam* openly given in Court, acquit the Prisoners indicted, in contempt of the King, *&c.*

The Court hath no knowledg by this Return, whether the Evidence given were full and manifest, or doubtful, lame, and dark, or indeed Evidence at all material to the Issue; because it it not return'd, what Evidence in particular, and as it was deliver'd, was given. For it is not possible to judg of that rightly, which is not expos'd to a man's Judgment. But here the Evidence given to the Jury is not expos'd at all to this Court, but the Judgment of the Court of Sessions upon that Evidence is only expos'd to us; who tell us it was full and manifest. But our Judgment ought to be grounded upon our own Inferences and Understandings, and not upon theirs.

It was said by a Learned Judg, *If the Jury might be fined for finding against manifest Evidence, the Return was good, tho it did not express what the Evidence particularly was, whereby the Court might judg of it, because returning all the Evidence would be too long.* A strange Reason! For if the Law allows me Remedy for wrong Imprisonment, and that must be by judging whether the Cause of it were good or not, to say the Cause is too long to be made known, is to say the Law gives a Remedy which it will not let me have, or I must be wrongfully imprison'd still, because it is too long to know that I ought to be freed. What is necessary to an end, the Law allows is never too long. *Non sunt longa quibus nihil est quod demere possis*, is as true as any Axiom in *Euclid.* Besides, one manifest Evidence return'd had suffic'd, without returning all the Evidence. *But the other Judges were not of his mind.*

If the Return had been, That the Jurors were committed by an Order of the Court of Sessions, because they did *minus juste* acquit the Persons indicted:

Or because they did *contra Legem* acquit the Persons indicted;

Or

Or becauſe they did *contra Sacramentum ſuum* acquit them.

The Judges cannot, upon the preſent, more judg of the legal Cauſe of their Commitment, than they could if any of theſe Cauſes, as general as they are, had been return'd for the Cauſe of their Commitment. And the ſame Argument may be exactly made to juſtify any of theſe Returns, had they been made, as to juſtify the preſent Return; they being equally as legal, equally as certain, and equally as far from poſſeſſing the Court with the Truth of the Cauſe: And in what condition ſhould all Men be, for the juſt Liberty of their Perſons, if ſuch Cauſes ſhould be admitted ſufficient Cauſes to remand Perſons to Priſon?

To thoſe Objections made by the Priſoner's Council againſt the Return, as too general;

1. It hath been ſaid, That *Inſtitutum eſt quod non inquiratur de diſcretione Judicis.*

2. That the Court of Seſſions in *London* is not to be look'd on as an *Inferior Court*, having all the *Judges Commiſſioners*. That the Court having heard the Evidence, it muſt be credited: that the Evidence given to the Jury of the Fact, was clear and not to be doubted.

As for any ſuch Inſtitution pretended, I know no ſuch, nor believe any ſuch, as it was apply'd to the preſent Cauſe: But taking it in another, and in the true ſenſe, I admit it for truth; that is, when the King had conſtituted any man a Judg under him, his Ability, Parts, and Fitneſs for his Place, are not to be reflected on, cenſur'd, defam'd, or vilify'd by any other Perſon, being allow'd and ſtampt with the King's Approbation, to whom only it belongs to judg of the Fitneſs of his Miniſters.

And ſuch ſcandalous Aſſertions or Inquiries upon the Judges of both Benches is forbidden by the Statute of *Scandalum Magnatum*, 2 R. 2. *c.* 5. Nor muſt we upon ſuppoſition only either admit Judges deficient in their Office, for ſo they ſhould never do any thing right; nor on the other ſide, muſt we admit them unerring in their Places, for ſo they ſhould never do any thing wrong.

And in that ſenſe the Saying concerns not the preſent Caſe.

But if any Man thinks that a Perſon concern'd in Intereſt by the Judgment, Action, or Authority exercis'd upon his Perſon or Fortunes by a Judg, muſt ſubmit in all or any of theſe to the imply'd Diſcretion or Unerringneſs of his Judg, without ſeeking ſuch Redreſs as the Law allows him; it is a Perſuaſion againſt *Common Reaſon*, the *received Law*, and *Uſage both of this Kingdom, and almoſt all others.*

If

If a Court Inferior or Superior hath given a false or erroneous Judgment, is any thing more frequent than to reverse such Judgments by Writs of false Judgment, of Error, or Appeals, according to the Course of the Kingdom?

If they have given corrupt and dishonest Judgments, they have in all Ages been complain'd of to the King in the Star-Chamber, or to the Parliament.

Andrew Horn in his *Mirror of Justices*, mentions many Judges punish'd by King *Alfred* before the Conquest for corrupt Judgments, and their particular Names and Offences; which cou'd not be had, but from the Records of those times. Horn's *Mirror*, fol. 296.

Our Stories mention many punish'd in the time of *Edward* the First. Our Parliament Rolls of *Edward* the Third's time, of *Richard* the Second's time, for the pernicious Resolutions given at *Nottingham* Castle, afford Examples of this kind. In latter times the Parliament Journals of 18 and 21 *Jac.* the Judgment of the Shipmony in the time of *Charles* the First, question'd, and the particular Judges impeach'd. These Instances are obvious, and therefore I but mention them.

In Cases of Returns, too general upon Writs of *Habeas Corpus*, of many I could urge, I will instance in two only.

One *Astwick* brought by *Habeas Corpus* to the King's Bench, was return'd to be committed *per mandatum Nicolai Bacon militis Domini Custodis magni Sigilli Angliæ virtute cujusdam Contemptus in Curia Cancellar. facti*; and was presently bail'd. 9 Eliz. *Moore* fol. 839.

One *Apsley* Prisoner in the *Fleet*, upon a *Habeas Corpus*, was return'd to be committed *per considerationem Curiæ Cancellar. pro contemptu eidem Curiæ illato*; and upon this Return set at liberty. 13 Jac. *Moore* fol. 839.

In both these Cases no Inquiry was made, nor Consideration had, whether the Contempts were to the Law-Court or equitable Court of Chancery; either was alike to the Judges, lest any man should think a difference might arise thence.

The Reason of discharging the Prisoners on those Returns, was the generality of them being for *Contempts* of the Court, but no particular of the Contempt express'd, whereby the King's Bench could judg whether it was a Cause for Commitment or not.

And was it not as supposable, and as much to be credited, That the Lord Keeper and Court of Chancery did well understand what was a Contempt deserving Commitment, as it is now to be credited, that the Court of Sessions did understand perfectly what was full and manifest Evidence against the

Persons

Persons indicted at the Sessions? and therefore it needed not to be reveal'd to us upon the Return.

Hence it is apparent, that the Commitment, and the Return pursuing it, being in it self too general and uncertain, we ought not implicitly to think the Commitment was, *re vera*, for cause particular and sufficient enough, because it was the Act of the Court of Sessions.

And as to the other part, That the Court of Sessions in *London* is not to be resembled to other Inferior Courts of *Oyer and Terminer*, because all the Judges are commission'd here (which is true) but few are there at the same time, and as I have heard when this Tryal was, none of them were present. However Persons of great Quality are in the Commissions of *Oyer* and *Terminer*, thro the Shires of the Kingdom, and always some of the Judges; nor doth one Commission of *Oyer* and *Terminer* differ in its Essence, Nature, and Power from another, if they be general Commissions; but all differ in the Accidents of the Commissioners, which makes no Alteration in their Actings in the eye of Law.

Another fault in the Return is, that the Jurors are not said to have acquitted the Persons indicted against full and manifest Evidence, *corruptly, and knowing the said Evidence to be full and manifest against the Persons indicted.* For how manifest soever the Evidence was, if it were not manifest to them, and that they believ'd it such, it was not a *finable Fault*, nor deserving Imprisonment; upon which difference the Law of punishing Jurors for false Verdicts principally depends.

A Passage in *Bracton* is remarkable to this purpose, concerning Attainting Inquests.

Bracton, l. 4. c. 4. f. 288. *b.* *Committit Jurator perjurium propter falsum Sacramentum ut si ex certa Scientia aliter juraverit quam res in veritate se habuerit, si autem Sacramentum fatuum fuerit, licet falsum, tamen non committit perjurium, licet re vera res aliter se habeat quam juraverat, & quia jurat secundum Conscientiam, eo quod non vadit contra mentem. Sunt quidam qui verum dicunt mentiendo, sed se perjerant—quia contra mentem vadunt.*

Fleta, l. 5. c. 22. f. 336. n. 9. The same Words, and upon the same occasion are in effect in *Fleta: Committit enim Jurator perjurium quandoque propter falsum Sacramentum, ut si ex certa Scientia aliter juraverit quam res in veritate se habuerit secus enim propter factum quamvis falsum.* And lest any should think that these Passages are to be understood only of *Jurymens* Perjuries in *foro Conscientiæ*, it is clearly otherwise by both those Books, which shew how by the discreet Examination of the Judg, the Error of the Jury not wilful, may be prevented and corrected, and their Verdict rectify'd.

And

And in another place of *Bracton*, in the same Chapter: *Judex enim sive Justiciarius ad quem pertinet Examinatio si minus diligenter examinaverit, occasionem prebet perjurii Juratoribus.* And after,

Et si examinati cum justo deducantur errore dictum suum emendaverint, hoc bene facere possunt, ante judicium & impune, sed post judicium non sine pœna.

Bracton, l. 4. f. 289. *a.*

After these Authorities, I would know whether any thing be more common than for two Men, Students, Baristers, or Judges, to deduce contrary and opposite Conclusions out of the same Case in Law? And is there any difference, that two Men should infer distinct Conclusions from the same Testimony? Is any thing more known than that the same Author and Place in that Author, is forcibly urg'd to maintain contrary Conclusions, and the Decision hard which is in the right? Is any thing more frequent in the Controversies of Religion, than to press the same Text for opposite Tenents? How then comes it to pass, that two Persons may not apprehend with Reason and Honesty what a Witness, or many say, to prove in the Understanding of one plainly one thing, but in the Apprehension of the other, clearly the contrary thing? Must therefore one of these merit Fine and Imprisonment, because he doth that which he cannot otherwise do, preserving his Oath and Integrity? And this is often the Case of the Judg and Jury.

I conclude therefore, That this Return, charging the Prisoners to have acquitted *Penn* and *Mead* against full and manifest Evidence first, and next without saying that they did know and believe that Evidence to be full and manifest against the indicted Persons, is no cause of Fine or Imprisonment.

Of this mind were ten Judges of eleven. The Ch. Baron Turnor *gave no Opinion, because not at the Arguments.*

And by the way I must here note, That the Verdict of a Jury and Evidence of a Witness, are very different things in the Truth and Falshood of them. A *Witness* swears but to what he hath heard or seen, generally or more largely to what hath fallen under his Senses: But a *Juryman* swears to what he can infer and conclude from the Testimony of such Witnesses, by the Act and Force of his Understanding, to be the Fact inquir'd after; which differs nothing in the Reason, tho much in the Punishment, from what a Judg, out of various Cases consider'd by him, infers to be the Law in the Question before him. Therefore *Bracton*:

Et licet Narratio facti contraria sit Sacramento & Dicto praecedenti, tamen falsum non faciant Sacramentum licet faciunt fatuum Judicium, *quia*

quia loquuntur secundum Conscientiam, quia falli possunt in Judiciis suis, sicut ipse Justiciarius. Bract. f. 289. a.

There is one Objection which hath been made by none, as I remember, to justify this general Return, I would give answer to.

A Man committed for *Treason* or *Felony*, and bringing an *Habeas Corpus*, hath return'd upon it, that he was committed for High Treason or Felony: and this is a sufficient Return to remand him, tho in truth this is a general Return. For if the specifical Fact, for which the Party was committed, were express'd in the Warrant, it might then perhaps appear to be no Treason or Felony, but a Trespass, as in the Case of the Earl of *Northumberland*, 5 H. 4. question'd for Treason in raising Power. The Lords adjudg'd it a Trespass; for the Powers rais'd were not against the King, but some Subjects.

Why then by like Reason may not this Return be sufficient, tho the Fact for which the Prisoners stood committed, particularly express'd, might be no Cause of Commitment?

The Cases are not alike; for upon a general Commitment for Treason or Felony, the Prisoner (the Cause appearing) may press for his Tryal, which ought not to be deny'd or delay'd. And upon his Indictment and Tryal, the particular Cause of his Imprisonment must appear; which proving no Treason or Felony, the Prisoner shall have the benefit of it. But in this Case, tho the Evidence given were not full nor manifest Evidence against the Persons indicted, but such as the Jury upon it ought to have acquitted those indicted; the Prisoner shall never have any benefit of it, but must continue in Prison, when remanded, until he hath paid that Fine unjustly impos'd on him, which was the whole end of his Imprisonment.

We come now to the next part of the Return, viz. *That the Jury acquitted those indicted against the Direction of the Court, in matter of Law openly given, and declar'd to them in Court.*

The words, *That the Jury did acquit against the Direction of the Court in matter of Law*, literally taken, and *de plano*, are insignificant, and not intelligible; for no Issue can be join'd of Matter in Law, no Jury can be charg'd with the Tryal of Matter in Law barely, no Evidence ever was or can be given to a Jury, of what is Law or not; nor no such Oath can be given to, or taken by a Jury, to try Matter in Law, nor no Attaint can lie for such a false Oath.

Therefore we must take off this Vail and Colour of words, which make a shew of being something, and in truth are nothing.

If

If the meaning of these words, *finding against the Direction of the Court in Matter of Law*, be, That if the Judg having heard the Evidence given in Court (for he knows no other) shall tell the Jury, upon this Evidence, the Law is for the Plaintiff or for the Defendant, and you are under the pain of Fine and Imprisonment to find accordingly, then the Jury ought of duty so to do. Every man sees that the Jury is but a troublesome Delay, great Charge, and of no use in determining Right and Wrong, and therefore the Tryals by them may be better abolish'd than continu'd: Which were a strange new-found Conclusion, after a Tryal so celebrated for many hundreds of years.

For if the Judg from the Evidence shall by his own Judgment first resolve upon any Tryal what the Fact is; and so knowing the Fact, shall then resolve what the Law is, and order the Jury penally to find accordingly: what either necessary or convenient use can be fancy'd of *Juries*, or to continue Tryals by them at all?

But if the Jury be not oblig'd in all Tryals to follow such Directions if given, but only in some sort of Tryals (as for instance, in Tryals for criminal Matters upon Indictments or Appeals) why then the Consequence will be, tho not in all, yet in Criminal Tryals, the Jury (as of no material use) ought to be either omitted or abolish'd: which were a greater mischief to the People, than to abolish them in Civil Tryals.

And how the Jury should in any other manner, according to the Course of Tryals us'd, find against the Direction of the Court in Matter of Law, is really not conceivable.

True it is, if it fall out upon some special Tryal that the Jury being ready to give their Verdict, and before it is given, the Judg shall ask whether they find such a particular thing propounded by him? or whether they find the Matter of Fact to be as such a Witness or Witnesses have depos'd? And the Jury answer, they find the Matter of Fact to be so; if then the Judg shall declare, the Matter of Fact being by you so found to be the Law, is for the Plaintiff, and you are to find accordingly for him:

If notwithstanding they find for the Defendant, this may be thought *a finding in Matter of Law against the Direction of the Court*; for in that case the Jury first declare the Fact, as it is found by themselves; to which Fact the Judg declares how the Law is consequent.

And this is ordinary, when the Jury find unexpectedly for the Plaintiff or Defendant, the Judg will ask, *How do you find such a Fact in particular?* And upon their Answer he will say, then it is for the Defendant, tho they found for the Plaintiff,

Plaintiff, or *e contrario*, and thereupon they rectify their Verdict.

And in these Cases the Jury, and not the Judg, resolve and find what the Fact is.

Therefore always in discreet and lawful Assistance of the Jury, the Judg's Direction is Hypothetical and upon supposition, and not positive, and upon coercion; viz. *If you find the Fact thus* (leaving it to them what to find) *then you are to find for the Plaintiff; but if you find the Fact thus, then it is for the Defendant.*

But in the Case propounded by me, where it is possible in that special manner, the Jury may find against the Direction of the Court in matter of Law, it will not follow they are therefore finable; *for if an Attaint will lie upon the Verdict so given by them, they ought not to be fined and imprison'd by the Judg for that Verdict:* For all the Judges have agreed upon a full Conference at *Serjeants Inn* in this Case. And it was formerly so agreed by the then Judges, in a Case where Justice *Hide* had fined a Jury at *Oxford*, for finding against their Evidence in a Civil Cause: *That a Jury is not finable for going against their Evidence, where an Attaint lies.* For if an Attaint be brought upon that Verdict, it may be affirm'd and found upon the Attaint a true Verdict, and the same Verdict cannot be a false Verdict; and therefore the Jury fined for it as such by the Judg, and yet no false Verdict, because affirm'd upon the Attaint.

Another Reason that the Jury may not be fined in such a Case, is, because until a Jury have consummated their Verdict, which is not done until they find for the Plaintiff or Defendant, and that also be entred of Record; they have time still of Deliberation, and whatsoever they have answer'd the Judg upon an *Interlocutory Question* or *Discourse*, they may lawfully vary from it, if they find Cause, and are not thereby concluded.

Whence it follows upon this last Reason, *That upon Trials wherein no Attaint lies, as well as upon such where it doth, no Case can be invented, wherein it can be maintain'd, that a Jury can find in Mattter of Law nakedly against the Direction of the Judg.*

And the Judges were (as before) all of opinion, That the Return in this latter part of it is also insufficient as in the former, and so wholly insufficient.

But that this Question may not hereafter revive, if possible, it is evident by several Resolutions of all the Judges, That where an Attaint lies, the Judg cannot fine the Jury for going against their Evidence or Direction of the Court, without other Misdemeanour.

For

For in such case, finding against, or following the Direction of the Court barely, will not bar an Attaint; but in some case the Judg being demanded by, and declaring to the Jury what is the Law, tho he declares it erroneously, and they find accordingly, this may excuse the Jury from the Forfeitures; for tho their Verdict be false, yet it is not corrupt, but the Judgment is to be revers'd however by the Attaint, for a Man loseth not his Right by the Judges mistake in the Law.

Ingersalls C. *Cr.* 35 El. f. 309. n. 18.

Therefore if an Attaint lies for a false Verdict upon Indictment not Capital (as this is) either by the Common or Statute Law, by those Resolutions, the Court would not fine the Jury in this Case, for going against Evidence, because an Attaint lay.

But admitting an Attaint did not lie (as I think the Law clear it did not) for there is no Case in all the Law of such an Attaint or Opinion, but that of *Thirnings*, 10 *H.* 4. Attaint 60 and 64. for which there is no Warrant in Law, tho there be other specious Authority against it, touch'd by none that argu'd this Case:

The Question then will be, Whether before the several Acts of Parliament which granted Attaints, and are enumerated in their order in the Register, the Judg by the Common Law in all Cases might have fined the Jury finding against their Evidence, and Direction of the Court, where no Attaint did lie, or could so do, yet if the Statutes which gave the Attaints were repeal'd.

Reg. f. 122. 3.

If he could not in Civil Causes before Attaints granted in them, he could not in Criminal Causes upon Indictment (wherein I have admitted Attaint lies not) for the Fault in both was the same, *viz. Finding against Evidence and Direction of the Court*, and by the Common Law; the Reason being the same in both, the Law is the same.

That the Court could not fine a Jury at the Common Law, where Attaint did not lie (for where it did, it's agreed he could not) I think to be the clearest Position that ever I consider'd, either for Authority or Reason of Law.

After Attaints were granted by Statutes generally; as by *Westminster* the first, *c.* 38. *in Pleas Real*; and by 34 *Ed.* 3. *c.* 7. *in Pleas Personal.* And where they did lie at Common Law (which was only in Writs of Assize) the Examples are frequent in our Books of punishing Jurors by Attaint.

But no Case can be offer'd either before Attaints granted in general, or after, that ever a Jury was punish'd by Fine and Imprisonment, by the Judg, for not finding according to their

 Evidence,

Evidence, and his Direction, until *Popham*'s time; nor is there clear proof that he ever fined them for that Reason, separated from other Misdemeanour. If Juries might be fined in such case, before Attaints granted, why not since? For no Statute has taken that Power from the Judg. But since Attaints granted, the Judges resolv'd they cannot fine where the Attaint lies, therefore they could not fine before. Sure this latter Age did not first discover, that the Verdicts of Juries were many times not according to the Judges opinion and liking.

But the Reasons are, I conceive, most clear, that the Judg could not nor can fine and imprison the Jury in such cases.

Without a Fact agreed, it is as impossible for a Judg or any other to know the Law relating to that Fact, or direct concerning it, as to know an Accident that hath no Subject.

Hence it follows, that the Judg can never direct what the Law is in any Matter controverted, without first knowing the Fact; and then it follows, that without his previous Knowledg of the Fact, the Jury cannot go against his Direction in Law, for he could not direct.

But the Judg, *quâ* Judg, cannot know the Fact possibly, but from the Evidence which the Jury have; but (as will appear) he can never know what Evidence the Jury have; and consequently he cannot know the Matter of Fact, nor punish the Jury for going against their Evidence, when he cannot know what their Evidence is.

It is true, if the Jury were to have no other Evidence for the Fact, but what is depos'd in Court, the Judg might know their Evidence, and the Fact from it, equally as they; and so direct what the Law were in the Case, tho even then the Judg and Jury might honestly differ in the Result from the Evidence, as well as two Judges may, which often happens.

But the Evidence which the Jury have of the Fact, is much other than that: For,

1. Being return'd of the Vicinage, whence the Cause of Action ariseth, the Law supposeth them thence to have sufficient Knowledg to try the Matter in Issue (and so they must) tho no Evidence were given on either side in Court; but to this Evidence the Judg is a stranger.

2. They may have Evidence from their own personal Knowledg, by which they may be assur'd, and sometimes are, that what is depos'd in Court is absolutely false; but to this the Judg is a Stranger, and he knows no more of the Fact than he hath learned in Court, and perhaps by false Depositions, and consequently knows nothing.

3. The

3. The Jury may know the Witnesses to be stigmatiz'd and infamous, which may be unknown to the Parties, and consequently to the Court.

4. In many Cases the Jury are to have View necessarily, in many by consent, for their better Information; to this Evidence likewise the Judg is a Stranger.

5. If they do follow his Direction, they may be attainted, and the Judgment revers'd for doing that which if they had not done, they should have been fined and imprison'd by the Judg, which is unreasonable.

6. If they do not follow his Direction, and be therefore fined, yet they may be attainted, and so doubly punish'd by distinct Judicatures for the same Offence, which the Common Law admits not.

A Fine revers'd *in Banco Regis* for Infancy *per inspectionem & per testimonium del.* 4. *fide dignorum.* After upon Examination of divers Witnesses in *Chancery*, the suppos'd Infant was prov'd to be of Age *tempore finis levati*; which Testimonies were exemplify'd, and given in Evidence after *in Communi Banco*, in a Writ of Entry in the *Quibus* there brought. And tho it was the Opinion of the Court, That those Testimonies were of no force against the Judgment in the *King's Bench*, yet the Jury found with the Testimony in *Chancery* against direction of the Court upon a Point in Law, and their Verdict after affirm'd in an Attaint brought, and after a Writ of Right was brought, and Battel join'd.

7. To what end is the Jury to be return'd out of the Vicinage whence the Cause of Action ariseth? To what end must Hundredors be of the Jury, whom the Law supposeth to have nearer Knowledg of the Fact, than those of the Vicinage in general? To what end are they challeng'd so scrupulously to the Array and Pole? To what end must they have such a certain Freehold, and be *probi & legales Homines*, and not of Affinity with the Parties concern'd? To what end must they have in many Cases the View, for their exacter Information chiefly? To what end must they undergo the heavy Punishment of the Villanous Judgment, if after all this they implicitly must give a Verdict by the Dictates and Authority of another Man, under pain of Fines and Imprisonment, when sworn to do it according to the best of their own knowledg?

8. A Man cannot see by another's Eye, nor hear by another's Ear; no more can a Man conclude or infer the thing to be resolv'd by another's Understanding or Reasoning: and tho the Verdict be right the Jury give, yet they being not as-

ſur'd it is ſo from their own Underſtanding, are forſworn, at leaſt *in foro Conſcientiæ.*

9. It is abſurd, a Jury ſhould be fined by the Judg for going againſt their Evidence, when he who fineth knoweth not what it is, as where a Jury find without Evidence in Court of either ſide; ſo if the Jury find upon their own knowledg, as the Courſe is, if the Defendant plead *ſolvit ad diem* to a Bond prov'd, and offers no proof. The Jury is directed to find for the Plaintiff unleſs they know Payment was made of their own knowledg according to the Plea.

14 H. 7. f. 29. *per Vavaſor in Camer. Scac. without contradiction Hob.* f. 227.

And it is as abſurd to fine a Jury for finding againſt their Evidence, when the Judg knows but part of it; for the better and greater part of the Evidence may be wholly unknown to him; and this may happen in moſt Caſes, and often doth, as in *Grave*'s and *Short*'s Caſe.

Grave *verſ.* Short, 40 *El.* Cro. f. 616.

Error of a Judgment in the *Common Bench.* The Error aſſign'd was, The Iſſue being whether a Feoffment were made? And the Jurors being gone together to confer of their Verdict, one of them ſhew'd to the reſt an Eſcrow *pro petentibus,* not given in Evidence by the Parties, *per quod* they found for the Demandant, upon Demurrer adjudg'd no Error; for it appears not to be given him by any of the Parties, or any for them, it muſt be intended he had it as a piece of Evidence about him before, and ſhew'd it to inform himſelf and his Fellows; and as he might declare it as a Witneſs that he knew it to be true. They reſolv'd, if that might have avoided the Verdict, which they agreed it could not, yet it ought to have been done by Examination, and not by Error.

That *Decantatum* in our Books *ad queſtionem facti non reſpondent Judices, ad queſtionem Legis non reſpondent Juratores,* literally taken is true. For if it be demanded, what is the Fact? the *Judg* cannot anſwer it: If it be ask'd what is the Law in the Caſe, the *Jury* cannot anſwer it.

Therefore the Parties agree the Fact by their pleading upon Demurrer, and ask the Judgment of the Court for the Law.

In Special Verdicts the Jury inform the naked Fact, and the Court deliver the Law: and ſo is it in Demurrers upon Evidence, in Arreſt of Judgments upon Challenges, and often upon the Judges Opinion of the Evidence given in Court, the Plaintiff becomes Nonſuit; when if the Matter had been left to the Jury, they might well have found for the Plaintiff.

But

But upon all general Issues; as upon *Not Culpable* pleaded in Trespass, *Nil debet* in Debt, *Nul tort, Nul Disseisin* in Assize, *Ne disturba pas in Quare impedit*, and the like; tho it be matter of Law, whether the Defendant be a Trespasser, a Debtor, Disseisor, or Disturber in the particular Cases in Issue; yet the Jury find not (as in a special Verdict) the Fact of every Case by it self, leaving the Law to the Court, but find for the Plaintiff or Defendant upon the Issue to be try'd, wherein they resolve both Law and Fact complicately, and not the Fact by it self; so as tho they answer not singly to the Question what is the Law, yet they determine the Law in all Matters where Issue is join'd and try'd in the principal Case, but where the Verdict is Special.

To this purpose the Lord *Hobart* in *Needler*'s Case, against the Bishop of *Winchester*, is very apposite——*Legally it will be very hard to quit a Jury that finds against the Law, either Common Law or several Statute Laws, whereof all Men were to take knowledg, and whereupon Verdict is to be given, whether any Evidence be given to them or not. As if a Feoffment or Devise were made to one imperpetuum, and the Jury should find* Cross *either an Estate for Life, or in Fee-Simple against the Law, they should be subject to an Attaint, tho no Man inform'd them what the Law was in that Case.* Hob. f. 227.

The legal Verdict of the Jury to be recorded is finding for the Plaintiff or Defendant: what they answer, if ask'd, to Questions concerning some particular Fact, is not of their Verdict essentially, nor are they bound to agree in such particulars; if they all agree to find their Issue for the Plaintiff or Defendant, they may differ in the Motives wherefore, as well as Judges in giving Judgment for the Plaintiff or Defendant may differ in the Reasons wherefore they give that Judgment, which is very ordinary.

I conclude with the Statute of 26 *H.* 8. c. 4. *That if any Jurors in* Wales *do acquit any Felon, Murderer, or Accessary, or give an untrue Verdict against the King, upon the Tryal of any Traverse, Recognisance, or Forfeiture, contrary to good and pregnant Evidence, ministred to them by Persons sworn before the King's Justiciar; That then such Jurors should be bound to appear before the Council of the Marches there, to abide such Fine or Ransom for their Offence, as that Court should think fit.*

If Jurors might have been fined before by the Law, for going against their Evidence in Matters Criminal, there had been no cause for making this Statute against Jurors for so doing in *Wales* only.

Objections out of the Antient and Modern Books.

8 *Aſſ. pl.* 35. 1. A Juror kept his Fellows a Day and a Night without any reaſon or aſſenting, and therefore awarded to the *Fleet*.

This Book rightly underſtood is Law, *That he ſtaid his Fellows a day and a night without any reaſon or aſſenting*, may be underſtood, that he would not in that time intend the Verdict at all, more than if he had been abſent from his Fellows, but wilfully not find for either ſide. In this ſenſe it was a Miſdemeanour againſt his Oath, *for his Oath was truly to try the Iſſue*: which he could never do, who reſolv'd not to confer with his Fellows.

34 E. 3. *Bra. Title Jurors*, n. 46. And in this ſenſe it is the ſame with the Caſe 34 *E*, 3. where *Twelve* being ſworn and put together to treat of their Verdict, one ſecretly withdrew himſelf, and went away, for which he was juſtly fined and impriſoned; and it differs not to withdraw from a Man's Duty, by departing from his Fellows, and to withdraw from it, tho he ſtay in the ſame Room, and ſo is that Book to be underſtood.

But if a Man differ in Judgment from his Fellows for a day and a night, tho his Diſſent may not be as reaſonable as the Opinion of the reſt that agree, yet if his Judgment be not ſatisfy'd, one diſagreeing can be no more criminal, than four or five diſagreeing with the reſt.

41 *Aſſ.* p. 11. 2. A Juror would not agree with his Fellows for two days, and being demanded by the Judges, if he would agree, ſaid, he would firſt die in Priſon; whereupon he was committed, and the Verdict of the eleven taken. But upon better Advice, the Verdict of the eleven was quaſh'd, and the Juror diſcharg'd without Fine; and the Juſtices ſaid, the way was to carry them in Carts until they agreed, and not by fining them. And as the Judges erred in taking the Verdict of the Eleven, ſo they did in impriſoning the Twelfth. And this caſe makes ſtrongly, that the Juror was not to be fined who diſagreed in Judgment only.

Much of the Office of Jurors, in order to their Verdict, is *Miniſterial*, as not withdrawing from their Fellows after they are ſworn, not withdrawing after Challenge, and being try'd in before they take their Oath, not receiving from either ſide Evidence, after their Oath, not given in Court, not eating and drinking before their Verdict, refuſing to give a Verdict, and the like; wherein if they tranſgreſs, they are finable: but the Verdict it ſelf, when given, is not an Act Miniſterial, but Judicial, and according to the beſt of their Judgment, for which they are not finable, nor to be puniſh'd but by Attaint.

26 *H*. 6. f. 27. *Br. Jurors*, 18.

3. The

3. The Case of 7 *R.* 2. Title *Coronæ Fitz* 108. was cited where, upon Acquittal of a common Thief, the Judg said, the Jury ought to be bound for his good Behaviour during his Life: But saith the Book, *quere per quel ley*, but that was only *gratis dictum* by the Judg; for no such thing was done, as binding them.

4. *Bradshaw* and *Salmon*'s Case was urg'd, where a Jury had given excessive Damages upon a Tryal in an Action of Covenant, and the Court of Starchamber gave Damages to the Complainant almost as high as the Jury had given upon the Tryal. But the Jury who gave the Damages were not question'd, *Tho*, saith the Book, *they might have been, because they receiv'd Briefs from the Plaintiff, for whom they gave Damages, which was a Misdemeanour*; but the express Book is, That the Jury could not be punish'd by Information for the excessive Damages, but only by Attaint, therefore not for their false Verdict without other Misdemeanour; which answers some other Cases alledg'd. *Hob. f.* 114.

Nor can any Man shew (tho it was said) that a Jury was ever punish'd upon an Information either in Law or in the Starchamber, where the Charge was only *for finding against their Evidence, or giving an untrue Verdict, unless Imbracery, Subornation, or the like were join'd.*

5. It was said, a Perjury *in facie Curiæ* is punishable by the Judg; and such is it, if Jurors go against their Evidence. Perhaps a Witness may be punish'd for Perjury *in facie Curiæ* (which I will not maintain to be Law) but a Jury can never be so punish'd, because the Evidence in Court is not binding Evidence to a Jury, as hath been shew'd.

6. Some Records were cited of Fines *pro concelamento*; no doubt it is an Article inquirable in every *Oyer* and *Terminer*, and one Jury may find it upon another.

7. *Brayne*'s Case was urg'd, but the Jurors were there fined for a manifest Combination to delude the Court, by agreeing upon two Verdicts, and concealing the latter, if the Court would be satisfy'd with the former.

8. *Wharton*'s Case reported by two Reporters. *Yelverton* saith, That the Judges, whereof *Popham* was one, and a Privy Counsellor, were very angry, and fined the Jury for their Verdict and finding against Direction.

In those Reports that pass under the Name of *Ney's*, the same Case is reported with this, *That the Judges conceiv'd the Jury had been unlawfully dealt with to give that Verdict*; which if true, the fining was lawful, and the Case therein reported short by *Yelverton.*

9. *Wagstaff*'s Caſe in the *King's Bench* lately was the ſame with the preſent Caſe; but by the Record it is reaſonable to think the Jurors committed ſome fault beſides going againſt their Evidence, for they were unequally fined.

But however, *all the Judges having upon this Return reſolv'd, that finding againſt the Evidence in Court, or Direction of the Court barely, is no ſufficient Cauſe to fine; the Jury anſwers all theſe Caſes, if not anſwer'd before.*

Lannoys C. Moore, f. 730.

10. There remains *Southwell*'s Caſe reported by *Leonard*; ſome Caſes out of the Court of Wards in *Lannoy*'s Caſe reported by Serjeant *Moore, f.* 730. where Jurors were ſent to the *Fleet*, or threatned to be ſent, for not finding Offices according to the Direction of the Court.

1. An Inqueſt of Office is not ſubject to an Attaint.

2. It neither determines any man's Right, nor doth any Party put any Tryal upon them.

3. They are only to find naked Matter of Fact, as the Books are of 3 *H.* 7. *f.* 10. *b.* and 2 *H.* 4. *f.* 5. *a.* but principally an Office for the King is in many Caſes as neceſſary, as an Entry for a common Perſon, without which he can never come by or try his Right, nor can the King without an Office know whether he hath a Right to a Ward, a Mortmain, or the like. And as it is an Injury to hinder a Man from his Entry, whereby his Right may be try'd, ſo it is not to find an Office for the King whereby his Right may be try'd; which concludes no Man, but enables the King to a Tryal of his Right; and in truth, is only a finding of Matter of Fact, and no more.

Therefore perhaps it may be an Offence, as of a Witneſs refuſing his Teſtimony, not to find an Office for the King, when clear proof is made of the Matter of Fact; but if proof be not made at all, or be altogether doubtful, or that the Matter be Matter of Law, the Inqueſt may find an *Ignoramus*, which a Jury upon a Tryal can never do. But of this I ſhall ſay no more, it concerning not the Caſe in queſtion.

Precedents. That the Court of *Common Pleas* upon *Habeas Corpus* hath diſcharg'd Perſons impriſoned by other Courts upon the Inſufficiency of the Return only, and not for Privilege.

5 Jac. *Sir* A. Roper's *Caſe*, 12 *Rep. Sir* W. Chanſey's *Caſe*, & Ed. Thickneſs *Ca.*

Sir *Anthony Roper* committed by the High Commiſſion Court, diſcharg'd abſolutely in the *Common Pleas* as unlawfully committed and detain'd, without any mention of Privilege.

George

George Milton imprison'd for Contempt, scandalous words of the Court, and convicted of Drunkenness; the Causes resolv'd insufficient, and therefore *demittitur a prisona*, and the Goaler discharg'd of him; but he gave Bail to attend the Pleasure of the Court. 12 *Rep.* 8 Jac.

Elizabeth Ash committed by the High Commission *pro Lenocinio*, in like manner discharg'd; the Cause being insufficient to detain her in Prison, or to hinder her from the Privilege of that Court, but no other mention of Privilege, put in Bail. 4 Car. 1.

Richard Hayes, for refusing to do Penance as injoin'd, committed by the High Commission, the Cause judg'd insufficient to commit, but gave Bail as before; he demanded a *Habeas Corpus* by reason of Privilege. 7 Jac.

But it is to be observ'd, That Privilege lies only where a Man is Officer of the Court, or hath a *Prior Suit* in the *Common Pleas* depending, and is elsewhere arrested to answer, and molested that he cannot prosecute his Suit; he is then privileg'd justly, and without wrong, because his Prosecutor elsewhere might have sued, if he pleas'd, in the *Common Pleas*.

All Privilege is either for Officers, Clerks, or Attorneys of the Court not to be sued elsewhere; or for Persons impleading or impleaded having priority of Suit in the *Common Pleas*, arrested or sued in other Jurisdictions; or for the menial Servants of such Officers.

These Privileges are not detrimental to any, because whoever hath occasion to sue an Officer, or any other having Priority of Suit, as before, is not restrain'd to sue them in the *Common Pleas*, but is restrain'd from suing elsewhere. *And this is the true Privilege of the Court.*

And the way of enjoying this Privilege, was by Writs of Privilege to supersede the Proceeding of other Courts against such who had the Privilege of the *Common Pleas*, as is yet ordinary in the Cases of Attorneys, Officers, and Clerks.

And in such Writs the Cause of Privilege is mention'd; and as to their menial Servants, if not true, may be travers'd. As 22 *H* 6. 38. Debt was brought against *Baron* and *Feme*, and a *Supersedeas* out of the *Chancery* was cast for the Baron as menial Servant to an Officer of *Chancery*; whereupon the Plaintiff said it was contain'd in the Writ that the Husband was menial Servant to *R. J. del Chancery*, whereas he was not his menial Servant; and

21 H. 6. f. 20. 22 H. 6. f. 38. 34 H. 6. f. 15. *Vid.* Dyer 12 Eliz. f. 287. pl. 48. Vid. *the Supersed. for Clerks of the Court, and for Attorneys antiently, and their great Difference*, Reg. Jud. f. 84. *a.*

But now Attorneys are inroll'd as well as Officers.

and thereupon Iſſue was taken: but Query of the Officers appearing of Record in the Court, may be Travers'd.

Hence it follows, Tho Proceeding in other Courts againſt a perſon privileg'd *in Banco* might be ſuperſeded, yet it was when the Matter proceeded upon in ſuch Courts might as well be proſecuted in the *Common Bench:* But if a privileg'd Perſon *in Banco* were ſued in the *Eccleſiaſtical Courts*, or before the High Commiſſion, or Conſtable, or Marſhal, for things whereof the *Common-Pleas* had no Cognizance, they could not ſuperſede that Proceeding by Privilege. And this was the antient Reaſon and Courſe of Privilege.

1. Another way of Privilege, by reaſon of Suit depending in a *ſuperior Court*, is, when a perſon impleading or impleaded, as in the Common Bench, is after arreſted in a Civil Action or Plaint in *London*, or elſewhere, and by *Habeas Corpus* is brought to the *Common-Pleas*, and the Arreſt and Cauſe return'd. If it appear to the Court, that the Arreſt in *London* was after the Party ought to have had the Privilege of the *Common-Pleas*; he ſhall have his Privilege allow'd, and be diſcharg'd of his Arreſt, and the Party left to proſecute his Cauſe of Action in *London*, in the *Common-Pleas*, if he will.

2. If the Cauſe of Impriſonment return'd be a lawful Cauſe, but which can't be proſecuted in the *Common-Pleas*, as Felony, Treaſon, or ſome Cauſe wherein the *High-Commiſſion*, *Admiralty*, or *other Court*, had power to impriſon lawfully; then the Party impriſon'd, which did implead, or was impleaded in the Common Bench before ſuch Impriſonment, ſhall not be allow'd Privilege, but ought to be remanded.

3. The third way is, when a Man is brought by *Habeas Corpus* to the Court; and upon return of it, it appears to the Court, that he was againſt Law impriſon'd and detain'd, tho there be no Cauſe of Privilege for him in this Court, he ſhall never be by the Act of the Court remanded to his unlawful Impriſonment; for then the Court ſhould do an Act of Injuſtice in Impriſoning him, *de novo*, againſt Law. Whereas the Great Charter is, *Quod nullus liber Homo impriſonetur niſi per legem terræ.* This is the preſent Caſe, and this was the Caſe upon all the Precedents produc'd, and many more that might be produc'd; where upon *Habeas Corpus* many have been diſcharg'd and bail'd, tho there was no Cauſe of Privilege in the Caſe.

This appears plainly by many old Books, if the Reaſon of them be rightly taken; for inſufficient Cauſes are as no Cau-

ſes

ses return'd; and to send a Man back to Prison for no Cause return'd, seems unworthy of a Court.

If a Man be impleaded by Writ in the *Common-Pleas*, and is after Arrested in *London* upon a Plaint, there upon an *Habeas Corpus* he shall have Privilege in the *Common-Pleas*, if the Writ upon which he is impleaded bear Date before the Arrest in *London*, and be return'd, altho the Plaintiff in the *Common-Pleas* be *Nonsuit*, Essoin'd, or will not appear, and consequently the Case of Privilege at an end before the *Corpus cum Causa* return'd: but if the first Writ be not return'd, there is no Record in Court that there is such a Defendant.

9 *H.* 6. 54, 58. *Br. n.* 5. 14 *H.* 7. *f.* 6. *n.* 19. 9 *E.* 4. 47. *n.* 24. 12 *H.* 4. *f.* 21. *n.* 11. *Br.*

The like where a Man brought Debt *in Banco*, and after for the same Debt arrested the Defendant in *London*, and became *Nonsuit in Banco*; yet the Defendant upon a *Habeas Corpus* had his Privilege, because he had Cause of Privilege at the time of the Arrest. 14 *H.* 7. 6. *Br. Privilege n.* 19.

The like Case 9 *E.* 4. where a Man appear'd *in Banco* by a *Cepi Corpus*, and found Mainprise, and had a Day to appear in Court; and before his Day was arrested in *London*, and brought a *Corpus cum Causa in Banco Regis*; at which Day the Plaintiff became *Nonsuit*, yet he was discharg'd from the Serjeant at *London*, because his Arrest there was after his Arrest *in Banco*, and consequently unlawful. 9 *E.* 4. *f.* 47. *Br. Privilege* 24. and a Man cannot be imprison'd at the same time lawfully in two Courts.

Coke Mag. Chart. f. 53. *&* 55.

The Court of *King's Bench* cannot pretend to the only discharging of Prisoners upon *Habeas Corpus*, unless in Case of Privilege, for the *Chancery* may do it without question.

And the same Book is, That the *Common-Pleas*, or *Exchequer*, may do it, if upon the Return of the *Habeas Corpus* it appear the Imprisonment is against Law.

An *Habeas Corpus* may be had out of the *King's Bench* or *Chancery*, tho there be no Privilege, *&c.* or in the Court of *Common-Pleas* or *Exchequer*, for any Officer or Privileg'd person there: upon which Writ the Goaler must return by whom he was committed, and the Cause of his Imprisonment; and if it appeareth that his Imprisonment be just and lawful, he shall be remanded to the former Gaoler: but if it shall appear to the Court, that he was imprison'd against the *Law of the Land*, they ought by force of this Statute to deliver him; if it be doubtful, and under Consideration, he may be bail'd.— The *King's Bench* may Bail, if they please, in all Cases; but the Common

Mic. C. 2. *Coke f.* 55.

Common Bench must remand, if the Cause of Imprisonment return'd be just.

The Writ *de Homine replegiando* is as well returnable in the *Common-Pleas* as in the *King*'s *Bench*.

All Prohibitions for incroaching Jurisdiction, issue as well out of the *Common-Pleas* as *King*'s *Bench*.

Quashing the Order of Commitment upon a *Certiorari*, which the *King*'s *Bench* may do, but not the *Common-Pleas*, is not material in this Case.

1. The Prisoner is to be discharg'd or remanded barely upon the Return, and nothing else, whether in the *King*'s *Bench* or *Common-Pleas*.

2. Should the *King*'s *Bench* have the Order of Commitment certify'd and quash'd before the Return of the *Habeas Corpus*, or after, what will it avail the Prisoners? they cannot plead *Nul tiel* Record in the one Case or the other.

3. In all the Precedents shew'd in the *Common-Pleas*, or in any that can be shew'd in the *King*'s *Bench* upon discharging the Prisoner by *Habeas Corpus*, nothing can be shew'd of quashing the Orders or Decrees of that Court that made the wrong Commitment.

Glanvill C. Moore, f. 836.

4. It is manifest where the *King*'s *Bench* hath upon *Habeas Corpus* discharg'd a Prisoner committed by the *Chancery*, the person hath been again re-committed for the same Cause by the *Chancery*, and re-deliver'd by the *King*'s *Bench*; but no quashing of the *Chancery*-Order for Commitment ever heard of.

5. In such Cases of re-commitment, the Party hath other and proper Remedy, besides a New *Habeas Corpus*; of which I shall not speak now.

6. It is known, That if a Man recover in Assize, and after in a Re-disseisin, if the first Judgment be Revers'd in the Assize, the Judgment in the Re-disseisin is also Revers'd. So if a Man recover in Waste, and Damages given, for which Debt is brought, (especially if the first Judgment be Revers'd before Execution) it destroys the Process for the Damages in Debt, tho by several Originals. But it may be said, That in a Writ of Error in this kind, the Foundation is destroy'd, and no such Record is left.

Drury's *Case*, *Rep.* 8.

But as to that in *Drury*'s Case 8 Rep. an Outlawry issued, and Process of *Capias* upon the Outlawry, the Sheriff return'd *Non est inventus*; and the same Day the Party came into Court,

Court, and demanded *Oyer* of the Exigent, which was the Warrant of the Outlawry; and shew'd the Exigent to be altogether uncertain and insufficient, and consequently the Outlawry depending upon it to be null. And the Court gave Judgment accordingly, tho the Record of the Outlawry were never Revers'd by Error; which differs not from this Case, where the Order of Commitment is Judicially declar'd illegal, tho not quash'd or revers'd by Error; and consequently whatever depends upon it, as the Fine and Commitment doth; and the Outlawry in the former Case was more the King's Interest, than the Fine in this.

The Lord Chief Justice deliver'd the Opinion of the Court, and accordingly the Prisoners were discharg'd.

Phe-

Phenix XIII.

An Apology or Defence of William *the First of* Naſſau, *Prince of* Orange, *&c. in anſwer to the Proclamation againſt, and Proſcription of him by the King of* Spain.

To which is prefix'd the ſaid Proſcription *at length, with ſeveral* Letters *and* Declarations *of the Prince of* Orange, *&c. relating thereunto.*

The Copy of a Letter written by the King with his own Hand, to the Prince of Orange.

I Have with great Affection receiv'd your Letter of the 27th of *May*, and ſince that other which you writ unto me the 14th of *June*: And by that which I have written to my Siſter, you have been able to underſtand the ſmall Occaſion that you have to think that which you write unto me in that Letter of the 27th of *May*, but rather the contrary. Alſo it is certain, that you ſhould much deceive your ſelf to think, that I would not have all Confidence and good Opinion of you: And albeit ſome certain one ſhould mean to perform a contrary Duty towards me; yet this ſhould remain, that

that I would not be so light, as to give credit thereto, having so great Experience of your Loyalty and Services. Wherefore you need not trouble your self therewith, but stay your self upon the Letters, which heretofore I have written unto you in this behalf, and upon your own Deeds, but at no hand rest upon that which some Enemies (it may be of my Service, and of your good Estate) would endeavour to cause you to understand. Touching the Liberty you demand, to leave off your Charges and Offices, it grieveth me, that your particular Affairs and Businesses are in such Terms and State as you say: And I cannot but tell you, that the Affairs of those Countries, standing in such sort and manner as they do, it is not reason that such persons, as yours is (to whom I trust, and upon whom I stay my self) should abandon and forsake the same, specially I my self being so far off from the said Countries: yea rather it were reason, that those that are in their own Houses, should speedily provide for, and help this present necessity, and imploy themselves upon that whereunto they are bound, as ye have presently done, in going to *Antwerp*, whereby I have receiv'd great Contentment and Joy; and am very well assur'd, that ye will there do whatsoever shall be most convenient for my Service, and for the quietness and peace of the said Town and Country, and for the avoiding of the Disorders that shall arise there. Which thing also I hope of you, and I know that ye will not declare your self to be any other, than such a one as ye have heretofore declar'd your self to be, all your life long. And to the end ye may perceive, that I do deal freely with you, I will not cease to advertise you, that there hath been in these Quarters a great Rumor concerning this; to wit, that your Brother hath been found to be a dealer in those things that are done there. And because I cannot cease much and often to think of this matter, I charge you strictly diligently to consider, how it may be remedied and redressed, that it proceed no further, and look that you do effectually perform it: and if it seem good unto you to remove, for a few days, your Brother far from you, do so. From the Forest of *Segovia* the first of *August*.

Subsigned

PHILIP,

And written upon the Back-side

To the Prince of *Orange*,

And seal'd with the King's Seal.

A

A Proclamation *and an* Edict *in Form of a* Proscription, *made by the Majesty of the King our Lord, against* William *of* Nassau, *Prince of* Orange, *as the chief Captain and Disturber of the State of* Christendom, *and especially of these* Low-Countries; *by which every one is authoriz'd to hurt him and to kill him, as a publick Plague; with a Reward to him that shall do it, and shall be assisting and aiding thereunto.*

PHILIP, by the Grace of God, King of *Castile*, *Leon*, *Arragon*, *Navar*, *Naples*, *Cicilia*, *Majorca*, *Sardinia*, of the *Isles*, *Indies*, *Firm Land*, and of the *Ocean-Sea*; Archduke of *Austria*, Duke of *Burgundy*, *Lothier*, *Brabant*, *Lemburg*, *Luxenburg*, *Gelderland* and *Milan*; County of *Hapsburg*, *Flanders*, *Artois* and *Burgundy*; Palatine both of *Haynault*, *Holland*, *Zealand*, *Namure* and *Zutphen*; Prince of *Suave*; Marquis of the *Holy Empire*; Lord of *Friseland*, *Salines* and *Malines*, and the City, Towns and Country of *Utrecht*, *Overyssel* and *Groningen*, and Governor in *Asia* and *Africa*. To all those that shall see these present Writings, Greeting.

It's known to all the World, how the late Emperor of most Excellent Memory, *Charles* the Fifth, my Lord and Father, whom God absolve, hath favourably handled and dealt with *William* of *Nassau*, for the Succession of the late *Rene* of *Chaalon*, Prince of *Orange* his Cousin: and how from that time forward, even from his first Age, he hath (altho he were a Stranger) greatly advanc'd him; which thing we our selves also have always successively continued, and daily augmented more and more; having made him first of our Order, afterward our Lieutenant-General in the Government of *Holland*, *Zealand*, *Utrecht* and *Burgundy*; and withal, of our Council of State, bestowing upon him sundry Benefits and Honours; whereby both by reason of the Oath of Fidelity and Homages, which he hath likewise made unto us, because also of the Fees, Pensions, Lands and Lordships, held of us in divers our Countries and Provinces, he was greatly subjected, and bound to obey us; to keep and hold his Faith given, and to procure the Good and Profit

Profit of our Affairs, and consequently to maintain all quietness and peace in our Estates and Countries. Notwithstanding every one knoweth, that we were not so soon departed out of those our *Low-Countries*, but that the said *William* of *Nassau*, made Prince of *Orange* by the means above-mention'd, did by his sinister Practices, Devices and Crafts, assay first to get the Good-wills of those whom he knew to be discontent, greatly indebted, haters of Justice, studious of Novelties, and especially such as were suspected to be of the Religion, banqueting them, provoking them, and drawing them after him by fair Words, Promises and vain Persuasions, even so far, that he was the principal Author, Promoter and Framer of the first Request, presented by certain Companies of young Gentlemen, who did daily frequent his House and Table: yea, that the very Plot thereof was laid in his said House, by and with the Assistance of Count *Ludovick* of *Nassau* his Brother, a great Heretick. And albeit, that he was the Director of all these Devices; yet, in that time, he daily haunted the Council of State, being present at all Consultations and Resolutions taken and made therein; insomuch that every Man may easily mark the faithful Trust that was in him, and the Observation of his Oaths. And afterward passing from the said Request, and proceeding further, he and his Adherents brought in Heretical Preachings, and Publick Assemblies in sundry places of our said Countries, whilst that the Dutchess of *Parma*, our most dear and best-belov'd Sister (then Regent and General Governor of our said *Low-Countries*) had sent unto us, that we might give order concerning the said Request. And also, by the Advice, Knowledg, and Partaking of the said Prince of *Orange*, the Hereticks (being guided by those Presenters of the aforesaid Request, who were favour'd by him) began tumultuously to break Images, Altars and Churches; to prophane all holy and sacred Things, yea, the Sacraments instituted by God. Nevertheless, by the Grace of God, and Foresight of the said Lady, the Matters were so well govern'd and remedied, that he was inforc'd to depart out of our Countries, and to leave his said Governments, yet not without being full of Wrath and Threatnings that he would be reveng'd therefore: which thing he thought the Year following to perform by Arms, but in vain; for he was so speedily pursu'd by our Army continually following him at his heels, that he was driven out of all our said Countries, without being able to remain in any part thereof. But as soon after there did in sundry places appear some Discontentment of our said Subjects, against the Government of the Duke of *Alva* (who succeeded the said Lady in the Government aforesaid) and amongst others, in the Pro-

 vinces

vinces of *Holland* and *Zeland*; so he practised, that he might return thither again. To which, notwithstanding he was not receiv'd, but that first he did holily swear to the Estates of the said Countries, and the Towns therein, that he would maintain the said Countries and Towns for us, and in our Obedience; and that he would not change any thing whatsoever, of the antient Catholick and Romish Religion, but as a Governor only, would assist and defend them against the said D. of *Alva*, if he would inforce, and by Violence draw them to that which he pretended; that is to say, to the payment of the ten and twenty peny of that Imposition, which he would charge them withal: a thing indeed which we never commanded him, neither ever understood to have been done, but with the good leave and liking of our said Subjects; and yet that also, in the stead of other Aids and Impositions, whereof we meant to unburden them. Notwithstanding, so soon as the said *Nassau* was enter'd and receiv'd into the said Government, he began by his Officers and Accomplices to bring in Heretical Preachings in every place where he could, persecuting all the good Pastors, Preachers, Religious Persons, and honest People; whereof he drove away a great Number, and amongst them he caus'd many of them to be murder'd, or else wink'd at the Murder that was made of them, by some of his Adherents, until such time as the said Estates, being greatly offended with this Cruelty, would have a Reason and an Account yielded thereof. But then he feign'd, that the thing did much displease and dislike him; and yet notwithstanding afterwards, he return'd to his first Purpose and Mark, ill intreating those whom he knew to be Catholicks, and contrary to his Attempts, aiding himself with the Counsel of Heretical Ministers, as well Strangers, as of the said Country; changing likewise the Magistrates, which he knew favour'd not his Enterprizes and Purposes, and afterwards proceeded to bring in Liberty of Conscience, or (to speak truly) Confusion of Religion. Whereupon immediately after it fell out, that the Catholicks were openly persecuted, cast down, and driven away; the Churches and Monasteries, both of Men and Women, broken down, ruinated, and made even with the Earth; the Religious Persons, both Men and Women, evil handled, banish'd and rooted out, unless they would play the Apostates, and become married; for in the other he had no confidence at all (as also he himself, being before a married Man, his second Wife yet living, did take a Religious Woman and an Abbess, solemnly blessed by the Bishop's Hand, whom he as yet keepeth with him, the most shame-fac'd and infamous thing that can be, not only according to Christian Religion, but

but alſo by the Laws of the *Romans*, and againſt all Honeſty) and at the laſt hath proceeded ſo far, that he hath not left any more place for the Catholick Religion, ſuffering all the Errors and Impieties of all other Sects and Hereſies, that he might thereby overthrow and root up (if he would) our Catholick and Holy Religion, which hath been always obſerv'd by the whole Eſtate of Chriſtians.

Furthermore, He hath caus'd our poor Subjects of *Holland* and *Zeland* to be ſo ſtiff, and brought them to ſtand upon ſuch terms, that almoſt all the Towns thereof, one after another, have been beſieg'd and taken, ſome by aſſault, and otherſome by compoſition and yielding: inſomuch that more than once he hath been almoſt utterly driven out by our Armies, until ſuch time that the great Commander of *Caſtile*, being dead, whom we alſo made Succeſſor in that Government after the ſaid Duke of *Alva*, whom we call'd back from thence, that we might make our Subjects more contented thereby; things came into ſome diſorder, and Diſobedience of Soldiers, who took the Town of *Zirickzee*; which Diſorder began to give ſome favour to the ſaid *Naſſau*: and immediately after the States-General of our ſaid Countries, in thoſe Quarters, (deſiring once to get out of theſe Miſeries of War, perſuaded by the ſaid *Orange*, ſaying and feigning, That he deſir'd nothing but the good Peace and Tranquillity of the Countries, and to ſet them free from ſtrange Soldiers, and to hold the Country under our Obedience, and withal, to preſerve therein the antient Catholick Religion, ſuch as it had always been exercis'd and practis'd amongſt them, and to keep the Privileges and Liberty of the ſaid Country) did make with him the Treaty of *Gaunt*, eſtabliſh'd expreſly upon theſe two Grounds; that is, to maintain the ſaid Religion, and Obedience to us.

While theſe things were in handling, we ſent our good Brother, the late Lord *Don John* of *Auſtria*, of bleſſed Memory, with Commandment and Intention to pacify, reconcile, and accord, all the Troubles of our ſaid Countries, by the moſt gentle means, and favourableſt way that could be: which thing alſo he did, yielding unto our Subjects every thing, which any manner of way might be granted unto them; ratifying and confirming alſo the ſaid Treaty of *Gaunt*, which he caus'd to be publiſh'd in every place, according to the accuſtom'd manner, which the foreſaid *Orange* did gainſay by all the Forces and Power he had; but not being able to hinder it, he would never afterwards cauſe the ſame to be publiſh'd in the Places of his Governments, (fretting, as is ſaid, becauſe he was not able to lett it) notwithſtanding that we our ſelves had afterwards approv'd, confess'd and confirm'd both the one and the other Agreement and Treaty: and notwithstanding that our said good Brother (together with the Deputies of the rest of the States) had sent divers great and good Personages to the said *Orange*, to persuade him to that, to the end effectually to accomplish on his part, that whereunto he was held and bound, by the Articles and Points of the said Treaty of *Gaunt*. And because, that he pleaded and alledg'd continually, that he ought to recover his whole Government; and withal, that the Towns which would not acknowledg him for Governor, or else those which afterwards we had taken by force of Arms, and brought by some other means into our Obedience, should be put under his said Government; he was even in that also satisfy'd, by the goodness and gentleness of our said States, who had not yet then sufficiently known his Deceits and Perjuries, yet so notwithstanding, that he should swear that he would change nothing at all of the Form of the said Antient, Catholick and Roman Religion; and that for this purpose he should give such Assurances and Satisfactions, as the Magistrates, Burgesses and Inhabitants of every Town might justly demand. Whereupon they, having reason'd a long while touching the Assurances which every Town did demand, to the end, that that which the said *Orange* promis'd them might be observ'd and kept, they were subjected under his Government; after that he had sworn to perform the Points aforesaid, and other Articles contain'd in the Instruments and Writings of the said Satisfactions and Assurances. But so far off was it, that he hath kept and observ'd his foresaid Promises and Oaths, that, on the contrary side, he immediately brought into the said Countries and Towns, his Ministers and *Calvinist* Preachers; he hath caus'd the Hereticks, that were banish'd, to return; he hath there practis'd Liberty of Conscience, and hath caus'd to be committed some Offences in some Churches, joining himself, first to the poorer sort, and afterwardss to the Magistrates; and hath by little and little persecuted the good Pastors, and caus'd them to fly away. Finally, he hath expel'd and banish'd the whole Catholick Religion, and forbidden the Exercise and Use thereof. In doing of which, he us'd his ordinary Hypocrisies, and accustom'd Counterfeiting; saying, That those things displeas'd him, and that he was not able to remedy the same. And yet notwithstanding he did, both by himself, and by his Officers secretly, and as it were, under-hand, provoke all the seditious and heretical Persons, to use and practise the mischief he had conceiv'd: And for this cause he did (by the Aid and Assistance of those of his side) place by little and little, Garisons within the Towns, against

his

his Covenants and Promifes fworn; and in the mean while ceas'd not to accufe our faid Brother *Don John*, that he privily practis'd many Mifchiefs againft the States: which thing, notwithftanding, our faid Brother hath always affur'd us not to be true. But rather, that feeing the Obftinacy and Malice of the faid *Orange*, he might be able to impart the fame matter with others, and to devife how they might bring him to Reafon, and hinder him from again troubling the whole publick Quietnefs of the faid Countries, as afterwards he did indeed.

All this notwithftanding, the aforefaid *Orange* left not off, until that by his practices and fubtil fleights (which are very proper to him) he had fet fuch great Diffidence and Diftruft between our faid Brother, and the Eftates of our faid Countries, that there appear'd nothing but a moft great, evident, and apparent Murder. Infomuch that, for the avoiding of that Diforder, or at the leaft to efcape the Imprifonment of his own Perfon, the faid *Don John* plac'd himfelf fafely in our Town and Caftle of *Namure*. Whereunto he was fo much the more mov'd, by how much he was not any whit at all arm'd; and on the other fide, becaufe it was manifeft and certain, that the faid *Orange*, by all his Pofting Meffengers and Officers, did not ceafe to provoke the factious perfons to practife the like thing upon his own Perfon, as he had the fame year caus'd to be practis'd upon thofe of our Council of State, appointed to the general Government of our faid Countries: As alfo, becaufe that then the faid *Orange*, thinking that he had gotten all, did begin to fhoot out all his Arrows, and to difcover his Sleights and Weapons, that he might draw our People into open War, againft our faid Brother and Lieutenant-General. Notwithftanding, by occafion of fome good Men being nigh about his Perfon, and of other vertuous People, on the State's fide; the Matters came fo far, that all was well agreed; and that for the avoiding of all Occafion and Diftruft, it was both on the one fide, and on the other concluded, that he fhould withdraw himfelf from his Government, and go into *Italy*; which thing alfo we our felves wifh'd and will'd: And there were with him the Deputies of the Eftates, mutually to accept and fign the Offers made on both fides, one of them to another. But in ill time, this Enemy, the common Difturber of publick Quietnefs (who knowing that from the place of *Holland* where he was, he could not with all his Devices any more hinder this Peace and Reconciliation) made hafte to come at that very time to *Bruxelles*; and feigning that he would have Peace, he procur'd War, fetting down new Conditions, not yet talk'd nor confer'd of, nor open'd; infomuch

 that

that he obtain'd his Purpose, breaking the whole Agreement, as every one very well knoweth. Afterwards, the Matter being come to a breaking out of open and most cruel War, he by Force and Tumult of the People, caus'd himself, against the Good-will of the Estates, to be declar'd *Rewart*; that is, the Protector or Defender of our Country of *Brabant*, and afterwards the second Lieutenant of all our *Low-Countries*: and also, in fine, he caus'd himself by the Tumults of *Gaunt*, and of some other places, to be chosen Governor of *Flanders*; having also caus'd to come thither, his Brother, and Brother-in-law, being Strangers, to take upon them some other Governments of our Provinces. And yet notwithstanding he and his partakers burden our People with all sorts of Impositions, Exactions, Demands, Levies and Taxes, so hard, barbarous and tyrannous, that the like hath never been heard of; which he hath executed by a strong Hand and Force of Arms, without the consent of our People, and without yielding any account thereof: And if any Man speak of these things, he layeth hand upon them, or causeth them to be spoil'd, evil intreated, imprison'd or slain.

On the other side it is manifest, what we have continually done to pacify and quiet (so soon as we understood thereof) the Evil that fell out, as hath been said, between our said Lieutenant-General and the Estates: But all the good that we have done, or our said Brother, hath been suppress'd and hid; instead whereof, the said *Orange*, and his partakers, have devis'd a thousand Slanders, the more to abuse our said Subjects. Even as in the obtaining of the Victory of *Gembloux*, when we sent the Baron of *Seelles* with most reasonable Conditions, that he might receive into favour our said Subjects, and accord the whole Matter; nothing for all that follow'd thereupon, by means of the hinderance and lett, which he knew to cast in the way: albeit, that all this while, our said Subjects, writing both to us, and to our good Brother and Nephew the Emperor, and other Potentates, to justify the Controversies which they had against our said Lieutenant-General, did openly protest, that they meant not to change any thing in the Antient, Catholick, and Roman Religion, such as it had always been observ'd in our said Countries; and withal, that under the practice thereof, they would yield us that Obedience which by God's Law and Man's Law was due unto us: which were the only two Points which we always demanded, and demanded then of them, and whereof also we were agreed. Notwithstanding the said *Orange*, fearing the Reconciliation of our Subjects with us, came so far, that he laid again new Devices, not only for to hinder that matter, but also to make (if (if he could) for ever the thing paſt hope of Recovery, and altogether remedileſs, by going about to corrupt all with Hereſy, whereunto he attain'd in divers places, both by Subtilties, Crafts, Miſchiefs, and Perjuries, well known to him and all Hereticks, and alſo by mere force, uſing the ſame that he had practiſed before, to waſt and deſtroy the Provinces of *Holland* and *Zeland*, caſting all into the Fire of popular Tumult; and of the ſacking of Churches, Prophanations of Sacraments, Murder or Impriſonment of Biſhops, Paſtors, Jeſuits, Religious Men, Religious Women, and of ſundry ſecular Perſons of Quality and Honour; breaking againſt all Order of Law the Privileges, Uſages, and antient Obſervations; depriving the Preſidents, Counſellors, Governours of Places, Bailiffs, Provoſts, Sheriffs, and other Catholick Officers, well affected to Us, and the Good and Quiet of the Country; placing in their ſtead, and that extraordinarily and by his own Authority, and oftentimes by the Tumult of the People provok'd by him (amongſt whom he reigneth and triumpheth) all Sectaries, ſeditious Men, and turbulent Perſons, living on Prey and Spoil, and others like unto himſelf: inſomuch that he hath brought all to the moſt tyrannous, barbarous, and bloody Confuſion, that ever yet was heard of. Wherewith certain Catholick Provinces being diſpleas'd, even to ſee the Conſciences of the Good ſo oppreſs'd and violently inforc'd, and the Churches, Cloiſters, Abbeys, Caſtles, and Houſes of Noblemen and Great Perſonages, laid flat with the Earth, and their Goods given for a Prey to all wicked Men, at the diſcretion and pleaſure of this Stranger, and the whole Eſtate of the Country ſubverted by him; yea, ſo far, that he meant to conſtrain whole Provinces, and that againſt their Oath and Good Will: they did willingly reconcile themſelves to us. Which thing he endeavour'd on all ſides to gainſay and hinder, but they were more ſtrong and conſtant than he; yea, which is worſe, albeit that the ſaid Lord Emperor, at the earneſt Requeſt of the ſaid Eſtates (who beſought him to be an Interceſſor, and to make a mean for a Pacification between Us and Them) was content to take the whole matter into his own hands, and to determine it if he could. Whereunto, for the Deſire that we have to ſee our People deliver'd from theſe Calamities, We did willingly condeſcend and agree. And indeed his Imperial Majeſty ſent to this purpoſe his Commiſſioners to *Cologn*, as well Princes Electors, as others very principal Perſons of the Holy Empire, to underſtand the Points in controverſy and diſpute between us; yet that hath no whit at all turn'd him aſide, nor with-held him from his wicked and perverſe Purpoſes. And indeed the ſaid Commiſſioners having heard the whole matter, and debated a good while together upon the Demands of the said Estates, and our Offers made thereto, resolv'd and concluded the Points and Articles which they caus'd to be publish'd and imprinted, that they might be accepted both of the one side and the other. Nevertheless the whole matter was without any effect or fruit, notwithstanding that the Articles themselves were so gracious, favourable, just and reasonable, that there is no Man of good Judgment, but confesseth that they are more than sufficient, and that we have offer'd more than by any reason our Subjects ought to demand at our hands.

Whilst this Conference and Communication endur'd and lasted, the said *Orange*, to the end that he might countermine and work aginst the Emperor and us, and so by that means make all the matter desperate and past hope, caus'd to be made in *Utrecht* a certain Assembly of the Deputies of sundry Towns and Countries, which he keepeth under his own power; there to practise a new League, or a manifest and notorious Conspiracy against the said Religion and Us, with execrable and detestable both Words and Oaths, not abstaining to injure the Commissioners of the said Lord Emperor. For which purpose he was assisted by his said Brother, and Brother in Law, and other Helpers; which thing he hath also wrested and wrung from sundry quarters, by great Provocation, Practices, Slanders, and importunate Promises; yea, almost by Force. And notwithstanding all the Duties perform'd by the said Commissioners, to cause the Provinces to understand their said good and holy Resolution, so profitable for our Subjects; he by his Adherents, and certain suppos'd Persons whom he useth for Instruments, hath brought to pass that the said Articles were a long while suppress'd and kept close; and when they could not any longer be hidden, he hath not only hinder'd that they should not be accepted, but hath procur'd that certain pernicious Books, stuff'd with all Lyes and Slanders, should be written against them. And moreover, at the last the Deputies that he hath in *Antwerp* nigh about him, being of the same Profession, have demanded Articles more grievous, impertinent, hurtful, offensive, and full of Impiety against God, and Us their Sovereign Lord and natural Prince; yea, such Articles as a Man cannot speak too much against them. Besides, when he perceiv'd that as yet he could not by all his cunning Persuasions and Labours wholly obtain the same, he determin'd at length to depart out of *Antwerp* (from whence he had not stir'd by more than two years space) and went into our said Town of *Utrecht*, to the end he might accomplish the Execution of the said damnable League, and make

for

for ever all the matters unremediable. And generally, he hath ſo behaved himſelf in all manner of Tyranny, that he hath driven from thence and routed out all the People of the Church; yea, he hath ſo handled the Lords, and the whole principal Nobility of our Countries, that they have been inforc'd to withdraw themſelves and to forſake their Countries, to the end that he may reign and rule there moſt abſolutely, amongſt the Furies and Tumults of the People, the good being chaſed away. And becauſe that all this Confuſion and Curſe, which our Countries ſuffer, is confeſs'd to proceed from the Counſel, Exhortation, Provocation, and doing of this wicked Hypocrite, by means of his unquiet Spirit, which alſo placeth the whole Felicity thereof in the trouble of our Subjects: And withal ſeeing that it is manifeſt, that ſo long as he is in our Countries, there cannot be Peace, Reſt, nor any Quietneſs, eſtabliſhing all upon a perpetual Diſtruſt, which he hath ever in his mouth (a very ordinary and common thing to wicked men, who have their Conſciences vexed and troubled, as had *Cain*, *Judas*, and ſuch-like) moreover, ſeeing that notwithſtanding the Intreaties and Offers that have been made him, even by the Emperor's Commiſſioners, offering him moſt great Profits, to the end that he would return to his native Country (where every one naturally ought to deſire to live moſt) he would not accept thereof; and being a ſtranger, delighteth rather to deſtroy our Countries, than to yield to that which is reaſonable and good, for the benefit of our natural Subjects, the Inhabitants thereof.

For theſe cauſes, which are ſo juſt, reaſonable, and lawful, uſing in this behalf the Authority that we have over him, as well by virtue of the Oaths of Fidelity and Obedience, which he hath ſundry times taken unto us, as alſo being the Abſolute and Sovereign Prince of the ſaid *Low Countries*; for all his perverſe and wicked Deeds, and becauſe he alone hath been the Head, Author, and Promoter of theſe Troubles, and the principal Diſturber of our whole Eſtate: to be ſhort, becauſe he hath been the publick Plague of *Chriſtendom*, we publiſh him for a Traitor and a wicked Man, the Enemy of Us and our Countries; and as ſuch a one have proſcrib'd him, and do perpetually and for ever proſcribe him out of the ſaid Countries, all other our Eſtates, Kingdoms, and Signiories; interdicting and forbidding all our Subjects, of what eſtate, condition, or quality ſoever they be, not to haunt, live, be converſant, ſpeak, or communicate with him openly or ſecretly, nor to receive him or lodg him in their Houſes, nor to miniſter unto him Meat, Drink, Fire, or any other Neceſſaries,

cessaries, in any sort whatsoever, on pain of incurring our Indignation and Displeasure, as hereafter shall be said. And so We permit all, whether they be our Subjects or others, for the Execution of our said Declaration and Edict, to stay him, let him, and safely to keep his Person, and to hurt him both in his Goods, and also in his Person and Life, giving the said *William* of *Nassau* over unto all Men as the Enemy of Mankind, granting unto every one all his Goods, movable and unmovable, that can take, occupy, or conquer the same, wheresoever they be, except those Goods which are at this present in our power and possession. And to the end indeed, that this matter may be the more effectually and readily perform'd, and so by that means our said People the sooner deliver'd from this Tyranny and Oppression, we willing to reward Virtue and to punish Vice, do promise in the word of a King, and as the Minister of God, that if there be any found, either among our own Subjects, or amongst Strangers, so noble of Courage, and desirous of our Service and the Publick Good, that knoweth any way how to execute our said Decree, and to set Us and Himself free from the aforesaid Plague, delivering him unto us quick or dead, or at least taking his Life from him, we will cause to be given and provided for him and his Heirs, in good Land or ready Mony, chuse him whether, immediately after the thing shall be accomplish'd, the Sum of twenty five thousand Crowns of Gold; and if he have committed any Offence or Fault, how great and grievous soever it be, we promise to pardon him the same, and from henceforth do pardon it; yea, and if he were not before Noble, we do make him Noble for his Courage and valiant Act: And if the principal Doer take with with him for his Aid, in the Accomplishment of this Enterprise, or Execution of this his Fact, other Persons beside himself, we will bestow upon them Benefits and a Reward, and will give to every one of them, according to their degree, and according to that Service which they shall yield unto us in this behalf; pardoning them also whatsoever theyhave ill done, and making them likewise Noble. And because that the Receivers, Favourers, and Adherents of such Tyrants, are they who cause them to continue, and do nourish and uphold them in their Naughtiness, without the which the Wicked could not rule any long time, we declare all them likewise for Rebels against us, and Enemies of the common Quiet; and as such do deprive them of all their Goods, Nobility, Honours, and Favours, present or to come, who within a month after the Publication of this present Edict, shall not withdraw themselves from taking part with him, but shall continue to shew him Favour, and to give him Aid, or otherwise

wiſe ſhall haunt, frequent, follow, aſſiſt, counſel or favour him, directly or indirectly, or from this time forward ſhall deliver him any Money; giving all the Goods and Bodies of ſuch Men, wheresoever they may be found, either in our Kingdoms or Countries, or out of them, to thoſe that ſhall occupy the ſame, whether they be Merchandizes, Mony, Debts, Actions, Lands, Lordſhips, and other things whatſoever, except that the ſaid Goods be already ſeiz'd in our power, as hath been before ſaid. And that they may the more ſpeedily come to have Sentence againſt their ſaid Perſon or Goods, it ſhall be proof ſufficient enough to declare, that they have ſeen them, after the time expreſs'd in this Proſcription, communicate, ſpeak, treat, haunt openly or ſecretly with the ſaid *Orange*, or have ſhew'd him particular Favour, Aſſiſtance, or Aid, directly or indirectly howſoever; pardoning notwithſtanding all Men whatſoever, even unto the ſaid time they ſhall have done to the contrary, if returning back, and ſubmitting themſelves again under the due and lawful Obedience which they owe unto us, they have accepted or ſhall accept the ſaid Treaty of *Arras*, concluded at *Mons*, or the Articles of the Deputies of the Emperor determined at *Cologn*.

Thus we give in charge and command, our moſt dear and faithful, the Heads, Preſidents, and Perſons of our Privy and Great Councils; the Chancellor and Perſons of our Council in *Brabant*; the Governour, Preſident, and Perſons of our Council at *Luxemburg*; the Governor, Chancellor, and Perſons of our Council in *Gelderland*; the Governor of *Lembourgh*, *Faulquemont*, *Daelhem*, and of others our Countries of *Oultremeuze*; the Governor, Preſidents, and Perſons of our Councils in *Flanders* and *Artois*; the great Bailiff of *Hainault*, and Perſons of our Council at *Mons*; the Governor, Preſident, and Perſons of our Council in *Holland*; the Governor, Preſident, and Perſons of our Council at *Namur*; the Governor, Preſidents, and Perſons of our Council in *Frieſeland*; the Governor, Chancellor, and Perſons of our Council in *Overyſſel*; the Lieutenant of *Groningen*; the Governour, Preſident, and Perſons of our Council at *Utrecht*; the Governor of *Liſle*, *Douay*, and *Orchies*; the Provoſt and Count of *Valenciennes*; the Bailiff of *Tournay*, and of *Tourneſſes*; the Rent-maſters of *Beweſt* and *Beoiſterſchelt* in *Zeland*; the Judg of *Malines*; and all other our Juſtices and Officers, and thoſe of our Vaſſals and Subjects, whom it ſhall concern, their Lieutenants, and every one of them, in reſpect of himſelf, and as tho it did appertain unto him, that they cauſe this our preſent Declaration, Edict, and Decree to be publiſh'd, every one in his Government,

ment, and in the Places and Bounds of his or their Jurisdiction, where they are accustom'd to make Cries and Proclamations, to the end that none may pretend any cause of the Ignorance thereof. And moreover, that they keep, observe, and maintain, and cause inviolably to be kept, observ'd, and maintain'd, all the Points and Articles therein contain'd, according to their Form and Tenor, proceeding, and causing to be proceeded therein respectively, to the Recompence, Reward, Pain and Punishment of the Persons above-mention'd, without any Favour, Love or Dissimulation: and for this purpose, and all things appertaining thereto, we give them, and every one of them, full Power, Authority, and special Commandment: and we charge and command all, that they obey them commanding the same, and that they understand it diligently. And neverthelefs, seeing that at this present the said Publications cannot be made in the Towns, Countries and Territories occupy'd by the Rebellion of the said *Orange*; we will that the Publications which shall be made in the Towns nearest thereunto, being under our Obedience, shall be wholly and altogether of such force and effect, as if they had been utterly done in the Circuits and Places accustom'd: And for such we have authoriz'd, and by these Presents do authorise them; yea, we will and command, that immediately they be printed in two sundry Languages, by the sworn Printers of our Universities of *Louvain* or *Douay*, to the end that it may more easily come to all mens knowledg; and this is our Pleasure, Appointment, and Good Will. In witness whereof we have caus'd our Great Seal to be put to these Presents, which were made in our Town of *Maestricht*, the 25*th* Day of the Month of *March*, and in the Year of Grace 1580. and of our Kingdoms, to wit, of *Spain*, *Sicilia*, &c. the 25*th*; and of *Naples* the 27*th*.

By the express Appointment of his Majesty.

Verreiken.

And the said Letters are seal'd with the Great Seal of his Majesty in Red Wax, and a double Lace hanging thereat.

The

The Letter of the Prince of Parma *to the Governors and Counsellors of the Provinces, commanding the publishing of this Proclamation.*

Alexander, *Prince of* Parma *and of* Plaisance, *&c. Governour and Captain General.*

MY Cousin, most Dear and Well-beloved Friends: Seeing the King my Lord hath by two several Letters of his, very plainly commanded us to cause forthwith to be publish'd in these his Countries, the Proscription and Proclamation annex'd hereto against *William* of *Nassau* Prince of *Orange*, for the Causes contain'd in the said Proclamation; we could not cease to obey his Majesty's Commandment, and to send the same unto you; requiring you, and nevertheless, in the name and on the behalf of his Majesty, appointing you, that immediately after ye have seen the same, you publish it, and cause it to be publish'd throughout all the Towns and Places of your Government and Jurisdiction, after the accustom'd manner, to the end that none may pretend any cause of the Ignorance thereof; and fail ye not herein. And thus my Cousin, most Dear and Well-beloved Friends, our Lord have you in his keeping. From *Mons*, the 15*th* Day of *June*, 1580.

Underneath was written, ALEXANDER.

And sign'd over-against it, VERREIKEN.

This was the Superscription of it,

To the Governors and Counsellors of the Provinses.

A Declaration made by my Lord the Prince of Orange *to my Lords the Estates General of the* Low Countries.

My Lords,

YE have heretofore seen a certain Sentence, in the Form of a Proscription, which was sent by the King of *Spain*, and afterwards publish'd by the Appointment and Order of the Prince of *Parma:* and how by the means thereof, mine Enemies have against all Right and Reason, attempted grievously to touch and to taint mine Honour, and to cause my former Actions to be thought evil and wicked; wherein I have been very willing and desirous to take the Advice and Counsel of sundry notable Personages, and Men of great Name and Calling, yea of the principal Counsellors and Wise Men of this Country. But by reason of the Quality and Form of the said Proscription, and the heinous and grievous Crimes wherewith I am charg'd, altho indeed wrongfully, I have hitherto staid; notwithstanding I have been advis'd and counsel'd by sundry my Friends, that I cannot otherwise defend my Honour, but to shew by publick Writing, how unjustly I have been accused and charged with many Faults; and also how I have been openly injur'd, and maliciously slander'd. According to which Advice and Counsel (my Lords) seeing that in this world I acknowledg you only for my Superiors, I offer unto you this my Defence, written against the Reprehensions of my Adversaries; by which, I hope, that I have not only discover'd all their Deceits and Slanders, but also lawfully justify'd all my Actions past. And because that their principal mark and purpose is, to seek out all the means they can, to take away my Life, or else to cause me to be banish'd out of these Countries, or at the least to diminish the Authority which it hath pleas'd you to give me, as if obtaining that thing once, all should fall out as they would wish it: and on the other side, because they slander me, that by unlawful means I keep and hold my Authority, I beseech you my Lords to believe, that albeit I be content to live amongst you so long as it shall please God, and to continue towards you my faithful Service; yet notwithstanding that, my own Life, which I have dedicated to your Service, and my Presence in the midst of you, are not so dear unto me, but that I can most willingly abandon

and

and forgo my Life, or else withdraw my self out of the Country, when you shall think or know, that either the one or the other may any manner of way serve your turn, to purchase unto you a more assured Liberty. And as concerning the Authority which it hath pleas'd you to give me, you know, my Lords, how many times I have besought you to content your selves with my Service, and to unburden me thereof, if you should think that it would stand well with the good Estate of your Affairs; which thing even as yet I do demand of you, offering notwithstanding (as I have always done) in all that wherein it hath pleas'd you to command me, still to continue to employ my self in the Service of the Country; in regard of which, I esteem nothing of all that is in the world, as I do more largely declare the same unto you in this my Defence. Which if you shall judg it convenient, I beseech you to think it good, and to take care that it may be brought to light and publish'd; to the end that not only you (my Lords) but also the whole World may judg of the Equity of my Cause, and of the unjust Dealing of my Adversaries.

Presented by my Lord the Prince of Orange, *to my Lords the Deputies of the Estates General, and of the Provinces united together, being assembled in the Town of* Delft, *the* 13th *of* December, 1580.

Underneath was written,

I *J. Houfflin* being present.

The Answer of my Lords the Estates General, made to the former Declaration.

THE Estates General having, not many days since, seen and read a certain Proscription, publish'd by the Enemies against your Excellency's Person, by which they charge the same with heinous Crimes, endeavouring to make it odious (as tho by unlawful means, and indirect ways, it had usurp'd the Place and Degree wherein it is set and establish'd) and to deliver your said Excellency's Person over for a Pary, and to take from it the Honour thereof: Having in like sort seen and view'd a Defence set out by your Excellency against the said Proscription, we find by the truth of that which hath pass'd in these Countries, and which is known and manifest also

alſo to every one of them, in reſpect of themſelves, that the ſaid Crimes, Faults, and Reproaches, have unjuſtly been laid upon the ſame. And as concerning the Offices, as well of Lieutenant General as of the particular Governments, they affirm that his Excellency, yea even when he was lawfully elected and choſen, did not accept them, but at our inſtant Requeſt, in which alſo he hath continued at our Intreaties, and that with the ſound Contentment and Satisfaction of the whole Country. And the ſaid Eſtates do yet again beſeech him, that it would pleaſe him to continue therein, promiſing him all Aid and Aſſiſtance, without ſparing any of the means they have, and alſo to yield unto him ready and willing Obedience. And becauſe they know the faithful Services that your Excellency hath yielded to theſe Countries, and thoſe alſo which they hope, in time to come, you will perform; they offer unto him, for the aſſurance of his Perſon, to maintain a Company of Horſemen for the Safeguard thereof, beſeeching him to accept it on the behalf, and at the offer of thoſe Perſons, which think themſelves much bound to the Preſervation thereof. And ſo much as toucheth the ſaid Eſtates (who think themſelves alſo charg'd by the ſaid Proſcription) they mind ſhortly in like ſort to juſtify themſelves, ſo far forth as they ſhall think it convenient. So concluded in the Aſſembly of my Lords the Eſtates General, in the Town of *Delft*, the 17*th* Day of *December*, in the Year of our Lord 1580.

By the expreſs Determination of the ſaid Eſtates.

Signed *J. Houfflin.*

An

An APOLOGY *or* DEFENCE *of my Lord the Prince of* Orange, *Count of* Nassau, *of* Catzenellenboghen, Dietz, Vianden, *&c. Burgrave of* Antwerp, *and Viscount of* Besanson, *Baron of* Breda, Diest, Grimbergh, Arlay, Nozeroy, *&c. Lord of* Chastelbellin, *&c. Lieutenant General in the* Low Countries, *and Governour of* Brabant, Holland, Zeland, Utrecht, *and* Frise, *and Admiral,* &c. *against the Proclamation and Edict publish'd by the King of* Spain; *by which he proscribeth the said Lord. Whereby shall appear the Slanders and false Accusations contain'd in the said Proscription.*

THis is the thing which I have always pray'd unto God for (my Lords) and desir'd with all my heart, that he would grant it me, from the time that I vow'd my Person, and all the means that I have in the World, for the recovering of your Liberty, and the safety of your Persons, Goods and Consciences: If, I say, I should at any time have prefer'd that which respecteth my self particularly, before your Health and Wealth generally, that I might in this behalf, bear an eternal Punishment, which I should have drawn upon my self, by mine own Good-will and Accord. But on the other side, if that which I have done heretofore, hath been by me attempted and taken in hand, only for the preservation of your Estate; and that I have born a great part of the burthen of this present War only for the common safeguard of the Country; and that the hatred conceiv'd by certain wicked persons, against the Country, against godly People and honourable Personages, having been for a certain time dissembl'd and cover'd in their hearts, cometh wholly, and that at once, to vomit and cast up it self upon me only, rather than upon so many good people, and especially upon the general Estate of the Commonwealth: Then, I say, this hath been the thing that I have greatly desir'd, that if my Good-will had been such towards you (my Lords) your Children, your Towns and Commonalties,

monalties, as indeed it hath been, I might one day carry away a solemn Testimony thereof, as well for the Peace of my own Conscience, as for the Defence of my own Honour, before all the People of the Earth, and before all Posterity. And now I do greatly rejoice my self, and yield immortal thanks unto our good God, and I have great occasion of Contentment and Quietness, seeing that he suffereth me to be made so rare, and so noble, and so excellent a Mark thereof, by this cruel and barbarous Proscription; yea such a one, as the like hath not been heard in these Countries, commended amongst all People and Nations for their singular and incredible Courtesy. For albeit that nothing be more to be wish'd of a Man, than the Race and Course of his Life to be sound, blessed, prosperous, and upright, without any dash, blow, stumbling, or any wicked incountring: notwithstanding if all things had fallen unto me as I would have wish'd, and that I had not incounter'd with the Hatred of the *Spanish* Nation and its Adherents, I should have lost the gain of this Testimony, which my very Enemies have yielded me, and which I take to be the most excellent Flower of Glory, that I had been able to have desir'd to have been crown'd with, before my death. For what in this world can be more acceptable, and that especially to him, who hath enterpris'd so great and excellent a Work, as is the Liberty of so good a People, oppress'd by so wicked People, than to be deadly hated of his Enemies; yea, such Enemies as are withal the Enemies of the Country; and by their own very mouth and confession to receive a sure Testimony of his Faithfulness towards his own People, and of Constancy against Tyrants and Disturbers of common Peace? Insomuch that the *Spaniards* and their Adherents, thinking indeed to do me displeasure, have done me many pleasures; as by this infamous Proscription they have thought to hurt me more than before, and yet they have made me more rejoice, and given me more Contentedness of mind. For I have not only thereby receiv'd that profit, but they have open'd unto me a more large field to defend my self, than I durst ever be bold to desire; that so I might cause all the world to know the Equity and Justice of my Enterprises, and by it leave unto my Posterity an Example of Virtue, meet to be follow'd by all those that would not dishonour the Nobility of their Ancestors, from whence we are descended, and of whom not so much as one only hath at any time favour'd Tyranny; but they have all loved the Liberty of the People, amongst whom they have born Office and had Authority.

I have no occasion to complain, that I had not had heretofore matter large enough to speak of my self, and to reprove the

the foul and heinous Faults of my Enemies; but neither would Shamefacedneſs ſuffer me my ſelf to ſing and ſet out my own Praiſes, which ſurely is a hard matter not to do, whatſoever Modeſty a man pretend in ſuch a matter: neither would publick Honeſty permit me to enlarge my ſelf to rehearſe the Faults of mine Enemies, liking much better to bury ſome part of their grievous Enterpriſes under ſilence, than in publiſhing them (albeit in truth) to caſt my ſelf into danger, to incur the Suſpicion to be a Slanderer.

Seeing then (my Lords) that in this Proſcription, the Queſtion is not only to tax my Perſon, and barbarouſly to make it a Prey; but alſo it is known to every one, that by my wounds they mind to wound the Commonwealth, and the State of all theſe Countries: As alſo this is no more now perform'd by ſmall defamatory Libels, made by People of no account, and whoſe Injuries done againſt me, ſhould no more move me, than the Tongue of ſome little Serpent, which a man muſt rather break in pieces with his foot, than endeavour to fight againſt it with Weapons. But that men of ſo great countenance, ſhould ſo far and ſo vilely debaſe their Greatneſs, as to buſy themſelves falſly to backbite and to ſlander; it hath ſeem'd unto me altogether neceſſary to ſpeak, to the end that our common Country (for which I am ready to give up my Life, as I have already loſt my Goods) may not feel herſelf damnify'd or hurt by my ſilence; and that on the other ſide, theſe famous Titles of ſo many Countries and Kingdoms, ſtretching themſelves ſo far as over *Africa* and *Aſia*, may not dazle the eyes of many, who judg the Affairs and Matters of this world rather by Shadows, Appearances, and outward Shows, than by Strength and Soundneſs of Reaſon. I know notwithſtanding all this, that thoſe who perſecute me, have in many points advantage againſt me, and principally in two points: the one is, that they make a ſhew and boaſting of their great Qualities and Eſtates, which do infinitely exceed my Condition: the other (which is alſo a natural thing to all men) willingly to open their ears to evil Speeches and Slanders. For I have oftentimes heard the moſt elegant of all the Poets to have very well ſaid, that there is not in any Feaſt any Sauce ſo ſweet to the Palate of the Mouth, as evil Speech and Backbiting is to the Ear: And on the other ſide, that nothing is heard ſo much againſt the heart, and with ſo great grief, as the Speech of him that praiſeth himſelf. Of theſe two points, that which bringeth pleaſure is given to my Enemy, and I have for my ſhare that which is hard and unpleaſant almoſt to the whole world. But I hope, that by means of your Favour and uſual Good

Will, neither the one or the other ſhall bring me any loſs or hurt; ſeeing ſo it is, that this long time ſince you have try'd that theſe great and famous States, if they be ſpotted and tainted with Tyranny, cannot gain much of free Hearts and noble Courages. And on the other ſide, knowing the ordinary trade and courſe of my Life, who love not more to blame another man, than to praiſe my ſelf; yet if it ſo fall out that I do either the one or the other, as it is a very hard thing not to do ſo (albeit that it ſhall be with the greateſt modeſty that I can) and if there be any thing that may ſeem not very ſeemly, it ſhall belong to you (my Lords) to attribute the ſame rather to the Neceſſity ſo to do (which mine Enemies have laid upon me) than to my Nature; and by that means to unburden me, and to lay the fault wholly upon their own Shameleſneſs and Importunity. And I will pray you (my Lords) to remember, that I am falſly accuſed to be *unthankful*, *unfaithful*, *an Heretick*, *an Hypocrite*, *like unto* Judas *and* Cain, *the Diſturber of the Country*, *Rebellious*, *a Stranger*, *an Enemy of Mankind*, *the publick Plague of the Chriſtian Commonwealth*, *a Traitor*, *and a wicked Perſon*, *that I am ſet out to be ſlain as a Beaſt*, *with reward to all Murderers*, *and to all Poiſoners which will attempt the ſame*; leaving you to judg (my Lords) whether it be poſſible to purge my ſelf from ſuch Slanders, without ripping up in ſome matters the ordinary courſe of my Life, and without exceeding my Cuſtom, in ſpeaking of my ſelf and other men.

In the mean while, I am ſo aſſur'd of the Juſtice of my Cauſe, and of my Soundneſs and Faithfulneſs towards you; and on the other ſide, of your Equity and Roundneſs, and of the knowledg that you have, how and after what ſort all things have paſs'd; that I demand no other thing of you, but only that you would judg and take notice of this matter, and determine thereof for your own Good, Health, and Preſervation, that which the Laws, Freedoms, Liberties, and Privileges of the Country command you, according to the Hope that the People have of your Wiſdom and Uprightneſs: which thing alſo I pray you to do, yea I earneſtly beſeech you, by all Holy and Sacred Things, and that by the Oath and Band which you bear to the Country; certainly aſſuring my ſelf, that as in many other matters I am leſs than mine Enemies, ſo I ſhall be in this behalf ſo much the more their Superior, as that by all means and crafts they have purpoſed to violate, break, and ſuppreſs your Laws, your Privileges, and Liberties: whereas on the other ſide, I have with a good Heart and all Faithfulneſs, imploy'd my ſelf to maintain and preſerve the ſame. And albeit (my Lords) that I am not in

ſuch

ſuch ſort an Enemy to my Renown and own good Name, but that I take delight and pleaſure (as alſo I hope my Actions and Deeds deſerve the ſame) to be in good account among all the Princes, Potentates, and Commonwealths of the world (excepting only amongſt the *Spaniards* and their Adherents, who perſevering in the purſuit of their Tyranny, I deſire not either Grace or Favour, or any Friendſhip at their hands) notwithſtanding ſeeing that you are the Men only in this matter, to whom I have taken an Oath, to whom alone I count my ſelf bound, who alone alſo have power to approve or improve my Acts and Deeds: I ſhall hold my ſelf very well ſatisfy'd, when on your part I ſhall have receiv'd a Teſtimony conformable and agreeable to my intents and purpoſes, which have always been join'd with your Good, Profit, and Service; and I ſhall patiently ſuffer other People and Nations to judg thereof according to their Paſſions and Affections, or rather (which thing alſo I moſt deſire) according to Equity, Right, and Juſtice; having firſt put off all Prejudice, and freed their own Underſtandings from the thick Clouds of theſe Greatneſſes and Glory, which might heretofore have ſomewhat dazled them.

Now if mine Enemies (my Lords) had come directly to the point and matter of the Proſcription, ſetting out the Reaſons upon which this barbarous Sentence is grounded (which Sentence indeed doth overmuch declare their mind very baſe, and much degenerating from the Virtue and Courage of their Anceſtors) I had not uſed likewiſe any Circuits or Compaſſings of words, but had at the very Entry declar'd both what my own Innocence is, and how weak and ruinous their Foundations and Groundworks are. But ſeeing that to make me odious, they have better liked to ſet, even at the entrance, before the eyes of all the world, a heap of Injuries, and in the courſe of this Speech, without purpoſe to interlace them, ſpeaking ſo ſhameleſly of me; I ſuppoſe it is neceſſary, yea indeed moſt juſt, that I anſwer to ſuch Slanders, to the end that ſome being mov'd or perſuaded by ſuch words, may not yet receive this my Defence with a Heart more eſtranged from me, than the Law allow'd amongſt People, and Juſtice it ſelf requireth.

As concerning then this heap of Injuries, by which I am ſo ſhameleſly rent in pieces, and which being taken out of this Proſcription, nothing ſhall remain therein but a Smoke. You ſee, my Lords, how plain and without painting Colours the Defence is that I uſe. If you know me to be ſuch a one as my Enemies publiſh me to be; if I carry either in my Body or in my Soul, ſuch Colours as the Forger of this Writing

 ſaith,

ſaith, that he hath painted me out withal (for, my Lords, ye have known me from my Youth, and I have not ſpent my Age elſewhere, but with you) ſhut immediately your ears, and refuſe to hear or underſtand, ſo much as one word coming out of my mouth. But if, on the other ſide, I have all my Life through been more honeſt, more ſound, more continent, and leſs covetous, than the Authors of this ſlanderous Writing, and than he who hath publiſh'd the ſame, to wit, the Prince of *Parma*, and his Predeceſſors, whoſe Facts are over-well known by Hiſtories: If, I ſay, you have known me and mine Anceſtors more virtuous People than theſe (for I ſpeak not as yet of the King) and their Anceſtors; then believe, that as they falſly ſlander at the very entrance, ſo they ſhall be no more meet to be believ'd in all the reſt of their ſhameleſs Accuſations. For to what end, I pray you, ſerveth this Recital of ſo many Injuries, but only to ſhew unto the world, that my Enemies are skilful to ſlander and backbite, and that he whom yet thro God's Goodneſs they have not been able to murder, neither by Poiſon nor Sword, nor yet to deceive by Promiſes, nor yet buſy him with vain and uncertain Hopes; they do at leaſt aſſay to wound him with the Venom of their Tongue, accuſtom'd even from their youth to ſo infamous an Occupation?

Of the good turns which ſome ſay the Ld Prince hath receiv'd of the Emperor Charles.

They at the beginning make a Recital of *many good Turns which I have receiv'd from the Emperor, in reſpect of the Succeſſion of my late Lord the Prince of* Orange, *my Couſin, that the King made me of his Order, Lieutenant General in the Government of* Holland, Zeland, Utrecht, *and* Burgundy, *and one of the Council of State.* To what end are theſe things alledg'd? To declare that I am greatly bound to the Houſe of *Spain*, and that I cannot ſhun this, but I muſt be condemn'd of Ingratitude: And moreover, that by reaſon of the Oath that I had taken, and of the Lands and Lordſhips that I hold in homage of the ſaid Lord, I am bound to procure the Profit and Advancement of his Affairs and Matters, thinking to make me likewiſe culpable and faulty of Unfaithfulneſs. Verily I confeſs and agree with the King, and the whole Houſe of *Spain*, that nothing is ſo much to be condemn'd in this world, as a Man defil'd with theſe two Spots and Stains, to wit, Unthankfulneſs and Unfaithfulneſs; and he that hath ſpoken theſe two Injuries to a Man, hath ſaid as much to him and againſt him, as if he had charg'd him with all the Accuſations and Slanders,

Accuſation of Ingratitude.

Accuſation of Unfaithfulneſs.

ders, that wiſe People and Fools, diſcreet and indiſcreet, could rake together: and ſpecially look, by how much a Lord is of a more noble and famous Houſe, by ſo much the more ſhall he be diſhonour'd, if he can be convinc'd of theſe or ſuch Faults. And I refuſe not to be hated of all the world, to be rooted out of the earth, and that the Memory of me and mine ſhould be wither'd for ever, if I may be found ſuch a one. But that ſhall be with this condition alſo, That if I declare, that there is no Prince in the world, more ungrat ful and unkind towards a poor Lord, than he that accus'd me, and would condemn me, is againſt me and mine: That the Unfaithfulneſs alſo which he hath uſed in reſpect of me (for I will not yet ſpeak of the open violating of his Faith towards the Country) is incredible, that then (I ſay) he alſo may be ſubject to the like Condition and State, and may be held for ſuch a one as he is, amongſt all living People, and all Poſterity to come: And I ſhall think the Puniſhment greater in his behalf, than he thinketh any in mine, as may appear by that which he maketh ſhew to ſeek for by this tragical Proſcription, which thro God's Grace and Goodneſs doth no more aſtoniſh me, than a vain Viſion or Dream. Firſt, my Lords, I proteſt, that the Remembrance and Memory of the Emperor *Charles*, ſhall always be in an honourable account with me, as well becauſe of his Acts, as that it pleas'd him to ſhew me ſo much Honour, as to have nouriſh'd me in his Chamber, by the ſpace of nine years; to whom alſo I yielded and perform'd moſt faithful and moſt willing Service. But if he, who by reaſon is moſt bound of all Men to maintain his Renown, come to accuſe me of Ingratitude and Unthankfulneſs, as that I have not acknowledg'd the good Turns, which he ſaith that I have receiv'd of the Emperor: I beſeech you to hold me excus'd, if being conſtrain'd for the Defence of my Innocence, I declare, in reſpect of good Turns alledg'd, that I have not receiv'd any at all from him, but that in doing him ſervice, I have receiv'd moſt great Loſſes, as you ſhall plainly underſtand, if it pleaſe you to hear me patiently.

An Anſwer to the Accuſation of Ingratitude.

Now then he ſaith, that in reſpect of the Succeſſion of the late Lord, the Prince *Rene* my Couſin, the Emperor handled me favourably. But wherein? Firſt, there was never any Lord as yet found ſo evil-adviſ'd, that would pretend Right againſt me for Succeſſion; inſomuch that if the Emperor hath not hinder'd me in that, what hath he done for me, that a Judg, the greateſt Enemy I could have, would not have done likewiſe? Was there yet any Party found ſo raſh, that durſt offer himſelf to ſpeak againſt it? And tho I had had adverſe Parties, if my Right were ſo clear and ſo well grounded, that nothing was ever yet hitherto able to be alledg'd againſt it, which was able to darken or to ſhake it: And that hereupon the Emperor had given forth a Decree for my Profit; what hath he done for me, but adminiſter'd me Juſtice, and would not take from me that, which the Laws, Reaſon, and very Nature it ſelf did give me? But if it pleaſe you (my Lords) to conſider the Nature and Quality of this Succeſſion, you ſhall find my Right and Title to have been ſuch, that the Emperor could not have depriv'd me of it, or taken it from me, without an extreme Injury, and a moſt manifeſt wrong.

The Succeſſion of Naſſau *and* Chaalons.

There were in the Succeſſion two principal Members or Branches: The firſt was that which came by our Houſe of *Naſſau*, which my Lords my Predeceſſors, the Grandfather and Great Grandfathers, Uncles by the Father's ſide, and Couſin German by the Father's ſide, enjoy'd; that is to ſay, the Goods which at this day belong unto me in *Brabant*, *Flanders*, *Holland*, and *Luxemburgh:* The other was, the Succeſſion of the Houſe of *Chaalons*. As concerning the Succeſſion of *Naſſau*, which Men commonly call *Breda*, becauſe it was the principal Place of my Lordſhips, and where I and my Predeceſſors had held our Chambers of Accounts, Council, and principal Inſtructions pertaining to us and ours; who was he that might moleſt me in that, unleſs it were my Lord my Father, who was the Uncle, and I the Couſin German, of my Lord the Prince *Rene*, the only Son of my Lord *Henry*, Count of *Naſſau*, my Uncle, and the Brother of my Lord my Father? But ſo far off is it that I was hinder'd in that Succeſſion by my ſaid Lord and Father, that he himſelf took pains to come and ſollicite the matter, that I might be put in poſſeſſion thereof: Neither was there ever found Man ſo ſhameleſs, that would ſet himſelf againſt it, but *Schoore* the Preſident or Judg, who in the Council ſaid, that the Son of an Heretick ought not to ſucceed, becauſe that my Lord my Father following the Examples of good Kings, as of *David*, *Joſias*, and others, had reform'd the Churches of his Countries, which he held and had in *Germany*, and had purg'd them from Abuſes, according to the Word of God, and that by the Permiſſion and Sufferance of the Emperor. And notwithſtanding all this, the Council ceaſeth not to give Advice, and to determine the matter according to Reaſon and Equity, as indeed it could not otherwiſe do, ſeeing that they had maintain'd my Lord the

the Count of *Kingstain* my Uncle in the Succession of the County of *Rochefort*, altho that he himself were a Protestant. Seeing then that this was in question (if that may be called a Question, which was in our own House, as whether the Succession aforesaid were adjudg'd to the Father or to the Son, pronounc'd notwithstanding always according to the Laws) none beside could justly pretend any Right thereto.

The Baronies of Burgundy *and of* Dauphine.

As concerning the House of *Chaalons*, first it cannot be said in respect of the Baronies, which I peaceably hold and possess in the Dutchy of *Burgundy*, and in *Dauphine*, of *Vienna*, that I am therefore bound to the Emperor, for he had not any more power therein, than I; all being under the power of the *French* King, who alike seiz'd the County of *Charolois*, appertaining to the Emperor, and my Baronies, when War was moved between them two; insomuch that I cannot otherwise be bound unto him therefore, but in this, that I was contain'd in the Treaty of Peace made at *Sessons*, which was the last Duty that he could yield to the Memory of my Lord my Cousin, who but a little while before died in the same Expedition, and that on Foot at the Siege of *Saint Disier*, after so many Deeds of Arms done for his Service. And less hath he been able to favour me in my Princedom of *Orange*, where he had nothing to see to, nor to do; no, neither he, nor any Prince whatsoever; I my self holding the same in a naked, bare, and absolute Sovereignty: which thing few other Lords are able to say. And there is no Prince, in respect of my said Princedom, whose Amity and good Grace I stand in need of, but the *French* King's, who I hope will not touch that which belongeth to a poor Prince, who is his most humble Servant; because Reason suffereth not that, beyond which Reason he will not go, and also because of the loyal and faithful Services that my Predecessors have done to the Crown of *France*, and the Dutchy of *Britany* (whereof he is descended, and is the Heir) with great Dangers of their Lives, great Expences, and infinite Travels.

Princedom of Orange.

There remaineth then that which belongeth unto me in the County of *Burgundy*, and whereof I have been so long time so unjustly and tyrannously spoil'd and dispossess'd; which by means of lone and borrowing, yieldeth unto me, even to this present time, two Millions at the least of loss. But I would in the first place, that they should remember, wherefore the Count

Possessions in the frank or free County.

County of *Burgundy* is call'd *frank* or *free*; to wit, amongst other Reasons, because that the Freedom and Liberty of the Lords, and such as hold Possessions in the said Country, is, That they have Power by Will to bequeathe and to dispose of their Goods, how and to whom they shall think good, without being either for their Wives or their Children, or other Heirs whatsoever, inforc'd otherwise to dispose of their Goods, but in such sort as shall be agreeable to their own Will and Pleasure. Seeing then that so it is, that my Lord the Prince *Rene*, mov'd of his own Good-will, did (without any other respect that he had to me, who was at that time a young Child, living in *Germany*, under the Power and Discipline of my Masters and Governors, and he having no other respect but that I was his Cousin-German) did, I say, appoint me his general Heir; which thing also he did, according to the Power that he had, even by the Laws and Customs of the Country: I say, that if I ought to yield Thanks to any, it is to the Memory of the said Lord Prince, who being the eldest of our House, meant also, that as I should succeed him in the Order of Age, so I should come in like sort to succeed him in his Goods and Possessions. I perceive not then as yet, even to this present time, that I am any thing at all bound for this Succession to the House of *Spain*; neither is there any Man in the World that can say it with Truth.

The Grant.

But the Emperor gave a Grant unto the said Lord Prince, by Will to bequeath it to whom he should think good; and by the Power of that Grant the Prince chose me for his Heir. This (my Lords) maketh very much for me, and can at no hand serve my Enemy's turn. For when the Emperor yielded to the Grant, he knew not who should be nominated Heir by the Prince; neither was it known of any Man, until the day of the opening the Will; which was done in the Presence of *Mary* the Queen, after the Death of the said Lord Prince: Insomuch that the Emperor consenting to the Grant, seeing that his Purpose was not to advance me, I do not think my self to be bound unto him, because the favour which was shew'd unto the Prince (which notwithstanding every mean person whatsoever may easily obtain, by ordinary Letters out of the Chancery) was not shew'd on my behalf, or in respect of me. Besides, to judg of the Grant by that which afterwards ensu'd thereupon, should be to judg against the Rules, which so oftentimes I have heard the Emperor repeat, who said, That Councils ought to be examin'd, lik'd or dislik'd, by the Causes, and not by the Effects. But let us put the Case, that he had not had

the

the Grant, yet nothing was appointed by the Will of my Lord the Prince *Rene*, but according to the Laws, as hath been before said.

But what will they answer, when, besides all these Reasons, I shall say unto them, That the Testament or Will of my Lord my Cousin is a Military Testament (which thing also they cannot gainsay nor darken) yea, and that made with very great Solemnity, ripe Judgment, and in good Season? Made, I say, and grounded by express Terms and Words upon this, That the said Lord Prince (who had before felt what were the Dangers of War, in so many Expeditions taken in hand for the Emperor's Service) was now on the way to go to a War so dangerous, and that with so great a Prince as King *Francis* was. And tho I be not a great Doctor in the Laws, yet so it is, that I do very well remember, that I have heard sundry learned Persons disputing of this matter in the Presence of my Lord my Father, who affirm'd, not only Military Testaments or Wills, but also little Scrips or Scrolls, to be of such value and force, according to the Laws of the Empire; that if a Man of War, or a Soldier, had before his Death made or given the least mark of his Will, yea the least sign that a Man can imagine or think of: As if he had but trac'd or drawn with his Blood upon his Target, his Name, whom he will institute, ordain and appoint to be his Heir; or with the print of his Halberd, or of his Sword, had written the same on the ground; that that Decree of his last Will is inviolable, and to be prefer'd before all other Ordinance, according to the antient Privileges of those who are honour'd with the War-like Chain or Collar. How much more then was this Privilege due to so valiant a Prince, and to so noble a Knight? For the Question is not here of some one simple Mark or other: but here is a Testament or Will well and advisedly made, and that not in haste, or by a simple Soldier wounded, and being ready to die, but by a vertuous Prince, and one worthy of immortal Honour, assisted by his Council, and somewhat forward in his way towards the Expedition; and the things bequeath'd not to a Stranger, but to his Cousin-German; and not to an importunate Flatterer, but to a young Child, being very far off from the Emperor's Army, which went to besiege St. *Disier*, and purpos'd to do the same even to *Paris*. But here is an Ordinance, I say, made not without the knowledg of the Emperor, but by his own Grant; yea, an Ordinance according to the Laws and Customs us'd in all places. This then being so strong, it was not in Man's power to reason against it, and much less to make it void, unless by some one way or other, which

Testament Military.

which ſhould have been over-tyrannous, and which (it may be) might have brought more hurt than profit, to the Renown and Credit of the Emperor, eſpecially if he had meant to offer any other thing than Reaſon. And as there have been amongſt my Predeceſſors ſome, who have indeed found means and ways to cauſe unjuſt and ungrateful perſons, who kept their Goods and Poſſeſſions from them, to yield them the ſame: So I hope, that God will yet ſhew me this Grace, to have a bleſſed Iſſue againſt him, who hath unjuſtly ſpoil'd me of my Goods, and would barbarouſly take from me my Life alſo. But ſeeing that I am inforc'd yet to ſpeak of the Succeſſion, I would fain have ſome tell me, whether the Emperor, ſuffering me to enjoy the Succeſſion, hath given it me of his own or no: For if I have receiv'd nothing from him, but that which before appertain'd to my Lord the Prince *Rene*, I perceive not how the King can in any manner upbraid me, that either he, or the Emperor his Father, have given me any thing, unleſs it be Liberality to give largely of another man's Goods.

But on the other ſide, albeit that at this preſent time, I ſay nothing of the Wrongs that have been done me in the ſaid County, in which I have ſuch Rights and Preheminences, and whereof they have ſpoil'd me, and whereof I ſpeak nothing at this time, leaving the Debate and Reaſon thereof, till Arms and Weapons ſhall have yielded me more Reaſon, than the Injuſtice of him that keepeth all from me. This I muſt needs ſpeak; I had no ſooner taken hold of the Succeſſion of the Seigniory or Lordſhip of *Chaſtell-bellin*, but I was even as ſoon ſpoil'd thereof, which is of ſo ſmall value, that at this preſent there are due unto me Three hundred and fifty thouſand Pounds of Arrearage by reaſon thereof. And this is the heap of Injuſtice that they charge me with, if I have done any. The Emperor was requeſted by my Lord my Father, that at the leaſt I might, according to the Laws, be firſt reſtor'd unto the Poſſeſſion, in which my Predeceſſor had been, but he would not ſuffer it: only he ſuffer'd me (being notwithſtanding ſpoil'd) to follow my Right by Juſtice and Law, wherein he left me at the leaſt ſome gap, becauſe he did not let me from debating my Right againſt him, when the Cauſe was call'd forth to the Parliament of *Malines*. But the Son (who notwithſtanding dares upbraid me with his good Turns) ſeeing the Cauſe ready to receive Judgment, the very ſelf-ſame Day that the Proceſs and Controverſy ſhould have been clear'd, and the Advice of the Preſident and Counſellors was already regiſter'd; and I had Advertiſement given me, to ſeek and

The Lordſhip of Chaſtel-bellin.

provide

provide for Silver for the Judges Fees: He, I ſay, forbid his Court to proceed any further, and left the Proceſs hanging upon the Hook or File, where it remaineth yet to this preſent. You ſee (my Lords) that Juſtice was well miniſter'd by him who had ſworn the ſame to me, and to the Barons of this Country. And theſe be the great Advantages and Profits that I have receiv'd from the Houſe of *Spain*: This is the Foundation and Ground-work of all their Reproaches; and upon this is this infamous Frame or Building of Proſcription ſtay'd and ſettl'd.

But if, on the other ſide, I ſhould come largely to lay out, how much the Houſe of *Spain* is bound to my Predeceſſors, (for concerning my ſelf I will as yet ſay nothing) I am afraid to enter into ſo great a Sea, which I cannot paſs over in many Months: Wherefore I will touch only the principal Matters, leaving unto you, my Lords, and to the Readers, the particular ſearching and finding out of the ſaid Bounds, in the Hiſtories and antient Records of this Country.

He that of the Houſe of *Auſtria*, firſt came into the *Low-Countries*, and that a long time after that my Predeceſſors held therein both Counties and Baronies, was the Emperor *Maximilian*, then Archduke of *Auſtria*. Now who knoweth not, that the Count *Engelbert*, my Great Uncle, was he who maintain'd and upheld the ſaid Emperor, imploying his Goods, his Life, and his Wit, for the Preſervation of him? Was it not the Count *Engelbert*, together with my Lord of *Romont*, that obtain'd the Victory of *Guinegaſte*, having by his Courage kept the Foot-men together, whenas the Horſemen had broken the Rank and Order (by means whereof, the great Conqueſt of King *Lewis* the Eleventh was ſtay'd and let, which thing dy'd afterwards) that aſſur'd *Maximilian*'s ſtate and condition? Was it not he, who upon his return out of Priſon in *France*, found *Maximilian* wonderfully troubl'd in *Flanders*, againſt my Lord of *Raveſtain*, and thoſe of *Bruges*, who alſo prevail'd ſo much by Arms and by Counſel, that a Truce and Concluſion was made? who was once again the Cauſe to uphold and maintain the ſaid Archduke, and who in like ſort caus'd the Accord made with the Inhabitants of *Bruges* to be maintain'd; whereof even yet at this day, there do remain notable Marks and Tokens, both of his Fidelity, and of the Thankfulneſs of the Inhabitants of *Bruges*. It is the very ſame *Engelbert* that ſubdu'd thoſe that rebel'd againſt him, about the Borders of the *Rhine*, and eſtabliſh'd the ſaid Emperor quiet in his Countries of *Oultremeuze*. That I may ſpeak no more of the dangerous Voyages attempted for the ſaid

My Lord Engelbert, *Count of* Naſſau.

Empe-

Emperor, as that Voyage into *Britain* for the Treaty of Marriage between the said Lord Archduke, and the Lady *Anne*, Heir of the Dutchy, and afterwards twice Queen of *France*: which matter he so well follow'd, that all was agreed, and further proceeding should have been made therein, saving that my Lord *John*, Prince of *Orange*, Father of my Lord *Philibert*, dash'd all, and procur'd the Marriage of the said Lady's Cousin-German with *Charles* the *French* King. And the Merits and Values of the said Lord Count, were in those Countries so great, that he was made Lieutenant-General throughout the *Low-Country*.

The said Count Lieutenant-General from the time of Duke Charles.

The Successor and Heir of the said Lord Count *Engelbert*, and of his Goods which he had in these Countries, was my Lord the Count *John* of *Nassau*, his Brother, and my Great Uncle; and after his Death, there succeeded him my Lord the Count *Henry* my Uncle, the eldest Son of the said Lord Count *John*, and his Heir, in the Goods and Possessions he had here in *Brabant*, *Luxenburg*, *Holland* and *Flanders*: and my Lord the Count *William* my Father, was his Heir, in the Goods and Possessions which he had in *Germany*.

My Lord Henry, *Count of* Nassau.

No Man can deny, that in his time there was any Lord in all these Countries, who labour'd more in the Service of the Emperor *Charles*, than he. And to the end I be not overlong in reciting that which is so well known, I will only in a word tell you, that it was he that put the Imperial Crown upon the Emperor's Head, having so earnestly follow'd this matter, even then, when the Emperor, in respect of his young Age, and by reason of his Absence (for he was in *Spain*) was not able to pursue the same, that he persuaded the Princes Electors to prefer the Emperor before the *French* King, who earnestly labour'd to obtain the said Election. And as every one knoweth, that this Imperial Crown was the Bridg, which afterwards made a passage to the Emperor to obtain so many Conquests; so none can deny, but that the acknowledgment thereof ought to be given to the said Lord Count.

But can any Man shew me at this present, so much as one Mark or Note of Recompence, or one only good Turn, that our Stock hath receiv'd from the House of *Spain*? Men may see in sundry places of these Countries, Pieces of Ordnance, with the Arms of *Hungary* upon them, which the King of *Hungary* gave to my Predecessors, in testimony and remembrance of that their vertue and strength, which they had imploy'd and shew'd in their Service against the *Turks*; certain of

which

which Pieces were violently taken from me, and carried away by the Duke of *Alva*, out of my House of *Breda*, when he play'd the Tyrant in this Country, and yet some of them remain there to this day. Which thing I put down to declare, that so long as these Pieces shall last, so long also shall the Notes and Marks of my Anceſtor's Vertue endure; and there shall remain also a notable Teſtimony, which the King of *Hungary* hath given them. But as my Predeceſſors have been so noble, and by the Grace of God, and the good Government of their things, were never yet poor; so they never yet demanded any thing of the Princes of these Countries, neither yet receiv'd any thing as a Free Gift: and yet I am sure, that the Imperial Crown at the leaſt, deserv'd some one Recompence or other. I confeſs, that the Succeſſion of *Chaalon*, and of the Princedom of *Orange*, was a great increase unto our House: but if we be bound to any for that, truly it is to the great King *Francis*, who gave in Marriage to the Lord mine Uncle, the Siſter of my Lord the Prince *Philibert*, the Daughter of my Lord the Prince *John*, who was nouriſh'd and brought up with Queen *Anne*, the Grandmother of the said Lord King, and whose Cousin the said Princeſs was.

And thus you here see (my Lords) the Honeſty and Good Behaviour of this Monarch of *France*. The Emperot got and receiv'd his Crown by the Pains and Travels of my Uncle: *Francis* the King (who knew all that the said Lord had done for his Competitor, that is, for him that sought to be Emperor as well as he) ceas'd not for all that to give him this Princeſs in Marriage, who was not the suppos'd Heir only, but the very Heir indeed of my Lord the Prince *Philibert*; the said King confeſſing, that he ought not to be displeas'd with him, who had conſtantly follow'd that part which he took upon him to follow: Insomuch that I may say of him, as the Hiſtoriographers of his time said, That it was an aſſur'd Teſtimony of a noble and liberal Heart in the Prince. And albeit, the Emperor had granted something to the Memory of my Lord the Prince *Rene*, and that (according to the laſt Appointment) he had granted some extraordinary Privilege and Benefit unto his Will: Should this, I beseech you, be a sufficient Recompence, yielded to so faithful and so excellent Services as he had perform'd, who was so valiant and so couragious a Prince, and had done for him so many Duties; having by Force of Arms, not only recover'd for the Emperor the Damage of a Battel loſt, but also having again conquer'd for him the Dutchy of *Gelderland*, and, in fine, he himself yielded up his Spirit at the Emperor's Feet, and that for his Service?

The Prince Rene.

What

What ſhall I need to ſpeak of Prince *Philibert*, who alone obtain'd for him *Lombardy*, and the Kingdom of *Naples*, and with my Lord the Duke of *Bourbon*, aſſur'd him of the State of *Rome*, and took the Pope for him as a Priſoner; and, to be ſhort, hath given him a heap of all Excellency and Bleſſedneſs? And yet now his Son will come, reproaching the Remembrance of ſuch Princes, and will ſay, That the Emperor hath executed Juſtice to their Succeſſor and Couſin. Now if they of *Naſſau* had not liv'd heretofore; if they of *Orange* had not done ſo many Deeds of Arms, before that the King was born, he would not have put ſo many Titles in the beginning of this Proſcription, by which he doth falſly and ſlanderouſly pronounce me a traitorous and wicked perſon, which as yet never hath fallen out, and I hope never ſhall fall out in any of my Race. But let them anſwer me, by whoſe Commandment the Cardinal of *Grandvelle* impoiſon'd the laſt *Maximilian* the Emperor, whilſt he was the King of the *Romans*: I know what he told me concerning that matter; and that afterwards he was ſo afraid of the King and the *Spaniards*, that he was altogether fearful, to make profeſſion of that Religion, which he knew notwithſtanding to be the beſt.

An Objection touching the Benefits and Honours beſtow'd by the King of Spain *upon the ſaid Lord Prince.*

He proceedeth and ſaith, *That he hath as it were in Order of Succeſſion, continu'd and increas'd more and more my State and Countenance, having made me of his Order, afterwards Lieutenant-General in the Government of* Holland, Zeland, Utrecht *and* Burgundy, *of his Council of State; and that he hath beſtow'd on me ſundry good Turns and Honours.* As concerning Benefits, I cannot at any hand confeſs it, unleſs a Man will call the great Expences that I have been at, as well for the Service of the Emperor, as of the King, Benefits. For they who liv'd at that time, and eſpecially in the King's time, may well remember, how the Court always was greatly accompanied with the Nobility of ſundry and divers Nations, and for the moſt part with the Nobility of *Germany*. Now, every one knoweth, that my Houſe lay always open, and that ordinarily I was to make the diſcharge and defraying of all Charges, bearing the Expences of the Court with a very little Allowance and Order, that was made on the King's behalf. Every one knoweth alſo, the great and exceſſive Expences, that I was of neceſſity to be at in the Voyage, in which both againſt my Will, and likewiſe againſt ſundry Proteſtations made to the Emperor, and alſo to the Queen of *Hungary*, I was conſtrain'd to carry the Crown of the Empire to *Ferdinando* the Emperor: and hereunto I was the more unwilling, becauſe it ſeem'd not rea-

ſonable

ſonable unto me that I ſhould carry from my Maſter's Head the Crown, which in times paſt had been ſet thereupon by my Predeceſſors. After this I made the Voyage into *France*, wherein I was ſent for one of the Pledges, appointed for the eſtabliſhment and execution of the Peace made at *Chaſteau* in *Cambreſis*, which brought unto me alſo great Expences and extream Charge; inſomuch that I can in theſe three Points (unto which add alſo the Charges that I was at in the laſt Wars, and eſpecially thoſe at the Town *Philippe* and *Charlemont*, where I was General) verily aſſure you, that I ſpent more than Fifteen hundred thouſand Florins: and yet notwithſtanding, the Chamber of Account or Exchequer, may eaſily aſſure Men of this, that I never had ſo much as one farthing in recompence for theſe Services; yea, that being Lieutenant-General of the Army, I did not receive for all Charges, but Three hundred Florins a month, which was not ſufficient to pay the Servants that pitch'd my Tents: Yea alſo, if the Queen of *Hungary* were yet alive, ſhe could yet remember, that which ſhe ſpake unto me, when the Emperor (perceiving himſelf to be in the greateſt extremity that ever he was, partly by the Power of Duke *Maurice*, and of *William* the Landgrave, and partly by the Power of the *French* King) made the Peace of *Paſſau*, with as great loſs to our Houſe, which ſerv'd him with our great Loſs and Charges, to preſerve the Empire for him, as it had before obtain'd the ſame for him. For, albeit in an open Aſſembly of the Empire, the Emperor being, by the Advice of the Electors, ſet in his Throne and Imperial Seat, had judg'd, and that by a definitive Sentence, that we ſhould have the County or Earldom of *Catzenellenboghen*, with more than two Millions of Florins for Arrearage; he made notwithſtanding his Peace with our loſs, putting by the Agreement of *Paſſau*, our adverſe Parties in the poſſeſſion thereof, without any recompence given to us. Which thing I propound not at this preſent, to ſtir up again any Contention, ſeeing that our Houſe hath ſince that time agreed with the moſt famous Houſe of the Landgraves of *Heſſe*, whoſe good Kinſmen and Servants we are; but to the end we may make the whole World to underſtand the great Benefits that we have receiv'd from the Houſe of *Spain*, and that every one may know who it is that, by good right, is to be tax'd for Ingratitude and Unkindneſs. And this (my Lords) is not the like firſt part that they have ſhew'd us: For my Lord the Prince *Rene*, being at that time the eldeſt of our Houſe, purſuing ſo courageouſly the War of *Cleveland*, the Emperor promis'd him, that he would never conclude Peace with the Duke of *Cleveland*, but upon condition,

The Peace of Paſſau.

tion, that he ſhould leave unto us peaceably the third part of the Dutchy of *Juliers*, which appertain'd unto us by the Succeſſion of my Lord, the Count *John* of *Naſſau*, my Great Uncle, and *Margaret* the Counteſs of *Juliers* and *Mark*: notwithſtanding, perceiving himſelf to be the Conqueror, he made Peace with him as pleas'd him, forgetting that this Victory was obtain'd to his hands, by the Travel and Valiantneſs of my ſaid Lord and Couſin.

Peace made with my Lord the Duke of Cleve.

The Honours.

As concerning the Honours, which he ſaith he hath done me, I will never deny, as I have ſaid heretofore, but that the Emperor did greatly honour me, whilſt he nouriſh'd me and made me of his Chamber, by the ſpace of nine years, and afterwards in my two firſt Wars, having appointed me and given me charge over all his Ordnance in theſe Countries.

My Lord the Prince made General of the Army at the Age of 21 years.

And albeit, that I was not then one and twenty years old, yea, tho I were abſent from the Court, at my Lordſhip of *Bueren*, notwithſtanding (the Duke of *Savoy* attempting a Voyage) the Emperor himſelf choſe me for General of the Army; albeit, that the Lords of the Council, yea and the Queen her ſelf, did preſent thereto ſundry other perſons, whoſe Capacity and Underſtanding was very great, as my Lords the Counts of *Boſſu*, of *Lalaing*, *Martin van Roſſem*, old Knights and Soldiers, and the Counts of *Arenbergh*, *Meghem*, and *Egmont*, who was twelve years elder than I.

All this notwithſtanding, albeit that no Man nam'd me (as afterwards they affirm'd to the Emperor) by reaſon of my Youth; yet ſo it was, that it pleas'd the Emperor to chuſe me, for the Reaſons which then he declar'd, and which the Queen of *Hungary*, inforcing me to take the Charge upon me, caus'd me afterwards to underſtand; which alſo I like better for this preſent time to conceal, than to declare, leſt I might ſeem over-much to praiſe, prize, and eſteem my ſelf. I ſay yet more, that it pleas'd the Emperor (my Lords) then to cauſe me to come from the Camp, when he declar'd unto you the Will and purpoſe that he had to make over his Kingdoms into the hands of his Son the King: and it pleas'd him yet further ſo much to honour me, that he would not perform this ſolemn Act in my abſence; yea, he preſented himſelf amongſt you in your Aſſembly, leaning upon me by reaſon of his infirmity; which thing ſundry at that time thought was a very great honour unto me. But be it ſo, that ſince that time the King had beſtow'd upon me ſome Honours, yet I

cannot

cannot ſee, how after any ſort he can prevail or get any thing thereby, ſeeing that contrary to all Right and Reaſon, yea contrary to his own Oath, he hath gone about to take them from me.

As concerning the Order, if the Emperor and the College or Company of the Knights thereof, have given me their Voice, I am no more bound to him therefore, than to other Knights, ſeeing it was neceſſary for him to allow of that which the College approv'd; even as he himſelf knoweth, that we, in the laſt Aſſembly of the Order held in theſe Countries, did, by Plurality of Voices, without his Advice, and againſt his Will, chuſe ſundry Knights of the Order, and caus'd them ſo to be receiv'd and accepted. But be it, that I were indebted to him therefore; yet ſo far off is it that he may reproach or upbraid me therewith, that on the other ſide, he himſelf is to be therefore greatly charg'd. He hath ſworn, and it is alſo contain'd in the Points that concern the Order, that the Knights of the Order ſhould be judg'd by their Brethren; that is, them of the ſame Order. Verily, it was never in the Power of Duke *Philip*, ſir-nam'd *the Good*, to inforce my Lord *John* of *Luxenburg* to forſake the Oath which he had made to the King of *England*, the ſaid Lord of *Luxenburg* committing the Determination of the Matter in Controverſy between them, to the College and Company of the Knights of the Orders. But the Brethren, which the King hath appointed to my Lords, the Counts of *Egmont* and of *Horn*, to the Marquis of *Bergues* and *Montigny* for their Tryal, were Porters, Pettifoggers, and People of no account; by which alſo he hath caus'd me to be condemn'd againſt all Order and Courſe of Law, even as I have heretofore proteſted, and have alledg'd the Inſufficiencys thereof in the Preſence of all *Europe*. Inſomuch that he himſelf having done againſt his own Oath, and againſt the Orders and Articles of the College or Company, he is at no hand to be heard in ſuch Reproaches as theſe are, wherein there are found the ingrav'd Marks of his own Oath being violated and broken. And beſide, if I ought to yield Thanks to any of the Order, for the Governments and other Dignities that I have, it muſt be to the Emperor, whoſe Mind it was, and who had ſo decreed the ſame, before he would depart out of this Country, having before known the Duties that I had perform'd, and my Faithfulneſs, namely, in reſpect of my Services yielded in the Government and Guiding of his Army, wherein I have for witneſs my Lord of *Nevers*, and the late my Lord of *Chaſtillon*, Admiral of *France*; who indeed made us afterwards to know, that he was our ad-

The Privileges of the Order.

verse Party: All which notwithstanding they gain'd nothing (thanks be to God) upon me; but I builded, in despite of their Beards, the Towns *Philippe* and *Charlemont*, albeit that the Plague did very strongly afflict our Army.

The Government of Burgundy.

As concerning the Government of *Burgundy* I can certainly assure all Men, that I have not receiv'd any thing, but that which my Predecessors have at all times maintain'd, as appertaining unto them by Inheritance; and indeed my Lady *Philibert* of *Luxenburg* (my Lord the Prince *Philibert* her Son being in *Italy*) caus'd the States of *Burgundy* to assemble and meet in the Town of *Nozeroy*. And because that some thought it not meet and convenient, because my said Town was upon one of the Frontiers of the County of *Burgundy*, she answer'd, That she meant to maintain the Possession of the Lords of the House of *Chaalon*, who were by Inheritance Governors of the County of *Burgundy*. But be it whatsoever it be, the Behavior of the King towards me do's sufficiently declare, that he cannot object unto me these Honours, which against all Rules of Honour he goeth about to take from me, together with my Life and Goods, having by Violence taken from me mine own Son, against all Law either of God or Man, yea, against the Privileges of the Country, which he sware to observe at his joyful entrance into it.

Counsellor of the Estate.

As concerning the Charge and Office of Counsellor of Estate, I have sufficiently enough declar'd in my Defence made heretofore, in the Year sixty-seven, that the Cardinal and others practis'd this matter, that I might be call'd thereto, thinking thereby to cloak and cover themselves only with my Authority before the People; and therefore I ought not to think my self bound unto them for this, because, that in doing this they sought not so much mine advantage, as their own profit. But if they be deceiv'd of their hope, they must attribute it, either to their own want of capacity, as not being able wisely enough to order and direct their Enterprizes, or else (which indeed is more true, for they did not want Wit and Understanding) that their Wickedness was grown so great, so apparent, and so palpable, that no Man was able to endure them, but that they were cast out of the Country as Venom or Poyson, yea as a publick Plague.

Now, forasmuch as they have not only directed themselves against my Person, accusing me of Unthankfulness and Unfaithfulness, but even as Rage and Madness doth equally bite the whole World, as well the innocent as he, whom Men judg culpable; so their Petulancy and Disorder hath been so great,

as

as that they have desir'd to touch and taint the Honour of my Wife, by the blame which they suppose to lay upon my last Marriage. I know not whether I may judg them more to be condemn'd in Impudence, or in Beastliness, whilst that these skilful Men, who boast themselves to be so good Painters, know not as yet to practise that Lesson, which is so often said and repeated by the meanest Scholars that be; that is, he that prepareth himself to speak Evil of another Man, ought to be exempted from all Crime and Fault. For this argueth great Impudence and Rashness, if Men know their notable Faults, and yet will notwithstanding pass over their own Thorns and Thistles, as if they were Roses: or if they know them not, what Beastliness and Blockishness doth this argue, not to perceive and see that, which every hour of a day offereth it self to their Eyes and Sight? They see every day before them an incestuous King, which is one only half degree, nigh unto *Jupiter*, the Husband of *Juno*, his own Sister; and yet they dare reproach me with a holy, an honest, and a lawful Marriage, made according to God's Word, and celebrated according to the Ordinances of the Church of God. And again, I am here inforc'd to beseech you (my Lords) not to think of me that, which as yet you have never seen in me; to wit, that by their wicked Speeches I am mov'd to lay open these abominable Boils, and to set before the Eyes of all the World, the benumbdness and hardness of such Consciences as these Men carry, but rather that it would please you to impute it to this Rage and desperate Madness of the Enemies of God, of the Enemies of all Christendom, and your Enemies particularly, who are inflam'd and set on fire against me, for no other reason but for this, That they know the great Care, Diligence and Faithfulness, that I have had for your Preservation. He then, that hath married his Niece, dare reproach unto me my Marriage; a Marriage, I say, very lawful, and according to God's Order.

Of the last Marriage of the said Lord Prince.

He, I say, dare upbraid me with my Marriage, who (to the end he might obtain such a Marriage) hath cruelly murder'd his own Wife, the Daughter and Sister of the Kings of *France*, (as I understand they have in *France* Informations and Instructions concerning that matter) yea, his lawful Wife, the Mother of two Daughters, the true Heirs of *Spain*, as I doubt not, but that the Crown of *France* (the which heretofore hath given the Crown of *Castile* to a Bastard, of whom *Philip* is descended, dispossessing a Tyrant thereof, tho he were lawfully born thereto) shall have no less Power to main-

The Murder of the Queen of Spain.

maintain and keep it for the true Heirs, if God, who is a just Judg, and never suffereth such Wickednesses unpunish'd, do not take Vengeance of it in his Life-time, depriving him of his Estate; which thing he hath most rightly deserv'd, altho he had not committed any other fault but this Incest, accompanied with so abominable a Murder. But you will say, he had a Dispensation for it. From whom? From the Pope of *Rome*, who is a God in Earth. Verily I believe that, for the God of Heaven would never have consented thereto. But what was the Ground-work and Foundation of this earthly, heavenly Dispensation? Forsooth this, that he must not leave so goodly a Kingdom without an Heir: and mark wherefore there was added to the former horrible Faults, a most cruel Murder, the Father unnaturally murdering his own Child and Heir, to the end that by that means the Pope might have a gap open to give a Dispensation for so execrable an Incest, abominable to God and Men. If therefore we say, that we do reject the Government of such an incestuous King, slayer of his Son, and the murderer of his Wife, who can justly accuse us therefore? How many Kings have there been, who have been banish'd and driven out of their Kingdoms, who had not committed such horrible Crimes? For as concerning *Don Charles* his Son, was he not to be, in all likelihood, our Lord and Master? And tho the Father could alledg against his Son a just Cause of Death, did not this Matter belong unto us, who had so great Interest therein, rather to judg thereof, than to three or four Friars and Inquisitors of *Spain?* But it may be, that he made Conscience to leave him for his Heir, whom he knew to be born in unlawful Marriage; because that at the time that he seem'd to marry the Daughter of *Portugal*, the Mother of *Don Charles*, he was married to the Lady *Isabella Osorius*, by whom also he had two or three Children; whereof the first was nam'd *Don Pedro*, and the second Son was nam'd *Don Bernardino*: of which Marriage *Rigomes*, the Prince of *Tuoli*, if he were living, could give a good and sufficient Testimony, for he was the procurer thereof; whereby also he obtain'd that great Credit, and so much Goodness in *Spain*, the which they do at this present unkindly suck and draw from his Widow, as it were with a Spunge. Now, if he have so well behav'd himself in that suppos'd Marriage, that Marriage also which he hath made with the Daughter of *France* hath not as yet been more happy. For beside the Murder of the Queen his Wife, it was also made noble by an Adultery excelling

The Murder of the Prince of Spain.

The Marriage of the K. of Spain *with the Lady* Isabella Osorius.

celling all other Adulteries, that is, that he kept ordinary and common Houshold with the Lady *Eufrasia*, who being become great with child by him, he inforc'd the Prince of *Ascoli* to marry her; and at the end of a certain time, the poor Prince (as the Ministers of the King's Tyranny say) died for grief, because that having too strong an Enemy, he was not able to remedy this, but that another man's Bastard should be his Heir. But they that speak more certainly of this matter, affirm, that he receiv'd a Morsel more easy to swallow down than to digest. And yet he, who is deck'd with a Crown of three such Marriages, being, I say, himself three times such a Husband, dare upbraid and reproach me with my Marriage.

The Adultery with the Lady Eufrasia.

But suppose that he were not so defiled, and that we might count him for a guiltless Person, yet for all that I fear him not, as tho he were able to reproach me with any fault; and thanks be to God, I have not done any thing, but very advisedly, and that by the Counsel of sundry honourable, wise, and discreet Persons. Neither is it needful, that he should travail much in that matter, wherein he hath no Interest, but to behold and see, and of which also I am not bound to yield him any account or reason. For as concerning my Wife that is dead, she was ally'd to Princes of very great Credit, to wise and honourable Princes, who, I doubt not, but they are fully satisfy'd in that behalf; and if I would enter further into that Discourse, I could easily make it appear unto him, that the most skilful of his Doctors condemn the same. As concerning the Marriage, by which I am ally'd at this present, albeit that they make the Zeal they would seem to have to the Traditions of the *Romish* Church, a Buckler and Defence for their Doings; yet so it is, that they shall never make any man in the world believe, that they are more zealous for that Church, than my Lord of *Montpensier*, my Lord my Father in Law, who maketh not profession of his Religion, as the Cardinal of *Grandville*, and such as he are, do; but as he thinketh, that his Conscience commandeth him. And notwithstanding, having well weigh'd that which is already past, and having heard the Advice of sundry principal Persons of the Court of Parliament at *Paris*, assembled at *Poictiers* for great and weighty Causes; having also heard the Advice of Bishops and Doctors, he hath found out at the last (as such is the truth indeed) that not only albeit there had been a Promise made on my Wife's behalf, yet it was none by Law, because it was made in the time under years, against the Canons and the Ordinances of *France*, and the Decrees of the High Courts, yea againſt the Canons of the Council *Trent*, to which my Enemy giveth and yieldeth ſo great Credit: but alſo that there was never any ſuch Promiſe made, but ſundry Proteſtations rather to the contrary, which is apparent by good Informations and Inſtructions made, even in the abſence of my Wife. And altho this were not ſo, yet ſo it is, that I am not ſo little converſant in good and holy Doctrine, but that I know that all theſe Bonds of Conſcience, laid upon us by men, cannot be any Bond at all before God. Neither can that hinder me which ſome ſay, that if ſuch a thing were permitted to a Lord of my countenance, yet at the leaſt the Pope ought to give a Diſpenſation for it. For it is long ſince (God be thank'd for it) that I know very well, of what value is this Traffick of the Diſpenſations from *Rome:* and ſo far off is it, that I will have recourſe unto him (who even unto this preſent hath procur'd againſt me all the miſchief he could) that I hope verily, that as this good Shepherd hath done to me and to all good People the worſt he could; ſo God will give me Grace to promote the Deſtruction of that myſtical Kingdom, which he hath ſet up in his Den of *Rome*, by means whereof he hath heretofore ruled over all the whole Earth, cauſing Princes and Kings to kiſs his Pantofle or Shoo, yea treading under his feet the Emperor.

That the ſaid Lord Prince is not a Stranger.

They object unto me alſo, that I am a Stranger, as if the Prince of *Parma* were a great Country-man, who was not born in this Country, nor hath not a farthing-worth of Goods here, nor any Title; who yet notwithſtanding doth with his White Staff command certain very evil-adviſed Perſons, and who yield themſelves obedient unto him, even as his poor Slaves. But what do they mean by the term *Stranger?* Verily ſuch a one as is born out of the Country. Then if that be ſo, he himſelf ſhall be a Stranger as well as I; for he was born in *Spain*, a Country which is naturally the Enemy of the *Low Country*; and I was born in *Germany*, a Country which is naturally a Friend and Fellow to this Country. They will anſwer, that he is a King; but I ſay to the contrary, that this Name of King is not allow'd of by me. Let him be a King in *Caſtile*, in *Arragon*, at *Naples*, amongſt the *Indians*, and in every place where he commandeth at his pleaſure; yea, let him be a King if he will in *Jeruſalem*, and a peaceable Governour in *Aſia* and *Africa*, yet for all that I will not acknowledg him in this Country for any any more than a Duke and a Count, whoſe Power is limited according to our Privileges, which he ſware to obſerve at his gladſom entrance. As concerning

cerning that which toucheth my ſelf, it is plain and manifeſt, that I and my Predeceſſors, from whom I am deſcended in the right Male Line, have begun more than two hundred Years ago to poſſeſs Countys and Baronies in the Countrys of *Luxemburg*, *Brabant*, *Flanders*, and *Holland*. For about the Year one thouſand three hundred and forty, my Lord the Count *Otho*, of whom I am deſcended in the ſeventh degree, and whoſe eldeſt Heir I am, marry'd the Counteſs of *Vianden*, and ſince that time the County of the ſaid *Vianden* departed not from our Houſe; but we have always peaceably enjoy'd the ſame, until ſuch time as the King had unjuſtly diſpoſſeſs'd me thereof. Afterwards, my Lord the Count *Englebert*, the firſt Son of the Son of the ſaid Count *Otho*, marry'd the Lady of *Leck* and *Breda*; from whom alſo I am in the right Male Line deſcended, and that in the fifth degree. May I therefore by any good Right be call'd a Stranger? And that I may ſay nothing at this preſent time of the Goods which I have in *Burgundy*, where I have (thanks be to God) a very good Portion, may I juſtly be counted a Stranger? And I leave it to you (my Lords) to judg, who know better our Laws than any People of the World, how our Anceſtors have uſed it time out of mind; and whether the Lords of *Raveſtain*, of *Luxemburg*, and of *St. Paul*, of *Nevers*, of *Eſtampes*, and other Lords, holding Counties and Baronies in this Country, were accounted for Strangers; and whether yet at this day, you account not as Naturals of the Country, all thoſe who poſſeſs ſuch Lordſhips, ſo that they will take part with theſe Countrys: And have we not for that indeed an expreſs Law amongſt us, as well in *Brabant* as in other places? For as concerning the Title of the Duke of *Brabant*, Count of *Flanders*, and others, which he beareth and braggeth of, albeit I confeſs theſe Dignities to be great, yet notwithſtanding, if he and his *Spaniards* know it not, they muſt learn this, that the Barons of *Brabant*, with the good Towns and Cities of the Country, have indeed (when the Dukes of *Brabant* have ſo far forgotten themſelves, that they have paſs'd the bounds of Reaſon) very well taught them, what was the Power of the Barons, and generally of the Eſtates of the Country of *Brabant*. Now it is manifeſt, that I am deſcended from ſuch Lords, as for ſundry Ages together have poſſeſs'd the principal Baronies and Lordſhips of *Brabant*, *Flanders*, *Holland*, and *Luxemburg*. But I hope, that my Lords the Eſtates have ſo well begun to declare unto him how much he hath fail'd in his Duty; and alſo that the ſaid Lords will hereafter take him forth ſo good a leſſon, that the poor People of *Sicilia*, *Calabria*, *Lombardy*, *Arragon*, and *Caſtile*, will learn

learn by our Example, that this Tyrant ought not to be fuffer'd on the earth ; yea that the poor People of *Granada* themfelves will know how they ought to handle fuch a Tyrant, who in the time of the War with the *Moors*, caus'd to be imprifon'd about an hundred Merchants, Inhabitants of *Granada*, all of them being Chriftians, of which the leaft was worth fifty thoufand Ducats; and afterwards by a Hurly Burly amongft the People, caus'd them to be flain; putting into his Coffers all the Goods of thofe poor People. And to be fhort, my Lords the Eftates (God aiding them) will teach them, how fuch muft be handled, that will falfify their Oaths made and given to fo good a People, at their joyful entranee.

But (my Lords) if I come to proceed further, and fhould begin largely to lay out before you the long time paft, in which my Predeceffors had not only their beginning here, but were alfo Lords, and poffefs'd great Goods, Titles, and Dignities in thefe Countries; I might fay unto you, that at the time that his Predeceffors were Counts of *Hapsburg*, and remain'd in *Swifferland*, mine were long time before Lords of the Country of *Gelderland*, whereof yet at this prefent there are remaining the Arms of our Houfe of *Naffau*, for the Arms of the Duke of *Gelderland*: And we have not (as it were paffing by it) kept the faid Country in poffeffion ; but after that my Lord the Count *Otho* had marry'd the Daughter and

The Counts of Naffau *were the Counts and Dukes of* Gelderland, *from the Year* 1039. *to the Year* 1350.

Heir of the *Voght* or Regent of *Gelderland* (for fo did Men name at thofe days the Lords of *Gelderland*) which continu'd from the Year 1039. until the Year 1350. my Predeceffors were the Lords, Counts, and Dukes of the Country of *Gelderland*, as yet even to this day men may behold the Monuments and Marks thereof. And I affure my felf, that fo far off is it, that he who calleth me a Stranger, can fhew fuch Marks that he had his Original and Beginning from thefe Countries; that, on the other fide, his Race in the faid time was altogether unknown in the faid Country.

And becaufe that he employeth himfelf to make a falfe, foolifh, and ridiculous Declaration, containing, as he faith, the Progrefs and Proceedings of my Enterprife; becaufe that many amongft you, when thefe matters were begun, were not of competent Age to underftand the fame, or elfe becaufe you having not then intermeddled in the publick Affairs, could not well fee how all things were directed and govern'd by the Craft of the Cardinal and his Favourers, and by the Council

Council coming out of *Spain*, which always meant to command this Country, as it had done others; *Spain* it ſelf being in their Opinion the Head of our Lordſhips, and we their Subjects and Slaves: I will for theſe cauſes recite unto you, how all things have been govern'd by theſe goodly Heads and wiſe Brains (who ſuppoſe that the reſt of the World are as Beaſts in reſpect of themſelves) until they had brought us within two fingers breadth of our Deſtruction, and of a miſerable Bondage, if God by his Providence had not watch'd over us, and deliver'd us from their cruel Counſels and bloody Hands.

The Inhabitants of the Low Countries *counted for the* Spaniards *Subjects and Slaves.*

And as I have here need, I do once again beſeech you (my Lords) of your patience to continue well and quietly to hear me, as you have already done: and I doubt not, but that as many among you have ſeen the whole, or elſe ſome part of my Acts and Behaviours, or elſe have underſtood it from their Fathers, and other good People, who have been Witneſſes thereof; ſo having heard me, ye will as eaſily judg my words to be as true, as thoſe of my Enemy are falſe and ſhameleſs. I will not (my Lords) recite unto you any thing of that, which I have ſeen in the Emperor's time, not becauſe I did not perceive ſundry matters ſet out and practis'd by the *Spaniards*, which I approv'd not as good, and of which I did not ſufficiently conceive, that the Diſeaſe in proceſs of time might grow ſo far, that in the end it ſhould be very neceſſary to uſe a ſtrong and powerful Medicine, and to purge the Country from theſe pernicious and hurtful *Spaniſh* Humours. But becauſe I was not able then, by reaſon of my Age, and the little Experience I had, to know the deep Malice of the *Spaniards* and their Adherents; I could hardly perſuade my ſelf, that we ſhould be inforc'd to bring a hot Iron to this Canker of *Spain*, or elſe to come ſo far as to root it out. But after that, together with my Age, I began to be of a more ſettled and ſound Judgment, I had indeed a contrary Opinion, and deliver'd the ſame to ſundry others, who never thought that the Rage and Cruelty of the *Spaniards* could proceed ſo far: for nothing fell out, by which I might have very particular knowledg of their cruel, covetous, and proud natural Diſpoſition, but I certainly and aſſuredly look'd for the ſame long time before. I will therefore let paſs that time, which cometh not alſo at any hand to be com-

The natural Diſpoſition of the Spaniards *was always cruel, but yet kept under for a time by the Wiſdom of* Charles *the Emperor.*

compar'd, in any manner of Diſorder and Tyranny, with that which hath ſince fallen out in the time of the King his Son: not that the *Spaniards* were then better than they are at this preſent; for amongſt the *Indies*, and in other places, where they commanded abſolutely, they yielded too evident a proof of their perverſe natural Diſpoſition, and tyrannous Affection and Will. But their Ambition and Pride was in ſome ſort reſtrain'd by the good Affection that the Emperor bare to the Subjects of this Country; and becauſe alſo that theſe Provinces were full of brave Lords, Wiſe and Valiant Men, favouring of their antient Nobility (and would to God they had Children like unto them) who ſerv'd in ſtead of a Bridle againſt their Inſolence, and of a Countermure againſt their Pride and Raſhneſs. I will then come to the time which enſu'd, becauſe alſo that he who was the Heir of the Goods, tho not of the Vertues of the Emperor, is he that cometh to aſſault me, after an Order more than barbarous and tyrannical.

The Emperor diſchargeth himſelf of his Kingdoms and Lordſhips, and committeth them to his Son.

The Emperor of moſt noble Memory, and the Queen *Mary*, ſeeing their Affairs and Buſineſſes ſo impair'd by the means of a clean contrary Iſſue of the Wars of *Germany* (which fell out otherwiſe than the Pope and the *Spaniards* had promis'd to themſelves) whilſt the *French* King was join'd in League with ſome of the chief Princes of *Germany*; his Majeſty, I ſay, was inforc'd to agree with his Enemy, his Affairs ſtanding in ſuch condition, that deſpairing of his Ability to keep his own Countries, he purpos'd to withdraw himſelf into *Spain*, and there to lead a private Life, after he had yielded up all his Kingdoms, Lands, and Lordſhips, and had laid them upon the Perſon of his Son. And albeit that the King, becauſe of the condition of his own Eſtate, had need to uphold his Subjects in good Will and Affection towards him (of which thing alſo he had moſt expreſs Commandment from his Father) ſeeing that of the Means and Valour that they had, there did wholly depend the Safeguard of the Country, and the Maintenance of his own Honour; yet, whether it were by reaſon of the Nouriſhment which he had in *Spain*, or by the Counſel of thoſe which then did, and even to this time have poſſeſs'd him, I know not, he hath always foſter'd in his heart a mind to make you ſubject to a certain ſimple and abſolute Bondage, which they call a full and intire Obedience, depriving you altogether of your antient Privileges and Liberties, that they may diſpoſe of you, your Wives, and your Children; and handle you, as his Officers

cers have done the poor *Indians*, or at leaſt as they do the People of *Calabria*, *Sicilia*, *Naples*, and *Milan*; whilſt they remember not, that theſe Countries are not Countries atchiev'd by Conqueſt, but come for the moſt part by the way of Patrimony, or elſe ſuch as willingly gave up themſelves unto his Predeceſſors under good and lawful Conditions. But it is likely that he did it by the Advice of ſuch as ſerv'd the Emperor his Father, and the King his great Uncle; inſtead of a Foundation, the better to rear up the Building of the Kingdoms and Lordſhips, to which we ſee the Houſe of *Auſtria* hath attain'd; it being at this day, without all controverſy, the greateſt and the mightieſt of all *Chriſtendom*.

The King's Heart always Enemy to theſe Countries.

And this Affection in him was but too much made manifeſt, immediately after the departure of the Emperor; as the Lords that then liv'd, did they yet remain amongſt us, could yield you ſufficient Teſtimony thereof. For even ſo ſoon as he was conſtrain'd to enter into War with the *French* King, conſidering the Power of his Enemy, and alſo the wiſe Advertiſements of the Emperor, if he had had but one only Spark of good and ſincere Affection towards theſe Countries, he ſhould at the leaſt have maintain'd his Subjects in good Devotion and Affection towards him. But in the midſt of his great Affairs (ſo diſorderly and unruly was the deſire he had to play the Tyrant) he gave forth a moſt plain and moſt certain Demonſtration of his evil Will. The Emperor, who (my Lords) knew better, than any Prince or Man in the World the arrogant and proud nature of the *Spaniards*, and it may be alſo the Inclination of the King his Son; and on the other ſide, the ſtate of this Country, and whatſoever might deſtroy and preſerve it; did ſeriouſly advertiſe his Son, that if he kept the Pride of *Spain*, he ſhould diligently foreſee that he would be the cauſe of the utter Ruin and Deſtruction of this Eſtate; which could not long ſuffer and endure this ſame proud Government, which the *Spaniards* exerciſe in every place where they can. And he gave him this Exhortation in the preſence of the late my Lord the Count of *Boſſu*, the Father of him that laſt deceas'd, and in my preſence alſo, and in the preſence of ſundry other Lords of his Chamber, of which ſome are yet at this day living. But neither the Authority and Commandment of his Father, nor the Profit of his own Affairs, nor Juſtice, nor his Oath (which yet notwithſtanding doth keep in the moſt barbarous Nations) were able in any thing to moderate and reſtrain the natural Diſpo-

The Emperor's Counſel given to the King his Son.

Diſpoſition and Affection that he had, to tyranniſe over us; but on the other ſide, as tho he had been above all Laws, Privileges, and Liberties of the Country, yea and above Equity and Juſtice it ſelf, he hath broken all Bonds, that he might outrage in all manner of irreconcilable Hatred and Cruelty.

The Aid call'd Novenale.

At the ſame time, you (my Lords) granted unto him the Aid which was call'd *Novenale*; by means of which Aid, and by the Valour and wiſe Government of the Lords and Nobles of this our Country, and of ſundry brave Lords and Soldiers of *Germany*, his Affairs were ſo well and ſo bleſſedly guided, that after the winning of two Battels, the taking of Towns, and Priſoners of great Calling, and that in great number alſo, he inforc'd his Enemy to accept a Peace, as unprofitable for the *French* King, as it was honourable and profitable for the King of *Spain*.

And if it be lawful for me to ſpeak any thing of my ſelf, if he have but one drop or ſpark of Gratitude and Kindneſs in him, he cannot deny, but that I was one of the principal Inſtruments and Means to cauſe him to come to ſo excellent and to ſo profitable a Peace; having privately treated thereof with my Lords the Conſtable, *Montmorency*, and the Marſhal of *St. Andrew*, at the inſtant requeſt of the King, who aſſur'd me, that the greateſt Service I could perform unto him in this world, was to make a Peace; and that he purpoſed to have it whatſoever it coſt him, becauſe he meant to go into *Spain*. But ſo far off was it, that either he or his Council, conſiſting of *Spaniards*, and of certain other Perſons of this Country (who always continued in hatred againſt you, your Liberty, and the whole Land) did take in good part either this ſo good an Aid, or the happy Execution that inſued thereof; that on the other ſide, they judg'd this Succour and Aid to be a Fault of high Treaſon againſt his Majeſty; and for the which you (and above all other the late Lord of *Lalaigne*) had incur'd, by good right, the Sentence of Puniſhment. And why ſo? Becauſe you (my Lords) would not agree to any thing, without the Aſſembly of the Eſtates General; and becauſe you meant to cut the Talents of theſe Harpies and Ravenors of *Barlemontes*, and ſuch-like, when you decreed that the Mony ſhould be diſtributed by your Commiſſioners, according to the Conditions propounded unto them. Behold indeed two great Faults! the one forſooth was, to demand a Meeting and an Aſſembly of the Eſtates.

The late Lord of Lalaigne, *and all the Eſtates appointed to death by the* Spaniards.

For

For inasmuch as it serveth for a Bridle and a Bar unto Tyranny, it is a crime so much the more hated of Tyrants (who are the Devourers of the People, and Enemies of their Subjects, and of their own Crown) as this noble Assembly is lov'd, honour'd, and reverenc'd of true Kings, true Princes, and such as are the good Fathers of the People, because it is indeed the true Foundation of an Estate, the Assurance of the Commonwealth, and the only Peace and Quietness of Princes. The other Fault will never be pardon'd; for these Biters of the People, living on the Blood of poor People, have so long time made account of their Thieveries and Sackings, that they suppose their Spoils to be as good, and as an assur'd Revenue (yet much more fruitful) as their Fields and Gardens; and dissembling the true Cause of the Mischief, which they hide from their Princes, they seek Pretexts and Clokes in flattering them, and in lying unto them, to harden and to set on fire their Hearts against their Subjects. I have seen (my Lords) their doings, I have heard their words, I have been a witness of their Advice, by which they adjudg'd all you to death, making no more account of you than of Beasts, if they had power to have murder'd you, as they do in the *Indies*, where they have miserably put to death more than twenty millions of People, and have made desolate and waste thirty times as much Land in quantity and greatness, as the *Low Country* is; with such horrible Excesses and Riots, that all the Barbaritys, Crueltys, and Tyrannys which have ever been committed, are but sport in respect of that which hath fallen out upon the poor *Indians*; which thing, even by their own Bishops and Doctors, hath been left in writing; and, to make the King without excuse before God and Men, the History thereof was dedicated to him by one of his own Subjects, in whom there remain'd, as it should seem, some Spark of Justice.

From that time then (my Lords) I and other Lords, and sundry of the best and wisest Personages, both of the Nobility and of the common People, thought it good to cause (if we could) the *Spaniards* to depart out of the Country; thinking indeed, that albeit there were yet remaining some corrupt Blood amongst us, as verily we see, there is more remaining than were meet, which did proceed from this infected Race of the Contagion of the Fathers, who serv'd at that time the Ambition of the *Spaniards*, and follow'd the Cardinal's businesses; yet notwithstanding, that the better number, and all the Lords of the greatest Credit and Countenance, would be Enemies to this *Spanish* Tyranny. But partly thro other Businesses, and partly by reason of my Voyage,

Voyage, and the going of ſome other Lords into *France*, whither we were ſent for Hoſtages, as alſo to be preſent at the *French* King's Daughter's Marriage; the Buſineſs it ſelf was interrupted, and the Performance thereof hinder'd. Now ſo far off is it (my Lords) that I will deny a great part of that which is ſet out againſt me, that I account it on the other ſide a great Praiſe for me, and will (it may ſo fall out) tell you more thereof than mine Enemies know; and the more that they ſhall write againſt me, and give a Teſtimony of their Fury and envious Heart againſt this Country, the more will I rejoice herein, that it hath pleas'd God to ſhew me this Grace, to be an Aider to cut off the courſe of this unmeaſurable Tyranny, and by that means alſo to have been an Aſſiſtant to the Manifeſtation and opening of the true Religion.

They ſay, *That from the time that the King turn'd his foot from theſe* Low Countries, *I have by ſiniſter Practices, Slights, and Subtilties, aſſay'd to get the Good Wills of the Malecontents, and of ſuch Perſons as have been greatly indebted, Haters of Juſtice, deſirous of Novelties, and ſpecially of thoſe that were ſuſpected to be of the Religion.* As concerning them that had the knowledg of the Religion, I confeſs that I never hated them. For ſeeing that from the Cradle I was nouriſh'd therein, and that my Lord my Father had liv'd and died therein, having driven out of his Lordſhips the Abuſes of the Church; who is he that will think it ſtrange, that if this Doctrine were after ſuch ſort ingraven in my Heart, and had taken ſuch deep root therein, it ſhould come in good time to bring forth her Fruits? For ſeeing that I was ſo long time brought up in the Emperor's Chamber, and being of the Age to bear Arms, I was even then preſently inwrap'd with great Charges in Armies: for theſe Reaſons I ſay (and conſidering the Scarcity of good Education that we had in reſpect of Religion) it was no marvel, tho I had then in my head the Feats of Chivalry, Hunting, and other Exerciſes which young Noblemen uſe, rather than thoſe things which concern'd my Salvation. And yet notwithſtanding I confeſs, that I have great occaſion to praiſe God, that he hath not ſuffer'd this holy Seed to be choked, which he himſelf hath ſown in me: And I ſay moreover, that I never liked of thoſe cruel Executions of Fire, of Sword, of Drownings, *&c.* which were at that time very common againſt thoſe of the Religion, as the Scrivener or Painter (for ſo he nameth himſelf) of this infamous Proſcription calleth them. Wherein, albeit he flatter, lye, and ſlander altogether in other places, he

The Love that the Ld Prince hath always born to them of the Religion.

he hath notwithſtanding ſpoken very well in this behalf, ſaying, thoſe whom he condemneth to be of the Religion, as indeed it only deſerveth this Name by Excellency; which thing alſo the Truth it ſelf hath wrung from his own mouth, ſo great is the Strength and Power of the ſame Truth. But whenas I being in *France*, had underſtood by King *Henry*'s own mouth, that the Duke of *Alva* ſought and ſpake of the means to root out all thoſe who were ſuſpected to be of the Religion in *France*, and in this Country, and throughout all *Chriſtendom*; and that the ſaid Lord King (who thought, that as I was one of the Commiſſioners for the Treaty of Peace, and had had Speech with him of ſuch great matters, ſo I was alſo of that Religion) had declar'd unto me the ground of the Counſel of the King of *Spain*, and of the Duke of *Alva*; I, to the end I might not be of leſs eſtimation with his Majeſty, as tho he would hide any thing from me, anſwer'd in ſuch ſort, that the ſaid Lord King was not deceiv'd in his Judgment: which alſo gave him occaſion ſufficiently enough to diſcourſe unto me ſo much, as that thereby I might underſtand the ground of the purpoſe of the Inquiſitors. I confeſs, that I was at that time in ſuch ſort mov'd with Pity and Compaſſion towards ſo many good People as were appointed to ſlaughter, and generally towards this whole Country, to which I was ſo much bound, and into which they meant to bring in an Inquiſition worſe and more cruel than that of *Spain*; yea that there were Nets laid to catch even the very Noblemen and the Lords of the Country, as well as the common People: Inſomuch that they whom the *Spaniards* and their Adherents were not able to ſupplant by any other way, might fall by this means into their hands; from whence it was impoſſible to eſcape; becauſe that a Man could behold nothing elſe, but a very Labyrinth, whereby they might be condemn'd to the fire. I ſeeing, I ſay, theſe things, do confeſs, that from that time forward I did earneſtly attempt to help to drive out of the Country this Vermin of the *Spaniards*; and I do not repent me that I have done it, but judg rather, that I and my Lords my Companions, who favour'd this ſo laudable an Enterpriſe, have done a Deed worthy of immortal Praiſe; and which indeed had been altogether accompliſh'd, and we by that means had atchiev'd the up-heap'd meaſure of Honour, if, after their gripes, we had as well

The Counſel of the King of Spain *and the Duke of* Alva, *to root out thoſe of the Religion, communicated to the* French *King, and by the ſaid King to the Lord Prince of* Orange.

The Enterpriſe of the Lords, to cauſe the Spaniards *to depart out of the Country.*

ſhut the gate againſt them, ſo that they might never after have enter'd in again upon us, as we have ſince found out, and had the means to purge the Country of them. And I ſay yet ſomewhat more unto you (my Lords) and I wiſh that the whole Council of *Spain*, yea that the whole World ſhould underſtand it, That if my Brethren and Companions of the Order, and of the Council of State, had liked rather to join their Counſels with mine, than to make ſo good and cheap a market of their own Lives, all of us would have employ'd our Bodies and Goods, that we might have hinder'd the Duke of *Alva* and the *Spaniards* from entring again into the Country. And I am yet even at this preſent content, that they ſhould underſtand, that as already one part of the Country is ſcour'd from this Filth, inſomuch that there is not therein any Remembrance thereof, except it be of their Bones: ſo I will not ceaſe, by the power of God, and by the aſſiſtance of your Favour (which I hope will never fail me) to imploy all the Power that I have with you (my Lords) to purge the whole Country in general from this Vermine, and to cauſe them and all their Adherents to paſs from hence over the Mountains, there to trouble their own Countries, if they will, and to ſuffer us to live here in peace and quiet poſſeſſion of Bodies, Goods, and Conſcience. Wherefore they are deceiv'd very much, when they think that I attempted this Work after their departure out of this Country. For I did it then when I was in *France*, even a hunting with the King, whilſt they themſelves were here; and I ceas'd not, till by the means of the late Lady of *Savoy*, of moſt noble Memory, I had obtain'd leave to come again into this Country, upon my Faith and Promiſe given to return again to *Rheims*, at the Coronation of King *Francis* the Second. And being come hither, I provok'd not Bankrupts, but good and honourable People, and of the chief and moſt Noble Perſonages of the Country, in the name of the Eſtates to demand that the *Spaniards* might be inforc'd to withdraw themſelves: which thing was at the laſt executed. And the Enemies may remember (if they will) who were thoſe good and honourable Perſonages, who brought them that moſt unpleaſant Meſſage; who when they ſhall ſhew themſelves, the Adverſarys ſhall know and confeſs their Impudences and Slanders.

The Requeſt preſented by the Nobility.

But as concerning that which they ſay, that I was the principal Author of the Supplication preſented and offer'd up, I will indeed tell you (my Lords) the whole matter; that is, That having once perceiv'd the Miſchief was grown ſo far, that there was not now any more queſtion of burning only the

poor

poor People, who suffer'd themselves to be cast into the fire, but that sundry of the best Nobility, and of the principal Men among the People, murmur'd thereat: I fearing some dangerous Issue, as I had seen before my eyes *France* it self to have endur'd a dangerous access of Civil War for the like occasion; and doubting lest we should be assail'd in this Country with the like Disease, which commonly hath most dangerous Accidents and Effects, more hard to heal than the Disease it self, as alas we do over-much see it at this day. Seeing, I say, these things, in respect of the Bond wherewith I was bound by reason of my Oath, and in respect of my Duty towards the Country, I besought my Lords my Brethren and Companions, the Knights and principal Counsellors of the State, to assemble together at *Hoochstraten*, with purpose to declare unto them the apparent Danger wherein the Country was; to wit, of falling into Civil War: and that this was the true and only mean to hinder it, That we, who by reason of our Degrees and Offices, had Authority in the Country, should take the matter into our hands, and so to use that Remedy, which we should find most agreeable for the Country's Good, and only to bring to pass, that the Cardinal's Creatures (who sought nothing but Effusion of Blood, Banishment, Confiscation of Goods, and to be short, Wounds and Murders) should not deal therein, which had brought an assured Destruction to the Country; but rather that those who thought it not meet, that men should burn others according to their accustom'd order, should not want a Guide, who might let and hinder him in his Attempts. And albeit I shew'd them very many Reasons, to cause them to condescend to my Counsel, and that I had added thereto (beside the Good Will which was between us) the Advice also of my Lord the Count of *Schwartzenbourg* my Brother in Law, and the Lord *George van Hol*, who had at that time very great credit with the Lords, for the evident and excellent Services which they had perform'd to these Countries: yet it was not in my power to obtain any thing; and this mutual sight one of another, did not profit me any whit at all, saving for a Testimony to all the world, that then seeing the Mischief afar off, which now we see present upon us, I did seek all the good means I could to prevent and turn away the same. But they of whom I have spoken, who thought these Persecutions hard, and who saw not, so long as they endur'd, any assured Rest in this Country (which thing always falleth out in such-like Affairs) began and labour'd to propound and broach new Enterprises; which by reason of the Offices I had, I found out a mean to discover: yet for all that, fearing left ſome moſt dangerous Event might enſue thereupon, and ſuppoſing that this way was the moſt mild, and very law-like or lawful, I confeſs I thought it not evil, that the Requeſt was preſented; which thing ſo far off is it that I mind to diſſemble or colour over, that I count it a moſt great Profit both for my own Honour and Reputation, and alſo for the Service of the King and the Country. For if the wiſe Counſellors of the King had been ſo well adviſed as to yield thereunto, there had not enſued ſo many Miſeries, by which there wanteth but a little that the whole Country had not been conſum'd. But if they deſire to know the true and the nigheſt cauſe of the ſaid Requeſt, and of that which follow'd thereupon, let them aſcribe it to their inſatiable Cruelty, which was not content with the intolerable Rigor of Placards and Licences; but following the Example of that Fool *Rehoboam*, and believing the Counſel of an unwiſe Woman, of a Cardinal the Pope's Creature, and other ſuch-like, they ſaid, *The Father hath corrected you with Rods, but the Son will chaſtiſe you with Scorpions.* Whereupon there was ſet out a moſt earneſt Purſuit, concerning the receiving of the new Biſhops, (who were ſet up but a little while before) that is to ſay, ſo many Tormentors, to burn the poor Chriſtians. Then were the Privileges trodden under feet, and by whom? Verily by a paſſionate Woman, who was yet notwithſtanding arm'd with the Vizard of a King's Power, and with the Treaſon, Perjuries, and Subtilties of a Cardinal. Behold, I ſay, the Anvil (my Lords) upon which was forg'd all the Evil that enſued, to wit, becauſe they yielded not (as requiſite and neceſſary it was) to the Requeſt preſented by the Nobility: wherein I know, and I may proteſt it before God and before you (my Lords) that I did not therein commit any thing againſt my Honour and my Oath; but I advertis'd the Dutcheſs, and all the Lords of the Council, of the great Inconveniences which afterwards fell out: inſomuch that all the Miſchief enſuing thereupon, muſt be imputed to themſelves. For ſo far off is it, that they would hearken to me, that they thought on the other ſide they had found a matter or mean fit for to execute that which they had a long time purpoſed and ſet before them; that is to ſay, that after they had deſtroy'd thoſe who were ſuſpected to be of the Religion, they might afterwards the more eaſily bring the reſt under a miſerable and intolerable Bondage. And not only were they admoniſh'd by me (my Lords) but alſo ſundry publick and particular Admonitions were given them by divers

The Dutcheſs of Parma *and the Card.* Grandville, *were the Cauſe of all the Miſchiefs in the* Low Countries.

divers others, both good People and Lovers of the Country, yea and Lovers of the King also more than he deserv'd; and they did in good time advertise him of the Danger to come, and what was the King's Duty by reason of his Oath, of his Obligations, or Bonds, and of the Conditions upon which he was receiv'd and admitted for Lord of these Countries, as also his Anceſtors were before him.

My Lord the Count of *Egmont* himſelf was ſent into *Spain*, to ſhew the ſaid Advertiſements unto the King's own Perſon; which notwithſtanding, ſo far was it from profiting any thing, that the ſaid Lord Count on the other ſide being deceiv'd, under the colour of the Word of a King (which afterwards coſt him very dear) brought Letters altogether contrary to that, which the King from his own mouth had given him in charge to ſpeak; inſomuch that then he was forced to confeſs, that I did before his Journy well foreſee what ſhould come thereof. And yet theſe Scholars of *Macchiavel* would here blear our eyes with theſe goodly ſhews of Loyalty, Fidelity, natural Clemency, and ſuch golden and glorious words; and yet notwithſtanding they make no difficulty to play with the Oaths which they take, and with the Words they give to Men of ſuch Quality and Countenance. Behold then the Authors, Promoters, and Framers of the Troubles, which have fallen out by reaſon of the firſt Requeſt or Supplication; and you have underſtood (my Lords) that this was the Counſel which I have given therein.

Touching my Ld the Count Lodowick *of* Naſſau.

As concerning that which they ſpeak of the late Lord the Count *Lodowick* my Brother, they ſhould do better to leave ſo good a Knight in Peace and unnamed, than to ſpeak of him, ſeeing that he was much more honeſt than they, and without compariſon a better Chriſtian; and I make no more of this, that they call him *Heretick*, than our Lord Jeſus Chriſt did, when as good People as our Enemies are, call'd him *Samaritan*.

Of the publick Aſſemblies of thoſe of the Religion.

As concerning Publick Preaching, which after their manner they call Heretical, you your ſelves (my Lords) do ſufficiently know, by whom and how they were brought in. And albeit that I had not at that time ſo much credit with them, as that they would demand my Advice therein, neither indeed did I ever counſel them; notwithſtanding the matters being come to ſuch terms, I confeſs I adviſed that the Dutcheſs of *Parma* ſhould yield unto them: Wherein if I have given ill Counſel, then that which follow'd afterwards, doth at the leaſt ſufficiently declare, whether thoſe

 who

who ſuppos'd my Counſel to be naught, have very well handled their Maſter's Affairs and Buſineſſes; but rather God hath manifeſtly ſhew'd, that albeit he do for a time correct his own Children, yet he never leaveth a Perjury, ſo well qualify'd and notorious, as that of the King and the Dutcheſs of *Parma* was, without grievouſly puniſhing it, to the end that all the world may know he ſaith not without cauſe, That he *will not hold him guiltleſs, who ſhall take his Name in vain.*

Concerning Images beaten down and overthrown.

As concerning the Beaters down of Images, and other Diſorders, I believe (my Lords) that there is none among you, but knoweth well enough, that ſuch Ways and Manners of doing pleaſe me not at all; and that many of them, who ſhould have aided and ſuſtain'd me, have on the other ſide with great injury torn me in pieces, becauſe I would never conſent that ſuch things ſhould be done, without ſome Ordinance and Decree of the Superiors and Governors.

Of the withdrawing of the Lord Prince into Germany.

They have no better Foundation, than ſuch as you have heard before. For this that they ſay, *That the Providence and wiſe Government of the Dutcheſs of* Parma *was ſo great, that I was inforced to depart out of the Country:* It may be, that they ſhould ſay ſomewhat, if they would ſay, That the Deceits of the Dutcheſs and her Perjuries were the cauſe thereof; or if they would ſpeak of the ſmall Reſolution, and of the over-great Eaſineſs to believe that ſome had, who look'd continually for the Hangmen and Tormentors, and of the over-great Affection which I and other great Lords had towards the King, who perſuaded my Lords of *Berghes* and of *Montigny* to go into *Spain*; ſuppoſing that for their good Services, and the Nobility of their Race, the King himſelf would be content to underſtand by their mouth, that which was neceſſary for the Preſervation of the Country, rather than to hear it by the *Spaniards:* But ſeeing that they were intreated in ſuch ſort as every one knoweth, I thought I had juſt occaſion more nighly to take heed unto my ſelf than before. If they would ſay theſe things were the Cauſe, they ſhould ſpeak ſome piece of the Truth. But I was reſolved a year before to depart and give up my Offices, as appeareth by Letters written with the King's own hand, and which I have alſo join'd to this preſent Writing; which doth ſufficiently ſet out the Falſhood of their Speech. And if any Man would know, why a year afterwards I withdrew my ſelf into *Germany*, my Defence publiſh'd in the Year Sixty Seven doth ſufficiently declare the Cauſes thereof; to wit,

ſpecially

ſpecially becauſe I would not conſent that the *Spaniſh* Inquiſition ſhould be receiv'd into my Governments. By reaſon whereof, I reſign'd them before into the hands of the ſaid Dutcheſs, with full purpoſe to live in Peace and Quietneſs with my Kinsfolks and Friends, looking when it would pleaſe God either to give the King better Counſel; or if he did yet wax worſe and worſe, when it would pleaſe God himſelf to open a gate to deliver this poor Country, which I ſaw plung'd into a bottomleſs Depth of Miſchiefs and Miſeries. For who can, without being wounded with wonderful grief, rehearſe the Baniſhments, the taking away of Goods, the Impriſonments, the Torments endur'd, the ſundry ſorts of horrible and miſerable Deaths, wherewith theſe bloody People (ſurmounting in Cruelty *Phalaris*, *Buſyris*, *Nero*, *Domitian*, and all Tyrants) have perſecuted the poor Subjects of this Country? And notwithſtanding theſe things, I ſeeing no mean to comfort them over this Miſery, did hold my ſelf peaceable and quiet.

The King of Spain *forced my Lord Prince, by all manner of Injuſtice, to take Arms.*

And becauſe, in this Proſcription, they ſay that I was at the leaſt offer'd it, whilſt that the laſt Treaty held at *Cologn* laſted; they ought to know, that they ſhould be contented with my voluntary Baniſhment, and not to purſue me any farther: ſeeing indeed I gave them to underſtand, by a Man of Countenance and Credit, who yet is living, that if they attempted to touch my Honour and my Goods, they would conſtrain me to take ſuch order for my Affairs as I might.

The Count of Bueren *taken in the Schools, and carried into* Spain, *againſt the Oath given and made at the King's joyful Entrance, and againſt the Privileges of* Brabant.

But, as mad People, after that they could not draw me by their honied and flattering words, the King alſo thinking to buſy me by over-honeſt Lettters, which yet notwithſtanding I did plainly perceive to be full of Deceit; they directed themſelves firſt to my young Son, a Child and a Scholar; and againſt the Privileges of the Univerſity, they took him violently from *Lovain*; yea, after the Exhortation and Declaration made by the Univerſity, that barbarous Fellow *Vergas* anſwer'd barbarouſly in falſe Latin: *Non curamus veſtros Privilegios*, We regard not your Privileges. After this they carried him out of *Brabant*, againſt the Privileges of the Country, and againſt the King's Oath, and they ſent him into *Spain*, that ſo they might remove him from me, who am his Father; and even unto this preſent, they keep this Innocent in hard and cruel Priſon:

 inſomuch

insomuch as if they had done me no other Injury, I should be unworthy not only of my Stock and the Name which I carry, but also of the Name of a Father, unless I did employ all the Wit and all the Means that God hath given me, to assay to deliver him out of this miserable Bondage, and to recover, if I could, such a Wrong. For I am not (my Lords) so unnatural, that I feel not the Affections of a Father; neither yet so wise, but that oftentimes the Grief of so long an Absence of my Son, doth present and offer it self to my Understanding. And yet they were not content, but against all order of Justice, they apprehended my Brethren, and pursued me with Summonings, Seizements of Goods; and thrust me on, even as it were by force, to attempt sundry things, whereof I my self never thought: they put the Process of me and my Companions (against the Articles of the Order, and against the Oath of the King, who was the chief thereof) into the hands of I know not what Porters and Pettifoggers, who were not meet to be Grooms or Pages to my Companions and me. They do degrade me: They do deprive me of my Goods: They do condemn me to Death. And is this any other thing than to free me from my Oaths? and to set me at liberty to come out, to assault my Enemy, by all the means that God shall give me?

Nota.

The unjust Proceedings against the Honour, the Life, and the Goods of the Lord Prince.

Behold then, how when I seek nothing but Quietness, they stir up Trouble; I seek Peace, and they provoke me to War. And what War? A War attempted to deliver my Child, to preserve my Life, to recover my Goods, and which is more dear than all, to defend my Honour. And yet I do not here propound unto you (my Lords) any thing of that which concerneth the common Cause, and belongeth unto the general State. This then (my Lords) is that which these Men slightly pass over, and under silence as it were, and which of set purpose they omit, as indeed not serving much for their purpose. If then, I not being the King's natural Subject (which thing also he himself saith) if I being absolv'd from mine Oaths by this unjust Proclamation and Sentence; if I having so just a Groundwork, by force to demand my Son and my Goods: If I say, I had driven him not only out of the *Low Country*, but also out of all his Lands and Lordships; yea and tho I did desire to make them mine own, seeing that against all Right and Equity, yea against his own Oath, he hath by force constrain'd me to attempt so necessary a War, even then when with all my power I did avoid it; and hath done me

all

all these Outrages, and that at the very self-same time, or a little after, when by his own Letters, written with his own hand, he yielded me so great and solemn a Testimony of Faithfulness, as no Man in the World could desire a greater, as appeareth by the Copy of the Letter hereafter inserted: who is he (the Premises being rightly consider'd) that can accuse me of any other fault than this, That I fram'd my self too much to the time, before that I would take Arms; and that I would not enjoy that which the Law of War, and of all Nations, yielded unto me; unto me, I say, who am born a free Lord, and who have this Honour to carry the Name and Title of an absolute Prince, albeit that my Princedom be not of any great length or largeness?

The justifying of the taking of Arms by my Lord the Prince.

But seeing that the special Foundation and Ground-work is this, That I have taken and born Arms against my Superior; I am likewise content to enter into this matter, where they shall find themselves to have as good Foundations as in other places. And in the first place, I would fain have them to tell me, by what Title King *Philip*, the Heir of the Bastard *Henry* of *Castile*, possesseth the Kingdom of *Castile*, and of *Leon?* For it is most manifest, that *Henry* his Predecessor was a Bastard, who rebell'd against the lawful Heir, who was his own Brother and Lord, whom also he slew with his own hand. What Right then or Title had this Bastard, being the King's great Grandfather? They answer, That *Don Pedro* was a Tyrant; and indeed I confess, that commonly they give him the Name of *Cruel*. But if by this Title *Philip* hold *Castile*, why doth he not perceive, that Men may by the same measure drive him out, that hath chased away others? And if there have never been any more cruel Tyrant, who hath more proudly, and with less consideration violated the Privileges of the Country, than *Philip* himself; shall not he be much more unworthy to bear, and to wear the Crown of *Castile*, than *Don Pedro?* For, at the least, *Don Pedro* was not an incestuous person, nor a slayer of his Son, nor a murderer of his Wife. And if some will say, that this concerneth me no whit at all, I am content to come yet somewhat more nigh, albeit that I have not purpos'd to stay my self upon that, which I shall presently speak unto you. But suppose that I did take up Arms against him, and that he were simply my Superior, and that I were born his Subject, (which yet is not so, even as he himself confesseth it) What should I do but that which his Predecessor had done, against the Emperor *Adolfus* of *Nassau*, his Superior? Every one that know-

Albert *Duke of* Austria *took Arms against* Adolfus *of* Nassau *the Emperor.*

knoweth ever so little in the Matters and Affairs of *Germany*, knoweth how *Albert* the first Duke of *Austria*, of that Name and Race (for before he bare the Title of the Count of *Hapsburg*) arm'd himself against the said Lord Emperor my Predecessor.

And albeit, it was God's Will that the said Emperor should die in the Battel; yet I know what the wisest Writers have judg'd thereof, albeit that *Gerrard*, then Bishop of *Maience*, the principal Author of that Conspiracy, meant to colour and darken the same. And verily, if a Man will somewhat more nighly look into the Story, he shall find, that this Faction was set up by Pope *Boniface* (of whom it is said, he enter'd into his Popedom as a Fox, he reign'd as a Lion, and dy'd as a Dog) because the Emperor would not acknowledg him for such a one as he said he was; and therefore he stir'd up against him *Albert*, who was already much displeas'd against him, because *Adolfus* was prefer'd before him in the Election to the Empire; and some Bishops also, over-much addicted to the Pope, did join themselves unto him, and aided him.

Pope Boniface *the 8th.*

But who is he that would willingly reverence so wicked a Man, who in his Jubilee, caus'd to be carried before him, in the manner of a Triumph, two Swords, causing him that carried one of them to cry, *O Christ, behold thy Vicar on Earth!* and the other to say, *O Peter, behold thy Successor!* And verily, having committed so wicked a Feat against the Emperor, and having *Albert* at his Command, he was purpos'd, for the like Consideration, to do as much to the *French* King, call'd *Philip the Fair*, giving his Kingdom to the said *Albert*, and caus'd him to be nam'd King of the *Romans*, and of the *French-men*. But he found the Priests of *France* less ready to serve him, and less able to help him, and the whole Kingdom stir'd up, by the learned Orations of Mr. *Peter Coignieres*, and a resolute King, who caus'd his Foolhood (for so the King call'd him in his Letters) to be taken at *Anania* by one of the Lords, and he the eldest of the noble House of *Colonnes*, and by a Gentleman of *Languedoc* nam'd *Nogaret*, who brought him to *Rome*; where also they put him to death, as he had most justly deserv'd the same. But, as I have said, I will not stay my self upon these Foundations, but mind to come to the mutual Bonds, which are between him and

King Philip *the Fair beginneth his Letter with these words,* Sciat fatuitas vestra; *That is, let your folly or foolhood know.*

and us. Let us then put the Caſe, that all this were neither ſo nor ſo. Doth not he very well know, that if he be Duke of *Brabant*, I, by reaſon of my Baronies, am one of the principal Members of *Brabant?* Doth he not know wherein he is bound to me, my Brethren and Companions, and the good Towns of the Country? Hath he forgotten upon what Conditions he keepeth this Eſtate? Doth he no longer remember his Oath? Or if he think upon it, doth he ſo little regard that which he hath promis'd to God and the Country, and that upon conditions tied to his Duke's Hat or Garland? It is not needful (my Lords) that I ſhould here ſet out unto you that which he hath promis'd us, before that we took any Oath unto him, for ſundry amongſt you know the ſame. But becauſe that others ſhall ſee this my Defence, I was very willing to call to your remembrance the ſum of his Oath. You know (my Lords) whereunto he is bound, and that it is not in his diſpoſition to do whatſoever he liketh of, as he doth in the *Indies*; for he cannot here amongſt us, by Violence inforce one of his Subjects only to any thing whatſoever, unleſs that the Cuſtom of the Bench of Juſtices, where they dwell, permit the ſame. He may not, by any Ordinance or Decree, alter or change, after any ſort whatſoever, the Eſtate of the Country. He muſt content himſelf with his ordinary and common Revenues; he may not cauſe to be levied, nor yet exact any Impoſitions or Taxes, without the Good-will and expreſs Conſent of the Country, and according to the Privileges thereof: He cannot bring Soldiers into the Country, without the conſent thereof: He may not touch nor deal with the decrying or imbaſing of Money, without the conſent of the Eſtates of the Country: He cannot cauſe any Subject to be apprehended, without Information made, and Knowledg firſt given, by the Magiſtrate of the place: Having any for a Priſoner, he cannot ſend him out of the Country. I beſeech you (my Lords) do you not ſee, hearing only this Sum rehears'd, if the Barons and Nobles of the Country, who by reaſon of the Preheminences, and the Charge of the Armies, do not oppoſe themſelves; I ſay, not only when theſe Articles are violated, but when they are tyrannouſly trodden under foot; and when not one Article, but all, and that not once, but a thouſand thouſand times, are broken and corrupted; not by the Duke only, but by barbarous and ſavage People: Do you not ſee, I ſay, that if the Nobles, according to their Oath and Bond, do not in-

The juſtifying of the taking of Arms by the Eſtates againſt Philip *Duke of* Brabant, *and Count of* Flanders.

The ſum of the Privileges of Brabant.

inforce the Duke to yield Equity and Justice to the Country, that they themselves should be condemn'd of Perjury, Unfaithfulness, and Rebellion against the Estates of the Country? And as concerning my self, I have indeed a particular Reason, and which toucheth me yet more nigh; that is, that contrary unto all the said Privileges, I was depriv'd of all my Goods, without observing any Form or Order of Justice therein. But that which fell out in the Person of my Son, the Count of *Bueren*, is so evident a Testimony of the Enemy's Disloyalty and Unfaithfulness, and of the Transgression or Breach of the Privileges, that no Man can, with any good reason, doubt why I have taken up Arms.

The first Army of the L. Prince.

And in that I was not able, at the first time, to take fast footing in the Country, which he upbraideth me withal, what new thing hath happen'd unto me, which hath not fallen out unto the greatest Captains of the World? Yea, even unto him himself, who hath so oftentimes enter'd, and that with so great and mighty Armies, into *Holland* and *Zeland*; and yet, with a handful of People, and by the Aid of my Lords the Estates of the said Provinces, he hath been shamefully driven out of the said Country, and that great Captain the Duke of *Alva* and his Successors, without having at this day, in the said Countries, one Foot of Land under his Disposition and Government, as, by your good Aid, I hope that shortly he shall not have any in all the rest of the Country. To be short, by his Oath he meaneth, that in the case of gain-standing him, we should be no longer bound unto him, neither yield him any Service or Obedience, as appeareth by the last Article. If then I be not bound unto him: If I owe him not any more Service or Obedience, why is he so rash as to say, that I have taken up Arms against my Lord? Certainly between all Lords and Vassals there is a mutual Bond; and this Saying of a certain Senator to a Consul, shall be always prais'd: *If thou do'st not account me for a Senator, I will not account thee for a Consul.* But between Vassals there is very great difference, some remaining, without comparison, in far greater liberty than othersome, as we are in *Brabant*; having such large Privileges and Rights, that we may freely make and give Grants in our Lands; so that, excepting the Homage which we owe, we cannot have any thing more than we have. And amongst other Rights and Privileges we have this, to stand our Dukes in that stead, that the *Ephori* at *Sparta* did their Kings; that is to say, to keep the Kingdom sure, in the Power of a good Prince, and to cause him to yield Equity, which stood against his Oath.

But

But ſome will ſay, that there is a Condition annex'd; that is, that we ſhall be ſo long freed from our Oath, till he have amended the fault. *An Objection.* But what if he will never amend it? If after the Emperor *Maximilian*, and the Princes of the Empire entreat him, and make interceſſion for us, that it would pleaſe him to unburden the Country: For a full Anſwer, ſome would ſay unto them, That they ſhould meddle with their own Matters; and that the King knoweth well enough how to govern his Subjects. If, after infinite Declarations, by the Meſſage of very noble Lords of this Country, we do requeſt him to do us Juſtice; he proudly rejects our Requeſts, and puts to Death the ſaid Lords, and ſuch as he can take, cauſeth them to paſs thorow the Hangman's hands, and purſue the reſt by all unworthy and cruel means: If he bring in upon us new Armies, utterly to deſtroy us; ſhall we tarry always looking for Mercy, until ſuch time as the *Spaniſh* Cruelty ſhall have cut off from us all hope of reſpite? But he will now amend the fault, and hath ſent means therefore by the Lord of *Selles*: alſo he hath diſallow'd the Duke of *Alva*. We ſhall ſee all theſe things in their Order. For the preſent, I am contented to declare, that by good Reaſon I have taken up Arms againſt him: Firſt, with the Eſtates of *Holland* and *Zeland*, and afterwards with you (my Lords) that he is forſworn againſt the whole Country, and in reſpect of me, againſt the Articles of the Rules of the Order, againſt the Privileges of *Brabant*, in taking away my Son, and carrying him into *Spain*, depriving me of my Goods and Dignities, having ſet me ſufficiently free from mine Oath towards him, and declaring at this preſent his very baſe Heart, and yet notwithſtanding tyrannous publiſhing this cruel and barbarous Proſcription as the heap of all Injuſtice and Unworthineſs. *Nota.*

Now (my Lords) ſince it hath pleas'd him to ſtretch out his Speech unto the Times which follow'd, I mind verily to enter thereinto alſo; and that the more willingly, becauſe that I have done nothing of that, whereof hereafter he accuſeth me: But firſt, by the Advice and Conſent of the Eſtates of *Holland* and *Zeland*, and afterwards by your Conſent in general; ſo that if there have been any fault committed, it ought not to be imputed to me, but rather I ſhould be greatly prais'd, becauſe I ſerv'd you ſo well and faithfully. I will then come to the Accuſations that remain, but it ſhall be with this condition (my Lords) that I may, as heretofore I have done, largely rehearſe, and plainly ſet out, that which he maliciouſly omitteth, to the end he might cover his wicked and cruel

cruel Heart; and yet neverthelefs ceafeth not to caufe it to be publifh'd by certain fmall flanderous Libels.

I have (my Lords) obferv'd, that all this Accufation, or ill Speech rather, which followeth afterwards, is divided into two parts: the one touching that, which was joyn'd with the coming of the Duke of *Alva*, and which follow'd thereupon, and efpecially concerning that, which after my coming into *Holland* and *Zeland*, was executed by my Government, and my Lords the Eftates of the faid Countries: The other is that which hath fallen out, fince that God opened your Eyes, by the means of the Pride and Outrages of the *Spaniards*; and that you publifh'd them, and their Adherents, for Rebels and Enemies to the Country, that fo you might at the laft deliver this poor Country from this accurfed Race. Wherefore I will follow the felf-fame Order. And firft, I render Thanks to God, that even by the very Silence of mine Enemy, you (my Lords) do know, and I hope that all the World fhall know, that I was not fo much as fufpected to have applied to mine own profit, fo much as one only penny of the publick Coin: For tho in other things, as you have already begun to fee, they have not ftuck at it, to fet out falfe Accufations, and to charge me with over-manifeft Slanders. Seeing alfo, that they do not object unto me the leaft fufpicion of Covetoufnefs, they do fufficiently thereby declare, not only how free I am from that fault, but alfo, albeit they themfelves be impudent, and in very deed my deadly Enemies; yet they durft never object againft me this fault, wherewith commonly the Governors of Provinces are either wrongfully or rightly charg'd. But, I thank God, I have long time ago learn'd, that he who governeth and commandeth others, ought above all things to have clean hands, and even void, if it may be, of all fufpicion; which was the Caufe, that even from my Youth I unburdned my felf of the Charge of the Treafures, which was moft gladly receiv'd and accepted of others. And albeit (my Lords) that it was at no hand needful, that I fhould make mention of thefe things, whilft I fpeak unto you, who know that I never had the handling of one only penny of the publick Treafure: And as concerning this, that it hath pleas'd you to appoint me fo much, as well in refpect of my Eftate, as in refpect of the extraordinary Charges of the War, you know how little I have receiv'd thereof; and of the means, which yet I have, how I have therewithal maintain'd and upheld fundry great Charges, fince that I entred into your Service: which I do not-

The Lord Prince was not fo much as fufpected by his Enemies to have touch'd or taken any of the Common Treafure.

notwithstanding not impute to the want of your Good-will towards me, but to the condition of the time wherein we live. But since that by the secret Confession of mine Enemy, I may have such an advantage; I mind not to pass it over under Silence, to the end I might cause certain small Serpents that are amongst us, to understand, that they ought to be asham'd to have spread abroad, either against their Conscience, or else thorow a certain extream Folly and Madness, that which the very Enemies, who have conspir'd against me and the Country, have as yet never been so impudent, as to object against me: perceiving indeed, that in propounding such a matter, the brightness of the Truth would discover the filthiness of their Life.

Seeing then, that they place me in so goodly a Field, as to declare not what I have done, but what the Estates of *Holland* and *Zeland* have done by my Aid and Service; I refuse not, even before you, my Lords, and before all the Men in the World, to enter into account with them: but also, since that you are the chiefest Judges of that which is done in this Country, it is more than reasonable that you should regard that which they have unjustly perform'd in all the other Provinces, whilst that my Lords, the Estates of *Holland*, *Zeland*, and I, did stand instead of Stays and Hinderances unto the Course of their Enterprizes and Attempts.

The Causes which mov'd the Lord Prince to come into Holland.

First they say, *That I practis'd to return into* Holland *and* Zeland. Tho it were so, what other thing did I, but that which my Duty requir'd? And if I did enter upon so good a Foundation, as I have heretofore laid out, into the Country with an Army; why should I have made any stay, to enter into that, which was of mine own Government, and whereunto I was more sworn and bound, and wherein I hold the chiefest degrees of Honour amongst the Nobility? But so far off was I from attempting such matters, that, on the other side, I am ready to shew the Letters both of the principal Governors of the Towns, and of the principal Towns themselves, by the which I was call'd, for the Deliverance of the Country against the Tyranny of the *Spaniards*, and namely of the Duke of *Alva*. And as concerning the Promises that I made at my entrance thereinto; and namely, that they say that I promis'd the said Estates to maintain them, if the Duke of *Alva* would press them with the tenth and twentieth Penny, shall never be found true; but this rather, that I came the second time, openly and in Arms, into the Country, that I might deliver it from that Tyranny which then oppress'd them, not only in respect of the tenth Penny, but

but for a thousand other sorts of more than barbarous Cruelty, and especially for the great Slaughter that the Duke of *Alva* then made of the poor Inhabitants of the said Countries. And as concerning what they say, that the Ecclesiastical *Romanists* were persecuted by me, and driven from their Goods, and another Religion brought in; I need, my Lords, for this no other defence, but that which you your selves know thereof; to wit, that the whole Change which ensu'd thereupon, was rather a work of God, than of Men. You know how often I have been accus'd, that I did over-coldly set my self against the Adversaries; that I did suffer them too much; and that I should be the cause of the Ruin of the Country, because I was over-slow to chase them away, and to root them out. And, when the Question was, to send some of them packing, you know the Duties that I perform'd, to the end that every one might live in peace, and one of them with another. But the Estates, which at the first thought it fit and profitable for the preservation of the Country, that both the one and the other Religion should be tolerated; learned afterwards, by the Insolences, Attempts and Treasons of the Enemies which were mingled amongst us; that their Estate was in danger of an unavoidable Ruin, unless they hinder'd the Exercise of the *Roman* Religion: and they perceiv'd, that those that made profession thereof, at least the Priests, had taken an Oath to the Pope, (as they do in every place where they come) which they prefer'd before the Oath they had made to the Country; insomuch, that in the Assembly of the Estates at *Leyden*, as also in the League of the Countries of *Holland* and *Zeland*, this Article was with one consent agreed upon. Neither could the Enemies be ignorant of these things, seeing that in the Treaty held at *Breda*, about the Question of Religion, (the Enemies there propounding this in their own behalf, that that change fell out by the guiding of certain particular persons) there was shew'd unto them the consent of all the Towns under their several Seals.

The Causes wherefore some of the Romish *Church withdrew themselves out of* Holland.

And now, I beseech you, what Bond could there remain unto me, seeing that they, unto whom I had made a promise, did not only discharge me thereof, but they themselves also did cut it in sunder, brake it, and made it of no force? And notwithstanding, I will leave it to the Judgment of the Wise, whether therein I have done well or ill. This only I say, that when such things were propounded, I desir'd them, that they would

The Establishment of one only Religion in Holland *and* Zeland; *and wherefore it was so done.*

would not proceed ſo far, and therefore much more when they did execute and perform the ſame: whereof not only my Lords of *Holland* and *Zeland*, but alſo certain troubleſome and way-ward perſons amongſt us (who alſo have ſpread abroad againſt me, in ſtrange Countries, their wicked Speeches) will give me ſo good a Teſtimony, that I hope I ſhall not need any great Defence againſt ſuch Accuſations, which being by me deny'd as falſe (for ſo they are indeed) I fear not that they ſhall be able to yield any proof thereof; leaving it to you (my Lords) to judg how fooliſh ſuch an Accuſation is, which may be beaten back with a ſimple denial; and yet notwithſtanding the greateſt part of the goodly Colours, wherewith this Painter boaſteth that he hath ſet me out, may be quite and clean defac'd with ſuch a Spunge only. If they will alledg, that yet notwithſtanding they who were driven out, have juſt occaſion to complain, becauſe that Promiſe was not kept with them: I anſwer, That albeit this is not directed againſt me; yet notwithſtanding, for the Defence of the Eſtates of *Holland* and *Zeland*, I will ſay thus much, That this Complaint ſhould have but a very ill Foundation, becauſe it is not reaſonable that any ſuch People ſhould enjoy a Privilege, by means of which they would deliver the Country into the Enemies hands. Their purpoſe was, to betray the Lives and the Goods of the Subjects; and not one, or two, or three Privileges only, but all the Franchiſes and Liberties, preſerv'd Time out of mind, and from Age to Age, by our Predeceſſors and Anceſtors.

They add withal, *That I have procur'd Liberty of Conſcience.* If they underſtand thereby, that I have made an open way to ſuch Impieties, as are commonly committed in the Houſe of the Prince of *Parma*, where *Atheiſm*, and other Vertues of *Rome*, are counted but ſport: I anſwer, That it is amongſt the Heirs of the Lord *Peter Lewn*, where a Man muſt ſeek and find ſuch Liberty, or rather unbridl'd Licence. But I will indeed confeſs, that the brightneſs of the Fires, wherein they have tormented ſo many poor Chriſtians, was never delightful or pleaſant to mine Eyes, as it hath rejoyc'd the ſight of the Duke of *Alva* and the *Spaniards*: and that I have always been of this mind, to wiſh and procure what I could, that the Perſecutions might ceaſe in the *Low-Countries*.

I will moreover confeſs unto you, to the end that the Enemies may know, that they have to do with one that ſpeaketh roundly, and without any Painting; to wit, that the King, when he departed out of *Zeland*, (which was the laſt place that he left in this Country) commanded me to put to death many godly and vertuous People that were ſuſpected to be of the Religion. Which thing I would not perform, but advertis'd them thereof, knowing indeed, that I could not do it with a good and safe Conscience, and that I was rather to obey God than Man. Let the *Spaniards* then speak what they themselves shall think good, I know that sundry Peoples and Nations, which are much better than they, who also have learn'd, that by Fire and Sword Men little or nothing prevail, would praise me, and approve my Fact.

But seeing that you (my Lords) together with the general Consent of the People, have since that time approv'd it, in condemning the Rigor of the Placards and Licenses, and in causing those cruel Executions to cease, I do no whit at all regard that which the *Spaniards* and their Adherents, do murmur and whisper concerning the same. Neither can I sufficiently wonder at their folly, when they are not asham'd to object unto me the Murderings of the People of their Church; seeing, that not only they know my natural disposition to be altogether estrang'd from such Violences; but also, that you and the whole World do very well know, that by Commandment and Appointment, some, in respect of such Outrages as these Men would charge me withal, were put to Death; and othersome, being of great Note, and noble Houses, were arrested by the principal Servants of my Houshold; and after that they had been kept Prisoners a long time, they were not deliver'd, but in respect of the House from whence they had the Honour to proceed and come; the long Imprisonment of their Persons being appointed unto them for the Punishment which they had deserv'd. But that which was done by my Charge and Appointment, is in such sort known to all the World, that they are not able, either to disguise or darken the same, only (as they have very well learn'd to speak Truth) that which I have done vertuously, they say, that I have feign'd that the thing did displease me. But who hath told them that I feign'd? Or who is he that hath reveal'd unto them so much of my Secrets? They see that which I have done; they cannot judg my Heart, neither is there any Man so malicious (except it be the Forger of this Writing, or some *Spaniard*) who ought not rather to give Judgment upon that which he seeth, than upon that which he maliciously and wickedly suspecteth.

They that ill intreated the Priests, were punish'd.

They cast also infinite Blames and Slanders upon our Religion, and they call us Hereticks: But it is such as a long time since they took upon them to prove it, and yet were never able to bring it to purpose or effect. And I say, that these

these Injuries (being like unto the Words of Women, provok'd and chaf'd with Choler) do not deserve any Answer, much less that Beastliness, to say, that I never trusted any, either Priest or Friar, unless he were married, and that I inforc'd them to marry. For, who is it that knoweth not, that without choice or discretion, they cast at my Head every thing that they find in the way, so great is their Fury, and their Passion so outragious and unmeasurable? And albeit that these things were true, as indeed they are not, neither yet reasonable (for we learn by our Religion, that Marriage ought to be free, and should not be either inforc'd or forbidden) yet so it is, that this fault should not be comparable with that Tyranny over Consciences, which hath forbidden Marriage to a great part of Christendom; against which Forbidding, not only the Eastern Churches oppos'd themselves, but also the Churches of *Germany* and *France*.

Concerning the Marriage of Priests.

But that (my Lords) which is greatly to be esteem'd in this Proscription, so true and well-grounded, is this, *That the King commanded not the Duke of* Alva *to impose the tenth and twentieth Penny, without the consent of the People.* If then the Duke of *Alva*, in a matter of so great importance, and which was the cause of the Death and Destruction of so many Thousands of Men, hath passed his Commission; what Punishment follow'd thereof? The Duke of *Alva*, for having perform'd to his own Son this Duty, to wit, that he might marry his Cousin, leaving another, whom under the colour of Marriage accomplish'd he had abus'd (even as *Rigomes* had before perform'd for the King, as before hath been declar'd) was cast into Prison, and put out of favour, and should not as yet have been deliver'd, if in all *Spain* they had been able to have found a Tyrant more fit to exercise Tyranny upon the poor *Portugals*, than he. He was then chastis'd for a small fault, and for such a great one he was honour'd, much made of, and fill'd with Rewards: And he that would press the King with the Death of my Lords of *Egmont* and of *Horn*, would say as much, and disallow again the Duke of *Alva* for it. Is not this a good mean, think ye, to discharge himself of all faults? But let them take which part they will, either the King commanded it, and then he cannot avoid the name of a Tyrant; or else he commanded it not; and yet for all that, the name of a Tyrant shall remain unto him, because he did not chastise and correct him, who, of his own private Authority, had usurp'd such a Tyranny upon a frank and free People, whereby it appeareth that he is culpable thereof. And albeit, that I have

Concerning the tenth and twentieth Penny.

have always esteem'd the Duke of *Alva* for the Enemy of the Country, and as one who hath willingly bath'd himself in our Blood, and in the Blood of all Christians, carrying closely a *Turkish* Heart within him: Yet so it is, that I have known him too well, and have been too too much practis'd to believe this, that he should be so sottish, and so presumptuous, as to dare to attempt to lay upon the People an Imposition of such consequence, and to pursue it so long time, and that by such extraordinary, yea and altogether insupportable means, to the Country, without good and sufficient Commandment directed unto him therefore; and that not once only, but sundry times. I beseech you (my Lords) to weigh this well, whether he, that in his own proper and private name, durst condemn, or favour them that did condemn, the Burgomaster of *Amsterdam*, in five and twenty thousand Florins of Amercement, because he set himself against the tenth Penny, was not well assur'd, and h d not sufficient discharge for the same from his Superior? Neither need we (my Lords) any other place than this, whereby to know the Frauds, Dissimulations and Crafts, wherewith the King hath so long a time led and deceiv'd us, and yet purposeth still to do, if we suffer him to wound us with the prick of his Tongue, or to astonish us with the Threatnings of his Armies. And because he will have the Bruit thereof sounded abroad, by reason of the Towns taken and surpriz'd in *Holland*; to wit, within these two, three, or four years, and that with more force than he hath fought against the *Turk* withal. I answer him, That, having the Advantages whereof he braggeth, he ought to consider, whether this tend not to his very great shame, that he is altogether driven out of that Country. And it standeth him not in any stead to alledg the Mutiny of the *Spaniards*: For a Governor, and especially such a one as had such great Means as he had, doth sufficiently bewray his Insufficiency and Unworthiness to command, when he is not able by such means to keep in Obedience his own Soldiers. On the other side, in excusing himself so foolishly, he seeth, whether he will or no, that he is inforc'd to confess, that I, and my Lords of *Holland* and *Zeland*, having slender means, as namely but four or five thousand Men, have broken his Attempts, and caus'd him to consume threescore thousand.

The shameful Losses of the Kingdom of Tunis and the Goulette.

And whilst (my Lords) he thus in this Country lost his Time, his Men and his Mony; he lost likewise, within two Months, the Kingdom of *Tunis* and the *Goulette*, with the greatest shame and confusion that ever any mighty Prince did, yea, tho he were driven

ven out of his own Land, albeit ſome would lay the fault hereof upon the Youth of *Don John*, and upon the Whoredom of the Cardinal. For whilſt he did ſo ill imploy his Forces here amongſt us, *Sinam Baſcha* took from him that Kingdom, and that Fortreſs, which Men ſuppos'd could never have been taken: and this he did in the ſight of *Spain* and of *Sicilia*, without that ever any of the King's ſide durſt ſo much as ſhew his Head to fight againſt him, or only to turn him aſide. And yet, if he had no regard to the good of Chriſtendom (which indeed he never had, as witneſſeth the painted League that he made, which alſo coſt the *Venetians* ſo much) nor reſpect to his own Honour, at leaſt the Memory and Name of the Emperor his Father (who did little or nothing regard all his notable Deeds and Feats of Arms, in reſpect of that Conqueſt) ought to have mov'd and thruſt him forward with a noble and earneſt deſire, wiſely to have maintain'd that which the Emperor his Father had ſo valiantly conquer'd for him and all Chriſtendom. But the Rage and Fury to deſtroy us, which carried him away, took both his Eyes from him, that he could not ſee that Evil; and his Underſtanding alſo, that he could not diſcern it; he loving over-much to make proof, rather of his Weakneſs againſt his own proper People, than of his Forces againſt the common and univerſal Enemy of Chriſtendom.

This (my Lords) is that which he objecteth againſt me, and which alſo fell out before our general Conjunction, and joyning together. Whereunto (it may be) it was not altogether neceſſary to anſwer, ſaving that it is requiſite, not only to ſatisfy you, but alſo to ſtop their mouths, and to make all the World to underſtand their Impudences and Slanders. For, if the Queſtion were but of that which concerneth your ſelves, and thoſe which heretofore were on our ſide, who have notwithſtanding very evilly, and without any cauſe, withdrawn themſelves from us: you, and thoſe with you, have heretofore ſufficiently declar'd, that you had a far better Opinion of me. For firſt, the Accord treated of by you, with me and my Lords of *Holland* and *Zeland* at *Gaunt*, hath ſufficiently juſtified me; ſeeing that if you had ſuppos'd me to be ſuch a one as this infamous Proſcription deſcribeth me, you neither would nor could have enter'd into Treaty with me: beſide, ſo many honourable Embaſſys, as you ſince that time have ſent unto me to *S. Gheertrudenburg*, and even yet to *Antwerp*, both to cauſe me to come into *Brabant*, and to cauſe me to come unto you to *Bruſſels*, that I might be aſſiſtant with you in Council; and alſo, that ye did honour me with the Title of Lieutenant-General: All theſe things, I ſay, do ſufficiently declare, what is is the Opinion and Judgment that ye have had of all these false and frivolous Accusations; which thing alone, I suppose, to be over-sufficient and strong to confute them.

But let us now see how, before that time, they on their behalfs govern'd themselves, with what Pride, Insolence and Disdain of our whole Nation. I will not repeat the Perjuries and Deceits of the Dutchess, nor of the King, in the behalf of my Lords the Counts of *Egmont* and *Horne*, nor the Baits and Allurements which they prepar'd for me; nor yet generally that which fell out before the Coming of the Duke of *Alva*, but that only which was done afterwards, until the time of our general Conjunction and joyning together; to the end, that as the Remembrance of the Mischiefs and Griefs past, shall bring unto you Pleasure and Contentment, and the same (as I hope) unto me, who with some delight have aided you therein: So that by the same you will more and more strengthen your selves in this Resolution, which is both Holy, and worthy of Immortal Praise, and which you also have taken upon you; that is, to oppose and set your selves against the *Spaniards* and their Adherents. Now, as well the said Duke of *Alva*, as those that Commanded under him and after him, have sufficiently made us to understand, what was at all times the Counsel of *Spain*; to wit, to root us out, and to bring us into Bondage. For, as *Hannibal*, even when he was but nine years old, did swear by the Altar of his Goddess, that he would be all his life long an Enemy to the *Romans*: So was this Duke of *Alva*, from his Childhood, nourish'd and brought up in an irreconcilable Hatred against this Country, which, by so much Blood as he hath spilt, could as yet never be satisfied; but so much the more hath he caus'd it to run out on every side, in all the Towns of this Country; yea, so far forth, that he hath caus'd to be put to death (which thing also he himself bragged of) eighteen thousand poor innocent Men and more, and that by the hands of the Hangman or Tormentor; and yet for all that, that cruel Lust of his could never be satisfied. So that if any would know, what are the Privy-Councils of *Spain*, what is the King's Good-will, and how much he loveth us, he shall find it all decipher'd and set out in the bloody Deeds of the Duke of *Alva*, as if it were set out before his Eyes, and lively painted in a Table of Painter's work. For there hath not been any kind of Dissimulation, Treason and Unfaithfulness, which he hath not us'd, that he might bring under his Subjection and Service the principal Lords of this Country, and that by Offers, Promises, and new Titles

The insupportable Pride of the Duke of Alva, *and other Officers being* Spaniards.

Titles of Honour bestow'd upon them. But the good and vertuous People that he could get into his hands, he hath cruelly put to death, without any respect either to their Innocency, or to the Privileges of the Country; and yet nothing was done, but by the King's Commandment. He committed the like against the Citizens and good Merchants, so proudly treading under feet our antient Liberties and Freedoms, yea every thing that was remaining amongst us of the Glory of our Ancestors, that it seem'd that he thought, that you were at no hand worthy to be reckon'd in the number of Men.

And where is it, that we can have a more certain and plain proof, and that so open, that it is as it were in the sight and beholding of all *Christendom*, concerning this matter; and withal, of his insupportable Contempt and Disdain of all these Countrys; than in that proud, ambitious, profane, heathenish, and withal foolish setting up of his own Image, in the midst of the Citadel at *Antwerp*; going impudently upon the Bellies of the Noblemen, of the Estates, and of all the People of this Country? Was not this, think you, a notable Monument of his Tyranny, and a Testimony of his Pride? What shall I need to speak of his Servants, and of all that Vermin which came out of *Spain*; who spake of us, not as it were of *Villacos* (as they use to say) or Villains, but even as it were of brute Beasts? You (my Lords) have, even as yet, your ears altogether beaten with such matters, and you are able to set out their Gestures, their Proceedings, their Words full of Boldness, of Pride, and of Contempt; also their unsupportable Acts, and how when they were within your Towns, with what Pride and Insolence they did command you. Wherefore if that be true which Wise Men report, that for the understanding of the natural Disposition of a Lord or Nobleman, Men must examine him by his Friends and Familiars; and for the knowledg of a Master, men must sift his Servants: you may (my Lords) by the Virtues of the Duke of *Alva*, his Master's principal Officer, and the Executor of all his Counsels, easily judg what good Affection and Will the King beareth you, who sent him to you to torment you: And also ye may know what ye ought to look for, unless ye provide for it in time, (as indeed ye ought) which thing also all the good People of this Land look for at your hands.

The profane and proud Erection of the Duke of Alva's *Image in the midst of the late Citadel at* Antwerp.

I will speak nothing of the Ravishings, Ransoms, and Exactions committed by the *Spaniards*, I will only stay my self

 upon

The Assembly of the Estates General ever refus'd.

upon the principal Point. Ye could never yet tell how to obtain a free Assembly of the Estates General; your Enemy very well knowing, that to hinder the calling together and meeting of them, was indeed to cut off by the foot the Tree of your Privileges, and utterly to dry up the Spring of your Liberty. For to what end serveth it the People, to have Privileges in fair Parchment, kept up in a Coffer, if by means of the Estates those Privileges be not maintain'd, and so Men feel the Effects thereof?

The King taketh a Dispensation from the Pope, for his Oath made at his joyful Entrance.

And indeed long time before, the King himself had receiv'd a Dispensation from the Pope for the Oath which he had made unto you, to keep your Privileges. Wherein he did not only violate and break his Faith, but also did over-easily, yea very hurtfully believe foolish Counsellors; whereby he too manifestly declar'd how great his own Wisdom was. For might he not very well understand, that counting himself free from the Oath which he had made to you, you also were freed and quit from your Oath towards him? Insomuch that he minding to be unburden'd of his Oath towards you, you ow'd not unto him any Obedience and Subjection. That I may at this time say nothing, but leave it unto others more exercis'd in such matters than I, to handle this Question, whether the Pope may justly vaunt that he hath any such Power and Authority, yea or no; and whether any thing in the world shall remain certain and sure, if Oaths so solemnly made, may, under such a pretext and cloke, be violated and broken. At the same time, Marriages made out of the Country were wholly forbidden, and that which was never practis'd was prohibited, to wit, that Youth might not go out of the Country to study in any other School of the world, but in that of *Rome*; and condemning by that means all other Schools (which is an over-great Arrogance) they did condemn (so unwary were they) even those of the Jesuits, without thinking any whit of them: and so (which is indeed the worst) they open'd a way to very Barbarousness. For as the meeting together of all manner of Learned Men, hath brought forth unto us in this Country, sundry Persons well qualify'd, who have greatly ennobled these Provinces; so this Interdiction and Forbidding, could not but in process of time cause a more than *Turkish* Ignorance: that I may speak nothing of this, that by that means they would make this Country

The Schools of all the World forbid, save that of Rome *only.*

subject

ſubject to ſuch Conditions as never were heard of. About the ſame time, the Council of *Trent* was publiſh'd; which Council hath ſeem'd, even to the *French*-men themſelves, ſo unjuſt, that even unto this day it could not as yet be publiſh'd in the Kingdom of *France*.

The publiſhing of the Council of Trent.

A little while before this time, there was eagerly purſu'd, and at the laſt obtain'd, the inſtalling of the new Biſhops, which had been ſo long time before debated, by reaſon of the Inconveniences which all wiſe People, and Lovers of the Country, and Haters of the tormenting of mens Conſciences, did foreſee would enſue thereupon. Which thing alſo I my ſelf writ even unto the King; that I may ſay nothing of the Warnings which I gave to the Dutcheſs, ſometime in open Council, and oftentimes elſewhere: All theſe their Purpoſes tending to no other end, but to ſet up the cruel Inquiſition of *Spain*, and to eſtabliſh the ſaid Biſhops, that they might ſerve inſtead of Inquiſitors, Burners of mens Bodies, and Tyrants over their Conſciences.

Biſhops newly made.

It is true, that at this day they deny that ever they meant to bring in this curſed Inquiſition; but if I bring forth unto them a man worthy of Credit, who was at that time a Penſioner of *Franck*, and who had the Rack twice ſhew'd him, to be tormented upon it, that he might confeſs who they were of the Lords of the ſaid *Franck*, which were purpos'd to refuſe the Inquiſition: Will they ſay that he is a forg'd Witneſs, who yet notwithſtanding is ſuch a one, as they are not able to object any thing againſt him? And beſide, if need were, I could find enough other plain and moſt manifeſt Proofs. There follow'd the moſt rigorous Placards and Licences, with expreſs Commandment to abate nothing of the old Rigour. And verily the Bull granted by the Pope, for the Erection of the ſaid Biſhops, doth plainly carry with it this much, that every Biſhop might give in his own Cathedral Church two Prebends: That every one of the Canons ſhould be bound to aſſiſt him in the matter of the Inquiſition: and that particularly two amongſt them ſhould actually and indeed be Inquiſitors. And as Princes or Tyrants, which poſſeſs new Kingdoms or Lordſhips, do lay upon them a Tribute, in ſign of their Victory; ſo the Duke of *Alva*, in teſtimony of his Conqueſt (for this was his common Speech, to wit, That theſe Countries appertain'd to the King, not in Title, or by Right or Patrimony, but as being conquer'd by Armour and Weapons) then I ſay, to the end he might make

Placards and Licences renew'd.

make all the world to understand the Condition whereon he had made subject this Country, laid upon the People, by the Commandment of his Master, the perpetual Payment of the tenth Penny, without the Consent of the Estates, without the Consent of the Towns and Provinces; and he resolv'd with himself and his People, to execute the same by Force. Insomuch that when he understood that certain noble and courageous Hearts began to be moved, even at the very hour (ye see, my Lords, how great God's Providence is) when he receiv'd News of the taking of the *Brill*; he was resolv'd to put to death the same night the principal Burgesses and Citizens of *Bruxelles*, because they set themselves against this Imposition, which was violently publish'd against their Privileges. The Hangman, named Mr. *Charles*, was commanded to have in a readiness seventeen Halters, and certain Ladders of ten or twelve foot high; the Soldiers were up in Arms; Don *Frederico* came into the House of *Viglius* the President, to conclude the Speech of the Condemnation, when these happy News, against the good Burgesses and Citizens of *Bruxelles*, arriv'd there. The Lieutenant of the *Amman* was one of them who should have been put to death, because he refus'd to execute those that set themselves against these Attempts; and indeed the Duke of *Alva* meant to keep the Promise with him, which but a little while before he had spoken unto him, saying, *By this* *, *if you will not do it, I will cause you to be hang'd.* And moreover, *the Judges are Knaves; it is sufficient that which I command you.* And I confess, that at the same time I being again provok'd, as well by sundry good People, as by mine own Oath, came again the second time with an Army; of which Expedition I will say no more at this time, because there is none amongst you, but he knoweth what then were, and what yet at this present are the Events and Successes thereof. Now then (my Lords) if it please you on the one side to consider that which the Duke of *Alva* did, before this War was begun; what just occasions he gave me, and the Estates of *Holland* and *Zeland*, to have recourse to Arms; and also that which he and the great Commandador did, until the day of the Revolting and Rebellion of the *Spaniards*: and on the other side, to weigh how since that time I have guided and govern'd my self, I refuse not to make ye Judges thereof, and to give ye leave to determine thereof, as ye your selves shall think con-

The Imposition of the tenth Penny, without the good Will and Consent of the Estates.

* *To wit, Beard, a Form of swearing used amongst the* Spaniards.

The second coming of the Ld Prince with an Army.

convenient and meet. But ye have already ſufficiently declar'd, what ye think thereof, by the Pacification of *Ghent*, by the Expulſion of *Don John*, and by ſo many Acts and Teſtimonies, that I need not to have any more; yea even by this, that ye would not diſcharge me of my Offices and Charges, altho that very oftentimes I requeſted the ſame of you.

Now I will come to that, which in the ſecond place they touch in their cruel Proſcription, to wit, that which follow'd the time wherein the *Spaniards* were declar'd Rebels, and Enemies to the Country.

The Pacification of Ghent, *and that the Enemies, both* Spaniards *and their Adherents, have broken the ſame againſt their Oath.*

About that time (my Lords) there was treated and concluded the Pacification of *Ghent*, and that with ſo great Joy and Contentment of the People, yea and of all the Provinces, both generally and particularly, that no Man alive is able to remember the like.

Every one may remember the mutual Promiſes of Friendſhip, of Intelligences, partaking of Counſel, and ſuch-like comprehended therein. But what? they themſelves, who afterwards did make manifeſt the great and inveterate Hatred of their Heart, and were notwithſtanding of the number of thoſe, who treated of the ſame matter with my Deputies, and with them of *Holland* and *Zeland*: they, I ſay, in treating thereof, did overthwartly caſt againſt it all the Hinderances that poſſibly they could, to cauſe it to die before it came to ripeneſs. Which thing, without controverſy, they had obtain'd, if they had not fear'd to fall into danger, and if the People, and all the Provinces (who perceiv'd, and ſaw before-hand afar off, that this Pacification ſhould be the Groundwork of their Liberty, and the Reſtitution of their antient Privileges) had not, as it were with one voice, inforc'd them to conclude the ſame. And becauſe (my Lords) oftentimes in this execrable Proſcription, and in their little, fooliſh, defamatory Libels, and ſecret Letters, they object unto me, that I have violated and broken the ſame; let us ſee how they, on their behalf, have maintain'd and kept it. It was no ſooner confirm'd by Oath, but that the Lord of *Hauſſi*, according to your Commandment, made ſundry Voyages into *Zeland* to me, that he might obtain Succour of Men and Munitions of War, for the Siege of the Caſtle of *Ghent*, one of the Neſts of the *Spaniſh* Cruelty; which thing he alſo obtain'd. But a certain Man, unworthy of his

Ld of Hauſſi *ſent to demand Succour of the Prince for the Siege of the Caſtle of* Ghent.

Stock,

Stock, and of his Country, could not contain himſelf, but at the ſame time began to vomit his Venom; charging with a Fault the ſaid Lord, in recompence of ſo good a Service, and which was indeed the very Gate to the Liberty of the Country and County of *Flanders*, and namely of the Town of *Ghent*, which had been ſo long time before kept under by Tyranny. And it was a matter of no great account to the ſaid *Sweveghen*, to the Count of *Rem*, *Mouqueron*, and others, that the *Spaniards*, yet all bloody with the Murder of *Antwerp*, and laden with the Spoils of good Burgeſſes and Citizens, ſhould perform a like Execution in the Town of *Ghent*, as they had committed in the moſt renown'd Town of *Antwerp*: which thing alſo they had executed and perform'd (as the Letters of *Rhoda* and others do ſufficiently prove) had not the ſaid Succour hinder'd them. Mark, I pray you, how that even then when the Trumpet ſounded to publiſh the Pacification of *Ghent*, theſe honeſt People began to break the ſame.

The coming of Don John.

Hereupon *Don John* arriv'd in theſe Countries; and albeit that mine Enemy would here play the Falſifier, and alter the matter, have not I yet the Letter ſign'd with the King's own Hand, and with the Hand of one of the Secretaries of his Eſtate, and ſeal'd with the Seal of his Arms, which yield Teſtimony concerning the Charge and Commiſſion given to *Don John*? Have not they been publiſh'd to all the world? Was there yet ever any *Spaniard* found, who durſt contend againſt him? By thoſe Letters we have known, That all the Difference between *Don John*, the Duke of *Alva*, and *Lewis* of *Requeſens*, was this, that he was more young and more fooliſh than the others, and that he could not ſo long time hide his Venom, diſſemble his Attempts, and with-hold his greedy Hands from the Deſire that he had to wet and waſh them in our Blood. I will not (my Lords) make in this place any recital of theſe matters unto you, for they are known unto little Children, and all the Land is as it were water'd therewith. Albeit then that theſe things were ſet out before the whole world; and albeit that the Pacifiers knew and underſtood the ſame: notwithſtanding the inveterate Hatred toward this poor People was ſo great (ſo much were they accuſtom'd to aid thoſe that oppreſs'd your Privileges, and to ſubject themſelves to Tyranny, was even become altogether natural unto them) that even like Horſe-Leaches, foaming with Rage, they themſelves came to lance themſelves upon the Thorn of the bloody Heart of *Don John*; and agreed with him againſt mine Advice, and the Advice of [illegible]em of *Holland* and *Zeland*, and againſt their own

Oath

Oath taken, against the Pacification of *Ghent*: and yet these Men dare object unto me the Pacification and mine Oath, as tho those Bands had been prepar'd only to shackle me, and my Lords of *Holland* and *Zeland*; whilst that those good and loyal Peacemakers having broken all Bond of Laws, of Loyalty, and of Fidelity, might have liberty to perpetrate, commit, and do whatsoever their disloyal Heart should put them in mind of. They will say, that they caus'd *Don John* to promise that the *Spaniards* should depart; as tho all our Agreement and League consisted in that only point. But before they had concluded with Don *John*, should not they have placed me in my Governments, and put me in possession of my Goods, and restor'd me my Son, who was one of the number of the Prisoners? Have they so much as only thought upon it, tho sundry amongst them were kin unto him? No whit at all indeed! For they had a far other Mark, which thing they themselves did sufficiently declare by so many Consultations as they made, that they might at the length find out a way to oppress me, and to bring *Holland* and *Zeland* under subjection; knowing that at the same time, I yet only, and the Estates of the said Countrys, were they who did openly hinder their pernicious Purposes; which was, to enter in the place of the *Spaniards*, to exercise the like Tyranny that the *Spaniards* had done; but yet, as they thought, with more Power and Authority, and also that they might remain in their own Countrys with greater Impunity. Concerning this matter, I refer my self to the Instructions given to those who came to treat with me at *St. Geertrudenberghe*; which I will bring to light, if need be thereof.

At the same time, they sent to the Queen of *England*, that they might fill her with all false matters against me, and also move her to arm her self against Me and my Lords the Estates of *Holland* and *Zeland*: But the Knowledg that she had of the Truth, and the singular Wisdom wherewith she is endued, made her to take a clean contrary Resolution than that which they hoped for. To be short, they devis'd as much as they could, to execute and perform against us, the same Practices that the *Spaniards* had done; and this (my Lords) was the Observation of the Pacification of *Ghent*, that these Men used even from the beginning. And as concerning the *Spaniards*, which *Don John* told them he had sent away, they saw (at the least if they had any Understanding, tho never so lttle, for they wanted not Advertisement and Intelligence) that some staid in *Luxemburg*, others in *Burgundy*, and others in *France*, under the Shadow of the

The Spaniards *licens'd by Don* John *to return.*

the Civil War, which was then rais'd up in *France*; looking only for their Watch-word, that they might return again in an instant, which they did. Beside this, they knew that Don *John* retain'd with him fourteen thousand *Germans*, of the old Soldiers, which he kept in garison in the principal Towns of the Country: that at *Malines* he treated with the said *Germans*: that he spake one thing to them, and another thing to you, my Lords: and did in the mean while take the Castle of *Antwerp* from the Power of the Duke of *Aerschot*, and of the Prince of *Chimay* his Son, and left it in the hands of *Treslon*. They saw, I say, these things, and did notwithstanding aid and favour him therein; and yet they will say that they kept the Pacification of *Ghent*. For as concerning that which my Enemies say, that Don *John* sware unto it, I confess further, that the King himself promis'd it should be observ'd; which maketh him so much the more vanquish'd, for even at the same time he commanded Don *John* to break it, as appeareth by his own Letters.

Fourteen thousand Lance-Knights left by Don John *in Garison in the principal Towns.*

And as concerning Don *John*, true it is, that he promis'd and sware to see the same perform'd, but that was with a Condition, which he spake of beforehand, in the presence even of some of your Deputies, which should be added, to wit, That it should be kept until such time as he repented him thereof, which Condition fell out very quickly afterward. For this young Man supposing that he was at the top of his Business, and that he had in his hands (by reason of the Garisons of *Germans*, and sundry Traitors taking part with them) the best Towns, took (but yet not without doing an unworthy Injury to the Queen of *Navarre*) the Castle of *Namur*, a Place which he thought was very fit and necessary for the *Spaniards* to go and come. But so soon as the Castle of *Antwerp* was by composition yielded up unto you, he found himself far from his reckoning, which caus'd him at one time to lose many Friends, who began even then to change their Copy and Countenance; and Don *John* was thereby made so perplex'd and doubtful, that he had no other Succour but this, That having corrupted some of your own Deputies, he might protract the time, and busy you with a painted Hope of Peace. And I would to God, that at that time ye (my Lords) had not been hinder'd by these good Observers of the Pacification of *Ghent*, from believing my Counsel; for then, by a very small Army, we might have been quit and rid of Don *John*, of his *Spaniards* and Adherents, and

Don John *swore to the Pacification of* Ghent.

and of so many Miseries as since have ensu'd. I would then yet further know in this place (my Lords) whether Don *John* did then keep this Pacification, and his Union so solemnly sworn (as they say) which he had made with these Favourers of the *Spaniards*. And why shall he come to upbraid me with the Pacification of *Ghent*, who yet hath caus'd this to be declar'd unto us by the Lord of *Selles*, that he would not keep it? Shall he, to my hurt, enjoy a Privilege, which he himself renounceth and forsaketh? And when we have said all, it is not with him that I and the Estates of *Holland* and *Zeland* have contracted and accorded, but it is with you, my Lords. Now if after so many Breaches of the Pacification, and that in such sundry sorts; if after that, contrary to the said Pacification, they have destroy'd the Towns, where they could exercise their Tyrannous Government, and the best Burgesses and Citizens therein, alledging against them false and wicked things: If then, I say, after these things you (my Lords) have judg'd, that for your own Security you ought to inlarge some of the Articles, yea and if need were, that you were minded altogether to break, cut in sunder, and revoke them: who is he that could accuse you therefore, if ye have used that which was your own, as you your selves thought it convenient for your own Profit, unless it be he, who would use his own Oath as a Net and Snare to catch you in? For as concerning that which they say, that the Change hath been on my behalf, tho that were true, yet so it is, that I am no more bound in respect of the Contractors with me, seeing that they have so many ways violated and broken the Contract it self: and seeing that on your part it was thought convenient that the Change should be made, you have as much Authority and Power to dispose thereof, as a Lord hath Right in his own Inheritance: For the Pacification was yours, which also you might use at your own pleasure and discretion.

But I have so often, both by Word and Writing declar'd, nothing to be broken on our parts, that I shall not need to bestow any more time to set out the same unto you; only I will confess this, that they of *Holland* and *Zeland* were indeed forbidden to innovate or change any thing in that Country: but that the other Estates might not in their Provinces, by some lawful Condition, provide for their Safety, it will never be found that there was yet any such Obligation or Bond: Which thing may be manifestly seen and known, by the reading of the eleventh and twelfth Articles. And indeed upon the making

Nothing was attempted by the Ld Prince, the Estates General, and those of the Religion, against the Pacification of Ghent.

ing of the ſaid Pacification, as one of thoſe who were Deputies on our ſide, did declare to ſome one principal Perſon of the other ſide, that ſome ſuch matter might fall out, and that therefore it was better to accord ſome Liberty for the poor Subjects of the Provinces, whoſe Cauſes they handled, and for whom they were to make agreement: ſo ſome other anſwer'd him again, that he needed not take care for ſuch matters, and that thoſe of *Brabant*, *Flanders*, and the other Countries, would not at any time demand a Change in the Matter of Religion. Now if they have been deceiv'd, what cauſe is there for them ſo furiouſly to direct themſelves againſt me? I give them alſo the ſame Anſwer, in reſpect of the Change which fell out in certain Towns of my Government; for I can indeed aſſure men before God, that I have not given any Advice or Conſent thereto; and that many things fell out there, as alſo in *Flanders*, which pleas'd me no whit at all. And I do defend it againſt them, that if there have been ſome Soldier-like Inſolence and Violence, that that was nothing but ſweet-ſmelling Roſes, in reſpect of the intolerable Exceſſes which they have committed: and alſo at the leaſt, that we have not had on our part any Infidelity, or Treaſon, or Intelligence with the *Spaniards*, as our Enemies on their part have had. For have not they, againſt their Faith and Promiſe, with an armed Power begun a War, and aſſaulted their Confederates, when we were within two days ready to give battel to our Enemies? Have not they purſu'd the Execution of their Complot and Conſpiracy againſt their Confederates, and declar'd their Defection and Falling away at that time, when the good Town of *Maeſtricht* was beſieg'd? Was there ever any deteſtable and vile Act in the world, and is it not this? Even then, when you your ſelves look'd for the Forces and Powers of your Confederates, to ſuccour a good Town beſieg'd, with which they were entred into a ſworn League; and of which they could not in any ſort either wrongfully or rightfully complain: even then I ſay, they did not only deſert and forſake you, but alſo made war upon you, and that as hotly and fiercely as they could.

The beginning of the War of the Malecontents, even then when they were ready within two days to drive away Don John.

The Hiſtories report, that *Suffetius* was drawn in pieces with four Horſes, becauſe he ſtir'd not, but only look'd on, when *Tullus Hoſtilius*, his Confederate, fought the Field. Then what Gibbets and what Puniſhments can a Man deviſe, which might be ſufficient to correct this Unfaithfulneſs and Treaſon?

And

And whoſe Treaſon? Thoſe (my Lords) who before had laid their hands upon the Count of *Mansfelt*, *Viglius*, *Fonc.* *Aſſonuille*, *Berti*, and others of the Council of Eſtate, then when I was not ſo ſtraitly bound unto them, as ſince I have been, and was not yet come into *Brabant*: Thoſe, I ſay, that by ſuch laying hands upon them, had given all the world to underſtand, what Judgments they had concerning the King and his Council: leaving it to you (my Lords) to judg, what great Conſideration there is in ſuch People, who, whilſt we make war, cannot foreſee that they ſharpen the Swords of thoſe whom they had taken Priſoners, to take away their own Heads. They will ſay, that I have not ſhew'd my ſelf to be an Enemy againſt them of our ſide, who have paſs'd the Bounds ſet them. Verily I have not approv'd the Exceſs of any; but do they think that I am ſo unwary, as that for to ſhew them a Pleaſure, I will open a gap to the Deſtruction of the Country, and ſo make *Eſcovedo* a Prophet? Have they ever heard that a wiſe Father, for the Contentment of his Enemy, would ſeek the Ruin of his Children? Nay, rather this is his Duty, to correct the Faults, and in amending of them, to labour the Preſervation of his Family and Houſhold.

The Continuance during the Siege of Maeſtricht.

But *Bours*, *Montigni*, and others, do not they know the Duties that I have perform'd, to eſtabliſh every thing in good order? Have they forgotten the Articles agreed upon, even ſuch as they themſelves demanded, and which ſince that time they have broken againſt their Oath? It is then Rage, Folly, Ambition, Hatred againſt the Religion, and Deſire to govern, which hath carry'd away their Hearts, and toſſed them as it were with madneſs; and which hath firſt moved them, and which ſince that time they have cover'd with the cloke of the Pacification of *Ghent*. For I know (my Lords) how hardly they were diſtreſs'd, and what labour they took to cloke and colour their Enterpriſe; and that a ſimple Captain, did in this Counſel open a Gap unto them, who was immediately follow'd.

I know, that ſundry will think it a new and ſtrange thing, that Children of ſo good a Houſe, iſſuing from ſuch Fathers, ſhould ſo far forget themſelves, as to heap up ſuch Reproaches upon their own Stock; yea ſome, I think, will think it unbelievable, that ever there could be found ſuch great Inconſtancy in them: and for my own part, I cannot chuſe but be greatly ſorry for it, by reaſon of the Good Will and Reverence which I have born to their Fathers, and the Deſire which I have had to ſee them advanc'd in all Virtue, Honour, and Reputation (which thing they might have attain'd, if they had only learn'd to forbear but a little while, and to bear some part of the Misery of their Country) and I would yet indeed desire, that they might become so wise, that by a good Repentance they might amend the Faults past. But to the end that I may not speak of sundry their particular Actions, which are not come to the sight of all the world, and are notwithstanding full of Inconstancy and Lightness; if we come to consider that which every one knoweth, and is laid out before the eyes of all the world, who is he that can sufficiently enough marvel at the Inconstancy and Vanity of their Resolutions? They served the Duke of *Alva*, and the great *Commandador*, as Servants or Pages, and they made war against me with all extremity. A little while afterwards they treated with me, and reconciled themselves; and then, lo, they were the *Spaniards* Enemies. Don *John* came, they follow him, they serve him, and they endeavour and practise my Destruction. Don *John* fail'd in his Enterprises concerning the Castle of *Antwerp*; incontinently they forsake him and call me: I was no sooner come, but contrary to their Oath, without communicating any thing thereof, either to you (my Lords) or to me, they call my Lord *Matthias* the Archduke. He being come, they saw that they could not come to their mark, therefore they left him, and without advertising him any thing at all thereof, they go to seek my Lord the Duke of *Anjou*: They bring him in, and they promise him wonderful things. They saw that they could not bring him to this point, to make him a Captain against you (my Lords) and them of the Religion; then they left him, and join'd themselves to the Prince of *Parma*. Are there any Waves of the Sea more inconstant? Is there any * *Euripus*, more uncertain than the Counsels of such People, who think that they are so highly set, so much lifted up, and so strengthned, that it should be lawful for them to play and dally in such sort with Princes of such Quality and Calling? If then they have done such things (as all the world knoweth they have) assure your selves, that there is nothing so light and vain, but they will enterprise and attempt it. And what could they have committed more grievous, than to have consented to this wicked Proscription, which was fram'd against his Head and Life, who had help'd and heal'd theirs, and caus'd their Possessions and Goods to be restor'd to the principal amongst them? And believe (my Lords) that this is not the last Prank they will

* *It is a part of the Sea, which flows seven times a day with such great force, that it carries Ships with full Sail against the Wind.*

will play. For tho they ſhould very quickly confeſs it (which thing I alſo deſire) yet ſhall you find them more than ten times change their Horſe and their Saddle, before this buſineſs be rid and ended.

As concerning that which they object againſt me, *That I cauſed my ſelf by Force and Tumult to be choſen Governour of* Brabant: You (my Lords) do remember, that I never ſpake to you thereof, and that I have not any manner of way provok'd you thereto. And on the contrary ſide, you remember, I hope, the great withſtanding that I uſed, and my plain Declarations and Speeches made to the contrary. And alſo as concerning the Eſtate of Lieutenant General, that I meant to have had the Advice and Conſent of the Governours which were in the Army, and which being very ſhortly after tumultuouſly and diſorderly handled (I mind not now to tell by whoſe fault) was ſent me, even as yet I have it, ſign'd with their own hands. Now, if ſome of the People prefer'd and promoted this Choice, and yet I neither intreated nor provoked them thereto, ſhall I miſlike them therefore? Nay, rather I am inforc'd to confeſs, that they were more wiſe, and better foreſeeing to the Affairs of this Country, than I was at that time. For they well underſtood, that if they ſhould leave the handling of the Matters, and the Adminiſtration of the publick Cauſe, in the hands of theſe Men, who were become *Spaniards* as it were, and ſo greatly affected towards them; it ſhould be nothing elſe, but to build upon the Quickſand, a Groundwork not ſtrong enough to ſet ſuch a Frame and Building upon. And it is as true that they ſay, That by the Tumults of *Ghent*, I was choſen Governour of *Flanders*; for it bewrayeth a very Ignorance of our Affairs: becauſe that the four Members or Parts of that Province did chuſe me, not once, but ſundry times; and that not while the Tumults laſted, but ſince that the Matters were well quieted: yea, and they themſelves have oftentimes ſued for it, both to me and to you, and yet at this preſent I have not minded to accept it.

The Eſtate of Governour of Brabant *and Lieutenant General.*

The Government of Flanders *offer'd to the Ld Prince, and yet not accepted.*

Alſo I do not (my Lords) think it reaſonable to anſwer concerning the Means and Mony levied by you; and which, according to your Advice, were govern'd under your Authority, by your Treaſurers, Commiſſioners, and Receivers, without that I, or any of mine, did ever ſee penny thereof. But if any muſt

Of the Monys levied by my Lords the Eſtates, and how they were diſtributed.

be blam'd for it, it is the Enemy himſelf, who hath inforc'd you to uſe and ſeek means for your own Defence. And if he, to the end he may execute miſchief, exerciſe Tyranny, and oppreſs your Liberty, do beſtow ſo great and exceſſive Charge and Expences; why ſhould not you beſtow ſome Coſt, to do good things, to repreſs the Tyrant, and to preſerve your Privileges and your Liberty, which cannot be valued? And if the matter be, to give up all that we have, even to the uttermoſt Farthing, and to the laſt drop of our Blood; what ſhould we do, but that whereunto we are holden and bound, and whereof we have in antient Hiſtories ſo many goodly Examples, as well of Strangers, as of our brave and valiant Predeceſſors and Anceſtors? But ſo far off it is, that we ſhould leave off, that on the other ſide, ſeeing we ſee that which pricketh and provoketh them, that that is it which we ſhould take unto our ſelves, thereby to endeavour and to encourage our ſelves to go forward. For to anſwer that which he ſaith, that I have committed to priſon, and caus'd to be ſlain, ſome of them that gainſaid theſe Contributions; I ſuppoſe it is not needful to anſwer them to this, before you (my Lords) who know that theſe are manifeſt Slanders; and who know alſo, that I have been more blam'd for my over-great Gentleneſs and Patience, in tolerating ſundry wicked Perſons, who by their Subtilties and ſecret Practices, hinder our Affairs, than I have been accus'd of mine Enemy, for my Rigor and Hardneſs. But if that which they object againſt me were true, there are ſundry which ſpeak at this day very high, and for whoſe ſake the Threds and Snares have been cut: and I do notwithſtanding as yet not repent me, that I have ſo uſed them, but will always rejoice, that I have had a Mind ready rather to receive Injury than do it; not doubting but that God, who is a juſt Judg, will bring upon the heads of theſe traitorous and diſloyal People (who did eat Bread with us, and were Partakers of our Counſels, and notwithſtanding at this preſent are in Counſel againſt us) the Reward and Recompence of their Wickedneſs, as already Vengeance purſueth them, with a perpetual Diſquietude, Vexation, and toſſing of Spirit.

The Negotiation of the Ld of Seelles.

As concerning the Buſineſs or Matter which the Lord of *Seelles* took upon him to deal for, and which alſo was known to be full of Diſſimulations and Deceits; to anſwer this, it appertaineth to you (my Lords) who have ſo wiſely diſcover'd his Frauds, and who have caus'd him to underſtand, that thoſe who have not ſeen *Spain*, are not for all that Beaſts, as he and ſuch as he are, do ſuppoſe: To you, I ſay, *it belongeth*

longeth

longeth to anſwer this, becauſe that this Accuſation is directed againſt you. I confeſs, that I was of the ſame mind that you are, that he was no more to be truſted, than a Beguiler and Deceiver; and that he was to be taken, as an Inſtrument choſen to bring all to Diviſion and Diſorder: upon which point to reſolve my ſelf, no man help'd me, ſo much as he himſelf. For in that he told me, that I was ſo much in the King's Favour, as that there was no Lord in theſe Quarters of whom he had better opinion than of me, and whom he would employ ſo much as me: this made me more and more to think, that they would gladly have taken away my Head and Life, if I would have let it gone ſo very cheap, as this Fellow ſo greatly affected to the *Spaniards*, would have perſuaded me.

I confeſs, I ſay, that I was of the ſelf-ſame opinion that you were; and that you have moſt wiſely reſolv'd upon this point, to wit, that according to the Example of that wiſe Captain, you have ſtop'd your ears againſt the Sirens or Mermaids of *Spain.* But what ſay I, that I have been of this Advice? Thoſe miſerable Men who have conſented to this curſed Proſcription, have not they alſo reſiſted his Attempts as well as I? The very ſelf-ſame Magiſtrates, who have caus'd this Proſcription to be publiſh'd, have not they alſo rejected the Lord of *Seelles*, and all his trifling Tales? which is ſufficient enough to anſwer that which they ſay, concerning *the changing of the Catholick Officers.*

The changing of the Officers.

And would to God that I had had power, or that by the Headlongneſs or Haſtineſs of ſome, I had not been lett and hinder'd from procuring and performing ſuch a Change in every place: for then there had not follow'd ſo great a Flood of Evils, as ſince we have ſeen, by reaſon of the Disjunction and Diſcord of the Provinces; which it is to be fear'd, leſt it will daily more and more grow, to the general Deſtruction of the Country: at the leaſt I hope, that if the Provinces, who have ſo wickedly forſaken us, do not repent them of ſo great a Fault, they ſhall perceive that there was never any Man better corrected for wicked Counſel, than they that have firſt given the ſame. And concerning this point, I will not ſtick at it to anſwer this Slander, that I have, and that by my own private Authority, put into Charge and Office the ſaid Officers; ſeeing that in every place, where I have been aſſiſtant in the changing of the Law, I have therein executed only that Charge and Office, which it hath pleas'd you to give me, and that as your Commiſſioner and Deputy, doing nothing therein againſt the Laws and Privileges. Indeed I will confeſs, that I ſought as much as poſſibly I could, to bring in and to place in theſe Offices virtuous People, honourable Perſonages, Men of good Conſcience, and above all Lovers of the Country. But I know what wringeth and pricketh them, that is, that I did not willingly favour thoſe, whom they had in their own Cord, People without Faith, without Godlineſs and Honeſty towards their Country; yea, bloody People, and Slaves to execute their Tyranny. And this is that (my Lords) which theſe Men call Confuſion, to wit, the good Rule and Government of our Commonwealth, according to our Laws, which alſo are as contrary to their barbarous Intents and Purpoſes, as the Day is to the Night. And indeed (my Lords) there is no great need to anſwer ſuch Objections, ſeeing that our own Enemy doth ſufficiently anſwer them for us. For who were theſe Officers, of whom they ſay, we have diſcharg'd and unburden'd our ſelves? *They were* (ſay they) *well affected to the King.* Which is as much as if they ſhould ſay, they were Enemies to the Country. And by this (my Lords) you underſtand, that it was very well done to change them in ſundry Places and Quarters.

Touching the Authority of the Ld Prince amongſt the People.

They upbraid me, *with the great Credit that I have amongſt the People.* So far off is it, that I am aſham'd of this, that I am very ſorry that I have not as yet attain'd more; that is to ſay, that I have not well known how to perſuade them to do that, which I have ſo oftentimes ſet before them, both by Word and Writing. For it is long time ſince, that I would, thro the Aid of God, have cleans'd the Country from theſe Filths of *Spain.* But if they be ſuch as they ſay they are, and that I am ſuch a one as they deſcribe me to be (for to ſhew them ſome pleaſure, I will eaſily grant them this point) they muſt of neceſſity confeſs, that their Tyrannies and Cruelties have been wonderfully exceſſive and outrageous in all ſorts, in that they have incur'd ſuch a general Hatred of all that People, who before were ſo well affected, and have been ſo loyal and faithful to their Predeceſſors, and even unto them, before ſuch Exceſſes were committed: and on the other ſide, that if the People ave willingly choſen me to be the Claimer and Challenger of their Liberty, what other thing can men ſay, what ſhall the ſtrange Nation ſpeak, and what ſhall Poſterity report, but this, That there was in me ſomething worthy of Favour and Friendſhip, and in them ſomewhat worthy of extreme Hatred? I confeſs then, that I am, and that I will all my Life long be popular; that is to ſay, that I will purſue,

ſue, maintain, and defend your Liberty and your Privileges. Thus you ſee, how theſe wiſe Brains are utterly void of common Wit and Underſtanding, and how that even then when they blame me, they praiſe me. True it is, that five or ſix ill-adviſ'd Perſons gather'd together, being the Enemies of your Liberty, whoſe Counſels, Imaginations, and ſecret Thoughts, tend altogether to this, to ſeek out the ways to make you ſubject to their Tyranny, which ſhould be more cruel, or at the leaſt more unworthy and more ſlaviſh, than that of the *Spaniards* hath been: that theſe Men, I ſay, meaſure the Brain of all the world by the Ell of their own Underſtanding, and think that every one will condemn that as evil, which they judg to be ſo. But when the whole matter ſhall be weigh'd at the common Beam and Balance, then they ſhall find that they have greatly miſreckon'd themſelves. For he whom they judg unworthy to live, that he might profit the Commonwealth (for what other thing is the Commonwealth than the Good of all the People) they will make him, thro their own Folly, ſo much the more honour'd, as the People themſelves will more eſteem of him who maintaineth them, than of him who would oppreſs them.

The regard that the Lord Prince hath always had of Nobility.

I cannot alſo ſufficiently wonder at that, which they themſelves have here forgotten; yet ſundry baſe, but wicked Writers, have lyingly put down, in their fond Libels of Defamation againſt me, to wit, *That I hate Nobility*: For ſhall I begin this Hatred at my ſelf, my Kinsfolks, and Friends, who are (thanks be to God for it) all deſcended of a noble and famous Race, and that ſo antient, and of ſuch great Riches and Dignities, that I am not afraid to affirm, that ſundry of mine Enemies cannot with any good right prefer themſelves before us, and few amongſt them ſhall be found, that may be made equal with us? But Experience hath declar'd, whether I do not that which is in my power for the Advancement of Noblemen. Now, if I have long time ago foreſeen, that certain ambitious Heads (who ſince that time have forſaken us) would go about to take poſſeſſion of certain Governments and Charges, that ſo they might afterward abandon the Country, and falſify their Oath: if, I ſay, I have known their Lightneſs, Vanity and Inconſtancy, and their Affection alſo tending to Tyranny, and therefore meant not to favour them, and ſo by that means I have help'd to preſerve the better and the greater, and the more ſound part of our Eſtate; I have not for all that hated and deſpis'd Nobility, but meant by good Counſel to prevent the Deſtruction of the Country, which

 might

might have follow'd. If their Fathers, who were more wise, more valiant, and more vertuous than they, and with whom I have liv'd in such good Friendship; if I say, they were now alive, they would die with grief, seeing their Stock so much degenerating from the Constancy and Vertue of their Anceſtors, who liv'd so honourably and without reproach; If they saw, I say, that there is at this day no Country, wherein they are not counted for inconſtant People, and great Coops-men: If they saw, even the *Spaniards* whom they serve, and the Cardinal (who is the Hinge, yea the Spindle whereupon the Mill turneth) to play with them, as it were with a Ball, to make them as it were little Children, to lead them by the nose like Beasts; and to uphold them, till it be time to demand again their Pictures, Inſtruments, Tapeſtry, and other Movables, which they have taken away; and even so far, till they come to the point to be led to the slaughter, even as it appeareth by his own Letters written with his own Hand, which you (my Lords) have seen and do know. If they saw these things, I say, what would they then do?

The Cardinal writeth to Morillon, *that it is not yet time to cause* Bourse *and others to yield an account.*

And because that mine Enemy (as tho he did diſtruſt his own Authority, and that he doubted whether the weight of his own Titles would be sufficient to intrap me) proceedeth yet further, and joineth the Emperor's Authority to them, and the Credit also of certain of my Lords the Eccleſiaſtical Electors; saying, *That they had propounded such reasonable Articles, as every man of good Judgment would deem them to be such*: he knew not (in a word, my Lords) to speak more than you. What, say I you? Nay, than all the Inhabitants of these Countrys, who did with one voice refuse the said Articles, as impertinent, captious, and unreasonable, being without Judgment, and void of Reason. But whom shall they be able to persuade, that a People beaten with such long War (which cannot be without a million of Inconveniences) would refuse a Peace, if it were reasonable? Or that good, yea very good Subjects, and suffering very much, would refuse to agree with their Superior, except it be, when they see that such Agreements are Baits to catch them? Such a Peace is worse than War, and such sweet Hony of the Tongue is more to be doubted than the ſteely Edg of Swords. It may be, that the Emperor, who thinketh such a Condition and State to be fit in his own Lands that come to him by Patrimony, holdeth an opinion that it should be likewise proper and fit for us here. The Emperor

The Treaty of Cologn.

was

was advertis'd of our State by our Enemies, and by the Traitors which were amongst us; who also under the colour of an Embassy to *Colen*, assay'd to destroy all our Matters. The Emperor inform'd other Princes, who trusted to his Report, thinking that that which came from this part, was an Oracle.

But you (my Lords) who know the depth of the State of these Countries, the Commodities or Discommodities, the true Causes of the upholding, or of the ruin thereof; who have also much to lose therein; who also are bound by all Laws to the Preservation thereof, have otherwise judg'd of those Articles: All the People was ask'd their Advice therein; and they did all, with one Consent, reject those Conditions as over-unreasonable: and this was done, not in one Town only, but in all. True it is, that we besought the Emperor's Majesty, the *French* King, the Queen of *England*, and the King of *Portugal*, to intreat for us, that a good Peace might be granted us: but to take that, as tho we had submitted our selves unto them, we suppose not that any Wise man would so think.

And as concerning *that forbidding, which they say was made, concerning the Publication of the said Articles:* Your Patience and Gentleness ought greatly to be prais'd, when you did not openly and for an Example cause such to be punish'd, who were so rash as to publish the same without your leave: and so far off is it, that we fear'd the communicating, divulging, and publishing of them, that on the contrary side, we caus'd them to be printed, with the Declarations of their insufficiency, and they were sent thorow all the Provinces and Towns, that they might be deliberated upon, and that the Advice and Resolution of all might be had. But there is great difference between a thing communicated in order, by the way of Right, and by the Authority of them, which have power so to do: and between this, that certain little Scouts should privily cast amongst the People, certain little Pamphlets, as some of them which were sent to *Colen* about your Service, caus'd under-hand, and closely to pass forth those things which they had negotiated, and treated of with the Enemy, wherein they betray'd both you and the Country, as more largely appeareth by their own Letters; whereof I will not speak any further, because that all is set abroad, and brought to every man's sight.

The Lord Prince hinder'd not the Communicating of the Articles of Colen *to the People.*

They

The Union of the Provinces made at the time of the separation of Artois *and* Haynault.

They think the Union of the Provinces, made at *Utrecht*, to be wonderfully wicked and evil. And why so? Because that all that which is good for us, is evil for them; and that which is healthful for us, is deadly for them. They had set all their hope upon a Discord and Disagreement; and they had provok'd thereto some of the Provinces, who have had as many Deliberations and Counsels, as there are months in a year: besides, they had at their Commandment certain pestilent Fellows amongst us. What Remedy then could a Man devise better against Dissension than Union? And what Counterpoison more certain against their Venom of Discord, than Concord? By means whereof, their Purposes, their Treacheries, their Night-Counsels, their Secret Intelligences, were all at one time scatter'd abroad; God (who is the God of Peace and Concord) declaring thereby how much he hateth such deceitful Tongues, and how he can easily overthrow such false and abominable Enterprizes.

You see (my Lords) that I give them a fair and large Field to cry out against me, and to scorn at me. I confess unto them, that I have procur'd the Union; that I have advanc'd and promoted the same; that I have endeavour'd to maintain it; and I tell you (my Lords) yet, and I speak it very plainly, and loud, that I like it well, that so not only they, but also all *Europe* should understand it. Maintain your Union; keep your Union, but do it, but do it indeed (my Lords) that so you may execute, not in Words, nor by Writing only, but in Effect also, that which your sheaf of Arrows, tied with one Band only, doth mean; which Sheaf you bear in your Seal. Let them go now and accuse me, that I have brought all to confusion when I procur'd the Union; for the doing of which matter, I will never blush. For if under the shadow of a Peace, they would bring forth unto us a Division; if they would assemble themselves, one while at *Arras*, another while at *Mons*, giving us always fair words; and that to this end, that they might sunder themselves from us, and so draw by their Cords unto themselves, light-headed Fellows like unto themselves: Wherefore should it not be lawful for us, on our own behalfs, to join and tie our selves together? Unless (as it may be) they think that they are permitted to do Evil, and to abandon the Country: And when, I pray you? Even when *Maestricht* was besieg'd (Will not ye, O ye poor People, feel, when ye shall read these things, the hot Iron which shall burn your Conscience?) and that it was not lawful for us then to do good, and to heal the Country. Let us then here (my Lords) learn

learn that which is profitable and neceſſary for us to learn; and let us learn it of the greateſt Enemy that ever the Country had, yea of the greateſt Tyrant of the whole Earth.

Concerning the Voyage of the Lord Prince into Overyſſel, An, 1580.

They object unto me afterwards a horrible Crime, and worthy forſooth of this more great Proſcription, than that which was pronounc'd by *Sylla* and *Carbo*; that is, *that I departed not out of* Antwerp *for two years ſpace, and that I went to* Utrecht. A Man may eaſily ſee, that they know very well what I do; as tho, that to their very great ſorrow and grief, I had not in thoſe two years ſpace travell'd twice into *Flanders*, where by the Aid of the four Members or Parts of that Province, I plac'd better Order in the ſaid Country, than they would or wiſh'd. But go to; let us grant that I did not for two years ſpace together go out of *Antwerp*: Was not this a great fault to be always nigh unto you, that I might the better ſerve you in every thing, which it pleas'd you to command me? But I went to *Utrecht*; behold (my Lords) the Evil; behold the Boil or Sore, for this is the Voyage that woundeth them, even to the Heart. They had before-hand ſo wiſely purpos'd their Matters: they had laid ſo ſure a Foundation for their Affairs and Buſineſs: they pleas'd themſelves ſo much therein: they writ thereof to their Friends: they held in their hands ſo many Countries and Governments: they had written ſo many Letters; and had us'd ſo many Hirings, ſecret Inticements, and open Practices, as they thought all to be ſure their own: and yet I coming only to ſhew my ſelf at *Utrecht*, with the good Aſſiſtance and Counſel of my Lords, the Deputies of the Provinces; behold that great Miſt or Fog was vaniſh'd away; ſo many Caſtles as they had reſerv'd for their Tyranny, were beaten down; and ſo many of our own Towns aſſur'd to us: they having for all, no other thing left unto them, but one only Town of Importance, wherein was the Captain of the Enterprize; Which Town, notwithſtanding he knew not how to ſubject to his Command, but by an abominable Murder of one whom he call'd his Father; who the Evening before had ſat at his Table, he, as a *Judas*, dealing with him under a falſe Kiſs. And this (my Lords) is the Cauſe that maketh them cry ſo loud, yea, this is the *Helena* for which they fight.

Touching the Prieſts driven out of the Country of Frieſeland.

And as concerning that which they object againſt me, *that I have driven out ſome of the Eccleſiaſtical Perſons or Church-men*; you (my Lords) know that this is not true. But when their Captain, who is in *Groningen*, had taken Priſoners ſome of the Religion, and

had

had murder'd otherſome; yea, the very Burgomaſter, and all this, contrary unto his Oath: having alſo before-time brought in, and ſworn unto, the New Religion (as they call it) and having ſolemnly, and that with his Oath, and his Sign, and his Seal confirm'd the Union of *Utrecht*. All theſe things conſider'd, who is he that will think it ſtrange, if thoſe on our ſide, meant what they could, on their own parts to aſſure themſelves, ſeeing that they ſaw the Enemies, without any reverence to their Oath taken, to tread under their feet all holy and ſacred Things, and with ſuch a perpetual Reproach to them and their Race, to have violated and broken whatſoever Juſtice and Equity doth as yet remain in the World? And this we may ſay at the leaſt, that no Man can juſtly charge us, that in the midſt of thoſe Troubles, which our Enemies themſelves have ſtir'd up, that ever any of our ſide proceeded or came to ſuch a heap of Injuſtice, as to wet their hands in the Blood of thoſe that were confederate to them, or of thoſe which ſtay'd themſelves upon their Fidelities: which thing their Captains have done, yea, and that with their own hands.

Concerning certain Noblemen that departed out of Frieſland.

Concerning the Nobles, which he ſaith, *have withdrawn themſelves out of the Country*; who is he which ever drove out ſo much as one of them? But if the Terrors of their own Conſciences have purſu'd them, and that they have been vex'd by their own feeling, which (as it were infernal and helliſh Furies) hath chas'd them from place to place, who ought to be accus'd therefore, but only they themſelves, who ſecretly, diſloyally and unfaithfully have practis'd the Deſtruction of their own Country? And would to God that they had ſooner felt this burden, and that they which remain, and are overtaken with the like madneſs, might follow them even at the heels; ſo ſhould they deliver us from great Travel, and the Commonwealth from Fear, leſt ſome one time or other they ſhould execute their pernicious Purpoſes.

The roundneſs and plainneſs of the Ld Prince.

It is a ridiculous and fond thing, that they call me Hypocrite, who never, in reſpect of them, have us'd any Diſſimulation. For while I was their Friend, I have freely foretold them, that they twiſted the Thread of their own Deſtruction, whilſt that they attempted and took theſe barbarous ways of perſecuting. And if their Rage and unmeaſurable Heat, joyn'd with a contempt of us, had not hinder'd them from following my Counſel, they had not been brought to that State, in which they are at this preſent. When

I

I was their Adverſary and Enemy for your Liberty, I know not what Hypocriſy they have found in me, unleſs they will call this Hypocriſy, to make open War upon them, to take Towns from them, to drive them out of the Country; and without diſſembling, to do againſt them whatſoever the Law of War ſuffer'd me. But, if it pleaſe you (my Lords) once again to read my Defence, which I publiſh'd three years ago, you ſhall ſee there the Letters of a King, who is a Deceiver and an Hypocrite, and who thought to catch me then in the Snare of his ſweet and deceivable Letters, as he ſuppoſeth at this preſent to aſtoniſh me with his Threats and Thunders of Words: But, thanks be to God, I have a Counterpoiſon againſt both the one and the other Venom.

The Lord Prince accus'd of Diffidence or Diſtruſt.

They proceed afterwards with a great heap of fooliſh Words to amplify this matter, *that I ſtay and ground my ſelf upon a certain Diffidence and Diſtruſt.* Tho I did ſo, ſhould I be for all that, like unto *Cain* and *Judas*, as he accuſeth me? No verily: For it is one thing to deſpair of the Promiſes, and of the Grace of God, who cannot lie; and another thing not to believe the Words of a ſubtle and deceitful Man, who keepeth not Faith or Loyalty, as the poor *Moors* of *Granada* may ſpeak too much thereof: And alſo, as the Death of the Lords, the Counts of *Egmont* and *Horne*, of bleſſed Memory, do give ſufficient proof thereof. But if theſe good Divines, ſuch as the Cardinal is (who is one of the Foundations of his Church) had thorowly ſounded for the true and nigh Cauſe of the Ruin and Fall of *Judas* and *Cain*, they ſhould have found, that it was Deſpair, to which by the Grace of God I have not been brought, and I hope never ſhall be. On the other ſide, if Men would look upon the monſtrous and thundring Speeches which are us'd, in this not Barbarous only, but more than Turkiſh Proſcription: ſhall they not find therein the very Stile of deſperate perſons, ſuch as we hear the Poets uſe, when they bring in furious and mad Men? They then have the ſear'd Conſcience of *Judas*, the aſtoniſh'd Conſcience of *Cain*, and the reprov'd Conſcience of *Saul*. You ſee notwithſtanding (my Lords) the great Wiſdom of theſe Wiſe Heads: Diffidence or Diſtruſt, ſay they, is a common thing to all wicked perſons. But I ſpeak unto thee (O Cardinal) who haſt ſpent ſo much time in the Schools; and I bid thee tell me, whether thou call not this Learning, to wit, to be from a man's Youth inſtructed to lie and deceive? I demand then of thee, what thou wilt anſwer to the moſt ſtrong and ſententious of all Orators, and to the greateſt Lover of his Country, who ſaith (as I have underſtood it from my Youth by by all learned Men) that the greateſt and ſureſt Fortreſs that a free People can have againſt a Tyrant, is Diffidence and Diſtruſt? And this Speech was directed againſt one call'd *Philip*, who had learn'd but a little Tyranny, in reſpect of thy Lord *Philip*, who exceedeth all other Tyrants, and for whom no Oration pronounc'd againſt *Philip* is ſufficiently worthy, no not that, which for the Excellency of it is call'd Divine. I know thou wilt adviſe and take counſel concerning this matter, and in the mean while I will ſpeak, I will write, and I will cauſe to be ingrav'd in every place this notable Sentence, worthy of eternal Remembrance: And would to God that I might be better believ'd, than that good Orator was amongſt his People, who ſuffering themſelves to be buſied and abus'd, by People like unto thy ſelf, and other ſuch wretched workers of Confuſion (which are at thy Command, and have ſet on Sale their Tongues and Pens) were at the laſt ſnar'd, and utterly brought to Confuſion. But I hope (my Lords) better things of your Conſtancy and Courage.

The Offers which the Enemies ſay have been made to the L. Prince, to cauſe him to depart out of the Country.

And as good Orators do always keep towards the end ſome ſtrong and piercing Reaſon; and as good Captains, leave their beſt Soldiers in the laſt Ranks; ſo theſe skilful and ſo much exercis'd Men, come at the laſt to entangle and ſnare me with the weight of a great and grievous Reproach. *They have offer'd me* (they ſay) *great Commodities, to the end that I might depart to the place where I was born, where every one ought to deſire moſt to live, to the which I meant not to conſent.* What could they ſay (my Lords) which might make more for me than this? Conſider, I pray you, their folly, or their ſhameleſneſs. For this muſt needs be, either that they ſpeak ſhameleſly, or elſe that they are ſo void of good underſtanding, that they praiſe me, when they think to blame me. *It is a pleaſant thing for every one to live in his own Country:* Wherefore then doth this curſed Race of *Spaniards* go from Country to Country, to torment and to trouble all the World? But if, in reſpect of ſo many Bonds, as I am bound unto you by, I prefer your Service (as I ought) before the Country wherein I was born: Am I therefore to be counted a Traitor, and a wicked Man, and the publick Plague of the World? And yet notwithſtanding you know, that ever ſince I was eleven or twelve years old, I have been nouriſh'd and brought up amongſt you, and not elſewhere, inſomuch that this Country is become as it were my natural Country. If then they have made me ſundry Promiſes; if they have offer'd me (as they ſay) great Commodities, and I have notwithſtanding refus'd

the

the ſame; what can they condemn in me, except it be my Conſtancy and Fidelity towards God and the Country, which I have prefer'd before all the Goods in the World? Think not (my Lords) that I love to be ſo continually occupy'd in Travel and Labour, or like to hear ſo many wicked Speeches and Slanders on the behalf of mine Adverſaries; and (which is more) that I would hear them of them that ought to be my Friends, and are bound unto me; or that I take delight to be ſo long time depriv'd of my Goods; to ſee my Son ſo long kept in cruel Priſon; to behold my ſelf charg'd with ſuch infinite Debts, and yet ſhould be able to put an end to ſo great Difficulties and Diſtreſſes, and would not; or that I ſhould not be like unto other Men of the Earth, who all prefer Quietneſs before Travel, and Proſperity before Affliction. But what? If I cannot obtain ſuch Bleſſings, and ſo bleſſed a condition without betraying you, without forſaking you, without giving you over (as much as might be) for a Prey into the Teeth of theſe bloody Wolves: Let the reſt of the World pardon me (for I know that you approve me, and that I need no excuſe before you) if I will not, either for Goods, or for Life, or for Wife, or for Children, mingle in my Drink one only drop of the Poiſon of Treaſon. But ſo long as it ſhall pleaſe God to give me any drop of Blood, one penyworth of my Goods, any Underſtanding, Induſtry, Credit and Authority, how ſmall ſoever it be; I will imploy, I will dedicate, and I will conſecrate the ſame wholly unto your Service. Notwithſtanding, ſeeing they upbraid me with ſuch things, I will yet tell you (my Lords) that they have not done any ſuch thing, without borrowing ſomewhat of the Truth, and going beyond it alſo, according to their good Cuſtom. For ſuch Offers as they ſpeak of, were as yet never made me; not but that I have been well and ſurely advertis'd, that I could not demand any thing in reſpect of mine own particular, but that they would yield the ſame unto me; that they would promiſe to ſet my Son at liberty; to leave him all my Eſtates; to aſſign unto me in *Germany* ſo much Goods as I have here, as well in reſpect of that which I poſſeſs, as of that which is held from me; to diſcharge me of my Debts, which are very great, and to give me in ready Coin a Million of Money, and good Aſſurances for all theſe things.

Theſe be (my Lords) the goodly Offers which have eaſily turn'd them aſide, which are departed away from us. But ſo far off is it, that ſuch Conditions were offer'd unto me, that on the other ſide, they never knew, either by the Letters of the Emperor's Ambaſſador, or by his ſecret Practices with ſome of my Servants, and ſundry of my neareſt Kinsfolks, or by the

the Letters of the Commissioners, how to get this only at my hand, to wit, that I should send particular Articles, and that in my own Name: But I have always answer'd, That if the Peace might be concluded, as you (my Lords) demanded it, I should be satisfied: I not minding to have any other condition, either Good or Evil, than that which you accepted of; nor yet minding, neither directly nor indirectly, to sunder my self from the common Cause; upon which I did judg, that either my Adversity, or my Prosperity, did depend.

Is not this a great fault to upbraid a Man with this, that he is a good Man? and that he is as much loyal, constant, and assur'd, against all the Winds of fair Promises, as by God's Grace he is against all the Floods of cruel Threatnings?

Hitherto (my Lords) you have heard the Accusations, or rather the Injuries, wicked Speeches and Slanders, which they have gather'd together against my Honour and Reputation. It shall belong to you (to whom only I think my self bound, by reason of my Goods, of the state wherein they are, and especially of my Oaths) to judg thereof as it shall please you: for I do not refuse, if I be found culpable, to receive Punishment; but if it fall out, as I hope it will, that you judg that I am accus'd by Tyrants and Slanderers, then I shall esteem my mean, yet (notwithstanding) my most loyal, and my most faithful Service, to have been very well imploy'd.

The Sentence of the Proscription.

NOW then (my Lords) upon these frail and weak Foundations, they come to build the Sentence of their Proscription; and here they lay out all their Tragical Eloquence; they thunder; they lighten; they storm and rage; they do as the *Corebæ*, or Furies do in Theatres; they dart out all execrable Words, and such as have been kneaded in *Cocyte*, *Styx*, and *Acheron*, against this poor Captain. But this, Thanks be to God, doth astonish me, as much as the Thunderings and Lightnings of Pope *Clement*, thrown out of the Mount *Tarpeius*, against my Predecessor, my Lord Prince *Philebert*, did astonish him; who ceas'd not for all that to make him his Prisoner. For, after that I have look'd round about me, I find that they are but Winds of Words and Noises, to make Children afraid, rather than a Man, who thorow God's goodness hath not lost his Courage; for the roarings of all their Canons, nor for their fourscore thousand Soldiers, who were always at the Duke of *Alva* his Command; nor yet for so many Armies by Sea; nor yet for so many Treasons of the said Duke, or of his Successor against me; nor for the Treasons of the Dutchess

of

of *Parma*, who was before them: and yet notwithstanding, this was indeed a more fearful thing, than a vain Noise of such a great Thunder, which so quickly vanish'd away, and hurt no Man. And it is sufficient for me shortly to say before you (my Lords) and before all *Europe*, that every *Spaniard*, or every one that favoureth the *Spaniards*, of what quality or condition soever he be (I respect not now any man's Person) who hath said, or shall say, (as this infamous Proscription hath publish'd it) *that I am a Traitor, and a wicked Man*; that he speaketh falsly, and against the Truth. In the mean while, let them forbid me as long as they will both Fire and Water, I, together with my Friends, will not leave off for all that, even in despite of their Rage, to live as long as it shall please God to give us Grace: For God only hath in his power, my Life and my Death, and hath number'd all the hairs of my Head; whose great Favour and Assistance I have felt, even until this present time, and I hope that he will preserve me even unto the end. As concerning the Goods which I possess, which also he giveth away (for hitherto he hath been so good a Husband, that he will give nothing of that which he hath violently taken from me) I hope (God aiding me) that it shall cost them so dear to have them, that they may get others elsewhere far better cheap. As concerning my other Goods, which he keepeth from me, I hope that God will give me grace, as well to dispossess them thereof wholly, as I have already done of a good part; and that they have never violently taken Goods from any poor Prince (albeit that they have spoil'd sundry thereof) which shall lie and weigh more heavy upon them.

The Answer of the Lord Prince, to the Sentence of Proscription.

He promiseth *five and twenty thousand Crowns, either in Lands, or in ready Money, to him that shall yield me up into his cruel hands, dead or alive, or to him which shall take my life from me.* But albeit, there hath heretofore no publication been made of such a matter, until this present time: thinketh he that I am ignorant, how oftentimes he and his have bargain'd with Murderers and Poysoners, to take away my Life from me? And if God have shew'd me such grace, as to make me able to preserve my self, even then when I was not advertis'd of any such danger; I hope that he will not shew me less favour at this time, wherein I am admonish'd, but rather, that as I have great occasion to look unto my self, so he will stir up sundry good and vertuous People, who shall watch for my assurance and safety. But albeit, that I know not in the World any impudence so shameless, which may be compar'd with the Impudence of the *Spaniards*: notwithstanding, I cannot sufficiently marvel, that they have been so shameless, as to dare to publish, before all *Europe*, not only that they set a Price upon a frank and free Captain, who (thanks be to God for it) did as yet never fear them; but also, that they annex thereunto such Recompences and Rewards, yea, and those so barbarous, and so estrang'd from all Rule of Honesty and Humanity, as the like hath not been heard of: That is to say, in the first place, *that they will make him Noble, if he were not noble before, who shall do so Gentle man-like, or so noble an act.* But, I beseech you, suppose that he which should execute so wicked an act, (which thing I hope God will never suffer) were of a noble Race and Stock; think you, that there is any Gentleman in the World, I mean amongst the Nations which know what Nobility is, who would so much as eat with so wicked, ungodly, and mischievous a Man, who for Money should kill another Man, yea, tho he were the least, and the most abject person that could be found?

Now, if the *Spaniards* account such people for Noblemen; and if this be the way to come to Honour in *Castile* and *Spain*, I will no more wonder at that which all the World believeth; to wit, that the greatest part of the *Spaniards*, and especially those that count themselves Noblemen, are of the Blood of the *Moors* and *Jews*, who also keep this vertue of their Ancestors, who sold for Ready-money, down told, the Life of our Saviour; which thing also maketh me to take patiently this injury laid upon me. In the second place, *they pardon him every offence and fault, how grievous soever it might be.* But what if he had pull'd up the Christian Religion out of one of his Kingdoms? what if he had ravish'd his Daughter? what if he had spoken evil of the Inquisition, which is the greatest Crime that can be in *Spain?* should he be pardon'd? But, seeing mine Enemy meant so far to forget himself, that he would attempt to take away my Goods, my Life, and mine Honour; and that he might have more Witnesses of his Injustice and Follies, to publish it so throughout the World, and that in so many Languages, I could not very well desire, in respect of most great advantage unto my self, that he should have enrich'd and adorn'd this his Proscription with any other Ornaments than these very same; to wit, that for killing of me, he should make noble, not only Villains and infamous Persons, but also the most wicked, and the most execrable People of the whole Earth; and to give such a great, yea so honourable a Reward, to so notable a Vertue. For what could be found out more fit, to justify my Righteousness and Innocency, than to go about to root me out by such means? and then this, to carry a Mind by Tyranny, Impoisonings, forgiving of grie-

vous

vous Crimes, making of wicked Men noble, and ſuch like, to oppreſs the Defender of the Liberty of a People that is cruelly and tyrannouſly vex'd.

I doubt not (my Lords) but that God, who is juſt, hath taken from him and his all Underſtanding; and that he hath ſuffer'd him to declare and ſet out to all the World matter enough, whereby they may know his poyſonful Heart againſt this Country, and againſt our Liberty, in as much as he maketh no account of any act, how wicked and deteſtable ſoever it may be, in reſpect of the Death of him, who hitherto hath ſo faithfully ſerv'd you. And further, he is not aſham'd to mingle with ſuch Sacrileges as theſe are, the Name of God, calling himſelf *his Miniſter or Officer*. Hath the Officer then this Power, not only to permit that which God hath forbidden; but alſo to reward it with Money, or Money-worth, with Nobility, and the forgiveneſs of Offences? And what Offences or Crimes I pray you? Verily of all Crimes, how grievous ſoever they can be. But I doubt not, but that God, through his moſt juſt Judgment, will cauſe to come down the juſt Vengeance of his Wrath upon the Captain and Head of ſuch Miniſters and Officers; and that on the other ſide, he will of his great Goodneſs maintain mine Innocency and mine Honour ſo long as I live, and amongſt my Poſterity after me. And as concerning my Goods and my Life, it is a long time ſince that I dedicated them to his Service; and I know that he will do therewith whatſoever he ſhall ſee to be good, for his own Glory, and for my Salvation.

And becauſe (my Lords) he proceedeth alſo to bring the Drops of this infamous Proſcription upon your Heads; ſo far off is it, that you ſhall be mov'd therewith, that ye ſhould rather think, that herein the *Spaniard* and his Adherents follow the natural diſpoſition of Women, who, after that they have wept, ſcratch'd and bitten, do for their laſt Remedy and Refuge, come to Injuries and Revilings: and even ſo doth your Enemy now yield out his laſt Barkings; and if we give them proof of our Conſtancy, Reſolution and Courage, behold they are at the laſt of their miſerable and wretched Enterprizes. For *Sylla*, *Carbo*, *Marius*, *Antonius*, and ſuch other Tyrants, the firſt Fathers of theſe abominable Proſcriptions, never gave Example to the *Spaniards*, to commit ſuch Folly and Beaſtlineſs; albeit, that they have trac'd out before them that Example of Cruelty and Barbarouſneſs, which theſe miſerable Wretches have accompliſh'd and perform'd: But they proſcrib'd ſuch only as were Fugitives, driven away, hidden in ſecret, and that within the Countries over which they had Power and Authority. And theſe Men are like unto them in this, that is to ſay, in Cruelty, becauſe they proſcribe good, vertuous, and honourable Perſonages: but yet in this point they ſhew themſelves ſottiſh and fooliſh, that they proſcribe him, whom they ſhould fight againſt with an armed Power. For to ſend a Poiſoner, as the Dutcheſs of *Parma* ſent one; or to ſend a Murderer, as her Son, the general Heir of the Vertues of his Anceſtors, did: this is not the Effect of a Proſcription, but of Bribery, and Thievery rather.

Behold, my Lords, not what I am able to ſay, againſt this tyrannous Proſcription, but what I have thought meet for this time: ſpeaking unto you, who have the knowledg of ſundry things that I omit, becauſe they are known unto you, and becauſe alſo that if I would attempt to ſpeak of the particular Enterpriſes of the King, and of his chief Officers, I ſhould aſſay to do that, which no Orator is ſufficiently able worthily to deſcribe; yea, that which no good Man was ever able to conceive: ſo great is their Cruelty, Tyranny, and all manner of unjuſt Dealing. Notwithſtanding I hope, that as well by the matter contain'd in this Proſcription (which is a ſufficient Teſtimony of their over-baſe and abject Courage) as by my Anſwer, you ſhall ſufficiently know, what are their pernicious Purpoſes and miſerable Attempts: and by this Knowledg you ſhall alſo learn, what it is neceſſary for you to caſt your eye upon, and diligently to underſtand; that is, that they deſpair that ever they ſhall be able to vanquiſh you by Force, and therefore they aſſay to ſow Diviſion amongſt us, magnifying chiefly thoſe, who have not only forſaken us againſt their Oath, but even have left us in perillous Times, and namely whilſt that one of our Towns was beſieg'd: whereof they are not able to make any juſt Complaint, nor alledg their accuſtom'd Pretext and Cloke; yea, (which alſo is the Heap of all Diſloyalty and Unfaithfulneſs) at the very ſame time they come to aſſault us in other Places and Quarters. As for the Threats annex'd in this Proſcription, they tend to no other end but to aſtoniſh you, to the end you might ſeparate your ſelves from me; and plainly to declare, that they make war againſt me, and not againſt you, even as the Wolf would perſuade the Sheep, that he had not war with any but with the Dogs, which being once diſcomfited, he would eaſily agree with the Flock of Sheep; for the Dogs were always the Authors of their Debate and Combating. But, my Lords, tho I were abſent, tho I were departed into *Germany*, would they burn no more? Would they ſpill no more Blood? Would they drown no more? Was the Liberty of the Country maintain'd by that gentle and mild Man the Duke of *Alva*? Did they not then wickedly

put

put to death in *Spain* your own Ambaſſadors, my Lords of *Bergues* and of *Montigni*? Did they not at the ſame time ſet before your eyes, upon Spears and Lances, the Heads of your principal Captains and Governours? The other Point, which they moſt ſet before them, is the Extirpation of Religion. I mind not here, my Lords, to enter into this Queſtion, which is the true Religion, wherein God is truly ſerv'd and call'd upon, and that according to his Word; but leave it rather to be declar'd by others, more exercis'd in that matter than I: and yet ſo, that every one may know by my Profeſſion, what I believe concerning the ſame. But this I cannot chuſe but tell you, that ſuch is the Eſtate of your Country, that without the Exerciſe and free Uſe of the ſaid Religion, it cannot ſtand three days. You ſee the number of them that profeſs it marvellouſly increas'd; you ſee that Hatred againſt the Pope is inrooted deeply in the Hearts of all the Inhabitants of the Country, becauſe that his damnable Practices againſt this whole Eſtate are manifeſtly diſcover'd.

Who is he then that can boaſt that he loveth the Country, and would give Counſel to drive away ſuch a great number of People, which once departing, ſhall leave the Country waſte, poor, and miſerable; and ſhall people and inrich the ſtrange Nations about us? But ſuppoſe that they will not depart, or void the Country, who is he that can inforce them ſo to do? Let us look upon our Neighbours; let us conſider our own Examples, and if we be not utterly void of Wit and Underſtanding, we will never chuſe ſuch pernicious and hurtful Counſels, as ſhall utterly, even from top to toe, bring to ruin and deſtruction this Eſtate. I will yet ſay ſomewhat more unto you, my Lords, that albeit that amongſt them which follow the *Roman* Church, there are ſundry good People, and Lovers of their Country; and that amongſt them there are ſome alſo, which have moſt honourably acquitted and behav'd themſelves: yet notwithſtanding thoſe of the Religion are very well aſſur'd of this, that there ſhall never be found any amongſt them, who hath had Intelligence, or made any practice with the Enemy, but all of them generally have been contrary unto him. And albeit that ſome have been found amongſt them, who being like unto wanton and proud Children, have brought, thro their Unheedineſs, ſome trouble into the Houſe; yet for all that, they have not had any dealing with the common Enemy. Seeing then, my Lords, that you know their Purpoſes and Attempts, there reſteth no other thing but this, that you do in time provide for them, and labour what ye can to redreſs the ſame. And how ſhall this be perform'd? Forſooth by this means, that ye perform in in effect that which ye have always in your mouth; and that which the Mark of your Sheaf of Arrows signifieth, which it hath pleas'd you to have graven in your Seal: that is to say, that no Member of this goodly Body respect that which is his own, but regard the whole Body altogether; that some one part of the Body take not unto it self that Meat which is prepar'd for the whole, but that it suffer the Stomach (which is the Council that ye shall ordain and appoint) to concoct and digest the same, and to send it by the Veins to all the Members of this Estate; and specially, that wheresoever any Disease or Sickness shall appear, the Physicians should speedily be sent thither, and that the Patients should quietly bear for a time the Miseries upon them, that so they may feel at the length a joyful Deliverance from their Disease and Evil. Shall not this be a just Reproach upon us and ours for ever, if that, having so glorious an Estate under our power, and so goodly means for our Defence, we do, thro a miserable Covetousness and greedy Desire to get unto our selves some Commodities, and that with the prejudice and hurt of our Country-men and Friends, whilst some draw one way, and some another; if we do, I say, find our selves, and that in a moment, snar'd and overwhelm'd by our deadly Enemies? Remember, my Lords, I pray you, the very great diminishing and weakning of this Estate, which came to pass after the Death of Duke *Charles*, which fell upon us for no other thing, but because that while the Provinces busied themselves, to contend and to fight against one another for certain pretended Privileges, and for certain Commodities, the rest was abandon'd and forsaken. Think not that it is in my power (the Affairs and Matters being in such Condition as they are) any long time to resist the Enemy with such small and slender means, as you (my Lords) know that I have had in my hand and possession. But on the other side, if I have any Experience or Practice of Government and War; if I know this Country, and the Means that the Enemy hath, tho that all the Armies and Powers, which they threaten shall come the next Year out of *Spain* and *Italy*, should come upon us and our Powers, they shall do no more, but much less rather, than the Duke of *Alva* did in *Holland* and *Zeland*. And if it be in your power to take order for this (as it is indeed) and yet notwithstanding ye do it not; by what name shall a man call this Fault, if it be committed by you, my Lords, who are here assembled, and upon whom all the good People of this Country stay themselves, esteeming you as their Fathers and their Protectors, who will also willingly embrace, as some joyful News sent from Heaven, any good

good Order which you ſhall decree and eſtabliſh? Wherefore take pity of your ſelves; and if that which concerneth your ſelves move you not, yet take pity, I pray you, of ſo many poor People already deſtroy'd, and more like to be; of ſo many poor Widows and fatherleſs Children; of ſo many Murders and Slaughters, committed within the Bowels of your own Country; of ſo many Churches deſtroy'd; and of ſo many Paſtors wandering up and down, together with their poor Flocks. Set before you that cruel and barbarous Execution committed at *Nivelle*, by the Count of *Mansfeld*. Which things you may eaſily avoid, and caſt all the Evil and Miſchief of this War upon the Enemy, if only you remove Partialitys and Partakings, and with one Courage and Heart, as it were, employ together all the means that you have, without ſparing, I ſay, not the bottom of your Purſes, but that which aboundeth therein.

And as concerning that which particularly toucheth my ſelf, you ſee (my Lords) that it is this Head that they ſeek for, the which by ſuch a Price, and ſo great a Sum of Mony, they have vow'd and appointed to death; and ſay, that ſo long as I ſhall be among you, the Wars ſhall have no end. Would to God, my Lords, either that my perpetual Baniſhment, or elſe my very Death it ſelf, might bring unto you a ſound and true Deliverance from ſo many Miſchiefs and Calamities, as the *Spaniards* (whom I have ſeen ſo many times deliberate in Council, deviſe, and ſpeak of particularly, and whom I know within and without) do deviſe againſt you, and prepare for you. O how ſweet ſhould this Baniſhment be unto me? O how delightful ſhould this Death be unto me? For wherefore is it, that I have given over, yea loſt all my Goods? Is it to enrich my ſelf? Wherefore have I loſt mine own Brethren, whom I lov'd more than mine own Life? Is it that I might find ſome other elſewhere? Wherefore have I ſo long time left my Son a Priſoner; my Son, I ſay, whom I ought ſo much to deſire, if I be a Father? Is it becauſe you are able to give me another, or becauſe you are able to reſtore him to me again? Wherefore have I put my Life ſo oftentimes in danger? What other Recompence, what other Reward, can I look for, of my long Travels, which have come upon me for your Service ſake, even ſo far, that they have brought upon me old Age, and the Ruin and Loſs of all my Goods, except it be to purchaſe and to procure you Liberty, and that, if need be, with the Price of my Blood? If you therefore, my Lords, do judg, either that my Abſence, or that my very Death it ſelf, may ſerve you, or ſtand you in any ſtead, behold I am ready to obey;

command me, yea ſend me even to the world's end, and I will obey you. Behold my Head, over which no Prince or Monarch hath any power, ſave you only; diſpoſe thereof, as ſhall make moſt for your own Good, and for the Health and Preſervation of your Commonwealth. But if you judg, that this mean Experience and ſmall Diligence that is in me, and which I have attain'd by ſo long and ſo continual Travel: if you judg that the Remainder of my Goods, and that my Life it ſelf, may as yet ſerve you (as indeed I do wholly dedicate and conſecrate the ſame unto this Country) reſolve then upon the Points which I propound unto you and ſet before you. And if you think that I bear any Love to the Country, and that I have any Sufficiency in me to give Counſel, believe that this is the only mean to aſſure, yea to deliver our ſelves from the Enemy. This being done, let us with one Heart and Good Will go together, and let us together embrace the Defence of this good People, which demandeth nothing elſe but to have good Counſels laid open before them, nor deſireth any thing elſe but to follow the ſame; And this doing, if you yet continue towards me the Favour which heretofore you have born me, I hope by your Aid and God's Grace (which I have ſo often heretofore felt, and that in very perplexed and doubtful Matters) that that which ſhall be reſolv'd upon by you, ſhall be for the Good and Preſervation of your Selves, your Wives and Children, and all Sacred and Holy Things.

The

The Prince of Orange's *Letter to the Estates.*

To my Lords the Estates General.

YOU have known, my Lords, by my Life past, and by my Behaviour, that I never minded to answer to any Libels of Defamation, which certain Slanderers had publish'd against me; insomuch as if the Quality and Greatness of the Wrong, which hath been done against me by the Proscription that the King of *Spain* hath caus'd to be publish'd, I had not as yet proceeded so far, especially had it not been that the Maintenance of mine Honour had requested the same of me, as I have more largely laid out the same in my Defence, which I have presented unto you. Since which time, there is come into my hands a Letter very false and counterfeit by mine Enemy, which they say they intercepted, and I sent to my Lord the Duke of *Anjou*, or (as they say) to the Duke of *Alanson*, whereof some Personages amongst them, and that of great Quality also, have sent Copies, as well to certain Towns of our side, and amongst us, as to sundry strange and foreign Princes. This Letter, my Lords, is so fondly written (whether a Man regard the Stile thereof, or will respect the matter therein contain'd, which by the bare reading thereof sufficiently bewrayeth that there is not in it any shew of Truth) that such an impudent Device deserveth no Answer: as also, God be prais'd, there is not found a Man amongst us, which is any whit at all mov'd therewith. On the other side, every Man hath known, that they had no other meaning hereby, but by such Mists and Smokes to darken the Brightness, by which their miserable and pernicious Intent against this Country hath been discover'd by the Letters of Cardinal *Grandville* and others, which you have commanded to be printed, after that you knew their Hands, their Signs, and their Seals; and withal thereby to take unto themselves an occasion and matter to cast up and spew out (according to the manner of shameless Women) slanderous and wicked Speeches, full of lying. But so far off is it, that by this means they have (in respect of me) obtain'd that which they pretended, that on the other side they have done me great pleasure, in publishing such Follies; because that thereby they do more and more justify and verify my De-

fence:

fence: sufficiently proving themselves to be shameless Lyars, most impudent Slanderers, and most fond Falsifiers, which serveth more and more to justify (as I have said) mine Innocency, and to give Approbation to all my Actions. For seeing that all Men know, that this should be the best News that they could receive or hear of, that I would forsake the Country, and leave it to them; I offer'd them (my Lords) and you under my Honour do promise them to accomplish it, if they be able to prove in your Presence, that I have at any time written, or commanded to be written, or sent such a Letter, that presently I will depart the Country, and withdraw my self from it, without ever setting my self against them: And I promise them, even upon a simple or bare Request, to send them such Passports and Safe-conducts, and they also pen'd in such order, as either they can or will demand. But yet this shall be with this Condition, that if they will not accept this so reasonable an Offer, all they who have been the Authors of such a Writing, or who have publish'd it, or who have sent it into the Towns amongst us, or to foreign Princes and strange Countrys, shall be held for Lyars, Slanderers, and wicked Speakers, as indeed such they are.

Given at Delft *the 25th of* January 1581.

A

A Copy of the Letter which my Lord the Prince of Orange *sent unto the Kings and Potentates of* Christendom.

SIR,

I Doubt not, but that your Majesty hath been advertis'd of a certain Proscription, which the King of *Spain* hath appointed to be publish'd against me, because he hath caused the same to be spread abroad in all Languages, and hath sent it also into divers quarters of *Christendom*. I and all my very good Friends have thought, that I could not sufficiently defend mine Honour (which I am advis'd and purpos'd not to hazard or indanger for any thing) but by setting a just Defence against this unjust Proscription. In regard whereof, I have presented unto my Lords, the Estates of these Countries, my Answer: which Answer also (for the maintenance of my Honour and Reputation amongst the Princes and Potentates of *Europe*, who in respect of their Preheminences and Dignities are the Succours of poor Princes and distressed Noblemen) I have been bold to send unto them, and to you, Sir, particularly; most humbly beseeching your Majesty, that after you have seen it, you would yield like Judgment thereof, as it hath pleas'd my Lords the Estates, who have been most faithful Witnesses of all my Actions, to do, and to esteem and judg thereof also (as it shall please your Majesty to take knowledg of it) by their Advice and Counsel, which also is annex'd to my said Defence. And because, Sir, your Majesty may think it strange, that the King of *Spain* having heretofore violently taken from me all my Goods, after that I had put my Governments into the hands of the Dutchess of *Parma*, then the Governess of this Estate, and had withdrawn my self into the Country of *Germany*, the Place of my Nativity, where I kept my self peaceably among my Brethren, Kinsfolks, and Friends, as also I had fully purpos'd so to continue: and that having at the same time convey'd or carry'd away from the Schools my Son the Count of *Bueren*, and both contrary to the Privileges of the Country, and against his own Oath, causing him to be carry'd Prisoner into *Spain*, where he is as yet cruelly kept captive: and besides, having procur'd me to be condemn'd to death, by the Duke of *Alva* his own Officer. Because, I say, your Majesty may think it strange,

strange, that for all these Reasons (which were nevertheless very great and weighty) I have not hitherto publish'd any Defence, which was directed to the said King, or might directly concern him: which thing notwithstanding I do at this present, and declare thereby, that the Faults wherewith the King of *Spain* mindeth to charge me, belong unto himself. I do therefore most humbly beseech your Majesty, Sir, that before you judg of this my Writing, you would consider the Quality both of the Crimes and Faults, wherewith I am charg'd by this Proscription, and also the Quality of mine own Person. For if the King of *Spain* was content to withhold from me my Son and my Goods, which he hath in his possession, and further to offer (as at this present he doth) five and twenty thousand Crowns for my Head, and to promise to make such noble as should murder me, and to pardon them all the Faults whatsoever that they could have committed before that time: no man should think it evil in me, that I have attempted by all the means I could (as indeed heretofore I have done) to preserve my self and mine, and to enable my self what I could, to enter again into that which is mine own; and that I have follow'd that Order and Course of Life that I have done. But further, the King of *Spain* having all the world thorow publish'd, that I am *a publick Plague, an Enemy of the World, Unthankful, Unfaithful, a Traitor, and a wicked Person*; these are such Injuries, Sir, that no Gentleman, no tho he were of the basest of the King of *Spain*'s natural Subjects, can or ought to endure: Insomuck, Sir, that tho I were one of his simple and absolute Vassals, who oweth Homage unto him by Honour, yet so it is, that by such a Sentence, and so unjust in all and every part thereof (I also having been by him spoil'd of my Lands and Lordships, in respect of which I should heretofore have taken an Oath unto him) I might have held my self absolv'd and free from all my Bonds towards him, and have assay'd also (which thing even Nature hath taught every one) by all the means I could to maintain mine Honour, which ought to be to me and to all Noblemen more dear than Life and Goods. Notwithstanding, seeing it hath pleas'd God to shew me this great Grace, that I am born a free Lord, not holding of any other but of the Empire, as do the Princes and other free Lords of *Germany* and *Italy*: and further, seeing that I bear the Title, and have the name of an *absolute and free Prince*, tho indeed my Princedom be not very great: yea whatsoever it be, I not being his natural Subject, neither having held any thing of him, but by reason of my Signiories and Lordships, of which notwithstanding he hath wholly dispossess'd me; it hath

seem'd

seem'd unto me, that I could not defend mine Honour, and satisfy or content my near Kinsfolks, sundry Princes (to whom this is my Honour that I am link'd) and my whole Posterity, but in answering by publick Writing to this Accusation, which in the presence of all *Christendom*, is publish'd and set out against me. And tho I have not been able to do it, without touching his Honour, I hope notwithstanding (Sir) that your Majesty will impute it, rather to the Inforcement that the Quality and Heinousness of this Proscription hath laid upon me, than to my Nature or Will. For as concerning this point, that some Men may think it strange, that I do after this sort defend my self, seeing that I have sometimes heretofore held of him sundry Lands and Lordships; for answer thereto, I will most humbly beseech your Majesty, to consider the Heinousness of the Injury that is done me, which a right Nobleman will never indeed abide: also that I am not his natural Subject, and as concerning my Fees and Pensions, that he hath spoil'd me of them. But suppose that I had always enjoy'd them, yet so it is, that the same Law which he useth towards others, should not be deny'd to me.

He holdeth of the *French* King in Loyalty and Homage, and even as the Vassal doth of his Lord, the County or Earldom of *Charolois*: and yet for all that he ceaseth not to make war against the Crown of *France*, yea he never leaveth off continually to practise and devise somewhat against the same. He taketh this as a sure Foundation or Rule, that being a Sovereign Governor in some other place, it is lawful for him to revenge himself of the wrong which he pretended was done unto him by the late *French* King *Henry* of most noble Memory. When he made war against the Pope *Caraffa*, because as a Vassal he held of him the Kingdoms of *Sicily* and *Naples*, he publish'd his Defence, by which he maintain'd that he was absolv'd from his Oath, because that the Pope kept not himself within the terms or points that the Lord oweth to his Vassal, according to the feodal Laws which are mutual, and respect as well the one as the other. Now, Sir, there is nothing so natural or kindly, as that every one should in his own cause, receive the very self-same Rule and Order, that he would have another Man to receive or allow of. Wherefore he should not think it strange, that I being so many ways revil'd and injur'd by him, and not being his Subject, that I, I say, do aid my self with the means that God hath given me, and with which he hath been willing to help himself against his Lords, who have not offended him in any thing what-

In the Letter sent to the French *King, it is written*, He holdeth of your Majesty.

whatsoever, that draweth nigh to the Wrong which I have suffer'd at his hand: yea, he should not think it strange, that I use against him that reproachful Note, by which he assayeth to mark as it were in the Forehead both me and my Race.

And because my Lords the Estates (who have more nearly known the truth of all that is contain'd in this my D fence, and have approv d the same) have yielded unto me sufficient Testimony touching my Life past; I do most humbly also beseech your Majesty (Sir) in approving this same mine Answer, to believe that I am not either a Traitor or wicked Person, but that I am (thanks be to God for it) a Nobleman, of a very good and most antient House, yea a good Man, and true in every thing that I promise; not unthankful, nor unfaithful, nor having committed any thing, whereby a Lord or Knight of my State and Countenance may receive any Reproach or Shame: most humbly beseeching you to hold and account me in the number of your most humble Servants. And thus having most humbly submitted my self unto your Majesty, I will pray God, Sir, to give you, together with a perfect Health, a most blessed and most long Life.

At Delft *in* Holland,
Febr. 4. 1581.

Your Majesty's most Humble

and Obedient Servant,

William of *Nassau.*

Phenix

Phenix XIV.

A Narrative of the Proceedings of a Great Council of Jews, *assembled in the Plain of* Ageda *in* Hungary, *about thirty Leagues from* Buda, *to examine the Scriptures concerning Christ, on the Twelfth of* October 1650.

By Samuel Brett, *there present.*

Also a Relation of some other Observations in his Travels beyond the Seas.

First Printed in 1655.

To the Reader.

THERE *was nothing I more desired than to travel beyond the Seas, and to know the various Manners of the Nations of the World: for which, thro God's Providence, I had an opportunity offer'd me, to my great Satisfaction, being Chirurgeon of an* English *Ship in the Straits, where, for a Cure that I did for* Orlando de de Spina *of* Gollipulo, *an eminent Man in those parts, I was by him prefer'd to be a Captain of a Ship of* Malta, *which was set out by the said* Orlando, *and committed to my Command against the* Turks *in the* Arches, *in assistance to the* Venetian *Service: in which Service I spent about nine months, till the tempestuous Season of the Year enforc'd me to return into Harbour again. And in this time of Employment, I made five Fights at Sea, and two at Land; being chosen by lot to invade the* Turks *Country, with a certain Company of Soldiers collected out of our Fleet, to do some execution upon the Borders of the Enemy, and to get some Provision for our Relief; in all which Fights (altho very perillous) God gave me the Victory.*

The whole time I spent beyond the Seas, before and after this Employment, was almost four years, not staying long in any one place. But first I travel'd to all the Sea-Towns of note for Merchandizing, to know the Trade of the places, and the Conveniency of their Harbours, that I might be able to do some profitable service in Merchants Affairs. Also I travel'd into several Countries, and the most eminent Cities and Towns therein; viz. Egypt, Macedonia, Dalmatia, Calabria, Apuleia, Sicilia, Assyria, Sclavonia, *some parts of* Spain *and* Portugal; *to the Islands of* Cyprus, Candia, Patmos, Delphos; *to* Carthage, Corinth, Troy, Constantinople; *besides many other Towns and Places: but my longest abode was in* Italy, *and therein at* Venice, Naples, Leghorn, Florence, Milan, Rome, Bolognia, Mantua, Genoa, &c. *And at last looking homeward, I came into* France; *taking a brief view of many eminent places in that Kingdom. And at* Paris *I found many of my Countrymen (of which, tho some be Persons of great Quality, yet) God knoweth they are in a low Condition. And now I shall give a brief Account of some of my Observations, during the time of my abode beyond the Seas.*

A Narrative of the Proceedings of a Great Council of Jews, *&c.*

AT *Paris* our Countrymen live peaceably, and enjoy our Religion without disturbance. There is a Place allow'd them, with necessary Accommodations for the Exercise of Religion. Dr. *Steward* did often preach to them; and for their Form of Worship, it is the same that was formerly in *England*, with the Book of Common Prayer, and the Rites therein used; and also they continue the Innovations that were practised by many of our Clergy, as Bowing at the Name of Jesus towards the Altar, *&c.* which I know giveth offence

offence to the good *French* Protestants, who to me did often condemn those Innovations for Romish Superstitions. Doubtless they would do our Church and our Religion more Credit there, if they did use less Ceremony. As for the *French* Papists, truly they are more civil to them than was expected: for the Opinion of the World, where I have been, is but mean of that Nation. And I believe the *Italian* may be their Cousin German, for both of them are false and faithless enough. And this Consideration (God having taken away *Orlando* my noble Friend, who did always much countenance me) did lessen my Affection to continue in that Service; for my Soldiers were all *Italians* (except a few *Greeks*) and I never saw much cause to be confident in their Fidelity; but it was chiefly for fear of him, that they were so tractable to me.

As for Religion, in most parts where I have been, it is generally the same with the Church of *Rome*; but for the *Grecians* (for amongst them I was) they are neither pure Protestants nor pure Papists; I mean, neither only Protestants nor only Papists, but their Religion is a mixture of both: For tho they hold some Fundamentals with us, yet they follow many of the *Romish* Superstitions; and (according to my Observation) they follow more the Religion of *Rome*, than the Protestant Church; and they are much poison'd with Heresys.

But of all Nations, according to my Observation, none are more zealous for the Religion of *Rome* than the *Spaniards*, who, I think, for this are more *Romanists* than the *Romans* themselves; for with them there is an Inquisition, and in *Rome* I never heard of the same dangerous Snare: there I had as much Freedom as I could desire, and more Courtesy than I could expect, without any Temptation to apostatize from my Religion.

As for the Occurrences that I met with, they were many: But these four were the most considerable.

First, The strangling of the great *Turk* by the Janizaries, at which time there was great Fear and Trouble in *Constantinople*; but they enthron'd his Son, and this brought a peaceable Settlement. And with him there were cut off divers *Basha*'s Heads; all whose Heads (excepting the Great *Turk*'s) lay three days in Chargers before the Palace-Gate, for the publick View of the People; which they say is the Custom for the Noblemen that are beheaded.

The next thing is, The flowing of the River *Nilus* in *Egypt*; the manner whereof is this: It beginneth to flow about the fifteenth of *June* every year: the People know the time thereof, and expect it accordingly; and this is after their Harvest, which is usually ended about the beginning of *May*. As for Rain, there seldom falleth any in *Egypt*. During the time the River is up, all the Country appeareth like Islands. Their Towns are seated upon Hills, and their lower Grounds are all cover'd with Waters; and the Inhabitants use small Boats to pass from place to place about their Affairs: and because they know the yearly flowing of *Nilus*, they provide for the Safety of their Cattel till the Waters are wasted away again. There are also certain Pillars of Stone set up, with divers Marks upon them, by which they know the degrees of the rising, and the usual height that the Waters do ascend unto; and if the Waters do ascend above the highest Mark, they do expect some strange Consequence thereof. But the greatest wonder is, the present Cessation of the Plague upon the flowing of this River. There died some thousands of the Plague the day before the flowing of *Nilus* in *Grandcairo*, as they certify'd me; and a day or two after, not one Person more died of the Infection. This I observ'd, that the Land is full of unhealthy Fogs, Mists, and Vapours, which cause the Disease; and it seems the Waters of *Nilus* do purify it again.

In the Kingdom of *Grandcairo*, alias *Pharaoh's Town*, is the City, and it is greater than any elsewhere I did behold; but *Memphis* is the neater City: and being there, I went to see the Land of *Goshen*, where the *Israelites* did inhabit. This is a very pleasant and fruitful Land for Pasture, such as I have no where seen the like. At this time also, I had an opportunity to see the *Red Sea*, and the place where (as they inform'd me) the *Israelites* did enter their Journy thro the same. There also they shew'd me the great Mountains that inclos'd them, when *Pharaoh* pursued them with his great Army; and the Hills where the two Armies lay in sight one of another. And there I found the true reason why it is call'd the *Red Sea*; not because the Water is red naturally, but because the Sand is red: And this was clear to me by plain Demonstration; for I put some of the Water into a clean Vessel, and there I did see it had the same colour of other Water; but the Sand is reddish, and giveth the same colour to the Water.

I shall omit many other things concerning *Egypt*; only this, It is under the *Turks* Dominion, and the Natives are his miserable Slaves.

Thirdly, You may expect some News from *Rome*, where also I was, and did behold their great Solemnity; it being then the *Anno Sancto*, as they there call it, that is, the Year of Jubilee.

There

There I beheld the Pope in his Glory, and how in great State he was carried about the City: the Streets were throng'd with the People; and as he pass'd by, they made them even ring with Acclamations and Rejoicings: He was carried by some eminent Men, having a rich Canopy over him. He made his Crosses in the Air with his fingers, and threw his Blessings amongst them. And truly these Delusions were so prevailing with the People, that (poor Souls) they seem'd to me to rejoice, as if Christ himself had been come to *Rome*, and brought them down the Felicities of Heaven.

At one time I beheld in *Naples* (perhaps it will seem strange, but it is true) about eight thousand Pilgrims going to *Rome* for their Absolution; all which the Vice-Roy of *Naples* maintain'd three days, at his own charge; and on the fourth day, they did present themselves before him at his Palace in Pilgrim Weeds, *viz.* with leaden Pictures of Saints in their Hats, with leather Collars about their Necks, which fell down half way over their Arms, and their Staves in their hands: and thus they march'd away from *Naples*, in the posture of an Army towards *Rome*; and so farewel *Rome*. *Vidi, satis est vidisse.*

I omit to recite many other Occurrences, which by conference I shall willingly communicate to my Friends, they being too many to commit to writing: only now the fourth remarkable thing remaineth to present you with; and that is,

The Proceedings of a great Council of *Jews*, assembled in the Plain of *Ageda* in *Hungary*, about thirty Leagues distant from *Buda*, to examine the Scriptures concerning Christ; on the twelfth of *October*, 1650.

It hath been much desir'd by many honest Christians, that this Narrative of the *Jews* Council should be publish'd, which I did intend only to communicate to private Friends. The chief Argument by which they have persuaded me to do it, is, because they do conceive it to be a Preparative and hopeful Sign of the *Jews* Conversion, and that it will be glad Tidings to the Church of Christ; and therefore I have yielded to satisfy their Desires therein. And thus it was:

At the place above-named there assembled about three hundred Rabbies, call'd together from several parts of the World, to examine the Scriptures concerning Christ; and it seems this Place was thought most convenient for this Council, in regard that part of the Country was not much inhabited, because of the continual Wars between the *Turk* and the King of *Hungary*; where (as I was inform'd) they had fought two bloody Battels: yet both Princes, notwithstanding their own Differences, did give leave to the *Jews* to hold their Council there.

there. And for their Accommodation there, the *Jews* did make divers Tents for their Repoſe, and had Plenty of Proviſion brought them from other Parts of the Country, during the time of their ſitting there. There was alſo one large Tent, built only for the Council to ſit in, made almoſt fourſquare; the North and the South part of it, being not altogether ſo large as the Eaſt and Weſt part thereof. It had but one Door, and that open'd to the Eaſt; and in the middle thereof ſtood a little Table and a Stool for the Propounder to ſit on, with his Face towards the Door of the Tent. The ſaid Propounder was of the Tribe of *Levi*, and was named *Zacharias*; and within this Tent round about were placed divers Forms for the Conſulters to ſit on. It was alſo incloſed with a Rail, that ſtood at a diſtance from it, to prevent entrance to all Strangers, and to all ſuch *Jews* as could not prove themſelves to be *Jews* by Record, or could not diſpute in the *Hebrew* Tongue, which many had forgotten, who liv'd in ſuch Countries, where they are not allow'd their Synagogues, as in *France*, *Spain*, and thoſe parts of *Italy* that do belong to the King of *Spain*, *viz.* the Kingdom of *Naples*, with the Province of *Calabria* and *Apuleia*; the Kingdom of *Sicilia* and *Sardinia*; in which places if a *Jew* be found, and he deny the Popiſh Religion, he is in danger to be condemn'd and executed for it; and yet Profit and Benefit allureth them to dwell in thoſe Countries, notwithſtanding their Fears and Dangers: and themſelves are willing to forget, and ſo neglect to teach their Children their native Language, rather than they will loſe their opportunity of Profit: and ſome have burnt the antient Records of their Tribe and Family, that they might not be diſcover'd by ſearching, or otherwiſe. And for this Defect, that they could not prove their Tribe or Family, they were not permitted to come within the Rail, but were commanded to remain without, with the Strangers that remain'd there, to ſee the Iſſue of their Proceeding, which were above 3000 Perſons, and they were for the moſt part *Germans*, *Almains*, *Dalmatians*, and *Hungarians*, with ſome *Greeks*; but few *Italians*, and not one *Engliſh*-man, that I could hear of, beſides my ſelf.

I was inform'd, that the King of *Hungary* not favouring the Reformed Religion, did give no encouragement to any Proteſtant Churches to ſend any Divines thither; but he did allow that ſome Aſſiſtants ſhould be ſent from *Rome*: and their coming thither did prove a great unhappineſs to this hopeful Council.

When the Aſſembly did firſt meet, they ſpent ſome time in their mutual Salutations; and, as their manner is, they kiſs'd one the other's Cheek, expreſſing much Joy for their happy Meeting. And all things being provided for their Accommodation,

dation, they consider'd of the *Jews* that were to be admitted Members of this Council; and they were only allow'd to be Members, which could by Record prove themselves to be native *Jews*; and for defect herein, I observ'd above Five hundred refus'd: tho doubtless they were True-born *Jews*, yet they could not by Record prove themselves so to be; and for this they were not admitted to be Members of the Council, but they did abide without the Rail with the Strangers that were there: and the number of them that were accepted to be Members, was about Three hundred *Jews*. And this was all that was done the first day.

On the second day, the Assembly being full, the Propounder stood up, and made his Speech concerning the end of their meeting: And, *This*, said he, *is to examine the Scriptures concerning Christ, whether he be already come, or whether we are yet to expect his coming.* In examining this Question, they search'd the Old Testament with great Care and Labour, to be resolv'd of the Truth thereof, having many Bibles with them there for this end. And about this Point there were great Disputes amongst them. The major part were of Opinion, That he was not come: and some inclin'd to think that he was come; being mov'd thereunto by their great Judgment, that hath continu'd now this Sixteen hundred years upon them.

I remember very well one of the Council in his Conference with me, seem'd to be very apprehensive of the great and long Desolation of their Nation, ever since their Destruction by the *Roman* Emperors; and he imputed this their Affliction to their Impenitency. And comparing their present Judgment, with their other Judgments they had suffer'd before, he ingenuously confess'd, that he did conceive it was for some great Wickedness; and that their Nation was guilty of the Blood of the Prophets sent from God to their Nation, and the many Massacres that had been committed by the several Sects and Factions amongst them. *For* (said he) *we are no Idolaters, neither do I think we were guilty of Idolatry since our Captivity in* Babylon; *and therefore* (said he) *I do impute this our Calamity and present Judgment to the fore-nam'd Causes.* And this was the sum of that which was disputed amongst them the second day of their meeting; and so they adjourn'd till the next Morning, which was the third day of their meeting.

When being assembl'd together again, the Point that was chiefly agitated was concerning the Manner of Christ's coming. And this, some said, shall be like a mighty Prince, in the full Power and Authority of a King, yea, in greater Power than ever any King had; and that he will deliver their Nation out of the Power of their Enemies, and their Temple shall be rebuilt again; and, that the Nations ſhall be of their Religion, and worſhip God after their manner. For they hold, That the *Meſſiah* will not alter their Religion, whenſoever he cometh. And further, concerning his Parentage, they did agree in this, That he ſhould be born of a Virgin, according to the Prediction of the Prophets; and they agreed alſo, that he may be born of ſuch a Virgin, which might be of mean Note amongſt their Nation, as was the Virgin *Mary*. And here ſome of them ſeem'd to me, to incline to think that Chriſt was come. Therefore when they came together again the next day, the Propounder demanded of them, if Chriſt were already come, and who they thought he was? and to this Demand they gave this Anſwer, That they thought *Eliah* was he, if he were come, becauſe he came with great Power, which he declar'd by ſlaying the Prieſts of *Baal*; and, for the fulfilling of the Scripture, he was oppreſs'd by *Ahab* and *Jezabel*: yet they eſteem'd him to be more than a mortal Man, becauſe he ſo ſtrangely aſcended up into Heaven. And becauſe this Opinion was contradicted by others, the day following they took into Examination the ſame Queſtion, to anſwer them that ſaid *Eliah* was not the *Meſſiah*. They of the contrary Opinion did urge the Care and Love of *Eliah* for the good of their Nation, in that he left them *Eliſha* his Diſciple to teach and inſtruct the People; which they expect to be the Care of their *Meſſiah*. Theſe were the chief Arguments they had to defend their Opinion: and the ſame day, towards night, it came into queſtion amongſt them, What he then was that ſaid he was the Son of God, and was crucified by their Anceſtors? And becauſe this was the great Queſtion amongſt them, they defer'd the further Conſideration thereof until the next day.

When meeting again, the *Phariſees* (for ſome of this Sect were amongſt them, that were always the Enemies of Chriſt) they firſt began to anſwer this laſt Night's queſtion; and theſe by no means would yield that he was the Chriſt; and theſe Reaſons they gave for their Opinion.

Firſt, Becauſe (ſaid they) he came into the World like an ordinary and inferior Man, not with his Scepter, nor Royal Power; wherewith they affirm'd the Coming of Chriſt ſhould be Glorious. Secondly, They pleaded againſt him the Meanneſs of his Birth, in that his Father was a Carpenter; and this they ſaid, was a Diſhonour that Chriſt ſhould not be capable of. Thirdly, They accus'd him to be an Enemy to *Moſes*'s Law, in ſuffering his Diſciples, and in doing Works himſelf that were prohibited on the Sabbath-day; for they believe that the *Meſſiah* will punctually and exactly keep the Law

Law of *Moses:* and where the Gospel doth testify of Christ, that he did fulfil the Law, they reject the Testimony thereof, because they do not own the Gospel. But I observ'd these Reasons of the *Pharisees* did not satisfy all that heard them, but there still remain'd some Doubt in some of them concerning Christ; for there stood up one *Rabbie* call'd *Abraham*, and objected against the *Pharisees*, the Miracles that Christ wrought whilst he was upon Earth, as his raising of the Dead to life again, his making the Lame to walk, the Blind to see, and the Dumb to speak. And the same *Abraham* demanded of the *Pharisees*, by what Power he did these Miracles? The Answer the *Pharisees* return'd to him, was to this purpose: They said he was an Impostor and a Magician; and blasphemously traduc'd him of doing all his Miracles by Magick: Thus, said they, he first caus'd them to be blind, to be dumb, to be lame; and then by taking away his Magical Charm, they were restor'd to their former condition. Neverthelesss, this Answer gave little Satisfaction to the said *Abraham:* but thus he reply'd, That he could not charm those that were born in that condition, as blind, *&c.* and born also before Christ himself was born; as it appeareth some of them were. This seem'd to him an absurd Paradox; and truly the pressing of this Argument did almost put them to a nonplus, till at last they had this Evasion (tho weak and vile) They were (said they) by other Magicians convinc'd to be so in their Mother's Wombs; and that altho himself were not then born when they were born with these Evils, yet he being a great Dissembler, and more cunning than any Magician before him, Power was given him by the Devil, to remove those Charms which others had plac'd. And there was one *Pharisee* nam'd *Zebedee*, who of the *Pharisees* there did most opprobriously revile him, and vehemently urge these things against him; but I conceive he did it not to the well-liking of many there that heard him, even Members of the Council. And as the *Pharisees* that day play'd their Parts against him; so did the *Sadduces* also endeavour (for some of that Sect were also of the Council) to render Christ vile and odious to the rest of the *Jews* that were assembl'd there. I observ'd it was with them, as it was once with *Herod* and *Pilate*; tho they two could not agree betwixt themselves at other times, yet they could agree together to crucify Christ: for the *Pharisees* and *Sadduces*, tho they be much divided in Opinion among themselves, yet did they at this time too much agree to disgrace and to dishonour Christ with their Lies, Calumnies and Blasphemies: for the *Sadduces*, as well as the *Pharisees*, did in other things accuse him for a grand Impostor, and for a Broacher of corrupt Doctrine; in that in his Gospel he teacheth the Resurrection from the Dead, which they there deny'd to be true Doctrine: but it is no new thing to see Factions dissenting, to agree in some evil design against others, as I found it by experience. Being at *Rome* in the Year 1650, which was the Year of their *Jubilee*, there was a great Strife between the *Jesuits* and the *Fryars* of the Order of St. *Dominick*, both which were against the Protestants: and altho their Differences have been by the care and vigilance of the *Pope* so smother'd, that the World hath not taken much notice thereof; yet this Fire broke out into a Flame greater than ever it was before, (as they certified me there) both by publick Disputings, and by bitter Writings one against another, opening the Vices and Errors of one another's Faction, thus seeking to disgrace one the other; which caus'd the *Pope* to threaten to excommunicate the Authors of all such black and libellous Books, that did tend to the dishonour of his Clergy and Religion, to make them infamous to the World. But this by the way.

We are come now to the seventh and last Day of their Council; and on this day, this was the main Query amongst them: If Christ be come, then what Rules and Orders hath he left his Church to walk by? This was a great Question amongst them: and because they did not believe the New Testament, nor would be guided by it, they demanded some other Instruction to direct and guide them in this Point: Thereupon six of the *Roman* Clergy (who of purpose were sent from *Rome* by the *Pope*, to assist in this Council) were call'd in, *viz.* two *Jesuits*, two *Friars* of the Order of St. *Augustine*, and two of the Order of St. *Francis*. And these being admitted into the Council, began to open unto them the Rules and Doctrine of the Holy Church of *Rome*, (as they call it) which Church they magnified to them for the Holy Catholick Church of Christ, and their Doctrine to be the infallible Doctrine of Christ, and their Rules to be the Rules which the Apostles left to the Church for ever to be observ'd, and that the *Pope* is the Holy Vicar of Christ, and the Successor of St. *Peter*: And for instance in some particulars they affirm'd the real presence of Christ in the Sacrament, the religious Observation of their Holy Days, the Invocation of Saints praying to the Virgin *Mary*, and her commanding Power in Heaven over her Son, the Holy use of the Cross and Images, with the rest of their Idolatrous and Superstitious Worship; all which they commended to the Assembly of the *Jews*, for the Doctrine and Rules of the Apostles. But so soon as the Assembly had heard these things from them, they were generally and exceedingly troubled thereat, and fell into high Clamors against them and their Religion, crying out, *No Christ, no Woman-God, no*

Intercession

Intercession of Saints, no Worshipping of Images, no praying to the Virgin Mary, *&c.* Truly their Trouble hereat was so great, that it troubled me to see their impatience: they rent their Clothes, and cast dust upon their Heads, and cryed out aloud, *Blasphemy, Blasphemy*; and upon this the Council broke up. Yet they assembled again the eighth Day; and all that was done then, was to agree upon another meeting of their Nation three Years after; which was concluded upon before their final Dissolution.

I do believe there were many *Jews* there that would have been persuaded to own the Lord Jesus; and this I assure you for a Truth, and it is for the Honor of our Religion, and the encouragement of our Divines: One eminent *Rabbi* there did deliver me his Opinion in conference with me, that he at first feared that those which were sent from *Rome*, would cause an unhappy Period to their Council; and professed to me, that he much desired the presence of some Protestant Divines, and especially of our *English* Divines, of whom he had a better Opinion, than of any other Divines in the World: For he did believe that we have a great Love to their Nation; and this Reason he gave me for their good Opinion of our Divines, because he understood that they did ordinarily pray for the Conversion of their Nation; which he did acknowledg to be a great Token of our Love towards them: And especially he commended the Ministers of *London* for excellent Preachers, and for their Charity towards their Nation; of whom he had heard a great Fame. As for the Church of *Rome*, they account it an Idolatrous Church, and therefore will not own their Religion: and by conversing with the *Jews*, I found that they generally think, that there is no other Christian Religion in the world, but that of the Church of *Rome*; and for *Rome*'s Idolatry, they take offence at all Christian Religion. By which it appeareth that *Rome* is the greatest Enemy of the *Jews* Conversion.

For the place of the *Jews* next Meeting, it is probable it will be in *Syria*, in which Country I also was, and did there converse with the Sect of the *Rechabites*, living in *Syria*. They still observe their old Customs and Rules; they neither sow nor plant, nor build Houses; but live in Tents, and often remove from one place to another, with their whole Family, Bag and Baggage. And seeing I find, that by the *Italian* Tongue I can converse with the *Jews*, or any other Nation, in all the parts of the world where I have been; if God give me an opportunity, I shall willingly attend their next Council. *The good Lord prosper it.* Amen.

Phe-

Phenix XV.

Certain LETTERS, *evidencing K.* Charles II's *Stedfastness in the Protestant Religion: Sent from the Princess of* Turenne, *and the Ministers of* Charenton, *to some Persons of Quality in* London.

A LETTER *from the Princess of* Turenne, *to a Noble Lady her Cousin-German, Madam* de Castelnaut, *at* London.

My Dear Cousin,

IF you had not been for a long time accustom'd to bear with, and to pardon my Laziness, I should be in pain for the Judgment you might make of my Silence, and that I have delay'd so long to answer the last Letter I receiv'd from you: But if your Goodness protects me from the Reproaches which you have reason to charge me with, it does not secure me from those which I ought to lay to my own charge, when I neglect to give you such Testimonies as I am able of the Tenderness I have for you. It is true, that I shall be more earnest to give you real and useful Proofs of it, than I am to let you see these weak Assurances; and you may be confident, my dear Cousin, that I shall ever cherish such Opportunities, and

and embrace them with all my heart as often as I am able. Yet I must complain of you to your self, because you have again written to me with Ceremony, and did not follow this Method which is more frank and more convenient; and truly this was the thing which did contribute to my Laziness: for I am so unacquainted with formal Writing, especially to those I love so heartily, that I know not how to set my self to it, and I was afraid that it would be too uncivil to use such freedom after all those Complements you gave me. Yet at last, Madam, my dear Cousin, I thought this should not make you suspect that I could fail to join to that Affection I have for you, all those Resentments of Honour and Respect which are due to you, and to which I am more particularly oblig'd than another, both by nearness in Blood, and by many other Reasons: Therefore I am fix'd to continue in this way in the Resolution to overcome you, and to oblige you to do so too; otherwise, I do declare, that I shall take a refusal for such a Complement as witnesses more Civility than Friendship, and for a kind of renouncing of this Commerce. I will therefore, Dear Cousin, expect a very kind Letter with little Ceremony; such a one I do desire, and that you would receive this with the same Affection wherewith I do write it. I long much for the Satisfaction to see you again in this Country, you have already seen many Revolutions in that where you are; and whatever my longing be for your return, I do avow it, That I wish with all my heart you may yet see there that Change, which the present condition of affairs gives us reason to hope very shortly, and which all good Men desire with an extreme Passion; that is, *The King's return into his former Lustre and Authority.* I have ever wish'd with great Passion the re-establishment of that Prince for divers Reasons, both for the desire which I think every one ought to have, that things be done according to Justice, and for the horror of the Crime committed upon the Person of the King his Father, which hath since drawn down such terrible Jugdgments on those Nations, and so fearful Confusions in those Churches, which God had gather'd there, and which he had made flourish with so much Lustre and Purity, that one cannot forbear to weep over their Ruin as bitterly as *Ezra*, *Nehemiah*, and *Daniel* did over that of *Jerusalem*, until it may please the Lord to hear us and settle them. I profess I cannot believe that that Sin can be expiated, nor the Interdict remov'd from among them, but by the re-establishment of their Lawful and Sovereign Lord, and by the rendring to him that Power which he receiv'd from God, and which for so long a time hath been usurp'd over him. The same who commands to give God the things which are God's, commands

mands us also to render to *Cæsar* the things that are *Cæsar's*: So that I believe that he who would content himself with one of these two Duties, and so separate the things which God hath join'd, should satisfy neither; and that so lame a Service should be less acceptable among Christians, than a lame Offering was among the *Jews*. These Considerations make me wish with great Passion that God would inspire those Nations to do their Duty; but I do avow it, that I double my Prayers and my Zeal, when I hear that the present Governours are no more those Sectarys, but Men of our Profession. They have had the misfortune to be slander'd by the Adversarys, as accessary to the Death of their Sovereign, and that infamous Accusation seems to have blackt all their Brethren. Blessed be the God of Mercy, who presents to them so fair an occasion to clear themselves, and to remove that Reproach from so holy a Profession as ours is, which we have ever brag'd to have this advantage above all others, in that it did teach us better than any other that which we owe to Sovereigns, and did not permit that Men should, under any pretext whatsoever, dispense themselves of the Oath of Fidelity which they have taken. I have so great an impatience to hear that they have there so re-establish'd it by so just and so lovely an Action, that I cannot tell you with how much Affection I beg'd it of God on the Fast day which we kept at *Charenton* last *Easter* Week, and how earnestly I do beg it every day: And I believe there be few Lovers of the Peace of *Jerusalem* who make not the same Prayer; and I see that all those of our Profession in this Kingdom are more earnest in this than ever, whether it be that God inspires this Motion to pray more earnestly in a time when he will do his work (as he is often pleas'd to make the Prayers of his Children meet with the Decrees of his Providence) or whether they have taken more notice of late of the *Effects of the Piety of the King of* England, which makes them interest themselves more sensibly in his Concerns. For my own part I profess it, that I was exceedingly satisfy'd when I had the Honour to pay my Respects to him the last time he past thro this Country, having heard him speak with so great Testimonys of Piety, that I was extremely edify'd. He was also pleas'd to give this Mark of his Communion with our Churches, as to go to Sermon at *Rochel* and at *Rouen* in his Passage; and if he had staid here, we had had the honour to have seen him at *Charenton*. There can nothing be added to the Regularity which this Prince keeps in assisting daily at those Exercises of Piety, which are kept Morning and Evening in his Family. *In a word, I bless God, because the Marks of God's Election are seen in him:* And I hope God will use his Service

for

for re-establishing what we have before seen with so much pleasure in his Dominions, and that his Subjects will have cause to bless the Lord for putting it into their Hearts, to render to their King his Crown, and as fair as ever he had it, and without spoiling or defacing it in setting it on his Head. I pray God with all my Heart that he may give them this Grace, and I do so lay it to heart, that I take the liberty to write you a long Letter of it, which looks like a little Volume. But it is, dear Cousin, because I believe that as you are on the place, it is a point of Duty to contribute always what one can to infuse these Thoughts into such as have them not, and that every one ought to be ambitious to bring their little Stone toward that excellent Work. As I do desire very much that those in whom I am concern'd may employ themselves toward what is excellent, I shall be very glad that my Lady your Sister in Law and You might contribute somewhat to this. Oblige me, by assuring her of my most humble Service, and by believing me altogether

Tuesday, 6 April, N. Stile, 1660. *Yours*,

Ox. Caumont.

A Letter of Monsieur Daille *to Monsieur* Le Roy.

SIR,

ONE of my Friends having desir'd me, a little while since, to send him a Copy of the great Bible printed at *London*, I remembred that the last Winter you propos'd to send one to Monsieur *Duret*, and my self, for fifty Crowns; so that I believ'd, that in this occasion I could not make an Address to any with more conveniency than to you, that my Friend might be provided. And I hope you will grant me the Favor which I request of you, to inform me, whether you can at present perform your Promise, and send me this Book for the price which you formerly exprest. Moreover, I cannot but rejoice with you for the happy News which is convey'd to us from the place where you are; whereby we are inform'd, that the universal Desire of the People seems with a common voice to recal their natural and lawful King. Besides that Generosity and Equity it self obliges us to wish, that this Prince may return into his own Kingdom and Inheritance, of which he hath been unjustly depriv'd; we ought also to desire it for the honour of our Religion, which should be more dear to us than any other Interest.

For

For when our Adversaries formerly would charge the Blame of the Death of the late King of *England* on our Religion, you know we could very well guard our selves from this Reproach, by casting it intirely upon the Sectaries, who indeed were only guilty of that horrible Crime. But at present we do not stand upon the same terms, since there is such a change of Affairs; the Sectarians having lost their credit, or at least being fallen from that Sovereign Power which they had graspt; and on the contrary the Presbyterian Party, which is ours, now governing in *England*. So that if they let slip the fair opportunity which God seems to open to them, for the re-establishing of the King of *Great Britain* in his Dominion, and to re-advance him to the Throne of his Ancestors, it is most apparent there will be no further ground to excuse themselves upon the Sectaries, nor to wash our holy Religion from that spot, from which, by the Grace of God, it hath always been preserv'd pure and clean to this present. I well know there are dispersed evil Rumors concerning the Religion of this Prince; and I doubt not, but there are some Persons at *London*, as well as at *Paris*, who endeavour to persuade the World, That he hath forsaken our Communion, to embrace that of *Rome*: But who can believe a thing that is so contrary to all probability? there is nothing of this appears to us. On the contrary we well know, That altho this Prince hath been constrain'd by the Circumstances of his present Condition, to reside sometimes in places where the Exercise of our Religion is not permitted, yet he hath always had his Chaplains near to him, who are nothing less than Papists, and who every where have regularly in his presence prayed, and perform'd the other parts of Divine Service. Moreover, all *Paris*, and all the World hath known the Anger and the just Indignation which he express'd, when he understood the Endeavours which have been used (tho ineffectively) for the Apostacy of the Duke of *Glocester*. And if this young Prince rendred his Piety and Constancy admirable, by that firm Resistance which he oppos'd in so tender an Age, to such a violent and dangerous Persecution; so also in that he retir'd to the King his Brother, and there sought for a Sanctuary to his Religion, it is a very certain Argument, that the King had not quitted that Religion: for if this had been true, the Duke of *Glocester* had found him an Enemy instead of a Protector, and had suffer'd the loss of his Conscience, where he had sought its Security, and where he really found it. It is objected against this, that during the whole space of time which the King of *Great Britain* past in the Court of *France*, he never came to our Religious Assemblies, and that amongst others he never came to

Cha-

Charenton in the days of our Worſhip. But altho this may at firſt view appear ſtrange to thoſe who know not the reaſon of it; nevertheleſs, as we are better inform'd of this than any one, we can teſtify that Religion was not the cauſe of it, and that he abſtain'd from coming upon politick and prudential Conſiderations, which may be peculiar to our Church. And the proof of this appears, in that when the King of *England* hath been out of *Paris*, he hath willingly gone to Sermon in the Churches of our Brethren; as for inſtance, in *Caen*, and ſome other Towns; and in *Holland* alſo, he hath ſeveral times heard the Sermons of the famous Monſieur *More*, who at preſent is our Colleague.

Thus, Sir, it is more clear than the Day, that whatſoever hath been reported till this time of the Change of his Religion, is a mere Calumny, ſcatter'd by the Artifice of his Enemies, for to vilify him in the Judgment of his Subjects, and to alienate their Affections and Good Will from him; and finally to render fruitleſs the juſt Prayers which they make at preſent for his happy Return into *England*.

God grant their Accompliſhment by his Almighty Juſtice; and as it is he who hath inſpir'd theſe good Deſigns into the Hearts of his People, and who ſeems to diſpoſe all things for the effecting them, may it pleaſe him to bleſs what remains of this Work, and to ſucceed it for his Glory, and the Honour of his Anointed, but eſpecially for the Edification of his Church. For this I pray to him with all my Soul, and recommend you particularly to his Grace, being,

Paris, 7 April, 1660.

Sir, Your moſt humble Servant.

DAILLE.

Raimond Gaches *Paſtor of the Reformed Church of* Paris, *to the moſt Famous Man and moſt Upright Paſtor*, Richard Baxter, *wiſheth all Health.*

THO I am neither by Face nor Fame known unto you (moſt Worthy Sir, and moſt Reverend Brother in Chriſt) yet I addreſs my ſelf to you with confidence, becauſe I know you very well, and am fully aſſur'd of your Piety. I have read again and again, not without admiration, thoſe learned Volumes

Volumes (little indeed, if we refpect the Bulk, but exceeding precious, and throughly dyed with the trueft Tinctures of Chriftianity) wherewith you have bleft your own Country, and with which *France* hath not been altogether unacquainted. Who can ferioufly read, tho but one Leaf of them, and not perceive how you felt the Breathing of God's Spirit, and were feafonably rais'd up for thefe unhappy times, as one who may with ftout Courage and invincible Arms undertake and curb outrageous Ungodlinefs? I folemnly profefs, I never faw any thing ftudied, and come from thofe, commonly call'd *the antient Fathers of the Church*, or from the Doctors of the latter times, which doth with equal Succefs breathe forth the Author's, and alfo kindle the Reader's Devotion. Thofe things which you have already put out concerning *Everlafting Reft, a Call to the Unconverted*, *Juftification* (in which if you leave the beaten Road a little, you do it, as far as I can underftand, not without Reafon and Scripture) *Infant-Baptifm*, *Peace of Confcience*, &c. do witnefs moft clearly both what your Learning is, and what your Love of Religion. Who then may forbid me to pour forth my careful and doubtful Thoughts into the Bofom of fuch and fo great a Man, and to declare what runs in my mind concerning the fad and fickle State of your Commonwealth? Truly I am no Pryer into other mens matters; and efpecially as to yours, I have been fo far from angerly thundring [*Virulent Declaiming*] againft them, that I have thought it an unfpeakable Fault to difpute curioufly of them. I will fay more, I could not but hope well of *Britain*; for I was, and am ftill of this opinion, that God hath referv'd to himfelf in *England* more Elect, and more Godly Men, than ever either flourifh'd of old, or can be fhewn now in any Realm of *Chriftendom*. Let both fearful Brethren and furious Enemies judg your Safety defperate, and ask in their Unbelief, who will give Salvation to *Ifrael* out of *Zion?* God will provide; there are not ten, not a thoufand Juft Men, but entire Millions of godly Men. I will hear what the Lord God will fay, for he will fpeak Peace to his People. But becaufe the moft high Ruler of the World (who can indeed without the intervening of means, both fcatter the Darknefs, and call back the Light, yet neverthelefs) wills not (for the moft part) to put forth his Power immediately; we ought (Reverend Sir) to lay together our Studies, and all Counfels to eftablifh firmly the Safety of *Britain*. I fuppofe its Condition will be perpetually tottering, until the Government return into one Man's hands (*Monarchy*.) As the Cuftoms of Nations and their Difpofitions are various, fo are their Manners of governing publick Affairs; they are not of the

fame

ame mind. One People chufes a popular Government; and neither is, nor can be accuftom'd to be ruled by one Man: Another People, being taken with the Splendor of Nobility, and hating the Madnefs of the Commonalty, prefers Monarchy. Your Country of *England* hath been a Lover of Kings for almoft innumerable Ages; neither do I know any Monarchy in the world more antient. The fame Sun fhines upon the prefent *Englifh*-men; the Afpects of the Stars, the Quality of the Soil hath the fame influence upon their Affections now as formerly: Who then can hope that either a Democracy or Ariftocracy, will eafily prevail in that Country, wherein Monarchy hath taken fuch deep rooting? But *England* (may fome man fay) hath already chang'd the Form of Government, and that (as it feem'd) with common Confent; who then can deny that may be commodioufly done, which hath been done commodioufly? I have a double Anfwer hereto. Firft, I will in like manner query, whether that Change prov'd very happy for *England?* Truly, if Taxes and Impofts be to be counted, they are not only doubled, but increas'd beyond almoft all meafure. If the State of Religion be to be confider'd, what a Common Sewer of Herefies is there! Who ever heard of *Ranters*, *Quakers*, &c. under the King? Secondly, Suppofe *Britain* hath been happy fince the Change, yet it was under the Government of One. What matters the Name? This One was a Protector, not a King, I grant; but he was One, and fuch a One, as was neither unskilful in the Art of Ruling, nor behav'd himfelf inferiour to a King in diffolving Parliaments; and from his Death, or at leaft from the cafting out of his Son, *England* never was quiet; Changes were continual: whom yefterday we reverenc'd, to day we loath; whom we fwore Fealty to but now, him foon after we damn with Curfes. Shall that moft noble Queen of *Iflands* always be fo tofs'd upon the Waves? And fhall no Halcyon fly thither, which may calm your Seas? Truly I fear you will never have Peace afcertain'd either againft Tumults at home, or the Attempts of Enemies abroad, till he, who is the Grandfon of fo many Kings, at length be reftor'd to his Grandfather's Throne. He hath every where by Right of Inheritance the Title of King of *Britain*, tho he yet poffefs not the thing defign'd by the Title. I know what *Odium* hath been caft upon him: Some, whether really or counterfeitly, are diffatisfy'd in his Conftancy to the true Religion; and alledg, that it concerns the Church very much, that he who is to rule others, fhould excel them in Godlinefs. I will not anfwer (which truly may be faid) that it belongs not to us to inquire into the Prince's Religion; Be he what he will, (if his Power be otherwiſe lawful, and the Right of Reigning belongs unto him) Obedience in Civil Matters muſt be perform'd to the King, and other Matters muſt be committed unto Divine Providence. Let the Biſhop of *Rome* luſt to juſtle Kings out of the Throne, unleſs they order Affairs of Religion according to his Beck; We may not be ſo proud. We give unto God the things that are God's, and to *Cæſar* the things that are *Cæſar*'s. But I paſs over all this; for (which is the thing chiefly to be conſider'd) this Prince being born, and duly educated in the true Religion, never departed from the publick Profeſſion of it; no, not even in thoſe places, in which he was likely to ſuffer loſs thereby: neither did he diſdain to be preſent at our Religious Aſſembly at *Roan* and *Rochel*. Moreover, he hath the Eſtimation of godly Uſe among thoſe that are about him. I confeſs he never graced our Church with his Preſence, while he was ſeated at *Paris*; which truly griev'd us: but becauſe the Caſe of thoſe call'd Presbyterians, ſeem'd to concern us who are Presbyterians; and becauſe the King's Death was aſcribed to the Presbyterians; he could not but be ſtrange to us, until the Event of things certify'd him that his Inſtalment was principally hinder'd not by our Brethren, but by the Anabaptiſts for the moſt part, or at leaſt the Independents; whom alſo he certainly underſtood to have before promoted his Father's ſad Death. I wiſh the Odium of that Fact, wherewith our Churches have ſo long been loaded, might now at length be removed both from us, and our *Engliſh* Brethren: which I know not how it can ever be, unleſs matters may be ſo compos'd as the Son may bear his Father's Scepter, not violently wreſted out of the Presbyterians hands, but friendly and freely proffer'd. Go on, Reverend Sir; prevent the Calamitys of imminent War. Do you, and the Brethren like you, embrace peaceable Counſels, and give the like to your Countrymen. Divine Providence will favour and bleſs your Endeavours, and will uſe you as ſacred Inſtruments for reſtoring Happineſs to your Country. But enough, and too much of this, for you may wonder that I ſpeak ſo familiarly to you; but I mention'd in the beginning what cauſe moved me thereto, *viz.* relying on your Piety and Charity, which will take all in good part. Further, God bleſs your Studies, your Labours, your Church, and all your, nay our *England*, which is the Flower and Glory of all the Kingdoms wherein God is truly worſhipped.

Paris, April 2. 1660.

Paris,

Paris, *April the third*, 1660.

SIR, my Honoured Brother,

NOthing hath happen'd more ſtrange in our days, than the Revolutions of *England*, *Scotland*, and *Ireland*. After the tragical Death of the late King, hopes were given that a Commonwealth might be eſtabliſh'd, that ſhould become the wonder and admiration of the whole World. But the ſeveral Changes that have happen'd ſince, from time to time, and the Confuſions that are to be fear'd, cauſe many to believe, that God will reduce Affairs to their firſt ſtate, and ſet the three Crowns united, upon the Head of one Monarch. That which in this doth moſt rejoice and comfort us, is, That it ſeems for the doing of this glorious Work, God will uſe the Service of thoſe with whom we have more ſtrict Communion in Doctrine and Diſcipline. For we underſtand, that ſuch as are call'd Presbyterians, are now poſſeſs'd of the greateſt Power, and ſit at the Helm of State. That illuſtrious Aſſembly, which would have preſerv'd to their King his Life and his Royalty, was without doubt very far from deſigning to rob his Children of that Right which is convey'd to them by a continued Succeſſion in their Royal Family for many Ages. A Report is here, that the thing which might hinder this King from being recall'd to the Inheritance of his Fathers, is the Opinion conceiv'd by ſome, of his being turn'd to the Roman Catholick Profeſſion; and the fear that in time he might ruin the Religion now flouriſhing in thoſe three Kingdoms. But, Sir, you know that we have ever deteſted the Doctrine of Popes and their Inſtruments, who teach that all Princes, call'd by them Hereticks, are incapable of Succeſſion of Crowns, and if in poſſeſſion, to be turn'd out. And more than this, I ſee not any ground there is for calling this Prince a Roman Catholick, he making no profeſſion of it; but on the contrary, hath rejected all the Advantages and all the Aids offer'd to him upon that condition. Charity is not jealous, and if it forbid us to ſuſpect on ſlight grounds private Perſons, how can it approve Jealouſys upon Perſons ſo ſacred? Experience hath taught us, how little reaſon hath in the end appear'd, for the like, and even the greateſt Apprehenſions of that kind: our Hiſtory doth furniſh us with a convincing Example. The *League* never pretended other cauſe for their Rebellion againſt King *Henry* the Third, but for his

 being

being an Heretick, and a Maintainer of Hereticks. And thence was infer'd, that he was no ways affected to the Roman, and a Favourer of our Religion. In the mean time, we never had a more potent Enemy; and to all mens knowledg he lived and died in the Communion of *Rome*, and therein shew'd as much Zeal as any of his Predecessors. But not to pass the Seas, you have in the midst of you an instance against all Contradiction: For what Jealousys have not been raised against the Religion of the late King of *Great Britain*, and yet at the hour when there was no place for dissembling, as being void of Fears and Hopes from Man, he made his Zeal to the true Religion appear; and even that Sweetness and that admirable Patience with which he suffer'd Death by the hands of his own Subjects, hath made it very visible that the Spirit of God reign'd in his Heart. True it is, that from my self I am not able to relate any thing touching the Religion of that Prince; because for Reasons of State, we had not the Honour of his Presence in our Assemblys of *Charenton*, the only place where in a formal Body we are able to witness the Respect we bear to stranger Princes in Communion with us. And as to my self, I am not considerable enough to have made a visit to so great a Prince, which was also the reason why I had not the Honour to see the Duke of *York*. But two years since being inform'd, how the Duke of *Glocester* had manifested his Ability to confound the false Doctors that had undertaken to seduce him, and that he had Courage and Generosity enough to resist those who would have placed him in the College of the Jesuits; I thought, considering how very young he was, that I might have the Honour to give him a visit, without apprehending any disadvantage. And I perform'd the Work freely, because I knew that not only he would accept it, but did also desire it. I cannot express how much I was satisfy'd with that young Prince. For besides the obliging manner wherewith he receiv'd me, he gave me several Proofs of his Zeal and Piety. I remember, that among other Discourses, he told me, how the late King his Father, a little before his death, had charg'd him with three things: Never to change his Religion: To obey his elder Brother, who was to be his King, in the same manner as he would have obey'd himself, if God had spared his Life: And to continue obedient to the Queen his Mother, in all, but what related to Religion. To which he added, that in persevering in his Religion, he did not only do his Duty towards God, and preserve the Peace of his Conscience; but also perform the last Will of the King his Father, and follow the Order of the King his Brother, who had sent for him, to free him of future Temptations.

This Discourse, which he deliver'd with a very good Grace, confirm'd me in the Belief I had of the late King's Religion, and made me see what I ought in Charity to believe of the King his Son. But over and above, there are in his Family among his Domesticks some Gentlemen of our Religion, and my antient Friends, who at several times have given me Assurances of the Piety of this Prince, and his Stability in the Profession he makes. True it is, *English*-men have unadvisedly done him great Wrong, for upon false Prejudices they have staid from Communion with us, and so have rais'd Jealousys, as if their King and all his Court were inclin'd to Popery. But the more discreet behave themselves otherwise; for knowing that the Belief of our Church, and that of the Church of *England* is the same, they willingly came to our Churches, and even Dr. *Cosin*, the King of *Great Britain*'s Chaplain, hath join'd with us with great Devotion. To return to my Discourse, God intrusts at this day your Presbyterians, the Gentlemen now in power, with the Honour and Reputation of our Churches: For if without the intervening of any foreign Power, they recal this Prince, and seat him in his Throne, they acquire to themselves and to their Posterity an immortal Glory, and stop their mouths for ever, who charge us falsly as Enemys of Royalty, and make appear, that the Maxim of, *No Bishop no King*, is injuriously imputed to us. For my part I confess, that as I have deplor'd with bitter Tears the bloody Death of the late King; so shall it be to me an exceeding Joy, to behold the Re-establishment of the King his Son, if perform'd with Circumstances not lessening the Splendor of Royal Majesty; and which may be to the Glory of God, and the Good and Rest of the three Kingdoms. 'Tis for this that I will offer up my hearty Prayers to God: and for you, Sir, that he will preserve and bless you. I have persuaded my self, that you would not take it ill that I open my Heart to you, and discover my Thoughts upon a Subject of such moment; since I am,

Sir, Your most humble and most affectionate

Brother and Servant,

DRELINCOURT,

Minister of the Church of *Paris*.

A Monsieur
Monsieur *Stroupe* f. M. D. S. E.
A Londres.

Phenix XVI.

A True Relation of the late King's Death. To which are added, Copies of two Papers written by the late King CHARLES II. *of Blessed Memory, found in the Strong Box.*

O*N Monday, being the second of* February, *the K. rose early, saying, that he had not slept well the last night; and about Seven of the Clock, coming from his private Devotions out of his Closet, fell down (and scarce any sign of Life remaining in him for the space of four hours) of a Fit of an* Apoplexy*: But with the loss of sixteen Ounces of Blood, and other Applications, came again to his Senses, and there was great hopes of his Recovery, till Thursday about One a clock; and at Five the Doctors being come before the Council, declar'd that the King was in great danger; and on Friday a quarter before Twelve, he departed this Life.* God have mercy on his Soul.

P. M. a C. F. came to the D. upon the Doctor's telling him of the State of the K. and told him, *That now was the time for him to take care of his Brother's Soul,* and that it was his Duty to tell him so. The D. with this admonishment went to the K. and after some private Discourse, the K. utter'd these Expressions; *O Br. how long have I wish'd? but now help me:* withal declaring, that he would have Mr. *Hud.* who had preserv'd him in the Tree, and now hop'd would preserve his Soul. Mr. *H.* was accordingly sent for, and desir'd to bring all

all Neceſſaries for a dying Man. But he not having the B. S. by him, went to one of the Qu. Ps. and telling him the occaſion, deſir'd his Aſſiſtance to procure it, and to bring it to the Back Stairs. The K. having notice that Mr. *Hud.* waited at the Door, deſir'd to be in private; the Biſhops and Nobles withdrew, the D. latching faſt the Door, the Lords *P. B.* and *F.* were going out alſo, but the D. told them they might ſtay. The K. ſeeing Mr. *H.* cry'd out, *Almighty God! what good Planet governs me, that all my Life is Wonders and Miracles! When, O Lord, I conſider my Infancy, my Exile, my Eſcape at* Worceſter, *my Preſervation in the Oak with the Aſſiſtance of this good Father, and now to have him again to preſerve my Soul! O Lord, my wonderful* Reſtoration, *my great danger in the late* Conſpiracy; *and laſt of all to be rais'd from Death to Life, and to have my Soul preſerv'd by the Aſſiſtance of this good Father, whom I ſee, O good Lord, that thou haſt created for my good!* The D. and Lds withdrew into the Cloſet for the ſpace of an hour: Then entring the Room again, the Father ask'd the K. whether he would be pleas'd to receive? He anſwer'd, *If I were worthy of it. Amen, Amen.* The Fa. remaining comforting and praying with him, he ſaid, *Father, if I am worthy of it, I pray let me have it.* The Fa. ſaid, it would be brought to him immediately, and ask'd his leave to proceed with the *Extreme Unction.* The King reply'd, *With all my heart:* the D. and Lords aſſiſting at the time. Fa. *H.* was call'd to the Door, where he receiv'd the B. S. and deſiring the K. to compoſe himſelf to receive, the K. would needs riſe (but was perſuaded to the contrary) he ſaid, *Let me meet my Heavenly Father in a better manner than lying on my back.* But being over-rul'd, they continue in Prayer: Amongſt others, the Fa. repeats an *Act of Contrition,* deſiring the K. to repeat it word by word after him. Having made an end, the K. receiv'd with the greateſt Expreſſions of Devotion imaginable. This being ended, they go on with the Prayers *de Anima.* That being done, the K. deſir'd the *Act of Contrition* to be again repeated, ſaying, *O Lord, good God, when my Lips fail, let my Heart ſpeak theſe Words eternally.* Amen.

The Biſhops and Lords enter the Room again, and deſire the K. to remember his laſt End, and to endeavour to make a good End. He ſaid he had thought of it, and hop'd he had made his Peace with God. They ask'd him whether he would receive; he ſaid he would not. So perſiſting in extolling the Qu. and D. ſaid, *He was not ſorry to leave the World, leaving ſo good a Brother to Rule behind him.*

The First Paper.

THE Discourse we had the other day, I hope, satisfied you in the main, *That Christ can have but one Church here upon Earth*; and I believe that it is as visible, as that the Scripture is in Print, That none can be that Church, but that which is call'd the *Roman Catholick Church*. I think you need not trouble your self with entering into that Ocean of particular Disputes, when the main, and in truth the only Question is, Where that Church is, which we profess to believe in the two Creeds? We declare there to believe one Catholick and Apostolick Church, and it is not left to every fantastical man's Head to believe as he pleases; but to the Church, to whom Christ left the Power upon Earth to govern us in matters of Faith, who made these Creeds for our Directions. It were a very irrational thing to make Laws for a Country, and leave it to the Inhabitants to be the Interpreters and Judges of those Laws: for then every man will be his own Judg, and by consequence no such thing as either Right or Wrong. Can we therefore suppose that God Almighty would leave us at those Uncertainties, as to give us a Rule to go by, and leave every Man to be his own Judg? I do ask any ingenious Man, whether it be not the same thing to follow our own Fancy, or to interpret the Scripture by it? I would have any Man shew me, where the Power of deciding Matters of Faith is given to every particular Man. Christ left his Power to his Church, even *to forgive Sins in Heaven*, and left his Spirit with them, which they exercis'd after his Resurrection: First by his Apostles in their Creeds, and many years after by the Council at *Nice*, where that Creed was made that is call'd by that name: and by the Power which they had receiv'd from Christ, they were the Judges even of the Scripture it self, many years after the Apostles, which Books were Canonical and which were not. And if they had this Power then, I desire to know how they came to lose it, and by what Authority men separate themselves from that Church? The only Pretence I ever heard of, was, because the Church has fail'd in wresting and interpreting the Scripture, contrary to the true Sense and Meaning of it, and that they have impos'd Articles of Faith upon us, which are not to be warranted by God's Word. I do desire to know who is to be Judg of that, whether the whole Church, the Succession whereof has continued to this day

day without interruption, or particular Men, who have rais'd Schisms for their own Advantage.

This is a true Copy of a Paper I found in the late King my Brother's Strong Box, *written in his own Hand.*

J. R.

The Second Paper.

IT is a sad thing to consider, what a world of Heresys are crept into this Nation: Every man thinks himself as competent a Judg of the Scriptures, as the very Apostles themselves. And 'tis no wonder that it should be so, since that part of the Nation which looks most like a Church, dares not bring the true Arguments against the other Sects, for fear they should be turn'd against themselves, and confuted by their own Arguments. The Church of *England* (as it is call'd) would fain have it thought they are the Judges in Matters Spiritual, and yet dare not say positively there is no Appeal from them; for either they must say, that they are Infallible (which they cannot pretend to) or confess, that what they decide in Matters of Conscience, is no farther to be follow'd than it agrees with every man's private Judgment. If Christ did leave a Church here upon Earth, and we were all once of that Church, how and by what Authority did we separate from that Church? If the power of interpreting of Scripture be in every man's Brain, what need have we of a Church or Churchmen? To what purpose then did our Saviour, after he had given his Apostles power to bind and loose in Heaven and Earth, add to it, *That he would be with them even to the end of the World?* These words were not spoken parabolically or by way of Figure: Christ was then ascending into his Glory, and *left his Power with his Church, even to the end of the World.* We have had these hundred years past, the sad Effects of denying to the Church that Power in Matters Spiritual, without an Appeal. What Country can subsist in peace or quiet, where there is not a Supreme Judg, from whence there can be no Appeal? Can there be any Justice done, where the Offenders are their own Judges, and equal Interpreters of the Law with those who are appointed to administer Justice? This is our case here in *England* in Matters Spiritual: For the *Protestants* are not of the Church of *England*, as 'tis the true Church from whence there can be no Appeal, but because the Discipline of that Church is conformable at that present to their Fancies;

Fancies; which as soon as it shall contradict or vary from, they are ready to embrace or join with the next Congregation of People, whose Discipline or Worship agrees with their own Opinion at that time: so that according to this Doctrine, there is no other Church, nor Interpreter of Scripture, but that which lies in every man's giddy Brain. I desire to know therefore of every serious Considerer of these things, whether the great Work of our Salvation, ought to depend upon such a sandy Foundation as this? Did Christ ever say to the Civil Magistrates (much less to the People) *That he would be with them to the end of the World?* Or did he give them the Power to forgive Sins? St. *Paul* tells the *Corinthians, Ye are God's Husbandry, Ye are God's Building; We are Labourers with God:* This shews who are the Labourers, and who are the Husbandry and Building. And in this whole Chapter, and in the preceding one, St. *Paul* takes great pains to set forth, that *They (the Clergy) have the Spirit of God, without which no man searches the deep things of God.* And he concludes the Chapter with this Verse, *For who hath known the Mind of the Lord, that he might instruct him? But we have the Mind of Christ.* Now if we but consider in human probability and reason, the Powers Christ leaves to his Church in the Gospel, and St. *Paul* explains so distinctly afterwards; we cannot think that our Saviour said all these things to no purpose. And pray consider on the other side, that those who resist the Truth, and will not submit to his Church, draw their Arguments from Implications, and far-fetch'd Interpretations, at the same time that they deny plain and positive Words: which is so great a Disingenuity, as 'tis not almost to be thought that they can believe themselves. Is there any other Foundation of the *Protestant Church*, but that if the Civil Magistrate please, he may call such of the Clergy as he thinks fit for his turn at that time, and turn the Church either to *Presbytery, Independency*, or indeed what he pleases? This was the way of our pretended Reformation here in *England*; and by the same Rule and Authority it may be alter'd into as many more Shapes and Forms, as there are Fancies in mens Heads.

This is a True Copy.

FINIS.